W9-DGB-457

*M*ulticultural Children's Literature

Through the Eyes of Many Children

DONNA E. NORTON
TEXAS A & M UNIVERSITY

Merrill
Prentice Hall

Upper Saddle River, New Jersey
Columbus, Ohio

Library of Congress Cataloging-in-Publication Data
Norton, Donna E.
Multicultural children's literature : through the eyes of many children / Donna E. Norton.
          p.   cm.
       Includes bibliographical references and index.
       ISBN 0-13-243122-X
         1. Children's literature, American—Minority authors—History and criticism. 2. Children's literature, American—Minority authors—Study and teaching. 3. Children—United States—Books and reading. 4. Children of minorities—Books and reading. 5. Pluralism (Social sciences) in literature. 6. Ethnic groups in literature. 7. Minorities in literature. 8. Ethnicity in literature.   I. Title.
       PS153.M56 N675   2001
       810.9'9282'08693—dc21

                                    00-028376

Vice President and Publisher: Jeffery W. Johnston
Editor: Linda Ashe Montgomery
Editorial Assistant: Jennifer Day
Production Editor: Mary M. Irvin
Design Coordinator: Diane C. Lorenzo
Text Design: STELLARViSIONs
Cover Design: Linda Fares
Cover Art: Steven Schildbach
Electronic Text Management: Marilyn Wilson Phelps, Karen Bretz, Melanie Ortega
Production Manager: Pamela D. Bennett
Director of Marketing: Kevin Flanagan
Marketing Manager: Amy June
Marketing Services Manager: Krista Groshong

This book was set in Usherwood by Prentice Hall and was printed and bound by Courier Kendallville, Inc. The cover was printed by Phoenix Color Corp.

Copyright © 2001 by Prentice-Hall, Inc., Upper Saddle River, New Jersey 07458. All rights reserved. Printed in the United States of America. This publication is protected by Copyright and permission should be obtained from the publisher prior to any prohibited reproduction, storage in a retrieval system, or transmission in any form or by any means, electronic, mechanical, photocopying, recording, or likewise. For information regarding permission(s), write to: Rights and Permissions Department.

10 9 8 7 6 5 4 3
ISBN: 0-13-243122-X

Preface

$\mathcal{T}$his text is intended for any adult who is interested in evaluating, selecting, and sharing multicultural literature written for children and young adults. The focus and organization of the text are designed for classes in departments of Education, English, and Library Science. The text focuses on the most outstanding literature in the following areas: African American, Native American, Latino, Asian, Jewish, and Middle Eastern. The text is written in the hope that those who share books with children will help them develop an appreciation for and an understanding of a varied and rich cultural heritage.

HIGHLIGHTS

Two-Part Chapter Organization

Each chapter focuses on two important areas related to multicultural literature. The first part of each chapter includes a discussion of specific literature, nonfiction, and fiction that develops a historical perspective of the culture, poetry, and contemporary literature. The second area in each chapter develops the techniques and methodologies that adults may use to help children develop an understanding for the culture.

Time Lines

Each of the chapters is introduced with a time line that highlights historical and literary milestones within the culture. These time lines encourage students to develop an in-depth understanding of the culture.

Criteria for Evaluating Literature

Each chapter discusses criteria that could be used when selecting and evaluating the literature. These criteria may be used in a historical perspective so that students understand the various changes in evaluation that may have occurred over time.

Issues

Each chapter discusses various issues that are associated with writing, publishing, selecting, and evaluating the literature. These issues are written in such a way as to encourage students to discuss or even debate various viewpoints.

Authentication

Examples are developed that show how students can authenticate the text and the illustrations in multicultural literature. Many of these authentication examples are research projects developed by university students.

Additional Activities for Developing Understanding of Each Literature

Each chapter includes lists of additional activities that university professors may use as assignments with their students. There are also lists of additional activities that may be used with each of the phases to be used with children.

Involving Children Sections with Each Chapter

Each chapter includes a five-phase procedure of activities and learning experiences that may be used to help children develop an understanding of culture. These activities progress in the following order: phase one, general approach to traditional literature; phase two, folklore from a narrower region; phase three, historical nonfiction; phase four, historical fiction; phase five, contemporary literature. The activities in these phases were developed during field research in which the activities were tested with school children.

Text Teaching Aids

Each chapter includes various charts, webs, and teaching strategies that increase understanding of and interest in the culture. For example, several chapters include modeling activities that help teachers develop understanding of the culture and the literature.

Annotated Bibliographies

Each chapter concludes with annotated bibliographies that describe the literature. These annotations provide a short description of the book, readability level, and an interest level.

ACKNOWLEDGMENTS

I would like to thank the reviewers of the manuscript for their insights and comments: Richard F. Abrahamson, The University of Houston; Mingshui Cai, the University of Northern Iowa; Rodney D. Keller, Ricks College; Janice V. Kristo, The University of Maine; Roberta Rosenberg, Christopher Newport University; and Masha K. Rudman, The University of Massachusetts–Amherst.

Contents

CHAPTER 3

Native American Literature   69

CHAPTER 4

Latino Literature   *133*

Involving Children in Latino Literature   *164*

Involving Children with Jewish Literature   266

CHAPTER 7

Middle Eastern Literature   285

1 | *Introduction to Multicultural Literature*

*T*he United States and Canada are multicultural nations, including Europeans, Native Americans, African Americans, Latinos, and Asians. The United States and Canada also include people from different religious groups such as Christian, Jewish, and Muslim. A heightened sensitivity to the needs of all people has led to the realization that literature plays a considerable role in the development of understanding across cultures.

The need for cross-cultural understanding that goes beyond the borders of the United States and Canada is emphasized in the following introduction to *The Dictionary of Global Culture*, edited by Kwame Anthony Appiah and Henry Louis Gates, Jr. (1996):

> In the year 2000, half the world's people will be Asian, and one eighth will be African; a majority, too, will be non-Christian. And of the world's twenty largest cities, none will be in Europe or the United States. . . . With the urgent awareness that we Americans can no longer afford to be limited to an understanding of culture that begins and ends in the West, Kwame Anthony Appiah and Henry Louis Gates, Jr., two of our most esteemed scholars, have compiled this important volume of information. (front flap)

The need for cross-cultural understanding also increases with the demographic shifts that are occurring in the United States. For example, Booth (1998) stresses that the United States is experiencing its second great wave of immigration. The first wave occurred between 1890 and 1920, when the immigrants came mostly from European countries such as Germany, Poland, Ireland, Hungary, and Russia. According to Booth, this immigration pattern has now changed: "The overwhelming majority of immigrants come from Asia and Latin America—Mexico, the Central American countries, the Philippines, Korea, and Southeast Asia" (p. 7). Educating the children of these immigrants requires cross-cultural understanding, just as it was needed in the past. According to Hoffman and Pearson (2000), "it is projected that between 2000 and 2020 there will be 47% more Hispanic children aged 5–13 in the United States than are there today" (p. 28). These authors conclude that educators must have knowledge about the cultural and linguistic diversity that is found in schools.

To aid in developing understandings of other cultures, many educators and researchers are currently emphasizing the need for high-quality multicultural literature. Hazel Rochman (1993) states the need for multicultural literature very well when she concludes: "The best books break down borders. They surprise us—whether they are set close to home or abroad. They change our view of ourselves; they extend that phase 'like me' to include what we thought was foreign and strange" (p. 9). This changing view of ourselves is especially important to researchers who are investigating minority children's responses to literature. For example, M. Liaw (1995), after analyzing Chinese children's responses to Chinese children's books, called for more cultural sensitivity in the stories and a need for researching children's responses to literature. Grice and Vaughn (1992), following research in which they analyzed responses to African American literature, also identified the need for culturally conscious literature.

Rena Lewis and Donald Doorlag (1995) present the following reasons for developing multicultural education:

1. Commonalties among people cannot be recognized unless differences are acknowledged.
2. A society that interweaves the best of all of its cultures reflects a truly mosaic image.
3. Multicultural education can restore cultural rights by emphasizing cultural equality and respect.
4. Students can learn basic skills while also learning to respect cultures; multicultural education need not detract from basic education.
5. Multicultural education enhances the self-concepts of all students because it provides a more balanced view of U.S. society.
6. Students must learn to respect others.

Eileen Tway (1989) argues, "In a country of multicultural heritage, children require books that reflect and illuminate that varied heritage" (p. 109). Bruce Sealey (1984) emphasizes that education should encourage children to accept and be sensitive to cultural diversity, to understand that similar values frequently underlie different customs, to have quality contact with people from other cultures, and to role-play experiences involved with other cultures. David Piper (1986) recommends using traditional stories and fables from various cultural sources and focusing on children's cultural backgrounds. Critics of literature for children and young adults maintain that readers should be exposed to multicultural literature that heightens respect for the individuals, as well as the contributions and values, of cultural minorities.

Positive multicultural literature has been used effectively to help readers identify cultural heritages, understand sociological change, respect the values of minority groups, raise aspirations, and expand imagination and creativity. This author has found that multicultural literature and activities related to the literature also improves reading scores and improves attitudes toward African Americans, Native Americans, and Latinos if the literature and literature-related activities are part of the curriculum and if adults know how to select this literature and develop strategies to accompany the literature (Norton, 1981, 1984, 1990, 1999). In contrast, merely placing the literature in a classroom or a library without subsequent interaction does not change attitudes.

Although we can find numerous authorities who identify the need for multicultural literature, the selection of literature that is of both high literary quality and culturally authentic is a formidable task. The tasks involved in the process are enormous. Universities are beginning to require that students in education, library science, and English take courses that focus on choosing, analyzing, evaluating, and effectively using multicultural literature. Library selection committees, university professors, public school teachers, librarians, and administrators must all become involved in this process of evaluating and choosing multicultural literature.

An example of the complexity of the problems facing the collection of multicultural literature is emphasized when we consider the evaluation of Native American literature. When developing the Native American collection, librarians and educators must meet the basic requirements for students, scholars, and general readers who are interested in the study of Native American people, their culture, and their literature. They must also, however, be equally concerned with the quality and authenticity of the literature and reference materials. A special sensitivity is required when approaching the selection of materials, the categorizing of the materials, and the possible issues related to those selections. A case in point is *The Education of Little Tree* written by Forrest Carter. When the book was reissued in 1991, it received that year's American Booksellers Association's ABBY award, given annually to the book that booksellers most enjoyed recommending directly to customers. At this point, it was advertised as a sensitive, evocative autobiographical account of a Cherokee boyhood in the 1930s and was on the *New York Times* best-seller list for nonfiction. After revelations about the author's background, the book was moved from nonfiction to fiction on the same best-seller list of the *New York Times*. The book has carefully developed characterizations, historical settings, and believable conflict, but it is not an autobiography of a Cherokee boy. Instead, it is historical fiction. Such distinctions are important for scholars and students who are studying Native American literature.

In addition to the sensitivity required in selecting materials, educators are also emphasizing the moral dimensions that are related to sharing and discussing literature associated with various cultures. Johnston, Juhasz, Marken, and Ruiz (1998) define morality as "judgments of what is right and what is wrong, what is good and what is bad. These judgments, moreover, are produced at the meeting point between personal values, beliefs, and standards, and their negotiation in social settings. Morality then crucially includes both individual and social judgments." (p. 162). Consequently, the nature of the discussions between students and adults, the questions asked, the reactions to responses, and the choices of materials to be read and discussed may reflect differences in cultural values and portray moral messages.

Johnston et al. (1998) conclude with the following advice to teachers or other adults who work in multicultural settings: "Observe classroom events carefully and reflect upon their significance while suppressing the urge to criticize or condemn. The overall message that emerges from our analysis is that what teachers do and say in class does matter—their words and their actions carry great moral weight. Teachers, unavoidably, act as moral agents; how they choose to direct this action is a crucial part of what it means to be a teacher" (p. 180). This is excellent advice for anyone who is selecting, evaluating, and using multicultural literature, especially if the literature reflects cultural values and beliefs that are different from those of the educator.

Numerous articles in newspapers and journals stress the importance of teacher education, especially after the recent violence in schools. For example, in an article in *The Denver Post* titled "Course Pushes Teachers to See Cultural Bias," Janet Bingham and Andrew Guy, Jr. (1999), highlight the efforts of Alameda High School in

Lakewood, Colorado, to provide cultural instruction. The authors state, "The district has made the course a centerpiece of its response to diversity issues that have come to the forefront since the Columbine High School shootings. The idea is to make teachers and administrators more aware of their own 'home cultures'—the traditions, habits and styles acquired from their families—and how they may contrast with the home cultures of their students" (p. 5B).

Author Naomi Shihab Nye (1989), in her introduction to *The Space Between Our Footsteps*, an anthology of poems and paintings from the Middle East, stresses the importance of overcoming negative stereotypes about a culture and providing a more balanced portrayal of a culture. She states, "I can't stop believing human beings everywhere hunger for deeper-than-headline news from one another. Poetry and art are some of the best ways this heartfelt 'news' may be exchanged" (p. vii). As we proceed through the various cultures developed in this book, we will try to locate literature that helps us develop this balanced portrayal of a culture.

DEVELOPING A STUDY OF MULTICULTURAL LITERATURE

My own interest in multicultural literature as a scholarly subject began over twenty years ago when I was attending a conference on researching and writing biography. One of the speakers, a Native American author, spoke about his difficulty in researching the life of a Native American chief who lived in the 1800s. As an example of the problems he encountered, he explained how there were three differing interpretations of the chief's last statement given before his execution. The interpretation by a military officer was that the chief called on his people to lay down their arms and live on the reservation. A missionary translated the same message to be one in which the chief asked his people to give up their own beliefs and worship the white-man's god. The third interpretation was given by the chief's brother. In this version, the chief reminded his people of his accomplishments and what he would like them to remember about his life. This example illustrates the need for careful research if the author is to present an authentic viewpoint.

Shortly after this experience, I began my own research into the authenticity of the multicultural literature used with children and young adults. I also developed a university course in which students who were mostly from the fields of education, liberal arts, and library science could gain insights into multicultural literature. After several years of trying different methods for teaching the course, I developed a five-phase multicultural literature study that proceeds from ancient to contemporary literature. The sequence of study is summarized in Chart 1–1. This procedure is based partly on the one described in Franchot Ballinger's article, "A Matter of Emphasis: Teaching the 'Literature' in Native American Literature Courses" (1984): he begins with a general study of the oral tradition associated with Native American folklore, extends the study to the literature from specific Native American cultures, continues with biography and autobiography, and concludes with contemporary writings. Throughout this study, he searches for the emergence of critical themes, basic symbols, and shared values that tie the ancient and contemporary literature together.

A modification of this approach proved to be the most valuable for my own students, both graduate and undergraduate, who chose to do in-depth studies of African/African American, Asia/Asian American, Latino, Native American, Jewish, or Middle Eastern literature or to develop instructional units to be used with children.

CHART 1–1   Sequence for Studying Multicultural Literature

Phase One: Traditional Literature (Generalizations and Broad Views)

A. Identify distinctions among folktales, myths, and legends.

B. Identify ancient stories that have common features and that are found in many regions.

C. Identify types of stories that dominate a subject.

D. Summarize the nature of oral language, the role of traditional literature, the role of an audience, and the literary style.

Phase Two: Traditional Tales from One Area (Narrower View)

A. Analyze traditional myths and other story types and compare findings with those in Phase One.

B. Analyze and identify values, beliefs, and themes in the traditional tales of one region.

Phase Three: Historical Nonfiction

A. Analyze nonfiction for the values, beliefs, and themes identified in traditional literature.

B. Compare adult autobiographies and children's biographies (if possible).

C. Compare information in historical documents with autobiographies and biographies.

Phase Four: Historical Fiction

A. Evaluate historical fiction according to the authenticity of the conflicts, characterizations, settings, themes, language, and traditional beliefs and values.

B. Search for the role of traditional literature in historical fiction.

C. Compare historical fiction with autobiographies, biographies, and historical information

---

Phase Five: Contemporary Literature

A. Analyze the inclusion of any beliefs and values identified in traditional literature and nonfictional literature.

B. Analyze contemporary characterization and conflicts.

C. Analyze the themes and look for threads that cross the literature.

As you read this book and conduct your own research, you will discover that the literature is discussed in a way that focuses on a five-phase approach. The conclusion of each chapter includes a section titled "Involving Children in _____ Literature," with the blank filled with the name of the culture covered in that chapter. These sections provide suggestions showing some of the ways that the literature from various cultures may be used with children and young adult audiences.

Five-Phase Approach for the Study of Multicultural Literature

Phase One   This phase is a broad introduction to the ancient myths, legends, and folktales of a culture. The literature, discussions, and assignments encourage students to understand the nature of the oral language in storytelling and to appreciate the role of oral tradition in transmitting the culture, the philosophy, and the language of the people.

Activities for Phase One.   Identify the ancient myths, legends, and folktales from a culture. Find the commonalties among them and identify those that are found in many regions within the cultural group. Also identify the types of stories that dominate, the characteristics of the traditional literature, and variants of the same tale. Consider the history of the recording of the tales and problems created by interpretations and translations. Finally, summarize the broad generalizations and understandings: What did you learn about the people, their belief and value systems, and their language?

Phase Two   This phase narrows the study to the ancient myths, legends, and folktales from one specific area. For example, this may involve the study of traditional literature from Native Americans of the Great Plains or the Southwest or the Inuit; tracing African tales from West Africa to Southern plantations in the United States, or comparing tales from the Aztec or Inca or Latino cultures to the tales of the Hispanic Southwest. The literature, discussions, and assignments encourage students to consider how the generalizations from Phase One apply to one specific segment of a wider culture, how and why the literature may diverge from the generalizations, and what traditional values are reflected in the literature.

Activities for Phase Two.   For one specific group or area, identify examples of ancient myths, legends, and folktales. Look for the characteristics and the story types that arose out of the study during Phase One. Identify stories that reflect differences from the characteristics identified in Phase One and consider any reasons for the differences. Comparative assignments are excellent ways to help students analyze literature. Identify examples of stories that reflect interference of an alien culture or changes that resulted because people were forced from their homelands: What are the changes? What might have caused these changes? Finally, summarize the philosophy, values, beliefs, and literary styles of the specific people as reflected in their myths, legends, and folktales.

Phase Three   This phase involves study of nonfiction selections such as biographies, autobiographies, and informational literature. The literature, discussions, and assignments should encourage students to understand the early experiences and the social and political history of the specific people. This is an opportunity to verify the beliefs, values, and traditions identified in Phase One and Phase Two and to evaluate the accuracy of literature by comparing biographies, autobiographies, and informational writing.

Activities for Phase Three.   Search for evidence that the philosophy, values, and beliefs depicted in myths, legends, and folktales are also depicted in biographies and autobiographies. Do the values, beliefs, and philosophies appear to be authentic? Use nonfiction informational texts to evaluate the authenticity of biographies. You may even be able to use autobiographies to evaluate the authenticity of both informational texts and biographies. If possible, compare an adult autobiography with a juvenile biography written about the same character. Or compare an adult biography with juvenile biographies that are written about the same character. What are the similarities and the differences? Evaluate the authenticity of the literature. Finally, summarize the historical happenings that influenced the culture and the people. Identify the literature that accurately presents this history.

The myths in this book include creation stories from many parts of the world.

Book Cover from *IN THE BEGINNING: CREATION STORIES FROM AROUND THE WORLD* by Virginia Hamilton, Illustrations copyright © 1988 by Pennyroyal Press, reproduced by permission of Harcourt, Inc.

Phase Four   This phase is a study of historical fiction selections based on characters from the specific culture or on interactions between the people and another cultural group. The literature, discussions, and assignments encourage students to use the background information gained during the previous readings and discussions to evaluate the authenticity of historical fiction.

Activities for Phase Four.   Analyze historical fiction for authenticity of settings, credibility of conflicts, and believability of characterizations, as well as for authenticity of the presentation of traditional beliefs, for the appropriateness of theme, and for the effectiveness of the author's style.

Phase Five   Phase Five is a study of contemporary literature including realistic fiction, poetry, biography, and autobiography. The literature, discussions, and activities encourage students to search for continuity among traditional literature, nonfiction, historical fiction, and contemporary writings and to consider the themes, values, and conflicts that emerge in contemporary writings.

Activities for Phase Five.   Search for any continuity within the literature as the literature proceeds from ancient to contemporary. Search for images, themes, values, style, and sources of conflict in writings by contemporary authors who are members of the group. Compare contemporary literature written for adult and juvenile audiences. Compare contemporary literature written by members of the group with contemporary literature that focuses on the group but is written by authors who are not members of the group.

My university students have found it helpful to detail some of their findings in chart form before they summarize their discoveries about the literature. They also find these charts to be extremely helpful when they are evaluating the authenticity of the literature. For example, you may find Chart 1–2 to be helpful in your own research.

Each of the following chapters includes examples of various assignments or research developed by my students. There will also be excerpts from the summaries of each phase of the literature developed by the students.

Authenticating the Literature

As can be inferred from this discussion, authenticity is very important in the selection of literature that depicts the values, beliefs, and cultural backgrounds of various groups. The need for accuracy and authenticity is emphasized in numerous articles about multicultural literature. For example, two articles by Betsy Hearne emphasize the importance of authenticity in picture books. In "Cite the Source: Reducing Cultural Chaos in Picture Books, Part One" (1993), Hearne states:

> How do you tell if a folktale in picture-book format is authentic, or true to its cultural background? What picture books have met the challenge of presenting authentic folklore for children? These two questions, which dominated a recent program at the Harold Washington Library in Chicago, are especially pressing in light of our growing national concern about multicultural awareness. And they generate even broader questions: How can an oral tradition survive in print? How do children's books pass on—and play on—folklore? (p. 22)

In her second article, "Respect the Source: Reducing Cultural Chaos in Picture Books, Part Two" (1993), Hearne discusses the importance of establishing cultural

CHART 1–2 Chart for Studying Multicultural Literature

Phase One			
Examples	Characteristics and types of folklore	Cultural knowledge gained	Beliefs and values of the people	Variants, interpretations, notes

Phase Two				
Examples	Values and beliefs	Commonalities, characteristics, and story types	Differences from Phase One	Interference of alien culture	Variants, interpretations, notes

Phase Three			
Examples	Values and beliefs from Phases One and Two	Historical happenings that influenced culture	Authenticity of historical information	Comparisons among biographies

Phase Four					
Examples	Setting	Conflicts	Character-ization	Traditional values, beliefs, and behaviors	Themes and style	Historical happenings and connections with previous phases

Phase Five				
Examples	Continuity and changes within literature	Images, themes, values, style	Sources of conflict	Comparisons between children's and adult literature	Comparisons between writings of members and nonmembers of group

authority, citing the sources for folklore, and training adults who select and interact with the literature. She concludes her article with the following statements:

> We can ask for source citations and more critical reviews; we can compare adaptations to their printed sources (interlibrary loan works for librarians as well as their patrons) and see what's been changed in tone and content; we can consider what context graphic art provides for a story; we can make more informed selections, not by hard and fast rules, but by judging the balance of each book. . . . We can, in short, educate ourselves on the use and abuse of folklore at an intersection of traditions. (p. 37)

Hearne's concerns about cultural authenticity are valid with any of the genres of literature. After reading this book and critically evaluating the literature discussed in the various chapters, you will be able to make critical decisions about choosing and evaluating the literature more effectively. Authenticating various examples of multicultural literature is one of the favorite assignments of both my undergraduate and graduate students. It has also been shown to be a favorite assignment when used with schoolchildren. Or like many of my students who express their own desires, you will be able to write your own stories that authentically depict a cultural group.

REFERENCES

Appiah, Kwame Anthony, and Henry Louis Gates, Jr., edited by. *The Dictionary of Global Culture*. New York: Knopf, 1996.

Ballinger, Franchot. "A Matter of Emphasis: Teaching the 'Literature' in Native American Literature Courses." *American Indian Culture and Research Journal* 8(1984): 1–12.

Bingham, Janet, and Andrew Guy, Jr. "Course Pushes Teachers to See Cultural Bias." *The Denver Post* (Sunday, July 25, 1999): 5B.

Booth, William. "Diversity and Division: America's New Wave of Immigration Is Changing Its 'Melting Pot' Image." *The Washington Post National Weekly Edition*. 15 (March 2, 1998): 6–8.

Grice, M., and C. Vaughn. "Third Graders Respond to Literature for and About Afro-Americans." *The Urban Review* 24 (1992): 149–164.

Hearne, Betsy. "Cite the Source: Reducing Cultural Chaos in Picture Books, Part One." *School Library Journal* (July 1993): 22–26.

Hearne, Betsy. "Respect the Source: Reducing Cultural Chaos in Picture Books, Part Two." *School Library Journal* (August 1993): 33–37.

Hoffman, James, and P. David Pearson. "Reading Teacher Education in the Next Millennium: What Your Grandmother's Teacher Didn't Know That Your Granddaughter's Teacher Should." *Reading Research Quarterly* 35 (January/February/March 2000): 28–44.

Johnston, Bill, Andrea Juhasz, James Marken, and Beverly Rolfs Ruiz. "The ESL Teacher as Moral Agent." *Research in the Teaching of English* 32 (May 1998): 161–181.

Lewis, Rena, and Donald Doorlag. *Teaching Special Students in the Mainstream*, 4th ed. Upper Saddle River, N.J.: Merrill/Prentice Hall, 1995.

Liaw, M. "Looking into the Mirror: Chinese Children's Responses to Chinese Children's Books." *Reading Horizons* 35 (1995): 185–198.

Norton, Donna E. "Changing Attitudes Toward Minorities: Children's Literature Shapes Attitudes." *Review Journal of Philosophy and Social Science* 9 (1984): 97–113.

_____. "The Development, Dissemination, and Evaluation of a Multi-Ethnic Curricular Model for Preservice Teachers, Inservice Teachers, and Elementary Children." New Orleans: International Reading Association, National Conference, April 1981.

_____. "Teaching Multicultural Literature." *The Reading Teacher* 44 (1990): 28–40.

_____. *Through the Eyes of a Child: An Introduction to Children's Literature*, 5th ed. Upper Saddle River, N.J.: Merrill/Prentice Hall, 1999.

Nye, Naomi Shihab. *The Space Between Our Footsteps*. New York: Simon & Schuster, 1998.

Piper, David. "Language Growth in the Multiethnic Classroom." *Language Arts* 63 (January 1986): 23–36.

Rochman, Hazel. *Against Borders: Promoting Books for a Multicultural World*. Chicago: American Library Association, 1993.

Sealey, Bruce. "Measuring the Multicultural Quotient of a School." *TESL Canada Journal/Review TESL du Canada* 1 (March 1984): 21–28.

Tway, Eileen. "Dimensions of Multicultural Literature for Children." In *Children's Literature: Resource for the Classroom*, edited by Masha Kabakow Rudman. Needham Heights, Mass.: Christopher-Gordon, 1989, 109–138.

African American Time Line

Late 1400s	Beginning of slave trade, which causes forced movement of slaves to the Americas
Early 1800s	Beginnings of the Underground Railroad (organized in 1838), which helps many slaves to escape to freedom in the North
1850	Passage of Fugitive Slave Act, which made it illegal to help runaway slaves
1852	*Uncle Tom's Cabin* published in book form
1861–1865	Civil War years
1863	Emancipation Proclamation, which abolishes slavery in the South
1882	First known collection of African tales published for European audiences
1932	Langston Hughes's *The Dream Keeper*
1933	Newbery Honor: Hildegarde Swift's *The Railroad to Freedom: A Story of the Civil War*
1948	Newbery Honor: Harold Courlander's *The Cow-Tail Switch, and Other West African Stories*
1949	Newbery Honor: Arna Bontemps's *Story of the Negro*
1951	Newbery: Elizabeth Yates's *Amos Fortune, Free Man*
1960s	Civil rights movement
1965	Nancy Larrick's article "The All-White World of Children's Books," which emphasizes lack of books about minorities
1969	Newbery Honor: Julius Lester's *To Be a Slave*
1970	Beginning of Coretta Scott King Award, which is given to writers and illustrators who make inspiring contributions to African American literature
1970	Newbery: William H. Armstrong's *Sounder*
1970s	Several Caldecott Honors Books about African and African American subjects: Illustrators Tom Feelings, Ezra Jack Keats, Gerald McDermott
1970s	Studies related to stereotypes in African American literature
1971	Caldecott: Gail E. Haley's *A Story—A Story: An African Tale*
1974	Newbery: Paula Fox's *The Slave Dancer*
1975	Newbery: Virginia Hamilton's *M. C. Higgins, the Great*
1976	Caldecott: to artists Leo and Diane Dillon for *Why Mosquitoes Buzz in People's Ears*
1976	Newbery Honor: Sharon Bell Mathis's *The Hundred Penny Box*
1977	Caldecott: to artists Leo and Diane Dillon for *Ashanti to Zulu: African Traditions*
1977	Newbery: Mildred D. Taylor's *Roll of Thunder, Hear My Cry*
1980s and 1990s	*The Adventures of Huckleberry Finn* attacked and frequently censored
1983	Caldecott: to artist Marcia Brown for *Shadow*
1985	Newbery Honor: Bruce Brooks's *The Moves Make the Man*
1987	Caldecott Honor: Ann Grifalconi's *The Village of Round and Square Houses*
1988	Caldecott Honor: John Steptoe's *Mufaro's Beautiful Daughters: An African Tale*
1992	Hans Christian Andersen Medal: Virginia Hamilton
1990s	Caldecott Honors: Carole Byard (*Working Cotton*), Jerry Pinkney (*The Talking Eggs*), Brian Pinkney (*The Faithful Friend* and *Duke Ellington*), Faith Ringgold (*Tar Beach*), and Christopher Myers (*Harlem*)
1990s	Newbery Honors: Patricia McKissack (*The Dark-Thirty*), Walter Dean Myers (*Somewhere in the Darkness*), Carol Fenner (*Yolonda's Genius*), Christopher Paul Curtis (*The Watsons Go to Birmingham—1963*), and Nancy Farmer (*A Girl Named Disaster*)
2000	Newbery and Coretta Scott King Award: Christopher Paul Curtis's *Bud, Not Buddy*

2 | *African American Literature*

Our journey through the study of African American literature includes both the literature from Africa and from the Americas. African American traditional literature, for example, cannot be understood and appreciated without also studying the literature that provides the foundations for it; namely, African folklore. In this chapter, we will discuss how the literature has evolved over time as we consider changing issues related to the literature. We will discuss historical and contemporary literature and analyze the contributions of outstanding authors and illustrators who create quality works and who write and illustrate with sensitivity and understanding. One of the ways to begin our journey is to consider the changing issues that have developed around the literature.

 ## ISSUES RELATED TO AFRICAN AMERICAN LITERATURE

An analysis of the various studies and issues surrounding African American literature provides insights into the changing scholarship and attitudes toward the literature that have occurred over time. Studies conducted in the 1970s and 1980s focused on issues related to stereotypes and images found in African American children's literature published in the past. Dorothy May Broderick (1971), for example, analyzed U.S. children's literature published between 1827 and 1967. She reports that the personal characteristics of African American people portrayed in these books suggested that they (1) are not physically attractive, (2) are musical, (3) combine religious fervor with superstitious beliefs, (4) are required to select life goals that benefit African American people, and (5) are dependent upon white people for whatever good things they could hope to acquire. Broderick concluded that in the 140-year period she studied, African American children would find little in literature to enhance pride in their heritage and that if these books were children's only contacts with African American people, white children would develop a sense of superiority. Likewise, Beryle Banfield (1985) discovered numerous negative stereotypes found in pre-Civil War literature. In 1985, author Eloise Greenfield presented a harsh evaluation of authors who still perpetuate racism and stereotypes in literature.

One of the issues frequently discussed by literature scholars is the changing attitudes toward the writings of Mark Twain (Samuel Clemens), especially *The Adventures of Huckleberry Finn*. In the 1800s, Twain was accused of going too far in advancing the cause of human equality and justice. In the 1980s and 1990s, *The Adventures of Huckleberry Finn* has been attacked and frequently censored from school libraries or English reading lists for being racially inflammatory or degrading.

Robert Scott Kellner (1982), a recognized Twain scholar, believes, however, that a "close examination of Twain's writing reveals an element of satire in his seemingly racist language, a satire directed at the reader who would choose to agree with the stereotyped image" (p. 1D).

The debate over the writings of Mark Twain is a continuing issue. You may want to read Twain's writings and search for his viewpoint. You might consider whether it reflects a belief in the inequality of human beings or whether it suggests that people of all races share a common humanity.

Books written for younger children have also been the subject of controversy. For example, in the 1960s, Garth Williams's *The Rabbit's Wedding* was criticized because the illustrations showed the marriage of a black rabbit and a white rabbit. The criticism at the time focused on a belief that there should not be marriages between black and white people.

In contrast, the issues around Helen Bannerman's *Little Black Sambo,* published in 1899, illustrate the changing sensitivities of Americans toward certain social issues. Although the book was popular for many years, eventually many people considered the crudely drawn features of the characters and the story line to be offensive, and the book was taken off many library shelves.

Controversy also surrounds Margot Zemach's 1982 book, *Jake and Honeybunch Go to Heaven*, a traditional tale with a "green pastures" depiction of heaven and African American characters. *The New York Times Book Review* found literary merit in the story. Public school library selection committees in Chicago, San Francisco, and Milwaukee, however, rejected the book for lacking literary merit and/or as containing racial stereotyping. The March 1983 issue of *American Libraries* focused on this controversy, presenting both positive and negative points of view. After reading the book, students of children's literature may decide for themselves if the images presented are positive or negative.

Changing viewpoints also surround Rachel Isadora's *Ben's Trumpet*. On the positive side, the book was awarded the 1980 Caldecott Honor Award. Opal Moore (1985), however, presents a more negative viewpoint by describing stereotypes that she found in the book.

As you read these books and ones like them and the various articles about the issues associated with the books, you may decide if you agree or disagree with the various conclusions.

As you evaluate picture books, consider which books might be controversial and the reasons for the controversy. Does controversy change with the times? What subjects might have caused controversy in picture books published in the 1950s, 1960s, 1970s, or 1980s? Are those subjects still controversial? Are any new areas of controversy developing today? This chapter discusses numerous selections of excellent African American literature that try to avoid stereotypes from the past.

There have been considerable changes in the availability of and the quality of multicultural literature since Nancy Larrick's article, "The All-White World of Children's Books" (1965). This article had considerable impact because Larrick's research disclosed that there was a lack of books about minorities and that stereotypes were found in the few available books. Many changes in U.S. social life and literature have occurred since then. This is especially true when evaluating the current availability and quality of African American literature.

By 1993, Hazel Rochman stated, "African American literature is flourishing. There is no way all the good titles—adult and young adult, fiction and nonfiction—could be included on any resource list. Autobiography, poetry, and historical fiction are especially rich genres here. There is also an increasing complexity in contemporary YA (young adult) stories, which reach beyond simple role models to confront issues of color, class, prejudice, and identity without offering Band-Aids of self-esteem" (p. 161).

As we progress through our study of African and African American literature, we will discover that there are also many excellent books written for children. Picture storybooks include all of the genres of literature from folklore through contemporary realistic fiction and nonfiction. Books written for slightly older readers include folklore, historical fiction, poetry, biography, and informational books.

Authors and Illustrators Who Write About the African American Culture and Experience

The quality of contemporary African American literature is reflected in the lists of books that have won Newbery Medals or Honor Awards and Caldecott Medal or Honor Awards. On these lists are African American authors and illustrators as well as non–African American authors and illustrators who write about the African or African American culture and experience.

A sampling of these books in recent years shows the availability of quality literature. For example, the 1997 Newbery Honor Awards include Nancy Farmer's *A Girl Named Disaster*. The 1996 Newbery Honor Awards include Christopher Paul Curtis's *The Watsons Go to Birmingham—1963* and Carol Fenner's *Yolonda's Genius*. The 1993 Newbery Honor Awards include Patricia McKissack's *The Dark-Thirty: Southern Tales of the Supernatural* and Walter Dean Myers's *Somewhere in the Darkness*. The 1989 Newbery Honor Awards include Virginia Hamilton's *In the Beginning: Creation Stories from Around the World* (the text includes stories from Africa) and Walter Dean Myers's *Scorpions*. The 2000 Newbery Award book is Christopher Paul Curtis's *Bud, Not Buddy*.

A sampling of the previous few years for the Caldecott Medal and Honor Awards includes 1998 Caldecott Honors for Christopher Myers's illustrations for Walter Dean Myers's *Harlem;* 1995 Caldecott Honors for Jerry Pinkney's illustrations for Julius Lester's *John Henry*; 1993 Caldecott Honors for Carol Byard's illustrations for Sherley Anne Williams's *Working Cotton*; 1990 Caldecott Honors for Jerry Pinkney's illustrations for Robert D. San Souci's *The Talking Eggs*; and 1989 Caldecott Honors for Jerry Pinkney's illustrations for Patricia McKissack's *Mirandy and Brother Wind*.

Since 1970, students may choose to read books that have won the Coretta Scott King Award. The award is made to one African American author and one African American illustrator for outstandingly inspirational contributions to children's literature.

Harlem

a poem by
Walter Dean Myers

pictures by
Christopher Myers

This book is a poem about growing up in Harlem.

Ilustration by Christopher Myers from *HARLEM: A POEM* by Walter Dean Myers. Published by Scholastic Press, a division of Scholastic Inc. Illustration copyright © 1997 by Christopher Myers. Reprinted by permission.

In her article "Writing for Children—A Joy and a Responsibility," African American author Eloise Greenfield (1985) provides an excellent introduction to the selection and evaluation of African American literature. Greenfield emphasizes the need for both literary merit and cultural authenticity when she states:

> The books that reach children should: authentically depict and interpret their lives and their history; build self-respect and encourage the development of positive values; make children aware of their strength and leave them with a sense of hope and direction; teach them the skills necessary for the maintenance of health and for economic survival; broaden their knowledge of the world, past and present, and offer some insight into the future. These books will not be pap—the total range of human problems, struggles and accomplishments can be told in this context with no sacrifice of literary merit. (p. 21)

Authors who make powerful statements communicate their ideas through the artistic and skillful use of language.

Accuracy and authenticity are emphasized as important selection criteria by the authors of *Multicultural Literature for Children and Young Adults* (Kruse, Horning, and Schliesman, 1997), a volume published by the Cooperative Children's Book Center of the University of Wisconsin. They state:

> We carefully considered books that were written or illustrated by people of color; we also looked carefully at books written or illustrated by individuals whose racial backgrounds are outside those of the experiences depicted in their books. We paid careful attention to issues of accuracy and authenticity, often seeking the opinions of content specialists when we were unsure about a certain historical or cultural matter, as well as listening to colleagues who pointed out significant features or cultural values that we, as outsiders, would otherwise have missed. (p. 2)

Johnson and Smith (1993) emphasize the importance of considering both the literary quality and the values and perspectives conveyed by the books. They believe that questions of literary quality should be "examined with a particular focus on the importance of authenticity in multicultural fiction" (p. 47). Consequently, when selecting books, they ask questions such as these: Does the book succeed in arousing my emotions?, Is the book well written?, Is the book meaningful?, and Have we examined the impact of stereotypes, if any, on the readers?

In addition to these questions concerning literary quality and personal responses, you may wish to consider the following criteria when evaluating the illustrations in picture books:

1. Are the illustrations authentic for both the time period and the geographical locations? Are the settings authentic so that readers can recognize the settings as rural, suburban, or urban?
2. Do the characters look natural?
3. Are the characters shown as individual people with characteristics in their own right?
4. Do the illustrations perpetuate stereotypes?
5. Do the illustrations across the books in a collection help the reader visualize the variety of socioeconomic backgrounds, educational levels, and occupations that are possible for African American characters?

The following provide additional evaluative criteria you may consider when evaluating the text in African American literature:

1. If dialect is used, does the dialect have a legitimate purpose and does it ring true?
2. Are social issues and problems depicted frankly, accurately, and without oversimplification?
3. Are the factual and historical details accurate? Does the book appear to be authentic for the culture?
4. Does the author accurately describe any contemporary settings and conflicts?
5. Does the author avoid offensive vocabulary?
6. Does the book reflect an awareness of the changing status of females within African American culture?

These evaluative criteria will be useful through the study of all of the genres of literature: traditional literature, historical fiction and nonfiction, contemporary realistic fiction, biography and autobiography, and poetry.

My own university students have selected some of their favorite illustrated texts, which they believe enhance an understanding of the African and African American cultures. In addition to the already listed Caldecott books, the students identified Leo and Diane Dillon's illustrations for Margaret Musgrove's *Ashanti to Zulu: African Traditions;* Tom Feelings' illustrations for Muriel Feelings's *Mojo Means One: Swahili Counting Book* and *Jambo Means Hello: Swahili Alphabet Book;* Gail Haley's illustrations for *A Story, A Story: An African Tale;* Ann Grifalconi's illustrations for *The Village of Round and Square Houses;* Molly Bang's illustrations for *Ten, Nine, Eight;* Jerry Pinkney's illustrations for Valerie Flournoy's *The Patchwork Quilt;* and John Steptoe's illustrations for *Mufaro's Beautiful Daughters: An African Tale* and *Stevie.* As we proceed through this chapter, we will discover many additional books that enhance an understanding of the culture. You may choose to develop your own lists of favorite literature.

TRADITIONAL LITERATURE

The traditional literature collected from the African continent and from the southern parts of the United States form the basis for many popular books. Some of these books provide highly illustrated versions of one tale, while others are anthologies in which authors retell numerous stories. In this section, we will consider the history of the recording of African folklore in writing, the types of stories that might be found in specific regions, the literary characteristics of the stories, and examples of folklore collected from African and African American sources.

History of Recording of African Folklore

Africa has a long and rich history of oral literature. In 1828, the first known collection of African tales was published for European audiences. This collection, *Fables Sénégalaises Recueillies de l'Oulof*, was translated into French by le Bon Roger, the French commandant of Senegal. More collections appeared as administrators, traders, and missionaries gathered and recorded traditional African stories for various purposes. A brief review of these purposes shows how important an understanding of folklore is for understanding people. Daniel Crowley (1979) states: "Linguists collected tales as samples of language usage, teachers as a means of inculcating local languages, missionaries to study local values and beliefs, African elites in pursuit of vindication against colonialism, diffusionists in the search of distribution patterns on which to base migration theories, litterateurs and journalists looking for 'authentic' themes. . . . " (p. 11).

Roger D. Abrahams (1983) warns, however, that early collections may not have been totally accurate: "There are well over a thousand major collections, most of these made by missionaries and colonial officials around the turn of the century. They often reflect the bias of such reporters, but recently, more 'objective' tellings have become available through the reports of anthropologists and folklorists" (p. xiv).

The collection of authentic folklore and artistic representations by ancient peoples is considered so important that Leo Frobenius and Douglas Fox (1983) state in the introduction to *African Genesis*: "Every fact, object, and belief which can help us to understanding the growth of human culture should be recorded and indexed for use. . . . We will find that there are peoples of whom we do not know enough, and so it will be necessary to send out expeditions to find and gather the material we lack" (p. 16). There are currently expeditions whose objective is to gather the oral stories and traditions of specific groups. For example, Kioi wa Mbugua's *Ink-ishu: Myths and Legends of the Maasai* (1994) is a result of an expedition with a team from OXFAM International who work with the Masai people of the Narok district (the Masai live in Kenya and Tanzania).

Knowledge about the original sources or means of collecting the stories is important to readers, especially useful for students of literature. When writing for adults, many collectors of the African folklore explain how they collected their stories, reveal their original sources, discuss problems they encountered in regard to translations, and provide reasons for any editing or changes made within the stories. Unfortunately, many retellers of African folktales for children do not provide this information. As we discuss the folklore collections and the highly illustrated individual stories, we will highlight the retellers' notes or any other information that allows readers to analyze and evaluate the authenticity of the retellings.

Types of Stories from Specific Regions

Africa is a huge continent with folklore that reflects not only the geography but the religions of the various peoples who live on the continent. As you read the stories from various African countries and their people you may look for some of the following types of stories. For example, if you are reading the tales from the various countries of West Africa, you may discover Hausa tales that reveal a Muslim influence; Yoruba tales that develop a rich mythology; and Ashanti tales that tell about the great trickster, Anansi the Spider. The Hausas tell about Spider or Jackal, and the Yoruba have Ajapa the Tortoise. The tales of southern Africa include marvels or Marchen. The human or animal tricksters may be called "Little Weasel" or "Little Hare." The Hottentots tell about Jackal.

The stories from Central Africa include tales about animals, stories about hunting and adventures in the bush. These stories may tell about greedy adults and unfaithful wives. Tshikashi Tsikulu is an old woman with strange powers who lives in the forest. The tricksters of Central Africa include Hare and Tortoise. Many of the stories from East Africa reflect Muslim influence especially the Swahili tales. Here are animal and trickster stories about Hare and Spider. There are also tales that show the influence of folktales from the Middle East and Europe.

Stories from the West Indies demonstrate the merging of European and African folklore. The story characters include trickster characters that are similar to the African Hare and the African Anansi. Stories collected from the United States show the interaction of the Plantation South and African culture. There are many animal stories and trickster tales. Sometimes Spider, Tortoise, or Hare merges into the cunning Brer Rabbit. There are also human trickster characters like the slave John who outwits Old Massa. Another character is John Henry, who characterizes the strength and beliefs of the African people. Many stories from the U.S. South reveal the slaves' passion to be free; consequently, there are stories that tell about "flying" to freedom.

Many of the African tales tell how the natural or tribal worlds began. These tales are explanatory tales that include both myths and *pourquoi* ("why") tales. Such tales reflect a deep interest in both the natural and supernatural. They tell how life began, how various tribes came to be, and how animals acquired certain characteristics. Most of the stories reveal various values, beliefs, and cultural patterns. Some of the stories focus on societal problems and suggest solutions. Dilemma tales are very popular for helping listeners reach solutions that reflect both acceptable moral and social behaviors.

Literary Characteristics of the Folklore

The art of storytelling, the role of the storyteller, and the participation of the audience are very important in African folklore and influence the literary characteristics of the tales. The original traditional settings in which the stories were told involved singing, acting, using a variety of voices, and audience participation in a way in which the audience and the speaker were intimately intertwined.

In forewords and authors' notes, many retellers of African folklore emphasize the importance of singing, acting, and audience participation as part of the stories that they are retelling. For example, Michael Rosen (1992) states that in Uganda "myths were told in song and dance by the elders as the tribe gathered around a fire" (p. 47). In the foreword of Geraldine Elliott's *The Long Grass Whispers* (1939), we learn that "at night the people gather round the flickering fire, within the dark circle of the hut, to hear the grandmother, as she leans against the hut pole, telling how the animals live and talk. Her imagination and her personality illuminate the ancient stories with her own turns and phrases. The story is the same, but its telling is ever changing" (p. vii).

In *Tales from the Story Hat*, Verna Aardema (1960) states that in addition to the old women of the tribes who have told stories to children, "there have been professional storytellers who have gone from place to place telling their tales and gathering new ones. They were the first historians and the first literary members of the tribe, and it was they who preserved and handed down the traditions" (p. 7).

Many of the African folktales include formulaic openings and closings. According to Jack Berry (1961), when a group in West Africa prepares for storytelling each storyteller begins a tale with an opening formula that serves to announce that a tale is about to be told, and the audience follows with a response. Such a story opener and audience response is presented by Philip Noss (1972), who relates the following common story starter from *Cameroon*:

> Storyteller: Listen to a tale! Listen to a tale!
> Audience: A tale for fun, for fun. Your throat is a gong, your body a locust; bring it here for me to roast!
> Storyteller: Children, listen to a tale, a tale for fun, for fun.

Rute Larungu's *Myths and Legends from Ghana* (1992) includes examples of both story openings and closing formulae. For example, "The Coming of the Golden Stool," opens with the following:

> "Let the voice of the drums stop talking;
> let them now be silent.
> Draw near and listen to my story, O my people;
> but you, O Sasabonsam, and all you evil spirits, stay away!
> You cannot come to touch me nor harm me
> for the words of my mouth:
> for hear! I say,
> 'I do not really mean, I do not really mean.'" (p. 51)

The closing of the story includes:

> "This is my story, which I have told you, if it be sweet, or if it be not sweet,
> take some with you and let some come back to me." (p. 61)

Just as African folklore may include specific types of openings and endings, the tales include other interesting linguistic styles. As might be expected from the oral tradition of the tales, the tales have a storytelling style that can be characterized as a lively mixture of mimicking dialogue, body action, audience participation, and rhythm. Storytellers mimic the sounds of animals, change their voices to characterize both animal and human characters, imitate dialogue between characters, and encourage their listeners to interact with the story. Consequently, the most effective stories have strong oral language patterns.

Verna Aardema (1994) describes the linguistic style of both the stories and the storytellers: "The African storyteller performs a story as if it were a play, taking all parts himself. He imitates the cries of the animals and gives each character a different voice. Also, he involves his listeners—eliciting clapping and noises, and letting them chime in on repeated refrains" (p. v Introduction).

By studying the various stories in Aardema's *Misoso: Once upon a Time Tales from Africa,* readers can discover many of the linguistic styles that are characteristic of the folklore. Many of the stories use repetitive words that are used to imitate sounds in nature. For example, the antelope coughs "kaa, kaa, kaa," the animals laugh "gug, gug, gug," the leopard binds the fly "kpong, kpong, kpong," and the banana hurries off "tuk-pik, tuk-pik, tuk-pik." Repetitive refrains are also found in many of the tales. These repetitive and sometimes cumulative refrains give the listeners ample opportunities to participate in the storytelling experience. For example, the tale "Half-A-Ball-Of-Kenki" includes the following repetitive refrain:

> It's I, the fly, tied
> By Leopard to this tree,
> Because the girls hated him,
> But they loved me.
> Please come here and set me free. (p. 28)

This refrain is repeated three times within the story. The repetitive language, the mimicking dialogue, and the strong rhythm found within the stories make them popular choices for sharing with children.

Notice how Ashley Bryan's introduction to "Ma Sheep Thunder and Son Ram Lightning," found in his retelling of Nigerian tales in *The Story of Lightning and Thunder,* reflects the oral storytelling style and a rich language tradition: "A long time ago, I mean a long, long time ago, if you wanted to pat Lightning or chat with Thunder, you could do it. Uh-huh, you could . . . "

By reading or listening to the language in the folklore, students of children's literature discover one of the important values reflected in the folklore: language and oral storytelling are important. As you read various examples of the folklore, select some of your favorite tales for oral retellings and practice them so that the stories sound authentic.

Examples of African Folklore

The examples in this section include folktales, legends, and myths. As we discuss the folklore, we will consider the motifs found in the tales, the values and beliefs reflected in the tales, and the literary characteristics of the tales. In addition, we will consider the importance of variant and incorporated tales that reflect the impact of other cultures on the content of the tales.

Folktales   The introduction to Kioi wa Mbugua's *Inkishu: Myths and Legends of the Maasai* (1994) emphasizes the importance of folktales in the cultural heritage of the people: "Traditionally, Maasai children are taught community customs, social values and history through stories. Like the fairy tales of Europe, the characters of giants, greedy animals and fierce warriors in Maasai literature serve to warn, prepare, and amuse children for their adult life to come" (foreword).

African folktales frequently explore societal problems and provide possible solutions to these problems. The stories may include a moral or a human truth that is taught through the story. The moral and social values reflected in the tales are emphasized by Mabel H. Ross and Barbara K. Walker (1979): "The measure of a narrator's skill is indicated in the degree to which he can leave with the listener a valid key to acceptable moral and social behavior, a guide to the making of a responsible choice, within the framework of his own culture" (p. 236). For example, Verna Aardema's *Bringing the Rain to Kapiti Plain: A Nandi Tale* shows that individuals have obligations for the betterment of the people, the environment, and the animals that provide their welfare. Ashley Bryan's "The Husband Who Counted the Spoonfuls," found in *Beat the Story-Drum, Pum-Pum*, develops a need for stability in marital relationships.

Ann Grifalconi's *The Village of Round and Square Houses* reveals how a social custom began. In this case, a volcanic eruption in the distant past leaves only two houses within the village: one round and one square. To meet the needs of the village, the women and children move into the round house while the men stay in the square house. According to the tale, the custom continues today because people "live together peacefully here—Because each one has a place to be apart, and a time to be together. . . . And that is how our way came about and will continue—Til Naka speaks again!" (unnumbered).

As you read collections of African folktales for children, notice how most of the values and beliefs identified by Ross and Walker in their adult collection are also found in folktales published for children: the importance of maintaining friendship, a need for family loyalty, the desirability of genuine hospitality, a strict code for ownership and borrowing, gratitude for help rendered, high risk in excessive pride, care for the feelings of those in authority, respect for individuality, appropriate awe of the supernatural, and the use of wit and trickery in the face of unequal relationships.

One of the ways that the folktales show the importance of the values and beliefs is through reward and punishment. Individuals who adhere to the values and beliefs of the culture are frequently rewarded, while individuals who reject the values and beliefs are usually punished.

An Ethiopian woman learns a strong lesson in how to treat others in Nancy Raines Day's *The Lion's Whiskers: An Ethiopian Folktale*. When a stepmother is met by the rejection of her stepson, she seeks advice from the medicine man. When he tells her that the magic potion that she desires requires three whiskers from a lion, she gradually tames the lion and eventually acquires the whiskers. Now the medicine man tells her that she does not need the magic potion because she should, "Approach your stepson as you did the lion, and you will win his love." The advice succeeds and there is a happy ending for a stepmother story.

African folktales are filled with stories of trickster characters. In many of these stories, wit and trickery are acceptable responses when the relationships among animals or people are unequal. For example, Verna Aardema's *Who's in Rabbit's House?* is a humorous Masai tale about tricky animals. This tale, written in play form and performed by villagers for the townsfolk, explains how Caterpillar, who is smaller, slower, and weaker than any of the other animals (including Rabbit, Jackal,

Leopard, Elephant, and Rhinoceros) must use wit and trickery to correct the imbalance. Repetition of words is part of the vivid descriptive language. The descriptions and dialogues among the animals suggest the richness of the African language. The jackal trots off "kpata, kpata," the leopard jumps "pa, pa, pa," and the frog laughs "dgung, dgung, dgung."

Wit and trickery are also appropriate actions in Gerald McDermott's retelling of *Zomo the Rabbit: A Trickster Tale from West Africa*. McDermott describes Zomo in this way:

> He is not big
> He is not strong
> But he is very clever. (p. 1, unnumbered)

In this tale, Zomo approaches Sky God because he wants more than cleverness—he wants wisdom. To acquire wisdom, however, he must earn it by bringing Sky God three items: the scales of Big Fish, the milk of Wild Cow, and the tooth of Leopard. Zomo is able to acquire these items through his wit and trickery. Consequently, Sky God tells him: "Three things in this world are worth having: courage, good sense, and caution. Little rabbit, you have lots of courage, a bit of sense, but no caution. So next time you see Big Fish, or Wild Cow, or Leopard . . . better run fast!" (p. 26, unnumbered). This is an example of a folktale in which the advice given by Sky God reflects the beliefs and values of the people. It is also an example of a tale in which a ruler gives an impossible request; consequently, wit and trickery are the only means for succeeding.

Another type of tale that is very common in African folklore is the *pourquoi* or "why" tale. *Pourquoi* tales answer a question or explain why animals, plants, or humans have certain characteristics. For example, Verna Aardema's *How the Ostrich Got Its Long Neck* is a *pourquoi* tale from Kenya. In it, a foolish ostrich tries to pull an offending tooth from a crocodile's mouth. Crocodile chomps down on Ostrich's neck to begin to eat it, and Ostrich's neck gets stretched during the animal's efforts to escape.

Two tales in Ashley Bryan's *Beat the Story-Drum, Pum-Pum* explain animal characteristics. "How Animals Got Their Tails" reveals not only how animals received their individual tails but also why there is animosity between rabbits and foxes. "Why Bush Cow and Elephant Are Bad Friends" reveals why animals fight in the bush. Verna Aardema's *Why Mosquitoes Buzz in People's Ears* explains why mosquitoes are noisy. The conclusion of *pourquoi* stories frequently depicts both a why explanation and a moral.

In addition to animal characteristics, African *pourquoi* tales may explain natural phenomena or the origin of human characteristics. Mary-Joan Gerson's *Why the Sky Is Far Away: A Nigerian Folktale* explains not only why the sky is far away but also why people have to plow the fields and hunt in the forests rather than take food from the sky. The story contains the theme that people will be punished if they waste resources and take more than they need to satisfy hunger. As you read the folktales from Africa, develop your own list of important themes and values found in the tales.

Legends   By reading legends, we discover the heroes of a culture and the characteristics that are considered important in leaders. Legends, although they may be exaggerated, are usually written about people who really lived in the historic past.

David Wisniewski's *Sundiata: Lion King of Mali* is such a legend, telling the story of a ruler who lived in the late 1200s. The tale begins in this fashion: "Listen to me, children of the Bright Country, and hear the great deeds of ages past. The words I speak are those of my father and his father before him, pure and full of truth. . . . " (p. 1, unnumbered). Sundiata's courage and leadership are especially valued in this tale. In addition, when he is returned to the throne, he tells his people that from that time on, no one shall interfere with another's destiny.

In endnotes, Wisniewski (1992) provides information about the source of this tale:

> The story of Sundiata has reached modern ears through the unbroken oral tradition provided by griots [storytellers]. Many African ethnic groups rely on the prodigious memories of these people, rather than written accounts, to preserve the history and wisdom of the past. This version of the Sundiata epic is distilled from the words of Djeli Mamoudou Kouyata, a griot of the Keita clan, in *Sundiata: An Epic of Old Mali*, a compilation written by Djibril Tamsir Niana and translated from the original Malinke by G. D. Pickett (London, 1965)." (endnote)

Notice in this endnote that Wisniewski presents enough source information that a reader could obtain the original source and compare the two versions.

Myths   Virginia Hamilton's *In the Beginning: Creation Stories from Around the World* includes several myths from Africa. In each of the myths, Hamilton provides information on places the myths were told and gives interpretations that improve readers' understanding. For example, in "Man Copies God: Nyambi the Creator" Hamilton informs readers that the myth is from the Lozi people of Zambia. She classifies the myth as a Divine Myth because in this type of myth, god is simply there and creates earth and all that is human. This tale is also an explanatory story that reveals such concerns as why god is separated from man. Spider plays an important role in the myth as it is through his web, or thread to the sky, that the God Nyambi is able to live away from humans and find peace in the sky.

The importance of Spider as part of mythology is also developed by Hamilton in "Spider Ananse Finds Something: Wulbari the Creator." In this tale, Spider Ananse is the captain of God Wulbari's court. He is also the boastful trickster character of folktale fame. The tale is an explanatory tale as it reveals how sun, moon, and darkness came to the earth and explains how blindness came to some humans.

"The Origin of Death" from *African Folktales and Sculpture* by Paul Radin (1952) includes influences of white people. The white person in it is referred to as a giant. The African must request food from the giant who demands a season of labor in return for the food given. This giant is also a cannibal who consumes the African's family. The giant's influences do not diminish with his death. When the giant is killed by fire, the magic powder at his hair roots brings back to life those who had been eaten. Unfortunately, the powder also revives the giant. Now, when the white man's eye blinks, a man dies.

Virginia Hamilton's *In the Beginning: Creation Stories from Around the World* includes a bibliography of mythology books. Several of these sources are from African mythology. For example, Hamilton recommends sources such as D. Arnott's *African Myths and Legends Retold* (1962), Ulli Beier's *The Origin of Life and Death: African Creation Myths* (1966), Susan Feldman's *African Myths and Tales* (1963), Geoffrey Parrinder's *African Mythology: Library of the World's Myths and Legends* (1986) and Paul Radin's *African Folktales* (1952).

Many more examples of African folklore could be added to this discussion. In summary, we have discovered that there are both commonalties and differences among folktales from different regions of Africa. The folktales are characterized by an oral storytelling style that encourages interactions with the audience. Stylistic elements in the folktales include story openings and story closings, as well as repetitive language. Many of the folktales, legends, and myths develop strong moral values and suggest the cultural values of the people.

Richard A. Waterman and William R. Bascom (Leach, 1972) provide an interesting conclusion to the discussion of African folklore and to the importance of the folklore. They state:

> [F]olklore is important in the process of transmitting culture through the education of the individual. Myths, legends, and secret formulae may be a part of the instructions given by a parent to a child or by a priest or chief to an initiate, while other forms of folklore may be learned informally in social situations not specifically directed toward education. Riddles, which are regarded as sharpening a child's wits, also teach lessons which must eventually be learned. In addition to the characteristics of animals, human beings, and other natural objects, they may refer to social distinctions and social etiquette. (p. 23)

Waterman and Bascom also present the sequence of folklore that might be used during the educational process of Chaga children. They state:

> Stories about monsters are told to the youngest children, with implied threats to those who misbehave. Later, these are gradually replaced by moral tales which indicate such attitudes as diligence and filial piety, and show the consequences of laziness, snobbishness, and rebelliousness. When the Chaga child reaches fourteen, folktales and riddles give way to proverbs. These are employed by parents to epitomize a lesson which they wish to teach their children, and they appear as a didactic device in the instructions given to Chaga boys during the initiation ceremonies. (p. 23)

African American Folklore

African American folklore includes many similarities to the folklore collected from Africa. For example, there are similar storytelling styles, values and beliefs, characters, and motifs. There are also differences, however, as the stories take on the characteristics of the new settings and situations. Virginia Hamilton (1985) highlights the relationships between the African folklore and the African American experience: "Out of the contacts the plantation slaves made in their new world, combined with memories and habits from the old world of Africa, came a body of folk expression about the slaves and their experiences. The slaves created tales in which various animals . . . took on characteristics of the people found in the new environment of the plantation" (p. x).

For example, the favorite Brer Rabbit was small and apparently helpless when compared with the more powerful bear and fox. However, he was smart, tricky, and clever, and usually won out over larger and stronger animals. The slaves, who identified with the rabbit, told many tales about his exploits.

Hamilton's collection of tales *The People Could Fly: American Black Folktales*, is divided into four parts: (1) animal tales, (2) extravagant and fanciful experiences, (3) supernatural tales, and (4) slave tales of freedom. The collection provides sources for listening, discussing, and comparing. For example, readers can compare the folklore elements, plot, and themes in Hamilton's "The Beautiful Girl of the Moon Tower," a folktale from the Cape Verde Islands, and elements and motifs found in European folktales.

Hamilton's *When Birds Could Talk and Bats Could Sing: The Adventures of Brush Sparrow, Sis Wren, and Their Friends* is a collection of retellings of eight folktales from the southern United States. The tales are written in the form of fables, with each fable ending with a moral. Like the African folktales, these tales are filled with rhyming and singing. Barry Moser's watercolors provide vivid visual characterizations of the animals. In *Her Stories: African American Folktales, Fairy Tales, and True Tales*, Hamilton retells nineteen tales about African American females. As in her other books, Hamilton provides notes on the stories that tell readers where the stories came from, how they traveled to new locations, and how they changed. The acrylic illustrations painted by Leo and Diane Dillon enhance the emotional impact of the tales.

The most famous collection of African American folktales originating in the southern United States are the stories originally collected and retold by Joel Chandler Harris's "Uncle Remus" in the late nineteenth century. Again, that "monstrous clever beast," Brer Rabbit, always survives by using his cunning against stronger enemies. William J. Faulkner's *The Days When the Animals Talked* (1977) presents background information on African American folktales about animals. Faulkner tells how the tales were created and what their significance is in American history.

Two authors, Van Dyke Parks and Julius Lester, have adapted highly acclaimed versions of the Uncle Remus stories originally written down by Joel Chandler Harris. Parks's text and Barry Moser's illustrations for *Jump! The Adventures of Brer Rabbit* and *Jump Again! More Adventures of Brer Rabbit* combine to provide a satisfying reading and visual experience. It is interesting to analyze the animal characters, to consider the social impact of slavery as depicted in the stories, to identify values that are similar to those found in African tales, to compare similar tales found in other cultures or various versions of the Uncle Remus stories, and to consider the impact of the authors' style.

For example, Brer Rabbit is considered a character who can use his head, outdo and outwit all other creatures, and rely on trickery if necessary. In this role, Brer Rabbit uses trickery if he is in conflict with bigger and more powerful characters, but Brer Rabbit also represents what happens when folks are full of conceit and pride. They "are going to get it taken out of them. Brer Rabbit did get caught up with once, and it cooled him right off" (*Jump!*, p. 19). Notice that both of these values are also found in African folklore. In addition, the tales reflect changes caused by the new environment, where the storytellers are influenced by slavery and European colonization and the need to protect their families and the tendency to develop friendships that are tempered with distrust.

Symbolism, onomatopoeia, and personification are essential aspects of Parks's storytelling style. For example, Parks uses symbolic meaning to contrast the length of night and day in *Jump!*: "When the nights were long and days were short, with plenty of wood on the fire and sweet potatoes in the embers, Brer Rabbit could outdo all the other creatures" (p. 3). Onomatopoeia is used to imitate sounds. Brer Rabbit relies on his "lippity-clip and his blickety-blick" (p. 3). Personification is found in descriptions of nature: "Way back yonder when the moon was lots bigger than he is now . . . " (p. 3).

By analyzing the various Brer Rabbit stories, you may make comparisons within and across cultures. For example, you might compare the stories retold in Parks's version with stories retold in Lester's *The Tales of Uncle Remus: The Adventures of Brer Rabbit*, and stories in earlier versions retold by Joel Chandler Harris. Make cross-cultural comparisons by analyzing "Brer Rabbit Finds His Match" (*Jump!*) and the Aesop fable "The Tortoise and the Hare."

Stories such as these Brer Rabbit tales are filled with symbolism and suggested meanings. For example, in *The Adventures of High John the Conqueror*, Steve Sanfield states:

> The slaves often told stories about Brer Rabbit, about how, through his cunning and his tricks, he would overcome all the might and power and meanness of Brer Fox and Brer Bear and Brer Wolf. Whites would hear those stories and think, "Oh, isn't that cute, little Brer Rabbit fooling big Brer Bear." But when the slaves told and heard them, they heard them differently. They saw themselves as Brer Rabbit and the slaveholders as Brer Wolf and Brer Fox, and the only way to defeat all that power and brute force was to be just a little bit more clever. (p. 5)

There are distinct oral storytelling styles in African American folktales. Current retellers of these tales frequently mention the influence of storytellers in their own youth. For example, Patricia McKissack introduces *Flossie and the Fox* by telling readers: "Here is a story from my youth, retold in the same rich and colorful language that was my grandfather's. He began all his yarns with questions. 'Did I ever tell you 'bout the time lil' Flossie Finley come out the Piney Woods heeling a fox?' I'd snuggle up beside him in the big porch swing, then he'd begin his tale. . . . " (author's note, unnumbered). As you read various African American tales, look for, compare, and analyze the influence of the storyteller's style in the selections.

Robert D. San Souci's *The Talking Eggs* is adapted from a Creole folktale collected in Louisiana. The tale shows that kindness is a respected value, while greed is not rewarded. William H. Hooks's *The Ballad of Belle Dorcas* is a tale set in the tidewater section of the Carolinas during the time of slavery. The protagonists are a freeborn woman and a slave who fall in love, but they are threatened with separation when the master wishes to sell the slave. In addition to showing the consequences of social injustice, the tale reveals the power of love and belief in the magical ability of the spells created by conjurers. Robert D. San Souci's *Sukey and the Mermaid*, collected from the Sea Islands off South Carolina's coast, is a melding of the story elements from West Africa and the Caribbean.

Robert D. San Souci's *The Faithful Friend* is set on the island of Martinique. The tale develops the values of friendship and sacrifice and includes a belief in supernatural beings. The author's note provides considerable information about the roots of the story and compares it with "Faithful John," a story retold by the Brothers Grimm.

Supernatural events are found in many of the folktales. Mary E. Lyons's *Raw Head, Bloody Bones: African-American Tales of the Supernatural* is a collection of stories about goblins, ghosts, monsters, and superhumans from the United States and the Caribbean countries. The author's introduction, notes, bibliography, and suggested readings provide useful information. Patricia McKissack's *The Dark-Thirty: Southern Tales of the Supernatural* is a collection of original tales that are rooted in African American history and the oral storytelling tradition. Lynn Joseph's *A Wave in Her Pocket: Stories from Trinidad* is a collection of stories, some of which originated in West Africa, some in Trinidad, and some in the author's imagination. You can compare the three books for the storytelling styles and subjects.

Robert D. San Souci's *The Hired Hand* is a folktale in which the following values and beliefs are clearly indicated: the value of hard work and the consequences of laziness; the need to show respect for one's fellow man; the consequences of

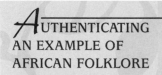

AUTHENTICATING AN EXAMPLE OF AFRICAN FOLKLORE

If enough information is provided, both the text and pictures of highly illustrated versions of folktales may be authenticated. For example, John Steptoe provides source notes that identify the original source, the culture, and the geographical location for *Mufaro's Beautiful Daughters: An African Tale*. He states:

> *Mufaro's Beautiful Daughters* was inspired by a story collected by G. M. Theal and published in 1895 in his book, *Kaffir Folktales*. The tale was collected from people living near the Zimbabwe ruins, a site that archaeologists now consider to have been a magnificent trade city built and occupied by indigenous Africans. Details in the illustrations for *Mufaro's Beautiful Daughters* are based on the architecture of the ruins and on the flora and fauna of the Zimbabwe region. (unnumbered back cover)

In addition, the author provides information about the names of the characters and scholars who provided assistance:

> The names of the characters are from the Shona language: Mufaro (moo-FAR-oh) means "happy man;" Nyasha (nee-AH-sha) means "mercy;" Manyara (mahn-YAR-ah) means "ashamed;" and Nyoka (nee-YO-kah) means "snake." The author wishes to thank Niamani Mutima and Ona Kwanele, of the Afro-American Institute, and Jill Penfold, of the Zimbabwe Mission, for their helpful assistance in the research of this book. (unnumbered dedication page)

Although Steptoe does not state whether or not he changed the text in his adaptation, he does provide enough information for literature students to authenticate the text by comparing it with the original source and to authenticate the illustrations by searching for sources that describe or illustrate the place and the time in which the story is set. This authentication task was completed by my student Diana Vrooman (1993).

A search for Theal's original source in *Kaffir Folk-lore* (1895, 1970) provides both important background information for understanding the values, the customs, and the beliefs of the people, as well as the text of the original source, "The Story of Five Heads." Theal provides the following background information that may also be used to authenticate Steptoe's version and to identify if any important differences are found in values, customs, and beliefs between the original story and Steptoe's adaptation. This background information may also be used to help authenticate the illustrations.

Theal states that each tribe was presided over by a chief, descendants of the ruling house had aristocratic rank, chiefs might have many wives, leopard skins were reserved for chiefs, people lived in villages in hemispherical huts thatched with reeds or grass, people were skilled potters, people lived in an agricultural society in which horned cattle and millet were important, men cared for cattle and women cultivated the ground, a taboo stated that women were not permitted to touch the milksack, people believed that spirits can and do influence their affairs, snakes were highly respected, fathers usually arranged marriages, and bridal processions were formed to escort brides to their new homes.

Comparisons between Theal's "The Story of Five Heads" and Steptoe's *Mufaro's Beautiful Daughters* illustrate both differences and similarities. One of the most obvious differences is in the names of the girls. Theal's Mpunzikazi is changed to Steptoe's Manyara; Theal's Mpunzanyana is changed to Nyasha. Steptoe expands the plot of the story to include Nyasha's tender interactions with the small snake. This addition allows Steptoe to develop the caring, loving nature of Nyasha, as well as show a kinder, gentler personality for the transformed king.

When characterizations are compared, however, both stories suggest that it is the arrogant, impatient sister who disregards customs and beliefs who is eventually punished (death in Theal, servitude in Steptoe). In contrast, it is the sister who honors the ways of her people and abides by tradition who is rewarded. Both Mpunzikazi and Manyara show disrespect for their elders and for the supernatural.

Theal's original version places more emphasis on traditions and taboos. The wedding party seems more important in Theal because the girl who enters the village of the chief without her family is chastised for coming alone. The girl in Theal's version touches a milksack which goes against women's roles in the society and she is dishonored because she cannot grind millet properly. Grinding millet is also one of the major roles of women in the culture.

Steptoe's adaptation places more emphasis on the personal characteristics of the protagonist and antagonist. Steptoe expands the characterizations of the two sisters by emphasizing the consequences of such undesirable characteristics as greed and such desirable characteristics as kindness and generosity. In both stories, it is despised traits found in the two female characters that justify their downfalls. These downfalls are also different. While both characters are either punished or rewarded, the punishment in Theal's version is harsher. The monstrous snake kills the girl, while in Steptoe's version she becomes the servant to her sister, the Queen.

These changes in personal characteristics and plot create different moods for the two folktales. Theal's harsher consequences produce a stronger feeling for the importance of cultural traditions and taboos. Steptoe's gentler version with the kind snake and the transformation of this small snake into the king, creates a "happier-ever-after" mood that is similar to a Cinderella story. Steptoe is writing for American audiences who are accustomed to magical folktales and who might not understand the harsher realities of the original version.

The source notes in Steptoe's *Mufaro's Beautiful Daughters* provide enough information to evaluate the authenticity of the illustrations. Because Steptoe identifies Zimbabwe as the location of the folktale, there are many sources that may be used to authenticate the illustrations. It is interesting to note that photographs taken of architectural sites in this region show almost identical characteristics to those found in the illustrations drawn by Steptoe. Ruins of an actual city in the region, Great Zimbabwe, are shown in photographs accompanying a *National Geographic* article titled "Rhodesia, A House Divided" by Allan C. Fisher (1975). The clay pots illustrated by Steptoe on page 2 (unnumbered) are similar to those shown in photographs in G. C. Thompson's *The Zimbabwe Culture: Ruins and Reactions* (1971). The huts illustrated on page 20 (unnumbered) are similar to the illustrations of mud huts with thatched roofs shown in Patricia Barnes-Svarney's *Places and People of the World: Zimbabwe* (1989). A chevron pattern on the great wall illustrated by Steptoe on page 20 is similar to one found in a photograph in Wilfrid Mallows's *The Mystery of the Great Zimbabwe* (1984). The soapstone birds illustrated by Steptoe on the throne of the king on page 22 (unnumbered) are shown in photographs in Patricia Cheney's *The Land and People of Zimbabwe* (1990). The conical tower shown by Steptoe on page 27 (unnumbered) is shown in a photograph in Richard Worth's *Robert Mugabe of Zimbabwe* (1990) and in a *National Geographic* article "After Rhodesia, A Nation Named Zimbabwe" (1981).

Many additional examples supporting the authenticity of the illustrations are available. Although Steptoe's text has been changed from the original, his illustrations are extremely authentic.

greed, dishonesty, and wastefulness; the power of forgiveness. Notice how the son's plea for forgiveness states the story's primary themes: "Don't be lazy an greedy an' wood-headed. 'Specially don' act high-handed and biggity with no one, 'cause if I didn't act that way to a man who's standin' in this here crowd, I'd be back at the sawmill, 'stead of headin' to a jail cell" (unnumbered).

John Henry, a real person and the great hero of African American folklore, is characterized as a "steel-drivin' man." Julius Lester's *John Henry* begins with the child's unusual birth when "[t]he bears and panthers and moose and deer and rabbits and squirrels and even a unicorn came out of the woods to see him. And instead of the sun tending to his business and going to bed, it was peeping out from behind the moon's skirts trying to get a glimpse of the new baby" (p. 2, unnumbered). The major focus of the text and illustrations is on John Henry's contest with the steam drill. Lester's language is filled with personification and poetic similes. For example, the sun yawns, washes its face, flosses and brushes its teeth, and hurries over the horizon; the wind is out of breath trying to keep up with John Henry. Jerry Pinkney's illustrations enhance the impact of the legendary tall tale. The introduction to the tale provides background information on the legend and lists the sources Lester used in his retelling.

Stories of another folk hero are retold by Steve Sanfield in *The Adventures of High John the Conqueror*. High John is similar to Brer Rabbit because he uses cleverness to outwit his more powerful adversary, the Old Master. The themes in these stories show that people's spirit cannot be taken away even if they are living in the worst conditions. Sanfield's text includes factual information to help readers understand and interpret the tales.

Spirituals provide another source for understanding the values in the African American folktales. Spirituals provide the text to accompany Ashley Bryan's colorful illustrations in John Langstaff's *What a Morning! The Christmas Story in Black Spirituals*. The format of the book includes a colorful illustration and appropriate biblical text followed by the words and music for the accompanying spiritual. Two other sources for spirituals are Bryan's *I'm Going to Sing: Black American Spirituals*, Volume Two, and *All Night, All Day: A Child's First Book of African-American Spirituals*.

 HISTORICAL NONFICTION AND FICTION

Violet J. Harris (1997) identifies two trends in current African American literature that influence both historical nonfiction and fiction, as well as other genres of literature. First, there is a general improvement in the quality and quantity of nonfiction including biographies and autobiographies. Second, there is a willingness of authors to create plots involving controversial topics.

Most of the historical literature, which includes nonfiction informational books, autobiographies and biographies, and historical fiction, focuses on a harsh time in U.S. history during which African Americans experienced slavery or discrimination. The philosophies, values, and beliefs depicted in the folklore, also appear in the historical literature. Here, however, pain and the consequences of prejudice frequently overshadow other concerns.

Authors who write about this period in the early centuries of American history, emphasize a time when white slave traders brought hundreds of thousands of black Africans to this continent in chains and sold them on auction blocks as field workers, house servants, and skilled craftspeople.

Many authors of historical literature focus their attention on conflicts. Authors who produce realistic biographies and create credible plots in historical fiction consider not only the historical events but also the conflicting social attitudes of the times. The themes developed in historical literature reflect a need for personal freedom, ponder the right of one person to own another, and consider the tragedies of both war and slavery. As we discuss the informational books, the biographies, and the historical fiction associated with this time period, we will also discover many of the same values and beliefs that were identified in the African and African American folklore. As you read historical literature, consider both the literary merit of the works and the authenticity of their content.

Informational Books That Develop Historical Perspectives

Some authors who chronicle the African American experience write nonfiction informational books about the forced passage of Africans from Africa to America or focus attention on the experiences of slaves. Informational books such as Milton Meltzer's *The Black Americans: A History in Their Own Words, 1619–1983* help students understand this time period. It includes firsthand accounts from African Americans of the past. This is also an excellent book to read before reading historical fiction such as Paula Fox's *The Slave Dancer*. The excerpt from Meltzer's text, which is titled "I Saw a Slave Ship," describes a slave ship. As you read historical fiction by authors such as Paula Fox, notice how closely descriptions in them match nonfiction descriptions like this one from Meltzer's text:

> The closeness of the place, and the heat of the climate, added to the number in the ship, which was so crowded that each had scarcely room to turn himself, almost suffocated us. This produced copious perspirations, so that the air soon became unfit for respiration, from a variety of loathsome smells, and brought on a sickness among the slaves, of which many died. This wretched situation was again aggravated by the galling of the chains, now become insupportable; and the filth of the necessary tubs into which the children often fell, and were almost suffocated. The shrieks of the women, and the groans of the dying, rendered the whole a scene of horror almost inconceivable. (p. 8)

Colin A. Palmer's *The First Passage: Blacks in the Americas, 1502–1617* provides a historical perspective on slavery that begins on the African continent, tells about the forced movement of slaves to the Americas, discusses the world of slavery, and concludes with an account of slaves' struggle for freedom. The text includes copies of handwritten documents, a chronology of important events, a glossary, a bibliography of further reading, and an index.

Steven Barboza's *Door of No Return: The Legend of Goree Island* presents both a historical and a contemporary view of this island, which was once a holding place for captured Africans who would eventually be sold to slave traders and placed on slave vessels bound for America. Labeled photographs show such structures as the House of Slaves and slave dungeons. A sign above one of the doors reveals the tragic impact of the dungeons and the door of no return: "Innocent child far away from the laugh and cry of your mother." This sign highlights the fact that in some of the slave dungeons, infants were separated from their mothers.

Tom Feelings's *The Middle Passage: White Ships/Black Cargo* is a picture book for older readers. The illustrations convey the pain of the slaves as they cross from Africa to the Americas. The scenes illustrated in the book range from raids on villages to the dungeonlike conditions in slave forts to the ships where treatment of the slaves included beatings and throwing corpses into the ocean.

Raymond Bial's *The Underground Railroad* is an informational book that chronicles the history of the Underground Railroad. Photographs show actual hiding places such as a false-bottomed wagon, a hand-dug tunnel, and homes that were stations on the Underground Railroad. The text also includes a map of the various routes, a chronology of America's antislavery movement, and a listing of additional books. Informational books such as those just described provide sources that may be used to authenticate the content of both biographies and historical fiction.

Biographies and Autobiographies About the Slavery Period

Many authors of nonfiction books choose to tell about this historical period through the biographies of slaves who sought freedom or of abolitionists who too fought hard for individual freedoms. The literature frequently stresses that many people in both the North and the South believed that slavery was immoral; therefore, unable to pass laws against it, they assisted slaves in their flight toward Canada and freedom.

In *Minty: A Story of Young Harriet Tubman*, Alan Schroeder develops a fictionalized account of Harriet Tubman's childhood on a Maryland plantation. The account of her childhood emphasizes the cruel experiences in slavery that caused her to become a leader in the Underground Railroad. Readers may become motivated to research Tubman's life and decide if the fictionalized account is close to the reality of Tubman's life. Jerry Pinkney's watercolors depict the harshness of Tubman's situation. An author's note provides historical background information. Many of the authors who write biographies about the slave experiences highlight conflict and difficulties as they describe the dangers related to helping runaway slaves, especially after the passage of the Fugitive Slave Act in 1850 made it a crime to assist in the escape of a slave.

Ann Petry's *Harriet Tubman: Conductor on the Underground Railroad* is an interesting biography to analyze because it contains many of the values and beliefs identified in the traditional literature as well as authentic historical information about the time period. For example, readers see exemplified in the book traditional values and customs such as storytelling, singing, respect for elders, integrity in family obligations, and family loyalty. Notice in the following quote how Petry develops both the importance of storytelling and the use of oral stories to pass down to children the more terrifying experiences on the slave ships:

> When she (the old woman on the plantation who served as a baby-sitter) was in good humor, she told them stories about what she called the Middle Passage. The mumbling old voice evoked the clank of chains, the horror of thirst, the black smell of death, below deck in the hold of a slave ship. (p. 13)

Notice that this quote also reinforces a vivid language style that encourages listeners to hear, see, and feel the storyteller's experience. One of the motifs that is found in some of the folklore from the Plantation South is the longing to fly in order to escape slavery and to acquire freedom. This motif is also found in Petry's biography.

When analyzing Petry's biography for literary merit, you will discover four types of conflict—all of which are consistent with the time period and the African American experience. For example, person-against-self conflict occurs when Tubman faces the inner problems of whether she should attempt an escape without her husband. Person-against-person conflict occurs when Tubman interacts with slave owners and with her own husband when she discovers that he is willing to betray her if she attempts to escape. Person against nature is indicated when Petry describes the icy rivers, the thick underbrush, and the harsh conditions Tubman overcomes as she escapes. The overwhelming conflict, however, is the person-against-society conflict that she faces as she struggles to change society's attitudes toward slavery.

Petry's biography may be compared with other biographies of Harriet Tubman such as Jeri Ferris's *Go Free or Die: A Story About Harriet Tubman*. The major conflicts in Ferris's biography center on the person against society as Tubman fights to free slaves and combat injustice. The theme developed through the book is that freedom is so important that it is worth risking one's life to gain freedom. A related theme is that we must help others to obtain their freedom. The values developed by the author suggest that people have obligations to family, it is important to use wits to overcome injustice, the use of trickery is necessary to overcome an imbalance, and people must show gratitude for help received from others. The setting is also based on historical facts related to slavery and the Underground Railroad, the 1850 Fugitive Slave Act, and the Emancipation Proclamation. Literary elements, underlying values presented, and accurate integration of historical happenings may be used when analyzing and comparing biographies. Ask, How effectively does each author develop these important elements?

Several biographies for juvenile audiences portray the life of nineteenth-century freedom fighter Frederick Douglass. For example, Lillie Patterson's *Frederick Douglass: Freedom Fighter* gives the reader a dramatic encounter with Douglass's life in slavery, protest against slavery, escape from the slave owners and then slave hunters, work on the Underground Railroad, and championing of the rights of not only black people but also the Chinese, the Irish, and females. Douglas Miller's *Frederick Douglass and the Fight for Freedom* covers similar events, and is interesting for comparative study. Miller, a professor of American history, includes a valuable list of additional readings and discusses some of the problems with previous biographies.

Some biographers use Frederick Douglass's own writings and speeches to portray his life. For example, Michael McCurdy's *Escape from Slavery: The Boyhood of Frederick Douglass in His Own Words* preserves Douglass's original writings. Milton Meltzer's *Frederick Douglass: In His Own Words*, a book for older readers, presents primary-source materials that portray Douglass's beliefs. The text is divided into three chronological sections: Before the War, The War Years, and After the War. Meltzer introduces each of the speeches or writings with a commentary that provides information about the occasion. It is interesting for readers to analyze the emotional impact of Douglass's language and to evaluate his oratorical skills.

Virginia Hamilton's *Anthony Burns: The Defeat and Triumph of a Fugitive Slave* covers the life of a slave who is less well known than Frederick Douglass. However, the escape of Burns to Boston, his arrest, and trial had much impact on the abolitionists and advanced the antislavery movement. Because of the lack of documentation, Hamilton draws from supporting materials to re-create the early life of Burns.

Hamilton uses an interesting technique to help readers understand the early life of Burns. After Burns is captured as a fugitive slave, he goes within himself and remembers his happier childhood days. In the following quotation, Hamilton transfers her character from his unhappy days of imprisonment to his memories: "Anthony was not aware Suttle had gone anywhere, for he had left first and gone deep inside himself, to his childhood. These days seemed endless, perfect. There mornings and waking up were the times he could hardly wait for, he loved them so" (p. 7).

In a later chapter, Hamilton returns to the current world as the innocent child of five slips away and Burns's more painful memories and experiences come to the fore. When Hamilton suggests that the character is having a vision or a dream, she gives credibility to her invented dialogues and happenings. Dreams and visions do not always reflect the exact happenings in a person's life.

Several authors provide shorter accounts of the people who were involved in the fight for freedom from slavery. Virginia Hamilton's *Many Thousand Gone: African Americans from Slavery to Freedom* provides short accounts of people who were involved in this fight. The book is divided into three parts: Slavery in America, Running-Away, and Exodus to Freedom, and it includes a bibliography and an index. Michele Steptoe's *Our Song, Our Toil: The Story of American Slavery As Told by Slaves* is another book that provides short biographies of specific people.

The lives of white abolitionists are also popular subjects for biographers. For example, Jean Fritz's *Harriet Beecher Stowe and the Beecher Preachers* tells about the life of an important abolitionist who also is the author of one of the most influential novels of the time period, *Uncle Tom's Cabin; or, Life Among the Lowly*. Fritz's biography presents a character who fights for both women's rights and the rights of slaves. The biographer describes Stowe's determined personality and unique personal abilities, as well as the challenges she faced. It also highlights her strong desire to provide changes in the laws governing slavery. Readers may follow Stowe's development as an author and her strong need to write a book that would influence the world. Fritz concludes her biography with the importance of Stowe's novel: "Yet in almost any list today of ten books that have changed the world, *Uncle Tom's Cabin* will appear. Harriet Beecher Stowe was a towering figure in her time, and although Lymann Beecher might not have admitted it, she was the best preacher of them all" (p. 131). Fritz includes notes on the text, a bibliography of primary and secondary sources, and an index.

Students of literature may read *Uncle Tom's Cabin* and decide for themselves why the book was so influential. The story first appeared as a serial that ran from June 1851 to April 1852 in *The National Era*, an abolitionist weekly publication. It was published in book form in 1852 by John P. Jewett of Boston. The book became so popular that it was translated into nearly forty languages.

Historical Fiction About the Slavery Period

According to Hazel Rochman (1993), historical fiction is a particularly rich genre in African American literature. Although this genre contains literature of high literary merit, there are particular difficulties for authors who write about slavery, including these: How accurately should historical fiction reflect the attitudes and circumstances of the times? Should authors use terms of the period that are considered insensitive and offensive today? For example, in their authors' note to *Jump Ship to Freedom*, James and Christopher Collier consider use of the word *nigger*. Although the word is considered offensive today, would avoiding it in a novel about slavery distort history? The Colliers chose to use the term in order to illustrate their main character's change in attitude as he develops self-respect and self-confidence and to highlight the social attitudes of the other characters in the book

In *Jump Ship to Freedom*, those who use objectionable language express racial bias toward blacks, and those who do not are concerned with the rights and self-respect of all humans. This historical fiction emphasizes the themes that prejudice and hatred are destructive forces and that people search for freedom.

A slave ship in which human cargo are chained together in cramped quarters provides the setting for Paula Fox's *The Slave Dancer*. The fiction book describes conditions similar to those described in the earlier quote from Meltzer's nonfiction book *The Black Americans: A History in Their Own Words*. Fox's story is told from the point of view of a thirteen-year-old white boy, Jessie, from New Orleans. He is kidnapped by slave traders because they want him to play his fife on their ship. When the ship reaches Africa, Jessie learns about the trade in human "Black Gold" and discovers that African chiefs, in their greed for trade goods, sell their own people, as well as people kidnapped from other tribes. The detailed descriptions of the conditions on the ship are realistic as the protagonist describes the holds as pits of misery, is horrified by the low regard for human life, and is shocked when prisoners who die are thrown overboard without any ceremony.

This book has also stirred much controversy. Some have criticized the fact that the slaves in the book are not treated like human beings or even given names. Many college students, however, say that while reading *The Slave Dancer*, they realized for the first time the true inhumanity of slavery. Fox reveals the impact of the experience on Jessie by having Jessie look back on his experiences after time has passed:

> At the first note of a tune or a song. I would see once again as though they'd never ceased their dancing in my mind, black men and women and children lifting their tormented limbs in time to a reedy martial air, the dust rising from their joyless thumping, the sound of the fife finally drowned beneath the clanging of their chains. (p. 176)

A book written for young children explains the purposes of the Underground Railroad. N. Monjo's *The Drinking Gourd* tells of a family that is part of the Underground Railroad and the role of that family in helping a fugitive slave family escape. Even though this is an easy-to-read book, it develops an important theme, illustrating the importance of one family's contributions in the wider historical movement. The dialogue between father and sons discloses the purpose of the Underground Railroad. Young readers also experience excitement and danger as Tommy accompanies his father and an escaping slave family on the next part of their journey. The book reinforces the theme that moral obligations must be met, and moral sense does not depend on skin color, but on what is inside a person.

Characters such as the slave in Gary Paulsen's *Nightjohn* show both the ordeals experienced by the slaves and the hope and perseverance that allowed them to survive. Even though he is cruelly treated, Nightjohn brings his gifts of teaching reading and writing to the young slave children. Notice in the following quote how the author reveals both Nightjohn's suffering and personal values:

> In the night he come walking. Late in the night and when he walks he leaves the tracks that we find in the soft dirt down where the drive meets the road, in the soft warm dirt in the sun we see his tracks with the middle toe missing on the left foot and the middle toe missing on the right and we know.
>
> We know.
>
> It be Nightjohn.
>
> Late he come walking and nobody else knows, nobody from the big house or the other big houses know but we know.
>
> Late he come walking and it be Nightjohn and he bringing us the way to know. (p. 92)

Literature that shows the slaves' struggle for learning is important according to Cecelia McCall (1989), because "[t]hough the majority of slaves remained illiterate, some defied the prohibitions that decreed education illegal for those who were only three-fifths of a person. The history of learning among African-Americans is as old as their roots in this country and runs parallel to the struggle for freedom" (p. 3). This need for and search for learning is also an important goal for many of the characters in biographies.

Even though Virginia Hamilton's *The House of Dies Drear* is set in contemporary times, she skillfully presents historical information about slavery and the Underground Railroad through the conversations of an African American history professor and his son. Both are interested in the history of the pre–Civil War mansion that the family is about to rent. Hamilton provides details for a setting that seems perfect for the mysterious occurrences that begin soon after the family arrives: "The house of Dies Drear loomed out of mist and murky sky, not only gray and formless, but huge and unnatural. It seemed to crouch on the side of a high hill above the highway. And it had a dark, isolated look about it that set it at odds with all that was living" (p. 26).

The author develops the history of the period as the professor tells his son about the wealthy abolitionist Dies Drear, who built the house and helped many slaves on their way toward freedom. Hamilton hints at the suspense to follow. Thomas learns that Dies Drear and two escaped slaves were murdered and that rumors say the abolitionist and the slaves haunt the old house and the hidden tunnels below. In an interview conducted by Hazel Rochman (1992), Virginia Hamilton discusses her interest in the Underground Railroad and mentions that her grandfather was a fugitive slave who came to Ohio from Virginia. She describes the houses in Ohio that are similar to the one in *The House of Dies Drear*.

Both the biographies and the historical fiction set during times of slavery have strong themes about the importance of freedom. When evaluating the literature, we need to decide if both the settings and conflicts are authentic for the time period. If the story is a biography, the authors have responsibilities for both factual accuracy and telling stories with literary merit. Accurate characterization is especially important for real-life people who lived during these historical time periods. As you read the literature discussed in this section, compare the various authors' abilities to illuminate the time period and to express the emotions that accompanied the conflicts.

 ## AFRICAN AMERICAN POETRY

African American poetry provides a bridge between historical and contemporary literature. Poetry is available that reflects both the historical and contemporary searching for freedom and questing for individual dreams. *Masterpieces of African-American Literature*, edited by Frank N. Magill (1992), provides both a listing of the works of notable African American poets and a discussion of their works. The text includes the following poets, whose writings will be of interest to students studying the works of African American poets: Amiri Baraka, Gwendolyn Brooks, Sterling Brown, Lucille Clifton, Countee Cullen, Owen Dodson, Rita Dove, Paul Laurence Dunbar, Nikki Giovanni, Michael S. Harper, Robert Hawden, George Moses Horton, Langston Hughes, June Jordan, Etheridge Knight, Audre Lorde, Claude McKay, Haki R. Madhubuti, Carolyn M. Rodgers, Sonia Sanchez, Melvin B. Tolson, Alice Walker, Phillis Wheatley, and Jay Wright.

As you read this list of poets, you will notice that several of the poets such as Gwendolyn Brooks, Lucille Clifton, and Nikki Giovanni write for both children and adult audiences. The poetry of other poets such as Langston Hughes is frequently included in children's anthologies of poetry.

Do the following task: Read a selection of the poetry by both adult and children's poets. What subjects and themes are developed in the poetry? Are there differences in the subjects between adult and children's poetry? Are there differences in the poetry between poets who wrote in the 1800s and those who are considered contemporary poets? How would you account for these differences?

The poetry of Langston Hughes is among the most famous of American poetry. Although Hughes is not considered primarily a children's poet, his poetry explores feelings, asks difficult questions, and expresses hopes and desires that are meaningful to readers of any age. Some of his poems—such as "Merry-Go-Round"—can be used to help children understand and identify with the feelings and experiences of African Americans in earlier eras of U.S. history. In another poem, Hughes vividly describes what life would be like without dreams.

Dreams

Hold fast to dreams

For if dreams die

Life is a broken-winged bird

That cannot fly.

Hold fast to dreams

For when dreams go

Life is a barren field

Frozen with snow.

Langston Hughes
The Dream Keeper, 1932

Poetry collections written for younger children frequently emphasize the universal feelings and desires of children. For example, the poems in *Meet Danitra Brown* by Nikki Grimes celebrate friendship. The setting for these poems is the inner city. *In Daddy's Arms I Am Tall: African Americans Celebrating Fatherhood* illustrated by Javaka Steptoe is a collection of poems that honor African American fathers. The poems reflect strong family values and the importance of developing lasting relationships. The collage art is especially appealing.

Several poetry collections have island settings. For example, Lynn Joseph's *Coconut Kind of Day: Island Poems* depicts the sights, experiences, and sounds associated with the Caribbean islands. Poems such as "Pullin' Seine" re-create the actions and rhythms of the workers as they pull in a net full of fish. "Night Songs" captures the sounds of the night as frogs sing "pung-la-la," the midnight manicou cries "shirr-ooo-ooo," and the mongoose goes "rill-dee-dee." Three other poetry books with island settings include *Not a Copper Penny in Me House: Poems from the Caribbean* by Monica Gunning and *Father and Son* by Denize Lauture. Lauture's poetry reflects the traditions of the Gullah people, who live off the coast of South Carolina.

Poetry frequently has close relationships with music. Toyomi Igus's *I See the Rhythm* encourages readers to explore poetry, music, art, and history. Each section in this book traces the history of a different type of African American music. The book gives information on the origin of traditional African griots, as well as on contemporary rap and hip-hop. Each section includes poetic verses about the type of music, lyrics from a representative song, an appropriate painting to depict the era associated with music, and a historical time line for that period. The rhythm of the poetry can be used to teach poetic elements while the time line places the music into a historic perspective.

CONTEMPORARY AFRICAN AMERICAN LITERATURE

Picture Books

Picture books with African and African American themes and content include both concept books and fictional stories.

Several concept books, while focusing on teaching the alphabet and counting, provide information about culture as well. In addition, some alphabet and number books are specifically designed to provide information to older students rather than to teach letter/sound relationships and numbers to younger ones. For example, two award-winning books present information about African life: Margaret Musgrove's *Ashanti to Zulu: African Traditions*, vividly illustrated by Leo and Diane Dillon, depicts the customs of twenty-six African peoples; *Jambo Means Hello: Swahili Alphabet Book*, by Muriel Feelings, introduces Swahili words and customs. Another book by Muriel Feelings, *Moja Means One: Swahili Counting Book*, with illustrations by Tom Feelings, depicts the East African culture. Each two-page spread provides a numeral from one to ten, the Swahili word for the number, a detailed illustration that depicts animal or village life in Africa, and a sentence describing the contents of the illustration. Ifeoma Onyefulu uses colorful photographs to depict both numbers and scenes from Nigeria in *Emeka's Gift: An African Counting Story*. In addition to numbers, Onyefulu provides information on what is depicted in the photographs. The beautiful books just described can encourage children of all cultural backgrounds to learn more about African people.

Some of the books written with an African perspective emphasize the struggle that people experienced in their fight for equality. In *The Day Gogo Went to Vote: South Africa, April 1994*, Elinor Batezat Sisulu creates a strong character in Gobo, Thembi's 100-year-old great-great grandmother. Gogo, who has not left her home in many years, explains to her great-granddaughter why she is going out to vote. The remainder of the book follows the process as the oldest woman in the township goes to vote and as the township celebrates the election of Nelson Mandela.

Rachel Isadora's *At the Crossroads* shows the consequences of segregated townships as the text follows South African children waiting to welcome their fathers, who are returning from working in the mines after being separated from their families for ten months. The text describes, and illustrations show, the loving relationships between fathers and children. On a more mundane level, they also show the shanties in which the families live. Hazel Rochman (1998) expresses the belief that with the end of apartheid and censorship there will be many additional books by and about South Africans.

Many of the picture storybooks written for younger children depict children facing situations and problems that are common to all young children: overcoming jealousy, adjusting to a new baby, expressing a need for attention, experiencing rivalry with siblings, developing personal relationships, and overcoming family problems.

Books for younger children frequently depict warm relationships between children and their mothers or positive interracial experiences. Irene Smalls-Hector's *Jonathan and His Mommy* depicts a mother and her son walking in the neighborhood. On this walk, they try various movements, such as zigzag walking and itsy-bitsy baby steps. Michael Hays's illustrations show the city neighborhood and the people who live there. The actions and the illustrations suggest warm interpersonal relationships.

Rosa Guy's *Billy the Great* develops two universal themes: parents frequently plan the future for their children, even when the children are very young, and developing interracial friendships is frequently easier for the children than for the parents. In a satisfying ending, two boys of different races show the strength of their friendship.

Sharon Bell Mathis depicts warm relationships between young children and elderly people in *The Hundred Penny Box*. In this book, Michael makes friends with his Great-Great-Aunt Dew and learns about the box in which she keeps a penny for every year of her life. "It's my old cracked-up, wacky-dacky box with the top broken," says Michael's Aunt Dew. "Them's my years in that box. . . . That's me in that box." (p. 19). *The Patchwork Quilt*, by Valerie Flournoy, tells the story of a developing relationship between a grandmother and granddaughter. Both books demonstrate the importance of intergenerational love and respect and of shared memories.

Clifton L. Taulbert's *Little Cliff and the Porch People* also describes close intergenerational relationships between a boy, his great-grandparents, and their friends and relatives. Strong characterization allows the author to develop the values of respecting one's elders, praying, practicing traditions, and helping one another. You might compare this book with Jacqueline Woodson's *We Had a Picnic This Sunday Past*. In it, a meal becomes the focal point for expressing cultural values and beliefs concerning families and traditions.

Imagination and desire to win a cakewalk combine to make a girl try to capture the wind as her dancing partner in Patricia McKissack's *Mirandy and Brother Wind*. The background of the story may seem so realistic because the author was influenced by a picture of her grandparents after they won a cakewalk. Imagination also plays a role in Faith Ringgold's *Tar Beach*. The illustrations show a girl lying on the rooftop of her apartment building and flying over Harlem in the late 1930s. Margaree King Mitchell's *Uncle Jed's Barbershop* is set in the 1920s South. The author develops the themes that it is important to make dreams come true and there is great value in perseverance even when the going becomes difficult.

Happy childhood memories form the background for Donald Crews's *Bigmama's,* a story about warm family relationships that increase as the children visit Bigmama's house in Florida. Crews uses the same Florida setting for *Shortcut*. In this story, the children have a frightening experience. On the railroad track that they choose for a shortcut home, they encounter an oncoming train that sounds "WHOO WHOO" and "KLAKITY KLAKITY KLAKITY KLAK" in the night. The story has a happy ending: the children reach the warmth of Bigmama's house and decide that they will not take the shortcut again.

Fiction for Middle-Elementary Grades

Many African American stories written for children in the middle-elementary grades are written by authors—black and white—who are sensitive to the African American experience. Some themes—such as the discovery of oneself, the need to give and receive love, the problems experienced when children realize that the parents whom they love are getting a divorce, and the fears associated with nonachievement in school—are universal and suggest that all children have similar needs, fears, and problems. Other themes, such as searching for one's roots in the African past, speak of a special need by African American children to know about their ancestry.

Virginia Hamilton's *Zeely* is a warm, sensitive story about an imaginative girl named Geeder who makes an important discovery about herself and others when she and her brother spend the summer on their Uncle Ross's farm. After seeing Zeely, her uncle's tall, stately neighbor who resembles a photograph of a Watusi queen, Geeder is convinced that Zeely has royal blood. Geeder is swept up in this fantasy and shares her beliefs with the village children. Her greatest discoveries occur, however, when she realizes that dreaming is fine, but being yourself is even better and that Zeely is indeed a queen, but not like the ones in books, with their servants, kingdoms, and wealth. Zeely is a queen because she understands herself and always does her work better than anybody else.

Another book that explores a character's personal discovery and strength of character is *Sister*, by Eloise Greenfield. Sister, whose real name is Doretha, keeps a journal in which she records the hard times—and the good times that "rainbowed" their way through those harder times. Doretha's memory book helps her realize "I'm me." The words of the school song sung in *Sister* are characteristic of the themes found in this and other books by Greenfield:

> We strong black brothers and sisters
> Working in unity,
> We strong black brothers and sisters,
> Building our community,
> We all work together, learn together
> Live in harmony
> We strong black brothers and sisters
> Building for you and for me. (p. 69)

Fiction for Older Children

Outstanding realistic fiction written for older children incorporates both strong characters and strong themes. The themes in these stories include searching for freedom and dignity, learning to live together, tackling problems personally rather than waiting for someone else to do so, survival of the body and the spirit, and the more humorous problems involved in living through a first crush. Contemporary realistic fiction for older readers frequently focuses on the destructive forces of prejudice.

Christopher Paul Curtis's *The Watsons Go To Birmingham—1963*, a 1996 Newbery Honor book, provides an excellent source for both literary analysis and examination of historic authenticity of a text. It is a book that changes mood at about the halfway point in the story. At the beginning of the book, the author describes a typical African American family, who happen to live and work in Flint, Michigan. The problems of the various characters are typical of those of many families. When they decide to travel to Alabama, the tone of the book changes. Since it is a time of racial tension, person-against-society conflict is the most prominent. The racial conflict is developed early in the story when the mother wants to go from Flint to Birmingham because life is slower in Alabama and the people are friendlier. Dad responds, "'Oh yeah, they're a laugh a minute down there. Let's see, where was that 'Coloreds Only' bathroom downtown'" (p. 5). The culmination of this person-against-society conflict occurs toward the end of the book when a church is bombed and several African American children are killed.

Curtis develops parallels between the person-against-society and person-against-self conflicts. As a ten-year-old, Kenny tries to understand the hatred that could cause such deaths. In addition, he, with the help of his older brother, reaches a point where he releases his personal feelings and begins to cry. At a moment of complete self-understanding, Kenny admits to his brother that he is no longer afraid in the aftermath of the bombing incident; instead, he is ashamed of himself because he ran from the church rather than try to find his sister, who he believed was still inside. His older brother helps him clarify the situation and makes him realize that he has no reason for embarrassment.

The themes in the book also relate to the person-against-society conflict. Through the actions of the various characters, we learn that prejudice and hatred are harmful. The harmful nature of prejudice is revealed when Kenny's brother, Byron, tries to explain the actions of the bombers to Kenny: "I don't think they're sick at all, I think they just let hate eat them up and turn them into monsters" (p. 200). By the end of the story, the boys conclude that the world is not necessarily fair, but they just need to keep going. This ending also relates to an earlier theme developed by the boys' father: growing up is not easy; we all must work to accomplish this task.

In *Bud, Not Buddy,* Curtis wins both the 2000 Newbery Award and the Coretta Scott King Award. Curtis places his ten-year-old protagonist in the setting of the Great Depression of the 1930s. By developing his main character as a mistreated orphan boy, Curtis describes a very dark side of the Depression as Bud experiences waiting in line for food at missions and living with other homeless people in "Hooverville," shantytowns made of cardboard and wood. There is also a very positive side to the story as Bud, clutching the few possessions left to him by his mother, searches for the man he believes is his father. This search takes Bud into the world of a famous jazz band. Throughout the book, Curtis uses Bud's "Rules and Things for Having a Funnier Life" to explore Bud's character and to add humor to the story. It is interesting to learn in the author's afterword that Curtis modeled two of his characters after his own grandfathers: one a redcap for the railroad and the other a bandleader for several musical groups including "Herman E. Curtis and the Dusky Devastators of the Depression."

In *Scorpions*, Walter Dean Myers's characters face person-against-society conflicts related to the contemporary world of drug dealers and gangs. They also face person-against-self conflicts created by inner fears and consequences related to owning a gun. The characters of Mama and her younger son, Jamal, are especially strong. Myers develops Mama's character through numerous contrasts. For example, when Mama thinks about her older son, who is in jail for robbery, she remembers looking at him as a baby and feeling great expectations: "You got a baby and you hope so much for it. . . . " (p. 54). Later, Mama is torn between her need to help this older son and to protect her younger children. Myers develops Mama's inner conflict as she discusses her problems with her minister: "And I know they convicted him of taking somebody's life, but that don't mean he ain't my flesh and blood." The minister replies: "Sometimes the herbs we take are bitter, sister, but we got to take them anyway. . . . You got to hold your family here together too. We can't let the bad mess up the good" (p. 153).

In Jamal, the younger son, Myers develops a character who is tortured by his feelings of being weak and small. At the beginning of the story, Jamal thinks about all of the people who make him feel this way, such as the big kids who laugh at him, the teachers who make him stand in class, and the shop owners who yell at his Mama. Later, Myers contrasts Jamal's earlier fears with his changing feelings after obtaining a gun.

In a tragic ending, Jamal discovers the consequences of having the gun and makes an even greater personal discovery. There was "the part of him, a part that was small and afraid, that still wanted that gun" (p. 214). This poignant story reveals the complex problems facing two generations of people who are fighting for personal and family survival in a dangerous world.

You may compare *Scorpions* with Nikki Grimes's *Jazmin's Notebook*, set in Harlem of the 1960s. In this book, the protagonist is a girl who retains her optimism even though she lives in a poor, dangerous inner-city environment. Through the use of techniques such as creating poetry written by the heroine, Grimes allows readers to understand the character. In the book, Grimes develops themes relating to the importance of dreams, holding onto hope, and expressing one's inner beliefs. The importance of self-esteem is a message developed by authors in many of the contemporary realistic novels.

Carol Fenner, the author of another of the 1996 Newbery Honor books, *Yolonda's Genius*, uses several techniques to develop the characteristics of two African American children: bright fifth-grader Yolonda and her slower, younger brother, Andrew. For example, the author reveals both Yolonda's intelligence and her ability to use this intelligence after she is teased about her size. During this incident, Yolonda responds to being called a whale by letting her fellow bus rider and the readers of the book know that she is very knowledgeable. Yolonda states, "Whales are the most remarkable mammals in the ocean—all five oceans" (p. 16). She then provides information about whales, such as "The whales sank, lifting their tales [sic] high above the water like a signal. Deep in the ocean, their voices sent out a high swelling cry, sharing their message of victory for a hundred miles" (p. 17). We learn later that Yolonda goes to the library each week to learn new facts.

Yolonda's positive attitudes and Andrew's possible musical genius are developed as Yolonda reviews what Andrew can do and not what he cannot do. Later, Yolonda's actions show both her respect for Andrew's talents and her dislike for those who torment her younger brother because he is a slower learner in school and gains his enjoyment primarily out of playing his harmonica. Yolonda takes vengeance on the three boys who destroy Andrew's harmonica. She does this while Andrew is watching because she wants it to be Andrew's vengeance as well as her own.

The author shows characterization through the symbolism of music. Andrew makes discoveries about people through sounds, he learns the alphabet after a teacher relates the alphabet to the instruments, and Andrew eventually plays his harmonica to celebrate Yolonda's character. Students may analyze the following quote to identify how the author describes Yolonda through Andrew's music: "Yolonda walking, a steady, strong beat—great big moves, slow, making waves of air pass by. Yolonda eating a chocolate eclair—full mouth—soft and happy. Yolonda reading to him, voice purring around the big words, Yolonda dancing. This is the sound of Yolonda's body—large, gobbling, space, powerful and protecting— great like a queen, frightening everyone with a scowl and a swelling of her shoulders" (p. 203). This book, like any good book of literature, shows the importance of carefully developed characters and the importance of developing self-esteem.

In another book that is also lighter in tone, *The Mouse Rap*, Walter Dean Myers uses a style that many readers enjoy. Students of children's literature can analyze the impact of the language as the main character, fourteen-year-old Mouse, presents many of his views in rap. *The Mouse Rap* is an excellent book to read aloud and enjoy the language and style.

Nonfiction

Many authors of nonfiction books create biographies about individuals who were or are active in the civil rights movement or who are leaders in such areas as the arts and the theater. Other authors develop historical perspectives about the fight for freedom.

Biographies about civil rights leaders encourage readers to examine historical, political, and social perspectives of the movement. For example, James Haskins's *Thurgood Marshall: A Life for Justice* presents the fight against racism and segregation waged by the first African American Supreme Court Justice. The text includes bibliographies of books, articles, other sources, and indexes that encourage older readers to conduct specific research.

There are several biographies of Martin Luther King, Jr., that may be used for comparative studies and analysis. James T. DeKay's *Meet Martin Luther King, Jr.* stresses the magnitude of King's work and his reasons for fighting against injustice. Lillie Patterson's *Martin Luther King, Jr. and the Freedom Movement* begins with an account of the 1955–1956 Montgomery, Alabama, bus boycott and King's involvement in the boycott. Patterson then explores King's earlier background and discovers some of the influences that caused King to become a leader in the boycott and the civil rights movement. James Haskins's *The Life and Death of Martin Luther King, Jr.* presents a stirring account of King's triumphs and tragedies. Haskins's *I Have a Dream: The Life and Words of Martin Luther King, Jr.* focuses on King's involvement with the civil rights movement. You may wish to compare these biographies of Martin Luther King, Jr., with the revised edition of *My Life with Martin Luther King, Jr.* by Coretta Scott King.

Interesting comparisons may be made between two highly illustrated biographies of Martin Luther King, Jr.: one by Faith Ringgold and the other by Rosemary L. Bray. Ringgold's *My Dream of Martin Luther King* develops the biography of the civil rights leader through a dream sequence. The text and illustrations present various stages in King's vision for a better world, tracing events in King's life such as joining demonstrations, being arrested, listening to his father's sermons, being influenced by the teachings of Mahatma Gandhi, becoming an adult minister, and finally dying from an assassin's bullet. The text and dream sequence ends as people in a crowd scene trade bags filled with prejudice, hate, ignorance, violence, and fear for Martin Luther King's dream for the promised land. The text includes a chronology of important dates in King's life.

Bray's biography, *Martin Luther King,* is illustrated with folk-art paintings by Malcah Zeldis. Bray's biography includes more details about King's life than the one by Ringgold. It also includes a chronology of dates. Neither book includes source notes. Students of children's literature can compare the impact of the illustrations and the depiction of King's life in these two highly illustrated biographies written to appeal to younger readers.

There are also several biographies of Malcolm X that lend themselves to comparative studies and analysis. For example, Arnold Adoff's *Malcolm X* stresses how and why Malcolm X urged African Americans to be proud of their heritage and themselves. In a book written for older readers, *Malcolm X: By Any Means Necessary*, Walter Dean Myers sets Malcolm X against the history of segregation and the civil rights movement. In the foreword to his biography of *Malcolm X: His Life and Legacy,*

Kevin Brown hints at the complexity of this historical figure when he states: "The story of Malcolm X is one of transformation and redemption. Without imposing an artificial unity where none exists, I have sketched a portrait that attempts to untangle the thread of Malcolm's various reincarnations from Little to Detroit Red to X to El-Hajj Malik El-Shabazz" (p. 9). The author also identifies his book as part biographical essay and part analysis of the Nation of Islam, of which Malcolm X was the spokesperson. The biography includes labeled photographs, boxed quotes by Malcolm X, an afterword, a bibliography, source notes, and an index.

Several biographies reflect the contributions of African Americans to the fine arts. James Weldon Johnson's *Lift Every Voice and Sing* is often referred to as the African American national anthem. This book combines the song with linocut prints that were originally created in the 1940s by Elizabeth Catlett. Andrea Davis Pinkney's *Duke Ellington* provides an introduction to the life and music of the jazz artist. Brian Pinkney's illustrations create the mood of the Jazz Era as well as support the theme that creating music and art is an important human endeavor.

The study of outstanding African American artists and writers would be enhanced through several books. For example, John Duggleby's *Story Painter: The Life of Jacob Lawrence* presents an interesting combination of biography and art. The text is illustrated with reproductions of Lawrence's paintings. Wade Hudson and Cheryl Willis Hudson compile profiles of African American authors and artists in *In Praise of Our Fathers and Our Mothers: A Black Family Treasury by Outstanding Authors and Artists*. This collection includes stories, poetry, interviews, and illustrations contributed by over forty African American authors and illustrators. Steven Otfinoski's *Great Black Writers* provides brief profiles of ten authors including Phillis Wheatley, James Weldon Johnson, and Langston Hughes. These books may also provide motivation for future authors and illustrators.

The contributions of African American people to the American theater are stressed in James Haskins's *Black Theater in America*. Haskins traces the American theater from minstrel shows through contemporary protest plays and drama, highlighting African American writers, actors, and musicians.

Several authors focus attention on the contributions of African Americans in the labor movement. Walter Dean Myers's *Now Is Your Time! The African-American Struggle for Freedom* includes short episodes that explore the African American experience from slavery through the civil rights movement and into contemporary times. Patricia and Frederick McKissack have written a second edition of *The Civil Rights Movement in America from 1865 to the Present*. This large book is supported with numerous photographs and descriptions of people who influenced the civil rights movement.

The experiences of young people following apartheid in South Africa are included in interviews by Tim McKee in *No More Strangers Now: Young Voices from a New South Africa*. The choice of interviews from numerous people presents a well-rounded view of the overall situation in South Africa for all the citizens. The interview with Pfano Takalani, the son of the chief, is especially interesting because Takalani stresses the values of his traditional life, which include respect for elders, learning traditional dances, and expectations for children. Takalani summarizes the importance of traditions when he states: "If these traditions are lost, we will lose a lot of human dignity" (p. 76).

Black Stars in Orbit: NASA's African American Astronauts by Khephra Burns and William Miles provides both historical background information and biographical information about the space program and the emergence of African American pilots and astronauts. The book is divided into two parts. The first section, Taking

Flight, provides historical information about African American pilots such as the beginning of the Black Eagles, the fighter pilots of World War II. This portion of the book emphasizes the early struggle of African Americans to be recognized and trained as pilots. The second section, Journey into Space, focuses on the recruitment and training of NASA's first African American astronauts. Black-and-white labeled photographs show all phases of the training. The text includes an index.

These biographies and other nonfiction works have broad appeal for children and juvenile audiences. Comparisons between the historical biographies and the contemporary one are especially interesting. They can lead to examining questions such as these: What are the values and beliefs expressed by the biographical characters from the earlier Civil War period and from the later civil rights movement? If there are similarities, what do you believe accounts for the similarities?

SUMMARY

The investigation of African and African American traditional literature indicates the strong values, beliefs, and themes of the cultures. Love, life, family commitment, respect for elders, cooperation, gratitude for help rendered, maintenance of friendships, respect for individuality, respect for heritage, respect for storytelling, community responsibilities, courage, hope, honesty, use of wit and trickery in unequal relationships, hard work, singing, and a respect for nature are values and beliefs that strongly link the traditional literature with more contemporary literature.

In the context of these broader conflicts, values, and beliefs, the themes developed in African American picture storybooks written for younger readers also reflect strong themes. We learn that life is precious, we are responsible for helping others overcome adversity, living involves changes, love is eternal, the past can be relived through memories in the form of stories, black is wonderful and powerful, honesty brings rewards, the dreams of our elders are passed on to us, nature/God sometimes intervenes in the affairs of people, and knowing one's past gives one's present meaning.

This chapter has discussed historical fiction and nonfiction as well as contemporary literature and poetry. The emergence of outstanding authors who write about the African and African American experience with sensitivity and honesty has provided many excellent books. There are many more books available than can be discussed in one chapter. Add new books to this discussion as you discover them in your own research and reading.

SUGGESTED ACTIVITIES FOR DEVELOPING UNDERSTANDING
OF AFRICAN AMERICAN LITERATURE

1. Read an article such as Ilene Cooper's "The African American Experience in Picture Books" (1992). According to the author,

   "Thirty years ago there were almost no picture books featuring African American children. Happily, this is no longer the case—throughout children's literature, there are now stories (and nonfiction) that examine the black experience, from both a particular and a universal perspective. This is especially true of picture books, where each publishing season seems to bring more titles featuring African American children. . . . " (p. 1036). Test Cooper's points by analyzing the copyright dates of African American picture books in a public, university, or school library. What changes do you find in the last thirty years?

2. Read a critical article that focuses on one of the issues in African American literature such as Michelle H. Martin's "'Hey, Who's the Kid with the Green Umbrella?': Re-evaluating the Black-a-Moor and Little Black Sambo" (1998). Do you agree or disagree with the author's points?
3. With a group of your peers or a group of students you teach, prepare for oral presentation one of the plays published in a collection such as Sylvia E. Kamerman's *Plays of Black Americans: The Black Experience in America, Dramatized for Young People* (1994).
4. With a group of your peers, create an oral storytelling experience using African and African American folklore. Try to use authentic openings, closings, and storytelling style.
5. Choose a well-known author of African American literature such as Virginia Hamilton or Walter Dean Myers. Read several books by the author. What makes the plots and characters memorable? What are the themes in the writer's work? Is there a common theme throughout the writing? What changes, if any, have occurred between the earliest books and those with later copyrights?
6. Read the works of several African American poets such as those listed in *Masterpieces of African-American Literature*, edited by Frank N. Magill (1992). Analyze the themes, subjects, and poetic styles developed by the poets. Are there differences depending on time periods and audiences? If there are differences, how do you account for the differences?

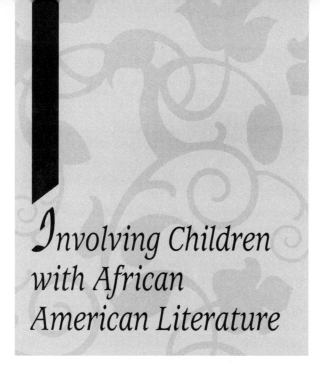

Involving Children with African American Literature

 ## PHASE ONE: TRADITIONAL LITERATURE

As we have discovered, the oral tradition was very important in transmitting the folktales, myths, and legends from Africa. To help students understand and appreciate the importance of oral language in transmitting cultural information, begin with a study of African folklore. Emphasize the role of oral storytellers in keeping alive the cultural past. Storytellers chanted and sang, interacted with the audience, and acted out story elements. The art of storytelling was so highly valued that storytelling competitions were held to encourage the most vivid and entertaining stories. Tell the students that they will be listening to oral storytellers, identifying oral storytelling styles, and creating their own storytelling experiences.

Discovering Oral Storytelling Styles from Africa

Listening to Ashley Bryan's tape, *The Dancing Granny and Other African Stories* (1985) is an excellent way to introduce storytelling styles. Ask the students to listen to the tape and then describe this very vivid style. Have them search other sources for descriptions of storytelling styles. They will discover that the style of the traditional African storyteller, still found in many African countries today, can be characterized as a lively mixture of mimicking dialogue, body action, audience participation, and rhythm. Storytellers mimic the sounds of animals, change their voices to characterize both animal and human characters, develop dialogue, and encourage their listeners to interact with the story. They may also add musical accompaniment with drums or other rhythm and string instruments such as thumb pianos.

Examples of African folklore suitable for storytelling include Gail Haley's *A Story, A Story: An African Tale*, a folktale that reveals how Anansi, the spider man, outwitted various animals and brought stories from the Sky God down to the people; Verna Aardema's *Anansi Does the Impossible: An Ashanti Tale*, a folktale about how Anansi and his wife outwit the Sky God to obtain stories; Aardema's *Who's in Rabbit's House?*, a folktale in play form that features players wearing masks to represent the various animals in the story; Aardema's *Why Mosquitoes Buzz in People's Ears*, a cumulative tale that reveals why mosquitoes make their specific noise; and Ashley Bryan's *Beat the Story-Drum, Pum-Pum* and *The Ox of the Wonderful Horns and Other African Folktales*, collections of folktales that are developed on strong oral language traditions.

After you have told several stories to the class, discuss possible advantages of telling a story rather than reading a story. Share information with the students about how traditional folktales were handed down from one generation to the next by oral storytellers. Tell the students that the art of traditional storytelling, cultivated in every culture by people from every level of society, reflects the culture, the nature of the land, the social relationships, and the traditional values of the people. African folktales, for example, arise out of a highly developed oral tradition. The influence of this oral language is shown in the repetitive language and the interaction between the audience and the storyteller.

Ask the students to identify the ways in which a storyteller may begin a story. (Most children and young adults will probably identify "Once upon a time.") If they cannot identify any common story openers, share several examples from folktales. Explain that many cultures used a beginning that introduced their listeners to an earlier time. African storytellers might begin a story with the examples discussed in this chapter. Read introductions to various folktales aloud and discuss what each one means. Explore the similarities between the introductions and identify the traditional values found in the African folktales.

As students read the various folktales recommended earlier, ask them to search the folktales to discover how interpreters and translators of traditional folklore introduced their stories. Are there differences in the type of tale or the people who told the stories? For example, they can find these story openers in Bryan's *The Ox of the Wonderful Horns and Other African Folktales*:

> We do not mean, we do not really mean, that what we are going to say is true.
> Listen, let me tell the story of . . .
> I never tire of telling the tale of . . .
> Listen, brothers and sisters, to the story of . . .

You may develop a comparative chart showing the locations of the stories and include examples of the story openers.

Ask the students to identify any endings that storytellers may use. Explain that African storytellers also used certain types of endings. For example, if the story was dramatic it might end with one of the following:

> Hausa Suza zona ("they remained")
> Mahezu ("finished)

An exaggerated story might end in the following way:

> Chase the rooster and catch the hen.
> I'll never tell a lie like that again.

If the story was humorous it might end in this way:

> They lived in peace, they died in peace
> And they were buried in a pot of candle grease.

Read the endings aloud and discuss what they mean. You may discuss which endings might be appropriate for a dramatic tale, an exaggerated tale, or a humorous tale. Ask the students to explore endings they find in the various African folktales.

To prepare students to develop their own storytelling, model a storytelling experience for them. Tell an African folktale with a traditional introduction and ending. Allow students to select African folktales and develop their own stories to share with a group. They may enjoy using musical instruments to accompany their stories.

Comparing Traditional Values in an African Folktale and an African Literary Folktale

Comparisons may be made among folktales to develop an appreciation of specific qualities, values, and beliefs found in the oral tales. Comparisons may also be made between traditional folktales and literary folktales to evaluate whether the author of the literary tale is building the tale on traditional values. For example, the following application is developed between Gail Haley's folktale *A Story, A Story: An African Tale* and Walter Dean Myers's literary folktale *The Story of the Three Kingdoms.*

Begin this activity by discussing various ways in which students can identify traditional values found in folktales. For example, they can read the folktale to discover answers to the following questions:

1. What reward or rewards are desired?
2. What actions are rewarded or admired?
3. What actions are punished or despised?
4. What rewards are given to the heroes, the heroines, or the great people in the stories?
5. What are the personal characteristics of the heroes, the heroines, or the great people in the stories?

After discussing the importance of these questions for folklore, read several examples of folklore and discuss the answers to each of the questions. Chart 2–1 indicates the values identified when a folktale and a literary folktale were compared:

CHART 2–1 Comparison of Values in a Traditional Folktale and a Literary Folktale

Questions for Values	Haley's *A Story, A Story*	Myers's *The Story of the Three Kingdoms*
What reward is desired?	Stories from powerful Sky God	Ability to share forest with elephant, sea with shark, and air with hawk
What actions are rewarded or admired?	Outwitting the leopard, the hornet, and the fairy	Learning from stories that encourage people to work together and conquer animals
What actions are punished or despised?	None given	None given
What rewards are given?	Oral stories to delight the people	Understanding that in oral stories can be found wisdom, and in wisdom, knowledge
What are the personal characteristics of heroes, heroines, or great people?	Small old man with intelligence and verbal ability	Humans with gift of stories who can learn to share wisdom

After students have identified the answers to the questions, ask them to compare their findings. Do they believe that *The Story of the Three Kingdoms* is based on values that are similar to those found in the oral traditional tales? Why or why not? Make sure that students understand that both stories reflect the value of oral stories and the need for wisdom and knowledge.

ADDITIONAL ACTIVITIES TO ENHANCE PHASE ONE

There are numerous oral language, writing, art, and library research projects that enhance students' understandings of the various phases. Some are listed in these Additional Activities sections, one of which follows each of the phases. The activities are ones for children or young adult students to do. For example, you might help students do any of the following activities for Phase One:

1. Read aloud and analyze the storytelling style in Verna Aardema's *How the Ostrich Got Its Long Neck* and *Anansi Does the Impossible: An Ashanti Tale*. Discuss the power of the repetitive language.
2. Prepare and present Verna Aardema's *Who's in Rabbit's House?* as a play.
3. Prepare and present folktales from Ashley Bryan's *Beat the Story-Drum, Pum-Pum* as a readers' theater.
4. Do the activities suggested by Margaret Lo Piccolo Sullivan in *Social Education* (1998), relating to the Epic of Sundiata (this is for older students).

PHASE TWO: FOLKLORE OF THE AMERICAN SOUTH

Webbing Traditional Values

Identifying and webbing the traditional values of folklore from the American South helps students identify similarities and differences between the African and the African American folklore. They will also discover the role of slavery in the adaptations of many of the tales that were brought across the ocean. Some of the stories such as the tales of a trickster rabbit are similar to those found in Africa. Other stories such as those found in Virginia Hamilton's *The People Could Fly: American Black Folktales* reflect the experiences of the people and their dreams for freedom.

Select a group of folktales from the American South such as Virginia Hamilton's *Her Stories: African American Folktales, Fairy Tales, and True Tales*, *The People Could Fly: American Black Folktales* and *When Birds Could Talk and Bats Could Sing*; Van Dyke Parks's adaptations of Joel Chandler Harris's *Jump! The Adventures of Brer Rabbit* and *Jump Again! More Adventures of Brer Rabbit*; Julius Lester's *John Henry*, *The Knee-High Man and Other Tales*, and his adaptations of Joel Chandler Harris, *The Tales of Uncle Remus: Adventures of Brer Rabbit*, and *More Tales of Uncle Remus: Further Adventures of Brer Rabbit, His Friends, Enemies, and Others*; Mary E. Lyons's *Raw Head, Bloody Bones: American Tales of the Supernatural*; Patricia McKissack's *Flossie and the Fox*; Steve Sanfield's *The Adventures of High John the Conqueror*; Robert D. San Souci's *The Faithful Friend* and *The Hired Hand*; and Janet Stevens's *Tops and Bottoms*.

Select several of the African American folktales to read and discuss as a group. Ask students to identify and discuss the traditional values found in the stories as they are placed on the web. Following the analysis and discussion of several folktales as a group, they can continue the activity in small groups or individually. The web in Figure 2–1 shows a partially completed web. The folktales used were the ones previously listed.

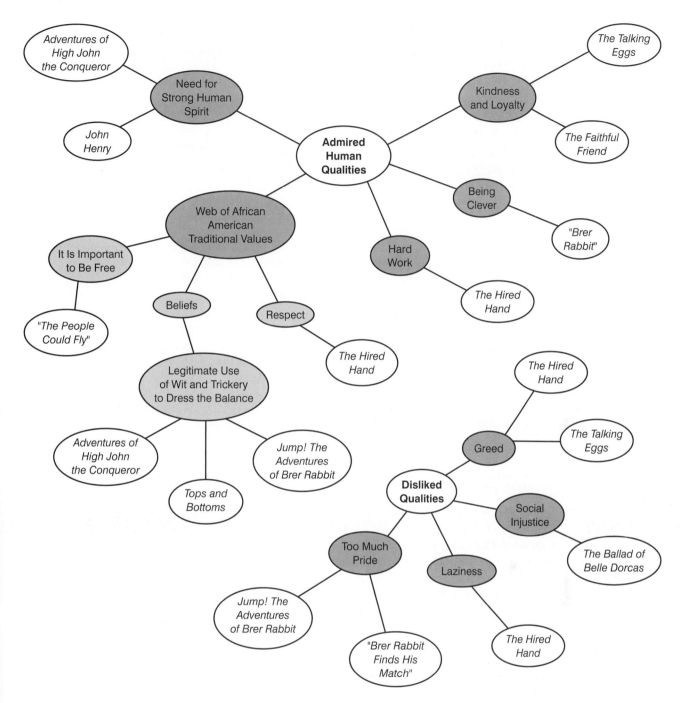

FIGURE 2–1   African American Traditional Values Web for Selected Folktales

Discussing African American Folktales That Show European Influences

There are also numerous African American tales that reflect European influences. Students can read and discuss these influences using books such as Robert D. San Souci's *Cendrillon*, *The Faithful Friend*, and *The Talking Eggs*; "Catskinells" in Virginia Hamilton's *Her Stories: African American Folktales, Fairy Tales, and True Stories* and "The Beautiful Girl of the Moon Tower" in *The People Could Fly: American Black Folktales*.

There is interesting information in the various authors' notes in these books that may be used for discussion and additional research. For example, the author's note in *Cendrillon* states:

> This story is loosely based on the French Creole tale "Cendrillon," in Turiault's nineteenth-century *Creole Grammar*. That version follows the basic outline of Perrault's "Cinderella," while incorporating elements of West Indian culture and costume. I have expanded the tale considerably, drawing on details of life on the island of Martinique, culled from such sources as Lafcadio Hearn's *Two Years in the French West Indies* (New York and London: Harper & Brothers Publishers, 1890) and Patrick Chamoiseau's *Creole Folktales* (New York: The New Press, 1994), translated from the French by Linda Coverdale. (author's note)

Students may use this information to compare various versions of the text, identify elements that would make the story seem French or West Indian, and evaluate any changes made by the author. They may also evaluate the illustrations in search of Caribbean characteristics. (I have used this type of activity to help students compare and authenticate texts with students ranging from the third grade up through university students.)

ADDITIONAL ACTIVITIES TO ENHANCE PHASE TWO

Here are some activities for children or young adult students related to this phase:

1. Compare the characteristics of African folktales with the characteristics of African American folktales. What are the similarities and what are the differences? How would you account for these similarities and differences?
2. Compare the oral storytelling style of African folktales with the oral storytelling style in African American folktales.
3. Prepare one of the folktales as a choral reading or readers' theater.
4. Write a literary folktale using the characteristics of African American folklore. Walter Dean Myers used a similar approach when writing his literary African tale, *The Story of the Three Kingdoms*.

PHASE THREE: HISTORICAL NONFICTION AND PHASE FOUR: HISTORICAL FICTION

Developing understanding of historical nonfiction and historical fiction may be enhanced through units that encourage students to compare the literature and to authenticate the fictional literature through the use of nonfiction materials.

Developing a Multicultural Study of African American Historical Fiction and Biography

Units using historical fiction and biography are a popular method for increasing students' understandings. The following unit is based on one developed in Donna E. Norton's *The Impact of Literature-Based Reading* (1992). The unit has been used with students in the upper-elementary and middle-school grades. The unit was also used with student teachers as a model to develop their own units.

UNIT OBJECTIVES

1. To analyze the role of African traditional values in historical fiction and biography
2. To evaluate the settings, conflicts, characterizations, themes, and authors' style in historical fiction
3. To authenticate historical fiction and biography by referring to historical events in informational books
4. To provide a personal response to the characters and the situations developed in historical fiction, biographies, and informational literature

Two time periods are reflected in the bulk of African American historical fiction and biographies. Powerful historical fiction and biographies have been written about overcoming problems associated with slavery and about the fight for civil rights in the 1900s. Teachers can use both periods or focus on one. For example, if choosing the topic of slavery, teachers could choose James and Christopher Collier's *Jump Ship to Freedom* (historical fiction), the story of a slave who obtains his freedom and that of his mother; Jed Ferris's *Go Free or Die: A Story About Harriet Tubman* (biography), Tubman's experiences during slavery and the Underground Railroad; and Meltzer's *The Black Americans: A History in Their Own Words, 1619–1983* (informational), a collection of writings of many people from different times. Additional historical fiction books about slavery include Paula Fox's *The Slave Dancer*, Belinda Hurmance's *A Girl Called Boy* (although there is a time-warp segment in this book, it presents a vivid picture of slavery), N. Monjo's *The Drinking Gourd*, and Gary Paulsen's *Nightjohn*.

Additional biographies about slavery include Virginia Hamilton's *Anthony Burns: The Defeat and Triumph of a Fugitive Slave* and Elizabeth Yates's *Amos Fortune, Free Man*. Additional informational books about slavery include Colin A. Palmer's *The First Passage: Blacks in the Americas, 1502–1617* and Dorothy and Thomas Hoobler's *The African American Family Album*.

Historical fiction books about later periods in African American history include Mildred Taylor's *Roll of Thunder, Hear My Cry; Let the Circle Be Unbroken;* and *The Gold Cadillac*.

Prepare the school environment by collecting pictures that show the various stages in African American history from freedom in Africa to slavery in earlier America to the contributions of contemporary politicians, authors, and musicians. Ask the students to bring to class any examples of music, writing, and art that reflects the African American culture.

Introduce one of the historical fiction books. Explain to older students that authors who write about slavery face special problems. How accurately should historical fiction reflect the attitudes and circumstances of the times? Should authors use terms of the period that are considered insensitive and offensive today? For example, you could read the authors' note in *Jump Ship to Freedom* in which James and Christopher Collier consider the use of some of the terminology. After students have read the book, ask them if they think the authors were successful in depicting conflict, characters, and changes in attitude. After students have read the book, ask them to debate the issue of using controversial words in historical fiction.

Use the same discussion and analysis structure as that shown for evaluating historical fiction about Native Americans in chapter 3, Involving Children with Native American Literature, Phase Three. Ask students to identify and discuss examples of setting, conflicts, characterizations, theme, and authors' style. You may follow a similar discussion procedure as the one described for Native American historical fiction.

After the students have read, responded to, and discussed several historical fiction selections, introduce the biographies. You may tell them that as they read each biography they will be searching for evidence of the values and beliefs found in traditional folklore, themes that are similar to those found in traditional folklore and historical fiction, and sources of conflict that might relate to the traditional values and the historical fiction. Finally, they will use nonfiction informational books to try to identify the historical events and evaluate the authenticity of the biographies. Place a shell of a chart on the board or on a transparency to guide the reading and discussions. See Chart 2–2 for an example of a shell to use.

For example, when using this chart to analyze Ferris's *Go Free or Die: A Story About Harriet Tubman*, students will find the following evidence of values and beliefs found in both traditional folklore and in the two examples of historical fiction:

1. The themes developed by the author show that freedom is worth risking one's life for and we must help others obtain freedom.
2. The values illustrated by the characters and their actions show that obligations to family and others are important, wit and trickery might be needed to influence the balance of power, responsibility is important, and expressing gratitude is essential.

Students will discover that the sources of conflict are person against society as Harriet fights to free the slaves and combat injustice. When they look to various nonfiction informational sources to identify the historical events, they will discover the following:

1. The setting is in the United States from the mid-1800s to the end of the Civil War.
2. The story is based on facts about slavery, the Underground Railroad, the 1850 Fugitive Slave Act, and the 1863 Emancipation Proclamation.
3. They will discover that Tubman freed more than 300 slaves in ten years.

CHART 2–2   Chart for Analyzing Historical Biography and Autobiography

Analyzing Historical Biography and Autobiography			
Literature	Evidence of Philosophy, Values, Beliefs, and Language from Phases One and Two	Sources of Conflict	Historical Happenings and Evaluations

Either in groups or individually, ask students to read and analyze additional biographies. After students have read biographies about those who were active during the antislavery movement, have them read biographies about contemporary people, ask them to consider any similarities between the themes, values, and conflicts. Ask students to think about why these themes, values, and person-against-society conflicts might be important in the lives of people today.

The following projects and other activities could be used with this multicultural unit:

1. *Creative dramatizations and role playing:* Ask students to choose a scene from one of the books and dramatize the scene or choose an issue and role-play the various responses that people might have as they try to decide the issue.
2. *Library research:* Ask students to choose one of the African countries from which slaves were sent to America. Compare the country during the time of slavery with the country today.
3. *Personal responses through writing and art:* Ask students to keep a writing journal and to respond to what happens to the characters in the historical fiction or biographical stories. For example, in Hurmance's *A Girl Called Boy*, they can respond to both the beliefs of the contemporary girl and what happens to her when she experiences slavery. They can create a collage that expresses their feelings as a historical character faces and overcomes conflict.
4. *Personal responses through writing and music:* Ask students to read Deborah Hopkinson's *A Band of Angels: A Story Inspired by the Jubilee Singers*. This is a story about how the daughter of a slave forms a gospel singing group and goes on tour to raise money in support of Fisk University. Ask students to consider how they would react in similar circumstances. They may also conduct research into the music played by the singers such as "Swing Low, Sweet Chariot," "Many Thousand Gone," and "Go Down, Moses."

ADDITIONAL ACTIVITIES TO ENHANCE PHASES THREE AND FOUR

Here are some activities for children or young adult students related to this phase:

1. Interview several African American families and develop a history similar to that developed by Dorothy and Thomas Hoobler in *The African American Family Album*.
2. Research the historical role of African Americans in your community, county, or state.
3. Compare Milton Meltzer's biography, *Frederick Douglass: In His Own Words* with other biographies about Frederick Douglass.

 ### PHASE FIVE: CONTEMPORARY LITERATURE

Developing Listening Comprehension Through ELVES

Many of the multicultural literature stories can be shared with children through reading them aloud. An approach such as ELVES (Levesque, 1989) may be used to focus listeners' attention on literary elements, to help them predict outcomes and verify predictions, to visualize mental images stimulated by listening to text, and to verbalize responses about a book.

ELVES is a five-part read-aloud strategy that progresses through the following sequence of activities: (1) excite, in which the discussion focuses on the listeners' experiences, the literary elements within the story, and the predictions about the story; (2) listen, in which students listen to verify predictions and to comprehend other story elements; (3) visualize, in which listeners share their mental images; (4) extend, in which the students gain new understandings by relating previous and new knowledge; and (5) savor, in which students reflect on the story, verbalize their responses, and become involved with follow-up activities such as writing or readers' theater.

The following example shows how the ELVES strategy may be developed with Ann Grifalconi's *Darkness and the Butterfly*, an African story about a girl who is afraid of the dark and learns to overcome her fear of, and even appreciate, the dark.

1. *Excite:* Begin the discussion by posing questions that encourage the students to relate to various elements within the story. For example, ask questions such as the following: Have you ever been really afraid of the dark? How did you feel when you were afraid? How did you get over your fear? Was it important that you got over your fear? Why or why not? Pretend that you live in rural Africa. What could you see and hear when it is light? What could you see and hear when it is dark? Does your imagination cause you to see and hear things that might not really be there? If you were this child living in Africa, do you think you would be more afraid of what you can see in the light or what your imagination lets you see in the dark? If you were this African child, how would you get over your fear? After students share experiences about being afraid in the dark, ask questions that encourage them to share additional responses and predictions about the title and the cover illustration. For example ask questions such as the following: Do you have different feelings when looking at the front cover than when looking at the back cover? What do you think will happen to the child on the cover? What kind of mood will be developed in the story?

2. *Listen:* Now read the story and ask students to listen so that they can confirm or reject their earlier responses and predictions. The students might use signals in particular places in the story to show that they were right or wrong.

3. *Visualize:* You may choose especially vivid sections of the book and ask students to close their eyes and describe what they see and feel as you read or reread these parts. For example, ask students, What do you see, feel, and hear in this part of the story: "Have you ever been afraid of the dark? Of being alone in the night when strange things float by that seem to follow you . . . with eyes that glow in the darkness?" (unnumbered). Or ask, What do you see, feel, and hear in this contrasting setting: "She was floating up through the air like a butterfly. Flying along with the moon. High in the night sky over her village! Then she looked about her and saw that the night was not really dark at all!" (unnumbered). You can extend this visualization by asking students to compare the girl in the first setting with the girl in the second setting.

4. *Extend:* Lead a discussion in which students make connections between their previous knowledge and any new insights they gain from listening to and reacting to this story. For example, ask them questions such as these: How did the illustrator let you know that the girl was afraid of the dark and then that she was no longer afraid? How did the author let you know that it is all right to have fears? How did the author let you know that we can overcome our fears? You can also extend this story into other settings. For example, ask, How might the story change if it took place in a city? How might the story be similar?

5. *Savor:* Students can savor the story by describing additional thoughts and feelings about the story. They could respond to the following proverb about the butterfly and discuss how the proverb relates to the story: "Darkness pursues the butterfly." Students could develop a readers' theater production using the book. They could also relate this story to several values found in African traditional literature. For example, the value of listening to advice from older people or the value of overcoming your own problems.

ADDITIONAL ACTIVITIES TO ENHANCE PHASE FIVE

Here are some activities for children or young adult students related to this phase:

1. *Personal responses through dialogue:* Choose an incident in the life of a contemporary worker for civil rights such as Martin Luther King, Jr. Pretend you can have a conversation with the person: What would you talk about? What questions would you ask? What advice might you give the person?
2. *Library research:* After reading a biography about an African American athlete such as Kathleen Krull's *Wilma Unlimited: How Wilma Rudolph Became the World's Fastest Woman*, an illustrated biography of Wilma Rudolph, research and discuss records set by the athlete.
3. *Literary and artistic expansion:* Read several works by an African American author or carefully examine the works of an African American illustrator. Analyze the types of stories the chosen people write or illustrate, consider how these authors or illustrators develop a cultural perspective in their works, and respond personally to their works. Wade Hudson and Cheryl Willis Hudson's *In Praise of Our Fathers and Our Mothers: A Black Family Treasury by Outstanding Authors and Artists* will help you select authors or artists.

BIBLIOGRAPHY

Aardema, Verna. *Misoso: Once upon a Time Tales from Africa.* New York: Knopf, 1994.

Aardema, Verna. *Tales from the Story Hat.* New York: Coward, McCann & Geoghegan, 1960.

Abrahams, Roger D. *African Folktales.* New York: Pantheon, 1983.

Arnott, D. *African Myths and Legends Retold.* London: Oxford University Press, 1962.

Banfield, Beryle. "Racism in Children's Books: An Afro-American Perspective." In *The Black American in Books for Children: Readings in Racism*, 2nd ed., edited by Donnarae MacCann and Gloria Woodard. Metuchen, N.J.: Scarecrow Press, 1985, 23–38.

Barnes-Svarney, Patricia. *Places and Peoples of the World: Zimbabwe.* New York: Chelsea House, 1989.

Beier, Ulli. *The Origin of Life and Death: African Creation Myths.* London: Heineman, 1966.

Berry, Jack, collected by. *West African Folk Tales.* Chicago: Northwestern University Press, 1961.

Brandehoff, Susan E. "Jake and Honeybunch Go to Heaven: Children's Book Fans Smoldering Debate," *American Libraries* 14 (March 1983): 130–132.

Broderick, Dorothy May. *The Image of the Black in Popular and Recommended American Juvenile Fiction, 1827–1967.* New York: Columbia University, 1971. University Microfilm No. 71-4090.

Bryan, Ashley. *The Dancing Granny and Other African Stories* [Tape]. New York: Caedmon, 1985.

Cheney, Patricia. *The Land and People of Zimbabwe.* New York: Lippincott, 1990.

Cobb, Charles E., Jr. "After Rhodesia, A Nation Named Zimbabwe." *National Geographic* (November 1981): 616–651.

Cooper, Ilene. "The African American Experience in Picture Books." *Booklist* 88 (February 1, 1992): 1036–1037.

Crowley, Daniel. Foreword to *"On Another Day . . . ": Tales Told Among the Nkundo of Zaire*, collected by Mabel Ross and Barbara Walker. Hamden, Conn.: Archon, 1979.

Elliott, Geraldine. *The Long Grass Whispers*. London: Routledge & Kegan Paul, 1939.

Faulkner, William J. *The Days When the Animals Talked*. Chicago: Follett, 1977.

Feldman, Susan, edited by. *African Myths and Tales*. New York: Dell, 1963.

Fisher, Allan C. "Rhodesia, A House Divided." *National Geographic* (May 1975): 641–671.

Frobenius, Leo, and Douglas Fox. *African Genesis*. Berkeley, Calif.: Turtle Island for the Netzahualcoyal Historical Society, 1983.

Greenfield, Eloise. "Writing for Children: A Joy and a Responsibility," In *The Black American in Books for Children: Readings in Racism*, 2nd ed., edited by Donnarae MacCann and Gloria Woodard. Metuchen, N.J.: Scarecrow Press, 1985, 19–22.

Hamilton, Virginia. *The People Could Fly: American Black Folktales*. New York: Knopf, 1985.

Harris, Violet J. "Children's Literature Depicting Blacks." In *Using Multiethnic Literature in the K–8 Classroom,* edited by Violet J. Harris. Norwood: Christopher-Gordon, 1997.

Johnson, Lauri, and Sally Smith. *Dealing with Diversity Through Multicultural Fiction: Library-Classroom Partnerships*. Chicago: American Library Association, 1993.

Kamerman, Sylvia E., edited by. *Plays of Black Americans: The Black Experience in America, Dramatized for Young People*. Boston: Plays, 1994.

Kellner, Robert Scott. "Defending Mark Twain." *The Eagle*. Bryan-College Station, Texas (April 11, 1982): 1D.

Kruse, Ginny Moore, Kathleen T. Horning, and Megan Schliesman. *Multicultural Literature for Children and Young Adults*. Madison: Cooperative Children's Book Center, 1997.

Larrick, Nancy. "The All-White World of Children's Books." *Saturday Review* 48 (September 11, 1965): 63.

Larungu, Rute. *Myths and Legends from Ghana*. Telcraft, 1992.

Leach, Maria, edited by *Funk & Wagnalls Standard Dictionary of Folklore, Mythology, and Legend*. New York: Harper & Row, 1972.

Levesque, J. "ELVES: A Read-Aloud Strategy to Develop Listening Comprehension." *The Reading Teacher* 43 (October, 1989): 93–94.

Magill, Frank N. *Masterpieces of African-American Literature*. New York: HarperCollins, 1992.

Mallows, Wilfrid. *The Mystery of the Great Zimbabwe*. New York: Norton, 1984.

Martin, Michelle H. "'Hey, Who's the Kid with the Green Umbrella?' Re-evaluating the Black-a-Moor and Little Black Sambo." *The Lion and the Unicorn* 22 (1998): 147–162.

Mbugua, Kioi wa. *Inkishu: Myths and Legends of the Maasai*. Nairobi, Kenya: Jacaranda Designs, 1994.

McCall, Cecelia. "A Historical Quest for Literacy." *Interracial Books for Children Bulletin* 19 (1989): 3–5.

Moore, Opal. "Picture Books: The Un-Text." In *The Black American in Books for Children: Readings in Racism*, 2nd ed., edited by Donnarae MacCann and Gloria Woodard. Metuchen, N.J.: Scarecrow Press, 1985, 183–191.

Norton, Donna E. *The Impact of Literature-Based Reading*. New York: Merrill/Macmillan, 1992.

Noss, Philip. "Descriptions in Gbaya Literary Art." In *African Folklore*, edited by Richard Dorse. Bloomington, Ind.: Indiana University Press, 1972.

Parrinder, Geoffrey. *African Mythology: Library of the World's Myths and Legends*. New York: Bedrick, 1986.

Radin, Paul, edited by. *African Folktales*. Princeton: Bollingen Series, Princeton University Press, 1952.

_____, selected by. *African Folktales and Sculpture*. New York: Pantheon, 1952.

Rochman, Hazel. *Against Borders: Promoting Books for a Multicultural World*. Chicago: American Library Association, 1993.

_____. "Apart from Apartheid: Children's Books About South Africa." *Journal of Youth Services in Libraries* 11 (Winter 1998): 139–142.

_____. "The Booklist Interview: Virginia Hamilton." *Booklist* 88 (February 1, 1992): 1020–1021.

Rosen, Michael. *How the Animals Got Their Colors*. San Diego: Harcourt Brace Jovanovich, 1992.

Ross, Mabel H., and Barbara K. Walker. *"On Another Day . . . ": Tales Told Among the Nkundo of Zaire*. Hamden, Conn.: Archon, 1979.

Sullivan, Margaret Lo Piccolo. "The Epic of Sundiata: Using African Literature in the Classroom." *Social Education* 62 (April/May 1998): 201–206.

Theal, George McCall. *Kaffir Folk-lore*. Conn.: Negro Universities Press, 1896, 1970.

Thompson, G. C. *The Zimbabwe Culture: Ruins and Reactions*. London: Frank Cass, 1971.

Vrooman, Diana. Authenticating *Mufaro's Beautiful Daughters: An African Tale*. Unpublished paper. College Station: Texas A & M University, 1993.

Wilms, Denise. "Focus: Jake and Honeybunch Go to Heaven." *Booklist*. 79 (January 1, 1983): 619.

Wisniewski, David. *Sundiata: Lion King of Mali*. New York: Clarion, 1992.

Worth, Richard. *Robert Mugabe of Zimbabwe*. New York: Messner, 1990.

CHILDREN'S AND YOUNG ADULT LITERATURE REFERENCES

Aardema, Verna. *Anansi Does the Impossible: An Ashanti Tale*. Illustrated by Lisa Desimini. Simon & Schuster, 1997 (I: 4-8 R: 4). Anansi brings stories to the people.

_____. *Bringing the Rain to Kapiti Plain: A Nandi Tale*. Illustrated by Beatriz Vidal. Dial, 1981 (I: 5-8). This is a cumulative tale.

_____. *How the Ostrich Got Its Long Neck*. Illustrated by Marcia Brown. Scholastic, 1995 (I: 4-7 R: 4). This *pourquoi* tale from Kenya explains an animal characteristic.

_____. *Misoso: Once upon a Time Tales from Africa*. Illustrated by Reynold Ruffins. Knopf, 1994 (I: 8 + R: 3). A collection of twelve tales.

_____. *What's So Funny, Ketu?* Illustrated by Marc Brown. Dial, 1982, (I: all R: 4). This is a tale from Sudan.

_____. *Who's in Rabbit's House?* Illustrated by Leo and Diane Dillon. Dial, 1977 (I: 7 + R: 3). A Masai folktale is illustrated as a play.

_____. *Why Mosquitoes Buzz in People's Ears*. Illustrated by Leo and Diane Dillon. Dial, 1975 (I: 5–9 R: 6). An African folktale explains why mosquitoes buzz.

Adoff, Arnold. *In for Winter, Out for Spring*. Illustrated by Jerry Pinkney. Harcourt Brace Jovanovich, 1991 (I: all). The poetry reflects the four seasons.

_____. *Malcolm X*. Crowell, 1970 (I: 7–12 R: 5). This is a biography of the African American leader.

Armstrong, William H. *Sounder*. Harper, 1969 (I: 10 + R: 6). Winner of the 1970 Newbery.

Bang, Molly. *Ten, Nine, Eight*. Greenwillow, 1983 (I: 3–6). A number game counts backward.

Barboza, Steven. *Door of No Return: The Legend of Goree Island*. Cobblehill, 1994 (I: 10 + R: 6). Photographs accompany a history of the slave trade on an island off Senegal.

Bell, William. *Zack*. Simon & Schuster, 1999 (I: 10 + R: 6). A boy discovers his heritage when he writes a history paper.

Berry, James. *Ajeemah and His Son*. HarperCollins, 1991 (I: 10 + R: 6). A father and son are taken from Africa and sold into slavery.

_____. *Everywhere Faces Everywhere*. Illustrated by Reynold Ruffins. Simon & Schuster, 1997 (I: 10 +). This is a collection of poems.

Bial, Raymond. *The Underground Railroad*. Houghton Mifflin, 1995 (I: 9 + R: 5). This history includes first-person accounts.

Bontemps, Arna. Story of the Negro. Knopf, 1948. Winner of the 1949 Newbery Honor.

I = Interest age range
R = Readability by grade level

Bray, Rosemary L. *Martin Luther King*. Illustrated by Malcah Zeldis. Greenwillow, 1995 (I: 7–10 R: 5). The biography is illustrated with folk-art paintings.

Brooks, Bruce. *The Moves Make the Man*. Harper, 1984 (I: 10 + R: 6). Winner of the 1985 Newbery.

Brown, Kevin. *Malcolm X: His Life and Legacy*. Millbrook, 1995 (I: 12 + R: 7). The biography is accompanied by photographs, a chronology, an index, and author's notes.

Bryan, Ashley. *All Night, All Day: A Child's First Book of African-American Spirituals*. Atheneum, 1991 (I: 3–8). Words and music accompany the illustrations.

_____. *Ashley Bryan's ABC of African American Poetry*. Atheneum, 1997 (I: all). Poems match the letters of the alphabet.

_____. *Beat the Story-Drum, Pum-Pum*. Atheneum, 1980 (I: 6 + R: 5). This is a collection of tales.

_____. *I'm Going to Sing: Black American Spirituals*. Vol. 2. Atheneum, 1982 (I: all). The text includes musical arrangements.

_____. *The Ox of the Wonderful Horns and Other African Folktales*. Atheneum, 1971 (I: 6 + R: 5). A collection of tales.

_____. *The Story of Lightning and Thunder*. Atheneum, 1993 (I: 6 + R: 5). A Nigerian folktale.

_____. *Turtle Knows Your Name*. Atheneum, 1989 (I: 6 + R: 5). This folktale is from the West Indies.

Burns, Khephra, and William Miles. *Black Stars in Orbit: NASA's African American Astronauts*. Harcourt Brace, 1995 (I: 10 + R: 7). This text is based on a 1990 television documentary.

Clifton, Lucille. *Everett Anderson's Good-bye*. Illustrated by Ann Grifalconi. Holt, Rinehart & Winston, 1983 (I: 6–9). The story describes a boy's pain after his father's death.

Collier, James, and Christopher Collier. *Jump Ship to Freedom*. Delacorte, 1981 (I: 10 + R: 7). A slave acquires his freedom.

Cooper, Floyd. *Coming Home: From the Life of Langston Hughes*. Philomel, 1994 (I: 6–9 R: 5). A highly illustrated picture book about the writer's life.

Courlander, Harold. *The Cow-Tail Switch and Other West African Stories*. Holt, 1947 (I: all). Winner of the 1947 Newbery Honor.

Crews, Donald. *Bigmama's*. Greenwillow, 1992 (I: 5–7). Children visit Bigmama in Florida.

_____. *Shortcut*. Greenwillow, 1992 (I: 5–7). Children have a frightening experience when they walk the railroad tracks.

Curtis, Christopher Paul. *Bud, Not Buddy*. Delacorte, 1999 (I: 10 + R: 6). The story is set during the Depression.

_____. *The Watsons Go to Birmingham—1963*. Delacorte, 1995 (I: 10 + R:6). A family experiences racial tensions and a church bombing.

Curtis, Gavin. *The Bat Boy and His Violin*. Illustrated by E. B. Lewis. Simon & Schuster, 1998 (I: 5–10 R: 4). Set in the 1940s, a boy proves the worth of his violin.

Day, Nancy Raines, retold by. *The Lion's Whiskers: An Ethiopian Folktale*. Illustrated by Ann Grifalconi. Scholastic, 1995 (I: 5–8 R: 5). A stepmother makes friends with her stepson.

Dee, Ruby. *Tower to Heaven*. Illustrated by Jennifer Bent. Holt, 1991 (I:6–9 R: 5). This is a *pourquoi* tale that explains why the god, Onyankopon, lives in the sky.

DeKay, James T. *Meet Martin Luther King, Jr.* Illustrated by Ted Burwell. Random House, 1969 (I: 7–12 R: 4). This biography stresses the magnitude of King's work.

Duggleby, John. *Story Painter: The Life of Jacob Lawrence*. Chronicle, 1998 (I: all). A biography set during the Harlem Renaissance.

Everett, Gwen. *Li'l Sis and Uncle Willie: A Story Based on the Life and Paintings of William H. Johnson*. Rizzoli, 1992 (I: all). A fictionalized story is built on the paintings of the artist.

Fairman, Tony, retold by. *Bury My Bones but Keep My Words: African Tales for Retelling*. Illustrated by Meshack Asare. Holt, 1993 (I: 8 + R: 5). The twelve tales are from Africa.

Farmer, Nancy. *A Girl Named Disaster*. Jackson/Orchard, 1996 (I: 10 + R: 6). Winner of the 1997 Newbery Honor.

Feelings, Muriel. *Jambo Means Hello: Swahili Alphabet Book*. Dial, 1974 (I: all). A beautiful book uses the Swahili alphabet.

_____. *Moja Means One: Swahili Counting Book*. Illustrated by Tom Feelings. Dial, 1971 (I: all). The book uses Swahili numbers.

Feelings, Tom. *The Middle Passage: White Ships/Black Cargo*. Dial, 1995 (I: 12 +). This wordless book expresses the horror associated with the slave trade.

Fenner, Carol. *Yolonda's Genius*. McElderry, 1995 (I: 10 + R: 6). A fiction book about a bright fifth-grade girl and her younger brother, who has a special musical talent.

Ferris, Jeri. *Go Free or Die: A Story About Harriet Tubman*. Carolrhoda, 1988 (I: 7 + R: 4). The biography describes Tubman's experiences during slavery and the Underground Railroad.

Flournoy, Valerie. *The Patchwork Quilt*. Illustrated by Jerry Pinkney. Dial, 1985 (I: 5-8 R:4). Constructing a quilt brings a family together.

Fox, Paula. *How Many Miles to Babylon?* Illustrated by Paul Giovanopoulos. White, 1967 (I: 8 + R: 3). Ten-year-old James discovers who he really is when he is abducted by a gang.

_____. *The Slave Dancer*. Illustrated by Eros Keith. Bradbury, 1973 (I: 12 + R: 7). A fife player experiences the slave trade.

Fritz, Jean. *Harriet Beecher Stowe and the Beecher Preachers*. Putnam, 1994 (I: 8 + R: 4). This is a biography of the abolitionist and author of *Uncle Tom's Cabin*.

Gershator, Phillis. *Rata-pata-scata, fata: A Caribbean Story*. Illustrated by Holly Meade. Little, Brown, 1994 (I: 4–9). The language provides a pleasant story for reading aloud.

_____, retold by. *Tukama Tootles the Flute: A Tale from the Antilles*. Illustrated by Synthia Saint James. Orchard, 1993 (I: 4–7). A young boy learns that there is hypnotic power in music.

Gerson, Mary-Joan, retold by. *Why the Sky Is Far Away: A Nigerian Folktale*. Illustrated by Carla Golembe. Little, Brown, 1992 (I: 4–8 R: 5). A *pourquoi* tale tells why the sky is separated from the earth.

Greene, Bette. *Philip Hall Likes Me. I Reckon Maybe*. Illustrated by Charles Lilly. Dial, 1974 (I: 10 + R: 4). Beth Lambert experiences her first crush.

Greenfield, Eloise. *Honey, I Love and Other Love Poems*. Illustrated by Jan Gilchrist. Harper-Collins, 1995 (I: 3–6). A highly illustrated poem.

_____. *Nathaniel Talking*. Illustrated by Jan Gilchrist. Black Butterfly Children's Books, 1989 (I: all). A boy's life is revealed through rap and verse.

_____. *Rosa Parks*. Illustrated by Eric Marlow. Crowell, 1973 (I: 7–10 R: 4). This biography is about the woman who refused to give up her bus seat in Montgomery, Alabama.

_____. *Sister*. Illustrated by Moneta Barnett. Crowell, 1974 (I: 8–12 R:5). A thirteen-year-old reviews memories.

_____. *Under the Sunday Tree*. Illustrated by Amos Ferguson. Harper & Row, 1988 (I: all). This poetry is about the Bahamas.

Grifalconi, Ann. *Darkness and the Butterfly*. Little, Brown, 1987 (I: 4–8 R: 4). A young African girl learns not to fear the dark.

_____. *The Village of Round and Square Houses*. Little, Brown, 1985 (I: 4–9 R: 6). A *pourquoi* tale explains why women live in round houses and men live in square houses.

Grimes, Nikki. *Jazmin's Notebook*. Dial, 1998 (I: 10 + R: 5). A fourteen-year-old presents her experiences.

_____. *Meet Danitra Brown*. Illustrated by Floyd Cooper. Lothrop, Lee & Shepard, 1994 (I: all). These poems are about family and friendship.

Gunning, Monica. *Not a Copper Penny in Me House: Poems from the Caribbean*. Illustrated by Frane Lessac. Boyds Mills, 1993 (I: all). The poems reflect island experiences.

Guy, Rosa. *Billy the Great*. Illustrated by Caroline Binch. New York: Delacorte, 1992 (I: 5–8 R: 3). Two boys develop an interracial friendship

Haley, Gail E. *A Story, A Story: An African Tale*. Atheneum, 1970 (I: 6–10 R: 6). An African tale tells about a spider man's bargain with Sky God.

Hamilton, Virginia. *Anthony Burns: The Defeat and Triumph of a Fugitive Slave*. Knopf, 1988 (I: 10 + R: 6). This is a biography of the escaped slave whose trial caused riots in Boston.

_____. *Her Stories: African American Folktales, Fairy Tales, and True Tales*. Illustrated by Leo and Diane Dillon. Scholastic, 1995 (I: 10 + R: 6). This collection includes nineteen tales about women.

_____. *The House of Dies Drear*. Illustrated by Eros Keith. Macmillan, 1968 (I: 11 + R: 4). A suspenseful story about a family who is living in a home that was a station on the Underground Railroad.

_____. *In the Beginning: Creation Stories from Around the World*. Illustrated by Barry Moser. Harcourt Brace Jovanovich, 1988 (I: all R: 5). Creation stories come from many cultures.

_____. *M. C. Higgins, the Great*. Macmillan, 1974 (I: 12 + R: 4) M. C. dreams of fleeing from the danger of a strip mining spoil heap.

_____. *Many Thousand Gone: African Americans from Slavery to Freedom*. Illustrated by Leo and Diane Dillon. Knopf, 1993 (I: 8 + R: 5). Short stories tell about people who were involved in fighting for freedom.

_____, retold by. *The People Could Fly: American Black Folktales*. Illustrated by Leo and Diane Dillon. Knopf, 1985 (I: 9 + R: 6). A collection of tales told by or adapted by African Americans.

_____. *The Planet of Junior Brown*. Macmillan, 1971 (I: 12 + R: 6). Three outcasts from society create their own world in a secret room.

_____. *When Birds Could Talk and Bats Could Sing: The Adventures of Bush Sparrow, Sis Wren, and Their Friends*. Illustrated by Barry Moser. Scholastic, 1996 (I: 10 + R:4). This collection includes eight tales from the southern part of the United States.

_____. *Zeely*. Illustrated by Symeon Shimin. Macmillan, 1967 (I: 8–12 R: 4). Geeder believes her stately neighbor is a Watusi queen.

Harris, Joel Chandler. *Jump! The Adventures of Brer Rabbit*. Adapted by Van Dyke Parks. Illustrated by Barry Moser. Harcourt Brace Jovanovich, 1986 (I: all R: 4). Five Brer Rabbit stories.

_____. *Jump Again! More Adventures of Brer Rabbit*. Adapted by Van Dyke Parks. Illustrated by Barry Moser. Harcourt Brace Jovanovich, 1987 (I: all R: 4). Five additional tales.

_____. *More Tales of Uncle Remus: Further Adventures of Brer Rabbit, His Friends, Enemies, and Others*. Retold by Julius Lester. Dial, 1988 (I: all R: 4). A collection of tales from the South.

_____. *The Tales of Uncle Remus: The Adventures of Brer Rabbit*. Retold by Julius Lester. Illustrated by Jerry Pinkney. Dial, 1987 (I: all R: 4). This book contains forty-eight Brer Rabbit tales.

Haskins, James. *Black Theater in America*. Crowell, 1982 (I: 10 + R: 7). The book stresses the contributions of African Americans.

_____. *Freedom Rides: Journey for Justice*. Hyperion, 1995 (I: 12 + R: 7). This is an informational book about the people who were part of the civil rights movement.

_____. *I Have a Dream: The Life and Words of Martin Luther King, Jr.* Millbrook, 1993 (I: 10 + R: 7). This biography focuses on the civil rights movement.

_____. *The Life and Death of Martin Luther King, Jr.* Lothrop, Lee & Shepard, 1977 (I: 10 + R: 7). This biography covers the life of the civil rights leader.

_____. *Thurgood Marshall: A Life for Justice*. Holt, 1992 (I: 10 + R: 7). Biography of the first African American Supreme Court Justice.

Hoobler, Dorothy, and Thomas Hoobler. *The African American Family Album*. Oxford University Press, 1995 (I: 10 + R: 5). Photographs, reproductions, a list of further reading, and an index are included in this pictorial history.

Hooks, William H. *The Ballad of Belle Dorcas*. Illustrated by Brian Pinkney. Knopf, 1990 (I: 8 + R: 5). A folktale from the Carolinas.

Hopkinson, Deborah. *A Band of Angels: A Story Inspired by the Jubilee Singers*. Illustrated by Raul Colon. Atheneum, 1999 (I: all). This fictional story is based on real events.

Hudson, Wade, edited by. *Pass It On: African-American Poetry for Children*. Illustrated by Floyd Cooper. Scholastic, 1993 (I: all). This anthology includes many African American poems.

_____, and Cheryl Willis Hudson, compiled by. *In Praise of Our Fathers and Our Mothers: A Black Family Treasury by Outstanding Authors and Artists*. Just Us Books, 1997 (I: 10 +). A collection of writings and art.

Hughes, Langston. *The Dream Keeper and Other Poems*. Illustrated by Brian Pinkney. Knopf, 1994 (I: all). This is a revision of a text first published in 1932.

_____. *The Sweet and Sour Animal Book.* Illustrated by students from the Harlem School of the Arts. Oxford University Press, 1995 (I: all). This is a collection of twenty-seven previously unpublished poems.

Hurmance, Belinda. *A Girl Called Boy.* Houghton Mifflin, 1982 (I: 10 + R: 6). A contemporary girl experiences slavery.

Igus, Toyomi. *I See the Rhythm.* Illustrated by Michele Wood. Children's Press, 1998 (I: 7 +). The text explores both poetry and music.

Isadora, Rachel. *At the Crossroads.* Greenwillow, 1991 (I: 3–8 R: 3). Children wait to welcome their fathers who were working in the South African mines.

Johnson, James Weldon. *Lift Every Voice and Sing.* Illustrated by Elizabeth Catlett. Walker, 1993 (I: all). Linocut prints accompany the song.

Jonas, Ann. *Splash!* Greenwillow, 1995 (I: 4–6). In this concept book, a young African American girl counts animals.

Joseph, Lynn. *Coconut Kind of Day: Island Poems.* Illustrated by Sandra Speidel. Lothrop, Lee & Shepard, 1990 (I: all). The poems re-create the sounds and sights of the Caribbean.

_____. *A Wave in Her Pocket: Stories from Trinidad.* Illustrated by Brian Pinkney. Clarion, 1991 (I: 8 + R: 5). A great aunt entertains children with frightening stories.

Kamerman, Sylvia E., edited by. *Plays of Black Americans: The Black Experience in America, Dramatized for Young People.* Plays, 1994 (I: 12 + R: 6). This collection ranges from plays about Harriet Tubman to Langston Hughes.

Knutson, Barbara, retold by. *How the Guinea Fowl Got Her Spots: A Swahili Tale of Friendship.* Carolrhoda, 1990 (I: 4–8 R: 4). This is a tale of friendship.

_____. *Why the Crab Has No Head.* Carolrhoda, 1987 (I: all R: 4). This is a *pourquoi* tale from Zaire.

Krull, Kathleen. *Wilma Unlimited: How Wilma Rudolph Became the World's Fastest Woman.* Illustrated by David Diaz. Harcourt Brace, 1996 (I: 8 + R: 5). This biography is about the track-and-field star.

Langstaff, John. *What a Morning! The Christmas Story in Black Spirituals.* Illustrated by Ashley Bryan. McElderry, 1987 (I: all). Five spirituals focus on the Christmas story.

Lauture, Denize. *Father and Son.* Illustrated by Jonathan Green. Philomel, 1992 (I: 4–8). This poem is about experiences of the Gullah people.

Lester, Julius. *Black Cowboy, Wild Horses.* Illustrated by Jerry Pinkney. Dial, 1998 (I: 5 + R: 5). Based on the story of Bob Lemmons.

_____. *John Henry.* Illustrated by Jerry Pinkney. Dial, 1994 (I: all R: 5). This is an illustrated version of the legend.

_____. *The Knee-High Man and Other Tales.* Illustrated by Ralph Pinto. Dial, 1972 (I: all R: 4). Six folktales from the South.

_____. *The Last Tales of Uncle Remus.* Illustrated by Jerry Pinkney. Dial, 1994 (I: all R: 4). The text includes thirty-nine stories.

Lewin, Hugh. *Jafta.* Illustrated by Lisa Kopper. Carolrhoda, 1983 (I: 3-7 R: 6). A South African boy is compared to animals in his environment.

_____. *Jafta's Mother.* Illustrated by Lisa Kopper. Carolrhoda, 1983 (I: 3–7 R: 6). Jafta's mother is compared to the South African environment.

_____. *To Be a Slave.* Dial, 1968 (I: 10 + R: 6). Winner of the 1969 Newbery Honor.

Lyons, Mary E., selected by. *Raw Head, Bloody Bones: African-American Tales of the Supernatural.* Scribner's, 1991 (I: 8 + R: 6). A collection of fifteen tales.

_____. *Sorrow's Kitchen: The Life and Folklore of Zora Neale Hurston.* Scribner's, 1990 (I: 10 R: 6). This is the biography of the first African American author to write a popular book of African American folklore.

_____. *Starting Home: The Story of Horace Pippin, Painter.* Scribner's, 1993 (I: 5–9 R: 5). This is an illustrated storybook about the artist.

McCurdy, Michael, edited by. *Escape from Slavery: The Boyhood of Frederick Douglass in His Own Words.* Knopf, 1994 (I: 9 +). This autobiography presents Douglass's original language.

McDermott, Gerald. *Anansi the Spider: A Tale from the Ashanti*. Holt, Rinehart & Winston, 1972 (I: 7–9). This is a folktale about the trickster.

_____. *Zomo the Rabbit: A Trickster Tale from West Africa*. Harcourt Brace, 1992 (I: 4–8 R: 4). This tale shows the importance of courage, sense, and caution.

McKee, Tim. *No More Strangers Now: Young Voices from a New South Africa*. Photographs by Anne Blackshaw. DK, 1998 (I: 10 +). A collection of interviews.

McKissack, Patricia. *The Dark-Thirty: Southern Tales of the Supernatural*. Illustrated by Brian Pinkney. Knopf, 1992 (I: 8 + R: 5). This is a collection of ghost stories.

_____. *Flossie and the Fox*. Illustrated by Rachel Isadora. Dial, 1986 (I: 3–8 R: 3). This is a tale of the rural South.

_____. *Mirandy and Brother Wind*. Illustrated by Jerry Pinkney. Knopf, 1988 (I: 4–9 R: 5). A girl enters a cakewalk contest.

_____. *Nettie Jo's Friends*. Illustrated by Scott Cook. Knopf, 1989 (I: 3–8 R: 3). Animals help a young girl find a needle so she can make a dress for her doll.

_____, and Fredrick McKissack. *The Civil Rights Movement in America from 1865 to the Present*, 2nd ed. Children's Press, 1991 (I: 10 + R: 6). This is a history of the civil rights movement.

Mathis, Sharon Bell. *The Hundred Penny Box*. Illustrated by Leo and Diane Dillon. Viking, 1975 (I: 6–9 R: 3). An elderly relative tells her story through the pennies in her box.

Mbugua, Kioi wa. *Inkishu: Myths and Legends of the Maasai*. Nairobi, Kenya: Jacaranda Designs, 1994 (I: 8 + R: 5). A collection of folktales from Kenya and Tanzania.

Meltzer, Milton. *The Black Americans: A History in Their Own Words, 1619–1983*. Crowell, 1984 (I: 10 + R: 6). Short writings provide a political and social history.

_____, edited by. *Frederick Douglass: In His Own Words*. Illustrated by Stephen Alcorn. Harcourt Brace, 1995 (I: 12 +). Each of Douglass's speeches or writings is introduced with a commentary.

_____. *Langston Hughes: A Biography*. Crowell, 1968 (I: 10 + R: 6). A biography of a famous poet.

Miller, Douglas. *Frederick Douglass and the Fight for Freedom*. Facts on File, 1988 (I: 10 + R: 6). A biography of the leader who escaped slavery.

Mitchell, Margaree King. *Uncle Jed's Barbershop*. Illustrated by James Ransome. Simon & Schuster, 1993 (I: 5–9 R: 3). A man retains his dreams.

Monjo, N. *The Drinking Gourd*. Illustrated by Fred Brenner. Harper & Row, 1970 (I: 7–9 R: 2). This is a history of the Underground Railroad for beginning readers.

Musgrove, Margaret. *Ashanti to Zulu: African Traditions*. Illustrated by Leo and Diane Dillon. Dial, 1976 (I: 7–12). Traditions of twenty-six African peoples are presented.

Myers, Walter Dean. *Harlem*. Illustrated by Christopher Myers. Scholastic, 1997 (I: all). This is a book of poetry.

_____. *Malcolm X: By Any Means Necessary*. Scholastic, 1993 (I: 10 + R: 6). A biography of the African American leader.

_____. *The Mouse Rap*. Harper & Row, 1990 (I: 10 + R: 5). A contemporary story has a large portion written in rap.

_____. *Now Is Your Time! The African-American Struggle for Freedom*, HarperCollins, 1991 (I: 10 + R: 6). The author chronicles the lives of numerous people associated with the struggle for freedom.

_____. *Scorpions*. Harper & Row, 1988 (I: 11 + R: 5). A boy faces problems with a gang.

_____. *Somewhere in Darkness*. Scholastic, 1992 (I: 10 + R: 5). Winner of the 1993 Newbery Honor.

_____. *The Story of the Three Kingdoms*. Illustrated by Ashley Bryan. New York: HarperCollins, 1995 (I: 7 + R: 4). This is an original tale that uses a folkloric style.

Onyefulu, Ifeoma. *Emeka's Gift: An African Counting Story*. Cobblehill, 1995 (I: 4–8). Photographs from a southern Nigeria market show counting from 1 to 10.

Otfinoski, Steven. *Great Black Writers*. Facts on File, 1994 (I: 12 +). The text includes examples of subjects' writings as well as information about their careers.

Palmer, Colin A. *The First Passage: Blacks in the Americas, 1502–1617*. Oxford University Press, 1995 (I: 12 + R: 10). This informational book provides a history of African Americans.

Patterson, Lillie. *Frederick Douglass: Freedom Fighter*. Garrard, 1965 (I: 6-9 R:3). This is a biography of the African American leader.

_____. *Martin Luther King, Jr. and the Freedom Movement*. Facts on File, 1989 (I: 10 + R: 6). This book chronicles King's nonviolent struggles against segregation.

Paulsen, Gary. *Nightjohn*. Delacorte, 1993 (I: 10 + R: 4). A slave teaches children to read.

Petry, Ann. *Harriet Tubman: Conductor on the Underground Railroad*. Crowell, 1955 (I: 10 + R: 6). This is a biography of a woman who led over three hundred slaves to freedom.

Pinkney, Andrea Davis. *Duke Ellington*. Illustrated by Brian Pinkney. Hyperion, 1998 (I: all). A highly illustrated biography.

_____. *Seven Candles for Kwanzaa*. Illustrated by Brian Pinkney. Dial, 1993 (I: 5–9 R: 4). The book details the preparation for the African American holiday.

Polacco, Patricia. *Pink and Say*. Philomel, 1994 (I: all). The story is about the author's great-great-grandfather

Ringgold, Faith. *Aunt Harriet's Underground Railroad in the Sky*. Crown, 1993 (I: 5–9 R: 4). This picture book tells about a girl who meets Harriet Tubman on a freedom train in the sky.

_____. *My Dream of Martin Luther King*. Crown, 1995 (I: 5–9 R: 4). This is a highly illustrated biography that develops as the author tells about King's life through a dream sequence.

_____. *Tar Beach*. Crown, 1991 (I: 4–7 R: 4). A girl imagines that she can fly over the city.

Rosen, Michael. *Elijah's Angel: A Story for Chanukah and Christmas*. Illustrated by Aminah Brenda Lynn Robinson. Harcourt Brace, 1992 (I: 7–10 R: 4). A Jewish boy learns about friendship through the gift of a black wood-carver.

Sanfield, Steve. *The Adventures of High John the Conqueror*. Illustrated by John Ward. Watts, 1989 (I: 8 + R: 4). The text includes sixteen southern folktales.

San Souci, Robert D. *Cendrillon*. Illustrated by Brian Pinkney. Simon & Schuster, 1998 (I: 5–10 R: 5). This is a Cinderella variant.

_____. *The Faithful Friend*. Illustrated by Brian Pinkney. Simon & Schuster, 1995 (I: 5–10 R: 5). A folktale from the West Indies.

_____. *The Hired Hand*. Illustrated by Jerry Pinkney. Dial, 1997 (I: 5–10 R: 5). The folktale is set in Virginia.

_____. *Minty: A Story of Young Harriet Tubman*. Illustrated by Jerry Pinkney. Dial, 1996 (I: 5–9 R: 5). This is a fictionalized account of Harriet Tubman's childhood.

_____. *Sukey and the Mermaid*. Illustrated by Brian Pinkney. Four Winds, 1992 (I: 5–10 R: 5). A folktale that has elements from West Africa, the Caribbean, and the Sea Islands of South Carolina.

_____. *The Talking Eggs*. Illustrated by Jerry Pinkney. Dial, 1989 (I: all). A folktale from the American South.

Schroeder, Alan. *Carolina Shout!* Illustrated by Bernie Fuchs. Dial, 1995 (I: 4-8). Set in Charleston, South Carolina, the language presents the musical shouts of street vendors and work crews.

Sisulu, Elinor Batezat. *The Day Gogo Went to Vote: South Africa, 1994*. Illustrated by Sharon Wilson. Little, Brown, 1996 (I:4–8 R: 6). This story takes place during the first election in which blacks were allowed to vote.

Smalls-Hector, Irene. *Jonathan and His Mommy*. Illustrated by Michael Hays. Little, Brown, 1992 (I: 3–8). A boy and his mother take a walk in the neighborhood.

Stanley, Diane, and Vennema, Peter. *Shaka, King of the Zulus*. Illustrated by Diane Stanley. Morrow, 1988 (I: 6–10 R: 6). This is a picture biography.

Steptoe, Javala, illustrated by. *In Daddy's Arms I Am Tall: African Americans Celebrating Fathers*, Lee & Low, 1997 (I: all). A collection of poems.

Steptoe, John. *Mufaro's Beautiful Daughters: An African Tale*. Lothrop, Lee & Shepard, 1987 (I: all R: 4). An African folktale has some Cinderella elements.

_____. *Stevie*. Harper & Row, 1969 (I: 3–7 R: 3). Stevie wants his own way.

Steptoe, Michele, edited by. *Our Song, Our Toil: The Story of American Slavery As Told by Slaves*. Millbrook, 1994 (I: 8 +). Text is developed around short biographies of slaves.

Stevens, Janet. *Tops and Bottoms*. Harcourt Brace, 1995 (I: 4–7). A folktale from the Plantation South.

Swift, Hildegarde. *The Railroad to Freedom: A Story of the Civil War*. Harcourt Brace Jovanovich, 1932 (I: 10 + R: 6). The book won the 1933 Newbery Honor.

Taulbert, Clifton L. *Little Cliff and the Porch People*. Illustrated by E. B. Lewis. Dial, 1999 (I: 5–9 R: 4). Set in Mississippi of the 1950s.

Taylor, Mildred. *The Gold Cadillac*. Illustrated by Michael Hays. Dial, 1987 (I: 8–10 R: 3). An African American family experiences racial prejudice during a drive into the segregated South.

_____. *Let the Circle Be Unbroken*. Dial, 1981 (I: 10 + R: 6). This is a sequel to *Role of Thunder, Hear My Cry*.

_____. *Roll of Thunder, Hear My Cry*. Dial, 1976 (I: 10 + R: 6). An African American family in Mississippi experiences humiliating and frightening situations in 1933.

Temple, Frances. *Taste of Salt: A Story of Modern Haiti*. Orchard, 1992 (I: 12 + R: 6). This story is set in the repressive environment of Haiti.

Turner, Glennette Tilley. *Take a Walk in Their Shoes*. Cobblehill, 1989 (I: 8 + R: 4). The text includes short biographies of fourteen African Americans.

Walker, Barbara K., retold by. *The Dancing Palm Tree and Other Nigerian Folktales*. Illustrated by Helen Siegl. Texas Tech University Press, 1990 (I: all). This collection of tales is from West Africa.

Walter, Mildred Pitts. *Brother to the Wind*. Illustrated by Diane and Leo Dillon. Lothrop, Lee & Shepard, 1985 (I: all R: 3). An African boy wishes to fly.

Williams, Karen Lynn. *When Africa Was Home*. Illustrated by Floyd Cooper, Orchard, 1991 (I: 4–8 R: 4). A family moves back to Africa after they miss their friends.

Williams, Sherley Anne. *Working Cotton*. Illustrated by Carole Byard. Harcourt Brace, 1992 (I: all). The memories of a migrant family working in California.

Williams, Vera B. *Cherries and Cherry Pits*. Greenwillow, 1986 (I: 3–8 R: 3). A girl uses her magic marker to tell stories about people who like cherries.

Wisniewski, David. *Sundiata: Lion King of Mali*. Clarion, 1992 (I: all). This is a highly illustrated legend.

Woodson, Jacqueline. *We Had a Picnic This Sunday Past*. Illustrated by Diane Greenseid. Hyperion, 1998 (I: 3–8 R: 3). Story of a family picnic.

Yates, Elizabeth. *Amos Fortune, Free Man*. Illustrated by Nora S. Unwin. Dutton, 1950 (I: 10 + R: 6). A slave becomes a free man in Boston.

Native American Time Line

50 000 B.C.	Shamanic religion and core Earth-Diver creation myths and trickster myths brought to North America by Native Americans
1823	*Poor Sarah . . .* , by Elias Boudinot (Cherokee), a fictionalized conversion story, possibly the first Native American fiction
1827	David Cusick (Tuscarora)'s *Ancient History of the Six Nations* published, which is cited as first historical work by Native American
1829	William Apes (Pequot)'s *A Son of the Forest* published, which is cited as the first autobiography written by a Native American
1831–32	Sovereignty of Native American tribes affirmed by the Supreme Court
1832	The first "as-told-to" autobiography, from Black Hawk (Sauk), published
1837	Beginning of enforcement of the Indian Removal Act of 1830 by President Andrew Jackson, driving southern tribes on the Trail of Tears
1839	Two volumes of Chippewa tales published by Schoolcraft
1868	John Rollin Ridge's (Cherokee) *Poems,* first volume of poetry published by a Native American
1871	Refusal of Congress to recognize tribes as independent nations
1876	Custer defeated at Little Bighorn
1890	Massacre of Ghost Dancers at Wounded Knee, South Dakota
1902	Charles Eastman's (Yankton Sioux) *Indian Boyhood* published
Early 1900s	Importance of Native American myths and folktales recognized
1924	Indian Voting Rights Act stressed by anthropologist Franz Boas
1929	Types and motifs of tales identified by Stith Thompson in *Tales of the North American Indians*
1942	Newbery Honor: Lois Lenski's *Indian Captive: The Story of Mary Jemison*
1952	Newbery Honor: Elizabeth Baity's *Americans Before Columbus*
1966	Canadian Book of the Year: Farley Mowat's *Lost in the Barrens*
1969	Pulitzer Prize: N. Scott Momaday (Kiowa)'s *House Made of Dawn*
1970s	Several Caldecott Honor Awards to artists of books about Native Americans: Tom Bahti, Peter Parnall
1970s	Several Newbery Honor Awards to books about Native American subjects: Scott O'Dell (*Sing Down the Moon*), Miska Miles (*Annie and the Old One*), Jamake Highwater (*Anpao: An American Indian Odyssey*)
1973	Newbery: Jean Craighead George's *Julie of the Wolves*
1974	James Welch's (Blackfoot/Gros Ventre) *Winter in the Blood* identified in *New York Times* as "best first novel of the season"
1975	Caldecott: Gerald McDermott's *Arrow to the Sun*
1977	Leslie Silko (Laguana) published *Ceremony;* later awarded MacArthur Foundation Fellowship (1981) for her achievement
1979	Caldecott: Paul Goble's *The Girl Who Loved Wild Horses*
1982	Caldecott Honor: Artist Stephen Gammell's *Where the Buffaloes Begin*
1980s	Newbery Honor Awards: Elizabeth George Speare (*The Sign of the Beaver*) and Gary Paulsen (*Dogsong*)
1984	Canadian Book of the Year: Jan Hudson's *Sweetgrass*
1994	Caldecott Honor: Gerald McDermott's *Raven: A Trickster Tale from Pacific Northwest*
1995	Newbery: Sharon Creech's *Walk Two Moons*

3

Native American Literature

*I*n our study of Native American literature, we will discover both traditional and contemporary literature that reflects many different groups. We begin our study with a historical perspective, extend the study to folklore, discuss the historical nonfiction and fiction, and conclude with contemporary literature, both fiction and nonfiction.

HISTORICAL PERSPECTIVE

The history of Native American literature extends thousands of years into the past. According to Ron Querry (1995),

> [W]hile the writings of the seventeenth century English colonists have traditionally been considered—and are taught—as the first works of American literature, the continent of North America already had a 28,000-year history of storytelling when John Smith and Anne Bradstreet first sat down to write of their experiences in the "new" world. The texts of that long Indian history were oral and communal. Because of that fact, it is often assumed that Indians had no literature or, at the very least, that its oral quality made that literature inferior. Early on, however, their oral traditions gave Indian people a rich literary heritage. (p. 1)

Stereotypes in Literature from the Past

What is a stereotype? Catherine Verrall and Patricia McDowell (1990) in a publication by the Canadian Alliance in Solidarity with the Native Peoples present a definition of stereotypes:

> A stereotype is a fixed image, idea, trait, convention, lacking in originality or individuality, most often negative. Noble savage, stoic warrior in noble defeat, drunken savage, heathen, lazy Indians, children of the forest, Indian princess, whore, dead and dying saints . . . how many others can you identify? Stereotypes rob individuals and their cultures of human qualities, and promote no real understanding of social realities. (p. 7)

Books about Native Americans written for juvenile audiences and published prior to the mid-1970s are frequently filled with such negative stereotypes. Researchers who analyze the images of Native Americans in these books have been especially critical of the common stereotypes. Laura Herbst (1977) found the most common stereotypes characterize Native Americans as savage, depraved, and cruel; noble, proud, silent, and close to nature; or inferior, childlike, and helpless. Terms and comparisons suggesting negative and derogatory images often reinforce such stereotypes. She also identified the stereotypical ways in which Native American culture has been portrayed in children's literature as inferior to the white culture; valueless, and not worthy of respect; and quaint or superficial, without depth or warmth. In the cultural stereotypes, the suggestion is made that life will improve if the Native Americans abandon their culture. Stereotypes of the Native American culture as valueless and not worthy of respect usually ignore the rich diversity of Native American cultures, spiritual beliefs and ceremonies, moral values, artistic skills, and life-styles in favor of the attitude that violence is the chief Native American value.

The changing attitudes toward stereotypes in Native American literature are apparent in the literary criticism of award-winning books. For example, in 1941, Robert Lawson's *They Were Strong and Good* won the Caldecott Medal. The book has since been criticized for having a stereotypical text and illustrations. Similarly, although *The Matchlock Gun* by Walter Edmunds won the 1942 Newbery Medal, the book has been criticized in later years for the stereotypical views of Native Americans. As you read these books and books like them, consider your own responses and the stereotypes they develop.

Any of the stereotypical portrayals described in this section is offensive. More current books, however, especially those written by Native American authors or other authorities on Native American culture, are usually sensitive to the heritage and individuality of the native peoples of North America.

 ## AUTHORS AND ILLUSTRATORS WHO WRITE ABOUT NATIVE AMERICAN CULTURE AND EXPERIENCE

According to Ron Querry (1995), many of the Native American authors

> trace their identities back to the voices of the continent's earliest storytellers. Unlike most of their ancestors, these contemporary Indian authors tell their stories in writing, but they continue an ancient tradition nonetheless. Like their ancestors, they tell distinctive stories about times and places that have shaped the identities of those who inhabit them. Like their ancestors, these modern storytellers provide challenging discoveries of America by showing what has happened here. (p. 1)

Querry traces the emergence of high-quality novels written for adult audiences to the 1968 publication of N. Scott Momaday's Pulitzer Prize-winning novel *House Made of Dawn*. Querry states that following this publication there have been more than one hundred novels written by Native American writers.

The same increase in Native American literature is apparent in the juvenile market. Books by both Native American authors and authors who write with a Native American perspective are available in picture books, traditional literature, and contemporary titles. A review of Caldecott Medal and Honor books for the 1990s, 1980s, and 1970s indicates the number of books relating to Native Americans is increasing from earlier periods and shows they are receiving recognition for their literary quality: *Raven: A Trickster Tale from the Pacific Northwest* by Gerald McDermott (1994 Caldecott Honor); Olaf Baker's *Where the Buffaloes Begin* (1982 Caldecott Honor, illustrated by Stephen Gammell); Paul Goble's *The Girl Who Loved Wild Horses* (1979 Caldecott); Byrd Baylor's *Hawk, I'm Your Brother* (1977 Caldecott Honor, illustrated by Peter Parnall); Byrd Baylor's *The Desert Is Theirs* (1976 Caldecott Honor, illustrated by Peter Parnall); Gerald McDermott's *Arrow to the Sun* (1975 Caldecott); and Byrd Baylor's *When Clay Sings* (1973 Caldecott Honor, illustrated by Tom Bahti).

The Newbery Medal and Honor books include Sharon Creech's *Walk Two Moons* (1995 Newbery); Virginia Hamilton's *In the Beginning: Creation Stories from Around the World* (this 1989 Newbery Honor book includes several Native American myths); Gary Paulsen's *Dogsong* (1986 Newbery Honor); Elizabeth George Speare's *The Sign of the Beaver* (1984 Newbery Honor); Jamake Highwater's *Anpao: An American Indian Odyssey* (1978 Newbery Honor); Jean Craighead George's *Julie of the Wolves* (1973 Newbery); Miska Miles's *Annie and the Old One* (1972 Newbery Honor); and Scott O'Dell's *Sing Down the Moon* (1971 Newbery Honor).

Many other authors are either Native American or write with a Native American perspective. For example, John Bierhorst, Joseph Bruchac, and Maurice Metayer retell Native American folklore. Michael Dorris and Jan Hudson write historical fiction. Dorothy Nafus Morrison and Jean Fritz write biographies. Virginia Driving Hawk Sneve and White Deer of Autumn are known for contemporary literature.

The works of Native American artists are beginning to be found in the illustrated texts. For example, Navajo artist Shonto Begay's illustrations are found in *Navajo: Visions and Voices Across the Mesa*. Cherokee artist's Murv Jacob works illustrate Joseph Bruchac's *The Boy Who Lived with the Bears and Other Iroquois Stories*. Cayuga/Tuscarora artists' works are found in Chief Jake Swamp's *Giving Thanks: A Native American Good Morning Message*. Cherokee artist Christopher Canyon's works illustrate Sandra DeCoteau Orie's *Did You Hear Wind Sing Your Name? An Oneida Song of Spring*. Cree artist George Littlechild's illustrations are found in *This Land Is My Land*. The paintings of Chief Lelooska from the Northwest Coast are found in *Echoes of the Elders: The Stories and Paintings of Chief Lelooska*. Throughout this chapter, we will discover many excellent books and illustrated texts written and illustrated by both Native Americans and non–Native Americans.

 ## ISSUES RELATED TO NATIVE AMERICAN LITERATURE

There are numerous influences on the interpretation, writing, and acceptance of Native American literature. A review of these influences and the associated issues includes the following major areas of concern (Norton, 1996): (1) authenticity of text and illustrations; (2) conflicts over sovereignty related to who may write, adapt, or interpret the stories and culture; (3) disputes over translations of poetry, folklore, and biography/autobiography; and (4) disagreements over literal versus metaphorical interpretations.

In *This Land Is My Land,* the author, a Plains Cree Indian from Canada, describes his experiences.

Source: Reprinted with permission of the publisher, Children's Book Press, San Francisco, CA. Copyright © 1993 by George LIttlechild.

Since the late 1960s, the numbers of literature selections identified as Native American have increased dramatically. Some of these books are of high literary and cultural quality; others however, are filled with stereotypes or inaccurate information about people, their culture, their beliefs, and their values.

Criteria for Evaluating Native American Literature

Criteria for evaluating Native American literature include both generic criteria related to Native American literature and criteria that apply to specific genres of literature. In addition, the literature should be evaluated for literary quality. You may use the following generic criteria when evaluating the literature (Norton, 1997):

1. Are the Native American characters portrayed as individuals with their own thoughts, emotions, and philosophies? The characters should not conform to stereotypes.
2. Do the Native American characters belong to a specific tribe, or are they grouped together under one category referred to as "Indian"?
3. Does the author recognize the diversity of Native American cultures? Are the customs and ceremonies authentic for the Native American tribes?
4. Does the author respect Native American culture?
5. Does the author use offensive and degrading vocabulary?
6. Are the illustrations realistic and authentic?
7. If the story has a contemporary setting, does the author accurately describe the life and situation of Native Americans today?

Beverly Slapin, Doris Seal, and Rosemary Gonzales (1989) emphasize the need to evaluate for stereotypes; to consider loaded words with insulting overtones, as well as racist adjectives; to look for distortions of history; to evaluate the life-styles and culture to make sure that the culture, religions, and traditions are described accurately; to evaluate the dialogue to make sure that it represents the skill of those who come from an oral tradition; to consider the role of women, who should be portrayed as an integral and respected part of society; to analyze the role of elders, who should be considered as valued custodians of the people's history, culture, and life-ways; to consider the effects of the story on children's self-images; and to analyze authors' or illustrators' backgrounds to ascertain if they have the background and skills that qualify them to write or illustrate books about Native Americans.

Analyzing, evaluating, and selecting Native American literature is a complex task. Several authors emphasize this complexity and problems associated with selection. For example, in a bulletin published by the National Council for the Social Studies, Karen D. Harvey, Lisa D. Harjo, and Jane K. Jackson (1990) identify the following facts that everyone should consider when evaluating and selecting materials about Native Americans. First, Native American cultures span twenty or more millennia, from before written history to today. Second, most of the Native American history is tentative, speculative, and written by European or Anglo-American explorers or scholars, and much of the oral history of the Native Americans was lost. Third, widely diverse physical environments influenced the development of ancient and contemporary Native American cultures, including Arctic tundra, woodlands, deserts, Mesoamerican jungles, prairies, plateaus, plains, swamps, and mountains. Fourth, linguists believe that at least two hundred languages were spoken in North America before European contact, and scholars estimate that seventy-three language families existed in North America at the time of European contact. Fifth, currently, there are about five hundred federally recognized tribes and about three hundred federal reservations. Sixth, no one federal or tribal definition establishes a person's identity as an Indian. Consequently, Harvey, Harjo, and Jackson conclude, "the subject is vast, complicated, diverse, and difficult" (p. 2).

Jon C. Stott (1992) focuses on another problem faced by people seeking literature written by Native American authors. He states, "Works by native authors generally appear on the lists of smaller, regional publishers, and, unfortunately, seldom reach a wide audience" (p. 374). Consequently some Native American literature is not easily available. Thankfully, as we analyze the literature, we will discover a considerable collection of newer quality literature that is available.

Authenticity of Text and Illustrations

There are numerous issues related to authenticity of both the text and illustrations. For example, Jon C. Stott (1990) contrasts two versions of the Sedna tale, an Inuit myth. After his analysis of Robert and Daniel San Souci's *Song of Sedna,* he states that the text is "so altered as to be virtually worthless as a reflection on Inuit Culture" (p. 199). Stott declares that throughout the book, the illustrations are inaccurate, the visual depictions of the setting are inappropriate, and the illustrations counteract the Inuit values found in the original story. Stott describes the illustrations as being appropriate for the Native Indians of southern Alaska and northern British Columbia rather than the Inuit peoples. Stott concludes, "The effect of these inaccuracies is to rob the accompanying story of its cultural background. More important, it implicitly reflects the attitude that cultural accuracy in portraying a story of these people is unimportant" (p. 200).

In contrast, Stott finds that Beverly Brodsky McDermott, the reteller and illustrator of *Sedna: An Eskimo Myth*, "combines art and text in a way that presents and amplifies the traditional meanings of the myth" (p. 199). Stott concludes his analysis of McDermott's text by stating, "McDermott clearly respects the culture and the story, as well as the young audience for whom it is adapted. Not only has she closely followed the outline of the Inuit myth, but also she has embodied the cultural dualities that are one of its essential aspects" (p. 201). The types of errors identified in *Song of Sedna* or the accuracy in *Sedna: An Eskimo Myth* also shows the importance of identifying authentic nonfiction informational books that allow readers to evaluate the authenticity of illustrations and settings.

Authenticity in text and illustrations is a major issue in books such as Susan Jeffer's *Brother Eagle, Sister Sky: A Message from Chief Seattle.* Critics are now questioning the authorship of the text. Was the text really written by the Suquamish Indian chief who lived in the Washington Territory in 1854 or was the text written by a playwright in much more recent times? Are the illustrations accurate for a tale supposedly about the people who lived in the Washington Territory?

Conflicts over Sovereignty of the Stories

Conflicts over sovereignty raise significant issues related to writing, publishing, and reading Native American literature. The major question is, Who should write or retell stories about Native American people and their culture? People who adhere to one viewpoint argue that the Native American people should have total sovereignty over their traditions, their culture, their past, and their present circumstances. Advocates of this viewpoint believe that Native American literature should be protected against the desecration committed by the imposition of alien cultures and American/European standards of literacy. In this viewpoint, only Native Americans can translate their traditions or write about their history and culture with an accurate perspective. The contrasting viewpoint encourages writing by knowledgeable and sensitive authors who are able to write with a Native American perspective even though they are not themselves Native American.

The debate in journals and among scholars has not as yet been resolved. Questions such as the following are frequently debated in journals, by publishers, and at scholarly meetings: Should anyone but a member of that specific Native American group write about the group? Who should be the intended audience for Native American literature? Must Native American writers be spokespersons for that group, or may they write about any subject?

Mary Jo Lass-Woodfin (1978) addresses both sides of the issue. She states:

> There is a need for books written by Indians, part-Indians, and non-Indians alike. For, while it is true that no one knows an experience as deeply as one who has lived it, it is equally true that an observer can sometimes see processes that the person involved in the events cannot see until later, if ever. Many of the Indian and Eskimo legends, myths, and speeches would have been lost forever if non-Indian anthropologists, writers, and ethnologists had not recorded them. (p. 4)

Disputes over Literary Styles and Translations

The issues related to disputes over literary styles and translation frequently focus on the desirability or undesirability of changing literature so that it is more accessible to, and able to be more easily understood by, a broader audience. Should the literature retain its total context within the Native American culture, or should it be changed to meet the standards and literary style of literature written from an American/European perspective?

Jamake Highwater (1981) emphasizes the communication differences between Anglo/European and Native American languages and literary styles that may interfere with translations and understandings. For example, in the Anglo/European cultures, words convey explanations and the question is "What does it mean?" In contrast, in Native American cultures, literature conveys a picture of an object or situation into the mind of the listener. The Native American perspective embraces all senses. Highwater states:

> I was once given advice by an Indian who was very much worried about my preoccupation with words. "You must learn to look at the world twice," he told me as I sat on the floor of his immaculately swept adobe room. "First you must bring your eyes together in front so you can see each droplet of rain on the grass, so you can see the smoke rising from an anthill in the sunshine. Nothing should escape your notice. But you must learn to look again, with your eyes at the very edge of what is visible. Now you must see dimly if you wish to see things that are dim—visions, mist, and cloud—people. . . . animals which hurry past you in the dark. You must learn to look at the world twice if you wish to see all that there is to see." (p. 75)

Differences in style affect the retellings of many types of literature. Changes in language and style are frequently found in the translations of folklore, poetry, chants, and autobiographies, especially the literature written for younger audiences. Native American scholars such as Michael Dorris (1979) argue against diluting the literature so that it can be understood by a broader audience; Dorris maintains that scholars and readers need to develop an understanding of Native American literature by taking part in a study that progresses from an awareness of the language and philosophy of creation stories; proceeds through reading myth cycles; continues to historical sagas; proceeds to reading riddles, songs, and religious chants; continues to treaties, diaries, and autobiographies; and concludes with modern authors from the culture. Donna Norton (1990) modifies Dorris's approach to identify appropriate Native American literature and suggest a sequence of study that helps children and adolescents understand Native American culture and literature. In this type of study, students need to read and have access to a wide variety of literature. This is also the sequence that is developed throughout this textbook.

Translations of early Native American autobiographies are also of concern when choosing Native American literature. The authenticity of these translations may be questioned. What is the influence of interpreters on the content of the autobiography? What is the consequence if editors add information to place the narrative in a context that will be better understood by their audiences? Is a book really an autobiography if it has been translated and rewritten? We will explore this issue in greater detail when we discuss biographies.

Disagreements over Literal versus Metaphorical Interpretations

Native American literature frequently includes visions such as those described by Black Elk in the autobiography *Black Elk Speaks: Being the Life Story of a Holy Man of the Oglala Sioux* (1932, 1979) and by Plenty-Coups in *Plenty-Coups: Chief of the Crows* (1962). Are these visions to be interpreted as literal experiences or should they be analyzed for their metaphorical meanings? The Native American authors of both books state their strong beliefs in the literal interpretations of their medicine dreams. They maintain that these dreams controlled their actions. Literary critics, however, debate these interpretations. Some critics maintain that seeking meaning subverts the integrity of the literature. Others believe that the images bear no real connection to the meaning of the experience. Still others argue that certain traditions make sense only in a metaphorical, not in a historical or literal, way. Finally, some believe that a literal interpretation should be used to limit misinterpretation and to encourage fundamental understanding of the Native American experience. These questions are debated, especially in children's and adolescent literature. As students of multicultural literature, we need to decide for ourselves, How do you believe that visions should be interpreted?

 ## TRADITIONAL LITERATURE

Ron Querry (1995) defines traditional Native American literature as "that which was composed in an Indian language for an Indian audience at a time when tribal cultures were intact and contact with whites was minimal. It was literature made up of sacred stories, myths, legends, and songs" (p. 2).

Native American tales show that the North American continent had traditional tales centuries old before the European settlers arrived. Traditional Native American tales make up a heritage that all North Americans should take pride in and pass on to future generations.

An authentic folklore collection is one of the most important elements in any Native American literature collection. This is especially true for myths, or narratives about gods, superhuman beings, animals, plants, and creation that are truths to the people who believe in them and that give the people spiritual strength and guidance. Critics and reviewers of multicultural literature emphasize the need for authenticity in texts and in illustrations. For example, Betsy Hearne (1993) emphasizes that not only should the reteller provide information about the original source for the tale but also a text adapted from folklore should be judged for its balance of two traditions: the one from which it is drawn and the one that it is entering. Consequently, both texts and illustrations should ring true for the culture from which they are adapted and be meaningful to the culture that is reading them. In an evaluation of children's literature about Native Americans, Clifford E. Trafzer (1992), the Director of Native American Studies at the University of California, Riverside, emphasizes the need for citing tribal sources and creating works that are culturally authentic for the tribe.

In this section, we will consider the history of the collection of Native American folklore in written form, discuss the importance of folklore in developing understanding of Native American cultures, and evaluate and discuss specific examples of Native American traditional literature. We will discover that there are numerous examples of folklore. In fact, in a review of Native American literature, Debbie Reese (1998) states: "Most of the good books about Native Americans are folktales" (p. 638).

History of European Recording of North American Folklore in Written Form

The Native American folklore that we now read or hear was told through generations of oral storytellers before it was collected in written form. As early as the 1600s, Jesuit missionaries recorded a few myths they collected in the regions east of the Great Lakes.

John Bierhorst, in *The Mythology of North America* (1985), provides specific information about the collection of the stories. He identifies the role of explorers and Indian agents:

> Modern appreciation of Indian myth and the idea of recording entire mythologies originated with the explorer and Indian agent Henry Rowe Schoolcraft whose diary entry for July 31, 1822, expresses his elation at having stumbled on something new: "Who would have imagined that these wandering foresters should have possessed such a resource? What have all the voyagers and remarkers from the days of Cabot and Raleigh been about, not to have discovered this curious trait, which lifts up indeed a curtain, as it were, upon the Indian mind and exhibits it in an entirely new character?" (p. 3)

The two volumes of Chippewa tales published by Schoolcraft in 1839 titled *Algic Researches* were compared with the collections of German folklore by Jacob and Wilhelm Grimm published in 1812–1815.

In the early 1900s, anthropologist Franz Boas recognized Native American myths and folktales as a source for deciphering Indian languages and learning about the Native American culture. Collections from such cultures and tribes as Navajo, Hopi, Caddo, and Kwakiutl were then published by scholarly presses. During this time, Boas described the basic tale types and motifs. In 1929, folklorist Stith Thompson analyzed Native American traditional literature. His *Tales of the North American Indians* (1929) analyzed the stories by types and motifs to identify common plots and incidents. Both Boas and Thompson looked at common types of motifs among all Native American tribes rather than characteristics of the folklore of one group.

By 1935, there was a changing attitude among anthropologists. Anthropologists began viewing myths as a means of analyzing a single cultural group such as the Cherokee or the Zuni. At that time, folklore was not considered to be generic. It was believed to belong to a particular people who had particular livelihoods, social organizations, and religions.

In the 1950s, the emphasis shifted to a cultural and personality approach to anthropology. At that time, collectors noted how characteristics such as sex, age, or psychology of the teller affected the story. By the 1960s, performance ethnographers and some collectors of mythology emphasized the narrator's art, which included such characteristics as tone of voice and comments made by listeners.

Currently, there is considerable interest in the publications of myths and other traditional narratives by Native American groups. Many groups are publishing their own traditional tales to retain their culture, their stories, and their histories.

Importance of Native American Folklore

Joseph Campbell (1988) provides compelling reasons for including mythology in the literature when he identifies four functions of myth. First, a mythical function allows people to realize and experience the wonder of the awe in the universe. Second, a cosmological dimension shows people the shape of the universe. Third, a sociological role supports and validates a certain order. Fourth, a pedagogical function teaches people how to live under any circumstances.

Clifford E. Trafzer (1992) emphasizes the importance of myths, legends, and folktales in transmitting the beliefs and values of the Native Americans. He states, "The words of the old stories are not myths and fairy tales. They are a communion with the dead—the Animal, Plant, and Earth Surface Peoples who once inhabited the world and whose spirits continue to influence the course of Native American history" (p. 381). Trafzer also emphasizes the importance of these stories for children, saying, "There is something sacred in the old texts, the ancient literature of America. . . . The accounts provide children with a better understanding of this land and its first people" (p. 393).

The importance of the oral tales is reinforced through the contemporary writings of many Native American authors. For example, Ray A. Young Bear, when writing his own autobiography, *Black Eagle Child: The Facepaint Narratives* (1992), includes creation myths and tales that depict his cultural history and influence his life.

Native American traditional literature is an excellent source for identifying and understanding tribal traditional values and beliefs. Several sources provide documentation for traditional Native American values and beliefs. For example, *Human Behavior and American Indians*, by W. D. Hanson and M. O. Eisenbise (1983), documents tribal traditional values and compares them to urban industrial values. *The Journal of American Indian Education* (Spang, 1965) identifies North American Indian cultural values and compares them to the values of the dominant non-Indian culture. The Coalition of Indian Controlled School Boards (Ross and Brave Eagle, 1975) identifies traditional Lakota values and compares them to non-Lakota values. This last source is especially valuable for analyzing the traditional literature of the Northern Plains Indians.

A review of these sources indicates that many of the traditional values, such as living in harmony with nature, viewing religion as a natural phenomenon closely related to nature, showing respect for wisdom gained through age and experience, acquiring patience, and emphasizing group and extended needs rather than individual needs, are also dominant themes in the traditional tales from various tribal regions. As you read various Native American traditional tales, see if you can identify these important values.

For example, living in harmony with nature is a dominant theme in Tomie dePaola's retelling of the Comanche tale, *The Legend of the Bluebonnet*. In the legend, selfishly taking from the land is punished by drought, while unselfishly giving of a prized possession is rewarded with bluebonnets and rain. The name change in the main character as she goes from She-Who-Is-Alone to One-Who-Dearly-Loved-Her-People supports the emphasis on extended family rather than the individual.

Paula Underwood Spencer's *Who Speaks for Wolf* develops the importance of living in harmony with nature through a "Native American Learning Story," told to the author by her Oneida father, Sharp-Eyed Hawk. The story chronicles the experiences of the Oneida as they move to a new location, only to discover that they have failed to consider the rights of the animals. At the end of the tale, the wise storyteller gazes slowly around the council circle and asks the ancient question:

Tell me now my brothers
Tell me now my sisters
Who speaks for Wolf? (p. 40)

The interactions between buffalo and Great Plains Indians are developed in Olaf Baker's *Where the Buffaloes Begin* and Paul Goble's *Buffalo Woman* and *The Legend of the White Buffalo Woman*. In *Where the Buffaloes Begin,* Stephen Gammell's marvelous black-and-white drawings capture the buffaloes surging out of a mythical lake after their birth, rampaging across the prairie, and eventually saving Little Wolf's people from their enemies. In traditional tales from the Great Plains, the buffalo people frequently save those who understand and respect them. Goble's *Buffalo Woman* ends with a statement of why the relationship between the Great Plains Indians and the buffaloes is so important:

The relationship was made between the People and the Buffalo Nation; it will last until the end of time. It will be remembered that a brave young man became a buffalo because he loved his wife and little child. In return the Buffalo People have given their flesh so that little children, and babies still unborn, will always have meat to eat. It is the Creator's wish. (unnumbered)

The Legend of the White Buffalo Woman shows another close spiritual relationship as the Buffalo Woman gives the Sacred Calf Pipe to the Lakota so that the people can pray and commune with the Great Spirit.

Showing respect for animals, keeping one's word, and listening to elders are interrelated themes in Frank Cushing's "The Poor Turkey Girl," found in *Zuni Folk Tales*. In this Cinderella-type tale, a Zuni maiden who cares for the turkeys is helped to go to a festival by the turkeys. When the girl does not heed old Gobble's admonition and return on time to feed the turkeys, she loses everything.

Traditional tales of legendary heroes reflect many important values and beliefs of the people. The legendary heroes may have many of the same characteristics found in heroic tales from other cultures. For example, like Beowulf in the Norse legend, an Inuit hero shows bravery, honor, and a willingness to avenge wrongs. In the introduction to one of the tales included in *Stories from the Canadian North*, Muriel Whitaker states:

In order to understand fully the ending of "The Blind Boy and the Loon," one must realize that the Eskimo hero was predominantly an avenger. Just as the spirits of weather, thunder, lightning, and the sea took vengeance on those who mistreated them, so too was the mortal hero expected to have the will and the power to exact retribution for evil. (p. 20)

According to Robin McGrath (1988), the traditional tales in Inuit folklore can be divided into six classifications: (1) creation myths or stories, which embody religious beliefs; (2) stories of fabulous beings such as trolls, giants, or ghosts; (3) tales of epic heroes; (4) stories of murder and revenge; (5) beast fables; and (6) personal memoirs. Stories in these classifications can be found in the adult resource *The Eskimo Storyteller: Folktales from Noatak, Alaska* by Edwin S. Hall, Jr. (1976).

Legends from the northwestern coast of the United States and Canada empha-size heroes who venture onto the unpredictable sea and overcome perils associated with the ocean wilderness. Christie Harris's *The Trouble with Adventurers* includes tales with representative themes. For example, "The Bird of Good Luck" shows that fame can arouse envy; "How Raven Gets the Oolikan" suggests that the deeds of heroes are not always to be admired; "Revenge of the Wolf Prince" suggests that heroes do not always survive to enjoy a happy future; and "Ghost Canoe People" shows that heroes often need supernatural help but that supernatural beings may not be inclined to offer assistance. Tales from British Columbia are found in *Kwaki-utl Legends*, retold by Chief James Wallas.

Native American peoples developed a rich heritage of traditional myths and leg-ends. John Bierhorst (1976) identifies the following four categories found in Native American folklore: (1) creation myths that emphasize "setting the world in order," in which the world is created out of the chaos of nature, or in which physical or social order is brought to the tribal world; (2) tales that deal with "family or tribal drama" by centering on conflicts and affinities rising out of the kinship unit; (3) "fair and foul" trickster tales such as the trickster cycle tales, in which the hero pro-gresses from being a character of utter worthlessness to one that displays a gradual understanding of social virtue; and (4) "crossing the threshold" tales that reflect major changes such as the passage from unconsciousness to consciousness, the ordeal of puberty, the passage into and out of the animal world, the passage into and out of death, and the transition from nature to culture. In a book for adults, *Red Swan: Myths and Tales of the American Indians* (1976), Bierhorst presents and discusses examples of these various categories of myths. Bierhorst's categories are similar to those used in other anthologies that include tales passed down in Native American cultures across the North American continent. Consequently, we will use Bierhorst's categories when discussing Native American folklore.

Setting-the-World-in-Order Tales   Creation myths that emphasize setting the world in order usually tell about the creation of the earth and animal and plant life. Earth creation myths are frequently "Earth-Diver" tales such as "Turtle Dives to the Bottom of the Sea: Earth Starter the Creator," a Maidu tale from California, and "The Woman Who Fell from the Sky: Divine Woman the Creator," a Huron myth from northeastern United States. Both of these stories are found in Virginia Hamil-ton's *In the Beginning: Creation Stories from Around the World*.

Creation stories from several tribes are found in Michael J. Caduto and Joseph Bruchac's *Keepers of the Earth: Native American Stories and Environmental Activities for Children*. "The Earth on Turtle's Back," an Onondaga tale from the northeastern woodlands, tells how Great Turtle gives his shell to hold Earth and the seeds brought to Earth by the Great Chief's wife. In "Four Worlds: The Dine Story of Creation," the Holy People move from the first world to the fourth world by way of a female reed. This tale is an excellent example of tales that depict the disastrous consequences of not taking care of Earth. The warning associated with Earth is characteristic of many of the setting-the-world-in-order tales: "So the Fourth World came to be. However, just as the worlds before it were destroyed when wrong was done, so too this Fourth World was destined to be destroyed when the people do not live the right way. That is what the Dine say to this day" (p. 34). A Cherokee myth "The Coming of Earth" is found in Caduto's *Earth Tales from Around the World*.

"The Great Flood" is one of the creation stories found in *The Serpent's Tongue: Prose, Poetry, and Art of the New Mexico Pueblos*, edited by Nancy Wood. In this Zia tale, the people and animals leave their underworld as Spider Sussistinnako places a huge reed upon the top of the mesa and the people pass through this reed until they reach Earth. The creation stories in this volume develop the strong relationship between the people and the spirit world because: "This connection, this belief in the spirit world, was all the Pueblo Indians needed to survive. Tribes do not accept the idea that their ancestors crossed the Bering Strait land bridge and moved southward during the Ice Age. We have always been here, they insist. Our world came with us" (p. xii).

In some of the creation tales, a creator intervenes to preserve animal life. In "The Battle of the Attiyiyi and Toqueenut," retold by Nashone in *Grandmother Stories of the Northwest*, Creator saves the last salmon egg after a battle between the Salmon Chief and five hostile North Wind brothers. In an ending that is typical of many northwestern tribal stories, the young hero faces and kills his enemies. Only the younger sister escapes. It is the younger sister of the five North Wind brothers who returns each winter to remind the people that her brothers lived in the Northwest. The story not only sets the world in order by preserving the salmon, but also explains why there are sometimes cold, windy winters in the Northwest.

Native American tales, such as Barbara Juster Esbensen's *The Star Maiden*, account for the creation of plant life. In this lyrical rendition of an Ojibway tale, Star Maiden and her sisters leave their home in the sky and become the beautiful star-shaped water lilies.

Several of the tales in George Bird Grinnell's adult texts *Blackfeet Indian Stories* (1993, 1926, 1913) and *Blackfoot Lodge Tales: The Story of a Prairie People* (1962) are creation stories. For example, "The Blackfeet Creation" is an Earth-Diver type of story. The origin of the medicine lodge is told in "Scarface: Origin of the Medicine Lodge." The section of "Stories of Ancient Times" also includes the origin of the medicine pipe.

Family Drama Tales   Family drama tales focus on various family needs and conflicts, such as learning from elders, providing protection, obtaining food, and overcoming problems, including rivalry and aggression. The family in these stories may be the smaller tribal unit or the greater cosmos. If the tale deals with the greater world family, the storyteller may refer to Earth as mother, Sky as father, and humanity as children. Many of these stories reveal tribal standards.

The importance of tribal stories in providing instructions for life is emphasized in several Native American folklore collections. For example, Tewa Vickie Downey's comments in *The Serpent's Tongue*, edited by Nancy Wood:

> Now people call our Instructions legends because they were given as stories. But to the Indian people, that was like a reality at some point in history. . . . The Instructions during that time, at the beginning, were to love and respect one another even with all the differences—different cultures, different languages. We were told we were all from the same source. We were coming from the same mother, same parents. The Instructions were to help us live in a good way and be respectful to everybody and everything. We were told if the Instructions were lost, then harm would come to the people. (p. 55)

In the introduction to *Echoes of the Elders: The Stories and Paintings of Chief Lelooska*, edited by Christine Normandin, Stephen Down Beckham states: "The stories were the primary means of passing on the tribal memory. They recounted how the world had come to be, why things were named as they were, and how humans should act. They speak through time to listeners and readers today" (p. 5). As we see from these comments, the stories are considered to be very important in Native American cultures.

The consequences of not caring for one's young is an important theme in Michael Rosen's *Crow and Hawk: A Traditional Pueblo Indian Story*. The lesson is developed when Crow becomes tired of sitting on her eggs and abandons the nest. Hawk finds the abandoned nest, hatches the eggs, and cares for the young birds. A confrontation develops when Crow returns and wants her growing children. The birds take their quarrel to Eagle, King of the Birds. Eagle decides in Hawk's favor after asking the babies who their mother should be. The babies respond: "Hawk is the only mother we know. . . . Hawk hatched us. Hawk fed us. You left us" (unnumbered). The learning lesson concludes when Eagle tells Crow not to cry because that is the way it must be, "You left the nest; you lost the children" (unnumbered). This story was originally included in Ruth Benedict's *Tales of the Cochiti Indians*, which was published in 1931 by the University of New Mexico Press.

The need for leading a balanced life is the theme created in *The Magic of Spider Woman* retold by Lois Duncan. When Wandering Girl is given the secret of weaving by Spider Woman, she is given both the name change of Weaving Woman and advice for herself and her people. Spider Woman tells her: "But there is one danger that you always must be aware of. The Navajo People must walk the Middle Way, which means that they must respect boundaries and try to keep their lives in balance. They should not do too much of anything. You must promise not to weave for too long, or a terrible thing will happen to you" (unnumbered). Unfortunately, when Weaving Woman becomes totally engrossed in weaving a beautiful blanket she forgets the warning and her spirit becomes trapped within the blanket. A shaman holds a Blessing Way during which he chants a prayer asking that Weaving Woman be restored:

> In the house made of dawn,
> In the house made of twilight,
> In the house made of dark cloud,
> May Weaving Woman be restored to us! (unnumbered)

Spirit Woman hears the prayer and creates a spirit pathway through the border of the blanket. Now Weaving Woman has learned her lesson as she cries out to Spirit Being: "Never again will I weave for too long at a sitting, and never again will I doubt the wisdom of my creators" (unnumbered). The story concludes with the information that since then every Navajo blanket is woven with a pathway so that the spirit of the weaver will not be imprisoned by its beauty.

Overcoming problems through the use of one's wit is the focus of Lois Ehlert's *Mole's Hill: A Woodland Tale*. This Seneca tale reveals how Mole saves her home by creating a hill that is too big to move and then uses her tunneling skills to solve the animals' problem. The medium of collage with abstract geometric designs used to illustrate text adds to the pleasure of the story. The depth of Mole's tunnels are suggested by two double-page spreads in which both the text and illustrations are turned sideways.

The need to share with others and to have respect for all living things is developed in Jennifer Berry Jones's *Heetunka's Harvest: A Tale of the Plains Indians*. In this tale, Hunka, the Spirit of Kinship, of Oneness-of-life reveals the lesson of sharing and caring for others when she develops the lesson through a dream: "You were wrong to take all of the Mouse-children's food. You must return some beans, or put corn in their place, or your own children will hunger and go without" (unnumbered). In this story first mentioned in a journal kept by Captain William Clark in 1804 and later published in Melvin R. Gilmore's 1925 article, "The Ground Bean and Its Uses" the woman learns the disastrous consequences of selfish actions and ignoring simple duties.

Why there is chaos in the sky, society, and family life is revealed in Jerrie Oughton's *How the Stars Fell into the Sky: A Navajo Legend*. In this tale, First Woman wants to write the laws for the people to see. First Man suggests that she take her jewels and write the laws in the sky. First Woman begins her mission by designing a pattern of stars so that all can read the laws. Coyote offers to help her complete her task, but he is unhappy when she tells him that writing the laws with the stars could take many moons. Coyote impatiently gathers the corners of First Woman's blanket and flings the remaining stars out into the night, spilling them in disarray. The tale concludes: "As the pulse of the second day brought it into being, the people rose and went about their lives, never knowing in what foolish haste Coyote had tumbled the stars . . . never knowing the reason for the confusion that would always dwell among them" (p. 30). According to Oughton, this is a retelling of a traditional tale told to the Navajo Indians by Hosteen Klah, their great medicine man.

Trickster Tales   Trickster tales are among the most common folklore throughout the world, and trickster characters are found throughout North America. Trickster tales reveal both good and bad conduct; they allow the narrator an opportunity to tell about immoral or antisocial temptations in humorous ways. On the northwestern coast of the Pacific Ocean, the trickster is called Raven. When evaluating the role of Raven, Bierhorst (1993) states:

> Raven is tough. Whatever is ascribed to him, he can survive it. And when we look back on what has been said of him, we may find that there is more wisdom to these tales than we had realized. As for Raven himself, he is always off on a new adventure. One of the old Tsimshian narrators used to say that after each scrape Raven doggedly "journeys on." Or as another of the old texts once phrased it, the trickster simply "put on his raven garment and flew away."

Raven the trickster is the central character in Gerald McDermott's *Raven: A Trickster Tale from the Pacific Northwest*. In this tale, to bring light from Sky Chief, Raven changes himself into a pine needle that is in a drinking cup of Sky Chief's daughter. After swallowing the needle, the daughter eventually gives birth to a child that is really Raven in human form. Thus, Raven is able to acquire the sun, which is in a set of nested boxes found in the sky lodge and bring light to the earth.

Iktomi is the Sioux name for trickster. In *Iktomi and the Boulder: A Plains Indian Story*, Paul Goble describes the fair and foul side of Iktomi:

> [Iktomi is] beyond the realm of moral values. He lacks all sincerity. Tales about Iktomi remind us that unsociable and chaotic behavior is never far below the surface. We can see ourselves in him. Iktomi is also credited with greater things: in many of the older stories, the Creator entrusts him with much of Creation. People say that what seem to be the "mistakes" and "irrational" aspects of Creation, such as earthquakes, floods, disease, flies, and mosquitoes, were surely made by Iktomi. (introduction)

In Goble's version of the Sioux tale, conceited Iktomi first gives his blanket to a boulder and then deceitfully takes the blanket back when he needs it for protection. Iktomi uses trickery to save himself from the angry boulder. Even though Iktomi eventually wins the confrontation, he is frightened and momentarily humbled by his experience. Goble's *Iktomi and the Berries* provides another humbling experience for the trickster character.

Another trickster character is Coyote, who may be a creator or a trickster in folklore. Native American author Simon Ortiz (1990) states that trickster characters are extremely important in Native American literature, both past and present. He discusses various trickster characters and concludes:

> Coyote, or Perruh, is a part of a tradition of literature of resistance, of struggling against what will overcome you, that is, Western colonialism. . . . In some stories Perruh is a figure who represents Indian people in their struggle against the Spanish soudarrhu, or the soldier, the Spanish troops who came among the people aggressively, destroying. Perruh is the spokesperson; he outthinks, outsmarts, the foolish soldiers; in that case he is a survivor. He's a figure important in a genre that can be called resistance literature. In a sense because Coyote in some other traditions—for example, in the Northern California traditions—is a shaper, or a maker even, by his wits and intelligence and creative nature, he overcomes odds or sets an example or is a teacher or comes to have people realize something about themselves; obviously, he is going to be a means of speaking for survival. (p. 106)

In *Coyote Steals the Blanket: A Ute Tale*, a tale retold by Janet Stevens, Coyote repeatedly declares, "I go where I want, I do what I want, and I take what I want." Consequently, when Hummingbird warns him not to touch the blankets that cover the rocks, he does it anyway. When Coyote brags and disobeys, he is humbled.

In Gerald McDermott's introduction to *Coyote: A Trickster Tale from the American Southwest*, the author describes Coyote's image in the Southwest as a troublesome trickster who is portrayed as a devious, gluttonous fool who is a victim of his own inquisitiveness. His desires to imitate others, to intrude on their lives makes him seem both very foolish and very human. McDermott emphasizes that the Pueblo of Zuni associate Coyote with the West and the color blue. Consequently, McDermott's illustrations picture coyote as blue. The theme of the story stresses that human vanity and misbehavior result in misfortune. In addition to being a trickster tale, this is also an explanatory tale as it reveals why Coyote is the color of dust, has a tail with a black tip, and finds trouble by following his nose.

Rabbit plays a trickster role in "Rabbit and Fox" in Joseph Bruchac's *The Boy Who Lived with the Bears and Other Iroquois Stories*. In this tale, Rabbit transforms himself first into an old woman and then into a medicine man. Through these disguises, Rabbit is able to strike Fox blows on the head and then escape in his animal form. Finally, Fox is convinced that Rabbit has transformed himself into an old log and eats the log. As a consequence, Fox learns a lesson: "don't like to eat Rabbits after all" (p. 21).

Threshold Tales   Threshold tales in Native American folklore depict many different types of thresholds: these include transformations that allow characters to go into and out of the animal world, to pass the threshold from childhood to adulthood, or to go into the spirit world. Paul Goble's *Buffalo Woman* presents transformations from the human to the animal world, but also illustrates the bond between Native Americans and the buffalo that were so important to the people of the Great Plains.

In *Beyond the Ridge*, Goble's main character goes from the land of the living to the spirit world. An elderly Plains Indian experiences the afterlife as believed by her people. On her way, she discovers Owl Maker. The spirits of individuals who have led good lives pass Owl Maker to the right, toward Wanagiyata, Land of Many Tipis. However, Owl Maker pushes the spirits of those who have led bad lives to the left, along a short path where they fall off, landing back on Earth to wander for a time as ghosts.

In Laura Simms's retelling of *The Bone Man: A Native American Modoc Tale,* the main character, Nulwee, goes from a frightened boy to a warrior whose strength comes from compassion. Along the way, he discovers the importance of both tradition and courage, confronts his fears, and transforms the evil monster into something that helps his people. According to the author's note, the story was recorded by Jeremiah Curtin around 1900.

Paul Owen Lewis's *Storm Boy* is an original story that uses Native American elements. This is a hero epic that develops the three rites of passage: separation, initiation, and return. The author's note provides information about each of these Northwest Coast motifs. For example, separation occurs when the boy in the story wanders too far from the village. This invites supernatural encounters and the boy finds a mysterious entrance to the spirit world, which allows him to enter the realm of the killer whales. Initiation occurs when the boy encounters animals in human form and there is an exchange of gifts and cultural information. Return occurs when the boy is given a dancing staff shaped like a dorsal fin and instructions on how to return to his own realm (the boy closes his eyes and visualizes his home). The return motif includes a time disparity between the two realms: for every day spent in the spirit world, a year passes in the earth realm. The return concludes with a reunion celebration in which the boy recounts his mysterious adventure and displays the killer whale staff and demonstrates the dance shown him in the other realm. Because he has been adopted by the Killer Whale People, he can now claim the killer whale crest. The illustrations for the text depict the art of the Haida and Tlingit people of the Northwest Coast.

Combination Tales   Many of the traditional tales combine several of the folklore types. For example, John Bierhorst's *The Ring in the Prairie: A Shawnee Legend* has elements related to fair and foul tricksters, to crossing thresholds, and to family drama. First, the Shawnee hunter plays the trickster, turning himself into a mouse and creeping close to a beautiful young woman who descends from the sky. Then he returns to his human form and captures the woman who is his heart's desire. The tale contains several crossing-the-threshold experiences. The hunter passes into and out of the animal world before he and his family are permanently transformed into animals. His captured bride crosses from the world of the Star People to the world of humans and back to the world of the Star People before she is permanently transformed into a white hawk. The story also reflects strong family ties. The hunter mourns the loss of his wife and son and then goes on a difficult quest so that he can be reunited with his family.

In *Keepers of the Animals: Native American Stories and Wildlife Activities for Children*, Michael J. Caduto and Joseph Bruchac discuss the various circles found in "Salmon Boy," a Haida tale from the Pacific Northwest. They state: "'Salmon Boy' is an allegory of great importance, revealing a series of interlocking circles which, as the story proceeds, run progressively deeper into the life ways of the Haida. . . . There is an important, independent relationship here: The salmon give people food and the people show their appreciation through prayer and reverence" (p. 97).

Barbara Juster Esbensen's *The Great Buffalo Race: How the Buffalo Got Its Hump* provides an excellent source for authentication. In the author's note, Esbensen identifies the source for the original tale as the Seneca people who were part of the Iroquois Nation. The source for the tale is identified as "The Buffalo's Hump and the Brown Birds" retold by Arthur C. Parker in his collection *Skunny Wundy: Seneca Indian Tales* (1926). Esbensen identifies the home of the Seneca people as New York State, although they fought campaigns that took them to the Mississippi River and beyond. She states: "The patterns and costumes found in the illustrations were inspired by traditional beadwork and clothing found in books on the Iroquois as well as the American Museum of Natural History and the American Indian Museum, Heye Foundation, both in New York" (note to the reader, unnumbered).

A search for the original source provides both Arthur C. Parker's background and information about the Seneca. Parker, whose Seneca name is Gawaso Wanneh, was an anthropologist as well as a member of the Seneca tribe. His career in anthropology included experiences at the American Museum of Natural History, the Peabody Museum, and the Rochester Museum of Arts and Sciences. His studies focused on the Iroquois and the League of the Iroquois, a confederation of five tribes or nations: the Mohawks, Oneidas, Onondagas, Cayugas, and Senecas who lived in what is now New York State.

The introduction to Parker's *Skunny Wundy: Seneca Indian Tales* provides additional information that may be used to authenticate tales about the Seneca. For example, the lands where they lived were in a region of forest and lakes in what is now New York state; the people lived on close terms with the animals; clan names, rituals, symbols, and stories reflect the importance of these animals; different creatures have special traits including the cleverness of the fox and raccoon, the easy duping of the rabbit, the bravery of the bear, the villainous nature of the wolf, and the special place for the turtle from whose back grew the Tree of Life with Sun at its top; the people lived in houses built of posts covered with elm bark; and the people not only hunted, but raised vast fields of corn, beans, squash, melons, and tobacco.

A textural comparison of the original "The Buffalo's Hump and the Brown Birds" and the retelling found in Esbensen's *The Great Buffalo Race: How the Buffalo Got Its Hump* shows a close similarity in characters, plot, and theme, although the language of the texts is different. In both versions, the major conflict is between Old Buffalo and Young Buffalo as they vie for leadership of the buffalo herd. The members of the buffalo herd are called followers in the original version and tribesmen in the adaptation. The spiritual being is called "The Masterful One" in the original and "Haweniyo, the Great Spirit" in the retelling. Both versions identify trickery as inappropriate behavior

Caduto and Bruchac identify the first circle as the great circle of life and death and as the reality of the spirit world. Another circle is transformation, depicted when Salmon Boy returns to his people as a healer and a teacher to instruct them in the ways of the Salmon People and to help them when they are sick. The circle shows the sense of interconnectedness between this world and the spirit world, and between animals and people. Finally, Salmon Boy's body is placed in the river, where it circles four times, a sacred number, and returns to the Salmon People. Notice how this tale includes a combination of the types of tales identified by Bierhorst.

in the eyes of the spiritual being. In both versions, Old Buffalo and Young Buffalo are punished because of their foolish actions when they ignore the rights of the small animals of the fields as the competing herds race westward toward what they believe is rain and green grazing grounds. In both versions, it is Brown Buffalo, son of Old Buffalo, who is rewarded because he had the wisdom to stay in the original grazing area and wait for the lush green grasses to return with the rain. Both versions explain why buffaloes have shoulder humps and heavy heads that almost touch the ground: it is so that they will remember the actions of the two herds that were punished and will remember to be careful in their dealings with the smaller animals who live or nest on the ground. This care for the smaller animals of the field reflects the close relationship between the Seneca Indians and the animals in the environment.

Additional authentication may focus on location of the buffalo, the setting in the illustrations, the name of the great spirit, and the patterns and costumes found in the illustrations. In the area in which the buffalo lived, the question arises, Would buffalo be common in the land of the Seneca, which is the eastern United States? A map showing the range of the buffalo, or bison, found in Bryan Hodgson's article "Buffalo: Back Home on the Range," published in *National Geographic* (1994), identifies the bison, circa 1500, as ranging east into what is now the southern portion of New York state. In addition, the Seneca traveled long distances on their war and hunting trips and may have seen buffalo herds grazing on the prairies. This speculation is especially important for authenticity because Helen K. Davie's illustrations for *The Great Buffalo Race: How the Buffalo Got Its Hump* reflect the prairies with their vast stretches of grass—and not the forests and trees of the Seneca homeland.

Instead of the original "The Masterful One," Esbensen's name for the spiritual being is "Haweniyo, the Great Spirit." According to Sam D. Gill and Irene F. Sullivan in *Dictionary of Native American Mythology* (1992), Hawenniyo (Gill and Sullivan have a different spelling for the name) is the main character in the Seneca origin story of the False Faces and also a Seneca term that later came to be used to refer to the Christian God.

The designs on the costumes in the illustrations in Esbenson's book are similar to designs in beadwork and porcupine-quill-embroidered buckskin in pictures of Seneca artifacts found in nonfiction texts such as Peter T. Furst and Jill L. Furst's *North American Indian Art* (1982) that show artifacts from earlier time periods in the Seneca culture.

You may choose to authenticate texts such as Kristina Rodanas's *Dance of the Sacred Circle: A Native American Tale* in which the author identifies the original source as Robert Vaughn's *Then and Now: Or Thirty-Six Years in the Rockies* (1900).

 ## HISTORICAL NONFICTION AND FICTION

Ron Querry (1995) identifies much of the historical nonfiction as transitional literature that is "generally represented by translations of the great Indian orators of the nineteenth century and by memoirs of the Indian experience as it related to white dominance" (p. 2). In this section, we will consider biographies written about earlier Native American peoples, informational literature that is about the earlier cultures, and historical fiction.

Biography About Early Peoples

Biographies and autobiographies of the earlier Native American figures are important for developing understanding of various Native American cultures. These texts provide a source for researchers, whether adult or children, who are investigating early U.S. or searching to discover the impact of an alien culture on native peoples. Books written for a juvenile audience, however, are frequently criticized for their lack of accuracy or their nonrealistic depiction of their Native American subjects. Autobiographies of Native Americans, biographies of Native Americans written for adults, and historical documents provide sources for comparisons with juvenile texts and sources to use when authenticating children's biographies.

My own research (Norton, 1987) investigated the authenticity of the conflicts described in Native American biographies intended for children and young adults by comparing information in juvenile biographies with information found in Native American biographies, autobiographies, and other historical documents written for adults. You may choose to complete a similar type of research in which you search for answers to questions such as these: Are the types of conflicts similar in adult and juvenile biographies? Are the depictions of cultural details similar for biographies of Native Americans from the same tribal areas? Are there differences in the Native American responses to an intrusion of an alien culture in biographies written for adults and those written for children?

First, a search of historical documents revealed two types of conflicts in historical studies about Native Americans who lived in the eighteenth and nineteenth centuries, during the period of European expansion and settlement in the United States: (1) conflicts over land and (2) conflicts resulting from cultural confrontation, which included differences in beliefs, values, customs, and religion. The historical documents also showed that the Native Americans responded to the intrusion of the Europeans in various ways that included the following (1) retreatism, in which the reservation and the traditional way of life served as a sanctuary; (2) rebellion, in which Native Americans fought rather than accommodated to the white culture; (3) ritualism, in which the Native Americans rejected white values and sought refuge in Native American rituals, religious beliefs, and cultural values; (4) innovation, in which the Native Americans retained some Native American identities and values while accepting some of the Anglo/European values, customs, and religion; and (5) conformity in which the Native Americans rejected Native American beliefs, values, customs, and religion, while totally accepting the alien culture.

In an analysis of adult biographies and autobiographies of Native Americans from the Great Plains, the Great Basin, and the Southwest, conflicts over land were found in all three areas. For example, 61 percent of the literature from the Great Plains emphasized the displacement of the people, 77 percent stressed the impoverishment of the people, and 38 percent told of the emergence of leaders because of these conflicts. The literature from the Great Basin showed 100 percent of the books emphasized the displacement and the impoverishment of the people; fifty percent of the literature developed the emergence of leaders. The literature from the Southwest did not emphasize as many conflicts over land. Fifty percent of the texts emphasized displacement of the people. Twenty-five percent stressed impoverishment and 38 percent developed emergence of leaders because of conflicts over land.

Results of this research showed that a majority of the adult texts written about Great Plains and Great Basin Indians emphasized conflicts over land, which resulted in both the trauma associated with displacement and the impoverishment resulting from greed and dishonesty. Comparisons between life before and after interaction with Anglo Europeans and visions depicting the consequences of interaction are common in autobiographies such as *Black Elk Speaks: Being the Life Story of a Holy Man of the Oglala Sioux* (1932, 1979), who compares his memories of an earlier idyllic summer with the actuality of his later life on the reservation.

Two types of leaders emerge in the adult texts as the Native Americans faced conflicts over land. There were Native American patriots such as Chief Joseph (1879), leaders who were considered good and brave by their people and who fought for their freedom, their right of conscience, or their personal security. The second type of leader was less hostile toward, or even friendly to, the settlers. Many of the Native Americans of this type tried peaceful solutions because they recognized the consequences of European expansion and wanted security for their people. For example, Sioux Charles Eastman's (1916) leadership emphasizes cooperation.

It is apparent from the literature that the closer the interaction with European settlers, with missionaries, and with the United States government, the harsher the resulting personal conflict between Native American beliefs, values, customs, and religions and those of the Europeans. Historian Gerard Reed (1984) highlights the importance of cultural interaction during the period of European expansion. This interaction was favorable to the Europeans and disastrous to the native populations. Reed states, "No economic development rivals the prosperity enjoyed by Europeans as a consequence of their conquest and its attendant technological development. No social devastation equals the destruction suffered by indigenous cultures in conquered lands where European invaders imposed their own customs and civilizations" (p. 4). We could assume that conflicts over customs and beliefs would be developed in biographies and autobiographies.

The resulting analysis of the adult texts showed that 46 percent of the Native American subjects from the Great Plains revealed conflicts over beliefs, 50 percent from the Great Basin showed these conflicts, and 50 percent from the Southwest described conflicts over beliefs. Conflicts over values were reflected in 85 percent of the Native American subjects from the Great Plains, 50 percent from the Great Basin, and 75 percent from the Southwest. Conflicts over customs were reflected in 54 percent from the Great Plains, 50 percent from the Great Basin, and 50 percent from the Southwest. Religion caused conflicts in 85 percent of the literature from the Great Plains, 0 percent from the Great Basin, and 63 percent from the Southwest.

In all of the texts, the autobiographers or biography writers emphasize and describe in detail responses to some type of cultural conflict. Conflicts over beliefs frequently center on beliefs over ownership of the land, characteristics of the earth, and visions that rule one's life. A Great Plains Indian, Lame Deer, in *Lame Deer: Seeker of Visions* (1972), states this conflict: "because deep down with us lingers a feeling that land, water, air, the earth, and what lies beneath its surface cannot be owned as someone's private property" (p. 46). Black Elk (1932, 1979) describes his conflict when he is forced to live in square, wooden houses when his people believed in the power of the circular tepis. Another Great Plains Indian, Edward Goodbird (1914), emphasizes the power of the medicine man when he states, "If our beliefs seem strange to white men, theirs seemed just as strange to us" (p. 33).

Conflicts over values caused the greatest concern for Native Americans in the Great Plains and the Southwest. Lame Deer (1972) describes his discomfort as the Native Americans' chasing the vision versus the white man's chasing the dollar. Carl Sweezy (1966), an Arapaho, discusses differences in attitudes toward time: "We enjoy time; they measure it" (p. 17). Charles Eastman (1916) describes his conflicts in values: "From childhood I was consciously trained to be a man; that was after all the basic thing; but after this I was trained to be a hunter and not to care for money or possessions, but to be in the broader sense a public servant . . .

to harmonize myself with nature" (p. 1). Later, Eastman acknowledges experiencing considerable conflict when his honor was questioned because his tribe "valued nothing except honor; that cannot be purchased!" (p. 47).

Conflicts over religion are apparently the most traumatic for Great Plains Indians and to a slightly lesser extent for Southwest Indians. Two different attitudes emerge as Native Americans either accept or reject the teachings of the missionaries. Most Native Americans, however, even if they finally accept Christianity, express considerable conflict. Charles Eastman (1916) expresses shock when he first hears prayers in school because he had been taught that the Supreme Being can be communed with only in the solitude of the wilderness. An Arapaho, Carl Sweezy (1966), states that for the Indian this conflict arises because everything they do or own is connected with religion. An Apache, Jim Whitewolf (1969), describes major conflicts because the Indian people interpreted the missionaries' Christianity through the various Indian religions. Belief in the Ghost Dance and the Peyote Cult and the conflicts with missionaries are emphasized.

Many Native American autobiographers express concern because they were expected to respect and understand the white man's God but the respect and understanding were not returned. Edward Goodbird (1914) expresses this bewilderment: "Worshipping as we did many gods, we Indians did not think it strange that white men prayed to another God; and when missionaries came, we did not think it wrong that they taught us to pray to their God, but that they said we should not pray to our own gods, 'Why,' we asked, 'do the missionaries hate our gods?'" (p. 33).

The autobiographical writers and subjects of biographies responded in different ways to the conflicts with alien cultures. For example, rebellion was a common method of responding to this alien culture. The causes of rebellion are closely related to conflicts over land. Chief Joseph (1879) states this position: "This land has always belonged to my people. It came unclouded to them from our fathers, and we will defend this land as long as a drop of Indian blood warms the hearts of men" (p. 418).

Ritualism was a response primarily used by Holy Men such as Sioux Lame Deer and Black Elk, and Crow Plenty-Coups. Black Elk (1932, 1979) states that he must use his power and his visions to bring the "people back into the sacred hoop, that they might again walk the red road in a sacred manner pleasing to the Powers of the Universe that are One Power" (p. 238).

The degree to which some Native Americans accepted European values is illustrated in responses characterized as either innovation or conformity. Innovation in the study sample is more common than conformity. Althea Bass, the recorder of Carl Sweezy's autobiography (1966), expresses the role of innovation:

> Unlike many of the Indians, Carl Sweezy never lost his way; he saw good along both roads and accepted something of both. The old Arapaho virtues, courtesy, and hospitality, and loyalty, and deep religious feelings, he found to be virtues among the best of the white people too; it was only the methods by which they practiced that differed. So he could sing Mennonite hymns with the missionaries and chants with the Sun Dance participants. (p. viii)

The greatest conformity with the new culture is reflected in the autobiography of Charles Eastman (1916), which is titled *From the Deep Woods to Civilization: Chapters in the Autobiography of an Indian*. Eastman chronicles his experiences in 1876: "I renounced finally my bow and arrows for the spade and the pen; I took off my soft moccasins and put on the heavy and clumsy but durable shoes. Every day of my life I put into use every English word that I knew, and for the first time permitted myself to think and act as a white man" (p. 58). This conformity, however, was not easy and it does include some retention of Indian values as Eastman concludes his autobiography: "I am an Indian; and while I have learned much from civilization, for which I am grateful, I have never lost my Indian sense of right and justice. I am for development and progress along social and spiritual lines, rather than those of commerce, nationalism, or material efficiency. Nevertheless, so long as I live, I am an American" (p. 195).

Finally, this study analyzed differences in texts written for adult and juvenile audiences. Table 3–1 shows the differences found in the extent and type of conflict between adult and juvenile texts with settings in the Great Plains.

As seen in Table 3–1, for some of the categories, readers of texts for adults and for juveniles would find different and often contradictory profiles for Native Americans who lived in the Great Plains. The profile developed through adult autobiographies and biographies suggests that while the Native Americans were alienated and impoverished because of their physical displacement, they suffered even greater conflicts because of cultural confrontation. Major conflicts resulted from conflicts with Christianity and alien value systems, customs, and beliefs. The Native Americans in the adult texts rarely responded through complete conformity to the alien culture, but were more apt to rebel, to reject European values and to practice traditional religion and ritualism, or to retain group identities while accepting some European values. The consequences of intrusion of an alien culture were both physically and psychologically detrimental.

TABLE 3–1 Comparisons Between Adult and Juvenile Biographies with Settings in the Great Plains

Conflicts Over Land		
People Displaced (%)	People Impoverished (%)	Leaders Emerge (%)
Adult 61	77	38
Juvenile 78	44	56

Cultural Confrontation			
Beliefs (%)	Values (%)	Customs (%)	Religion (%)
Adult 46	85	54	85
Juvenile 22	22	33	0

Acculturation Continuum				
Retreatism (%)	Rebellion (%)	Ritualism (%)	Innovation (%)	Conformity (%)
Adult 0	30	30	34	6
Juvenile 0	33	1	33	33

In contrast, the profile developed through juvenile texts suggests that displacement of people caused the greatest conflict. Cultural conflicts between two value systems were viewed as of minimal significance. In addition, the majority of biographical subjects and autobiography writers either conformed to the alien culture or combined aspects of the two cultures. Only biographies of the great war chiefs suggest rebellion. Retaining Native American religious practices was not a significant factor in the juvenile biographies. The consequences of intrusion of an alien culture are seen as detrimental because of loss of land, but could be inferred to be beneficial because of the acceptance of superior value and belief systems.

As we discuss biographies written for younger audiences, we will consider these conflicts and the responses of Native Americans who are their subjects. How closely do the biographies written for younger people reflect some of the same concerns as those developed by Native Americans who write about their own experiences? Unlike adult autobiographies and biographies, few juvenile biographies develop conflicts over both land and culture. Biographies of Crazy Horse and Red Cloud tend to emphasize conflicts over land. Dorothy M. Johnson's *Warrior for a Lost Nation: A Biography of Sitting Bull* is an exception to this trend. Johnson presents a profile of a leader who not only fought for his land, but also experienced personal conflicts because of alien beliefs and customs. In general, conflicts in juvenile biographies are simplified, and cultural conflicts experienced by many Native Americans are absent.

There are also discrepancies between the information presented in the adult texts and the juvenile biographies. The consequences of forced education and the practice of hiding children so that they could not be educated are frequently emphasized in adult texts. If the descriptions in adult autobiographies are representative, the seeking for white people's learning is incorrect for many Native Americans of this time period. Native Americans are frequently shown as seeking education in white schools in juvenile biographies. In a more accurate depiction, Johnson's juvenile biography of Sitting Bull chronicles his final battle with the United States government to retain Sioux customs and his arguments with the educational system that repudiated the values of his people. After Sitting Bull reluctantly accepts the reservation for his people, he remains suspicious about the motives of educators. He tells a congressional mission that his people needed a medicine woman. He wanted her to teach them to read, but he did not want her to try to convert them to her religion. This depiction seems more accurate when comparisons are made with the attitudes in adult texts.

Many of the juvenile biographies are less candid than the adult sources and imply different consequences for the Native Americans who interacted with the European settlers. The reasons for these differences between adult and juvenile texts may reflect a belief that children are not able to understand the more complex issues associated with cultural confrontation. In the evaluation of the literature written for the two groups, however, several questions emerge that you may want to consider: By ignoring confrontation with values, are biographers lying to children or are they only focusing on content that children can understand? By placing less emphasis on cultural conflict are biographers implying that Native Americans living in the eighteenth and nineteenth centuries did not have a culture worthy of preservation? By emphasizing conformity and innovation as the two most frequent responses to intrusion, are biographers again lying to children, or are they only presenting content that is necessary if children are to develop a respect for governmental authority and a belief in the heroic deeds of all U.S. leaders from the past? There are educators and other individuals who will argue on different sides of these issues. It may happen that biographers and historians will eventually write juvenile biographies that present a truthful profile of this turbulent period in U.S. history.

Several juvenile biographies are exceptions and provide historically accurate depictions of the time period and the people. For example, Dorothy Nafus Morrison's *Chief Sarah: Sarah Winnemucca's Fight for Indian Rights* is one of the strongest biographies as the author develops the numerous conflicts the biographical character faces as the character tries to gain rights for her people and preserve their culture. Morrison develops conflicts through contrasts when she describes Sarah's confusion: "The whites killed—but they had made her well. They took the Indians' meadows—but gave them horses and presents. They burned stores of food—but they gave food, too. Would she ever understand these strange people who were overrunning the land?" (p. 31). Throughout the biography, Morrison shows Sarah's battle for retention of the Paiute culture.

As you read various juvenile biographies of Native Americans, you may use the findings from adult autobiographies and biographies to compare the types of conflicts depicted in the literature.

Several juvenile biographies look at famous Native Americans who interacted with white settlers of the continent. For example, *Sacajawea, Wilderness Guide*, by Kate Jassem, is the biography of the Shoshone woman who guided the Lewis and Clark expedition across the Rocky Mountains to the Pacific Ocean.

Dennis Brindell Fradin's *Hiawatha: Messenger of Peace* is written for younger children. Fradin uses information that is known about the Iroquois who lived about five hundred years ago to re-create the role of Hiawatha as one of the founders of the Iroquois Confederacy. Fradin clearly separates what is actually known from the legend of Hiawatha. For example, Fradin states:

> It is also said that around this time the Peacemaker chose the pine tree as a symbol of peace between the five Iroquois tribes and that Hiawatha invented a way to record important events. Hiawatha took large numbers of purple and white wampum beads and used them to make pictures that told a story. The Iroquois then began to record their major events on wampum belts in picture form. Some of these belts are now in museums, but they are not our main sources of information about Hiawatha. Other primary sources are the stories that the Iroquois elders have handed down to their young people for generations. (p. 30)

Conflicts between worlds provide numerous opportunities for character and plot development in Jean Fritz's *The Double Life of Pocahontas*. Fritz effectively develops a character who is torn between loyalty to her father's tribe and to her new friends in the Jamestown colony. As in her other biographies, Fritz documents her historical interpretations. Notes, a bibliography, an index, and a map add to the authenticity.

Brandon Marie Miller's *Buffalo Gals: Women of the Old West* includes a chapter on "Clash of Cultures" that focuses on the lives of Native American women. Instead of providing biographical information on specific women, the author focuses on the role of women in Native American cultures and changes caused by white settlement. For example, notice in the following quote how Miller describes both the culture and the role of women within the culture. Also notice that unlike many of the biographies, this author stresses the role of religion within the culture:

> Religion was woven into the very fabric of an Indian woman's life. The forces of life and death were everywhere to be seen—in the seasons, the hunt, the planting, and the harvest. Prayers asked for food and good health for the tribe. In some tribes,

women, as well as men, hoped for a vision or special dream to show them the road to a good life. Many native cultures revered female spirits, like White Buffalo Calf Woman, who brought the sacred pipe to the Lakota and taught them to live as one with all creatures, the earth, and the sky. (p. 71)

Laurie Lawlor's *Shadow Catcher: The Life and Work of Edward S. Curtis* documents the life and work of the man who photographed and researched the cultures of Native Americans. The biography is illustrated with photographs that exemplify the thirty years of Curtis's work. Both the photographs and the text provide insights into the lives of Native Americans. Each photograph is labeled and is accompanied by interpretive text. For example, a photograph of a clam digger includes the following information: "Clams, an important food source for Northwest Coast tribes, are gathered using a wooden digger called a dibbler. Many of Curtis's earliest Native American photos were of clam diggers from the nearby Tulahip Reservation in Washington State" (p. 26). The text includes a listing of the twenty volumes of Curtis's works, the sources of the photographs, an index, and a bibliography of books for children. This biography is divided into three parts: Books About Indians, Books by and About Edward S. Curtis, and Books About Photography.

Informational Books About Earlier Time Periods

Nonfiction books about early Native American cultures provide information about the various groups. They can serve to authenticate literature about Native Americans. Books, both adult and juvenile sources, with authentic paintings and illustrations, may be used to authenticate the art in picture storybooks. Books with detailed descriptions of settings, cultures, and conflicts are valuable for authenticating historical fiction and biographical settings.

The symbolism in Native American folklore, biography, fiction, and poetry may be difficult to understand without some background information. One of the informational sources that is excellent for this interpretative purpose is the *Dictionary of Native American Mythology* (1992) by Sam D. Gill and Irene F. Sullivan. Each entry in this adult reference source includes an entry title, a tribal or cultural area association, a definition of the entry, cross-references that provide related information, and bibliographic references. The dictionary also includes maps of tribal or cultural areas, a bibliography, and an index by Native American group.

Sources that depict the Americas prior to Columbus or detail the lives and cultures of people who lived in North America at that time are valuable parts of Native American literature. Some of these sources encourage readers to compare life and culture on different continents during the fifteenth century. For example, *The World in 1492*, written by Jean Fritz, Katherine Paterson, Patricia and Fredrick McKissack, Margaret Mahy, and Jamake Highwater, includes information on the history, customs, beliefs, and accomplishments of people living in Europe, Asia, Africa, Australia and Oceania, and the Americas. Photographs and illustrations add to the readers' understandings. A bibliography of sources divided according to these areas adds references for further research. The adult text *Circa 1492: Art in the Age of Exploration* (1991), edited by Jay A. Levenson and published by the National Gallery of Art in Washington, D.C., includes detailed commentaries and photographs of art and other cultural sites. There is a large section titled "The Americas."

Books that chronicle the lives of Native Americans prior to the Age of Exploration are popular subjects for young audiences. In *People of the Breaking Day*, Marcia Sewall takes readers back to the Wampanoag nation of southeastern Massachusetts before the English settlers arrived. The text, which is divided into sections, presents information about the tribe, the belief in the Great Spirit, the celebrations, the role of warriors and other members of the tribe, and the family.

Caroline Arnold's *The Ancient Cliff Dwellers of Mesa Verde* takes readers back to the world of the Anasazi. The text details the lives of the Anasazi, or ancient ones, through color photographs and text describing the cliff dwellings found in Mesa Verde National Park. Topics covered by Arnold include the discovery of Mesa Verde, uncovering the past, the history of the Anasazi, the daily life of the Anasazi, and speculations about why the Anasazi left Mesa Verde. David Lavender's *Mother Earth, Father Sky: Pueblo Indians of the American Southwest* begins with the prehistoric Anasazi and continues through the study of modern Pueblos. Jennifer Owings Dewey's *Stories on Stone: Rock Art: Images from the Ancient Ones* uses drawings of petroglyphs in the Southwest to explain characteristics of the people and reasons behind their art. The text includes a map of Anasazi country with locations of the various cliff dwellings and canyons. You may compare these books with George Ella Lyon's fictional *Dreamplace*. The setting for Lyon's text is an Anasazi ruin. In *Dreamplace*, a modern girl dreams of what the location must have been like when the tribe lived there.

In *Only the Names Remain: The Cherokees and the Trail of Tears*, Alex W. Bealer presents a history of the people before the arrival of the Europeans, as well as the historical consequences on the people of their removal from their homeland. You might compare these conflicts with the ones presented in some of the biographies and autobiographies.

Paul Goble's *Death of the Iron Horse* and Russell Freedman's *Buffalo Hunt* and *An Indian Winter* also provide historical perspectives. Goble uses an actual incident in 1867, when a Union Pacific train was derailed by the Cheyenne. In this fictionalized story, Goble shows that the Cheyenne fought the encroaching white culture by attacking the railroad. In *Buffalo Hunt*, Freedman shows the importance of buffaloes to the Native Americans living on the Great Plains. His text includes descriptions of the hunts, attitudes of the Indians toward the buffaloes, and the consequences to the Indians when the white culture all but eliminated the buffaloes. The text is illustrated with reproductions of paintings by such artists as George Catlin and Karl Bodmer, who actually saw the buffalo hunts. The titled and dated illustrations add interest to the text. Freedman uses a similar approach in *An Indian Winter*, accompanying his description of traditional Mandan life in the 1800s with paintings and drawings created by Karl Bodmer, a young Swiss artist who traveled through the Missouri River Valley in 1832. Many authors of informational books rely on reproductions of paintings completed during earlier times in Native American history to add a sense of authenticity to their texts.

Historical Fiction

Themes and conflicts in historical fiction about Native Americans often emphasize the survival—either of the body or of the spirit. Some authors emphasize periods in history in which contact with white settlers or cavalry resulted in catastrophic changes. Others emphasize growing interpersonal relationships between Native American and white characters. Four award-winning books provide examples for these two types of historical fiction.

Scott O'Dell's Newbery Honor book, *Sing Down the Moon*, focuses on the mid-1860s, when the U.S. Cavalry forced the Navajo to make the three-hundred-mile Long Walk from their beautiful and productive home in Canyon de Chelly to stark Fort Sumner. O'Dell effectively develops the resulting conflict through descriptions of the contrasting settings. He provides detailed descriptions of Canyon de Chelly, a place of miracles. This idealistic setting does not last. It is followed by horror when Colonel Kit Carson's soldiers first destroy the crops and livestock in the canyon and then force the Navajo to walk through desolate country to a setting that is inconducive to physical or spiritual survival. Fifteen hundred Navajo die, and many others lose their will to live. O'Dell's protagonist, a Navajo woman named Bright Morning, retains an inner strength based on hope for the future. While she is a captive, she hoards food and plans for the day when she and her husband will return to their canyon.

Jan Hudson's *Sweetgrass*, a winner of the Canadian Library Association's Book of the Year Award, develops the harmful influences of an expanding white population. Hudson focuses on the struggle for maturity of a young Blackfoot girl as she faces a life-and-death battle in 1837. Smallpox, the "white man's sickness," results in hunger and death. The themes in *Sweetgrass* are that it is important to honor moral obligation toward others and that it is important to retain one's dreams.

Hudson employs figurative language involving signs and omens that are meaningful to the characters and that reinforce themes related to retaining one's identity and meeting obligations toward family members. For example, the main character considers the importance of her name. She believes that it is appropriate because sweetgrass is "ordinary to look at but it's fragrant as the spring" (p. 12). Later, her grandmother tells her that sweetgrass has the power of memories. As Sweetgrass considers her future, readers discover that she is joyfully approaching womanhood. She says, "I felt mightier than a brave. . . . I felt I was holding the future like summer berries in my hands" (p. 26). Instead of allowing the signs and omens to control her life, Sweetgrass uses them to overcome taboos and to help her family in a time of great trouble. She decides, "I would make Father do what I wanted. I would use the signs, the power to control my own days. I would make my life be what I wanted" (p. 15).

A Canadian Library Association Book of the Year, Farley Mowat's, *Lost in the Barrens* takes place in the twentieth century in a remote arctic wilderness, hundreds of miles from the nearest town. The main characters are Awasin, a Woodland Cree, and Jamie, a white Canadian orphan who moves north to live with his uncle. The setting becomes hostile to both boys when they accompany the Crees on a hunting expedition and then become separated from the hunters. Mowat vividly describes the boys' searching for food and preparing for the rapidly approaching winter. Through long periods of isolation, the boys develop a close relationship and an understanding of each other.

A Newbery Honor Book, Elizabeth George Speare's *The Sign of the Beaver* focuses on the friendship between a Native American boy and a white boy in the Maine wilderness of the 1700s. Themes of friendship, faith, moral obligation, working together, and love for the land are developed in this book—in which the wilderness can be either an antagonist or a friend. Matt, the thirteen-year-old main character, faces a life-and-death struggle when his father leaves him alone to guard his family's frontier cabin through the winter. Without food or a gun, Matt confronts a harsh natural environment, fear of the local Indians, and the possibility that he may never see his parents again. In spite of conflicts about the ways in which white settlers are changing their land, a Penobscot boy befriends Matt and teaches him how to survive. For the Penobscot tribe, the wilderness is a friend rather than an antagonist.

In his last book, *Thunder Rolling in the Mountains*, Scott O'Dell, with the assistance of his wife Elizabeth Hall, again develops a story based on the removal of Indian peoples from their land. This time, the narrator is Chief Joseph's daughter, who tells, from her point of view, the story of the forced removal of the Nez Percé tribe from their homeland in 1877. In the foreword to the book, Hall describes O'Dell's fascination with this subject: "At the time of his death, Scott O'Dell was immersed in the story of Chief Joseph and his people. Their courage and determination in the face of cruelty, betrayal, and bureaucratic ignorance moved him deeply. So deeply that he continued to work on the manuscript in the hospital until two days before he died" (p. ix). Readers will also experience O'Dell's fascination with this time period and the plight of these brave people.

One of the strengths of Diane Matcheck's *The Sacrifice*, the story of a girl from the Apsaalooka (Crow) tribe, lies in the effective development of a character who is experiencing a personal struggle. The author first develops a protagonist who is angry, heartless, and guilt ridden until she realizes that she did not kill her brother and begins to forgive herself. By the conclusion of the story, she realizes her personal worth and seeks a life worthy of being a Great One. The author's note provides historical information about the 1840s and 1850s and the setting that is now Montana, Wyoming, and Nebraska.

The five hundredth anniversary of Columbus's voyage resulted in the publication of several books written from the viewpoint of the native peoples. Jane Yolen's picture storybook *Encounter* develops the hypothetical interaction between a Taino Indian boy and Columbus and his men on the island of San Salvador in 1492. The text is based on the premise that dreams forewarn the boy about the disastrous consequences of interacting with the explorers, whom the people believe have flown down from the sky. Yolen includes descriptions of the Taino people and their beliefs, details about the loss of culture and human life that resulted because of the exploration and colonization by the Spanish, and details describing trade between the explorers and the Taino people. Information provided in the author's notes indicate how disastrous this encounter was for the Taino people, who went from a population of 300,000 at the time of Columbus's landing to 500 only fifty years later. Yolen's book develops a common theme found in contemporary books: Interaction with people who do not respect your culture can have terrible consequences for the native people. The final illustration by David Shannon depicts a much older Taino Indian, whose body is literally disappearing just as his culture disappeared. As a result of this encounter, the Taino people lost their language, religion, and culture.

In *Morning Girl*, Native American author Michael Dorris sets his story on a Bahamian island at the time of Columbus's landing. The unique quality of this book is the alternating points of view developed by the author as he describes the day-to-day activities of Morning Star and Star Boy, two Taino children. Through this approach, Dorris encourages readers to understand the nature of the Taino people and to realize that they had individual identities and a culture worth preserving. Unlike Yolen, Dorris concludes his book at the time of the first sighting of the Spanish sailors. Dorris includes an epilogue that quotes Columbus's journal on October 11, 1492, the day he first encounters the Taino people. You may also find it interesting to compare *Encounter* and *Morning Girl*.

In *Sees Behind Trees*, Dorris sets his historical fiction novel in sixteenth-century America. Dorris's choice of Walnut, a Powhatan boy who has a physical handicap, allows the author to stress the importance of "seeing" with senses other than just sight. Throughout the book, the author develops Walnut's character as the boy learns to use his other senses and receives the honor of a new name, Sees Behind Trees. The boy's special abilities allow the author to depict the setting through senses such as smelling and hearing. Notice in the following quote how these senses are used to depict the setting:

But the longer we didn't talk, the more separate parts announced themselves: the hush of a brook just behind me and, further beyond that, the rush of a river. The buzz of a beehive on a tree not far over to my right. The beat of a hummingbird's wings as it dove in and out of a cluster of . . . what was that smell? . . . roses near, where my mother—who, I could tell, had just oiled her hair this morning—sat." (p. 6)

Throughout the book, Dorris encourages readers to hear the various activities of the village such as the stacking of firewood, the approaching hunters, and the peeling of bark from saplings and to smell the environment through descriptions of stewing venison, pemmican scent of berries mixed with dried meat, and smoke from the campfire. Sees Behind Trees develops his unique capabilities as he learns to believe in himself and discovers the importance of looking within himself and respecting the dreams of others. In addition to setting, readers will discover many values and beliefs associated with the Powhatan tribe. This book provides an excellent source for discovering the symbolic and cultural meanings associated with name changes, especially the tests that are given prior to the name change and the differences in expected behaviors that follow the name change.

Sally M. Keehn's *Moon of Two Dark Horses* is the story of friendship between Coshmoo, a Delaware boy, and Daniel, a white boy—a story that begins in 1776, during the time of the American Revolution. The author develops the theme of loyalty and friendship between the two boys. Both the loyalty and friendship are tested, however, as the conflict increases between the British army and the American colonists. The book ends on a strong note as both boys face a gauntlet, and run free.

Through all of these stories, children can experience Native American characters who have personal thoughts and emotions and who live within a family as well as within a tribal group. In addition, children will begin to understand the impact of white people on the Native American way of life. Interesting comparisons may also be made between the themes, settings, and conflicts in biographies and historical fiction.

Characteristics of Contemporary Native American Authors

According to Paula Gunn Allen (1994), tradition remains important in Native American fiction:

> Native American fiction in the twentieth century has two sides: The Oral Traditions of the Native Nations, and Western fiction and its antecedents. As does the Bible for the thought and literature of the West, ceremonial texts provide a major source of the symbols, allusions, and philosophical assumptions that inform our world and thus our work. It is a mistake to believe that ceremonial texts are "dated" and thus irrelevant to the work of modern writers. . . . They interact, as wings of a bird in flight interact. They give shape to our experience. They signify. (p. 7)

Some contemporary Native American authors have described the characteristics of Native American writing and its distinguishing features. Many also emphasize the need to read and analyze Native American literature in ways that are quite different from mainstreamed American literature. In this section, we will discuss some of these characteristics identified by Native American authors and then search for these characteristics in poetry and contemporary writing.

Laura Coltelli in her introduction to *Winged Words: American Indian Writers Speak* (1990), a collection of interviews with contemporary Native American authors, contends that the Native American author's voice of protest, of resistance, of literary creativity has only begun to receive attention from readers and literary critics. She maintains that memory, language, and storytelling tradition—so closely intertwined—are crucial to Native American authors. Throughout the subsequent interviews conducted by Coltelli, the Native American authors emphasize important characteristics of, and influences on, their writing. Of recurring emphasis is the importance of the oral tradition, geographic locations, and tribal backgrounds. Most authors maintain that the oral tradition is central to all forms of Native American expression. For example, N. Scott Momaday, of Kiowa and Cherokee descent and the author of the Pulitzer Prize–winning *House Made of Dawn*, discusses the importance of the oral tradition and the sense of place within the oral tradition. Momaday states, "The understanding of the landscape is one of the most important aspects of Indian oral tradition" (p. 90). Momaday places special emphasis on prose poetry because he maintains that it is very close to the Native American oral tradition.

The importance of place in the oral tradition and the Native American heritage is also emphasized by Simon Ortiz, who is of Acoma Pueblo descent. He maintains that the spirit of place informs his writing. Ortiz qualifies the spirit of place, "Place is more than just a physical or geographical place, but obviously a spiritual place, a place with the whole scheme of life, the universe, the whole scheme and power of creation. Place is the source of who you are in terms of your identity, the language that you are born into and that you come to use" (p. 105). Ortiz, like many other Native American authors, emphasizes the link between historical stories, recent historical stories, and older stories from the oral tradition. He maintains that these older stories and profiles are used in his writing because "they often refer to certain values that Indian people hold precious and dear. Whether the stories are tragic or happy, they are examples of values Indian people should follow, or see in reflections" (p. 108).

Native American authors may emphasize the role of struggle and conflict in their writing. Paula Gunn Allen discusses the problems associated with keeping a sense of self as she moves from one world to another. Simon Ortiz maintains that struggle is hopeful and optimistic because, "As long as people do not stop struggling, they do not become cynical; they may get pessimistic sometimes, but not cynical or hopeless" (p. 112).

By reading a collection of adult literature such as those found in *Voice of the Turtle: American Indian Literature, 1900–1970*, edited by Paula Gunn Allen (1994), you will discover many of the symbols, allusions, and philosophical assumptions of the authors. For example, in "The Great Vision," Black Elk and John G. Neihardt focus on the importance of sacred herbs and colors. Zitkala-Sa in "The Widespread Enigma Concerning Blue-Star Woman" emphasizes the cultural values associated with the old teachings and the importance of visions. John Joseph Mathews in "Sundown" decries the spiritual poverty brought on by Western values. Don C. Talayesva in "School off the Reservation" includes a soul traveling to the House of the Dead, belief in a Guardian Spirit, learning lessons from the Guardian Spirit, and the symbol of the eagle prayer feather. N. Scott Momaday in "Feast Day" emphasizes supernatural power.

Louis Owens's *The Sharpest Sight* (1992) provides many examples of characteristics of contemporary writing. For example, he includes belief in visions, dreams, spirit walking, ancient tribal memories, the panther or soul-eater, the medicine pouch, and unbroken circles. The author uses traditional stories to develop values and stress history. Contemporary conflicts include racism, comparing historic and contemporary feelings, and the need to stay on a straight path and know who you are. Notice how many of these contemporary Native American authors discuss the values and beliefs found in the traditional literature discussed earlier in this chapter. As you read contemporary Native American literature written for children, you may search for these characteristics, values, and beliefs, which are emphasized by outstanding Native American authors.

NATIVE AMERICAN POETRY

In this section and the next sections on contemporary fiction, we will analyze the contemporary Native American literature written for children by both Native American authors and non–Native American authors. In these sections, we will search for the previously identified characteristics, values, and beliefs.

Songs, chants, and poems are very important in the various Native American cultures. Many of the poems express reverence for creation, nature, and beauty. Native Americans created poetry for a purpose; they believed that there was power in the word. Songs were often part of ceremonial rituals, with their symbolism portrayed through dance. The author's note in Edward Field's *Magic Words*, poems inspired by traditional Inuit stories, contains a definition of poetry that relates the words in poems to songs: "Songs are thoughts, sung out on the breath, when people are moved by great feelings, and ordinary speech is no longer enough" (Note About the Poems). In this section, we will consider both historical and contemporary poetry. Also notice as you read the poetry discussed in this section, that many of the poems have a close relationship to the values and beliefs found in the traditional literature.

The beauty of both ancient Native American poetry and contemporary poetry about Native American experiences can be shared with children. An interesting resource book that shares the music of Native Americans with children of many cultures is John Bierhorst's *A Cry from the Earth: Music of the North American Indians*. According to Bierhorst, people throughout North America shared a belief in the supernatural power of music to cure disease, bring rain, win a lover, or defeat an enemy.

Many Native Americans today sing the songs for pleasure and to express pride in their heritage. Bierhorst's book contains words and music for many songs, including songs of prayer, magic, and dreams, songs to control the weather, and music to accompany various dances. There are greeting songs, love songs, a Hopi flute song, a Hopi sleep song, a Cherokee lullaby, and a Kwakiutl cradlesong. Music, words, and dance steps are included so that children can re-create, experience, and respect this musical heritage. The text includes extensive commentaries on the sources and meanings of the selections. Each selection is also identified according to tribal origin.

In "Law of the Great Peace," adapted from the Iroquois Book of the Great Law, John Bierhorst presents a poem that reflects the values of the original League of Five Nations which included the Mohawk, Oneida, Onondaga, Cayuga, and Seneca. The poem expresses a strong desire for unity among all peoples because the "Great Creator has made us of one blood, and of the same soil."

Native American author, Virginia Driving Hawk Sneve, emphasizes the importance of spoken words as they are developed through ceremonial prayers and chants, lullabies and tribal songs, and other forms of poetry. Her collection of both ancient poetry and contemporary works in *Dancing Teepees: Poems of American Indian Youth* provides poetry from a variety of tribal sources such as Lakota Sioux, Hopi, Zuni, and Ute. Many of the poems reflect the traditional beliefs of the people as suggested in these titles, "The Life of a Man Is a Circle" (Lakota Sioux). "Farewell, My Younger Brother" (Navajo poem about death), and "The Four Corners of the Universe" (Mescalero Apache).

The importance of the oral tradition, geographic locations, and tribal backgrounds are especially meaningful in poetry collections such as *Spirit Walker* by Nancy Wood. Wood's poetry reflects the values of the Taos Indians, especially their interconnections with nature and spirituality. The oral tradition is exemplified in poems such as "Generations" in which she retells the story of creation and emphasizes the importance of Grandfather, who created the people; Grandmother, who issued the stars and moon; Father, who is the Living Sun; and Mother, who is the Enduring Earth.

The poetry of Byrd Baylor reflects the oral traditions, the geographic locations, the history, and the values of various Southwest Indian tribes. For example, *Moon Song* has mythological references that retell in poetic form a Pima Indian story about the birth of Coyote. The history and the southwestern geography are reflected in her poetic renditions in *When Clay Sings*, a poem in which she ponders on the secrets of prehistoric people as seen through their drawings on pottery. The designs on ancient shards of pottery created by the Anasazi, Mogollon, Hohokam, and Mimbres cultures of the Southwest provide inspiration for both the poetry and the illustrations. A closeness to nature and reverence for both plant and animal life form the basis for Baylor's *The Other Way to Listen* and *The Desert Is Theirs*. In both books, Peter Parnall's illustrations suggest the majesty of the desert and the respect of the Papago Indians for nature.

Both the poems and the paintings in Shonto Begay's *Navajo: Visions and Voices Across the Mesa* explore the beliefs, values, struggles, and settings of the Navajo world. Through the poetry, Begay presents the "constant struggle for balance—balance in living between the 'New World' and the ancient world of my people, the Navajo. And ever present, there are the voices of my elders—warning us to guard and protect our mother the earth" (p. 7). Poems such as "Echoes" and "Creation" tell about the ancient spirits, the arrival of beings into the Fourth World, and the power of First Man and First Woman. Poems such as "Mother's Lace," "Reflections After the Rain," and "Early Spring" reflect the beauty of the earth. Poems such as "Into the New World," "Storm Pattern," and "Down Highway 163" express the modern struggle of the Navajo people. This collection represents an excellent view of traditional beliefs and shows how traditional beliefs and values are still important even in a world that includes struggle.

Inuit traditional beliefs are reflected in the poems in Edward Field's *Magic Words*. Poems such as "The Earth and the People," "Magic Words," and "Day and Night: How They Came to Be" reflect traditional stories told in poetic form.

A poem by an Apache Indian child in Arizona, published in C. Cazden's *Classroom Discourse: The Language of Teaching and Learning* (1988), reflects the cultural differences among students. This child laments the long, hard work hours of her family and the hurt she feels at school when she is forced to learn words that are not her words.

The roles of struggle and conflict are current themes in contemporary poetry written by Native American poets for older audiences. Many of these poets develop themes related to inner conflicts as the poets try to retain their Native American values in a white culture. Poetry collections such as *Songs from This Earth on Tur-*

tle's Back: Contemporary American Indian Poetry, edited by Joseph Bruchac, allows readers and researchers to understand these present-day conflicts. For example, poems by Maurice Kenny (Mohawk) develop the poet's strong love for nature. Poems by Simon Ortiz (Acoma), Carrol Arnett/Gogisgi (Cherokee), and Karoniak-tatie (Turtle Clan) explore contemporary conflicts with society. As you read the poetry discussed in this section, try to identify both the traditional values and the contemporary conflicts expressed by the poets. Ask this question: Do the poems reflect characteristics of Native American literature identified by contemporary Native American authors?

CONTEMPORARY REALISTIC FICTION

Contemporary realistic fiction about Native Americans develops many of the same themes and conflicts found in the poetry and the Native American literature previously discussed in this chapter. In books for younger children, Native American characters frequently explore nature or develop close ties with their traditional roots. Native American characters often express conflict between the old ways and the new ones. Characters must frequently decide whether to preserve their heritage or abandon it. Many of the stories allow Native Americans to honor the old ways but live with the new ones. Some stories show life on modern reservations; others depict families who have left the reservation to live in cities.

Picture Story Books

The need to live in harmony with nature and the importance of ancestral beliefs are themes in White Deer of Autumn's *Ceremony—In the Circle of Life*. The conflict develops because Little Turtle cannot accept the terrible environmental destruction that surrounds him in his city environment. Through a vision, the author allows Little Turtle to learn about the wisdom and knowledge of his ancestors. This contemporary story written in picture-book format is closely related to traditional values and beliefs. Little Turtle discovers the importance of the nuclear family as found in Mother Earth, Grandmother Moon, and Father Sky. He discovers that the Circle of Life requires listening to Mother Earth if people are to prosper. The symbolic importance of the four directional parts of the circle are developed in both the text and in Daniel San Souci's illustrations.

Reverence for nature is an important theme in picture books by both Sandra De Coteau Orie and Chief Jake Swamp. Orie's *Did You Hear Wind Sing Your Name?: An Oneida Song of Spring* is a celebration for all the forms of life in the sacred circle of spring. The author's note prepares readers for the text and illustrations that follow by discussing the symbolism of the pine tree, which represents the unity of the nations of the Iroquois Confederacy; the importance of Hawk as the bringer of good news; the sustaining influence of Elder Brother Sun; the ceremonial purposes for Cedar and Sweet Grass; the importance of the Three Sisters—Corn, Beans, and Squash—in sustaining the people; the trilliums that announce spring's arrival; and the strawberries that bring the first fruits of the season. The author states that the book is a celebration of the circle of life, "the return of morning to night as well as of each cycle of the seasons" (unnumbered). Readers may search for these symbols in both the text and the illustrations and develop a closer understanding of their importance in Native American cultures.

Chief Jake Swamp, a member of the Mohawk Nation, also praises the natural world in *Giving Thanks: A Native American Good Morning Message*. This is a tribute to Mother Earth, to the life sustaining foods and to the animals, to the Four Winds that bring clean air, to Grandfather Thunder Beings for bringing rain, to Elder Brother Sun for light and warmth, to Grandmother Moon for lighting the darkness, to Spirit Protectors of past and present, and to the Great Spirit for giving all of these wonderful gifts.

In *The Seasons and Someone*, Virginia Kroll uses a question-and-answer format to allow readers to vicariously accompany a young Inuit girl as she explores what happens during each of the seasons in the Arctic. For example, she asks in the spring: "What will happen when Wind's roars change to whispers and icicles grow thin?" (unnumbered). The text and illustrations indicate: "Lichen will dapple rocks, imitating snowflakes. Ground Squirrel will scurry from her burrow. Ptarmigan's feathers will blend with brown brush again. Fox and Lemming will try to outrun each other. And Someone will laugh aloud to see buds on the berry bushes" (unnumbered). The text develops both descriptions of the environment and the importance of family life.

The importance of relationships between a Yup'ik Eskimo boy and his grandfather are developed in Margaret Nicolai's *Kitaz Goes Ice Fishing*. The colors in the illustrations used by Alaskan artist David Rubin reflect the bright color of the exterior and the warmth of the interior settings.

In *This Land Is My Land*, Cree author and artist, George Littlechild, presents a historical preview of his people and his own experiences. The importance of both nature and the ancestors are found in his introduction:

> I paint at night. I'm inspired to paint at night. I stand outside staring at the night sky and I begin to dream. The sky is like a doorway into the other world, the Spirit World. I am inspired by the ancestors. When I look back on our history and see all the difficulties our ancestors had to face, I can only honor them. Through the wisdom of our Elders and the courage of all our people we have survived the past 500 years. I thank the Creator for Wahkomkanak, our ancestors (unnumbered).

Littlechild then provides brief histories that develop a chronology of his people and his own life. Through the dedication in which Littlechild pictures his own ancestors, readers receive a very personal message from the author.

Like other contemporary realistic fiction written for younger children, stories about Native Americans frequently develop themes related to love and family relationships. In *Mama, Do You Love Me?* by Barbara M. Joosse, a young child tests her mother's love. Through satisfactory responses, the girl discovers that her mama loves her. Each of the questions and responses relates to the culture.

A loving relationship between a Navajo girl and her grandmother provides the foundation in Miska Miles's *Annie and the Old One*. The conflict in the story develops because Annie does not want to accept the natural order of aging and death. In an effort to hold back time, Annie tries to prevent her grandmother from completing the rug that she is weaving because her grandmother has said, "My children, when the new rug is taken from the loom, I will go to Mother Earth" (p. 15). The author emphasizes the way that Annie's inner conflict ends, and the theme that we are all part of nature emerges when Annie finally realizes: "The cactus did not bloom forever. Petals dried and fell to earth. She knew that she was a part of the earth and the things on it. She would always be part of the earth, just as her grandmother had always been, just as her grandmother would always be, always and forever. And Annie was breathless with the wonder of it" (p. 41). Annie's actions show that she has accepted nature's inevitable role. Annie picks up the weaving stick and begins to help her grandmother complete the rug. These stories reflect a respect for older people as well as a respect for the natural order.

Books for Older Readers

Authors of contemporary stories with Native American characters frequently have characters develop understandings about the past to help them respect their heritage. For example, in *High Elk's Treasure*, Virginia Driving Hawk Sneve ties the past to the present with a flashback to the year 1876, when the Sioux were taken to the reservation following the defeat of General Custer at the Battle of Little Big Horn. One hundred years later, High Elk's descendants excitedly discover a pictograph of the Battle of the Little Big Horn. This pictograph is later authenticated by an expert from the university. Throughout her book, Sneve develops a strong feeling for the past and pride in Native American heritage. In *Bearstone*, Will Hobbs uses an ancient turquoise bear to help a Ute Indian boy clarify his beliefs and overcome his personal problems. Joseph Bruchac uses symbols, beliefs, and legends in *Eagle Song* to help a boy clarify his beliefs after he moves with his family from a Mohawk reservation to Manhattan. Through his experiences, he learns to take pride in himself.

In *Walk Two Moons*, Sharon Creech's heroine, thirteen-year-old Sal, is proud of her Native American heritage through her mother. Now she faces conflicts because her mother has left her. The author develops two parallel stories as the heroine tells the story of her best friend, Phoebe, and her experiences when Phoebe's mother left.

Sal makes discoveries about her own life and learns to accept her own mother through a series of mysterious messages. The answers to the messages allow the author to show characters' actions and motivation as Sal and her grandparents trace the route of her mother's disappearance. For example, the first message is, "Don't judge a man until you have walked two moons in his moccasins" (p. 51). On page 61, father interprets the message. The second message, "Everyone has his own agenda" (p. 60), is interpreted by Gramps (p. 70), tied into the actions of Sal and her sister (p. 104) and Phoebe's thoughts about her own agenda. The third message, "In the course of a lifetime, what does it matter?" (p. 105), is interpreted when Sal thinks about the meaning of the message (p. 106). The meaning of the fourth message, "You can't keep the birds of sadness from flying over your head, but you can keep them from nesting in your hair" (p. 154), is developed when Phoebe thinks about her mother and tries to tell a story about her mother in London (p. 155), through Phoebe's father (p. 162), during Sal's response to Phoebe's crying (p. 169), when telling a story of Pandora's box (pp. 174–175), and describing the birds of sadness around Phoebe's family (p. 189). The meaning of the fifth message, "We never know the worth of water until the well runs dry" (p. 198), is revealed through Mrs. Cadaver (p. 221). The final message is the same as the first: "Don't judge a man until you have walked two moons in his moccasins" (p. 152). It is interpreted when Gramps and Sal play the moccasin game in which they take turns pretending they are walking in someone else's moccasins (p. 275) and through Grams and Gramp's gift to Sal when they let her walk in her mother's moccasins.

Ancient traditions, symbolism, and personal conflicts are important in Jean Craighead George's *The Talking Earth*. In this book, a Seminole girl who lives on the Big Cypress Reservation questions the traditions of her people and searches for her heritage as she travels alone through the swamp. Through her journey of self-discovery, she learns the importance of her ancient traditions.

Journeys that allow Native American characters to search for their ancient traditions and cultural heritages are important themes in much of the Native American literature for children and adolescents. In Jean Craighead George's *Water Sky*, a boy from Massachusetts journeys to Barrow, Alaska, in search of his uncle and his Inuit heritage. During his quest, he lives in a whaling camp, where he learns to respect his Inuit heritage and discovers Inuit values and beliefs. In Gary Paulsen's *Dogsong*, a contemporary Inuit boy leaves the modern world to discover the ways and beliefs from the days of dogsleds. The protagonist discovers his traditional heritage through his interactions with an elderly Inuit and by journeying alone on a 1,400-mile dogsled trek across the isolated ice and tundra. The author uses many traditional references through dreams and visions that allow the boy to travel back to earlier times.

In Scott O'Dell's *Black Star, Bright Dawn*, an Inuit girl drives a dogsled team in the Iditarod Trail Sled Race from Anchorage to Nome. Through her experiences, the girl learns to depend on her dogs and herself. In addition, she discovers the strength in her Inuit heritage, values, and beliefs.

Conflicts involving settings are often used to develop the plots in contemporary realistic fiction written for older readers. The conflict frequently occurs when a protagonist leaves the reservation and lives in urban environments. The protagonist in Robert Lipsyte's *The Brave* leaves the reservation and the support of his people to try to become a boxer in Manhattan. In the city, he experiences the harsh underworld of violence, drugs, gangs, and prison. It is his heritage, however, and the teachings of his uncle about the Running Braves, that make it possible for him to face his problems and control his life. Knowing oneself and relying on traditional teachings and cultural heritage are frequently shown as sources for personal strength.

Symbolism, traditional values, tribal customs, and conflict with contemporary society are common elements in Native American books written for older readers. For example, Jamake Highwater's Ghost Horse Cycle, that includes *Legend Days*, *The Ceremony of Innocence*, and *I Wear the Morning Star*, is a series of three books that follow three generations of a Northern Plains Indian family as they progress from a proud and powerful people to a people who are alienated from both their roots and the encroaching white culture. The cycle focuses on the life of Amana, a woman of power, courage, and tragedy, who symbolizes the fate of her people.

The importance of believing in the traditional ways of one's people is an important theme in *Legend Days*. This theme is developed through the "legend days" motif used throughout the book. Omens, powers, visions, and close relationships with animals and nature are important in both the plot and Amana's characterization. That alienation will result if one loses his or her identity is a strong theme developed in both *The Ceremony of Innocence* and *I Wear the Morning Star*. This theme is developed as Amana finds herself alienated from both her tribal ancestors and her half-French, half-Indian daughter. As she confronts her daughter, she reveals the importance of her tribal heritage and the depth of her alienation. The theme of the destructive force of alienation is reinforced through the unhappiness of two of Amana's children. When the characters try to deny their Native American heritage and struggle to become part of the white culture, they do not know their own identities. It is only Amana and her son, Sitko, who eventually obtain acceptance of self and peace of mind. Amana succeeds by escaping into her earlier visions and reuniting with Grandfather Fox through death. Sitko learns the myths of his grandmother and recaptures her visions through art.

The historical perspective of Highwater's *Legend Days* is based on accounts of life in the Northern Plains as found in the oral history of the Blackfoot Confederacy. The book is grounded in mythological foundations typical of the mythology of the Great Plains. The social context of Highwater's *Ceremony of Innocence* and *I Wear the Morning Star* is similar to the context of Native American authors writing for adult audiences. For example, N. Scott Momaday (Kiowa) in *House Made of Dawn* (1968) focuses on the alienation of a returning Native American soldier as he feels separated from both urban society and tribal ways. Many of the short stories of Simon J. Ortiz (Acoma Pueblo) and his poems, such as "From Sand Creek" in *Songs from This Earth on Turtle's Back: Contemporary American Indian Poetry*, reveal how difficult it is to face stereotypical attitudes and be accepted as an individual. Louis Owens (Choctaw/Cherokee/Irish) uses visions and belief in traditional values and mythology to allow his protagonist to discover who he is in *The Sharpest Sight* (1992). The themes by these Native Americans writing for adult audiences are quite similar to the themes in contemporary realistic fiction written for juvenile audiences.

 ## NONFICTION INFORMATIONAL BOOKS

Native American author Paula Gunn Allen (Coltelli, 1990) expresses concern that many people do not realize that Native Americans are active participants in not only the history, but also the culture and arts of contemporary America. To overcome this problem the Native American informational literature should include sources that describe the lives, contributions, and problems of contemporary Native Americans.

The juvenile sources in this area tend to portray both the promises and the conflicts faced by Native Americans as they live in two worlds. Arlene Hirschfelder's *Happily May I Walk: American Indians and Alaska Natives Today* is a comprehensive text, discussing such contemporary topics as tribal governments, education, economic life, and organizations. The text includes photographs, further reading lists, and an index. A map of Native American lands and communities helps readers find locations identified in the text. It is interesting to compare this map with the maps showing the historic tribal lands of the 1600s.

Tricia Brown's *Children of the Midnight Sun: Young Native Voices of Alaska* provides a unique perspective by focusing on the lives of eight children who each represent a different culture: Eskimo—Yuk'ik and Inupiat; Aleut; and Indian—Athabascan, Tlingit, Tsimshian, and Haida. Through their stories, readers understand how these young people meld the contemporary world with the traditional cultural values and beliefs. Roy Corral's photographs add considerable interest. The text includes a glossary and a list of recommended reading.

Highly illustrated informational books for young readers follow the lives of children growing up in the culture or provide insights into characteristics of the culture. For example, Marcia Keegan's *Pueblo Boy: Growing Up in Two Worlds* is a photographic essay that accompanies a boy as he engages in activities in his pueblo and in his school. The contrasting environments of ceremonial dances in the pueblo and computers in the school are shown through the photographs. Diane Hoyt-Goldsmith's *Arctic Hunter* is a photographic essay that follows the activities of a contemporary Inupiat boy in Kotzebue, Alaska. Normee Ekoomiak's *Arctic Memories* illustrates and discusses the Inuit artist's own memories of life in the Arctic. The illustrations provide information about the culture, including the igloo, ice fishing, traveling, games, and ancestral hunters. This interesting text is written in both English and Inuktitut.

Through text and photographs, Diane Hoyt-Goldsmith's *Buffalo Days* covers not only the history of the buffalo (bison), but also focuses on the celebration of the Crow Fair and Rodeo, which is held during the third week of August on the Crow Reservation in Montana. Lawrence Migdale's photographs add to the cultural understanding. Jacqueline Left Hand Bull and Suzanne Haldane's photo essay *Lakota Hoop Dancer* follows the activities of Kevin Locke, a Hankpapa Indian and member of the Lakota Nation, as he prepares for and performs the traditional dance. Both text and photographs emphasize the importance of retaining the Lakota culture. The text includes a glossary and a list of recommended reading.

SUMMARY

Through the study of Native American literature, we discover that there is a continuum that begins with the traditional literature and extends through the contemporary literature. The traditional literature is of vital importance because it reflects the values and beliefs of the people that are still important in the contemporary literature. For example, a review of traditional literature of the Northern Plains Indians indicates that traditional values include living in harmony with nature, showing respect for wisdom gained through age and experience, viewing religion as a natural phenomenon closely related to nature, acquiring patience, and emphasizing group and extended needs rather than individuals needs.

Themes and conflicts in historical fiction about Native Americans often emphasize survival during periods in history in which contact with settlers or cavalry resulted in catastrophic changes. Another theme emphasized is growing interpersonal relationships between Native American and white characters.

Many of the contemporary works discussed in the chapter indicate that oral tradition remains important in Native American fiction. Native American authors may emphasize the role of struggle and conflict in their writing. Some authors use traditional stories to develop values and recall history. The importance of the spoken word is reflected in both ancient and contemporary Native American poetry.

Native American literature is a complex subject. An understanding of the literature requires an in-depth study of both the history and the contemporary role of the people.

SUGGESTED ACTIVITIES FOR DEVELOPING UNDERSTANDING OF NATIVE AMERICAN LITERATURE

1. Compile a bibliography of illustrated books that develop a Native American perspective. Emphasize the strengths in both the text and the illustrations.
2. Using the evaluation criteria identified in this text, evaluate a selection of Native American literature available in a university, public, or school library. What conclusions do you reach about the quality of the books available? Or choose two time periods and use your evaluation criteria to compare the quality of the books.
3. Consult recent journal articles that deal with issues related to Native American literature. What are the current opinions about authenticity, sovereignty, translations, and literal versus metaphorical interpretations? With a group of your peers, choose one of the topics and conduct a debate on the subject.

4. Read "The Beaver and the Porcupine Woman" in Michael Dorris's "Native American Literature in an Ethnohistorical Context," *College English*, 41 (October 1979): 147-162. Try to interpret the example of Athapaskan folklore given in the article before you read Dorris's background information or the interpretation. How does your interpretation of the tale change after you have this background information? What message did you gain about the importance of background information when interpreting or comprehending Native American folklore?

5. Choose a highly illustrated version of Native American folklore that you can authenticate through other sources. Authenticate both the text and the illustrations.

6. Choose a Native American tribal or cultural area. Compile a list of the values and beliefs that are developed in the folklore of that area. Use examples of folklore to prove your points.

7. Read an adult biography or autobiography of a Native American subject and read a children's biography written about the same figure. Compare the two texts, using some of the same characteristics as discussed in this text.

8. Using the characteristics of contemporary Native American authors discussed in this text, do a literary analysis of a contemporary realistic fiction book or a collection of poetry by a Native American author. Use quotes from the literature to identify and support any of the characteristics discussed.

9. Choose a Native American tribal or cultural area. Develop an annotated bibliography of nonfiction informational sources that can be used to add understanding of that tribal group.

Involving Children with Native American Literature

 ## PHASE ONE: TRADITIONAL LITERATURE

Before beginning a study of traditional Native American literature and culture, students need to understand the diversity of locations for Native American peoples. John Bierhorst's *The Mythology of North America* (1985) includes a map of North American mythological regions. A map is also located in Michael J. Caduto and Joseph Bruchac's *Keepers of the Animals: Native American Stories and Wildlife Activities for Children* (1991). According to the authors, this map indicates the cultural areas and tribal locations of Native North Americans as they appeared around 1600. Students could begin their study of Native American folklore with an investigation of the oral language as reflected in storytelling.

Developing Oral Storytelling Styles

You could begin the study of storytelling by explaining to students that Native American storytellers developed styles of telling stories over centuries of oral tradition. Storytelling was an important part of earlier Native American life, and stories were carefully passed down from one generation to the next. It was quite common for Native Americans to gather around a fire or sit in their homes and listen to stories. Each tribe member told a story, and storytelling sessions frequently continued for long periods. Several collectors of tales and observers of storytellers have identified opening sentences, storytelling styles, and endings that characterize the storytelling of various tribes. Copying and implementing the techniques may be used to make the storytelling experience more authentic for students of literature.

For example, Navajo storytellers frequently opened their stories with one of these openings:

In the beginning, when the world was new . . .
At the time when men and animals were all the same and spoke the same language . . .

White Mountain Apache frequently opened their stories with

> Long, long ago, they say . . .

Discuss the meanings of each introduction and consider how the introduction relates to traditional Native American values.

Now you may select a collection of Native American folklore suitable for storytelling. The following texts provide a few suggestions: Joseph Bruchac's *Tell Me a Tale: A Book About Storytelling* includes tales from various tribal areas as well as suggestions for telling the stories; Chief Lelooska's *Echoes of the Elders: The Stories and Paintings of Chief Lelooska* includes tales from the Northwest Coast; Nancy Wood's *The Serpent's Tongue: Prose, Poetry, and Art of the New Mexico Pueblos* includes stories divided according to such categories as creation, childhood, a lasting way of life, hunting, and ceremony. You may also select examples of individual stories that are appropriate for storytelling such as Barbara Juster Esbensen's *The Star Maiden,* which is an Ojibway tale about the creation of water lilies; Paul Goble's *Iktomi and the Berries* and *Iktomi and the Boulder: A Plains Indian Story,* which are trickster tales from the Lakota Sioux; and Laura Simms's *The Bone Man: A Native American Modoc Tale,* which explores the values of courage, wisdom, and compassion.

Students may use these folktales to discover how interpreters and translators of traditional folklore introduce their stories. They can ask: Are there differences according to tribe or region? For example, students can find the following examples in Chief Lelooska's *Echoes of the Elders* (Northwest Coast):

> Many generations ago, there lived . . .
> Our ancestors believed there were . . .

These examples of story openers are in Nancy Wood's *The Serpent's Tongue* (from the nineteen Pueblos of New Mexico):

> Many, many years ago, all things came to be.
> In the beginning, long, long ago, there was but one being in the lower world.
> It seems—so the words of the grandfathers say . . .

You may share with the students information about various Native American storytelling styles. For example, storytellers from the Northwest used a terse, staccato, and rapid style to tell their stories. Coeur d'Alene storytellers used gestures to increase the drama of their tales. Hopi children responded to the story by repeating the last word of the sentence, and Crow children responded with "E!" (yes) following every few sentences. Jicarilla Apache storytellers gave kernels of corn to children during story time. (It was believed that if children ate corn during the storytelling, they would remember the content and the importance of the stories.) Kiowa Indians did not tell trickster tales during daylight hours because when trickster was about ready to leave our world, he told the people never to tell stories about him in the daytime.

To help students develop an understanding of story endings, you may discuss the following examples:

> Clackama storytellers ended many of their stories with words that meant "myth, myth" or "story, story."

The Kiowa ended many of their stories with "That's the way it was—and is—down to this day."

Students may now want to search Native American folklore to discover how interpreters and translators ended their stories. For example, the following are from Nancy Wood's *The Serpent's Tongue*:

> . . . the People shall continue.

> I will pass here again, with other stories. Go home to your parents and sleep well. Songe-de-ho, goodbye!

They may discuss the meaning of each ending and consider how the ending might relate to Native American traditional values.

You may divide the students into groups according to a Native American tribe or a region of the country. Ask them to develop appropriate storytelling techniques for that tribe and ask them to practice and present their stories to the rest of the group. In *Tell Me a Tale*, Bruchac stresses the importance of introducing folktales by telling information about the story. Students could provide background about the tribe, when and why the story was told, and any other background information that could increase understanding and enjoyment. Bruchac also recommends using objects that help storytellers remember the stories. He identifies devices such as wampum belts and storytelling bags that were used by Native Americans in the Northeast. These mnemonic devices add interest as well as provide help remembering the story. Wampum belts have patterns that symbolize important events. Bruchac describes how he uses a wampum belt to tell stories based on the designs depicted in the belt. The storytelling bags contain objects related to various stories. These bags could be held out to the audience. Someone would reach into the bag and pull out an object; the storyteller would relate a story associated with the object.

Identifying Types of Tales Found in Native American Folklore

You may want to collect as many examples of Native American folklore as possible. Ask the students to categorize the tales according to John Bierhorst's (1985) story types discussed earlier in this chapter and repeated below. The following are a few tales that exemplify these types:

Setting the World in Order: The creation stories in Michael J. Caduto and Joseph Bruchac's *Keepers of the Earth: Native American Stories and Environmental Activities for Children,* Nancy Wood's *The Serpent's Tongue,* and Barbara Juster Esbensen's *The Star Maiden.*

Family Drama Tales: Tribal stories that provide instruction in Nancy Wood's *The Serpent's Tongue,* Michael Rosen's *Crow and Hawk: A Traditional Pueblo Indian Story,* Lois Duncan's *The Magic of Spider Woman,* and Jennifer Berry Jones's *Heetunka's Harvest: A Tale of the Plains Indians.*

Trickster Tales: Gerald McDermott's *Raven: A Trickster Tale from the Pacific Northwest* and *Coyote: A Trickster Tale from the American Southwest,* Paul Goble's *Iktomi and the Boulder: A Plains Indian Story* and *Iktomi and the Berries.* And "Rabbit and Fox" in Joseph Bruchac's *The Boy Who Lived with the Bears and Other Iroquois Stories.*

Threshold Tales: Paul Goble's *Buffalo Woman* and *Beyond the Ridge* and Laura Simms's *The Bone Man: A Native American Modoc Tale.*

Have students discuss the various types of tales found in North American folklore. Before leaving Phase One, students can summarize generalizations about Native American folklore and review discoveries about oral storytelling.

ADDITIONAL ACTIVITIES TO ENHANCE PHASE ONE

Here are some activities for children or young adult students related to this phase:

1. Collect trickster tales from as many tribes as possible. What are the characteristics of the various tricksters? Why do you believe that a trickster character is associated with that tribe?
2. On a map of North America, label the locations of various tribal regions. Compare the tribal regions in the early 2000s with the tribal regions identified by Bierhorst or Caduto and Bruchac. How have the regions changed? What might account for these changes?

 ## PHASE TWO: FOLKLORE FROM SPECIFIC PEOPLES

During this second phase, the emphasis is narrowed to the study of the folklore of one or two Native American peoples or tribal regions, and students do an in-depth study of the folklore of that region. Colleen Wilson (1996), a teacher on the Blackfoot Indian Reservation in Browning, Montana, uses a literature-based approach in which she has students examine Native American literature from various regions of the United States. She states:

> We examine literature for the cultural significance of beliefs, traditions, history, and geography of other Native tribes, past and present. For example, I developed a sequence of lessons designed to improve literacy skills as well as increase students' interest in their own culture. We also worked to develop an appreciation for and social awareness of the lifestyles of other Native peoples across North America, helping students to connect these tribal characteristics to locations in North America. (p. 20)

For these extensive learning experiences, Wilson uses folklore, historical fiction and nonfiction, informational books, biographies, and contemporary literature. She also includes books by Native authors such as Joseph Bruchac and Simon Ortiz as well as non-Native authors such as Paul Goble and Scott O'Dell "who have made the effort to immerse themselves in Native sources and write sensitively about them" (p. 21). (At the conclusion of this chapter you will find a list of books from different genres that you could use to develop such a study about various regions.)

There are numerous folklore collections and individual stories retold from the Plains Indians, from the Southwest Pueblo peoples, and from Indians of the Pacific Northwest. Ask the students to search for examples of the story types found in Phase One and analyze the literature for values and beliefs of the specific people. Ask them to consider the importance of variants in the story types and search for cultural and geographical reasons for these variants. For example, students might choose literature from the Great Plains tribal areas such as "How the Spider Symbol Came to the People" (Osage—Plains), "The First Flute" (Sioux), "How the Fawn Got Its Spots" (Sioux), and "The Passing of the Buffalo" (Kiowa—Plains) in Michael J. Caduto and Joseph Bruchac's *Keepers of the Animals: Native American Stories and Wildlife Activities for Children*; "Tunka-Shila, Grandfather Rock" (Lakota), "How Turtle Flew South for the Winter" (Sioux), and "The White Buffalo Calf Woman and the Sacred Pipe" (Sioux) from Caduto and Bruchac's *Keepers of the Earth: Native American Stories and Environmental Activities for Children*; George Bird Grinnell's *Blackfeet Indian Stories* and *Blackfoot Lodge Tales: The Story of a Prairie People;* Paul Goble's *Buffalo Woman*, *The Legend of the White Buffalo Woman* (Lakota), and *The Gift of the Sacred Dog*; Kristina Rodanas's *Dance of the Sacred Circle: A Native American Tale* (Blackfoot). There are many additional sources from various tribal regions identified in the beginning of this chapter and in the list at the conclusion of the chapter.

Students should summarize the values, beliefs, and themes found in the traditional literature of a specific people and compare the types of stories found in Phase One and Two. You may also use the activities described in detail below: locating traditional values in folktales, comparing variant versions of a story, and webbing to discover additional information about the Native Americans (see Figure 2–1 for an example done for African American literature).

Identifying Traditional Values in Native American Folklore

Native American folklore can be used to develop an appreciation of a cultural heritage that places importance on oral tradition; respect for nature; understanding between animals and humans; knowledge of elderly people; and passing on cultural and tribal beliefs. An examination of folklore shows the rich diversity of Native American folktales, cultures, and customs.

You may introduce the same questions as were used to identify and compare traditional values in African folktales:

1. What reward or rewards are desired?
2. What actions are rewarded or admired?
3. What actions are punished or despised?
4. What rewards are given to the heroes, the heroines, or the great people in the stories?
5. What are the personal characteristics of the heroes, the heroines, or the great people in the stories?

You may develop a chart with the questions, listing books that include various values. (Using the same chart with different cultures helps students compare the traditional values across cultures.)

Table 3–2 shows how these values might appear when analyzing Tomie dePaola's *The Legend of the Bluebonnet*, a Comanche tale that shows how unselfish actions are rewarded, and Paul Goble's *Star Boy*, a Blackfoot tale that reveals the importance of courageous and wise actions. (These books are both from the Great Plains.) You may ask students to listen for answers to the questions printed in the table.

You may discuss any similarities and differences identified in the values. You may use additional Native American folklore and compare the values in various Native American groups living on the Great Plains, the Southwest, the Northwest Coast, and the Arctic regions.

Comparing Variants of the Cinderella Story

Students enjoy comparing stories that include elements with which they are familiar. Frank Hamilton Cushing's *Zuni Folk Tales* (1901, 1986) includes a Cinderella

TABLE 3–2   Chart with Values Identified in Native American Folklore

Questions for values	The Legend of the Bluebonnet (Comanche)	Star Boy (Blackfoot)
What reward is desired?	To end the drought and famine To save the land and the people	To remove a scar To marry the chief's daughter
What actions are rewarded or admired?	Sacrifice of a loved object to save the tribe	Courage Obedience to the Creator
What actions are punished or despised?	Selfishness Taking from the earth without giving back	Disobedience (cast out of Sky World; son's face marked with scar)
What rewards are given to heroes, heroines, or great people?	Bluebonnets, beautiful flowers A sign of forgiveness Rain Honored name change	Scar removed Married chief's daughter Life in Sky World after death
What are the personal characteristics of heroes, heroines or great people?	Unselfishly loved her people Willing to give her most prized possession	Poor Courageous Respect for wisdom of animals Wisdom, purity, honoring Creator

variant, "Poor Turkey Girl." Penny Pollock uses Cushing's retelling in her variant *The Turkey Girl: A Zuni Cinderella Story*. Consequently, these two versions provide interesting examples for comparisons, for searching for Cinderella elements, for analyzing Native American elements, and for identifying references to time and place. For example, the following details are found from an analysis of Cushing's "Poor Turkey Girl".

The Cinderella elements include the following:

1. A humble girl wears old clothing and works very hard.
2. A girl longs for kindness.
3. A dance or festival is announced.
4. A girl is not allowed to attend the dance.
5. A girl is helped to attend the dance.
6. A promise is demanded.
7. Fine clothes change back to rags at a given time.

Native American elements in Cushing's tale:

1. Zuni Indians
2. Belief in Middle World
3. Dance of the Sacred Bird
4. Respect for elders
5. Importance of keeping a vow
6. Close relationships between humans and animals
7. Reference to Maiden Mother
8. Theme: God disposes of people according to how the people are fitted; and if the poor be poor in heart and spirit as well as appearance, how will they be anything but poor to the end of their days?
9. Birds that sing are using their orenda, or magical power.
10. Birds with magical power will give favors if they are honored.
11. The tale accounts for phenomena in nature.
12. The Turkey Girl is a favorite character in Pueblo tales.

References to time and place in Cushing's tale:

1. Matsaki or Salt City
2. Southwest, North America
3. Thunder Mountain and mesas beyond
4. Plains
5. Canon Mesa
6. Time of the ancients
7. Zuni Mountains
8. Land where turkeys are plentiful

Now students may analyze Penny Pollock's text and Ed Young's illustrations for *The Turkey Girl: A Zuni Cinderella Story*. Identify the Cinderella elements, the Native American elements, and references to time and place. Students should focus on these questions: What are the similarities and differences between Cushing's tale and Pollock's retelling? How would you compare the two stories?

Webbing the Literary and Cultural Elements in Native American Folklore

There are numerous versions of folklore that may be used for a webbing activity. For example, you may read Lois Duncan's *The Magic of Spider Woman* and ask students to identify the elements that would be included under setting, characters, conflict, theme, and cultural beliefs and values. For this activity, draw a web with *The Magic of Spider Woman* placed in the center. Now on arms extending from the center draw the following categories: setting, characters, conflict, theme, and cultural beliefs and values.

You may approach this activity in several ways. You may read the tale and ask students to fill in all of the parts. Alternately, you may assign specific categories to certain students: those students are only responsible for identifying setting, or one of the other categories.

If students are responsible for certain categories, after they have filled in their category, ask them to share their responses with each other before you lead a whole-group discussion. This early sharing helps them develop more in-depth analysis of the book. After they have shared their responses, lead a whole-group discussion in which you develop a detailed web on the board or on overhead transparencies. Students may use both the text and illustrations in the text to develop their webs. When students discuss their listings on their webs, they should refer back to the text and illustrations to provide evidence for why they included specific details on the web. Figure 3–1 is a partially completed web following a discussion of the book *The Magic of Spider Woman*.

After completing a web together as a group, students may develop individual webs to accompany other books and share them with the group. If the books are chosen from a specific tribal area, students will gain considerable information about that group.

ADDITIONAL ACTIVITIES TO ENHANCE PHASE TWO

Here are some activities for children or young adult students related to this phase:

1. Summarize the major types of tales found in the folklore from each of the tribal regions of North America.
2. Compare the motifs in tales from the Northwest and the Southwest. How would you account for any similarities and differences?
3. Compare Rafe Martin's Cinderella variant *The Rough-Face Girl*, with the two Cinderella variants discussed earlier. Locate Cinderella elements and elements that relate to a Native American culture.

 ### PHASE THREE: HISTORICAL NONFICTION

Historical nonfiction includes biographies, autobiographies, and other informational books. Students may analyze biographies and autobiographies and search for evidence of philosophy, values, beliefs, and language discovered in Phases One and Two. They may identify the sources of conflict in the biographies and autobiographies and use other examples of nonfiction informational books to evaluate the authenticity of the historical happenings and sources of conflict. You may also use the information presented earlier in the chapter that analyzed biographies and autobiographies of Native Americans from the Great Plains, the Great Basin, and the Southwest to evaluate the probable authenticity of the conflict developed in the biographies.

Some of the biographies that you might use in Phase Three include Dorothy M. Johnson's *Warrior for a Lost Nation: A Biography of Sitting Bull*, Dorothy Nafus Morrison's *Chief Sarah: Sarah Winnemucca's Fight for Indian Rights*, Dennis Brindell Fradin's *Hiawatha: Messenger of Peace*, and Kate Jassem's *Sacajawea, Wilderness Guide*.

Nonfiction sources such as Peter Aleshire's *Reaping the Whirlwind: The Apache Wars*, Paul Goble's *Death of the Iron Horse*, Russell Freedman's *Buffalo Hunt* and *An Indian Winter*, and Rayna Green's *Women in American Indian Society* provide historical perspectives and sources for information about the conflicts and historical happenings.

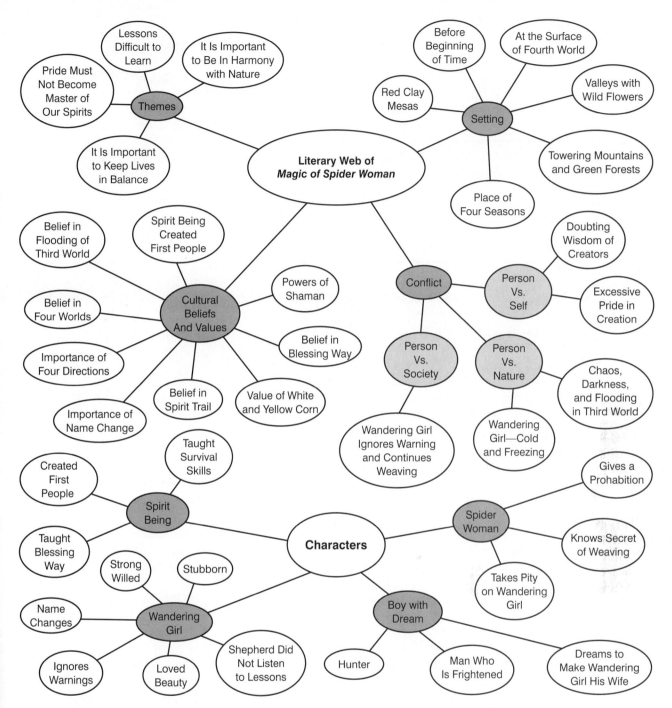

FIGURE 3–1 Literary Web for *The Magic of Spider Woman*

ADDITIONAL ACTIVITIES TO ENHANCE PHASE THREE

Here are some activities for children or young adult students related to this phase:

1. Using Phase Three literature, locate any of the references to folklore and folk-loric themes and motifs that were found in Phases One and Two.
2. Compare Johnson's biography of Sitting Bull with Judith St. George's *To See with the Heart: The Life of Sitting Bull*. Encourage students to speculate about the meaning of the title of St. George's biography.
3. On a Native American tribal map of North America, place the locations of the various tribal leaders read about in the biographies.

PHASE FOUR: HISTORICAL FICTION

There are several historical fiction books about Native Americans that have won Newbery Awards or Canadian book awards: Jan Hudson's *Sweetgrass* and Farley Mowat's *Lost in the Barrens* have won the Canadian Library Association's Book of the Year; Scott O'Dell's *Sing Down the Moon* and Elizabeth George Speare's *The Sign of the Beaver* have won as Newbery Honor books. Consequently, these books provide excellent sources for evaluating historical fiction and identifying authors' techniques that result in believable and accurate historical fiction. The books also develop themes, values, and beliefs that may be compared with those found in the traditional literature depicting a similar group of Native Americans.

Evaluating Historical Fiction About Native Americans

You may explain to the students that they will be reading historical fiction set during the time when many Native Americans experienced great changes in their lives. They will be evaluating the books for each author's ability to produce believable historical fiction and to create authentic depictions of Native Americans living during that time period. You may use the following criteria for evaluating historical fiction found in Norton's *Through the Eyes of a Child: An Introduction to Children's Literature* (1999):

1. The setting must be authentic and encourage readers to understand time, place, and conflict.
2. The conflict must accurately reflect times and attitudes of the people.
3. The characters' actions, beliefs, and values must be true to the time period without depending on stereotypes.
4. The theme should be worthwhile, as relevant today as in the historical time.
5. The Native American culture, values, and beliefs should be respected.
6. The language should be authentic for the time.
7. The style should vividly depict setting, characters, and culture.

Ask students as they read the historical fiction either in a group or individually to identify examples from the books that they believe are either good or poor examples of the author's ability to develop believable historical fiction. When this activity was completed with a group of fifth- and sixth-grade students, they identified and discussed some of the following examples: For setting, Farley Mowat in

Lost in the Barrens developed a believable person-against-nature conflict by describing foaming rapids, searching for food, and preparing for winter. Scott O'Dell in *Sing Down the Moon* developed settings by contrasting the beautiful and peaceful Canyon de Chelly with the harsh, dry Fort Sumner.

For conflict, Jan Hudson in *Sweetgrass* developed a believable conflict by describing how Sweetgrass fought to save her family from the small pox epidemic of 1837. This epidemic really happened. Elizabeth George Speare in *The Sign of the Beaver* developed conflict with nature by describing the setting that is an enemy of the inexperienced white boy and a friend to the Penobscot Indians. A believable person-against-society conflict develops because the Indians must move west to get away from the settlers.

For characterization, Jan Hudson *Sweetgrass* describes Sweetgrass's emotions and concerns about growing up. The girl's actions show that she respects the traditions of her people and believes in their values. For theme, Farley Mowat of *Lost in the Barrens* showed that working together is important for survival. This is developed by a believable theme as a white boy and a Cree both struggle to survive in the wilderness. In *Sing Down the Moon*, Scott O'Dell suggests that the loss of spiritual hope might be the greatest tragedy, that hatred and prejudice are destructive. These themes are developed as the Navajo try to survive the march to Fort Sumner. In *Sweetgrass*, Jan Hudson develops the theme that it is important to have moral obligations toward others. It is also important to keep one's dreams and to respect one's family and one's tribe. In the area of language, the author of *Sweetgrass* uses figurative language and prairie symbolism to describe Sweetgrass—when picking strawberries, "Her little hands pulled at them as daintily as a deer plucking grass in a meadow."

As each example is identified and discussed, ask the students to consider why this is a good (or bad) example to be used in a book reflecting the Native American culture. After they have completed their analysis of the literary elements in historical fiction, ask them to look carefully at the conflicts developed in the books. Have students answer the following questions: Do you think these conflicts were authentic for the time period? Why or why not? How could we find out? Do you think the settings and the characterizations were accurate for the time period? Why or why not? How could we find out?

You may ask the students to remember the beliefs and values they learned about when they read the Native American folklore. They may consider whether the beliefs and values are also shown in the historical fiction. They may speculate about what might happen to them if they experienced conflict between their own culture and one that is imposed on them from outside. They may discuss the characterizations, conflicts, and values identified earlier, and whether the themes developed in historical fiction relate to the traditional beliefs and values found in Native American literature. They may place themselves in the position of a character who is in conflict with a strong belief or value. Ask them to consider how they would respond in that situation. Ask the students to do additional research to authenticate the historical fiction.

ADDITIONAL ACTIVITIES TO ENHANCE PHASE FOUR

Here are some activities for children or young adult students related to this phase:

1. Choose an informational book that covers the same time period and setting as a historical fiction text. Use the informational book to authenticate the historical fiction.

2. Investigate the life and writings of one of the award-winning authors of historical fiction about Native Americans. Try to discover why the author chose to write about the subject and time period.
3. Compare the authors' development of setting, characterization, and themes in Mowat's *Lost in the Barrens*, O'Dell's *Sing Down the Moon*, Hudson's *Sweetgrass*, and Speare's *The Sign of the Beaver* with the development of the same literary elements in Dorris's *Sees Behind Trees*. What are the similarities and the differences? How do you account for either the similarities or the differences in these historical fiction novels? How do the differences in locations and time periods influence the development of the literary elements and the lives of the Native American people?

 ## PHASE FIVE: CONTEMPORARY LITERATURE

Developing Understanding of Author's Style

Byrd Baylor's *The Desert Is Theirs* is an excellent choice for developing both an understanding of the author's style and the values and beliefs developed through contemporary literature written in a poetic style. In the area of author's style, ask students to respond to and to identify the various poetic elements that are found in the story. For example, Baylor uses numerous examples of personification, comparisons, mythological references, and symbolism. A few examples of personification include the following: spider people who sew the sky and earth together, coyotes who dance in the moonlight, and hawks who call across the canyons. Examples of comparisons include the following: women weave grass into baskets and birds weave grass into nests; men dig earth to make homes and lizards dig burrows to make homes; and desert people are patient and toads wait months to sing songs and weeds wait years to bloom. Students should notice that all of these comparisons compare human actions and actions that occur in nature. Examples of mythological references include these: references to creation when Buzzard made mountains, Gopher led people from the underworld, and Earthmaker created the desert; and references to legendary heroes when Elder Brother taught the desert ceremonies to the people and Coyote gave advice and scattered Saguaro cactus seeds. Examples of symbolism include referring to Earth as the Papago Indians' mother who nurtures them and the patience of the desert animals and plant life who are like the people, strong and patient.

The Desert Is Theirs also provides an excellent source for developing an understanding of the values and beliefs reflected in the literature. Students may identify lines from the text, identify the values reflected in the lines, and discuss how they would interpret these lines as they relate to an understanding of this Native American culture. Before reading the text and looking at the illustrations, students should understand that this book is about the Papago Indians of Arizona. They should also understand that the Papago Indians live in a desert climate. Table 3–3 provides a guide for this discussion.

Students who have read considerable folklore from the Southwest may search for examples of similar values and beliefs found in the folklore to gain a better understanding of how many of the values and beliefs of the people are reflected in both the folklore and in contemporary literature.

TABLE 3-3   Chart Showing Values Reflected in a Piece of Literature

Lines from Text:	Value Reflected:	Interpretation:
"...Desert People...call earth their mother." (p. 3)	Respect for nature	Many tribes refer to the earth as mother because it provides sustenance.
"They have to see deserts every day."	Harmony with nature	Papago Indians believe they are part of nature.
"They sing...songs. They never hurt it" (p. 3).	Respect for nature	The earth is a major part of life. Earth means all creatures, plants, and water.
"He gave the...ceremonies ..." (p. 10).	Respect for nature	Many tribes have dances that are held to ask for rain. Dances, songs, and ceremonies are used as prayers for rain to help plants grow. Rain nourishes animals and people.
"Papagos try not to anger their animal brothers" (p. 15).	Respect for nature	The Papago have a kinship with animals.
"They say, 'we share...only share'" (p. 15).	Respect for nature	Sharing of the earth's gifts is a major aspect of many tribal ceremonies.
"They share the feeling of being brothers in the desert..." (p.17).	Cooperativeness Respect for nature	The Papago do not try to abuse, destroy, or change the land. They live in harmony with their environment.
"The desert has its own kind of time..." (p. 21).	Present-time orientation	The Papago believe that time is always with us. There is no need to rush. Things will come. Things will happen by and by.

ADDITIONAL ACTIVITIES TO ENHANCE PHASE FIVE

Here are some activities related to this phase for children or young adult students:

1. Compare the themes of living in harmony with nature and the importance of ancestral beliefs in the contemporary story by White Deer of Autumn, *Ceremony—In the Circle of Life*, with the themes found in traditional literature.

2. The importance of nature and the close relationships between a Native American boy and a hawk may be analyzed in Byrd Baylor's contemporary story from the Southwest, *Hawk, I'm Your Brother*. Discuss the importance of point of view in literature. Rewrite the story from the point of view of the hawk.

3. Search for the evidence of continuity in the themes in Native American literature in the writings of Virginia Driving Hawk Sneve and Jamake Highwater. For example, search for any of the themes, values, and conflicts found in Phases One through Four in Jamake Highwater's *Legend Days*, *The Ceremony of Innocence*, and *I Wear the Morning Star*. Highwater's books contain many examples of symbolism, traditional values, tribal customs, and conflict with contemporary society.

4. Trace the emergence of conflict, characterization, and theme in Sharon Creech's *Walk Two Moons* as the character receives mysterious messages and searches for the answers to the messages, thus allowing the author to relate characters' actions and motivation to the developing plot and resolution.

5. Choose a book such as Tricia Brown's *Children of the Midnight Sun: Young Native Voices of Alaska,* and ask children to compare their own lives with the children profiled in the book. What are the similarities? What are the differences? Why are there similarities and differences? Then use this book as a model to interview students in your own school or people in your neighborhoods.

At the conclusion to Phase Five, have students do the following: Summarize the findings and the threads discovered across the ages of literature. Review examples of continuity and evidences of change. Analyze how what they know about the literature of Native Americans will make a difference in their lives. Have them review their tribal maps and summarize what they know about specific tribes. Ask them to list areas of interest or questions that they would like to use for continued study.

BIBLIOGRAPHY

Allen, Paula Gunn, edited by. *Voice of the Turtle: American Indian Literature, 1900-1970.* New York: Ballantine, 1994.

Ballinger, Franchot. "A Matter of Emphasis: Teaching the 'Literature' in Native American Literature Courses." *American Indian Culture and Research Journal.* 8 (1984): 1–12.

Bierhorst, John. "Children's Books." *New York Times Book Review* (May 23, 1993).

_____. *The Mythology of North America.* New York: Morrow, 1985.

_____. *The Red Swan: Myths and Tales of the American Indians.* New York: Farrar, Straus & Giroux, 1976.

Black Elk, as told through John G. Neihardt. *Black Elk Speaks: Being the Life Story of a Holy Man of the Oglala Sioux.* New York: Morrow, 1932; Lincoln: University of Nebraska Press, 1979.

Campbell, Joseph. *The Power of Myth.* New York: Doubleday, 1988.

_____. *Transformations of Myth Through Time.* New York: Harper & Row, 1990.

Cazden, C. *Classroom Discourse: The Language of Teaching and Learning.* Heineman, 1988.

Coltelli, Laura. *Winged Words: American Indian Writers Speak.* Lincoln: University of Nebraska Press, 1990.

Cushing, Frank Hamilton. *Zuni Folk Tales.* Tucson: University of Arizona Press, 1986 (first printing 1901).

Dorris, Michael. "Native American Literature in an Ethnohistorical Context." *College English* 41 (October 1979): 147–162.

Eastman, Charles. *From the Deep Woods to Civilization: Chapters in the Autobiography of an Indian.* Boston: Little, Brown, 1916.

Edmonds, Walter. *The Matchlock Gun.* New York: Dodd, Mead, 1941.

Furst, Peter T., and Jill L. Furst. *North American Indian Art.* New York: Rizzoli, 1982.

Gill, Sam. D., and Irene F. Sullivan. *Dictionary of Native American Mythology.* New York: Oxford University Press, 1992.

Goodbird, Edward, retold to Gilbert L. Wilson. *Goodbird the Indian: His Story.* New York: Fleming H. Revell, 1914.

Grinnell, George Bird. *Blackfeet Indian Stories.* New York: Scribner's, 1993, 1926 (first published 1913).

_____. *Blackfoot Lodge Tales: The Story of a Prairie People.* Lincoln: University of Nebraska Press, 1962.

Hall, Edwin S., Jr. *The Eskimo Storyteller: Folktales from Noatak, Alaska.* Knoxville: The University of Tennessee Press, 1976.

Hanson, W. D., and M. O. Eisenbise. *Human Behavior and American Indians*. Rockville, Md.: National Institute of Mental Health, 1983. ERIC Document Reproduction Service, ED 231–589.

Harvey, Karen D., Lisa D. Harjo, and Jane K. Jackson. *Teaching About Native Americans*. Washington, D.C.: National Council for the Social Studies, 1990.

Hearne, Betsy. "Cite the Source: Reducing Cultural Chaos in Picture Books, Part One." *School Library Journal* 39 (July 1993): 22–27.

Herbst, Laura. "That's One Good Indian: Unacceptable Images in Children's Novels." In *Cultural Conformity in Books for Children*, edited by Donnarae MacCann and Gloria Woodard. Metuchen, N.J.: Scarecrow, 1977.

Highwater, Jamake. *The Primal Mind: Vision and Reality in Indian America*. New York: Harper, 1981.

Hodgson, Bryan. "Buffalo: Back Home on the Range." *National Geographic* (November 1994): 64–89.

Chief Joseph, edited by Allen Thornkike Rice. "An Indian's View of Indian Affairs." *The North American Review* (1879): 412-433.

Lame Deer, J. Fire,, and E. Richard. *Lame Deer: Seeker of Visions*. New York: Simon & Schuster, 1972.

Lass-Woodfin, Mary Jo, edited by. *Books on American Indian and Eskimos: A Selection Guide for Children and Young Adults*. Chicago: American Library Association, 1978.

Lawson, Robert. *They Were Strong and Good*. New York: Viking, 1940.

Levenson, Jay A., edited by. *Circa 1492: Art in the Age of Exploration*. Washington, D.C.: National Gallery of Art, 1991.

McGrath, Robin. "Words Melt Away Like Hills in Fog: Putting Inuit Legends into Print." *Children's Literature Association Quarterly* 13 (Spring 1988): 9–12.

Momaday, N. Scott. *House Made of Dawn*. New York: Harper & Row, 1968.

Norton, Donna E. "Dimensions of Native American Literature for the Library Collection." *Encyclopedia of Library and Information Science* 57 (Supplement 20, 1996): 123–154.

_____. *The Effective Teaching of Language Arts*, 5th ed. Columbus, Ohio: Merrill/Prentice Hall, 1997.

_____. "The Intrusion of an Alien Culture: The Impact and Reactions As Seen Through Biographies and Autobiographies of Native Americans." *Vitae Scholasticae* 6 (Spring 1987): 59–75.

_____. "Teaching Multicultural Literature in the Reading Curriculum." *The Reading Teacher* 44 (September 1990): 28–40. Reprinted in *Literacy Instruction for Culturally and Linguistically Diverse Students*, edited by Michael F. Opitz, pp. 213–228. Newark: International Reading Association.

_____. *Through the Eyes of a Child: An Introduction to Children's Literature*, 5th ed. Upper Saddle River, N. J.: Merrill/Prentice Hall, 1999.

Ortiz, Simon, in *Winged Words: American Indian Writers Speak*, edited by Laura Coltelli. Lincoln: University of Nebraska Press, 1990.

Owens, Louis. *The Sharpest Sight*. Norman: University of Oklahoma Press, 1992.

Parker, Arthur C. *Skunny Wundy: Seneca Indian Tales*. Chicago: Whitman, 1926.

Plenty-Coups, edited by Frank B. Linderman. *Plenty-Coups: Chief of the Crows*. Lincoln: University of Nebraska Press, 1962.

Querry, Ron. "Discovery of America: Stories Told by Indian Voices." In *American Diversity, American Identity: The Lives and Works of 145 Writers Who Define the American Experience*, edited by John K. Roth. New York: Holt, 1995.

Reed, Gerald. "The Significance of the Indian in American History." *American Indian Culture Research Journal* 8 (1984): 1–21.

Reese, Debbie. "'Mom, Look! It's George, and He's a TV Indian!'" *The Horn Book Magazine* (September/October 1998): 636–643.

Ross, A. C., and D. Brave Eagle. *Value Orientation—A Strategy for Removing Barriers*. Denver: Coalition of Indian Controlled School Boards, 1975. ERIC Document Reproduction Service, ED 125–811.

Slapin, Beverly, Doris Seal, and Rosemary Gonzales. *How to Tell the Difference: A Checklist for Evaluating Native American Children's Books*. Berkeley: Oyate, 1989.

Spang, A. "Counseling the Indian." *Journal of American Indian Education* 5 (1965): 10–15.

Stott, Jon C. "In Search of Sedna: Children's Versions of a Major Inuit Myth." *Children's Literature Quarterly* 15 (Winter 1990): 199–201.

_____. "Native Tales and Traditions in Books for Children." *The American Indian Quarterly* 16 (Summer 1992): 373–380.

Sweezy, Carl, told to Althea Bass. *The Arapaho Way: A Memoir of an Indian Boyhood*. New York: Clarkson N. Potter, 1966.

Talayesva, Don C., edited by Leo W. Simmons. *Sun Chief: The Autobiography of a Hopi Indian*. New Haven, Conn.: University Press, 1942.

Thompson, Stith. *Tales of the North American Indians*. Bloomington: Indiana University Press, 1929.

Trafzer, Clifford E. "The Word Is Sacred to a Child: American Indians and Children's Literature." *The American Indian Quarterly* 16 (1992): 381–395.

Vaughn, Robert. *Then and Now: Or Thirty-Six Years in the Rockies*. Minneapolis: Tribune Printing, 1900.

Verrall, Catherine, and Patricia McDowell. *Resource Reading List 1990*. Quebec, Canada: Canadian Alliance in Solidarity with the Native Peoples, Kahnawake Mohawk Territory, 1990.

Whitewolf, Jim, edited by Charles S. Bryant. *The Life of a Kiowa Apache Indian*. New York: Dover, 1969.

Wilson, Colleen. "Exploring the United States with Native American Literature." *Primary Voices K–6* 4 (August 1996): 19–30.

Young Bear, Ray A. *Black Eagle Child: The Facepaint Narratives*. Iowa City: University of Iowa Press, 1992.

CHILDREN'S AND YOUNG ADULT LITERATURE REFERENCES

Ackerman, Ned. *Spirit Horse*. Scholastic, 1998 (I: 8+ R: 6). The story is set more than 200 years ago in the Great Plains.

Aleshire, Peter. *Reaping the Whirlwind: The Apache Wars*. Facts on File, 1998 (I: 12+ R: 8). This informational book focuses on wars between the government and the Apache people.

Ancona, George. *Powwow*. Harcourt Brace, 1993 (I: all). Photographs and text present the Crow Fair in Montana.

Arnold, Caroline. *The Ancient Cliff Dwellers of Mesa Verde*. Photographs by Richard Hewett. Clarion, 1992 (I: 8+ R: 6). This nonfiction book is about the Anasazi people.

Baity, Elizabeth. *Americans Before Columbus*. Viking, 1951 (I: 8+), A 1952 Newbery Honor book.

Baker, Olaf. *Where the Buffaloes Begin*. Illustrated by Stephen Gammell. Warne, 1981 (I: all R: 6). The story tells about the lake where the buffaloes were created.

Baylor, Byrd. *The Desert Is Theirs*. Illustrated by Peter Parnall. Scribner's, 1975 (I: all). The life of the Papago people is captured in illustrations and text.

_____. *Hawk, I'm Your Brother*. Illustrated by Peter Parnall. Scribner's, 1976 (I: all). A boy would like to glide like a hawk.

_____. *Moon Song*. Illustrated by Ronald Himler. Scribner's, 1982 (I: all). Written in poetic style, this Pima Indian tale tells how coyote was born of the moon.

_____. *The Other Way to Listen*. Illustrated by Peter Parnell. Scribner's, 1978 (I: all). If one listens carefully, nature is heard.

_____. *When Clay Sings*. Illustrated by Tom Bahti. Scribner's, 1972 (I: all). A poetic telling of the ancient life of peoples in the southwestern desert.

I = Interest age range
R = Readability by grade level

Bealer, Alex. W. *Only the Names Remain: The Cherokees and the Trail of Tears*. Illustrated by Kristina Rodanas. Little, Brown, 1996 (I: 9 + R: 6). Provides a history of the Cherokee people.

Begay, Shonto. *Navajo: Visions and Voices Across the Mesa*. Scholastic, 1995 (I: all). Navajo philosophy is reflected in poetry and illustrations.

Bierhorst, John. *A Cry from the Earth: Music of the North American Indians*. Four Winds, 1979 (I: all). A collection of songs.

_____, edited by. *The Dancing Fox: Arctic Folktales*. Illustrated by Mary K. Okheena. Morrow, 1997 (I: 8 +). Bierhorst includes notes on the Inuit tales.

_____, edited by. *The Deetkatoo: Native American Stories About Little People*. Illustrated by Ron Hilbert Coy. Morrow, 1998 (I: 10 + R: 6). A collection of tales from fourteen Native American tribes.

_____, adapted by. "Law of the Great Peace" in *The Book of Peace*, edited by Ann Durell and Marilyn Sachs. Dutton, 1990 (I: all). This poem reflects the values of the Iroquois.

_____. *The Ring in the Prairie, A Shawnee Legend*. Illustrated by Leo and Diane Dillon. Dial, 1970 (I: all R: 6). One of the most skilled hunters discovers a mysterious circle.

_____, edited by. *The Sacred Path: Spells, Prayers, and Power Songs of the American Indians*. Morrow, 1983 (I: 8 +). This is a collection of poems, prayers, and songs.

Brown, Tricia. *Children of the Midnight Sun: Young Native Voices of Alaska*. Photographs by Roy Corral. Graphic Arts Center, Alaska Northwest, 1998 (I: 8 + R: 6). The author focuses on the daily lives of children.

Bruchac, Joseph. *The Arrow over the Door*. Illustrated by James Watling. Dial, 1998 (I: 8-11) This is historical fiction.

_____, retold by. *The Boy Who Lived with the Bears and Other Iroquois Stories*. Illustrated by Murv Jacob. HarperCollins, 1995 (I: 8 + R: 6). Six Iroquois tales.

_____. *Eagle Song*. Illustrated by Dan Andreasen. Dial, 1997 (I: 7–10 R: 4). A boy moves to Brooklyn from the reservation.

_____. *Lasting Echoes: An Oral History of Native American People*. Illustrated by Paul Morin. Harcourt Brace, 1997 (I: 10 + R: 8). This history is presented through viewpoints of Native Americans.

_____, edited by. *Songs from This Earth on Turtle's Back: Contemporary American Indian Poetry*. Greenfield, 1983 (I: 10 +). A collection from many poets.

_____. *Tell Me a Tale: A Book About Storytelling*. Harcourt Brace, 1997 (I: all). He discusses the components of storytelling.

_____, and James Bruchac. *When the Chenoo Howls*. Walker, 1998 (I: 8 + R:5). A collection of scary tales from the woodlands of the Northeast.

Burks, Brian. *Walks Alone*. Harcourt Brace, 1998 (I: 10 + R: 6). The book focuses on Apache Indian life in the late 1800s and the massacre of Apaches by the United States Army.

Caduto, Michael J. *Earth Tales from Around the World*. Illustrated by Adelaide Murphy Tyrol. Fulcrum, 1997 (I: 10 + R: 6). The text includes several Native American tales.

_____, and Joseph Bruchac. *Keepers of the Animals: Native American Stories and Wildlife Activities for Children*. Illustrated by John Kahionhes Fadden. Golden, Colo.: Fulcrum, 1991 (I: all). The text includes folklore and activities.

_____, and Joseph Bruchac. *Keepers of the Earth: Native American Stories and Environmental Activities for Children*. Illustrated by John Kahionhes Fadden and Carol Wood. Golden, Colo.: Fulcrum, 1989 (I: all). Folklore and activities about the earth.

Chanin, Michael. *The Chief's Blanket*. Illustrated by Kim Howard. H. J. Kramer, 1998 (I: 4–8). A picture book about Navajo life in the 1800s.

Cohlene, Terri. *Turquoise Boy: A Navajo Legend*. Watermill, 1990 (I: 5–9 R: 4). Tale reveals how a boy brought horses to his tribe.

Cohn, Amy L., compiled by. *From Sea to Shining Sea: A Treasury of American Folklore and Folk Songs*. Scholastic, 1993 (I: all). The collection includes Native American folklore.

Cornelissen, Cornelia. *Soft Rain: A Story of the Cherokee Trail of Tears*. Delacorte, 1998 (I: 9 + R: 8). A novel about the forced march in 1838.

Creech, Sharon. *Walk Two Moons*. HarperCollins, 1994 (I: 10 + R: 6). A thirteen-year-old girl makes discoveries about herself and her Native American mother.

Crook, Connie Brummel. *Maple Moon*. Illustrated by Scott Cameron. Stoddart Kids, 1998 (I: 6 + R: 4). Tale reveals how sap was discovered.

Cushing, Frank Hamilton. *Zuni Folk Tales*. University of Arizona Press, 1901, 1986. An adult source contains many tales that may be retold to or read by older students.

Dabcovich, Lydia, retold by. *The Polar Bear Son: An Inuit Tale*. Clarion, 1997 (I: 5–8 R: 4). A woman adopts a polar bear cub.

DeArmond, Dale, retold by. *The Boy Who Found the Light*. Little, Brown, 1990 (I: all). A collection of Inuit folklore.

dePaola, Tomie. *The Legend of the Bluebonnet*. Putnam, 1983 (I: all R: 6). Unselfish actions are rewarded.

Dewey, Jennifer Owings. *Mud Matters: Stories from a Mud Lover*. Photographs by Stephen Trimble. Cavendish, 1998 (I: 8 + R: 3). The text describes uses of mud in activities such as making pottery and dancing.

_____. *Rattlesnake Dance: True Tales, Mysteries, and Rattlesnake Ceremonies*. Boyds Mills, 1997 (I: 9 + R: 6). The author witnesses a Hopi snake dance ceremony.

_____. *Stories on Stone: Rock Art: Images from the Ancient Ones*. Little, Brown, 1996 (I: all R: 6). The author explores petroglyphs in the Southwest.

Dixon, Ann, retold by. *How Raven Brought Light to People*. Illustrated by James Watts. Macmillan, 1993 (I: all R: 5). A story about how the trickster brings light from the Sky Chief.

Dorris, Michael. *Morning Girl*. Hyperion, 1992 (I: 8 + R: 5). This historical fiction book is set in the Bahamas in 1492.

_____. *Sees Behind Trees*. Hyperion, 1996 (I: 8 + R: 5). A partially sighted boy earns his name through his senses.

Dudley, William, edited by. *Native Americans*. Greenhaven, 1998 (I: 12 + R: 10). This is part of the Opposing Viewpoints American History series.

Duncan, Lois. *The Magic of Spider Woman*. Illustrated by Shonto Begay. Scholastic, 1996 (I: all R: 5). This is a Navajo myth.

Eckert, Allan W. *Return to Hawk's Hill*. Little, Brown, 1998 (I: 10 + R: 7). This is a sequel to *Incident at Hawk's Hill*.

Ehlert, Lois. *Mole's Hill: A Woodland Tale*. Harcourt Brace, 1994 (I: 5–8 R: 4). A Seneca tale in which Mole uses her wits.

Ekoomiak, Normee. *Arctic Memories*. Holt, 1990 (I: all). The text is written in both Inuktitut and English.

Esbensen, Barbara Juster, retold by. *The Great Buffalo Race: How the Buffalo Got Its Hump*. Illustrated by Helen K. Davie. Little, Brown, 1994 (I: all). A Seneca tale reveals a characteristic.

_____. *The Star Maiden*. Illustrated by Helen K. Davie. Little, Brown, 1988 (I: all). Tells about the creation of water lilies.

Field, Edward. *Magic Words*. Illustrated by Stefano Vitale. Harcourt Brace, 1998 (I: all). These poems are based on Inuit folklore.

Fitzpatrick, Marie-Louise. *The Long March: The Choctaw's Gift to Irish Famine Relief*. Beyond Words, 1998 (I: 9 + R: 6). The story is based on the potato famine in 1847.

Fradin, Dennis Brindell. *Hiawatha: Messenger of Peace*. Macmillan, 1992 (I: 10 + R: 5). This is a biography of the Iroquois leader.

Freedman, Russell. *Buffalo Hunt*. Holiday, 1988 (I: 8 + R:6). Text shows the importance of the buffalo.

_____. *Indian Chiefs*. Holiday, 1987 (I: 10 + R: 6). Short biographies of six chiefs.

_____. *An Indian Winter*. Illustrated by Karl Bodmer. Holiday, 1992 (I: 8 + R: 6). A detailed description of the Mandan and Hidasta tribes.

Fritz, Jean. *The Double Life of Pocahontas*. Illustrated by Ed Young. Putnam, 1983 (I: 8–10 R: 7). A biography of Pocahontas.

_____, Katherine Paterson, Patricia McKissack, Fredrick McKissack, Margaret Mahy, and Jake Highwater. *The World in 1492*. Illustrated by Stefano Vitale. Holt, 1992 (I: 8 +). The section "The Americas in 1492" is written by Jamake Highwater.

George, Jean Craighead. *Julie of the Wolves*. Illustrated by John Schoenherr. Harper & Row, 1972 (I: 10 + R: 7). An Inuit girl survives with the help of wolves.

_____. *The Talking Earth*. Harper & Row, 1983 (I: 10 + R: 6). A Native American girl tries to discover her heritage.

_____. *Water Sky*. Harper & Row, 1987 (I: 10 + R: 6). A boy discovers his Inuit heritage.

Goble, Paul. *Beyond the Ridge*. Bradbury, 1989 (I: all R:5). An elderly Native American woman experiences death and goes to the afterlife.

_____. *Buffalo Woman*. Bradbury, 1984 (I: all R: 6). A bond is developed between animals and humans.

_____. *Death of the Iron Horse*. Bradbury, 1987 (I: 8 + R: 5). This story is based on an incident in 1867 between the Union Pacific Railroad and the Cheyenne people.

_____. *The Dream Wolf*. Bradbury, 1990 (I: all R: 6). This tale from the Plains tells how a wolf saves two children.

_____. *The Gift of the Sacred Dog*. Bradbury, 1980 (I: all R: 6). This Sioux tale tells how the horse was given to the people.

_____. *The Girl Who Loved Wild Horses*. Bradbury, 1978 (I: 6–10 R: 5). A Native American girl's attachment to horses is described.

_____. *Iktomi and the Berries*. Watts, 1989 (I: 4–10 R: 4). Iktomi is a trickster from the Lakota Sioux.

_____. *Iktomi and the Boulder: A Plains Indian Story*. Orchard, 1988 (I: 4–10 R: 4). Iktomi learns a lesson.

_____. *The Legend of the White Buffalo Woman*. National Geographic, 1998 (I: 8 + R: 4). A sacred legend of the Lakota Indians.

_____. *Star Boy*. Bradbury, 1983. (I: 6–10 R:5). A Blackfoot Indian returns to the sky world.

Goldin, Barbara Diamond, retold by. *Coyote and the Fire Stick: A Pacific Northwest Indian Tale*. Illustrated by Will Hillenbrand. Harcourt Brace, 1996 (I: 8 +). Trickster brings fire to the people.

_____, retold by. *The Girl Who Lived with the Bears*. Illustrated by Andrew Plewes. Harcourt Brace, 1997 (I: 8 +). A tale from the Northwest Coast.

Goodman, Susan E. *Stones, Bones, and Petroglyphs: Digging into Southwest Archaeology*. Photographs by Michael J. Doolittle. Simon & Schuster, 1998 (I: 8 + R: 6). A class works with archaeologists during a field trip.

Green, Rayna. *Women in American Indian Society*. Chelsea, 1992 (I:12 + R:7). The text presents the history of Native American women.

Hamilton, Virginia. *In the Beginning: Creation Stories from Around the World*. Illustrated by Barry Moser. Harcourt Brace Jovanovich, 1988 (I: all R: 5). This collection includes several Native American myths.

Harris, Christie. *The Trouble with Adventurers*. Illustrated by Douglas Tait. Atheneum, 1982 (I: 10 + R: 6). A collection of stories from the Northwest Coast.

Highwater, Jamake. *Anpao: An American Indian Odyssey*. Illustrated by Fritz Scholder. Lippincott, 1977 (I: 12 + R: 5). Anpao journeys across the history of North American traditional tales.

_____. *The Ceremony of Innocence*. Harper & Row, 1985 (I: 12 + R: 6). This is part two of the Ghost Horse Cycle.

_____. *I Wear the Morning Star*. Harper & Row, 1986 (I: 12 + R:6). This is part three of the cycle.

_____. *Legend Days*. Harper & Row, 1984 (I: 12 + R: 6). This is the first part of the Ghost Horse Cycle.

Hirschfelder, Arlene. *Happily May I Walk: American Indians and Alaska Natives Today*. Scribner's, 1986 (I: 10 + R: 6). This informational book is about contemporary life.

Hobbs, Will. *Bearstone*. Atheneum, 1989 (I: 10 + R: 6). A troubled Ute boy is helped by an elderly rancher.

Hoyt-Goldsmith, Diane. *Arctic Hunter*. Photographs by Lawrence Migdale. Holiday, 1992 (I: 8 + R: 5). A photographic essay follows the life of an Inuit boy and his family.

_____. *Buffalo Days*. Photographs by Lawrence Migdale. Holiday, 1997 (I: 7 + R: 5). The book is a photo essay.

_____. *Lacrosse: The National Game of the Iroquois*. Photographs by Lawrence Migdale. Holiday, 1998 (I: 8 + R: 5). Includes a history of lacrosse and the Iroquois Confederacy.

Hucko, Bruce. *A Rainbow at Night: The World in Words and Pictures by Navajo Children*. Chronicle, 1997 (I: all). Twenty-three reproductions of paintings are included.

Hudson, Jan. *Sweetgrass*. Philomel, 1989/Tree Frog, 1984 (I: 10 + R:4). A Blackfoot girl grows up during the winter of a smallpox epidemic in 1837.

Hunter, Sally M. *Four Seasons of Corn: A Winnebegao Tradition*. Photographs by Joe Allen. Lerner, 1997 (I: 8 + R: 5). A twelve-year-old learns about his people's relationship with corn.

Jaffe, Nina. *The Golden Flower*. Illustrated by Enrique O. Sanchez. Simon & Schuster, 1996 (I: all). A Taino tale explains the creation of water and vegetation.

Jassem, Kate. *Sacajawea, Wilderness Guide*. Illustrated by Jan Palmer. Troll Associates, 1979 (I: 6–9 R: 2). This is an illustrated biography of the Shoshone woman who guided the Lewis and Clark expedition.

Jeffers, Susan. *Brother Eagle, Sister Sky: A Message from Chief Seattle*. Dial, 1991 (I: all). A poetic retelling of the message.

Johnson, Dorothy M. *Warrior for a Lost Nation: A Biography of Sitting Bull*. Westminster, 1969 (I: 10 +). A biography of the Native American leader.

Jones, Jennifer Berry. *Heetunka's Harvest: A Tale of the Plains Indians*. Illustrated by Shannon Keegan. Roberts Rinehart, 1994 (I: 6–9 R: 5). The tale develops the theme of the need to share with others.

Joosse, Barbara M. *Mama, Do You Love Me?* Illustrated by Barbara Lavalle. Chronicle, 1991 (I: 3–7). A young child tests her mother's love.

Keegan, Marcia. *Pueblo Boy: Growing Up in Two Worlds*. Cobblehill, 1991 (I: 6-10 R: 5). A photographic essay depicts the life of a contemporary boy.

Keehn, Sally M. *Moon of Two Dark Horses*. Philomel, 1995. (I: 10 + R: 5). This historical fiction is set at the time of the American Revolution.

Kirkpatrick, Katherine. *Trouble's Daughter: The Story of Susanna Hutchinson, Indian Captive*. Delacorte, 1998 (I: 10 + R: 6). A historical novel set in the 1600s.

Kroll, Virginia. *The Seasons and Someone*. Illustrated by Tatsuro Kiuchi. Harcourt Brace, 1994 (I: 4–8). A young Inuit girl witnesses the changes in the seasons.

Lavender, David. *Mother Earth, Father Sky: Pueblo Indians of the American Southwest*. Holiday, 1998 (I: 8 + R: 5). An informational book about Pueblo Indians.

Lawlor, Laurie. *Shadow Catcher: The Life and Work of Edward S. Curtis*. Walker, 1994 (I: 12 + R: 7). This biography is illustrated by photographs of Native Americans taken by Curtis.

Left Hand Bull, Jacqueline, and Suzanne Haldane. *Lakota Hoop Dancer*. Dutton, 1999 (I: all). The book follows the activities of the dancer.

Lelooska, Chief. *Echoes of the Elders: The Stories and Paintings of Chief Lelooska*. Edited by Christine Normandin. Callaway, 1997 (I: all). The stories and paintings focus on the Northwest Coast.

Lenski, Lois. *Indian Captive: The Story of Mary Jemison*. Lippincott, 1941 (I: 10 + R: 5). A 1942 Newbery Honor book.

Lewis, Paul Owen. *Storm Boy*. Beyond Words, 1995 (I: 8 + R: 5). The tale includes Northwest Coast motifs.

Lipsyte, Robert. *The Brave*. HarperCollins, 1991 (I: 12 + R: 6). A young Native American man desires to become a boxer.

Littlechild, George. *This Land Is My Land*. Children's Book Press, 1993 (I: 8 + R: 5). The text presents a historical viewpoint of Native Americans.

Luenn, Nancy. *Nessa's Fish*. Atheneum, 1990 (I: 4–8 R: 4). An Inuit girl and her grandmother go ice fishing.

Lyon, George Ella. *Dreamplace*. Orchard, 1993 (I: 5–9 R: 4). A young girl dreams about the original people who lived on the site of the Anasazi.

McCaughrean, Geraldine. *The Bronze Cauldron: Myths and Legends of the World*. Illustrated by Bee Willey. Simon & Schuster, 1997 (I: 8 + R: 5). Includes several Native American legends.

McDermott, Beverly Brodsky. *Sedna: An Eskimo Myth*. Viking, 1975 (I: 8 + R: 5). This is a tale from the Eskimo people.

McDermott, Gerald. *Arrow to the Sun*. Viking, 1974 (I: 3–9 R: 2). Strong shapes and colors complement a Native American tale.

_____. *Coyote: A Trickster Tale from the American Southwest*. Harcourt Brace, 1994 (I: all). Coyote's vanity brings him misfortune.

_____. *Raven: A Trickster Tale from the Pacific Northwest*. Harcourt Brace & Jovanovich, 1993 (I: all). This trickster tale tells how light was brought to the people.

McMillan, Bruce. *Salmon Summer*. Houghton Mifflin, 1998 (I: 4–7). Numerous photographs show an Aleut boy in Alaska.

Marrin, Albert. *Plains Warrior: Chief Quanah Parker and the Comanches*. Simon & Schuster, 1996 (I: 10 + R: 6). The biography includes a history of the Comanche relationship with the settlers.

Martin, Rafe. *The Boy Who Lived with the Seals*. Putnam, 1993 (I: 10 + R: 5). This Chinook Indian tale is about a boy who was raised by seals.

_____. *The Rough-Face Girl*. Illustrated by David Shannon. Putnam, 1992. (I: All R: 5). An Algonquin Indian Cinderella tale.

Matcheck, Diane. *The Sacrifice*. Farrar, Straus & Giroux, 1998 (I: 10 + R: 5). An historical novel about a Crow girl set in the mid-1900s.

Metayer, Maurice, edited by. *Tales from the Igloo*. Illustrated by Agnes Nanogak. Hurtig, 1972 (I: all R: 5). This is a collection of Inuit tales.

Miles, Miska. *Annie and the Old One*. Illustrated by Peter Parnall. Little, Brown, 1971 (I: 6–8 R: 3). Annie's love for her Navajo grandmother causes her to prevent the completion of a rug, which would signal her grandmother's death.

Miller, Brandon Marie. *Buffalo Gals: Women of the Old West*. Lerner, 1995 (I: 10 + R: 6). The text includes a section on Native American women.

Morrison, Dorothy Nafus. *Chief Sarah: Sarah Winnemucca's Fight for Indian Rights*. Atheneum, 1980 (I: 10 + R: 6). Sarah was a leader of the Paiute people.

Mowat, Farley. *Lost in the Barrens*. Illustrated by Charles Geer. McClelland & Stewart, 1966, 1984 (I: 9 + R: 6). A Cree boy and his friend are lost in northern Canada.

Nashone. *Grandmother Stories of the Northwest*. Sierra Oaks, 1988 (I: all). Five stories from the Northwest.

Nicolai, Margaret. *Kitaz Goes Ice Fishing*. Illustrated by David Rubin. Alaska Northwest, 1998 (I: 4-8 R: 4). A Yup'ik Eskimo boy goes fishing with his grandfather.

Norman, Howard, retold by. *The Girl Who Dreamed Only Geese and Other Tales of the Far North*. Illustrated by Leo and Diane Dillon. Harcourt Brace, 1997 (I: 9 +). Includes ten tales from Inuit folklore.

O'Dell, Scott. *Black Star, Bright Dawn*. Houghton Mifflin, 1988 (I: 8 + R: 6). An Inuit girl enters the Iditarod Trail dog sled race.

_____. *Sing Down the Moon*. Houghton Mifflin, 1970 (I: 10 + R: 6). A young Navajo girl tells of the forced march of her people in 1864.

_____, and Elizabeth Hall. *Thunder Rolling in the Mountain*. Houghton Mifflin, 1992 (I: 10 + R: 6). This historical novel is told from the point of view of Chief Joseph's daughter.

Orie, Sandra DeCoteau. *Did You Hear Wind Sing Your Name? An Oneida Song of Spring*. Illustrated by Christopher Canyon. Walker, 1995 (I: 4–8). The text and illustrations present the Oneida view of the cycle of spring.

Oughton, Jerrie. *How the Stars Fell into the Sky: A Navajo Legend*. Illustrated by Lisa Desimini. Houghton Mifflin, 1992 (I: 4–8 R: 5). Coyote's impatience causes problems.

Paulsen, Gary. *Dogsong*. Bradbury, 1985 (I: 10 + R:6). An Inuit boy journeys 1,400 miles on dogsled.

Pollock, Penny. *The Turkey Girl: A Zuni Cinderella Story*. Illustrated by Ed Young. Little, Brown, 1996 (I: 5–10 R: 5). A story first retold by Frank Hamilton Cushing.

Rodanas, Kristina. *Dance of the Sacred Circle: A Native American Tale*. Little, Brown, 1994 (I: all R: 5). A Blackfoot tale about the first horse.

Rosen, Michael. *Crow and Hawk: A Traditional Pueblo Indian Story*. Illustrated by John Clementson. Harcourt Brace, 1995 (I: 5–9 R: 5). A family drama tale that depicts the consequences of not caring for one's young.

Roth, Susan. *The Story of Light*. Morrow, 1990 (I: 6–10). This is a retelling of a Cherokee myth about the bringing of light.

San Souci, Robert D., and Daniel San Souci. *Song of Sedna*. Doubleday, 1981. This may be used for comparisons with other Sedna tales from the Inuit.

Santiago, Chiori. *Home to Medicine Mountain*. Illustrated by Judith Lowry. Children's Press, 1998 (I: 8 + R: 5). This book recounts a year at a government boarding school in the 1930s.

Sewall, Marcia. *People of the Breaking Day*. Atheneum, 1990 (I: 8 + R: 5). This is a nonfiction description of the Wampanoag nation of southeastern Massachusetts.

Simms, Laura. *The Bone Man: A Native American Modoc Tale*. Illustrated by Michael McCurdy. Hyperion, 1997 (I: 6–8 R: 4). The author includes information to help authenticate the tale.

Sneve, Virginia Driving Hawk, selected by. *Dancing Teepees: Poems of American Indian Youth*. Illustrated by Stephen Gammell. Holiday, 1989 (I: all). This is a collection of ancient and contemporary poems.

_____. *High Elk's Treasure*. Illustrated by Oren Lyons. Holiday, 1972 (I: 8–12 R: 6). A dream beginning in 1876 is renewed in the 1970s.

Speare, Elizabeth George. *The Sign of the Beaver*. Houghton Mifflin, 1983 (I: 8–12 R: 5). A white boy survives through the help of a Native American friend.

Spencer, Paula Underwood. *Who Speaks for Wolf*. Illustrated by Frank Howell. Austin: Tribe of Two Press, 1983 (I: all R: 5). This is a Native American learning story.

Steptoe, John. *The Story of Jumping Mouse*. Lothrop, Lee & Shepard, 1984 (I: all R:4). This is a Great Plains Indian legend.

Stevens, Janet. *Coyote Steals the Blanket: A Ute Tale*. Holiday, 1993 (I: all). This tale is from the Southwest.

St. George, Judith. *To See with the Heart: The Life of Sitting Bull*. Putnam, 1996 (I: 10 + R: 6). A biography of the Sioux Chief.

Swamp, Chief Jake. *Giving Thanks: A Native American Morning Message*. Illustrated by Erwin Printup, Jr. Lee & Low, 1995 (I: 5–8). An ancient message of peace and appreciation for Mother Earth.

Swann, Brian. *Touching the Distance: Native American Riddle-Poems*. Illustrated by Maria Rendon. Harcourt Brace, 1998 (I: all). The text includes fourteen riddle poems.

Swanson, Diane. *Buffalo Sunrise: The Story of a North American Giant*. Little, Brown, 1996 (I: 10 + R: 6). A section includes how the buffalo provided for the Blackfoot families.

Tompert, Ann. *How Rabbit Lost His Tail*. Illustrated by Jacqueline Chwast. Houghton Mifflin, 1997 (I: 7 + R: 4). This is a Seneca tale.

Van Laan, Nancy, retold by. *Buffalo Dance: A Blackfoot Legend*. Illustrated by Beatriz Vidal. Little, Brown, 1993 (I: 7 + R: 4). A story about respect between humans and animals.

_____, retold by. *Shingebiss: An Ojibwe Legend*. Illustrated by Betsy Bowen. Houghton Mifflin, 1997 (I: 7 + R: 4). Wisdom and persistence prove to be important values.

Viola, Herman J. *It Is a Good Day to Die: Indian Eyewitnesses Tell the Story of the Battle of the Little Bighorn*. Random, 1998 (I: 10 +). The book includes the accounts of thirteen witnesses.

Waboose, Jan Bourdeau. *Morning on the Lake*. Illustrated by Karen Reczuch. Kids Can, 1998 (I: 5–9 R: 4). The story emphasizes the Ojibwa respect for nature.

Wallas, James. *Kwakiutl Legends*. Recorded by Pamela Whitaker. Hancock, 1981 (I: all R: 4). Tales from British Columbia are told by Chief Wallas of the Quatsino tribe.

Whitaker, Muriel, Ed. *Stories from the Canadian North*. Illustrated by Vlasta VanKampen. Hurtig, 1980. (I: 12 + R: 7). This is a collection of short stories.

White Deer of Autumn. *Ceremony—In the Circle of Life*. Illustrated by Daniel San Souci. Raintree, 1983 (I: all R: 5). A nine-year-old boy discovers his ancestors' beliefs.

Wood, Nancy. *Sacred Fire*. Illustrated by Frank Howell. Doubleday, 1998 (I: 10 +). The author uses poetry and prose to emphasize the Pueblo world.

_____, edited by. *The Serpent's Tongue: Prose, Poetry, and Art of the New Mexico Pueblos*. Dutton, 1997 (I: 8 +). A large collection of tales.

_____. *Spirit Walker*. Illustrated by Frank Howell. Doubleday, 1993 (I: all). Native American poetry.

Yolen, Jane. *Encounter*. Illustrated by David Shannon. Harcourt Brace, 1992 (I: 6–10 R: 5). This is a hypothetical story of a Taino boy who tells about the landing of Columbus.

Latino Time Line

1400 B.C.	Probable beginning of Mesoamerican culture
1400 B.C. to A.D. 1000	Flourishing of Mayan civilization in southeastern Mexico and Central America (A.D. 200–800 classic Mayan Period)
1150 B.C. to A.D. 500	Flourishing of Olmec culture
200 B.C. to A.D. 1200	Rise of Toltec cultures rise in the central valley of Mexico
1000	Beginning of Inca culture in South America
1200	Aztecs arrive at central plateau of Mexico
1400s	Height of Aztec imperial conquest and construction of great temple and pyramid to God of War
1492	Columbus arrives at San Salvador
1519	Cortes takes Montezuma prisoner
1531	Apparition of Our Lady of Guadalupe to Juan Diego
1560s	Recording of Aztec oral literature by Fra Bernardino de Sahagún
16th century	Early Aztec and Mayan folklore recorded for Europeans by Spaniards
1947	Caldecott Honor: Leo Politi for *Pedro, the Angel of Olvera Street*
1950	Caldecott Medal: Leo Politi for *Song of the Swallows*
1953	Newbery Medal: Ann Nolan Clark's *Secret of the Andes*
1954	Newbery Medal: Joseph Krumgold's *. . . And Now Miguel*
1959	Newbery Honor: Francis Kalnay's *Chucaro: Wild Pony of the Pampa*
1960	Caldecott Medal: Marie Hall Ets and Aurora Labastida for *Nine Days to Christmas—A Story of Mexico*
1961	Newbery Honor: Jack Schaefer's *Old Ramon*
1965	Newbery Medal: Maia Wojciechowska's *Shadow of a Bull*
1966	Newbery Medal: Elizabeth Borton de Trevino's *I, Juan de Pareja*
1967	Newbery Honor: Scott O'Dell's *The King's Fifth*
1968	Hans Christian Andersen International Medal: Jose Maria Sanchez-Silva (Spain)
1982	Hans Christian Andersen International Medal: Lygia Bojunga Nunes (Brazil)
1992	Nobel Prize to Mexican poet and essayist Octavio Paz, who becomes Mexico's first Nobel laureate for literature
1999	Americas Award given by the Consortium of Latin American Studies Programs to books published in 1998 that portray Latin America, the Caribbean, or Latinos in the United States, with winners including George Ancona's *Barrio: José's Neighborhood* and Amelia Lau Carling's *Mama and Papa Have a Store*

4 Latino Literature

In this chapter, we will discover the rich and varied literature of peoples whose ancestry originates in such diverse areas as Mexico, Puerto Rico, Cuba, and other Latin American and South American countries. As might be expected, there is no clear preference for names to be applied to this literature. Terms such as Hispanic, Latino, and Chicano are frequently used. There are authorities who will argue for the use of each of these terms. In a *New York Times* article, David Gonzalez (1992) points out that the United States Census Bureau uses the term Hispanics. He argues, however, that "the term of choice is often Mexican, Puerto Rican, or something that specific" (p. 6). In the same article, author Sandra Cisneros states that she prefers being called Latino. She maintains, "To say Latino is to say you come to my culture in a manner of respect. . . . To say Hispanic means you're so colonized you don't even know for yourself or someone who named you never bothered to ask what you call yourself" (p. 6). The National Association of Hispanic and Latino Studies (2000) uses both terms to identify the organization. In this chapter, we will try, whenever possible, to identify the literature with the specific area of the setting and the people.

The literature discussed in this chapter also includes stories set both in the United States and in other countries. Hazel Rochman (1993) states that Latino literature lists should include both because "[p]eople don't come to America blank: their memories and stories and poetry stay with them and enrich us all, even as new experience changes them, and they change us. And many Latinos go back often to the places and peoples they came from, and that returning and leaving is part of their story" (p. 207).

In addition to crossing contemporary borders, the literature includes influences from numerous cultures. When discussing folklore, Jose Griego y Maestas and Rudolfo A. Anaya (1980) emphasize the importance of cultural infusion on Latino literature:

> The stories reflect a history of thirteen centuries of cultural infusing and blending in the Hispano mestizaje, from the Moors and Jews in Spain, to the Orientals in the Philippines, Africans in the Caribbean, and the Indians in America—be they Aztec, Apache or Pueblo. . . . The Native American influences create ambients of folk healers

and other levels of reality that are not often dealt with by Western man. The popular legends about Death, kings and queens, and country rogues come to us directly from the Middle Ages—and the Spanish Golden Age that spread its influence as far away as New Mexico" (p. 4).

As we read and discuss the literature, we will try to locate examples of this cultural infusion.

Even though there are 22.4 million U.S. residents who, according to the 1990 census, are of "Spanish/Hispanic Origin" (Gonzalez, 1992) and this number is growing rapidly, there are fewer children's books about Latinos than there are books about either African Americans or Native Americans. Cecilia Silva-Diaz (1997) accounts for some of this shortage of books when she states:

> Latin American children's literature has had a slow development that can be traced to social inequities, mediocre educational systems, inadequate publishing infrastructure, and difficult access to books and reading. The increase in the number of publishing companies, especially those dedicated to original works, a reading public ready to welcome the works of regional authors, as well as the growing professionalism of authors demonstrate that a new phase is beginning. (p. 21)

To further emphasize the shortage of books, Rosalinda B. Barrera and Ofalia Garza de Cortes (1997) compare publication of Mexican American books across time:

> [F]ormerly, the average number published per year was about 6 books; now the annual average is 19 books. While this threefold publishing increase by itself might seem encouraging, it is still depressingly low in light of the increased production of multicultural children's literature in this country during the '90s, in general, not to mention the marked growth of the Mexican American population in recent years. (p. 130)

In addition to the fewer numbers of books published, the books tend to go out of print faster than do the books about the other cultures. This phenomenon is readily seen between the third edition of Norton's *Through the Eyes of a Child: An Introduction to Children's Literature* (1991) and the fourth edition of the same text (Norton, 1995). A search of *Books in Print* disclosed that the following percentage of books from the 1991 text were no longer in print in 1995: 14 percent of African American, 25 percent of Asian American, 35 percent of Native American, and over 50 percent of Latino books.

Sally Lodge (1997) identifies another concern that may contribute to the shortage of books, especially those that are published in English and Spanish. Lodge states: "Finding good translators is one of the major hurdles publishers of Spanish language translations face. Many publishers admitted to scrapping one or more translations they had commissioned because of unacceptable quality, a dilemma that is both costly and time-consuming" (p. 549). Lodge is hopeful for the future of books that focus on Latino populations and Spanish-language texts. She indicates, however, that authors must be encouraged by publishers if there is to be an increase in high-quality books.

Lack of research in the area of cultural and linguistic diversity may also relate to the shortage of books. For example, Luis C. Moll (1999) states: "We currently have this huge emphasis on diversity, but during this past 10 years only 3% of all literacy research has dealt with cultural or linguistic diversity" (p. 227).

Most children's books about Latinos depict people of Mexican or Puerto Rican heritage, although the United States population contains numerous other groups such as Cuban Americans and the many new Americans from Central American countries. There is also an imbalance in the types of stories available. Many award-winning novels are about a small segment of the American population, the sheep herders of Spanish Basque heritage, whose ancestors emigrated to parts of North America before those parts came under United States control. Although collections of folktales and poetry are available for adults, a shortage of children's literature exists. In addition, there is a lack of balance in the settings for the literature. For example, the majority of books about Puerto Ricans overuse a New York City ghetto setting.

In this chapter, we will investigate historical perspectives including stereotypes in literature from the past, discuss Latino values identified by researchers, consider criteria for evaluating the literature, and discuss examples of the literature from various Spanish-speaking countries and literature that reflects a Latino perspective in the United States. The chapter includes the following: the ancient literature of the Aztecs and Maya; the more recent folklore that reflects interaction with other cultures; historical nonfiction that helps readers understand the ancient people and their cultures; the historical fiction; and the contemporary literature including biography, informational books, realistic fiction, and poetry.

 ## HISTORICAL PERSPECTIVES

Latino educators are particularly critical of the previous educational systems in the United States that tended to ignore their heritage and identity. For example, Rosalinda B. Barrera (1999) states:

> I think our own professional development is a topic that we need to address as Latino teachers and teacher educators. So many of us are in need of healing from the cultur-alectomies that we endured as children in U.S. schools. There are many scars left from this process. For example, many currently practicing Latino educators in the U.S. Southwest, in particular those of Mexican American heritage, never saw their culture, language, and history reflected in the school curriculum as they moved through the elementary and secondary grades. In fact, some faced school biases related to both English and Spanish language learning. . . . Consider what something like this does to identity formation and self-concept. (p. 217)

If we add to these concerns the issues related to stereotypes in the literature from the past, we begin to understand the historical conflicts faced by Latinos who did not read books that valued their cultures. We also begin to understand the reasons for carefully evaluating the literature that we present to children.

 ## AUTHORS WHO WRITE AND ILLUSTRATE LATINO LITERATURE

A search of the books winning Caldecott and Newbery awards again points to the shortage of books with Latino characters and about Latino cultures. For example, the Caldecott book winners with Latino characters and cultures are older titles such

The examples of stereotypes in this discussion related to Mexican Americans but the general issues may apply to all Latino groups.

The Council on Interracial Books for Children (1977) has been especially critical of the depictions of Mexican Americans in children's literature of the past. After analyzing two hundred books, the council concluded that little in the stories would enable children to recognize a culture, a history, or a set of life circumstances. The council criticized the theme of poverty that recurs as if it is a "natural facet of the Chicano condition" (p. 57) and the tendency for Mexican American problems to be solved by the intervention of Anglo Americans. The council also maintained that Mexican Americans' problems had been treated superficially in the books it studied. For example, many books suggest that if children learn English, all of their problems will be solved.

Isabel Schon (1981) is critical of the literature of the recent past because the "overwhelming majority of books incessantly repeat the same stereotypes, misconceptions, and insensibilities that were prevalent in the books published in the 1960s and the early 1970s" (p. 79). Schon supports this contention by reviewing books published in 1980 and 1981 that develop the stereotypes of poverty, embarrassment of children about their backgrounds, distorted and negative narratives about pre-Columbian history, and simplistic discussions of serious Latin American problems.

In a recent review of the images depicted by the media of Mexican immigrants and Latinos living in the United States, Lucila Vargas and Bruce De Pyssler (1998) conclude that the stereotypes of Mexican immigrants are overwhelmingly negative and "U.S. Latinos are regularly presented as uneducated immigrants who are unable or unwilling to help or speak for themselves" (p. 408). They found the following media stereotypes: "(1) dark lady, (2) Latin lover, (3) female clown, (4) male buffoon, (5) half-breed harlot, and (6) bandit." (p. 410). This evaluation of the media is of particular concern because "Research suggests that teen attitudes toward current affairs derive more from the mass media than from teachers, parents, or peers" (p. 410).

Vargas and De Pyssler recommend that teachers counter these negative images through activities that explore and discuss the biases that might be operating in the media stories. They conclude, "Using a media literacy approach, the social studies teacher has a unique opportunity to guide students to a rich appreciation of immigration generally, and Mexican immigration specifically. With this approach, the social studies teacher can help future citizens in our democracy make well-informed, objective, and morally sound decisions" (p. 411).

As you read the literature try to identify these stereotypes found in both older books and more recent media and consider the possible influences the stereotypes might have on juvenile or adult audiences. You may try the suggestions presented by Vargas and De Pyssler to guide students to a better understanding of Latino literature and culture.

---

as Marie Hall Ets and Aurora Labastida's *Nine Days to Christmas,* a winner in 1960; Leo Politi's *Song of the Swallows*, a winner in 1950, and Politi's *Pedro, the Angel of Olvera Street,* a winner in 1947.

A list of the Newbery Award and Honor books includes the following: Walter Dean Myers's *Scorpions* (this 1986 award includes a Puerto Rican character—the story is set in Harlem); Scott O'Dell's *The Black Pearl* (1968 award, set in Baja, California); Scott O'Dell's *The King's Fifth* (1967 award, set in the Southwest); Elizabeth Borton de Trevino's *I, Juan de Pareja* (1966 award, set in Spain); Maia Wojciechowska's *Shadow of a Bull* (1965 award, set in Spain); Jack Schaefer's *Old Ramon* (1961 award, set in the Southwest); Francis Kalnay's *Chucaro: Wild Pony of the Pampa* (1959 award, set in South America); Joseph Krumgold's *. . and Now Miguel* (1954 award, set in New Mexico); and Ann Nolan Clark's *Secret of the Andes* (1953 award, set in South America). As you will notice from the titles, the majority of the books are historical fiction. In addition, several of the books reflect settings in Spain.

My own university students have selected some of their favorite authors and illustrators whose works they believe enhance an understanding of various cultures. In addition to the already listed books, the students identified the following favorite illustrated books: Barbara Cooney's illustrations for John Bierhorst's *Spirit Child: A Story of the Nativity* and for Margot C. Griego's *Tortillitas para Mama and Other Spanish Nursery Rhymes*; Tony Chen's illustrations for Verna Aardema's *The Riddle of the Drum: A Tale from Tizapan, Mexico*; Tomie dePaola's *The Lady of Guadalupe*; Leonel Maciel's illustrations for Francisco Hinojosa's *The Old Lady Who Ate People*, Scott Taylor's photographs for June Behren's *Fiesta!*; photographs in Milton Meltzer's *The Hispanic Americans*; and photographs in Carolyn Meyer and Charles Gallenkamp's *The Mystery of the Ancient Maya*. (Unfortunately, some of these books are no longer in print.)

The students also identified some of their favorite Latino authors: Rudolfo A. Anaya, Pura Belpre, Sandra Cisneros, Nicloa DeMessieres, Francisco Hinojosa, Jose Griego y Maestas, Nicholasa Mohr, and Gary Soto.

Another source for identifying Latino children's literature is the Américas Award. These books are identified as outstanding books by the Consortium of Latin American Studies Program. The books are chosen from selections "in English or Spanish that authentically and engagingly portray Latin America, the Caribbean, or Latinos in the United States. . . . The award winners and commended titles are selected for their (1) distinctive literary quality; (2) cultural contextualization; (3) exceptional integration of text, illustration, and design; and (4) potential use" (Américas Award, 1999, p. 38).

The award recognizes books at three levels: Américas Award winners, Honorable Mention, and Commended List. The two Américas Award winners are George Ancona's *Barrio: José's Neighborhood* and Amelia Lau Carling's *Mama and Papa Have a Store*. The Honorable Mention book is Robert D. San Souci's *Cendrillon: A Caribbean Cinderella*.

There are nineteen books on the Commended List. A sample of these books includes Alma Flor Ada's *Under the Royal Plans: A Childhood in Cuba;* Francisco Alarcon's *From the Bellybutton of the Moon and Other Summer Poems* (also in Spanish); Veronica Chambers's *Marisol and Magdalena: The Sound of Our Sisterhood;* Phillis and David Gershator's *Greetings, Sun;* Gerald Hausman's *Doctor Bird: Three Lookin' Up Tales from Jamaica;* Rachel Isadora's *Carribean Dream;* Gary Soto's *Big Bushy Mustache* and *Petty Crimes;* and Nancy Van Laan's *The Magic Bean Tree: A Legend from Argentina.*

As you read the various books discussed in this chapter, try to develop your own favorite list and the reasons that you believe the books or illustrations enhance an understanding of the cultures and the people.

 ## VALUES IN LATINO CULTURE

How important is it that we not reinforce the stereotypes in Latino literature discussed earlier? How important is it that we identify books that develop values and beliefs that are authentic for the culture and then use those books with children?

One way to answer the question of the importance of using positive Latino literature with children is to identify the percentage of people who are members of the Hispanic/Latino cultural groups in the United States. For example, David E. Rosenbaum (2000) identifies the percentage of Hispanic people (*The New York Times* uses the term *Hispanic*) in various states. California has one of the highest percentages of Hispanic people with 31%; New York has 14.4%, while Massachusetts has 6.1%. Although not identified in Rosenbaum's article, Texas, Arizona, and Florida also have large percentages of Hispanic populations.

These current percentages and estimates of population trends in the future highlight the importance of multicultural literature in the United States. Kathryn H. Au (1993) states:

> Clearly there is a need for schools to improve the literacy instruction of students of diverse backgrounds. This need is becoming even more urgent given the population trends in the United States. In 1982 only one of 10 young people was Hispanic, while it is estimated that this figure will change to one of four in 2020. (p. 3)

These estimates highlight the need for not using literature that projects stereotypes and for selecting literature that highlights cultural values.

Denise Ann Finazzo (1996) is emphatic about the issue of stereotypes in children's literature when she states:

> It is important in multicultural children's selections that the characters not be depicted in stereotypical fashion. Stereotypical, flat characters are those cast in images that are commonplace and predictable. The danger in character development is to portray certain groups of people in certain ways—for example, strong males and weak females; athletic and rhythmic African-Americans; intellectual Asians; lazy and unpunctual Latinos; hot-tempered Italians; savage Native Americans; frugal Jews; inactive, failing elderly people. It is crucial for readers to examine characters for well-roundedness and to recognize the limited extent to which the author has developed certain characters. (p. 123)

In addition to stereotyping characters, authors of Latino literature frequently emphasize superficial cultural aspects such as holidays, food, and dances rather than the rich body of oral tales that are available throughout Mexico, Central America, and South America.

Kathryn H. Au (1993) identifies four values in using multicultural literature that benefit all students. First, when students from diverse backgrounds read literature that highlights the experiences of their cultural group, they learn to feel pride in their identify and heritage. This literature may give students the inspiration and confidence to write about and to value their own experiences. Second, all students learn about the diversity and complexity of U.S. society. They potentially will develop tolerance and appreciation for other cultural groups. Third, students gain a more balanced view of the historical forces that shaped U.S. society. Fourth, students can explore issues of social justice.

As we read the literature in this chapter, we will discover some of the values and beliefs identified in the literature. For example, there is a strong integration of religious beliefs that is developed throughout daily life; consequently, religion is important. There is strong respect for both the immediate family and the extended family. As part of the extended family, godparents are extremely important. The family is of primary importance throughout much of the literature. Within the family and the culture, there is respect for elderly members of the family. Mutual cooperation is important within the family as each family member contributes to the family's welfare. This cooperation is especially important in the definition of behavioral expectations for children. Within this close family, children are expected to be polite, cooperative, and respectful.

Both the shortage of books on Latinos and Latino culture and the possible stereotypes found in the literature make the evaluation of Latino literature especially important. You may want to use the following criteria when evaluating the literature (Norton, 1997):

1. Does the book suggest that poverty is a condition for *all* the people? This is a negative stereotype suggested in some literature.

2. Are problems handled individually, allowing the main characters to use their efforts to solve their problems? Or are all problems solved through the intervention of Anglo Americans?
3. Are problems handled realistically or superficially? Is a character's major problem solved by learning to speak English?
4. Is the cultural information accurate? Are Mexican American, Mexican, Cuban, Puerto Rican, or other Latin American and

South American cultures realistically pictured? Is the culture treated with respect?
5. Do the illustrations depict individuals, not stereotypes?
6. Is the language free from derogatory terms?
7. If the author portrays dialects, are they a natural part of the story and not used to suggest a stereotype?
8. If the author uses Spanish language, are the words spelled and used correctly?

In addition to strong family ties, there are also traditional cultural values related to personal characteristics. For example, when analyzing the literature, we find a great value on cleverness, while wasting time is punished. Both cleverness and sharing are rewarded, while greed and evil actions are punished.

As we read the literature, we will discover strong cultural values that are very different from the stereotypical characters that were in many of the early books.

FOLKLORE

The wide cultural areas for Latino folklore encompass Mexico, South and Central America, Cuba, and the American Southwest. The folklore incorporates the ancient tales of the Aztecs, Maya, and Incas. The Spaniards colonized the areas, and many different groups such as the Apache and Pueblo Indians, interacted with the Spanish and other groups in the Spanish colonies. As in other cultures, there are myths that explain (*ejemplo*), as well as folktales and fairy tales (collectively called *cuento*). Jose Griego y Maestas and Rudolfo A. Anaya (1980) emphasize that we need to understand the traditional literature in order to understand the culture because the tales "are a great part of the soul of our culture, and they reflect the values of our forefathers" (p. 4), as well as the cultural infusion that occurred over thirteen centuries as different cultural groups influenced both different peoples and their folklore.

Maria Perez-Stable (1997) emphasizes the importance of Latino folklore in helping children learn about the people. She contends that although folklore should not replace nonfiction books, the traditional tales "provide readers with unique insights into cultures, attitudes, and national mores" (p. 30). Perez-Stable identifies the following categories that are found in Latino folklore: (1) creation and religious stories, (2) magical tales based on historical events, (3) folktales about animals, (4) *pourquoi* tales, (5) stories that present moral lessons, and (6) trickster and noodlehead stories. Notice how these categories are very similar to those identified in other cultures. As we discuss the various forms of folklore, try to identify both the categories of the tales and the cultural values and beliefs found in the literature.

Ancient Mayan, Aztec, and Inca Folklore

The ancient roots of the early cultures and their folklore are emphasized by Roberta H. Markman and Peter T. Markman (1992):

> The Aztec culture confronted by the Spanish was a very late-flowering and relatively short-lived development of the tradition of which it was an integral part; the Aztec myths and gods are but the very tip of the iceberg that is the mythological tradition of Mesoamerica, the high culture area comprising the southern two-thirds of today's Mexico, all of Belize and Guatemala, and portions of Honduras and El Salvador, a culture reaching back at least to 1400 B.C. In its history of urban civilizations, with the earliest village-culture roots of those civilizations going back at least another thousand years. (p. 4)

Within these thousands of years prior to Spanish conquest are such cultures as the Olmec, the Toltec, and the Maya.

Markman and Markman (1992) discuss problems related to the collection and translation of the tales associated with these early people. For example, there are mythic images carved in stone, formed in ceramic, and painted on books made of bark paper or skin called codices from each of the cultures. Markman and Markman state: "Unfortunately, very few of the narrative myths that recounted the exploits of these flayed gods, feathered serpents, were-jaguars [animals similar to European werewolves], obsidian butterflies, and snake women have survived, and those that do remain are almost all from one area—the Basin of Mexico—and in the form in which they were recorded after the conquest" (p. 25). Unfortunately, at the time of the conquest, some Christian priests burned many of these codices that they believed were the "books of the devil."

Fortunately for current scholars, some of the early Aztec and Mayan tales were recorded for European audiences by Spaniards in the sixteenth century. For example, Bernardino de Sahagún, a Franciscan priest, recorded Aztec history and folklore in *La Historia General de las Cosas de Nueva España*, which was a twelve-book collection of stories and history that he collected from the Aztec people. Other tales and histories were written down by Aztecs who learned to read and write in the Texcoco Seminary. These early collections by both Spaniards and Aztecs provide many of the sources used by current folklorists and retellers of the tales. Other adult sources such as John Bierhorst's translation of *History and Mythology of the Aztecs: The Codex Chimalpopoca* (1998) provide sources for early tales, which may be told to children or used for comparative purposes.

Mayan Folklore   During the classic period from A.D. 200 to 800 the Maya in southeastern Mexico and Guatemala perfected the arts of painting, sculpture, and architecture, and developed a system of writing. They also told myths that explained the creation of the earth, humans, and animals.

The mythology includes references to the early gods such as the Lord of the Hills and the Valleys, also called Lord of the Thirteen Hills. The Rain God, Chac, has a frog orchestra because frogs when they croak are believed to be calling for rain. A major deity, known as Hackakyum, made the sun, but his elder brother, Sukunkyum, carries it through the sky each day. At night, Sukunkyum goes to his house in the underworld, feeds the sun, and spends time with his wife until the sun is again brought up to the sky. Kisin (Death Maker) lives permanently in the underworld. Later myths identify Death Maker with the devil of Christianity.

The underworld ruler of the dead is a traditional Mayan concept, illustrated in paintings that are more than 1,000 years old.

The creation of life in an empty world is the focus of Mary-Joan Gerson's *People of the Corn: A Mayan Story.* The two gods, Plumed Serpent and Heart of Sky, create oceans, forests, animals, and wooden people. Unfortunately, these wooden people have no hearts and do not satisfy the gods. After the gods destroy these unsuccessful people through a flood, the gods discover corn and believe that corn is the source of life. From the corn, they create humans who have hearts and voices that allow them to honor the creators.

Roberta H. Markman and Peter T. Markman's adult source *The Flayed God: The Mythology of Mesoamerica* (1992) includes several Mayan creation myths: "The Birth of the Uinal" (the awakening of the world); "The Birth of All of Heaven and Earth"; "The Creation of Animals"; "The Human Made of Earth and Mud"; "The Human Carved of Wood"; "The Creation of Humanity"; and "The Creation of the Sun and Moon." In order to assist the researcher, the authors include the sources for each of the translations. The text includes both examples of stories appropriate for storytelling and background information about the stories. My students use this book as the basis for oral storytelling with both children and adults.

Virginia Hamilton's *In the Beginning: Creation Stories from Around the World* includes a creation story from the Popol Vuh, the sacred history and ancient Book of Wisdom of the Quiche Maya of the highlands of Guatemala. Hamilton states that the earliest authors for the story, "Four Creations to Make Man: Maker and Feathered Serpent the Creators," were "ancient Mesoamericans who lived in Central America in 950–1500 A.D. These were wise men and priests and members of ancient nobility. The theme of the whole Popol Vuh, written over many centuries, tells of the greatness of the Quiche Mayan peoples, their sacred religion, and the rise and fall of things Quiche" (p. 99). This Mayan creation story proceeds through four creations until humans are finally created in their final form.

One of the better sources for juvenile folklore is John Bierhorst's *The Monkey's Haircut and Other Stories Told by the Maya,* collected from the Maya in Guatemala and southeastern Mexico. Bierhorst's collection includes "Notes on Sources and Variants" and a bibliography. Both of these sections are useful for readers who wish to conduct their own research. The tales indicate many of the traditional Mayan values and cultural characteristics. For example, tales such as "Rabbit and Coyote" and "Tup and the Ants" depict champion riddlers who place great value on cleverness. In "Rabbit and Coyote," a double meaning allows Rabbit to dupe Coyote and escape from his cage. In "Tup and the Ants," the plot hinges on a pun when the old man says, "Cut trees," which Tup interprets to mean "clear the forest." His foolish brothers waste time cutting into the trees trying to hollow them out.

Numerous cultural characteristics are also emphasized in Bierhorst's retelling of the tales. For example, husbands must pay a "bride service" of from several weeks to a year or two. During this time, husbands live with their wife's families and work for their fathers-in-law. Later the couple lives with his parents until they can build a house of their own. In "The Mole Catcher," the main character works for his father-in-law, the Death Maker. Another cultural characteristic is the importance of corn, which is considered the flesh and blood of mankind, and may be called "divine grace" or "Our Lord's sunbeams."

Although David Wisniewski's *Rain Player* is an original story created by the author rather than a tale retold from an oral source, the author uses Mayan history and legend to develop his characters and the plot. Wisniewski's extensive author's note provides considerable background about the Mayan culture. The themes in the story are very similar to those found in other folklore—for example, the belief that the future was divinely decreed. The cut-paper illustrations are stunning and artistically and colorfully depict the early culture.

Following your reading of Mayan folklore, develop a list of the characteristics you discover. For example, a summary of the books included in this discussion indicates that the Mayan people had a well-developed mythology that accounted for the creation of the earth and the people. They expressed strong beliefs in their gods and deities including the Lord of the Thirteen Hills and Chac, the Rain God. Death Maker, the underworld ruler of the dead, was also a strong personage. The belief in their deities led to a belief that the future was divinely decreed. In addition to the deities, the characters in the folklore include demons, monsters, and witches. The folklore also reveals additional values of the people. For example, cleverness was valued, and wasting time was not. Corn was considered so important that it was believed to be the flesh and blood of mankind. The folklore also reveals the importance of such cultural practices as paying a bride price through service to the bride's father.

As you read additional Mayan folklore, add to your lists of values and beliefs. You may also use your study of Mayan folklore to authenticate an illustrated version of a tale or to compare values and beliefs across cultures. The following example is an authentication of a retelling of a Mayan folktale that was completed by one of my university students after she had read a number of tales and referred to numerous sources.

Aztec and Other Mexican Folklore   John Bierhorst's *The Hungry Woman: Myths and Legends of the Aztecs* provides an interesting source for analyzing Aztec literature. Myths in the collection such as "The Hungry Woman" and "The First Sun" illustrate the importance of the spirits and the gods Quetzalcoatl and Tezcatlipoca. Both stories depict creation. In "The First Sun," the gods create the first world but then destroy this world because it is faulty. Consequently, the myth shows the power of the gods and desire for a better world. Many other cultures such as the Native Americans of the Southwest also relate stories about destroying worlds that are faulty. In stories such as "The Hungry Woman," readers discover that gods and goddesses must be appeased. A belief in the flood story is developed in "Monkeys, Turkey, and Fish," which describes the creation and destruction of subsequent worlds. In this myth, the second world is destroyed by fire and the third by water. This creation story also explains many aspects of nature.

Harriet Rohmer and Mary Anchondo's *How We Came to the Fifth World* is another retelling of a creation story that develops the theme that deities will destroy a world that is faulty, especially when the people become greedy and selfish. In this Aztec tale, the worlds are destroyed by elements of nature including water, air, and fire. In the fifth world, the people experience peace and happiness, but destruction is always possible if humans have evils in their hearts.

The author's note in Gerald McDermott's *Musicians of the Sun* states that the tale is a fragment from the mythological tradition of the Aztecs. The text, according to McDermott, survived in a 1543 French translation. The tale reveals how Tezcatlipoca, Lord of the Night, commands Wind to fly to the house of the Sun and free the four musicians who are held prisoner: Red, Yellow, Blue, and Green. This becomes a creation myth as Wind overcomes Sun's power, frees the musicians, and brings color and music to Earth. The importance of the four directions is emphasized as each color faces a different direction. The myth concludes as the

AN EXAMPLE OF AUTHENTICATION OF A RETELLING OF A MAYAN FOLKLORE

In *Song of Chirimia: A Guatemalan Folktale*, Jane Anne Volkmer retells the story of a young man who goes on a quest to win a Mayan princess. When Nancy Carolyn Marek (1994) evaluated and authenticated this book, she found that the author did not give specific sources or references for the translations, versions, or interpretations; consequently, my student could not compare an original text with the retelling. Instead, she used sources such as John Bierhorst's *The Mythology of Mexico and Central America* (1990), Michael Coe's *The Maya* (1992), and Carolyn Meyer and Charles Gallenkamp's *The Mystery of the Ancient Maya* (1985).

A portion of Marek's conclusions is included in the following discussion. As you read her interpretations, compare Marek's conclusions with your own interpretations:

> Pages 1–2 text: The naming of a newborn was very important in Mayan culture. Parents gave the baby a name of something in nature. The spirit of the object was considered the child's protective spirit throughout its life. The number 20 was important in the Mayan calendar. The month had twenty days. This textual page appears to be authentic for the culture.

> Page 2 illustrations: The Clear Sky's dress shown in the illustrations is almost identical to that of a Maya king shown on a throne on a carved wooden lintel from Temple IV at Tikal (Coe, 1992). Clear Sky is wearing the elaborate headdress, earplugs, and necklace (which appears to be jade), and jaguar cloak of a person of high status. The stylized moon with four circles might be a representation of the ancient Mayan ball court with four sacred directions and center hole leading to the underworld (Meyer and Gallenkamp, 1985). Both people have flattened foreheads and prominent noses as found in the Mayan tradition. Shortly after birth, the Mayan mother would bind the infant's head between two boards, front and back, to flatten the baby's forehead (Meyer and Gallenkamp, 1985).

> Pages 3–4 text: The text states that Clear Sky would take Moonlight out in a boat on a nearby lake to watch the fishermen throw their nets into the water. According to Coe (1992), canoes enabled the Maya to fish with nets for gar, snook, porgy, and catfish. But, the canoes look like reed boats with upturned ends rather than the dugout canoes used by the Maya.

> Pages 5–6 text: The story tells that the King and his daughter walked through the market to see the merchants' displays and enjoy the fragrance of the cacao beans. Cacao beans were used to make chocolate and for money in exchange for goods (Coe, 1992). It seems unlikely, however, that people of the ruling class would wander through the market. Glyphs show rulers being carried on litters or in baskets (Coe, 1992).

> Pages 7–8 text: The father tries to make the girl happy again by giving her jade beads and quetzal birds and by allowing her to watch a ball game in the ball court. Jade beads were valued by the Maya and worn by ruling classes as earplugs, necklaces, and noseplugs (Coe, 1992). Quetzal birds were a symbol of authority in Maya mythology and were valued for their brilliant feathers. Games were played with a rubber ball in a special court (Coe, 1992). Played since pre-classic times (2,000–300 B.C.), the Mayan ballgame symbolized the movements of the heavenly bodies.

AN EXAMPLE OF AUTHENTICATION OF A RETELLING OF A MAYAN FOLKLORE
continued

Pages 15–16 text: In the text the King orders all unmarried young men to come to the central plaza so that Moonlight can choose her husband. In Mayan culture, priests conducted a coming of age ceremony (Meyer and Gallenkamp, 1985). There is no mention of a ceremony. Instead the story is like a Cinderella in reverse. There is a princess who is looking for a husband. Marriage in the Mayan society was arranged by parents and there were strict rules about whom one could marry. There would be a "bride price" and the matchmaker would work out the details (Meyer and Gallenkamp, 1985).

Pages 21–22 illustrations: As before, the elaborate dress of the ruler and his daughter indicate royalty. The plain dress of the young man, Black Feather, suggests lowly status. The glyphs on page 21 are similar to glyphs carved on stelae, calendar stone, and bone, and painted on pottery (Coe, 1992). Glyphs appear to be animals such as jaguars and monkeys. The glyph on page 22 is similar to the glyph which represents the quetzal bird (Coe, 1992).

Pages 23–24 text: Ceiba trees lead Black Feather into the woods and down a steep path to where the birds never cease their singing. The Maya believed that all things in nature have a spirit. The Ceiba tree was a large tropical tree which was the source of the silky fiber kapok.

Pages 27–28 text: The Great Spirit tells Black Feather to cut a branch from the tree. After setting the treetop afire, the Great Spirit fashions the branch into a hollow pipe. When the flames are extinguished, the Great Spirit floats down to Black Feather. The Maya believed that the gods are in control of all events in human lives. Nothing happens that is not predetermined. Everything that is created comes from the gods. The wood of trees is believed to have magical powers. Fire is used to create the pipe, symbolizing creation from fire (Bierhorst, 1990).

Conclusion: The story has elements of the Mayan beliefs, values, and customs. Overall, the illustrations seem close to actual carvings in stone stelae, temples, and statuary from the Maya people. The story is pleasantly told; however, there are some discrepancies between the evidence found in adult references and this story. I could not help but compare the quality of the author's notes and the illustrations to the more thorough accounts presented by Paul Goble in his Native American retellings of folklore.

world is now filled with color and happy people: "All gave thanks to Lord of the Night, King of the Gods, Soul of the World" (unnumbered).

Music is an important feature in Aztec life. Hal Ober's *How Music Came to the World* tells how the sky god and the god of wind bring musicians and singers to the earth and fill the land with music. The book's illustrations reflect botanical motifs and codices of the Aztecs.

Additional Mexican folktales are found in Francisco Hinojosa's *The Old Lady Who Ate People*, a collection of frightening stories from Mexico. The illustrations by Leonel Maciel, one of Mexico's leading artists, give an added interest to these stories told by various Mexican Indian tribes. Many of the tales reflect a time before Christianity, a time when the people worshipped the elements of rain, sun, wind, and fire. The illustrations correspond to the frightening characterizations such as the one given in this introduction to "The Old Lady Who Ate People": "Suddenly, her nails would begin to grow and curve into claws, her arms and legs would become the limbs of a tiger, her teeth the fangs of a lion, and her body would curl and slither like a snake's" (p. 43). The stories included in this collection reflect the value of cleverness and the importance of battling evil. In these stories, good prevails over evil. Fear may also be a tool used to maintain obedience.

Pourquoi tales are popular among Mexican folktales. For example, Vivien Blackmore's *Why Corn Is Golden: Stories About Plants* reveals why the sunflower exists (to remind you of the light) and why corn has a golden color (gold from the sun god was deposited into the roots). In both of these tales about plants notice how the stories reflect the importance of the sun's light and the golden corn. Blackmore's tales suggest that because gods gave plants to humans, humans are now responsible for caring for the plants and for retaining their beauty. In one of the tales, "Chiapaneco," the villagers discover that if they help the needy they will be rewarded with good crops; if, however, they do not, the crops will be destroyed.

As you conclude your study of Aztec folklore, you will discover that the mythology details the creation of the world and the people. There is a belief in spirits and gods such as Ometecutli, Lord of Duality, and Quetzalcoatl, the Plumed Serpent. These gods are jealous and must be appeased. In the agricultural society, corn is of great value. The people, however, are responsible for caring for the land and the plants. Cleverness and sharing are rewarded, but greed and evil actions are not. It appears that the people enjoyed frightening stories about fearful monsters as well as the stories of the great gods.

Inca and Other South American Folklore   Legends, myths, and riddles from South America are found in collections by John Bierhorst and Natalia M. Belting. Bierhorst's *The Mythology of South America* provides scholarly background and selections that reflect the creation of the world and the origins of civilization, as well as the conflicts between people. Bierhorst divides the stories and the discussions according to Greater Brazil, Guiana, Brazilian Highlands, Gran Chaco, Far South, Northwest, and Central Andes. Extensive notes on sources and references add to the value of the text. Bierhorst's *Lightning Inside You and Other Native American Riddles* includes 150 riddles from several North and South American cultural regions, including southern Mexico and western South America. An annotated list of sources is helpful for students of children's literature.

Belting's *Moon Was Tired of Walking on Air* is a collection of creation myths told in South American Indian cultures. Belting introduces her selections by describing the scattering of the Ancestors, who did the following:

[They] looked at the earth and wondered at the sky, and the animals, the birds and the fishes. How was the earth made? How did Sun and Moon, how did the stars, get into the sky? Where did they themselves come from, and where had the animals lived before? How was night made, and the seasons? Why was Rainbow bent? They wondered, dreamed, asked one another, told their children what they knew, what they learned: this is the way, they told them, that things came to be. (introduction)

Belting includes a map of South America, in which she locates the places where the tales originated.

Lois Ehlert's *Moon Rope* is adapted from a Peruvian tale called "The Fox and the Mole," in which Fox convinces Mole that they should try to climb to the moon on a rope woven of grass. The story ends as a *pourquoi* tale because, after falling off the rope, Mole prefers to stay in the earth and come out only at night, avoiding other animals and never having to listen to Fox. Fox, however, may have made it to the moon because "[t]he birds say that on a clear night they can see him in the full moon, looking down on earth. Mole says he hasn't seen him. Have you?" (unnumbered). The text, written in both English and Spanish, is illustrated with pictures that were inspired by ancient Peruvian textiles, jewelry, ceramics, sculpture, and architectural detail.

Tales from the Rain Forest is a collection of stories from the Amazonian Indians of Brazil retold by Mercedes Dorson and Jeanne Wilmot. The theme developed in many of these myths is the need to respect the jungle:

> The message common to so many of the tales retold in these pages is the importance of respecting the needs of the formidable jungle. . . . The tales of the Brazilian Indians are dominated by animals, humans of animal ancestry, and even humans transformed into plants. Time is not linear. It is marked by the cycles of nature such as the ripening of fruit or the season of flood waters. Anything can be transformed or metamorphosized into anything else. A star can turn into a woman, a boy into a plant, a serpent can have a human daughter, and a jaguar can be more civilized than a man. The animate and inanimate are interchangeable in a way that resists logical comprehension. (p. xix)

These creation stories reveal the beginnings of night, fire, rain, thunder, and plants. Each of the tales concludes with a comment that helps readers interpret the tales and place them into the culture.

Two highly illustrated books written by Nancy Van Laan and Pleasant DeSpain present Brazilian folktales for younger readers. Van Laan's *So Say the Little Monkeys* uses a rhyming text that incorporates the sounds of the mischievous and active monkeys with the sounds of the jungle. DeSpain's *The Dancing Turtle: A Folktale from Brazil* develops the theme that survival requires courage and wit.

Jane Kurtz's *Miro in the Kingdom of the Sun* is an Ecuadorian Inca tale about a poor heroine who cures a sick royal prince by successfully bringing water from a lake at the pachap cuchun cuchun, one of the corners of the earth. She is helped in her quest by birds. David Frampton's woodcuts add to the sense of time and place.

Folklore that Reflects Interaction with Other Cultures

Many of the folktales from Mexico, South and Central America, and the southwestern part of the United States reflect a blending of cultures. Many of the values, beliefs, and characteristics of ancient literature are found in more recent traditional literature. The most dramatic additional factor affecting traditional literature coincides with the arrival of Cortes and the Spanish. A large body of folklore reflects the interactions between the ancient peoples and Christianity or the Spanish culture or African cultures. Some tales show the clash of cultural values, while others are examples of stories that changed because of a different setting.

For example, "The Man Who Knew the Language of the Animals," a folktale in Jose Griego y Maestas and Rudolfo A. Anaya's *Cuentos: Tales from the Hispanic Southwest* (1980), is based on a Moorish tale from "A Thousand and One Nights." The tale is also similar to Verna Aardema's African tale *What's So Funny, Ketu?* Differences between the African and Hispanic tales reflect cultural values. The main character in the Hispanic tale portrays a stronger masculine role than is developed in the African tale. From your reading of the folklore, can you account for these differences?

John Bierhorst's *Doctor Coyote: A Native American Aesop's Fables*, a retelling, also indicates cultural infusion. Bierhorst identifies the text as Mexican in origin and

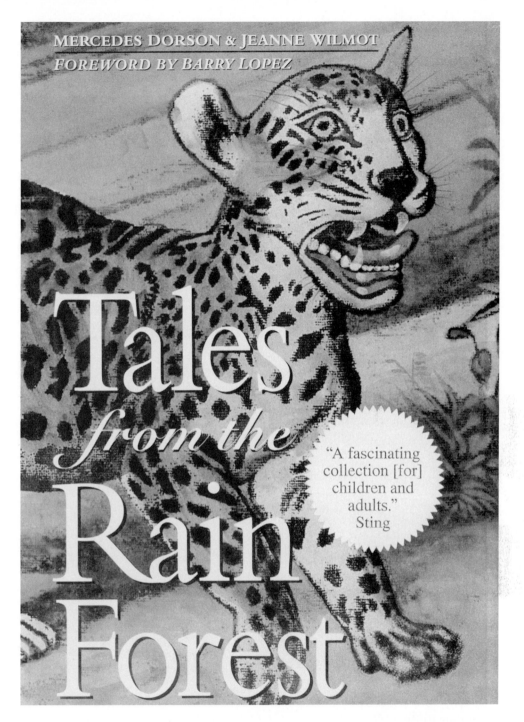

MERCEDES DORSON & JEANNE WILMOT
FOREWORD BY BARRY LOPEZ

Tales from the Rain Forest

"A fascinating collection [for] children and adults."
Sting

Tales from the Rain Forest is a collection of myths and legends from the Amazonian Indians of Brazil.

Source: Tales from the Rain Forest, Mercedes Dorson and Jeanne Wilmot, Ecco Press, 100 West Broad Street, Hopewell, NJ 08525.

shows the strong Spanish-Aztec connection. The fables were adapted in the 1500s by Indian retellers, who used a Spanish collection of fables. Several of the fables reflect the Spanish obsession with gold. Resulting morals about gold include conclusions such as if you have gold, you had better keep it hidden. The message appears to be that it is not good to be obsessed with gold. In contrast, hard work is a better way of obtaining true riches.

Pat Mora's *The Race of Toad and Deer* is a Guatemalan variant of the tortoise and the hare. It is interesting to compare these fables with Aesop's fables and with coyote trickster tales. Comparisons may also be made between stories that contain trickster rabbit characters. Stories similar to "The Tar Baby" are believed to be imported from Spain or Africa. Maria Cristina Brusca and Tona Wilson's *Pedro Fools the Gringo and Other Tales of a Latin American Trickster* includes trickster tales in which Pedro Urdemales uses wits to overcome rich and powerful characters including politicians, priests, and even the devil. The text includes an author's note and a bibliography.

Bierhorst's *Spirit Child: A Story of the Nativity* shows the infusion of Christian and Aztec beliefs. The text describes and Barbara Cooney's illustrations depict an Aztec setting for the birth of the Christ Child. Extensive Aztec beliefs are infused within the Christian story. For example, after reading this book and analyzing the pictures, readers will discover a belief in the supernatural and in the devil who plots our deaths, a belief that gods can take human form and that people are servants of all gods and must do their bidding, and a knowledge that Jesus does not demand human sacrifice and blood. Now even though the devil plots deaths, the people are saved because Jesus is the redeemer of humans who have faith.

Likewise, various versions of the story of the Virgin of Guadalupe represent the merger of Spanish-Catholic and Aztec heritages. Tomie dePaola's *The Lady of Guadalupe*, a retelling of a Mexican story, develops the connection between the people and their religious faith. The tale develops such values as a belief in God, trust and faith in the Lady of Guadalupe, respect for people in authority, and the need to do God's bidding. According to legend, the Lady of Guadalupe, now the patron saint of Mexico, appeared to a poor Mexican Indian on a December morning in 1531. Juan Diego, "He-who-speaks-like-an-eagle," was walking toward the Church of Santiago when he saw a hill covered with a brilliant white cloud. Out of the cloud came a gentle voice calling Juan's name and telling him that a church should be built on that site so that the Virgin Mary could show her love for Juan's people, the Indians of Mexico. On Juan's third visit to the bishop to ask for the church to be built, Juan's story is finally believed because he brought with him a visual sign from the Lady of Guadalupe: his rough cape had a painting of the lady on it. The church was built on the location, and the cape with its miraculous change was placed inside the structure. The author dePaola says that he has had a lifelong interest in the legend of the Lady of Guadalupe. His drawings, based on careful research, depict the dress and architecture of sixteenth-century Mexico.

Several of the tales in Bierhorst's *The Monkey's Haircut and Other Stories Told by the Maya* are adaptations that reflect cultural infusion. For example, "How the Christ Child Was Warmed" and "How Christ Was Chased" reflect the influences of Christianity on the Mayan culture. "The Lost Children" is a Hansel and Gretel variant that reflects the influence of European folklore.

Additional Hansel and Gretel variants from Spain and Mexico are found in James M. Taggart's article, "Hansel and Gretel in Spain and Mexico" (1986). These variants are more complex because they include changes in the tales as the result of male or female storytellers. Taggart's interpretation of the Nahuat variants from

Mexico are especially interesting for scholars investigating the impact of cultural values on a folktale.

Two traditional tales adapted by Harriet Rohmer, Octavio Chow, and Morris Vidaure originate with the Miskito people of Nicaragua. *The Invisible Hunters* reflects the impact of European cultures on the Miskito people. Three hunters are punished when they break their promise and forsake their people. European traders influence the hunters' actions, playing on their greed. The theme developed in the story shows that a trader culture threatens the values and beliefs respected by the villagers. *Mother Scorpion Country* is a tale of love. In this tale, a husband tries to accompany his wife into the land of the dead.

Both of Rohmer's texts include information about the author's research. For example, Rohmer began her research for *The Invisible Hunters* in anthropological archives, visited the Miskito communities in the company of an Afro-Indian Catholic priest, learned more details of the story from an elder Miskito Catholic deacon, and finally met a Miskito bishop of the Moravian Church who provided many additional details. During this final contact, Rohmer was told, "According to the stories I heard as a child the Dar has a voice. I can take you to people who say they have heard that voice" (p. 31). In *Mother Scorpion Country*, Rohmer traces the story to the endeavors of a young Moravian minister who recorded the stories and customs of the Miskito Indians in the early 1900s.

The understandings gained from the folklore may be used to authenticate Deborah Lattimore's *The Flame of Peace: A Tale of the Aztecs*. This literary folktale is based on the Aztec nine evil lords of darkness and the god of peace. Lattimore uses information from Aztec myth and hypothesizes about what might have caused the Alliance of Cities during the time of Itzcoatl. In the resulting story, a young boy uses his wits against the evil lords and brings peace to the cities. The illustrations reflect Aztec settings and characters.

 ## HISTORICAL NONFICTION AND FICTION

High-quality informational books about Latino peoples for adults and children include books on history, geography, culture, and people from various places. There are also numerous adult sources that provide illustrations and background information that can be used to authenticate juvenile literature. The historical fiction often depicts the early Spanish presence in the Americas.

Informational Books That Develop Historical Perspectives

Several books appropriate for young people discuss accomplishments of the ancient native cultures of the Western Hemisphere. Carolyn Meyer and Charles Gallenkamp's *The Mystery of the Ancient Maya* (1985) provides a thoroughly documented presentation of Mayan history and accomplishments. The lively writing style creates interest in the subject, and early photographs and drawings add to the authenticity. In *The World in 1492*, Jean Fritz, Katherine Paterson, Patricia and Fredrick McKissack, Margaret Mahy, and Jamake Highwater discuss the history of various parts of the world at the time of Columbus. The section titled "The Americas in 1492" is written by Jamake Highwater. This chapter includes information on the Aztecs, the Incas, and other native peoples. Readers will discover information about social classes and religious ceremonies and festivals. Maps show the Aztec and Inca empires, and illustrations show art from the time period. Albert Prago's *Strangers in Their Own Land: A History of Mexican-Americans* traces the history of Mexican Americans and explores reasons for difficulties that Mexican Americans face today.

Johan Reinhard's *Discovering the Inca Ice Maiden: My Adventures on Ampato* provides a fascinating glimpse into the search for Inca antiquities by describing the true experiences of the author as he discovers a Peruvian mummy that was 500 years old. The photographic essay provides knowledge about the ancient culture, as well as the people who still live in the area. Readers will also gain an understanding of the scientific method as they follow how the discovery is handled at both the original site and later in the laboratory.

Information on the history and contributions of Puerto Ricans, Mexican Americans, and Cubans is discussed in Milton Meltzer's *The Hispanic Americans*. Meltzer explores Spanish influences resulting from exploration and colonization. Then he considers the development of the political, economic, and cultural status of Hispanic Americans.

Several adult sources provide information and illustrations that are worthwhile for background and authenticate information about a culture. Both my undergraduate and graduate students use these sources to provide background information either for sharing the culture with children or for conducting their own research. For example, *The Olmec World: Ritual and Rulership*, published by the Art Museum at Princeton University and Abrams (1996), develops an in-depth look at the people who lived in Mexico and Central America between about 1400 and 400 B.C. The text includes essays by leading authorities, maps, photographs of art works, and drawings. For example, the topics discussed include the following: "Olmec Archaeology" (Richard A. Diehl and Michael Coe); "Art, Ritual, and Rulership in the Olmec World" (F. Kent Reilly, III); "Art in Olmec Culture" (Carolyn E. Tate); "Shamanism, Transformation, and Olmec Art" (Peter T. Furst); "The Rainmakers: The Olmec and Their Contribution to Mesoamerican Belief and Ritual" (Karl A. Taube); and "The Olmec Mountain and Tree of Creation in Mesoamerican Cosmology" (Linda Schele). The text includes 252 labeled photographs, many in color, showing examples of Olmec art including sculptures, masks, glyphics, and ornamental pieces. In addition, there are numerous drawings.

The Gods and Symbols of Ancient Mexico and the Maya: An Illustrated Dictionary of Mesoamerican Religion by Mary Miller and Karl Taube (1993) provides an illustrated source for information about the gods and symbols of the Olmecs, Zapotecs, Maya, Teotihuacanos, Mixtecs, Toltecs, and Aztecs. The text includes almost 300 entries.

The Incas and Their Ancestors–the Archeology of Peru by Michael E. Moseley (1992) traces the Incas from the first settlement in Peru over 10,000 years ago to the Spanish conquest. The text includes 225 illustrations. Another adult source, *Maya Cosmos: Three Thousand Years on the Shaman's Path* by David Freidel, Linda Schele, and Joy Parker (1993), provides extensive information about religious beliefs of the Maya. The book includes drawings, photographs, detailed chapter notes, and references.

Circa 1492: Art in the Age of Exploration, edited by Jay A. Levenson (1991), is an adult source that includes topics similar to those found in Fritz's juvenile text, *The World in 1492*. This large adult text includes sections on both Spain and the Americas. The sections on the Americas include reproductions of art from the Aztec and Inka (text spelling) Empires. This extensive book also provides a source for comparative study.

Maps found in various adult sources are useful for indicating the locations of the various people. For example, maps of Mexico and Central America indicating the locations of the Aztec and Mayan peoples are found in *Atlas of Ancient America*, by Michael Coe, Dean Snow, and Elizabeth Benson (1986); *The Maya*, by Michael Coe (1992); and *The King Danced in the Marketplace*, by Frances Gillmor (1977).

Historical Fiction

Historical fiction includes several books that deal with the Spanish conquest. An understanding of history is important for readers to analyze historical fiction about this time period. Consequently, some of the previously mentioned informational books provide useful background information.

Award-winning authors Elizabeth Borton de Trevino and Scott O'Dell have written historical fiction novels set in either seventeenth-century Spain or in the Americas at the time of the Spanish conquest. For example, de Trevino's *I, Juan de Pareja* is set in Spain in the 1600s. The story focuses on two quite different people: the court painter Diego Rodriguez de Silva y Velázquez and his slave Juan de Pareja. The author's "Afterword" provides interesting information for students of children's literature who are interested in the techniques an author uses to gather information and to write an historical novel about personages who really lived.

The author de Trevino states that her book is fictional because "Whenever one tells a story about personages who actually lived, it becomes necessary to hang many invented incidents, characters, and events upon the thin thread of truth which has come down to us. The threads of the lives of Velázquez and Pareja are weak and broken; very little, for certain, is known about them" (p. 177). Next, de Trevino states that only one direct quote can be authenticated. But, notice how much character information can be inferred from this quote: "I would rather be first in painting something ugly than second in painting beauty" (p. 178).

The writer also reveals that she relied heavily on portraits painted by Velázquez. For example, she states that the portrait of Pareja "shows a man intelligent, loyal, proud, and tender; the only self-portrait known of Velázquez (in 'Las Meninas') shows detachment, sensitivity, sobriety. Biographies of many painters are constructed by scholars from a study of their works, plus known facts. In fiction, then, I think the author may be pardoned for making her own interpretations of some of the paintings that have come down to us over the centuries, Velázquez's only recorded 'conversations'" (p. 178).

This book develops both views of the Spanish culture and the human interactions between a caring master and the slave who becomes his friend. Students of children's literature will gain insights into the culture of the time, as well as discover ways that authors develop historical novels from threads of the past.

Person-against-self and person-against-society conflicts, settings that depict Mayan and Aztec cultures, as well as themes that illustrate the consequences of greed, are found in O'Dell's novels based on the Spanish conquest of Mexico in the early 1500s. *The Captive*, *The Feathered Serpent*, and *The Amethyst Ring* focus not so much on the events of the time as on the moral dilemmas that a young priest faces in the New World. The books are told through the point of view of a young idealistic Jesuit seminarian, Julian Escobar, who leaves his secure home in Spain and joins an expedition to Central America, inspired by the prospect of saving the souls of native peoples in New Spain.

Through the three books, O'Dell creates both Escobar's character and his changing conflicts: Escobar is shown as a scholar who is interested in Mayan history and restoring their city, a Christian who is open to other cultural beliefs, and a man who experiences great conflicts as he is taken for a Mayan god. O'Dell explores changes in Julian by stressing the changing conflicts in Julian's life: Should he take on the role of the mythical Kukulcan in order to save his life and make his views palatable to people with their own ancient beliefs? Should he advise attacking a neighboring city before his own Mayan city is attacked? How should he respond to the Mayan rites of sun worship? Why does God permit both good and evil? Julian's defense of his inability to change the Maya and of his own eventual grasping for power demonstrate changes in his character. Much of the conflict is person against society and person against self as Escobar struggles with differences between Mayan and Spanish beliefs and then struggles with his own desires to convert the Indians to Christianity.

O'Dell's series of books are rich in cultural information, including values, beliefs, and customs. Students of children's literature will discover in O'Dell's books many beliefs and values that are similar to those found in the traditional literature of the Mayan people. For example, there are beliefs in the legend of Quetzalcoatl's return and in the importance of the ancient gods and the accompanying religious ceremonies. The people value an honorable life and expect to pay the consequences if they do not live such lives. Detailed settings provide extensive cultural information. O'Dell's themes also reflect the time period. For example, there are themes that greed is a powerful force that can ruin lives and people have moral obligations that must be met.

O'Dell's descriptions of Mayan and Aztec cities and temples and other aspects of the cultures encourage readers to understand that an advanced civilization inhabited the Americas long before European exploration and settlement. Readers may also ponder the right of one culture to destroy another culture whose people worship different gods and possess riches desired by a foreign power.

In *The King's Fifth*, O'Dell sets his story in the American Southwest. As in the previous books, O'Dell's characters reflect the conflicts of the time period. There is Esteban de Sandoval, an adventurous cartographer who accompanies Coronado and the conquistadors on their search for the cities of gold. There is arrogant and ambitious Captain Mendoza, who is drawn to the Southwest because of his greed for treasure. There is also Father Francisco, who goes on the journey in the hopes of saving souls. As would be expected from this cast of characters, there are both person-against-society and person-against-self conflicts as the various characters try to achieve their goals. O'Dell's themes suggest that strong beliefs require strong commitments, people have moral obligations that must be met, and greed is a powerful and dangerous force. Notice how all four of O'Dell's books about the Spanish conquest develop very similar themes. Students of children's literature can speculate about why these themes are so important for this time period.

Two other books by O'Dell are set in later times. *Carlota* is set in Spanish California in the mid-1800s. O'Dell explores the conflicts that occur between people who expect females to play a traditional female role and others who encourage a different type of behavior. Carlota is the strong and independent daughter of Don Saturnino, a native Californian whose ancestors came from Spain. Her father supports her brave and adventurous inclinations.

O'Dell's *The Black Pearl* is set in La Paz, a small, mountainous town in Baja California. The characters include Ramon, a boy who tries to please his father and also dreams of finding the magnificent Pearl of Heaven; Manta Diablo, the fearsome, giant, sea monster that is bigger than a ship; Blas Salazar, the strong proud pearl diver who is ashamed of his son's lack of size; Sevillano, the finest diver in the fleet who is a troublemaker and an antagonist; and Soto Luzon, the old, wise Native American who teaches the old ways of pearl diving.

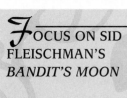

FOCUS ON SID FLEISCHMAN'S *BANDIT'S MOON*

Bandit's Moon is especially good for exploring changes in characters that reveal developing understanding between people of two cultural groups. Fleischman accomplishes this task by placing his characters in the days of the California Gold Rush, a time in the 1850s that is often characterized by lawlessness and in which people are shown as motivated by greed and even racial hatred.

The two major characters are Annyrose, a newly orphaned girl who finds herself on this lawless frontier, and Joaquín Murieta, a Mexican bandit who some believe to be notoriously cruel, while others believe to be a Robin Hood type of character whose major role is to right the wrongs against the Mexican settlers.

Fleischman first develops the character of Annyrose by describing her reactions to the villainous O. O. Mary. Fleischman compares O. O. Mary to a black widow spider and describes Annyrose's reactions to the loss of her violin and classical music when they are taken by the thieving woman. Through these descriptions, readers get a clear understanding of Annyrose's values and beliefs and learn about the frequent instances of greed and cruelty that are part of the setting. It is into this environment that Fleischman places Joaquín as he first saves Annyrose from O. O. Mary by taking Annyrose with him as part of his group of bandits. It is Annyrose's request to accompany the bandits that provides a foreshadowing of the relationships that may develop.

Through the interactions between Annyrose and Joaquín, readers obtain a vicarious experience that allows them to understand the differences between the two individuals and then to accompany them on their road to understanding. For example, notice their attitudes toward each other as Fleischman develops this early dialogue between the two characters:

> "You are not frightened?" he asked. "Don't you believe the stories about me?"
>
> "Some of them," I said. "But no man could be that heartless and cruel."
>
> "But the gringos are."
>
> "What are gringos?"
>
> "You," he said. "You Yankees who try to drive us Mexicans off this land."
>
> "I'm not a Yankee," I said. "I'm from Vermilion Parish, Louisiana."
>
> "You are all Yankees. You steal our gold and shoot at us for target practice."
>
> (p. 11)

From this early beginning that introduces the conflict among the various groups, Fleischman develops understanding as the characters become friends, help each other obtain some of their goals, and even rescue each other from dangerous circumstances.

The degree of their changing attitudes toward each other is especially revealing at the close of the book when Fleischman describes Annyrose's heartbroken reaction when she believes that Joaquín has been killed and then expresses her relief when she discovers that it is an impostor and not Joaquín who has been captured and killed. Readers can feel her relief as she "paused for a deep breath, taking in the fresh, fresh air. Somewhere in the California hills, I thought, there stood a patient oak tree still waiting for Joaquín" (p. 132). By the end of the book, she understands that Joaquín will probably still be hunted by the law. But she also knows that her actions had nothing to do with the possible capture of her friend.

By analyzing this book, students of children's literature will discover value systems that reflect the interaction of the old traditions and the newer Christian traditions. For example, there are both strong superstitions and suggestions that God favors those who are generous. O'Dell develops themes that are similar to his books set in an earlier time period. For example, people have moral obligations to themselves, to their community, and to the spirits and to God; greed and wrong doings will be punished; and honorable actions result in a clear conscience.

Marian L. Martinello and Samuel P. Nesmith's *With Domingo Leal in San Antonio 1734* takes a documentary approach to Spanish American history and life in the United States. Published by the University of Texas Institute of Texas Cultures in San Antonio, this carefully researched book describes a day in the life of a young eighteenth-century Spanish boy who lives in what is now Texas. The boy has traveled with his family from the Canary Islands through Mexico to the Villa de San Fernando on the banks of the Rio San Antonio de Padua. This historical novel can strengthen children's understanding of a long Spanish heritage in the southwestern United States. It also demonstrates that people of Spanish ancestry were living on the North American frontier before English-speaking settlers claimed it.

As you conclude your reading of historical fiction, notice how many of the values and beliefs are similar to those expressed in the earlier folklore. Also notice how the authors of historical fiction develop many of their plots and conflicts by showing person-against-society and person-against-self conflicts. Also notice how the authors of historical fiction develop settings, plots, conflicts, and themes that reflect the major happenings of the time periods.

CONTEMPORARY REALISTIC FICTION AND NONFICTION

Contemporary Latino literature includes picture books for young children that reflect many of the feelings and desires expressed by all children. Poetry reflects traditional beliefs and values and contemporary concerns. Realistic fiction for older children frequently presents problems related to growing up and to racial tensions. Many of the nonfiction titles are photographic essays that follow the lives of various families or groups or describe the geography of a region or festivals. The biographies reflect the lives of people who have made contributions to the Latino culture.

Poetry

Listening to and saying rhymes from various cultures encourage children to interact with language, as well as to discover the joy in language and in word play. Margot C. Griego's *Tortillitas para Mama and Other Spanish Nursery Rhymes* and Lulu Delacre's *Arroz con Leche: Popular Songs and Rhymes from Latin America* are written in both English and Spanish. The texts provide sources for sharing literature in either language. *Ten Little Fingers and Other Play Rhymes and Action Songs from Latin America* selected by Jose-Luis Orozco includes musical accompaniment as well as lyrics in both Spanish and English. Nancy Van Laan's *So Say the Little Monkeys* is written in poetic form. The tale is based on folklore from the Brazilian rain forest. The repetitive language is especially appealing to young children.

Many of the poems in Brian Swann's *Touching the Distance: Native American Riddle-Poems* are from groups including Aztec of Mexico, Chipawa of Southwest Bolivia, Amizgo of Mexico, and Mayan of Mexico. According to the author, the riddles are new poems drawn from a list of seven sources found in the author's acknowledgments. The riddles include both a poem and an illustration that helps readers identify the answers. The answers to the riddles are given at the back of the book.

Two poetry collections by Francisco Alarcon include poems written in both English and Spanish. *Laughing Tomatoes and Other Spring Poems* is a collection of twenty humorous poems. Many of the poems are about the importance of nature, plants, and family members. In the afterward, the poet provides information that could be used to either introduce the poetry or to motivate children to write poetry: "A collection of poetry is like a tomato plant. From a small seed it sprouts, then grows and grows. Poems need good soil, sunlight, water, air, and lots of care and tending. . . . Poems, like tomatoes, grow in many forms and shapes. And somehow they change every time you read them. This is the magic of poetry" (p. 31).

Alarcon's *From the Bellybotton of the Moon and Other Summer Poems* is, according to the poet, a celebration of life the way it was when he visited relatives in Mexico during summer vacations. As you read the poems, try to visualize the poetry through the viewpoint of the poet: "This collection of poetry is a celebration of this life when there were no radios or t.v. sets and the day's best entertainment came from the fantastic stories and incredible anecdotes told at night with the family seated around the kitchen table" (p. 32). Gary Soto's *Neighborhood Odes* is also a celebration of life. Soto's book is a collection of twenty-one poems about a Latino neighborhood and the people who live in the neighborhood.

Tun-ta-ca-tun: More Stories and Poems in English and Spanish for Children edited by Sylvia Peña is a collection of both poems and stories written for a wide range of ages. As might be expected from the title of the book, the poems have a linguistic style that appeals to children. As you read the poetry, try to imagine the celebration of life that is found in many of the selections.

Picture Books

Several of the contemporary picture books written for young children present the text in both English and Spanish. The purpose for many of these books is to provide instruction in languages. For example, a series of picture dictionaries by Rebecca Emberley provide illustrated vocabularies in the two languages. *Let's Go: A Book in Two Languages* introduces words associated with topics such as animals at the zoo, camping, going to the beach, and going to the circus. *My Day: A Book in Two Languages* pictures activities that a child might do during the day. The book begins with clocks showing different times and proceeds through vocabularies associated with activities such as getting dressed, eating breakfast, walking to school, and attending various classes. *My House: A Book in Two Languages* includes captioned illustrations showing items found in and outside the house. The book begins with labeled colors and proceeds from the inside of the house, to the family members, to various rooms in the house, to objects and activities associated with the outside of the house. *Taking a Walk: A Book in Two Languages* presents labeled illustrations showing objects a child might see while taking a walk. The book begins with labeled shapes. It includes many items a child might see such as the neighbor's house, the school, the playground, and the library.

My First Book of Proverbs by Ralfka Gonzalez and Ana Ruiz is also written in both English and Spanish. The text includes simple proverbs such as "A good listener needs few words." Each of the proverbs is illustrated with a colorful picture that has the flavor of folk art. An analysis of the proverbs also indicates some of the traditional values that are important in the Mexican culture such as the importance of experience, love, and singing.

Campbell Geeslin's *On Ramon's Farm: Five Tales of Mexico* includes both rhymes and stories about animals on the farm. Although not written completely in Spanish, the author does use numerous Spanish words. The humorous stories are about animals such as sheep who weep when they are shorn, a rooster who sees his reflection in a pail of water, and a goat who climbs the windmill.

Values related to the importance of family are central to Latino literature. These values are reflected in Benjamin Alire Saenz's *A Gift from Papa Diego*. This story, written in both English and Spanish, highlights the importance of family relationships through the story of a young boy who wishes to spend his birthday with his grandfather who lives far away. The story has a happy ending and reinforces the importance of family values.

Leo Politi has written and illustrated a number of award-winning picture storybooks about Mexican American children living in southern California. His *Song of the Swallows* tells the story of a young boy whose dear friend is the gardener and bell ringer at the mission of San Juan Capistrano. Politi shares Mexican American history with readers as the gardener tells Juan the story of the mission and of las golondrinas, the swallows who always return to the mission in the spring, on Saint Joseph's Day, and remain there until late summer. Politi's illustrations re-create the Spanish architecture of the mission and demonstrate a young boy's love for plants and birds.

Song of the Swallows is a good source for searching for values and themes that may be similar to those found in traditional literature and historical fiction. For example, you will discover that Politi develops values such as respect for elders, love of history and nature, responsibility for care of the Earth, and a belief in God. The themes developed in the book show the importance of living in harmony with nature, respecting the past because history provides many lessons, and respecting people who have this knowledge of the past.

Marie Hall Ets and Aurora Labastida's *Nine Days to Christmas: A Story of Mexico* tells of a kindergarten child who is excited because she is going to have her own special Christmas party, complete with a piñata. In the midst of numerous other everyday activities, Ceci chooses her piñata at the market, fills it with toys and candy, and joins the La Posada procession. After Ceci sees her beautiful piñata being broken at the party, she is unhappy until she sees a star in the sky that resembles her piñata. Children relate to the girl's feelings and learn about the Mexican celebration of Christmas when they read this book. This story depicts a middle-class family that lives in an attractive city home. Children can see that poverty is not the condition of all people with a Spanish heritage.

Richard Garcia's *My Aunt Otilia's Spirits*, a fictional story set in contemporary San Francisco, includes elements of the supernatural. Garcia bases the story on a visit from a Puerto Rican relative. Consider the relationships among reality and fantasy as Garcia describes the story in the endnotes:

> Like all stories, this one is based on a kernel of fact—that is that my Aunt Otilia was accompanied by bed shakings and wall knockings wherever she went. However, this was not regarded as unusual in my family, or a cause for much concern. The supernatural had a natural place in our life. Most of the time we ignored it—sometimes it meant something—as in the case of an omen or a dream. We had a large and well-worn copy of an old dream book—and this was often consulted in the morning if a dream seemed significant. . . . And those who had died were never thought of as being very far away—and were often spoken to as if they were in the room. (p. 24)

Fiction for Middle-Elementary Grades

The fiction written for students in the middle-elementary grades deals with problems such as gaining feelings of self-worth and solving problems that are common for children of that age. Some of the stories that have inner-city settings develop tensions related to racial issues. Maia Wojciechowska's Newbery Award winner set in Spain, *Shadow of a Bull,* develops two important themes: it is important to be true to oneself, and facing death is not the only way to demonstrate courage. In this realistic book, the son of a famous and supposedly fearless bullfighter learns that a male does not have to prove his manliness through acts of physical daring or violence. Manolo's village expects him to follow in his dead father's footsteps. As the men of the village begin training him in the art of bullfighting, Manolo believes that he is a coward because he has no interest in being a bullfighter. Manolo eventually learns that in order to be truly brave, he must be true to himself and not attempt to satisfy others' expectations. Wojciechowska effectively resolves Manolo's person-against-self conflict when Manolo tells the waiting crowd in the bullring that he prefers medicine to bullfighting.

Another Newbery Award book, Joseph Krumgold's . . . *And Now Miguel,* also has ties to Spain. This book, based on a full-length documentary film feature, is the story of the Chavez family, which has been raising sheep in New Mexico since before their region became part of the United States. Their ancestors raised sheep in Spain. Krumgold tells the story from the viewpoint of the middle child, Miguel, who unlike his older brother, is too young to get everything he wants and, who unlike his younger brother, is too old to be happy with everything he has. Miguel has a secret wish to accompany the older family members when they herd the sheep to the summer grazing land in the Sangre de Cristo Mountains. With the help of San Ysidro, the patron saint of farmers, Miguel strives to make everyone see that he is ready for this responsibility. When he is allowed to accompany his elders on the drive and reaches the summer camp, he feels pride in his family's traditions and in his own accomplishments.

The eight-year-old in Nicholasa Mohr's *Felita* has lived in her Puerto Rican neighborhood of New York City for as long as she can remember. Mohr depicts the reasons for Felita's great love of her neighborhood. When Felita walks down the street, she can greet everyone by name. Her dearest friends live in the apartments on the block, and her grandmother, Abuelita, lives nearby. Conflict results when Felita's father decides that the family must move to a neighborhood where the schools are better and the threats of gang violence are fewer. In the new neighborhood, Anglo children call Felita names, tear her clothes, and tell her to move away. Felita's mother is shocked by the attitudes of the children and tells Felita that she must not hate, because that could make her as mean inside as the people who are attacking her.

When violence against the family continues and no neighbors offer help, Felita's family moves back to the old neighborhood. Felita experiences anger, sorrow, and humiliation, but she finally regains her feeling of self-worth. With her grandmother's help, Felita returns to her happy, lively self, secure in the surroundings of her warm, loving family and friends. Perhaps the neighborhood and the people in *Felita* seem so real because Mohr herself was born and grew up in a similar neighborhood in New York City.

Although the problems faced in *Felita* began to stress person-against-society conflict, the majority of the books written for this age group tend to include conflicts that are more family orientated such as the conflict resulting for Gary Soto's heroine in *Too Many Tamales* when she faces a dilemma on Christmas Eve when she misplaces her mother's diamond ring.

Fiction Written for Older Readers

Many of the conflicts developed in books for older readers express a harsher and even a dangerous world. Some of the stories express conflicts as main characters try to cross borders or survive in the streets of major cities. Authors who set their stories in other countries may place their protagonists in conflicts against governments. Now the protagonists must escape or lose their lives.

Nicholasa Mohr's *Going Home* provides additional adventures for Felita, who is now twelve years old. Now Felita finds that she must face and overcome new person-against-self and person-against-society conflicts. During a trip to visit relatives in Puerto Rico, Felita finds that she is the object of attack because she is the gringa and not accepted by some of the Puerto Rican girls.

It is interesting to compare the setting in *Going Home* with the setting in *Danza!* by Lynn Hall. Hall's story takes place on a farm in Puerto Rico and emphasizes the interaction between Paulo, a Puerto Rican boy, and Danza, a Paso Fino stallion. Hall develops characters with believable emotions and actions.

Gary Soto has several current books that appeal to readers. *Taking Sides* is a realistic fiction story about a boy who moves from the barrio to the suburbs. The protagonist, who is a basketball player, must decide how he will respond when his new team plays his old team in a league game. Soto develops themes related to loyalty and friendship. In *Pacific Crossing*, the boys from the barrio participate in an exchange program in Japan.

The harsher, brutal realities of a border-town existence are developed in two books for older readers written by Gary Paulsen. In *The Crossing*, the protagonist, Manny, dreams of crossing the border to live in America. In this story of a teen-age boy who must use his wits to stay alive, Paulsen develops harsher themes such as you may need to lie as well as use your wits to survive in the streets; life is not always fair, but you should keep up the struggle; and one person can make a difference. *Sisters Hermanas* also deals with the realities of a harsh border town including prostitution, prejudice, and explicit language. By telling the story of a young illegal immigrant and an Anglo girl from a wealthier family, Paulson develops a person-against-society struggle that reflects some of the inequalities of life. Even through these conflicts, Paulsen's characters develop positive values such as striving for success, believing in dreams, and working hard.

Sandra Cisneros's *The House on Mango Street* is another book that reflects the complexities of a neighborhood and a family and the conflicting feelings that may be found within a character. Through Esperanza's experiences, readers discover that the same place may be loving and cruel, safe and dangerous, and liked and hated. All of these emotions about a place are expressed as Esperanza struggles with life and the problems associated with growing up. Through the Latino girl's struggles, Cisneros develops strong themes such as dreams and goals are always important; family ties are important; and be proud of your culture, your family history, and your success.

A girl and her Mexican American family prepare for the traditional celebration marking a girl's fifteenth birthday in Diane Gonzales Bertrand's *Sweet Fifteen*. The novel shows both strong family values and the conflicts that occur within the family. This book was selected as a commended title for the 1995 Américas Award for Children's and Young Adult Literature.

Stories that take place in foreign settings frequently show the protagonists engaged in dangerous conflicts. For example, Ben Mikaelsen's *Sparrow Hawk Red* is a story of survival in the streets and drug trafficking milieu of Mexico. Thirteen-year-old Ricky Diaz discovers that his mother was murdered by drug smugglers because of his father's work for the Drug Enforcement Agency. In an effort to avenge his mother, Ricky disguises himself as a Mexican street urchin. With the help of Soledad, another street urchin, he enters the smugglers' compound, steals a plane, and narrowly escapes. Through his adventures, Ricky discovers the importance of his heritage.

Surviving in the dangerous world of political turmoil is another popular plot device found in books written for older readers. James Watson's *Talking in Whispers*, a 1983 British Carnegie Honor book for older children, is a political thriller and a survival story in which the main character is hunted by the security forces of a South American government that denies basic human rights. The book develops a strong statement about what humans will do to retain their rights and their freedom.

A similar plot is developed in Anilú Bernardo's *Jumping Off to Freedom* when a Cuban father and son must escape from the political rulers of the dictatorship. This book develops both person-against-society and person-against-nature conflicts as the protagonists first escape from the authorities and then face the stormy ocean as they try to reach the Florida coast on a raft. This is another survival story that suggests that humans will face great obstacles in order to retain their freedom. The author is a Cuban American who now lives in Florida after her family escaped from the Communist government.

Grab Hands and Run by Frances Temple is another survival story set in El Salvador. The plot follows a family who tries to leave El Salvador after the father disappears.

To authenticate the nature of the harsher settings and conflicts described by the authors in some of these survival stories, search current newspapers for stories that might clarify the conflicts. For example, Larry Rohter's article in *The New York Times* "Driven by Fear, Colombians Leave in Droves" (2000) describes civil conflict and political violence that caused 800,000 people to leave Colombia in a period of four years.

Joan Abelove, the author of *Go and Come Back*, is a cultural anthropologist who placed her fictional work for older readers in a Peruvian jungle village. By telling the story from the viewpoint of a villager who is interacting with an anthropologist, the author encourages readers to understand cultural conflicts and respect differences. Through conversations and various experiences, the author shows clashing cultural values, differing views about the roles of men and women, contrasting attitudes about sex and babies, and opposing views about healing and medicine. As you read this book, consider Betsy Hearne's (1998) evaluation of the book:

> The viewing of the norm through an outsider's eyes is a perennially appealing device that should draw teens right in as well as give them some food for cultural thought. Reading this novel is like feeling wind rush through a stuffy room. We are taken by surprise. We breath deeper for the freshness of observing our own culture from the outside, for seeing two characters so like and unlike ourselves begin to expand, and for experiencing new possibilities of vision. (p. 272)

Contemporary Nonfiction

Informational books for young children are frequently highly illustrated books that depict various holidays or are photographic essays about families or people. For example, Cinco de Mayo, the commemoration of the Mexican army's defeat of the French army on May 5, 1862, is a major holiday for Mexican Americans. June Behren's *Fiesta!* is an informational book describing the modern-day celebration of this holiday. Photographs show a Mexican American festival in which music is played by a mariachi band, costumed dancers perform traditional Mexican dances, and young and old enjoy the celebration.

Several nonfiction books provide information about children and families. Tricia Brown's *Hello, Amigos!* is a photo essay for younger children. It chronicles a special day in the life of six-year-old Frankie Valdez, a Mexican American boy whose family lives in San Francisco's Mission District. Fran Ortiz's photographs show the boy as he goes to school, attends classes, plays with friends, reacts to a classroom birthday cake, goes to the Boys' Club, and shares his birthday celebration with his family.

Carmen Lomas Garza's *Family Pictures* is a highly illustrated book. Its drawings depict the memories of the author as she was growing up in Kingsville, Texas, near the border with Mexico. The detailed illustrations provide many insights into her life as she remembers activities and various family and neighborhood occasions.

Two books for younger children explore life in foreign countries. Maria Cristina Brusca's *On the Pampas* is a highly illustrated book that describes a girl's experiences during a summer spent with her grandparents on their ranch in Argentina. The watercolor paintings provide images of the settings. Douglas Keister's *Fernando's Gift* is a photographic essay that shows the life of a boy who lives in the rain forest of Costa Rica. The photographs depict many of the characteristics of the rain forest and the daily activities of people who live in this region. The text is written in both English and Spanish. You may compare this description of the rain forest with the one developed in Lynn Cherry and Mark J. Plotkin's *The Shaman's Apprentice: A Tale of the Amazon Rain Forest.*

Photographs are very important in Michele Sola's *Angela Weaves a Dream: The Story of a Young Maya Artist*. The text provides both photographs of various designs and interpretations of their meanings.

The lives of migrant children are depicted in several books. Beth Atkin's *Voices from the Fields: Children of Migrant Farmworkers Tell Their Stories* presents insights into the lives of children of migrant laborers. Atkin uses interviews to recount the stories of the children, who tell about their dreams and the joys of family relationships, as well as their hardships. In *Calling the Doves*, Juan Felipe Herrera tells a story about his childhood as a migrant farmworker. The story reflects a strong relationship between the family and the land, as well as depicting the grueling nature of farm labor.

Two books were written as school projects and provide interesting insights. Judy Cozzen's *Kids Explore America's Hispanic Heritage* was written as a school project and provides interesting ideas for a study of Hispanic cultures. *Hispanic, Female and Young: An Anthology*, edited by Phyllis Tashlik, is a collection of stories written by female authors and interviews collected by a group of eighth-grade girls. In her introduction, Tashlik presents some of the reasons for editing this book. For example, after the students surveyed textbooks, they reached the following conclusion: "We knew that good literature, stories that really appealed to us, was available, but publishers were excluding them from their books. Our main purpose has been to make the Hispanic woman noticeable, not only to other girls our age, but to many people. So, it's going to take a long time and hard work to get literature by Hispanics into students' textbooks" (p.12).

Students of children's literature can analyze both the selections chosen by the students and read and respond to the interviews reported in the text. The interviews provide insights into the feelings, beliefs, and values expressed by Latino authors. In addition, many of the interviews are with relatives of the girls who collected the stories. An interview with children's author Nicholasa Mohr will be of particular interest. Tashlik's book could be used as a model as students select their own favorite stories and collect and publish interviews with members of the Latino community.

Biographies of Latino figures provide interesting sources for analysis and comparisons. This is especially true if biographies are available about the same person but written for different age levels. For example, students of children's literature can compare the coverage, characterizations, and conflicts developed in three biographies about the artist Diego Rivera. Jeanette Winter's *Diego* is written for younger children. James Cockcroft's *Diego Rivera* is written for adolescent audiences, and Cynthia Newman Helms's *Diego Rivera: A Retrospective* (1986) is an adult biography.

By studying all three biographies, readers may find characterizations, values, and beliefs that are similar to those found in other genres of Latino literature: for example, the importance of fiestas, the role of women in sustaining religion, a belief in healers, a belief in the supernatural, a belief that people should be good and work hard, and a pride in one's heritage.

Each of the books, however, has a slightly different point of view about Rivera. Winter's biography, written for younger readers, portrays Rivera as a hero of the people whose mural paintings were influenced by the cultural events around him and the economic depression in Mexico. There is a strong theme in the book that one must be proud of one's heritage. Cockcroft's biography written for adolescent audiences includes more information about Rivera's personality, his character flaws, and his political affiliations. As in the biography written for younger readers, there is a strong theme about being proud of one's heritage. The adult biography explains the inspirations of Rivera's artistic works. This biography presents a chronology of his art and life, as well as discussing Rivera's influences on other artists. The text includes reproductions of Rivera's murals and gives explanations about his artwork. All of the biographies emphasize that Rivera was considered an artistic genius.

Another highly illustrated biography presents insights into Rivera's life and his influence on other artists. Robyn Montana Turner's *Frida Kahlo: Portraits of Women Artists for Children* presents the life and work of another great Mexican artist—Frida Kahlo. The text tells how Kahlo was influenced by Diego Rivera and eventually became his wife. Many of the large colored reproductions of her paintings "symbolize Kahlo's strong sense of being rooted in the land and culture of Mexico" (p. 27). As you look at Kahlo's paintings, try to identify the influence of the Mexican culture. It is interesting to compare Kahlo's artwork with that of other great artists from Mexico.

 SUMMARY

Folklore from South and North American cultures was emphasized in this chapter. For example, Mayan people developed a complex mythology that accounted for the creation of the earth and the people. They expressed strong beliefs in the gods.

The characters in the folklore also include demons, monsters, and witches. Folktales suggest that cleverness is valued, while wasting time is not. Aztec folklore also details the creation of the world and a belief in the spirits and gods. In the agricultural society of the Aztecs, corn is of great value; consequently, people are responsible for caring for the land and the plants. Cleverness and sharing are rewarded, but greed and evil actions are not. Folktales from other South American cultures were also discussed.

Many of the nonfictional books develop historical perspectives by presenting the history of the ancient peoples and the contributions of people from various countries. The discussion of books includes adult sources that could be used to authenticate books written for children or to provide background information.

Award-winning authors, such as Scott O'Dell, have written excellent historical fiction that depicts earlier settings and views of earlier cultures. Many of values and beliefs depicted in historical fiction books are similar to those developed in the folklore.

Contemporary literature includes poetry, picture books written for young children, fiction written for middle-elementary grades, and fiction written for older readers. Many of the contemporary books develop themes that show the importance of overcoming problems within oneself or conflicts created by society. Some of the fiction written for older readers may place the protagonists in situations where they must survive in dangerous circumstances.

SUGGESTED ACTIVITIES FOR DEVELOPING
UNDERSTANDING OF LATINO LITERATURE

1. Read James M. Taggart's "'Hansel and Gretel' in Spain and Mexico" (1986). How are the versions of folktale the same? How are they different? How do the versions compare with the Grimms' version? Why are the versions different? How does each version relate to traditional cultural values?

2. Choose one of the traditional groups discussed in this chapter such as the Aztec, the Maya, or the Inca. Read a number of myths, legends, and folktales from that culture. Summarize group's traditional beliefs and values. Provide quotations from the tales to show the beliefs and values. Try to identify those same beliefs and values in other genres of literature depicting the same culture. What conclusions can you reach about the importance of traditional literature?

3. Choose several selections of folklore that show the impact of Spanish culture on the earlier traditional beliefs of the people. Analyze the tales for evidence of the infusion of the alien culture.

4. Compare Jose Griego y Maestas and Rudolfo A. Anaya's "The Man Who Knew the Language of the Animals" in *Cuentos: Tales from the Hispanic Southwest* with Verna Aardema's *What's So Funny, Ketu?*, which is based on an African tale. Identify the similarities and differences and note ways in which the differences reflect cultural differences.

5. Choose an outstanding author of historical fiction such as Scott O'Dell, and read several books by that author. What makes the plot and the characters memorable? What are the themes in the writer's work? Is there a common theme throughout the writing?

6. Many stories, such as Sandra Cisneros's *The House on Mango Street*, express the pain and fear of characters who struggle to find themselves in a world that is often alien. In books such as Nicholasa Mohr's *Going Home*, analyze the

forces that cause an American girl from Puerto Rican ancestry to not be accepted by Puerto Rican girls.

7. Develop a time line showing the chronology of famous Latinos or historical happenings that reflect the culture. Identify literature that may be used with the time line.

8. Choose an illustrated book from the area of Latino literature and authenticate both the text and the illustrations. Provide sources for your authentication activity.

Involving Children in Latino Literature

*B*efore exploring Latino literature and the culture, students should understand that Latino culture is very complex. This complexity results from the infusion of numerous influences. Also, the literature covers a wide time span. The literature extends from the ancient Aztecs and Maya to the recent poetry and fiction set in the contemporary world.

PHASE ONE: ANCIENT AZTEC AND MAYAN FOLKLORE

Show the students the locations of the Aztec and Mayan peoples on a map of Mexico and Central America. *Atlas of Ancient America* (Coe, Snow, & Benson, 1986) and *The Maya* (Coe, 1992) include useful maps and information about the cultures of these peoples. For additional background information, share and discuss Deborah Lattimore's *The Flame of Peace: A Tale of the Aztecs*.

Read and discuss several selections of Aztec folklore such as those found in John Bierhorst's *The Hungry Woman: Myths and Legends of the Aztecs*, C. Shana Greger's *The Fifth and Final Sun: An Ancient Aztec Myth of the Sun's Origin*, and Gerald McDermott's *Musicians of the Sun*. Discuss the values and beliefs reflected in the stories. After reading and discussing these tales, ask students to look again at the illustrations and text in Lattimore's *The Flame of Peace: A Tale of the Aztecs*. Ask student to answer this question: What, if any, are the similarities between the folklore and the plot, characters, and illustrations in *The Flame of Peace: A Tale of the Aztecs*?

Next, share and discuss several sources of Mayan folklore. Explain to the students that John Bierhorst in *The Monkey's Haircut and Other Stories Told by the Maya* identifies several characteristics of Mayan folklore that reflect the group's values. As the students listen to or read these stories ask them to identify those characteristics. Bierhorst identifies the following recurring characteristics: (1) cleverness, as shown by stories that include riddles, puns, double meanings, and tricksters; (2)

culture and customs, such as paying a bride service and being godparents; and (3) corn and farming practices. Students should also listen for and identify additional traditional values in the stories. Either share or have students read independently tales such as Francisco Hinojosa's *The Old Lady Who Ate People*, Geraldine McCaughrean's "The Monster with Emerald Teeth" in *The Bronze Cauldron*, Harriet Rohmer and Dornminster Wilson's *Mother Scorpion Country*, and Vivien Blackmore's *Why Corn Is Golden: Stories About Plants*.

Have students develop and discuss webs of the Aztec and Mayan folklore. Figure 4–1 illustrates a web developed around the cultural values discovered in Mayan folklore. Ask students to compare the values found in Aztec and Mayan folklore and to summarize the cultural values discovered from reading the literature.

ADDITIONAL ACTIVITIES TO ENHANCE PHASE ONE

Here are some activities for children or young adult students related to this phase:

1. Research the early Aztec or Mayan cultures or one of the cultures that influenced the Aztec or Mayan cultures. If you choose one of the cultures that influenced the people, emphasize the time that the culture had the greatest influence and detail the influence.
2. Read *Tales from the Rain Forest: Myths and Legends from the Amazonian Indians of Brazil* by Mercedes Dorson and Jeanne Wilmot. Carefully consider the authors' comments at the end of each of the tales. These stories and comments could be used in a study of geography and science. Try to answer these questions: How do the myths and legends about plants and animals compare with the geography of the Amazon? How does the theme, the need to respect the jungle, found in many of the tales correspond with geography and science? How and why were the people prepared to take care of nature and to live in close relationship to both plants and animals?
3. Do an artistic investigation. Choose a folklore text with illustrations that reflect strong Mexican influences. Some of the texts such as Francisco Hinojosa's *The Lady Who Ate People*, illustrated by Leonel Maciel, and Vivien Blackmore's *Why Corn Is Golden: Stories About Plants*, illustrated by Susana Martinez-Ostos, are illustrated by well-known Mexican artists. Investigate other works by these artists.

 ## PHASE TWO: STORIES THAT REFLECT INTERACTION WITH OTHER CULTURES

Many of the folktales from the Southwest, Mexico, and South and Central America reflect a blending of cultures. There are numerous folktales that reflect interactions with other cultures and show the clash of cultural values.

Analyzing Folklore That Reflects Interactions with Other Cultures

Introduce a series of folktales that reflect interactions with other cultures and show the clash of cultural values. Ask the students to consider at what point in history they would expect the greatest changes. Encourage the students to identify the

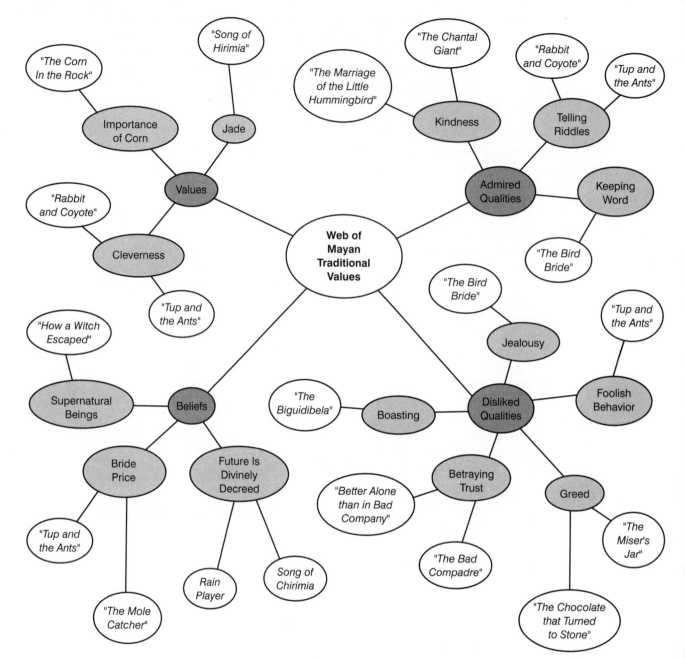

FIGURE 4–1 Web Showing Traditional Mayan Values Found in Folklore

arrival of Cortes and the Spanish as one of the greatest influences on the cultures and folklore. Ask them to think about how this occurrence changed the lives of the people and might have influenced their folktales, fables, myths, and legends.

Choose tales such as Verna Aardema's *The Riddle of the Drum: A Tale from Tizapan, Mexico*; John Bierhorst's *Doctor Coyote: A Native American Aesop's Fables* (this tale is retold from an Aztec manuscript) and *Spirit Child: A Story of the Nativity*; Harriet Rohmer, Octavio Chow, and Morris Vidaure's *The Invisible Hunters*; Tomie dePaola's *The Lady of Guadalupe*; and Jose Griego y Maestas and Rudolfo A. Anaya's

Cuentos: Tales from the Hispanic Southwest. As students read the tales ask them to identify both the cultural values and the influences that are incorporated in the tales. For example, both *The Riddle of the Drum: A Tale from Tizapan, Mexico* and *Doctor Coyote: A Native American Aesop's Fables* are easily analyzed according to the influences of physical setting and architecture. Comparisons can also be made showing the influence of Spanish folktales and Aesop's fables.

Students can share and discuss what happens when cultures clash in *The Invisible Hunters* and the interactions of the people and Christianity in *The Lady of Guadalupe* and *Spirit Child: A Story of the Nativity*. These books also develop strong cultural patterns through their illustrations.

Folktales in Jose Griego y Maestas and Rudolfo A. Anaya's *Cuentos: Tales from the Hispanic Southwest* are especially good for identifying cultural values and the influence of other cultures. For example, share "The Man Who Knew the Language of the Animals," and ask students to identify the plot of the story. Next, ask the students to identify the values and beliefs stressed in the folktale and then compare it with a similar African folktale, Verna Aardema's *What's So Funny, Ketu?* Ask the students to draw a plot structure of the African tale and identify the emphasized values and beliefs. Next, ask them to identify the similarities and differences between the two tales, Ask, "What do the similarities tell us about human values? How might the differences reflect cultural differences between the Hispanic and African peoples?"

ADDITIONAL ACTIVITIES TO ENHANCE PHASE TWO

Here are some activities for children or young adult students related to this phase:

1. For a creative writing activity, choose one of the Aesop's fables or another European folktale. Pretend that you heard this story from one of the early Spaniards who came to your country. Retell and adapt the story to reflect the southwestern setting, culture, and beliefs.
2. Create a museum that shows important artifacts from the cultural groups that influenced the literature. The museum can have drawings of art, clothing, and architecture. Develop an introduction to their museum and to create a multicultural festival including such activities as storytelling, musical features, slide shows, and guest experts.

 ### PHASE THREE: HISTORICAL NONFICTION

Choose books for discussion that will help students understand the ancient cultures and the changes that occurred because of interactions with other cultures. These can included books such as Carolyn Meyer and Charles Gallenkamp's *The Mystery of the Ancient Maya*, Albert Marrin's *Aztecs and Spaniards: Cortes and the Conquest of Mexico*, and Albert Prago's *Strangers in Their Own Land: A History of Mexican-Americans*. Ask the students to compare their knowledge of the cultures gained from the nonfiction books with their knowledge gained from the folklore. What are the similarities and differences?

Encourage students to read nonfiction books that describe contemporary explorations and discoveries that authenticate the lives of earlier peoples such as Johan Reinhard's *Discovering the Inca Ice Maiden: My Adventures on Ampato*. Ask student to answer this question: What did you learn about the earlier periods from reading this book? Reinhard's text includes a time line of history beginning with the Inca Civilization in A.D. 1200–1438 and extending to the landing of the Pilgrims in 1620. Ask students to identify nonfiction books that could be used to add information about the various cultures of South, Central, and North America.

ADDITIONAL ACTIVITIES TO ENHANCE PHASE THREE

Here are some activities for children or young adult students related to this phase:

1. On maps of North America, Central America, and South America, show the locations where the various people lived. Tell how their lives were influenced by other cultures.
2. Create a collage depicting some of the mysteries of the ancient Maya, Aztec, or Inca.
3. Develop a time line for a famous Latino historical figure.

 ### PHASE FOUR: HISTORICAL FICTION

Searching for Cultural Beliefs and Historical Happenings in the Writings of Scott O'Dell

Scott O'Dell's historical novels *The Captive, The Feathered Serpent*, and *The Amethyst Ring* provide many opportunities for students to search for cultural values and beliefs, customs, Mayan history, and consequences of Spanish intervention. For example, they will discover the belief in the legend of Quetzalcoatl's return and the importance of the ancient gods and the accompanying religious ceremonies. They will also find evidence that the people valued an honorable life and expected to pay the consequences if they did not live such lives. Through reading other history texts, they can authenticate the historical happenings described by O'Dell.

O'Dell provides descriptions of Mayan and Aztec cities and temples and other aspects of the culture. These descriptions may be used to motivate students to illustrate sections of his books. They can search for photographs and drawings in informational books to help them with their illustrations. For example, David Freidel, Linda Schele, and Joy Parker's adult source *Maya Cosmos: Three Thousand Years on the Shaman's Path* (1993) includes drawings and photographs.

Modeling Comprehension of Characterization with Fleischman's Bandit's Moon

Before developing a modeling activity, review the background for modeling presented in Chapter 6, Involving Children with Jewish Literature, Phase Four, pages 271–274 Review with the students the requirements needed for effective reasoning related to characterization, the objectives for modeling, and the sequence that will be used in a lesson. The following modeling example has been used with middle- and upper-elementary students.

Objectives: To be involved in a modeling activity designed to show students how to analyze evidence from the text and to speculate about the characters. To understand the requirements for effective reasoning. To appreciate and understand the author's use of implication when developing characterization. To respond to the themes developed in the book.

Source Materials: Sid Fleischman's *Bandit's Moon*. Background material for the time period about the Gold Rush. Sources of criticism about the book including *School Library Journal* (September 1998) and *Publishers Weekly* (August 3, 1998).

Procedures: First, identify and review the requirements for effective reasoning. Second, review characterization by asking students to identify how authors develop three-dimensional, believable characters. Share examples of each type of characterization as part of this review. Third, explain to the students that in this modeling activity, they will listen to you read a selection, ask a question, answer the question, provide evidence from the story that supports the answer, and share the reasoning process used to reach the answer. Tell the students that after they have listened to you proceed through the sequence, they will use the same process to answer questions, identify evidence, and explore their own reasoning processes. As part of this introduction, discuss the meanings of evidence and reasoning. Encourage the students to identify evidence about characters in literature and to share how they would use this evidence.

Develop an introduction to the story *Bandit's Moon,* which has a setting in California during the Gold Rush of the 1850s. Show the students a map of California and help them locate the region associated with the Gold Rush. Provide background information about the Gold Rush. To help students understand that part of this book is based on factual information and on a real character, read and discuss the author's note on pages 133–136. To provide background information related to some of the themes in the book, read the reviews found in *Publishers Weekly* (1998) and *School Library Journal* (1998). You may discuss such comments as "he expertly crafts a fictionalized tale that takes a clear-eyed look at bigotry and racism" (p. 86, *Publishers Weekly*) and "Fleischman makes Joaquín a sympathetic central character as he shows the injustice suffered by minorities during this time of greed and lawlessness. This is classic Sid Fleischman; a quick read, with lots of twists, wonderful phrasing, historical integrity, and a bit of the tall tale thrown in" (p. 203, *School Library Journal*).

Provide the first modeling example. Read orally the first paragraph of the book, which is told from the viewpoint of Annyrose, one of the novel's main characters:

> I had hardly got three miles down the road when O. O. Mary herself caught me running away and locked me up in the harness room off the barn. It was infernally dark, and I knew there were black widow spiders in there. I tried to keep my mind off them except to think that O. O. Mary could give black widows lessons in meanness. (p. 1)

Ask: "What do you know about Annyrose's character and Mary's character from this introductory paragraph?" My answer: "Annyrose is probably very frightened and living in dangerous circumstances. She is an independent character even though she is frightened about being in an environment inhabited by black widow spiders. O. O. Mary is a very nasty, mean, and dangerous character." Provide the evidence from the text: "Annyrose ran away from her environment and is now being forced to live in a locked-up space with insects she hates. O. O. Mary is compared to something that Annyrose fears. The author develops a description in which the setting is filled with both darkness and spiders." Provide the reasoning you used to reach your answer: "I believe Annyrose is an independent character because she ran away even though she probably realized that she would be punished. She is also living in a region that is not familiar to her. The way the author describes the setting as dark and filled with spiders allows me to envision a very frightening and even dangerous environment. I can feel Annyrose's fear and dislike for the location. I would be afraid if I were in a similar setting. Annyrose compares the black widow spiders to O. O. Mary. I know that a black widow spider is very poisonous and a bite could be extremely dangerous. This would be especially true if I lived a long way away from doctors. Consequently, I think that O. O. Mary has many of the characteristics that Annyrose dislikes and fears. Also the thought of O. O. Mary does not allow Annyrose to forget her circumstances. I believe that these thoughts must be very bad if they are not pleasant enough to take her mind off of O. O. Mary. I wonder what O. O. Mary must be like to be compared to a black widow spider."

Provide the second modeling example. At this point verify that the students understand the process, let them join the discussion by providing an answer, the evidence, and the reasoning. It is advisable to allow students to jot down brief answers to the questions, evidence, and reasoning. These notes increase the quality of the discussion that follows each question.

The next logical discussion point comes in the middle of page 4 after "She'd sold my New Orleans petticoats and dresses months ago. She had me walking around in some boy's castoffs, shirt and pants, and brown boots as curled up as a dead fish" (p. 4). Ask a question such as: "What additional characteristics are being implied about O. O. Mary? What characteristics does O. O. Mary suggest about the bandits? What might Annyrose's behavior suggest about the bandits?" Ask the students to answer the questions, provide their evidence for the answer, and discuss their reasoning.

Chapter 1 includes many additional places that lend themselves to discussion centering on inferring characterizations. For example, read through page 7 to discuss additional characteristics about Annyrose and O. O. Mary. Students will discover that Annyrose comes from an educated background because of her reactions to the loss of her violin and music by Mozart and Schubert. Additional characteristics of O. O. Mary are also discovered by her actions when she takes letters, horses, and even Annyrose's hair.

The characteristics of Joaquín, the bandit, are introduced through the author's physical descriptions on pages 8 and 9, his reactions to a Yankee on page 11, his reactions to Annyrose's request to accompany him on pages 13 and 14, and his request that Annyrose teaches him how to read. At the close of chapter 1, students should summarize what they now understand about the characters of Annyrose, O. O. Mary, and Joaquín. They could also consider what they believe will happen in the remainder of the story.

Longer stories, such as *Bandit's Moon*, lend themselves to discussions by chapters. Students can read and discuss several chapters each day. After each session, ask the students to summarize what they know about Annyrose, O. O. Mary, and Joaquín.

The following is a list of a few of the logical places in *Bandit's Moon* to ask questions about implied characterization, and some questions that might be asked and answered. Remember to have students provide evidence for their answers and explore their reasoning.

End of page 16: "What do Annyrose's actions reveal about herself, O. O. Mary, and Joaquín?"

Close of Chapter 2: "What do Joaquín's actions with the stolen horses reveal about him?"

Chapter 3: "Compare what you discovered about both the bandits and Annyrose through their actions and responses related to survival."

Close of Chapter 4: Ask questions about and discuss Joaquín's desires to learn to read and his responses to the reward poster that asks for $1,000 and his increasing the amount to $10,000.

Continue discussing characterization as revealed by the author's use of descriptions, characters' actions, characters' thoughts, and dialogue. By the end of the book, summarize Annyrose's changing responses to Joaquín. This book also includes several important themes that students could discuss. For example, "Injustice and greed are dangerous actions," "There is no honor in mistreating others," and "Revenge is a harmful human motivation."

A comparative study could also be accomplished after the completion of this book. A newspaper headline identifies Joaquín as "The Robin Hood of the Mountains." Students could compare Joaquín's character with that of the British legendary character Robin Hood. Ask students to examine these questions: How are they alike? How are they different? What might have motivated each character to take on his respective role?

ADDITIONAL ACTIVITIES TO ENHANCE PHASE FOUR

Here are some activities for children or young adult students related to this phase:

1. Search additional historical fiction stories to identify any references to traditional folklore, values, and beliefs of the culture. What influences do these traditional beliefs have on the characters and conflicts in the historical fiction?
2. As a creative writing activity, choose a character who might have lived during earlier periods of Latino history. Create a fictional story about the character. Refer to the informational books to create believable setting, characterization, and conflict.
3. Using a "You Are There" format, choose an incident from one of Scott O'Dell's books and recreate it as a drama.

 ### PHASE FIVE: CONTEMPORARY LITERATURE

Responding to the Language in Nursery Rhymes and Poetry

There are several highly illustrated picture books that encourage children to interact with the language and discover the joy of playing with words. Choose several of these books and share them with an appreciative audience. For example, Margot C. Griego's *Tortillitas para Mama and Other Spanish Nursery Rhymes*, Lulu Delacre's *Arroz con Leche: Popular Songs and Rhymes from Latin America*, Ralfka Gonzalez and Ana Ruiz's *My First Book of Proverbs*, and Jose-Luis Orozco's *Ten Little Fingers and Other Play Rhymes and Action Songs from Latin America* are written in both English and Spanish.

Read various nursery rhymes to lower elementary students. Encourage them to dramatize the language of the nursery rhymes. Read the rhymes to middle- and upper-elementary students and ask them to analyze how the rhymes are similar and different and how they relate to the culture.

Stimulate older children's aesthetic development and appreciation for the cultural relationships between the illustrations and the rhymes or poetry collections.

After sharing the nursery rhymes and poems with children, have them look at the illustrations and discuss the relationships among the illustrations, the cultural content of the illustrations, and the literary content of the nursery rhymes or poems. Older students may consider how effectively the illustrator creates the setting for the rhymes and uses colors or artistic technique to support the cultural motif. Are the illustrations and text placed effectively within the pages of the book? For example, in *Tortillitas para Mama and Other Spanish Nursery Rhymes*, illustrator Barbara Cooney re-creates the varied settings associated with Spanish nursery rhymes. Warm browns depict the interior of a Mexican home, cool blues warmed by the shining moon suggest a village by the water, and warm fuchsias reflect the emotional tone of a mother and father sharing a quiet time with their baby. Francisco X. Alarcon's *Laughing Tomatoes and Other Spring Poems* and *From the Bellybutton of the Moon and Other Summer Poems* may be used for a similar activity.

Responding to Courage in Literature

Numerous multicultural literature books develop themes related to the importance of individual courage. These books provide excellent springboards for students to develop a carefully detailed argument and develop a written or oral position about the meaning of courage. This type of activity is designed to help students define, for themselves and the class, the elements of courage. As a consequence of reading a book and debating the subject, they will write a paper that documents what they believe courage is. They will share their ideas and write a group paper that defines courage. Begin the activity by brainstorming the following questions with students: What is courage? When do we know that a person has courage? What are the characteristics we would look for? Write a list of attributes related to courage on the board or on a transparency on an overhead projector.

Select a book to share with students in which courage is an important element; for example, Maia Wojciechowska's *Shadow of a Bull,* which is set in Spain. The book develops a person-against-self conflict as a boy struggles with his own feelings when the men of the village begin training him to become a bullfighter like his father. The boy, however, prefers to be a doctor, but does not know if he has the courage to go against the wishes of the townspeople.

Tell the students that they will be reading or listening to a book about a boy who has a special problem. As they read the book or listen to the book, they will explore these questions: What is courage? Does the boy demonstrate courage? Introduce the book so that students become interested in the subject. For example, you might say the following to students:

> Imagine that you live in Spain. Your father was a famous and fearless bullfighter and the whole town expects you to be just like your father. What would you feel if you were afraid of bulls and if you thought that you were a coward? How would you work it out if you had a dream for a career that was different from that of your father? How would you convince people that it was all right for you to follow your own dream? This is the problem that you will read about in *Shadow of a Bull*. As you read this book, place yourself in Manolo's position. You have your own preferences, but everyone believes that you will follow in your dead father's footsteps. Try to imagine Manolo's inner conflicts as he learns to be true to himself. What do you think Manolo learns about himself? What do you think the people in his town discover about Manolo?

When you finish this book, try to decide what courage is. Do you believe that Manolo is courageous? Why or why not?

As the students read or listen to the book, ask them to be thinking about the question, What is courage? For example, is it courageous or cowardly to admit fear of the bull? Is it more courageous to face the bull in the bullring or to face the crowd and to tell them that you prefer being a doctor? After students have finished the book, ask them to write a paragraph on the question, What is courage? They should decide if they believe that Manolo is courageous or cowardly. They should document their answers by providing support from the text.

After students have finished their paragraphs, divide them into writing groups and ask them to share their paragraphs with their peer group. Ask someone in the group to list the various definitions of courage and to list the pros and cons of Manolo's actions that make him either courageous or cowardly. After the group has shared and recorded all of their thoughts, ask them to write a joint paragraph that develops the beliefs of the majority of the students. Make sure that they carefully develop their arguments with evidence from the book. After these group papers are completed, share each of the group papers with the total class.

Students may extend this activity into an oral debate as they discuss the various definitions of and attributes related to courage. Again, they should support their arguments with details and evidence. Another extension activity would be to ask students to identify other real-life or literary characters that the students believe demonstrate the characteristics of courage and that meet their definitions of What is courage? They can develop a cross-cultural study by identifying and analyzing the theme of the importance of courage in stories from different cultures. For example, courage is important in Gary Paulsen's Native American story *Dogsong*, in Laurence Yep's Chinese American story *Dragon's Gate*, and in Karen Cusman's novel set in early England *The Midwife's Apprentice*.

ADDITIONAL ACTIVITIES TO ENHANCE PHASE FIVE

Here are some activities for children or young adult students related to this phase:

1. Read a book such as Carmen Lomas Garza's *Family Pictures*. Create your own book that develops the ideas of family pictures.
2. Read, analyze, and discuss several of the books listed in "Americas Award," *School Library Journal*, August 1999. Consider why the committee might have chosen the books and how they meet the following criteria: distinctive contextualization; exceptional integration of text, illustration, and design; and potential for classroom use.
3. Investigate the background of and the literature written by Gary Soto, one of the prolific authors of Latino literature. What are the recurring themes in the literature?
4. Complete a project similar to one of the ones in Judy Cozzen's *Kids Explore America's Hispanic Heritage*.
5. Perform a play found in Joe Rosenburg's *¡Aplauso!* (the book includes plays for preschool, elementary, and young adult audiences for you to perform). There are plays in English and Spanish. The plays are from a variety of genres. Each play includes background information and guides for staging the plays.

BIBLIOGRAPHY

"Américas Award" by The Consortium of Latin American Studies Programs. *School Library Journal* 45 (August 1999): 38–39.

Au, Kathryn H. *Literacy Instruction in Multicultural Settings.* San Diego: Harcourt Brace, 1993.

Barrera, Rosalinda B. "Latina and Latino Researchers Interact on Issues Related to Literacy Learning: Conversations." *Reading Research Quarterly* 34 (April/May/June 1999): 217–230.

_____, and Oralia Garza de Cortes. "Mexican American Children's Literature in the 1900s: Toward Authenticity." In *Using Multiethnic Literature in the K-8 Classroom*, edited by Violet J. Harris. pp. 129–153. Boston: Christopher Gordon, 1997.

Bierhorst, John, translated by. *History and Mythology of the Aztecs: The Codex Chimalpopoca.* Tucson: University of Arizona Press, 1998.

_____, *The Mythology of Mexico and Central America.* New York: Morrow, 1990.

Coe, Michael. *The Maya.* New York: Thames and Hudson, 1992.

_____, Dean Snow, and Elizabeth Benson. *Atlas of Ancient America.* New York: Facts on File, 1986.

Council on Interracial Books for Children. "Chicano Culture in Children's Literature: Stereotypes, Distortions and Omissions." In *Cultural Conformity in Books for Children*, edited by Donnarae MacCann and Gloria Woodard. Metuchen, N.J.: Scarecrow, 1977.

Finazzo, Denise Ann. *All for the Children: Multicultural Essentials of Literature.* Albany, N.Y.: Delmar, 1997.

Freidel, David, Linda Schele, and Joy Parker. *Maya Cosmos: Three Thousand Years on the Shaman's Path.* New York: Morrow, 1993.

Gillmor, Frances. *The King Danced in the Marketplace.* Salt Lake City: University of Utah Press, 1977.

Gonzalez, David. "What's the Problem with 'Hispanic'? Just Ask a 'Latino.'" *The New York Times* (Sunday, November 15, 1992): 6E.

Griego y Maestas, Jose, and Rudolfo A. Anaya. *Cuentos: Tales from the Hispanic Southwest.* Santa Fe: The Museum of New Mexico Press, 1980.

Hearne, Betsy. "The Big Picture." *The Bulletin, 51,* (April 1998): 271–272.

Helms, Cynthia Newman, edited by. *Diego Rivera: A Retrospective.* Founders Society, Detroit Institute of Arts, 1986.

Levenson, Jay A., edited by. *Circa 1492: Art in the Age of Exploration.* New Haven: Yale University Press and Washington, D.C.: National Gallery of Art, 1991.

Lodge, Sally. "Spanish-Language Publishing for Kids in the U.S. Picks Up Speed." *Publishers Weekly* (August 25, 1997): 48–49.

Marek, Nancy Carolyn. "Authenticating *Song of Chirimia—A Guatemalan Folktale*." Paper presented at Texas A&M University, 1994.

Markman, Roberta H., and Peter T. Markman. *The Flayed God: The Mythology of Mesoamerica.* New York: HarperCollins, 1992.

Meyer, Carolyn, and Charles Gallenkamp. *The Mystery of the Ancient Maya.* New York: Atheneum, 1985.

Miller, Mary, and Karl Taube. *The Gods and Symbols of Ancient Mexico and the Maya: An Illustrated Dictionary of Mesoamerican Religion.* New York: Thames and Hudson, 1993.

Moll, Luis. "Latina and Latino Researchers Interact on Issues Related to Literacy Learning: Conversations." *Reading Research Quarterly* 34 (April/May/June 1999): 217–230.

Moseley, Michael. *The Incas and Their Ancestors: The Archaeology of Peru.* New York: Thames and Hudson, 1992.

National Association of Hispanic and Latino Studies. National Conference. February 21–26, 2000, Houston, Texas.

Norton, Donna E. *The Effective Teaching of Language Arts*, 5th ed. Upper Saddle River, N.J.: Merrill/Prentice Hall, 1997.

_____. *Through the Eyes of a Child: An Introduction to Children's Literature*, 5th ed. Upper Saddle River, N.J.: Merrill/Prentice Hall, 1999.

_____. *The Olmec World: Ritual and Rulership*. Princeton, N.J.: The Art Museum and New York: Abrams, 1996.

Perez-Stable, Maria. "Keys to Exploring Latino Culures: Folktales for Children." *The Social Studies* 88 (January/February 1997): 29–34.

Publishers Weekly. "Review of Sid Fleischman's *Bandit Moon.*" (August 3, 1998): 86.

Rochman, Hazel. *Against Borders: Promoting Books for a Multicultural World*. Chicago: American Library Association, 1993.

Rohter, Larry. "Driven by Fear, Colombians Leave in Droves." *The New York Times* (International, March 5, 2000): 8.

Rosenbaum, David E. "Coast to Coast: Troves of Delegates at Stake on Tuesday." *The New York Times* (Sunday 5, 2000): 22.

Schon, Isabel. "Recent Detrimental and Distinguished Books About Hispanic People and Cultures." *Top of the News* 38 (Fall 1981): 79–85.

School Library Journal. "Review of Sid Fleischman's *Bandit Moon.*" (August 3, 1998): 86.

Silva-Diaz, Maria Cecilia. "Rites of Initiation in Recent Latin American Narratives." *Bookbird* 35 (Summer 1997): 21–26.

Taggart, James M. "'Hansel and Gretel' in Spain and Mexico." *Journal of American Folklore* 99 (1986): 435–460.

Vargas, Lucila, and Bruce DePyssler. "Using Media Literacy to Explore Stereotypes of Mexican Immigrants." *Social Education*. 62 (November/December 1998): 407–412.

CHILDREN'S AND YOUNG ADULT LITERATURE REFERENCES

Aardema, Verna. *The Riddle of the Drum: A Tale from Tizapan, Mexico*. Illustrated by Tony Chen. Four Winds, 1979 (I: 6–10 R: 5). o.p.[*] The man to marry the king's daughter must guess the kind of leather in a drum.

Abelove, Joan. *Go and Come Back*, DK, 1998 (I: 14+ R: 6). Set in a Peruvian jungle, the story is told by a cultural anthropologist.

Ada, Alma Flor. *Under the Royal Palms: A Childhood in Cuba*. Simon & Schuster, 1998 (I: 8+ R: 5). The stories tell about growing up in Cuba during the 1940s.

Alarcon, Francisco X. *From the Bellybutton of the Moon and Other Summer Poems*. Illustrated by Maya Christina Gonzalez. Children's Press, 1998 (I: all). A collection of poems written in Spanish and English.

_____. *Laughing Tomatoes and Other Spring Poems*. Illustrated by Maya Christina Gonzalez. Children's Press, 1997 (I: all). A collection of poems written in Spanish and English.

Anaya, Rudolfo. *Maya's Children: The Story of La Llorona*. Illustrated by Maria Baca. Hyperion, 1997 (I: 5–9 R: 4). The tale of the crying woman who wanders through the night.

Ancona, George. *Barrio: José's Neighborhood*. Harcourt Brace, 1998 (I: 6+ R: 4). Photographic compositions enhance a story set in the Mission District of San Francisco.

_____. *Fiesta Fireworks*. Lothrop, Lee & Shepard, 1998 (I: 6+ R: 4). The text features the festival honoring the patron saint of Tultepec, Mexico.

Anzaldua, Gloria. *Prietita and the Ghost Woman*. Children's Press, 1966 (I: 5–8 R: 5). A girl searches for herbs.

Atkin, S. Beth, edited by. *Voices from the Fields: Children of Migrant Farmworkers Tell Their Stories*. Little, Brown, 1993 (I: 10+). The text includes interviews with nine children.

Beals, Carleton. *Stories Told by the Aztecs: Before the Spaniards Came*. Illustrated by Charles Pickard. Abelard, 1970 (I: 10+ R:7). o. p.[*] A collection of tales has footnotes and a bibliography.

Behrens, June. *Fiesta!* Photographs by Scott Taylor. Children's Press, 1978 (I: 5–8 R: 4). This book contains photographs of the Cinco de Mayo fiesta.

I = Interest age range

R = Readability by grade level

o.p. = Books that are out of print but too good to eliminate.

Belting, Natalia M. *Moon Was Tired of Walking on Air.* Illustrated by Will Hillenbrand. Houghton Mifflin, 1992 (I: all). A collection of traditional tales from the Native Americans of South America.

Bernardo, Anilú. *Jumping Off to Freedom.* Pinata, 1996 (I: 10+ R: 5). A boy and his father flee from Cuba on a raft.

Bertrand, Diane Gonzales. *Sip, Slurp, Soup. Soup/Caldo, Caldo, Caldo.* Illustrated by Alex Pardo DeLanga. Pinata, 1977 (I: 4–7). Four children watch as soup is prepared.

_____. *Sweet Fifteen.* Pinata, 1995 (I: 11+ R: 6). A family prepares for Stephanie's fifteenth birthday.

Bierhorst, John, edited by. *Black Rainbow: Legends of the Incas and Myths of Ancient Peru.* Farrar, Straus & Giroux, 1976 (I: 10+ R: 7). The text includes twenty traditional tales.

_____. *Doctor Coyote: A Native American Aesop's Fables.* Illustrated by Wendy Watson. Macmillan, 1987 (I: all). This fable is from Native Americans in Mexico.

_____, edited by. *The Hungry Woman: Myths and Legends of the Aztecs.* Morrow, 1984 (I: 12+ R: 6). o. p.* The tales include creation myths and legends about the conquest.

_____, edited by. *Lightning Inside You and Other Native American Riddles.* Illustrated by Louise Brierley. Morrow, 1992 (I: 8+). Text includes riddles from southern Mexico and western South America.

_____, edited by. *The Monkey's Haircut and Other Stories Told by the Maya.* Illustrated by Robert Andrew Parker. Morrow, 1986 (I: 8+ R: 6). o. p.* This book contains twenty-two tales.

_____. *The Mythology of South America.* Morrow, 1988 (I: 12+ R: 7). o.p.* This is a good resource for information.

_____, translated by. *Spirit Child: A Story of the Nativity.* Illustrated by Barbara Cooney. Morrow, 1984 (I: 8–12 R: 6). Pre-Columbian illustrations accompany an Aztec story.

Blackmore, Vivien. *Why Corn Is Golden: Stories About Plants.* Illustrated by Susana Martinez-Ostos. Little, Brown, 1984 (I: all R: 5). This book contains folklore about corn.

Brimner, Larry Dane. *A Migrant Family.* Lerner, 1992 (I: all). The text and photographs describe the life of Mexican American migrant workers in California.

Brown, Tricia. *Hello, Amigos!* Photographs by Fran Ortiz. Holt, Rinehart & Winston, 1986 (I: 3–8 R: 3). Photographs tell the story of a boy on his sixth birthday.

Brusca, Maria Cristina. *On the Pampas.* Henry Holt, 1991 (I: 6–9 R: 5). A nonfiction book provides details of life on the pampas in Argentina.

Carling, Amelia Lau. *Mama and Papa Have a Store.* Dial, 1998 (I: 3–8 R: 4). A Chinese family have a store in Guatemala City.

Carlson, Lori Marie, selected by. *Sol a Sol* Holt, 1998 (I: all). A collection of bilingual poems.

Chambers, Veronica. *Marisol and Magdalena: The Sound of Our Sisterhood.* Hyperion, 1998 (I: 10+ R: 5). Two girls of Panamanian heritage live in New York.

Charles, Donald. *Chancay and The Secret of Fire: A Peruvian Folktale.* Putman's, 1992 (I: all). The hero brings fire to the people.

Cherry, Lynn, and Mark J. Plotkin. *The Shaman's Apprentice: A Tale of the Amazon Rain Forest.* Harcourt Brace, 1998 (I: 6–8 R: 4). A boy learns the importance of the shaman's wisdom.

Cisneros, Sandra. *The House on Mango Street.* Arte Publico, 1983 (I: 12+ R: 7). A girl records her feelings about her world.

Clark, Ann Nolan. *Secret of the Andes.* Illustrated by Jean Charlot. Viking, 1952, 1980 (I: 8+ R: 5). A boy learns about the traditions of his Inca ancestors.

Cockcroft, James. *Diego Rivera.* Chelsea House, 1991 (I: 10+ R: 6). A biography of the artist written for adolescent readers.

Conord, Bruce W. *Cesar Chavez.* Chelsea, 1992 (I: 4–6 R: 5). A biography of the union leader.

Cozzen, Judy, edited by. *Kids Explore America's Hispanic Heritage.* John Muir, 1992 (I: all). This is a report of a school project.

Delacre, Lulu. *Arroz con Leche: Popular Songs and Rhymes from Latin America.* Scholastic, 1989 (I: all). This text includes a variety of songs and poems.

dePaola, Tomie. *The Lady of Guadalupe.* Holiday House, 1980 (I: 8+ R: 6). This is a traditional Mexican tale.

DeSpain, Pleasant. *The Dancing Turtle: A Folktale from Brazil*. Illustrated by David Boston. August House, 1998 (I: 5–8 R: 4). An animal uses its wits.

de Trevino, Elizabeth Borton. *I, Juan de Pareja*. Farrar, Straus & Giroux, 1965 (I: 10 + R: 6). The story is set in Spain in the seventeenth century.

Dorros, Arthur. *Radio Man: A Story in English and Spanish*. HarperCollins, 1993 (I: 6-10). This book focuses on migrant farm workers.

Dorson, Mercedes, and Jeanne Wilmot. *Tales from the Rain Forest: Myths and Legends from the Amazonian Indians of Brazil*. Ecco, 1997 (I: 8 + R: 7). A collection of folktales.

Ehlert, Lois. *Cuckoo: A Mexican Folktale*. Translated in Spanish by Gloria de Aragon Andujar. Harcourt Brace, 1997 (I: 4–8). A *pourquoi* tale.

_____. *Moon Rope*. Harcourt Brace, 1992 (I: all). This Peruvian tale is about two animals that try to reach the moon.

Emberley, Rebecca. *Let's Go: A Book in Two Languages*. Little, Brown, 1993 (I: 4–8). A picture dictionary of concepts related to places children might go.

_____. *My Day: A Book in Two Languages*. Little, Brown, 1993 (I: 4–8). A picture dictionary of concepts related to daytime activities.

_____. *My House: A Book in Two Languages*. Little, Brown, 1990 (I: 4–8). A picture dictionary shows captioned illustrations of things found in the house.

_____. *Taking a Walk: A Book in Two Languages*. Little, Brown, 1990 (I: 4–8). A picture dictionary showing items a child sees while on a walk.

Ets, Marie Hall, and Aurora Labastida. *Nine Days to Christmas: A Story of Mexico*. Illustrated by Marie Hall Ets. Viking, 1959 (I: 5–8 R: 3). Ceci is going to have her first Posada with her own piñata.

Fleischman, Sid. *Bandit's Moon*. Illustrated by Jos. A. Smith. Greenwillow, 1998 (I: 8 + R: 5). Historical fiction set in the time of the California Gold Rush.

Fritz, Jean, Katherine Paterson, Patricia McKissack, Fredrick McKissack, Margaret Mahy, and Jake Highwater. *The World in 1492*. Illustrated by Stefano Vitale. Holt, 1992 (I: 8 +). The section "The Americas in 1492," written by Jamake Highwater, includes information about the Aztecs and the Incas.

Garcia, Richard. *My Aunt Otilia's Spirits*. Illustrated by Robin Cherin and Roger Reyes. Children's Press, 1987 (I: 5–8 R: 2). An aunt from Puerto Rico visits her family in the United States.

Garza, Carmen Lomas. *Family Pictures*. Children's Book, 1990 (I: 4–8). The illustrations and text in English and Spanish show family scenes.

Geeslin, Campbell. *On Ramon's Farm: Five Tales of Mexico*. Illustrated by Petra Mathers. Atheneum, 1998 (I: 4–8). A collection of five stories.

Gershator, Phillis, and David Gershator. *Greetings, Sun*. Illustrated by Synthia Saint James. DK, 1998 (I: 3–7 R: 2). The text tours a Caribbean island.

Gerson, Mary-Joan. *People of the Corn: A Mayan Story*. Illustrated by C. Golembe. Little, Brown, 1995 (I: all). The illustrations are based on Mayan art.

Gonzalez, Lucia. *The Bossy Gallito*. Scholastic, 1994 (I: all). A Cuban folktale.

Gonzalez, Ralfka, and Ana Ruiz. *My First Book of Proverbs*. Children's Book, 1995 (I: all). A collection of sayings in English and Spanish.

Greger, C. Shana. *The Fifth and Final Sun: An Ancient Myth of the Sun's Origin*. Houghton Mifflin, 1994 (I: 8 + R: 5). A myth about the creation of the sun.

Griego y Maestas, Jose, and Rudolfo A. Anaya. *Cuentos: Tales from the Hispanic Southwest*. Illustrated by Jaime Valdez. Museum of New Mexico, 1980 (I: 9 + R: 5). This is a collection of tales.

Griego, Margot C. *Tortillitas para Mama and Other Spanish Nursery Rhymes*. Illustrated by Barbara Cooney. Holt, Rinehart & Winston, 1981 (I: 3–7). Nursery rhymes appear in Spanish and English.

Hall, Lynn. *Danza!* Scribner's, 1981 (I: 10 + R: 6). A boy and his horse share life on a farm in Puerto Rico.

Hamilton, Virginia. *In the Beginning: Creation Stories from Around the World*. Illustrated by Barry Moser. Harcourt Brace, 1988 (I: all R: 5). The text includes a creation story from the Mayan people of Guatemala.

Hausman, Gerald. *Doctor Bird: Three Lookin' Up Tales from Jamaica*. Illustrated by Ashley Wolff. Philomel, 1998 (I: 3–8 R: 3). These tales show how the national bird of Jamaica interacts with animals.

Heide, Florence Parry, and Roxanne Heide Pierce. *Tio Armando*. Illustrated by Ann Grifalconi. Lothrop, Lee & Shepard, 1998 (I: 5–8). An older man becomes part of an extended family.

Herrera, Juan Felipe. *Calling the Doves*. Illustrated by Elly Simmons. Children's Press, 1995 (I: all R: 5). The story of an immigrant family.

Hinojosa, Francisco, adapted by. *The Old Lady Who Ate People*. Illustrated by Leonel Maciel. Little, Brown, 1984 (I: all R: 6). o.p.* These four frightening folktales are from Mexico.

Isadora, Rachel. *Carribean Dream*. Putnam's, 1998 (I: 5–8). Watercolors show the Caribbean background.

Jaffe, Nina. *The Golden Flower: A Taino Myth from Puerto Rico*. Simon & Schuster, 1996 (I: all). A creation tale shows how vegetation came to the land.

Jenkins, Lyll Becerra de. *The Honorable Prison*. Lodestar, 1989 (I: 10+ R: 5). Marta and her family are prisoners of a Latin American country because of the actions of her father.

Jiménez, Franciso. *La Mariposa*. Illustrated by Simon Silva. Houghton Mifflin, 1998 (I: 8+ R: 5). The son of immigrant workers has difficulty in school.

Kalnay, Francis. *Chucaro: Wild Pony of the Pampa*. Harcourt, Brace, 1958 (I: 8+). Winner of the 1959 Newbery Honor.

Keister, Douglas. *Fernando's Gift*. Sierra Club, 1995 (I: 6+). Text and photographs show the life of a young boy who lives in the rain forest of Costa Rica.

Kroll, Virginia. *Butterfly Boy*. Illustrated by Gerardo Suzan. Boyds Mills, 1997 (I: 5-8 R: 4). A boy tries to ensure the return of the butterflies.

Krumgold, Joseph. *. . . And Now Miguel*. Illustrated by Jean Charlot. Crowell, 1953 (I: 10+ R: 3). Miguel Chavez is a member of a proud sheep-raising family.

Kurtz, Jane. *Miro in the Kingdom of the Sun*. Houghton Mifflin, 1996 (I: 6-9 R: 5). An Inca tale about a poor girl.

Lattimore, Deborah. *The Flame of Peace: A Tale of the Aztecs*. Harper & Row, 1987 (I: all R: 6). This story is based on Aztec mythology.

Luenn, Nancy. *A Gift for Abuelita: Celebrating the Day of the Dead*. Illustrated by Robert Chapman. Rising Moon, 1998 (I: 7+ R: 4). A girl and her grandfather spend time learning together.

Marrin, Albert. *Aztecs and Spaniards: Cortes and the Conquest of Mexico*. Atheneum, 1986 (I: 12+ R: 7). This book is a history of the Aztecs and tells about the influence of Cortes.

_____. *Empires Lost and Won: The Spanish Heritage in the Southwest*. Simon & Schuster, 1997 (I: 12+ R: 7). This history begins with the first stories of cities of gold.

Martinello, Marian L., and Samuel P. Nesmith. *With Domingo Leal in San Antonio 1734*. The University of Texas Institute of Texas Cultures at San Antonio, 1979 (I: 8+ R: 4). This book tells the results of research investigating the lives of Spanish settlers who arrived in Texas in the 1730s.

Martinez, Victor. *Parrot in the Oven: Mi Vida*. HarperCollins, 1996 (I: 12+ R: 6). A Mexican American family struggles against poverty.

Matthew, Gollub. *The Twenty-five Mixtec Cats*. Tambourine, 1993 (I: 6 R: 4). This folktale is from Oaxaca, Mexico.

McCaughrean, Geraldine. *The Bronze Cauldron: Myths and Legends of the World*. Illustrated by Bee Willey. (I: 8+ R: 4). Includes a Mayan myth.

McDermott, Gerald. *Musicians of the Sun*. Simon & Schuster, 1997 (I: all). An Aztec myth.

Meltzer, Milton. *The Hispanic Americans*. Photographs by Morrie Camhi and Catherine Noren. Crowell, 1982 (I: 9–12 R: 6). Puerto Ricans, Chicanos, and Cubans have influenced the United States.

Meyer, Carolyn, and Charles Gallenkamp. *The Mystery of the Ancient Maya*. Atheneum, 1985 (I: 10+ R: 8). This book tells about early explorers and discoveries.

Mikaelsen, Ben. *Sparrow Hawk Red*. Hyperion/Little, Brown, 1993 (I: 10+ R: 6). A thirteen-year-old boy tries to avenge his mother's murder by drug smugglers.

Mohr, Nicholasa. *El Bronx Remembered: A Novella and Stories*. Harper & Row, 1975 (I: 10+ R: 6). Twenty short stories are set in the inner city.

_____. *Felita*. Illustrated by Ray Cruz. Dial, 1979 (I: 9–12 R: 2). Felita is unhappy when her family moves to a new neighborhood.

_____. *Going Home*. Dial, 1986 (I: 10+ R: 6). Twelve-year-old Felita spends the summer with relatives in Puerto Rico.

_____. *Nilda*. Harper & Row, 1973 (I: 10+ R: 6). This is the story of a Puerto Rican girl living in Harlem during the 1940s.

Mora, Pat. *The Race of Toad and Deer*. Orchard, 1995. (I: all) An adaptation of a fable.

Myers, Walter Dean. *Scorpions*. Harper & Rowe, 1998. (I: 11+ R:5). A boy has difficulties with a gang.

Ober, Hal. *How Music Came to the World*. Houghton Mifflin, 1994 (I: all R: 4). This is an Aztec myth.

O'Dell, Scott. *The Amethyst Ring*. Houghton Mifflin, 1983 (I: 10+ R: 6). This is the final story of Julian Escobar.

_____. *The Black Pearl*. Illustrated by Milton Johnson. Houghton Mifflin, 1967 (I: 10+ R: 6). A boy dreams of finding a wonderful pearl while pearl diving.

_____. *The Captive*. Houghton Mifflin, 1979 (I: 10+ R: 6). A young Spanish seminarian named Julian Escobar witnesses the exploitation of the Maya during the 1500s.

_____. *Carlota*. Houghton Mifflin, 1981 (I: 10+ R: 6). A high-spirited Spanish American girl fights beside her father during the days of the Mexican War in early California.

_____. *The Feathered Serpent*. Houghton Mifflin, 1981 (I: 10+ R: 6). This book is the sequel to *The Captive*.

_____. *The King's Fifth*. Houghton Mifflin, 1966 (I: 10+ R: 6). Esteban de Sandoval accompanies Coronado's army in search of the cities of gold.

Orozco, Jose-Luis. *Ten Little Fingers and Other Play Rhymes and Action Songs from Latin America*. Illustrated by Elisa Kleven. Dutton, 1997 (I: 4+). Music and words in Spanish and English.

Paulsen, Gary. *The Crossing*. Doubleday, 1987 (I: 12+ R: 6). The harsh realities of a border town are developed as a boy longs to cross into the United States.

_____. *Sisters Hermana*. Harcourt Brace, 1993 (I: 12+ R: 6). Two girls, one Mexican and one Anglo, discover that they have many similarities.

Peña, Sylvia, edited by. *Tun-ta-ca-tun: More Stories and Poems in English and Spanish for Children*. Illustrated by Narciso Peña. Arte Publico Press, 1986 (I: all). The collection of poems and stories are written for children from preschool to older levels.

Politi, Leo. *Pedro, the Angel of Olvera Street*. Scribner's, 1946 (I: 5–8 R: 4). Winner of the 1947 Newbery Honor.

_____. *Song of the Swallows*. Scribner's, 1949 (I: 5–8 R: 4). Juan lives in Capistrano, California.

Prago, Albert. *Strangers in Their Own Land: A History of Mexican-Americans*. Four Winds, 1973 (I: 10+ R: 7). This book traces both the history and the difficulties of Mexican Americans.

Reeve, Kirk. *Lolo and Red-Legs*. Rising Moon, 1998 (I: 8+ R: 5). An eleven-year-old boy has adventures after he captures a tarantula.

Reinhard, Johan. *Discovering the Inca Ice Maiden: My Adventures on Ampato*. National Geographic, 1998 (I: 8+ R: 4). Photographs show the discovery.

Roberts, Maurice. *Henry Cisneros: Mexican American Mayor*. Children's Press, 1986 (I: 8+ R: 5). This is the biography of a former mayor of San Antonio.

Rohmer, Harriet, and Mary Anchondo. *How We Came to the Fifth World*. Children's Book Press, 1988 (I: all R: 5). This is an Aztec version of creation.

_____, Octavio Chow, and Morris Viduare. *The Invisible Hunters*. Illustrated by Joe Sam. Children's Press, 1987 (I: all R: 5). The tale reflects the impact of European traders.

_____, and Dornminster Wilson. *Mother Scorpion Country*. Illustrated by Virginia Steams. Children's Press, 1987 (I: all R: 4) A Central American tale is written in both English and Spanish.

Rosenberg, Joe. *¡Aplauso!*. Pinata, 1995 (I: all). Hispanic children's plays.

Saenz, Benjamin Alire. *A Gift from Papa Diego*. Illustrated by Geronimo Garcia. Cinco Puntos, 1998 (I: 7 +). A story in English and Spanish about a boy's love for his grandfather.

San Souci, Robert D. *Cendrillon: A Carribean Cinderella*. Illustrated by Brian Pinkney. Simon & Schuster, 1998 (I: all). Creole words are included in this variant.

Schaefer, Jack. *Old Ramon*. Houghton Mifflin, 1960 (I: 8 + R: 5). Winner of the 1961 Newbery Honor.

Slate, Joseph. *The Secret Stars*. Illustrated by Felipe Davalos. Cavendish, 1998 (I: 6–8 R: 4). Set in New Mexico, the text focuses on the Three Kings.

Sola, Michele. *Angela Weaves a Dream: The Story of a Young Maya Artist*. Photographs by Jeffrey Jay Foxx. Hyperion, 1997 (I: 8 + R: 5). Photographs show the weaving process and symbols in designs.

Soto, Gary. *Baseball in April and Other Stories*. Harcourt Brace Jovanovich, 1990 (I: 11 + R: 6). This is a collection of stories about Mexican American youth in California.

_____. *Big Bushy Mustache*. Illustrated by Joe Cepeda. Knopf, 1998 (I: 5–8 R: 4). The story focuses on Cinco de Mayo.

_____. *Neighborhood Odes*. Harcourt Brace Jovanovich, 1992 (I: all). This collection of poems is about a neighborhood.

_____. *Pacific Crossing*. Harcourt Brace Jovanovich, 1992 (I: 10 + R: 6). In a sequel to *Taking Sides*, boys from the barrio in San Francisco participate in an exchange program in Japan.

_____. *Petty Crimes*. Harcourt Brace, 1998 (I: 10 + R: 6). Stories featuring Latino characters show overcoming various emotional conflicts.

_____. *The Skirt*. Illustrated by Eric Velasquez. Delacorte, 1992 (I: 6–8 R: 4). A Mexican American girl leaves her folkloric skirt on the school bus and tries to retrieve it.

_____. *Taking Sides*. Harcourt Brace Jovanovich, 1991 (I: 10 + R: 6). A boy faces problems of loyalty as his new basketball team meets the old team from the barrio.

_____. *Too Many Tamales*. Illustrated by Ed Martinez. Putnam, 1993 (I: 6–8 R: 4). This family story is set on Christmas Eve.

Swann, Brian. *Touching the Distance: Native American Riddle-Poems*. Illustrated by Maria Rendon. Harcourt Brace, 1998 (I: all). Riddles are written in the form of poems.

Tashlik, Phyllis, edited by. *Hispanic, Female and Young: An Anthology*. Arte Publico, 1993 (I: 12 +). This is both an anthology of stories and a collection of interviews conducted by a group of students.

Temple, Frances. *Grab Hands and Run*. Orchard, 1993 (I: 10 + R: 6). Twelve-year-old Felipe tells about his family's attempts to leave El Salvador after the disappearance of his father.

Turner, Robyn Montana. *Frida Kahlo: Portraits of Women Artists for Children*. Little, Brown, 1993 (I: all). A biography of a great Mexican artist.

Van Laan, Nancy, retold by. *The Magic Bean Tree: A Legend from Argentina*. Illustrated by Beatriz Vidal. Houghton Mifflin, 1998 (I: 4–8 R: 4). The people are saved from drought.

_____. *So Say the Little Monkeys*. Illustrated by Yumi Heo. Atheneum, 1998 (I: all). A rhythmic text set in Brazil.

Vidal, Beatriz. *The Legend of El Dorado: A Latin American Tale*. Knopf, 1991 (I: all R: 5). The treasures of the gilded man are believed to be at the bottom of Lake Guatavita.

Volkmer, Jane Anne, retold by. *Song of Chirimia—A Guatemalan Folktale*. Carolrhoda, 1990 (I: 6-10 R: 5). A Mayan folktale in English and Spanish tells how a man tries to win the hand of a Mayan princess.

Watson, James. *Talking in Whispers*. Victor Gollancz, 1983 (I: 12 + R: 7). In a political thriller, a boy survives against an oppressive military government.

Winter, Jeanette. *Diego*. Scholastic, 1991 (I: 8 + R: 5). A biography of the artist written for younger readers.

Wisniewski, David. *Rain Player*. Clarion, 1991 (I: 5–8 R: 5). Paper constructions enhance this Mayan tale.

Wojciechowska, Maia. *Shadow of a Bull*. Illustrated by Alvin Smith. Atheneum, 1964 (I: 10 + R: 5). Manolo discovers that true bravery is not always in the bullring.

Asian Time Line

3000–1500 B.C.	Development of many of the great Hindu stories found in the Mahabharata	1939	Caldecott: Thomas Handforth's *Mei Li*
563–483 B.C.	Period in which Gautama Buddha lived and taught in India	1941	Bombing of Pearl Harbor and start of World War II for the United States
100 B.C. to A.D. 1500	Silk Route main trade link between East and West	1951	Newbery Honor: Jeanette Eaton's *Gandhi, Fighter Without a Sword*
Circa 2000 years ago	Jataka tales, or stories of Buddha's former birth, with teachings, beliefs, and values associated with the Buddhist religion	1956	Caldecott Honor: Taro Yashima's *Crow Boy*
		1973	Caldecott: Artist Blair Lent's *The Funny Little Woman*
681	Order by Emperor Temmu to place Japanese traditions into writing	1976	Newbery Honor and Children's Book Award: Laurence Yep's *Dragonwings*
Circa 800	Tuan Ch'eng Shih's *Yu Yang Ts a Tsy,* early Chinese "Cinderella"	1980	Hans Christian Andersen International Medal: Illustrator Suekichi Akaba (Japan)
1100–1350	Many Japanese tales collected	1983	Mildred L. Batchelder Award: Toshi Maruki's *Hiroshima No Pika*
1160	Birth of Mongol leader, Ghengis Khan, who conquered Persia and China	1984	Hans Christian Andersen International Medal: Illustrator Mitsumasa Anno (Japan)
Late 1600s	Tales of the supernatural collected in Shandong (Shantung) province (*The Beggar's Magic*)	1986	Newbery Honor: Rhoda Blumberg's *Commodore Perry in the Land of the Shogun*
Late 1800s	2,000 tales collected, translated, and published by Indian scholars, civil servants, and foreign missionaries	1989	Nobel Peace Prize awarded to Dalai Lama
		1989	Caldecott Honor: Artist Allen Say's *The Boy of the Three-Year Nap*
1926	Newbery: Arthur Bowie Chrisman's *Shen of the Sea*	1994	Caldecott: Allen Say's *Grandfather's Journey*
1933	Newbery: Elizabeth Forman Lewis's *Young Fu of the Upper Yangtze*	1994	Newbery Honor: Laurence Yep's *Dragon's Gate*
1935	Newbery Honor: Elizabeth Seeger's *Pageant of Chinese History*	1994	Hans Christian Andersen International Medal: Illustrator Michio Mado (Japan)
		1997	Mildred L. Batchelder Award: Peter Sis's *Tibet: Through the Red Box*

5 *Asian Literature*

*A*sian literature encompasses the rich and diverse cultural and ethnic heritage that is found in such countries as China, India, Japan, Vietnam, and Korea. Asian American literature also shows the impact of immigrating to a new country, with the Asian characters trying to retain their previous culture and adjust to new situations.

Asian literature provides readers with opportunities to explore various cultures through a wide variety of literary genres. For example, the folklore of India includes the Jataka tales, which are fables associated with Gautama Buddha. The folklore collected from Chinese Americans indicates how the people brought their beliefs, values, and stories with them when they came to a new land. Informational books about China take readers back to the time of the Silk and Spice routes and encourage them to understand how the routes supported the movement of ideas, industry, and religious beliefs. Historical fiction set in feudal Japan or in early China encourages readers to grasp such important themes as the need for people to overcome racial and cultural conflicts if they are to gain self-respect. Historical fiction set in an earlier United States develops the importance of the Chinese Americans as they worked on the transcontinental railroad or shows how people acculturate to a new land while maintaining their ethnic identities. Through contemporary literature, readers discover how characters develop cross-cultural understanding, as well as face and overcome conflicts in their own lives.

In addition to reading the Asian American literature for the pleasure and appreciation, students need to develop an understanding of the literature and the cultures. The increasing numbers of Asian immigrants to the United States—and high numbers of Asian Americans in the overall population—make an understanding of Asian culture and the literature very important. Dugger (1996) reports in an article in *The New York Times* that by the year 2000, "1 in 10 New Yorkers, and almost 1 in 5 Queens residents, will be of Asian origin" (p. 18).

In this chapter, we will investigate values that are part of the cultures, discuss stereotypes in literature from the past, consider criteria for evaluating Asian and Asian American literature, and discuss examples of the literature from various Asian countries, as well as literature that reflects an Asian American perspective.

Before we consider the inappropriateness of stereotypes of Asian in literature from the past or evaluate and discuss the literature from various Asian cultures, it is helpful to identify some of the values from those cultures. Scholars who investigate traditional values provide us with important information for analyzing the values and beliefs embedded in folklore and historical literature. Those who analyze the values in contemporary Asian cultures provide helpful sources for analyzing contemporary literature, as well as more traditional stories.

Donald Holzman (1998) provides a very useful analysis of the importance of filial piety in China since the earliest times and as part of the Confucian canon. Holzman traces the importance of this respect for ancestors and the utmost regard for parents when he states: "That a son should love his parents is fate—you cannot erase this from his heart—to serve your parents and be content to follow them anywhere—this is the perfection of filial piety" (p. 190). Holzman identifies a twofold structure for filial piety in early China: "piety within the family (toward one's parents) and in society (towards the emperor and towards the official hierarchy), and filial piety as exalted throughout as the root of all virtue" (p. 192). Filial piety was so important in the early stories that extreme cases of filial piety provoked supernatural intervention in favor of such children, as well as rewards for this behavior. In addition to filial piety, Holzman identifies the values of reaching the gods through one's ancestors; punishing unfilial conduct; and respecting and developing the virtues of righteousness, love, goodness, and truth.

In an interview with Leonard Marcus (2000) in *Publishers Weekly,* Laurence Yep discusses his difficulty in his writing when he tries to bridge two cultures. He states:

> Now, though, I am not so sure that it is possible to blend two cultures together. Asia cultures are family- and cooperation-oriented. American culture on the other hand emphasizes the individual and competition. The two cultures pull in opposite directions. So I see myself now as someone who will always be on the border between two cultures. That works to my benefit as a writer because not quite fitting in helps me be a better observer. (p. 101)

Violet H. Harada (1998) searches for, and identifies, authentic Japanese cultural values in the writings of the Japanese American author Yoshiko Uchida. For example, Harada identifies the importance of the family hierarchy and the acceptable social behaviors associated with one's place in the hierarchy; the importance of maintaining family and community traditions; the belief in filial obligations, duty, and loyalty; the power of persistence and endurance; and the legacy of the Japanese spirit and soul.

Additional contemporary values are identified by Gail M. Hickey (1998) and Nancy K. Freeman (1998). Hickey identifies the following cultural values as exemplified by recent Southeast Asian immigrants to the United States: respect for parents, family, and elders and emphasis on children's academic success as a way to elevate personal and family status. Freeman stresses that Eastern cultures emphasize community, cooperation, and interrelatedness. She compares these values with Western cultural values that are apt to foster individualism, competition, and personal possessions. She believes that such differences in cultural values may result in cultural conflicts.

As we proceed with the analysis of literature from various Asian cultures, try to identify the importance of these cultural values. Which are found in traditional literature? Which are found in more contemporary literature? Which values may be found in both traditional and contemporary literature? How do the values reflect the various Asian cultures? Are there differences in the values depicted in some of the earlier children's books about Asian cultures and more recent editions?

 ## CONCERNS OVER STEREOTYPES IN LITERATURE FROM THE PAST

Fortunately today there are many more excellent books written from an Asian or Asian American perspective than there were in the past. In 1976, the Asian American Children's Book Project (Council on Interracial Books for Children, 1977) identified 66 books with Asian American central characters, and most of these books were about Chinese Americans. The members of the project concluded that with only a few exceptions the books were grossly misleading. They presented stereotypes suggesting that all Asian Americans look alike, choose to live in "quaint" communities in the midst of large cities, and cling to "outworn, alien" customs. The project also criticized the books because they tended to measure success by the extent to which Asian Americans have assimilated white middle-class values and because they implied that hard work, learning to speak English, and keeping a low profile would enable Asian Americans to overcome adversity and be successful.

It is interesting to compare the older books and the stereotypes with the image of Asians and Asian Americans in the more recent books. As you read contemporary books about Asian Americans, you may consider the impact of Asian Americans on the U.S. educational system and their potential for influencing all aspects of U.S. life. Recent studies on affirmative action in U.S. universities and colleges point to the high levels of achievement among Asian Americans. In an article in *The New York Times*, Onishi (1996) discusses the high achievement of Asian Americans, "who generally have the highest grades and test scores of any racial group" (p. 26). Onishi points out that "in California, Asian Americans account for only 10 percent of the population but make up about one-third of the undergraduates in the University of California system" (p. 33).

 ## ASIAN FOLKLORE

Folklore collected from Asian cultures, like other folklore, portrays the feelings, struggles, and aspirations of common people; depicts the lives of the well-to-do; and reflects the moral values, superstitions, social customs, and humor of the times and societies in which they originated. Like medieval Europe, ancient Asia contained societies in which royalty and nobles led lives quite different from those of peasants. Females had less freedom and social influence than did males. Asian tales tell about the rich and the poor, the wise and the foolish, mythical quests, lovers, animals, and supernatural beings and powers, common to all folklore, but they also reflect the customs and beliefs of specific cultures. In this section on Asian folklore, we will explore in-depth the folklore from China, India, and Japan. We will also review some of the folklore from other Asian countries.

Following their study in the stereotypes found in the earlier Asian American literature, the Council on Interracial Books for Children (1977) recommended the following criteria for evaluating Asian American literature:

1. The book should reflect the realities and way of life of Asian American people. Is the story accurate for the historical period and cultural context? Are the characters from a variety of social and economic levels? Does the plot exaggerate the exoticism or mysticism of the customs and festivals of the Asian American culture? Are festivals in the perspective of everyday activities?
2. The book should transcend stereotypes. Do the Asian American characters handle their own problems, or do they require benevolent intervention from a white person? Do the characters have to make a definite choice between two cultures, or is there an alternative in which the two cultures can mingle? Do the characters portray a range of human emotions, or are they docile and uncomplaining? Are there obvious occupational stereotypes—do all Asian-Americans work in laundries or restaurants?
3. The literature should seek to rectify historical distortions and omissions.
4. The characters in the book should avoid the model minority and super minority syndromes. Are the characters respected for themselves, or must they display outstanding abilities to gain approval?
5. The literature should reflect an awareness of the changing status of women in society. Does the author provide role models for girls other than subservient females?
6. The illustrations should reflect the racial diversity of Asian Americans. Are the characters all look-alikes, with the same skin tone and exaggerated features, such as slanted eyes? Are clothing and settings appropriate to the culture depicted?

Suzanne Lo and Ginny Lee (1993) maintain that many of the older stereotypical books should be placed in an historical collection rather than used with children. They provide guidelines for evaluating the literature that are very similar to those listed above.

In a recent study of the images of Chinese and Chinese Americans found in seventy-three picture storybooks, Cai (1994) concluded:

Most of the picture books that have been subjected to scrutiny in this survey present quite positive images of Chinese and Chinese Americans and give the reader a sense of the Chinese culture. A number of authors and illustrators have turned out many artistically commendable and culturally authentic works. While biased stereotypical portraits have not been eliminated, cultural inauthenticity is the main flaw of many books exhibited in both the content of the texts and the details of the illustrations. To transmit accurate information and to maintain the integrity of the culture, authors and illustrators are obligated to undertake earnest research in that culture. Imagination alone cannot help them to cross cultural gaps. Inexact scholarship will inevitably lead to ridiculous misrepresentation. (p. 188)

As you conduct your own research in Asian literature and read and evaluate the literature, be aware of the necessity of evaluating the literature for both stereotypes and for authenticity of text and illustrations.

Chinese Folklore

Chinese folktales are of ancient origin. For example, Maria Leach (1972) maintains that complete versions of many of the Marchenforscher (folktales) were published in China hundreds of years before they were published in Europe. "Thus Des Perrier's story of Pernette in Nouvelles Récréations, 1558, the first European version of one of the complete Cinderellas, was anticipated in China by 700 years in Tuan Ch'eng Shih's *Yu Yang Tsa Tsy*, published in the middle of the T'ang Dynasty" (p. 228).

Moss Roberts (1979) maintains that the stories are important because they "bear the stamp of the society and traditions that originally produced them. They illuminate the Chinese social order through the structured relationships that defined it: emperor and subject, father and son, husband and wife (or wives), official and peasant, human and beast" (p. xv).

Difficulties Associated with the Study of Chinese Folklore   Long before published versions appeared, the folklore of China had stratified into the lore of the aristocrats and the lore of the populace. During the centuries, Chinese folklore had been modified by the rise of various philosophical schools, the migration of religious systems, and changes in politics. The influences of philosophical schools, religious systems, and politics all cause difficulties for those who are studying the folklore. Leach (1972) identifies the following causes for some of the difficulties associated with the study of Chinese folklore:

1. Chinese folklore extends over a long period of time and was collected from vast territories without clearly defined boundaries.
2. The Chinese nation includes a mixture of many cultures.
3. Stories were borrowed and adapted among many cultures.
4. The scholarly class had great power and prestige and consequently influenced the collection, telling, and publishing of the tales.
5. The Chinese written language is considered the property of the scholars, and thus the written materials may be distorted. The priestly class reworked and rationalized the folklore.
6. Extensive collections were gathered by missionaries who were eager to demonstrate the evil effects of the superstitions of others or by ethnographers attempting to impose European standards on Chinese data; consequently, some of the stories are incomplete and fail to demonstrate the variations of custom and belief in the various parts of China.

As we read and interpret the folklore, we must remember the possible influences of each of these factors.

Early Beliefs That Influence the Folklore   As in any other folklore, an understanding of the early beliefs and customs of the Chinese people is necessary before we try to analyze and understand the folklore. For example, "yin-yang" is a basic concept in early Chinese cultures. The yin-yang provides a balance among positive and negative forces of the universe such as male-female and heaven-earth.

During early periods in the history of China, the priests and cults formed powerful influences. A belief in the use of oracle bones to tell the future was part of the aristocratic cult in the Shang Dynasty (1766–1122 B.C.). The wu priests were part of the Shang culture; they operated in both the aristocratic and the popular cults. The priest kings had their own cults involving heaven, earth, soil, grain, and ancestor worship. Ancestor worship was highly developed in the earliest records.

Beliefs about the soul influenced the early culture. The cults maintained that humans had two souls: an animal soul, p'o, which is created at the moment of conception, and the spirit soul, hun, which enters the body at birth. P'o follows the dead body to its tomb and is nourished by the sacrifices of descendants, and is dissipated as the body disintegrates. In the early historic times in China, the soul of the aristocrat was followed by the sacrifice of his wives and retainers. In later times, papier-mâché figures were burned at the grave. It is not only human souls, however, that deserve homage. Homage is also paid to the spirits of rivers and mountains.

Several philosophies also influenced Chinese folklore. For example, during the Chou Dynasty, the philosophers, historians, and theologians preserved and reinterpreted the ancient beliefs and customs. Confucianists maintained that the Chinese must return to the practices of the wise rulers of earlier times. Tales that illustrate the Confucian philosophies frequently reflect the superior orders of emperor, father, husband. In contrast, the Taoist philosophers were social critics who opposed the Confucians. Their populist view found their way into many of the tales. Moss states that one of the purposes for Taoist literature was to publicize the crimes of the mighty and the injustices suffered by the ordinary people including children and women—and even injustices suffered by animals. The Taoists had a central leader and thousands of priests and nuns who devoted their lives to the attainment of The Way. As you read the folklore, try to identify the philosophy that is being developed through the story.

Types of Tales and General Elements in Chinese Folklore   Karl S. Y. Kao (1985) in his collection of *Classical Chinese Tales of the Supernatural: Selections from the Third to Tenth Century* identifies several types of tales: tales that show cosmological significance, tales that reveal manifestations of ghosts and spirits, tales that include animal transformations, tales that focus on fairies and deities and their interactions with humans, tales of magic feats, and tales of divine retributions and miracles related to the Buddhist faith and native Chinese beliefs.

The important plots and themes in these Chinese tales include transformations of humans into beasts; trials involving perilous encounters with humans or supernatural creatures; dragon lore that features human involvement in the family feuds of dragon clans; revelations of what is in store for humans in the future and dream phenomena; and supernatural, fantastic elements. According to Kao (1985), these tales are especially important because they influenced later fiction and served as a source of allusions for poetry and often provided the plots for the dramas of the Yuan and Ming dynasties.

There are certain elements and motifs that may be found in much of the Chinese folklore. For example, the universe is governed by Shang Ti, thought to be the Supreme Ruler or Heaven, or Yu Huang, the Jade Emperor, the highest of all things, physical or spiritual. Gods such as the Gods of the Cities and Villages control life. The Kitchen God controls life in the home and reports once a year on the behavior of each family. These deities are very important. Temples of the Gods of Place or Locality are scattered throughout the fields and are believed to allow the peasants to have a direct approach to Heaven. Heaven decrees the moment of death, when the soul is judged according to the Book of Destiny, which contains a record of all the acts of an individual. Following a family member's death, the disposition, repose, and happy journey of the soul are matters of great importance to the family.

Demons, spirits, and ghosts are important in the folklore. The two souls of a person may mingle with the throng of demons, spirits, and ghosts. During sleep, the superior soul leaves the body and goes about its own affairs—which become the substance of dreams. The souls of humans, animals, and things enjoy the pleasures and vices enjoyed by living human beings.

Fortune-telling, oracle bones, and astrology are considered complex sciences. The results of these sciences influence lives. In addition, there are strong beliefs related to locations of various dwellings. Houses, tombs, and palaces should face toward the south and be located near the veins of strength so that they may absorb the yang (male) influences, which produce strength. They should be protected at the back by high mounds of trees, which screen off the yin (female) influences from the north. The importance of the male is also found in the family because the line is carried through the male, and the head of the house performs as priest during the ceremonies for the ancestors of the group. Consequently, male offspring are essential.

Additional elements include the role of scholarship in obtaining life goals and the family in arranging marriages. Scholarship is highly valued in the Chinese culture and is considered the means for success. Much of the folklore illustrates respect for knowledge and learning. Marriage brokers make arrangements between the families of two young people. This is a common practice found in the literature. An understanding of the importance of these elements is useful in the analysis of folklore. The same elements may be found in historical fiction and poetry.

Examples of Chinese Folklore   Song Nan Zhang's retelling of *Five Heavenly Emperors: Chinese Myths of Creation* begins with the separation of sky and earth, the emergence of the two creative forces yang (male) and yin (female), and the creation of the universe by Pangu. The remainder of the myths are about the five heavenly emperors and other gods who created humankind and taught them how to live. The collection of myths ends with a discussion of the Taichi map invented around 1000 B.C. and used by fortune tellers to read both the past and the future, examples of Chinese words presented in the Chinese written language, and a depiction of the symbols for the various heavenly gods. A tale about the misuse of power, Eric A. Kimmel's *Ten Suns: A Chinese Legend,* reveals how the earth was saved from blazing heat and brought back to a balance between earth and sky.

Traditional Chinese sayings frequently suggest Chinese values and express philosophical viewpoints found in Chinese folktales over the centuries. For example: "A teacher can open the door, but the pupil must go through it alone" and "The home that includes an old grandparent contains a precious jewel." These sayings suggest the value of scholarship and respect for older people. The importance of sayings and proverbs are reflected in Ed Young's *The Lost Horse.* Young based his story on a Chinese proverb: it teaches trust in ever-changing fortune and the belief that things are not always as bad or as good as they seem. These two themes provide the key for developing harmony between father and son.

As you read the following descriptions and analysis of some of the Chinese folktales, try to identify some of the early beliefs that might have influenced the tales and the common elements that may be found in the tales. Can you identify any possible philosophies that might have influenced the tales?

The conflict between nobility and commoners is a popular topic in Chinese tales. A dislike for imperial authority is evident in several Chinese equivalents to the cottage tales of medieval European peasants. In these tales, the dragon, the symbol of imperial authority, is usually evil and is overcome by a peasant's wit. "The Golden Sheng," included in Louise and Yuan-hsi Kuo's *Chinese Folk Tales* (1976), tells the story of a little girl captured by a malevolent flying dragon:

> Your sister is suffering; your sister is suffering,
> In the evil dragon's cave.
> Tears cover her face;
> Blood stains her back;
> Her hand drills the rock;
> Your sister is suffering; your sister is suffering. (p. 18)

A common folktale theme, reward for unselfish action, and a common folktale motif, a magical object, allow the girl's brother to rescue her and dispose of the beast.

Marilee Heyer's *The Weaving of a Dream: A Chinese Folktale* reveals rewarded behavior: bravery, unselfish love, understanding, respect for one's mother, faithfulness, and kindness. In contrast, disrespect for one's mother and selfishness are punished. This tale also shows the power of a dream and the perseverance that may be required to gain the dream. Ed Young's *Lon Po Po: A Red-Riding Hood Story from China* shows the cleverness of the eldest daughter, and the cooperation of the three sisters are powerful enough to outwit the intentions of the evil wolf.

Caryn Yacowitz's *The Jade Stone: A Chinese Folktale* reveals the importance of inspiration and adhering to the soul that is within jade. The importance of dreams is emphasized as the Great Emperor of all China allows his dreams to decide the stone carver's fate. *The Cricket's Cage* retold by Stefan Czernecki reveals how a wise cricket helps his owner design a tower for the Forbidden City and gain respect and recognition from the emperor. The close relationship between humans and nature is a frequent element in Chinese folklore. The importance of really seeing what is around us in nature is developed in Ed Young's *Mouse Match*. The tale is presented to resemble a Chinese scroll and is written with Chinese text on the reverse side.

The defeat of an evil ruler is the main conflict in Rosalind C. Wang's *The Treasure Chest: A Chinese Tale*. The hero in this tale is a poor widow's son who rescues a fish and earns the gratitude of the Ocean King. The gift from the King of three bamboo sticks helps the young man save the woman he loves from Funtong, the evil ruler who desires the young woman.

In *Two of Everything*, Lily Toy Hong develops the importance of both humor and wisdom. A poor farmer and his wife discover the unusual characteristics of a brass pot that the farmer unearths in his garden. If one item is placed in the pot, two identical items appear. This happy situation continues until the wife falls headfirst into the pot, but the woman uses her wits and solves the problem.

In *Tiger Woman*, Laurence Yep uses a rhyming format to retell a Shantung folktale in which selfishness is punished and sharing is rewarded. When a beggar approaches a selfish woman and asks for some of her bean curd, she replies that she will not give up any of her food because she is a tiger when she is famished. The beggar then casts a spell so that whatever the selfish woman says she becomes. At the point when she almost becomes a pork roast, she repents and turns back into a human. At the end, she realizes the importance of sharing her food.

Margaret and Raymond Chang's *The Beggar's Magic: A Chinese Tale* also develops the theme that selfishness will be punished. In it, a greedy farmer refuses to give a holy man food. An author's note states that his tale of the supernatural was collected in Shandong (Shantung) province in the late 1600s.

Moss Roberts's large collection titled *Chinese Fairy Tales and Fantasies* is divided into tales about enchantment and magic, folly and greed, animals, women and wives, ghosts and souls, and judges and diplomats. Linda Fang's *The Ch'i-lin Purse: A Collection of Ancient Chinese Stories* includes a helpful preface and a list of source notes.

The Chinese American experience is emphasized in folktales collected by Laurence Yep. *The Rainbow People* is a collection of twenty Chinese folktales from Chinese Americans in the United States. The text is divided according to tales about tricksters, fools, virtues and vices, Chinese America, and love. Yep has included introductory comments for each of the sections. Many of the values and vices found in folklore from China are also found in these tales. Notice how a sampling of these values and vices could be used to summarize many of the values and vices discussed previously. For example, values highlighted in the stories include the importance of loyalty and wits and punishment for treachery found in "Natural Enemies," the importance of luck as found in "The Professor of Smells," the value of learning in "The Butterfly Man," the value of kindness to animals in "We Are All One" and "The Superior Pet," the punishment for impatience and the value for patience in "Snake-Spoke," the value of faithful service in "The Old Jar," the punishment for greed in "The Boasting Contest," and the virtue of obedience in "Dream Flier."

Folklore from India

Like China, India is a huge country with diverse people, languages, and religions. It is also an ancient country with folklore that goes back to ancient civilizations. An early record of Indian mythology is contained in the Rigveda, or "Hymn Veda." These myths along with the Yajurveda (Formula Veda), the Atharvaveda (Veda of the Atharvan priests), and the Brahmanas, or explanatory prose texts attached to them, date from the first and second millennium before Christ.

Much of the folklore from India is influenced by two great religions: Hindu and Buddhist. Many of the great Hindu stories are found in the Mahabharata, which dates anywhere from 3000 B.C. to about 1500 B.C. Donald A. Mackenzie (1987) reinforces the importance of myths and legends for the Hindus when he states:

> In no other country have the national poets given fuller and finer expression to the beliefs and ideals and traditions of a people, or achieved as a result a wider and more enduring fame. At the present day over two hundred million Hindus are familiar in varying degrees with the legendary themes and traditional beliefs which the ancient forest sages and poets of India invested with much beautiful symbolism, and used as mediums for speculative thought and profound spiritual teachings. The sacred books of India are to the Hindus what the Bible is to Christians. Those who read them, or hear them read, are believed to be assured of prosperity in this world and of salvation in the next. (pp. iii–iv)

One of the oldest and most important collections of folktales from India are Jataka tales, or stories of the Buddha's former births. These stories were first told more than 2,000 years ago and reveal many of the teachings, beliefs, and values associated with the Buddhist religion.

In the late nineteenth century there was a major thrust toward collecting and publishing the folktales from India. According to A. K. Ramanujan (1991), "some of the finest folktale collections were compiled then, and published in journals like *The Indian Antiquary*, *The Journal of the Royal Asiatic Society of Bengal*, and *North Indian Notes and Queries*" (unnumbered preface). During this time, about 2,000 tales were collected, translated, and published by Indian scholars, civil servants, and foreign missionaries.

Many of the tales found in the various religious sources and in other collections such as the Pancatantra, a collection of fables, are included in collections of tales for children. According to Meena Khorana (1991),

> Nationalistic concerns have led to the publication of biographies of national and religious leaders and collections of folktales in order to inculcate pride in India. Moreover, it is feared that the oral tradition is being lost due to changing family patterns, technology, rapid urbanization, mass media, and western-style education. Hence, all the major publishers have focused on stories based on the Pancatantra, Jatakas, epics, mythology, and history. (p. xix)

Types of Tales As would be expected from our discussion about the role of religion in Indian folklore, there are many tales about the gods, goddesses, and legendary heroes. Felix Guirand (1987) in the *New Larousse Encyclopedia of Mythology* identifies the following as subjects of myths in Indian folklore: royalty and the priestly caste, gods and goddesses, Brahmanas (the most ancient texts of Hindu sacred literature), heroes, and Buddha.

A. K. Ramanujan (1991) categorizes folktales into the following seven types: male-centered tales, in which a hero searches for adventure; women-centered tales, in which women may solve riddles that men cannot answer and thus rescue the men; tales about families that emphasize various types of family relationships; tales about fate, gods, and demons; humorous tales about rogues, jesters, and fools; and animal tales, especially those from the Jatakas and the Pancatantra, which are often didactic fables.

Examples of Folklore from India Numerous myths and legends from India are found in two books published for adults. These texts provide background information as well as examples of tales. Sister Nivendita and Ananda K. Coomaraswamy's *Myths and Legends Series: Hindus and Buddhists* (1987) includes chapters on the mythology of the Indo-Aryan races, the Ramayana, the Mahabharata, Krishna, Buddha, Shiva, and additional stories from the Puranas, epics, and vedas. Donald A. Mackenzie's *Myths and Legends Series: India* (1987) includes many tales about the deities. The following section describes some books for children and young adults.

Aaron Shepard's *Savitri: A Tale of Ancient India* is a Hindu myth that appears in the Mahabharata. This epic tale begins, "In India, in the time of legend, there lived a king with many wives but not one child. Morning and evening for eighteen years, he faced the fire on the sacred altar and prayed for the gift of children. Finally, a shining goddess rose from the flames. 'I am Savitri, child of the Sun. By your prayers, you have won a daughter'" (p. 1, unnumbered). This tale includes a righteous hero who is rich in virtue and intelligence. The plot includes the importance of both prayers and fasting and female loyalty and wit. The tale has a characteristic ending, "They lived long and happily, blessed with many children. So they had no fear or tears when Yama came again to carry them to his kingdom" (p. 33, unnumbered).

Madhur Jaffrey's *Seasons of Splendour: Tales, Myths, and Legends of India* is a collection of tales reflecting the Hindu religion. The tales are arranged in a sequence as they might be told at religious festivals during the course of the Hindu calendar year, which begins in April.

Diksha Dalal-Clayton's *The Adventures of Young Krishna: The Blue God of India* is a collection of myths about the Hindu deity. In the introduction, the author tells readers, "In India, people believe that whenever things are badly wrong in the world, a very brave and special person is born on Earth to fight evil and help the good. They believe that such people are the human form of God, or incarnations of God. This is why Krishna was born in India a long, long time ago" (p. viii). Children may like stories about Krishna because even though he fought demons and monsters and always won, he also behaved like any other child, having good and bad characteristics.

Debjani Chatterjee, an Indian-born storyteller and poet, retells several of the Hindu myths in *The Elephant-Headed God and Other Hindu Tales*. Notice in the following introduction to "The Elephant-Headed God" how the oral storyteller's style provides interest in the character.

Just look at the picture opposite this page. Take a good long look. You cannot help smiling, can you? Look at that elephant head sitting quite casually, and absurdly, on a fat boy's neck—he's so fat in fact that I think his neck's disappeared! Have you ever heard of a boy with an elephant's head? You will notice too that one of the tusks is broken. Can you see it? If you look carefully, you may spy a small rat in the picture too. (p. 10)

Hanuman, the tale of the monkey-hero found in an ancient text called *Ramayana* (The Path of Rama), is retold by Erik Jendresen and Joshua M. Greene. According to the authors' note the original text was written thousands of years ago in Sanskrit. The story follows Prince Rama's childhood, his marriage, his exile, his wife's abduction by the demon king, and Rama's final victory. The retelling employs an interesting storytelling style as revealed through this opening: "Listen now while I tell you a tale of a time long past when the world was menaced by a ten-headed beast whom the gods could not control. He was called Ravana: He who makes the universe scream" (p. 1, unnumbered). As you read the book, try to identify the characteristics of a hero as revealed in this tale from India.

The Jataka tales, which were passed down orally, are among the most important for revealing stories about Buddhist beliefs and values. The tales are attributed to Gautama Buddha, who lived and taught in northeast India between 563 and 483 B.C. Many of these tales develop the importance of cooperation, understanding, creativity, and wisdom—uniquely human potentials—as the key to life. The tales demonstrate the benefits derived from cooperation, friendship, respect, independent thought, responsible behavior, courage, humility, and education. They also reveal the problems caused by greed, ambition, foolishness, bad company, environmental damage, and disrespectful language.

Demi's *Buddha Stories* includes twelve of the tales that reveal moral values. These moral values are strengthened because Demi concludes each of the tales with a moral such as "When one person tells a falsehood, one hundred repeat it as true," "Treat others with kindness and your deeds will be rewarded," "It is easier to make a promise than to keep it," and "Pride leads to a fall, but humility is rewarded in the end." As you read the tales and the accompanying morals, what values do you discover related in the Buddhist tales?

The importance of helping others and living in harmony are themes found in many of the Jataka tales. In Lama Mipham's *Great Gift and the Wish-Fulfilling Gem: A Jataka Tale*, the son of a wealthy minister of a great king is saddened when he sees the needy in the land. To overcome this problem, he goes on a dangerous quest for a gem. The story concludes with the values taught by the Buddha: "Then a great assembly of people gathered, and Great Gift taught them how to be happy and live together in harmony. Following his teachings, they were kind and generous to each other for the rest of their lives" (p. 26, unnumbered).

The themes of unswerving devotion to truth, integrity, and friendship are developed in *Courageous Captain: A Jataka Tale,* retold by the Dharma Publishing Staff. When young sailors are saved by the captain's knowledge and virtue, the youths discover that the most important treasures are wisdom, compassion, and mindful action. Throughout the story, the captain illustrates the importance of wisdom, strength, determination, and unselfish actions, which allow one to take command of one's fate.

Selfless generosity and actions are also the powerful force of goodness that opens hearts in *The Rabbit in the Moon: A Jataka Tale* also by the Dharma Publishing

Staff. In this tale, a great being in the form of a rabbit possesses such a pure heart that even the greedy learn to share, the sly do not steal, and the mischievous forget to tease. Not only does the ending of the tale present the theme, but it also reveals why there is the shape of a rabbit in the moon: "Then in order to remind the world of the power of selflessness, he placed the rabbit in the moon, where he has dwelt from that day forward. Every month when the moon is full, the shape of the rabbit with the pure heart can be seen in the silvery moon" (p. 20, unnumbered). In Judith Ernst's retelling of *The Golden Goose King: A Tale Told by the Buddha,* the storyteller uses another tale told by the Buddha to reveal how a king and queen should rule wisely. Another source for Buddha tales is *The Wisdom of the Crows and Other Buddhist Tales,* retold by Sherab Chodzin and Alexandra Kohn.

As you read the folklore of India, notice the importance of the Hindu and Buddhist religions. Also try to discover the types of folktales—especially the male-centered tales, the women-centered tales, the family relationship tales, the tales about gods and demons, the humorous tales, and the animal tales. The folklore we have discussed develops such values as devotion to truth, integrity, friendship, and selfless actions.

Folklore from Japan

The folklore of Japan presents a complex subject because the early Japanese were influenced by the peoples of China, Korea, and other countries of the Asiatic continent. The myths were preserved by oral tradition through the Katari-be, a group of reciters whose function was to recite the ancient myths and legends during the Shinto festivals. The Katari-be were believed to be closely linked with the priests and priestesses who related ancient tales about the gods or the tribe during religious services.

In 681, Emperor Temmu ordered a committee to place the old traditions into writing. At the beginning of the eighth century, Japanese folklore was used as a source to compile the old histories of Japan. In 711, the Empress Gemmyo ordered the collection of old legends. This work was completed in 712 under the title of *Kojki.* In 720, *Jindaiki* was presented to the Emperor.

Royal Tyler (1987) states that many of the tales in his large collection of folklore titled *Japanese Tales* were gathered beginning in the early 700s, although most of the tales were collected between A.D. 1100 and 1350. Many of the tales in this collection tell about things that happened between 850 and 1050, a classic period in Japanese civilization.

Like the folklore of India, the folklore of Japan is influenced by religion. Medieval Japan was as steeped in religion as medieval Europe. Buddhism was dominant, but other religions or magical traditions were important too. Buddhism emphasized honoring of nature—mountains, valleys, and rivers play a great part in enlightenment. The treatment of the dead is also influenced by Buddhism. Buddhist rites had to be performed daily for the first seven days after death, then every seventh day thereafter until the forty-ninth day. Without this care, spirits were miserable and could easily linger on as harmful or unhappy ghosts.

The folktales of Japan also include supernatural monsters and beasts such as demons, tengu, foxes, badgers, dragons, turtles, snakes, and boar. The greatest trickster in Japanese folklore is the fox. Foxes are famous in Japanese folklore for masquerading as beautiful women. Dragons and snakes are closely associated in Japanese folklore with the water. The dragon may be associated with the energy of the water cycle: rain, river, sea, vapor, and rain. Dragon symbols are common in both folklore and in East Asian painting.

Examples of Japanese Folklore Japanese folklore is influenced by the folklore of India and China. The importance of the teachings of the Buddha illustrates the impact of this religion on Japanese culture. Two of the tales in Royal Tyler's *Japanese Tales* provide sources for understanding the importance of meditation, contemplation, and nature. For example, in the tale "Paradise in the Palm of the Hand," the hero discovers that he must contemplate the Buddha's countenance and the beauty of paradise if he is to enter paradise. In "Among the Flowers," a monk discovers the beauty and religion found in nature when he finds a man who lives in reverence in a field of flowers.

The Buddha plays an important role in Fiona French's *Little Inchkin*. After bravely protecting Prince Sanjo's daughter from two fiery demons, the small hero is rewarded by Lord Buddha, who grants his dearest wish: to be as tall as other men. The story ends with a moral that emphasizes both the importance of his brave actions and the honoring of the samurai warriors because small or tall he becomes "the most honored samurai swordsman in the land" (unnumbered).

Ellen S. Shapiro (1987) in her introduction to Grace James's *Green Willow and Other Japanese Fairy Tales* summarizes some of the characteristics of Japanese folktales. According to Shapiro, the stories include appreciation for the beauty and mystery of life, belief in the power of the spirit to accomplish its will, and ridicule for pretensions. In her discussion of style associated with Japanese folktales, Shapiro emphasizes that short phrases and repetitive sentences have great emotional impact, as in this quote from "The Wind in the Pine Tree" " . . . the heavenly deity descended. Lightly, lightly he came by way of the Floating Bridge, bearing the tree in his right hand. Lightly, lightly his feet touched the earth" (p. x).

Chinese culture influenced Japanese culture, and many Japanese tales are similar to Chinese tales. Dragons, for example, are common in tales from both countries. The tiger, usually considered a symbol of power, is a creature often found in Japanese tales. The cat is important in Arthur Levine's *The Boy Who Drew Cats: A Japanese Folktale*. When a boy paints cats on screens after he is trapped in an abandoned temple, the cats come alive to save him from a giant rat.

Japanese folktales reflecting respected values and disliked human qualities include Katherine Paterson's *The Tale of the Mandarin Ducks*. Paterson develops strong messages, such as kindness will be rewarded, creatures cannot survive when held captive, honor is important, and sharing helps people through trouble. These respected values are developed when two servants help a coveted mandarin duck that has been captured by a greedy lord. When the kitchen maid releases the duck against the lord's command, she and another servant are sentenced to death. The grateful drake and his mate, however, outwit the lord and reward the kindness of the servants. In Yoshiko Uchida's *The Magic Purse*, a courageous act brings rewards.

Cranes are frequently important in Japanese folktales. Anne Laurin's *The Perfect Crane* suggests the desirability of friendship between humans and supernatural creatures. In this story, a lonely magician develops a strong friendship with a crane that he creates from rice paper. Molly Bang's *The Paper Crane* has a similar theme. A hungry man rewards a restaurant owner with a paper crane that can be brought to life by clapping hands, and this attraction creates many customers for the business. A sadder outcome is developed in Odds Bodkin's *The Crane Wife* when the husband makes selfish demands on his wife, who is a crane transformed into a woman.

Dianne Snyder's *The Boy of the Three-Year Nap* has a strong female protagonist who outwits her lazy son. The tale is a humorous match of wits. The lazy son tries to trick a wealthy merchant into letting him marry the merchant's daughter. The mother, however, shows that she is the equal of the son. She not only convinces the merchant to repair and enlarge her house but also tricks her son into getting a job. Other strong female protagonists are found in *Three Strong Women*, retold by Claus Stamm and in Robert D. San Souci's *The Samurai's Daughter: A Japanese Legend*.

Respecting the wisdom of older people is an important value in Japanese folklore, as it was in other Asian traditional literature. Yoshiko Uchida's *The Wise Old Woman* is set in medieval Japan. A cruel lord declares that people over the age of seventy should be abandoned in the mountains. The value of older people is established, however, when a young farmer with the help of his mother is able to arrive at the solutions to meet three seemingly impossible tasks. The story develops the strong theme that wisdom comes with age.

Strong associations with nature and ecology are developed in Sheila Hamanaka's *Screen of Frogs*. A landowner responds favorably when a large frog appears in a dream and asks the man not to sell his home. Through the dream, the frog stresses the disasters that will occur if the frogs do not retain their land. As a reward for not selling the land, a tattered white screen belonging to the man is transformed into a beautifully painted screen of frogs.

Other Asian Folklore

The Asian Cultural Centre for UNESCO has published a series of five books called *Folktales from Asia for Children Everywhere*. The series contains stories from many Asian countries. For example, a story from Burma, "The Four Puppets," stresses the harm that wealth and power can bring if they are not tempered with wisdom and love. "The Carpenter's Son," a tale from Afghanistan, is similar to the Arabian story of Aladdin and his magic lamp. Additional collections of tales are found in David Conger's *Many Lands, Many Stories: Asian Folktales for Children*. Conger's text is a collection of stories from China, India, Japan, Korea, and Thailand. Conger has retold the tales for young readers. In *The Golden Carp and Other Tales from Vietnam*, a collection of six folktales, Lynette Dyer Vuong includes sources for the tales, interpretive notes, and pronunciation guides.

Nami Rhee's *The Magic Spring: A Korean Folktale* uses humorous irony to illustrate the consequences of greed. When a poor, older couple discover a magic spring in the forest, they learn that a drink returns them to their youth. When their rich, greedy neighbor learns about their secret, he goes in search of the spring. Unfortunately, his greed causes him to drink too much water and he becomes an infant. The rejuvenated couple find him in the forest and raise him as their child.

The rewarding of goodness and the punishment of cruelty are the themes developed in Nina Jaffe's *Older Brother, Younger Brother: A Korean Folktale*. When the father dies, the greedy elder brother inherits his father's property and banishes the good younger brother and his family. The younger brother's continuing generous nature is rewarded, however, and he eventually shows the older brother the errors of his ways.

Suzanne Crowder Han uses a format in which she writes the text of her tales in both Korean and English. *The Rabbit's Escape* is a tale in which a rabbit uses his wits to escape death, and a loyal turtle is rewarded for his fidelity with a ginseng cure for the king. Han's *The Rabbit's Judgment* is a Korean variant of "The Tiger, the Brahmin, and the Jackal."

Eastern folktales contain such universal motifs as reward for unselfishness, assistance from magical objects, cruel adversaries, and punishment for dishonesty. The tales also emphasize the traditional values of the specific people: homage is paid to ancestors, knowledge and cleverness are rewarded, and greed and miserly behavior are punished. The in-depth view of the folktales from the various cultures shows us how important are the traditional values of that culture as reflected in the folklore.

Fantasy Selections That Have Threads with Folklore

Authors of modern fantasy frequently use settings, themes, and motifs that are very similar to ones in folklore. For example, in *The Bird Who Was an Elephant,* author Aleph Kamal uses a thread of Hindu belief. In his author's note, he asks, "How could a bird have been an elephant?" He then explains that the Hindus in India believe that we have many lives and that when we do we become another human being, or an animal. Both the illustrations and the text are based on Hindu's beliefs.

Florence Karpin's fantasy picture storybook *The Prince in the Golden Tower* is another book that develops themes and plots similar to those in folklore. As you read the following summary of the book, notice how its plot and themes are similar to those in folklore. The author emphasizes the themes of keeping promises and caring for the poor through a story about an emperor who wishes for a son. After the son is born, the emperor places him in a high tower where he keeps him secure since the boy is the heir to his golden empire. A mythical tiger enters the picture: the prince sees a pure white tiger emerge in the moonlight. The prince unlatches the window, climbs out, and descends on leafy vines. He gets astride the tiger's back and is taken on a journey through the night where he sees many things, including land afflicted with drought and poverty and overcrowding. Through these experiences the prince feels compassion for the land and the people. His father, however, does not keep a promise made to share his gold with the poor. Consequently, the prince once again rides the white tiger's back, his father is punished, and Prince Sanjay becomes king and rules with justice and charity all of his days.

Jennifer Armstrong's *Wan Hu Is in the Stars* is a picture storybook whose hero is so absentminded that he writes verses with water instead of ink. He is also preoccupied with the stars. The plot follows the hero as he tries to travel to the stars with such techniques as harnessing geese and cranes. When this technique is unsuccessful, he can only imagine being pulled toward the stars until he discovers the power possible by sitting on forty-seven lit rockets. The book ends in a way common in folkloric tradition, with a new star formation appearing in the sky: "And some believe Wan Hu achieved his only hope and one desire. The gardener is sure that he did" (unnumbered).

 ## EARLY HISTORY OF THE PEOPLE AND THE CULTURE

Informational books, biographies, and historical fiction present information about the early history and cultures of the people from China, India, Japan, and other Asian countries.

Informational Books That Depict Asian History

The Silk and Spice routes that ran from China to European cities from about 100 B.C. to A.D. 1500 are popular subjects for informational books. These books illustrate the importance of the routes for transferring not only goods but also knowledge. The routes promoted culture exchange and exchange of religious beliefs as well.

Paul Strathern's *Exploration by Land: The Silk and Spice Routes* presents information about the ancient routes that linked China in the East with Europe in the West. According to the author, the interlocking paths covered a distance of more than 5,000 miles. The text highlights the importance of the routes for exchanging of goods such as silk, jade, and spices; the spreading of technologies such as printing and papermaking; and the expanding of religions and other beliefs. The text includes a map of the Silk and Spice routes and chapters that discuss topics such as a bridge between East and West, the opening of the Silk Route, controlling the Silk Route, the paths to new beliefs, and the Silk Route and the Mongols.

In the following quote from Strathern's text, notice how the author introduces the importance of the route: "It was around the start of the first century before the birth of Christ (100 B.C.) that the many different links in a long trading chain came together to form what we now call the Silk Route . . . from its early origins until its final decline around A.D. 1500, when the sea routes took over as the main trade links between East and West" (p. 7).

Other books about the trade routes include Struan Reid's *Cultures and Civilizations: The Silk and Spice Routes* and John S. Major's *The Silk Route: 7,000 Miles of History*. The focus of Major's text, as well as Stephen Fieser's illustrations accompanying the text, are the cities along the way and explanations about the importance of the cities to the caravan's progress. Readers receive a feeling of the different cultures as the author discusses topics such as religion, industry, and daily life of people who lived along the route. Readers may authenticate the impact of the trade routes on the expansion of religious beliefs by reading Reza's "Pilgrimage to China's Buddhist Caves" (1996). This article in *National Geographic* shows the impact of Buddhism's influences on the cave paintings dating from A.D. 400 to 700 along China's Silk Route.

As sea travel became more common, the traders began to use the oceans rather than the land. In 1853, Commodore Matthew Perry traveled to Japan in an attempt to open Japan to U.S. trade. Rhoda Blumberg's *Commodore Perry in the Land of the Shogun* depicts the attempts of the American naval officer Matthew Perry to open Japanese harbors to U.S. trade. This book, an excellent choice for multicultural studies, strongly emphasizes the dramatic interactions between Perry and the Japanese. Reproductions of the original drawings that recorded the expedition, contemporaneous Japanese scrolls and handbills, and photographs from the period enhance children's understanding of the setting and Japanese culture.

In the following introduction to *Commodore Perry in the Land of the Shogun,* notice how Blumberg creates interest in the informational book; she uses a folktale reference to suggest the profound effect Perry's arrival might have had on the Japanese who witnessed it:

> If monsters had descended upon Japan the effect could not have been more terrifying.
> People in the fishing village of Shimoda were the first to spot four huge hulks, two streaming smoke, on the ocean's surface approaching the shore. "Giant dragons puffing smoke," cried some. "Alien ships of fire," cried others. According to a folktale, smoke above water was made by the breath of clams. Only a child would believe that. Perhaps enemies knew how to push erupting volcanoes toward the Japanese home-

land. Surely something horrible was happening on this day, Friday, July 8, 1853. (p. 13)

The author includes several appendices, including some with firsthand sources. There is a letter from the president of the United States, Millard Fillmore, to the emperor of Japan; a translation of the answer to the president's letter, signed by Yenosuke, the chief interpreter; a list of some of the American presents for the Japanese; a list of some of the Japanese presents for the Americans; and the text of the Treaty of Kanagawa, a treaty designed for "a perfect, permanent, and universal peace, and a sincere and cordial amity between the United States of America, and on the one part, and the Empire of Japan on the other . . . " (p. 131). The text also includes author's notes, a bibliography, and an index.

In a book titled *In the Land of the Taj Mahal: The World of the Fabulous Mughals,* author Ed Rothfarb takes readers on an extended tour through the history, architecture, art, and literature of India. Numerous labeled drawings, a glossary, sources listed by chapter, and an index provide considerable assistance to the reader who wants to learn more about Indian history.

Biographies About Figures from Early Culture

Many biographies of early personages are about the Buddha. For example, Susan L. Roth's *Buddha* presents the early life of Prince Siddhartha. Readers discover that before the prince's birth, a wise man predicts that the child to be born will become a very holy man. Readers discover that, during the prince's early years, he learns to read, write, ride, and shoot, but he cannot learn to kill. The author focuses on experiences that led Prince Siddhartha to become a holy man and try to find a way to end the suffering in the world. The author's afterward discusses information about Siddhartha's life. It covers the time after he renounces his earthly possessions, living in the forest studying and meditating. Near the city of Benares, India, he delivers his Deer Park sermon, one of the most sacred events in the history of Buddhism. During this period, he presents his Noble Eightfold Path and Doctrine of the Four Truths, all of which emphasize gentleness, kindness, and love. It is interesting that 2,500 years later Buddhism is one of the world's major religions with more than 250 million followers. A biography of Buddha may be read in association with the various Jataka tales that are related to the early teachings of the Buddha.

Demi's *Chingis Khan* is a highly illustrated biography of the Mongol leader, born in 1160, who conquered Persia and China. In this biography that combines both history and legend, Demi recounts the Khan's early experiences, which help make him into a great leader. The story also present the details about the selection of the Khan's four commanders. The text includes mythical characters such as Bei Ulgan, the Everlasting Blue Sky God, and emphasizes the influences of such characters on Khan's life. Demi's illustrations depict both the Oriental splendor of the time period and the natural environment of the northern steppes.

Historical Fiction About Asian Cultures

Fascinating historical fiction books about ancient Asian cultures are available about time periods such as feudal Japan and early China. In this section, we will progress on an historical time line from books set in the earlier time periods to later time periods. We will conclude with the historical fiction books about Asian cultures that are set in the United States.

Jean Merrill's *The Girl Who Loved Caterpillars* is one of the most interesting picture storybooks: it is set in twelfth-century Japan. According to the author's note, the story is adapted from an anonymous Japanese story found on a scroll. The author also provides sources for three English translations that were used as the basis for the adaptation. The story presents a strong, clever female character, Izumi, who resists social and family pressures as she develops her own interests. The author contrasts Izumi's interests with those of a noblewoman called "The Lady Who Loved Butterflies," who was considered to be "The Perfect Lady" because "she dressed exquisitely, wrote poetry in a delicate script, and played with skill on the lute and the sho" (unnumbered). In contrast, Izumi loves caterpillars and other living creatures that most people dislike to touch. In addition, Izumi does not blacken her teeth or trim her bushy eyebrows. The story ends with a mystery because, according to Merrill, the original scroll inferred that this was part of a longer story that would be found in the second chapter. Unfortunately, the second chapter has been lost. Interesting speculations could be made, however, as readers consider what might have happened to this wise woman who was so interested in nature. Would she become a scientist, a philosopher, or did she become alienated from her family and society, or have some other fate?

Erik Christian Haugaard's *The Boy and the Samurai* is set in feudal Japan during the period of civil wars in the late 1400s and 1500s. As do the authors of many other stories with wartime settings, Haugaard emphasizes the search for peace and the painful realities resulting from war. Haugaard's settings and characters allow readers to visualize the world of street orphans, warlords, samurai, and priests.

Haugaard uses several techniques to help involve his readers and make the story seem more immediate. For example, in the preface, Haugaard introduces the book in the first person, as if he is telling his own autobiography: "As I wrote the tale of my youth, I relived it with each stroke of the brush. When I had finished I felt that a burden had been taken from me. . . . I felt at ease with myself" (p. xxi).

Another technique used by Haugaard is the inclusion of cultural traditions and beliefs throughout the text. For example, as the young boy thinks to himself, he also reveals his belief in the god, Oinari-sama:

> Oinari-sama is the god of rice and has two foxes who serve him. The foxes carry messages and one of them has a roll of paper in his mouth. It is well known that foxes, as well as Tanuki the Badger and the Crane, can change themselves into human beings if they want to. I liked the little fox god and felt that he was nearer to being a child like myself, so I would sometimes pray to him. (p. 8)

As you read Haugaard's book, you might try to locate examples of important symbols and beliefs such as the following: the symbol of the monkey (p. 42), the belief in signs of luck (p. 45), belief in ill omens (p. 49), the importance of being able to compose poetry (p. 136), the belief that writing poetry is the noblest of the arts (p. 137), the belief in benefits of honor and disadvantages for greed (p. 162), and the importance of bravery (p. 168).

In addition to a belief in Oinari-sama, Haugaard stresses the importance of Buddha. Notice in the following exchange between the boy, Saru, and the priest, Jogen, how the author develops the importance of searching for the right way:

> "Maybe each man has to find his own way." The priest smiled. "Maybe, Saru, it is the searching which enables you to get to Buddha. Maybe no one can tell anyone how to get to Buddha." Then he laughed. "But you, Saru, are a follower of Oinari-sama.

You do not want to become a Buddha—you want to become a fox. . . . Buddha belongs to those who search for him." Priest Jogen looked solemn. "That is the only thing that I am sure of. Everything else is like a man's thoughts: little fluffy clouds in the sky which might disappear any moment." (p. 124)

The Boy and the Samurai provides an interesting historical fiction text to use as the basis for searching for beliefs and values that are also depicted in the traditional folklore and in the art of ancient Japan.

Haugaard has written another historical fiction novel about the days of the samurai, titled *The Revenge of the Forty-Seven Samurai*. In this book, the author explores the ethical implications of the suicidal mission of honor of the samurai. In an epilogue, he encourages readers to ponder the mores of the culture when one of the characters is asked, "Would you have done it?" He responds, "No, I would not. . . . But then I am not a samurai."

The Ghost in the Tokaido Inn by Dorothy and Thomas Hoobler is set in eighteenth-century Japan. The authors include considerable detail about the culture, values, and beliefs of this time period as they tell a story about a fourteen year old who longs to become a samurai even though he was not born into the class that allowed him to become one. The authors use the solving of a mystery to help the hero prove his ability and prove himself to be worthy to the shogun. Through the solving of the mystery, the authors develop the theme that it is important to search for, and to follow, the correct path.

Laurence Yep's *The Serpent's Children* and Katherine Paterson's *Rebels of the Heavenly Kingdom* are set during the time of the Taiping Rebellion in nineteenth-century China, a time when many Chinese were fighting both British invaders and Manchu domination.

History and legend are both important in *The Serpent's Children*. Yep describes the setting, the British invaders, and the conflicts of the period. Yep explains the meaning of his title, *The Serpent's Children*, by telling a folktale to show the belief in snake spirits and the relationships of the heroine and hero, Cassia and Foxfire, with the serpent clan. The importance of the serpent clan and the related characteristics of those who belong to the clan are used throughout the book.

Yep effectively uses serpent characteristics to reveal Cassia's character. For example, the following is from an argument she uses at one point in the book.

As usual, though, I tried to turn my bloodline to my advantage. "Serpents may crawl on their bellies, but they aren't cowards. They always get their revenge even if they have to die. We'll show you what honor means at least to one family. We'll drive them out single-handed if we have to. Do you think the warriors in our family end with Father?" (p. 97).

In addition to building plots on the basis of history and characterization on the basis of folklore, Yep develops additional Chinese values such as oneness with ancestors, a belief in the spirits of the dead, the importance of shaping women's feet to make them small, the preference for boys because of the need for a male heir to provide food and money for the family and ancestors, respecting the harmonies of nature, and creating peace within oneself.

Paterson's *Rebels of the Heavenly Kingdom* focuses on Wang Lee and a secret group called the God-worshipping Society, which is dedicated to overthrowing the Manchu emperor. Paterson, like Yep, uses many Chinese values in the development of the plot and characterizations. For example, learning to read and write is of the greatest value because a scholar is given the highest esteem. Numerous conflicts are created by Paterson as her characters consider conflicts between Confucius and Christianity and conflicts created by killing and the revolution.

Elizabeth Foreman Lewis's Newbery Medal book, *Young Fu of the Upper Yangtze*, is set in the turmoil of China in the 1920s, a time of warlords, bandits, artisans, and scholars. As in the books by Yep and Paterson, the book describes historical incidents, as well as beliefs and values of the times. Throughout the book, Lewis highlights values and beliefs, such as valuing good artisans, respecting learning and knowledge, understanding the importance of not losing face, using storytelling to reveal history, understanding the richness in books, believing in omens, and building character by rising above one's misfortunes. The book concludes with a series of notes that contrast the life in China then and now. The notes are divided into subjects: transportation, education, coinage, streets, superstitions and "The Four Old Ones," foot binding, beggars and bandits, sanitation, floods, reverence for age, and marriage customs. These notes written for a 1973 edition expand on notes written for the 1932 edition. Students could make interesting comparisons by bringing the notes up to date as if they were written for a current edition.

Authors of historical fiction books with Chinese American heroes and heroines frequently develop themes about the difficulty of acculturation. In these books, the main characters frequently assimilate the mainstream culture while retaining their Chinese identity and value systems.

There are several award-winning historical fiction books with Chinese protagonists set in the United States. Both Laurence Yep's *Dragon's Gate* and *Dragonwings* were awarded the Newbery Honor Book award. Yep's characters do not reflect the stereotypes associated with literature about Asian Americans, and his stories integrate information about Chinese cultural heritage into the stories of everyday lives of his characters.

Mingshui Cai (1994) discusses examples of the acculturation found in Yep's novels: "They cover themes like poverty, racial discrimination, marginalization, and loss of identity, which are typical of multicultural literature; and most significantly, they represent Chinese Americans' process of acculturation as a way out of the dilemma of being caught in two worlds" (p. 108). Cai argues that Yep's novels contain two aspects of acculturation, "assimilating to the mainstream culture while maintaining Chinese identity" (p. 109).

Yep's *Dragon's Gate* is set in the Sierra Nevada mountains in 1867 when Chinese immigrants are working on the transcontinental railroad. Yep begins his story in China and provides a historical perspective that allows readers to understand the viewpoint of the Chinese and to understand some of the reasons that Chinese people might have desired to immigrate to America. As the story progresses, Yep shows the economic need of the characters to learn English and to go to the United States. He also develops the characters' beliefs in the freedom found in United States when Father explains that the Civil War in America is being fought to free slaves because, "Everybody there, they free. Everybody, they equal" (p. 3).

Yep tells the story through the point of view of a Chinese boy named Otter. Through his experiences on the cold mountain and in the dangerous tunnel, Otter makes discoveries about cooperation, the importance of life, and courage. Through a dream and growing self-realization, Otter discovers the real reason for coming to American: "I remembered his advice (Uncle Foxfire) when I had failed my first test of courage: I could learn to change things or go on being changed by events. That was the real point of coming to America. He would want me to become like him and not remain like the others—even if it meant he had to stay here forever. My

Grandfather's Journey

ALLEN SAY

In *Grandfather's Journey*, a Japanese American tell about his grandfather's voyage to North America.

Source: Illustration from GRANDFATHER'S JOURNEY. Copyright© 1993 by Allen Say. Reprinted by permission of Houghton Mifflin Co. All rights reserved.

uncle wouldn't want me to waste my life up here" (p. 267). Retaining one's dream and one's identity are important in this novel.

Yep's *Dragonwings*, set in 1903 San Francisco, is based on a true incident in which a Chinese American built and flew an airplane. The characters are people who retain their values and respect for their heritage while adjusting to a new country. The "town of the Tang people" is eight-year-old Moon Shadow's destination when he leaves his mother in the Middle Kingdom (China). He is filled with conflicting emotions when he first meets his father in the country that some call the "Land of the Demons" and others call the "Land of the Golden Mountain."

As the story progresses, Moon Shadow learns that his stereotype of the white demons is not always accurate. When he and his father move away from the Tang men's protection, Moon Shadow meets and talks to his first demon. Instead of being ten feet tall, with blue skin and a face covered with warts, the "demon" is a petite woman who is very friendly and considerate. As Moon Shadow and his father get to know this Anglo-Saxon woman and her family, all learn to respect people of different backgrounds as individuals. And when they share what they have learned, the father concludes: "We see the same thing and yet find different truths."

Readers also discover that many stereotypes about Chinese Americans are incorrect. This book is especially strong in its coverage of Chinese traditions and beliefs. For example, readers learn about the great respect that Chinese Americans feel for the aged and the dead. Family obligations do not end when a family member has died. As Moon Shadow seeks to educate his non-Chinese friend about the nature of dragons, readers discover traditional Chinese tales about a benevolent and wise dragon who is king among reptiles and emperor of animals. Readers realize the value of honor as the doubting Tang men pull *Dragonwings* up the hill for its maiden voyage. They do not laugh even though they may doubt the plane's ability to fly. To laugh would be an insult to Moon Shadow's father. Children who read this story learn about the contributions and struggles of the Chinese Americans and the prejudice that they still experience.

Stories about early immigrant experiences in the United States are popular subjects in children's books. Allen Say's *Grandfather's Journey* is an immigration story that includes two journeys: one to California and then, many years later, one back to visit the Japan of his youth. The story also covers the time of World War II, when Grandfather cannot return to California again, but he tells his grandson, Allen Say, stories about the United States. *Grandfather's Journey* is an excellent companion for Say's *Tree of Cranes*, which is set in Japan. The story shows the melding of two cultures. The boy's mother, who was born in the United States, prepares a Christmas celebration that combines the Japanese and U.S. cultures.

Paul Yee's *Tales from Gold Mountain: Stories of the Chinese in the New World* includes eight stories about Chinese immigrants in the United States and Canada. You may find it helpful to compare Yee's stories with those developed in Yep's *Dragonwings*.

POETRY

Poetry forms a bridge between the older and more contemporary literature. Poetry by Asian and Asian American poets reflects the ancient values and beliefs as well as contemporary concerns. Many of the poems are found in both highly illustrated volumes for younger children and anthologies that may be enjoyed by all ages.

The universality of nursery rhymes is found by reading Demi's *Dragonkites and Dragonflies: A Collection of Chinese Nursery Rhymes*. The rhymes, many using rhythmic and rhyming language, focus on topics such as playing games, seeing dragon boats, beating the drums for a bride carried in a chair, and contemplating fireflies lighting up the sky. Demi's illustrations depict a colorful setting that makes the subjects of the nursery rhymes come to life. Japanese artist Satomi Ichikawa includes a Hindu and a Japanese prayer in *Here a Little Child I Stand: Poems of Prayer and Praise for Children*. The Hindu prayer glorifies God in fire, water, and plants. The Japanese prayer asks the Creator to help us love one another and bring peace to the world.

Several poems in *Eric Carle's Animals Animals*, selected by Laura Whipple, are Japanese haiku that provide images of leaping flying fish, dancing butterflies, and galloping ponies. A series of haiku poems are also located in *Talking to the Sun: An Illustrated Anthology of Poems for Young People* selected by Kenneth Koch and Kate Farrell. This anthology also includes poems from ancient India and China. A poem written in China during the first century B.C. provides a theme of friendship.

Poems in Naomi Shihab Nye's *This Same Sky: A Collection of Poems from Around the World* include ones from China, India, Japan, South Korea, and Vietnam. As students of children's literature, you may analyze and compare the content of these poems and search for underlying themes. As you make this search, try to discover both similarities and differences across the cultural groups. There are poems about dreams and desires such as "My Life Story," written by Lan Nguyen of Vietnam, in which the poet wishes she could do something for her people. There are poems about the beauties found in nature such as "House of Spring," written by Muso Soseki of Japan, in which the poet views hundreds of open flowers and the colors that appear in the garden. There are poems about creating a future such as "A Headstrong Boy," written by Gu Cheng from China, in which the poet wants to draw a future that has never been seen and paint out every sorrow. There are poems about the joys of reading such as "Companion," written by Manjush Dasgupta from India, in which the poet grows from a player with butterflies who does not read to a person whose constant companions are books. There are poems of longing for remembered scents and people associated with them such as "Jasmine" by Kyongjoo Hong Ryou of South Korea, in which the poet associates the fragrance of the scents with a mother who is now dead.

The subjects in Janet S. Wong's *Good Luck Gold and Other Poems* reflect the experiences of a contemporary Asian American. Some of the poems such as "Bound Feet" and "Jade" provide glimpses into traditional values and beliefs. Other poems such as "Waiting at the Railroad Cafe," "Speak Up," and "All Mixed Up" suggest the inner conflicts experienced by many Asian Americans. The themes found in Wong's poems are also found in many contemporary literature selections.

CONTEMPORARY LITERATURE WITH ASIAN ROOTS

Nonfiction writing that focuses on various Asian cultures frequently presents both histories of, and contemporary practices associated with, religious beliefs. Other informational books present general information about Asian people, their countries, and their cultures. Several informational books describe the importance of Asian American culture. Biographies are about the important leaders and artists.

Informational Books

Many of the informational books on Asian cultures provide information about religious beliefs common in the cultures. For example, Catherine Hewitt's *Buddhism*, part of the World Religions Series, is an illustrated history that provides explanations of the beliefs and practices of Buddhism. The text begins with a discussion about the Four Noble Truths (there is suffering, the cause of suffering is wanting, suffering can end completely, and the Eightfold Path is the cure) and the importance of the Eightfold Path (right understanding, right thought, right speech, right action, right work, right effort, right mindfulness, and right meditation). The text includes considerable information about the background of Buddha and Buddhism and the importance of various Buddhist teachings. The text includes maps showing major locations of Buddhist populations. Color coding helps readers locate areas where Buddhism is the main religion and to identify countries where there are significant numbers of Buddhists. A glossary, a book list, and an index increase the usefulness of the book.

Hinduism is another major religion of Asian populations. Madhu Bazaz Wangu's *Hinduism: World Religions* informs readers that Hinduism is the third largest religion in the world, with over 650 million Hindus throughout the world. The text and labeled photographs cover topics such as "The Modern Hindu World," "The Roots of Hinduism," "The Late Vedic Period," "The Gods and Devotion," "Political and Social Change," "The Hindu Temple," and "Social Duty and Rites of Passage."

Anita Ganeri's *Benares,* in the Holy Cities series published by Dillon, discusses various aspects of one of India's holy cities. The text, which is illustrated with color photographs, covers such topics as Hindu beliefs, gods and goddesses, temples, legends and traditions, festivals and celebrations, daily life, language and literature, learning, and important events. The text includes a list of further readings and an index. As you read books such as *Benares,* notice the importance of many of the traditional beliefs, which are also developed in the folklore.

Another book in the Holy Cities series emphasizes the Sikhs and their holy city of Amritsar. Beryl Dhanjal's *Amritsar* describes this most holy city, which is located in Punjab in northwest India. The text includes photographs and text on subjects such as gurus and their teaching, temples and shrines, art and architecture, legends and traditions, festivals and celebrations, and important events. There are also a list of further reading and an index.

Sikhism is also described in Nikky-Guinder Kaur Singh's *Sikhism: World Religions.* The text describes the origins and history of the religion, central beliefs, and rituals of the approximate 12 million Sikhs. The text includes labeled black-and-white illustrations, glossary, a list for further reading, and index. If you are doing research in feminist studies, you will be interested to learn that according to the author, women are considered equal in this culture. Sikh literature contains women characters who display physical, intellectual, and spiritual strength.

In addition to texts that focus mainly on religious beliefs, there are numerous informational sources that focus on general information about a country. For example, Anita Ganeri's *Exploration into India* describes the history of the country, beginning with ancient India and continuing in chronological order to the India of today. The text includes a useful time chart comparing India, Europe, and other locations. The text also includes a glossary and an index. Anita Ganeri and Jonardon Ganeri's *India* is another source of general information about the country's geography, climate, weather, natural resources, population, daily life, rules and laws, food and farming, trade and industry, transportation, environment, and the future. Each section includes about four key facts that may be used as a rapid source for information. Some of the sections include maps and graphs.

Jules Hermes's *The Children of India* describes the daily lives of children from different regions in the country and from different social levels. Captioned photographs help readers visualize the daily lives of children from different backgrounds, including a young princess who lives in a palace, a boy born into the Shudra (laborer caste), a Hindu girl who lives in a large city and sells oil lamps to tourists, and a boy who is studying to become a Buddhist monk.

The "Enchantment of the World" series includes texts on many of the Asian cultures. Robert Zimmermann's *Enchantment of the World: Sri Lanka* introduces the island off the southern coast of India that was once called Ceylon. The text includes chapters that introduce the island's geography, history, religion, people and their daily life, interesting cities, art, economics, and politics. Captioned color photographs and maps that show the locations of the cities discussed enhance the text. Sylvia McNair's *Enchantment of the World: India*, and Jason Laure's *Enchantment of the World: Bangladesh* use a similar format.

In *I Remember India*, Anita Ganeri writes about her own experiences and memories of living in India. The author is now living in the United States. This book provides a brief introduction to India's land, people, and daily life. The style of the book is written in a way to interest children. For example, the introduction shows the picture of a girl and the text reads as follows:

> My name is Renu. I am from India. I was born in Calcutta, India's second largest city. When I was very young, my father decided to leave India. He could not find work there. My mother and I came with him. Now, I have two brothers who were born here. . . . Come with me, and find out about India. I'll help you learn all about the land, the people, and the Indian daily life. (p. 3)

This book written for younger readers includes captioned color photographs, a fact file, and an index.

Two authors have focused on the Ganges River. In *Sacred River*, Ted Lewin uses watercolors and text to introduce readers to the Ganges River as it passes through the holy city of Benares. This book, which presents most of its information through the illustrations, may be compared with David Cumming's *The Ganges*, in which the author provides a more comprehensive coverage of the topic. Cumming's text includes captioned color photographs, a glossary, a list of additional readings, addresses for additional information, and an index.

Informational books may explore the multicultural nature of United States and the Asian American cultures. Lauren Lee's *Korean Americans* focuses on the group's culture, family and community, religion and celebrations, various customs and expressions, and the contributions of Koreans to U.S. culture.

Biographies

The life of Indira Gandhi of India is the subject of several children's biographies as well as adult biographies. In addition, Gandhi wrote an autobiography. Consequently, these texts provide excellent sources for comparisons of biographical writing. You may choose to first read Indira Gandhi's autobiography, *My Truth* (1980). It provides information about her childhood and her feelings, how her personality was shaped, and how she came to govern one-sixth of the world's population. To broaden your understanding of the life of Indira Gandhi, her autobiography may be compared with an adult biography such as Paul Swaraji's *Indira Gandhi* (1985). The focus of Swaraji's biography is not on Gandhi's childhood, but on her political life after she becomes the prime minister. Swaraji explores the qualities that made Gandhi a dynamic leader including her understanding of people and politics and her worldwide vision. The biographer states, "Indira Gandhi's combination of coolness and poise under pressure contrasted sharply with the feebleness of many of her more senior colleagues" (p. 26). By examining both the autobiography and biography, readers can gain a clearer understanding of both her youth and her experiences as prime minister.

The information in several biographies of Indira Gandhi written for children may be compared with the information found in the adult texts. When Nandita Gurjar (1995), one of my graduate students from India, compared and authenticated the various biographies about Gandhi, she concluded that Shakuntala Masani's *The Story of Indira,* written for children, was authentic and written in an interesting style. When she analyzed Carol Greene's *Indira Nehru Gandhi: Ruler of India*, however, she concluded that the book written for younger children lacked authenticity. For example, Gurja found differences in statements about the location of Gandhi's birth, inaccuracies in information about Gandhi's father, and inaccuracies in statements about relationships between Mohandas Gandhi and Indira Gandhi. There are no sources listed in Greene's text; consequently, readers cannot identify the primary sources that may have been used by the author.

Additional biographies of Indira Gandhi that you might use for a similar activity include the following: Francelia Butler's *Indira Gandhi*, a biography written for older students that emphasizes the history, politics, and culture that shaped her life; Trevor Fishlock's *Indira Gandhi*, an illustrated biography written for younger readers that places Gandhi's life in the context of Indian history; and Manorama Jafa's *Indira Priyadarshini,* an illustrated biography that won the Children's Choice Award. Texts such as James Haskins' *India Under Indira and Rajiv Gandhi* chronicle the history of India under two leaders. The text includes a list of further readings of books and articles.

There are also numerous biographies of Mohandas Gandhi that may be used for comparison. For example, Victoria Sherrow's *Mohandas Gandhi: The Power of the Spirit* describes the life of the man who led a thirty-year struggle to free India from British rule. The author emphasizes the bitter conflicts between religious groups, including the conflict between Muslim Pakistan and Hindu India. The author presents a person whose deep moral sense gradually transforms him from an insecure young lawyer to a national leader whose influence transcended his time and place. Throughout the biography, readers discover a man who believed that social and political goals could be won without violence—through peaceful resistance, marches, demonstrations, and strikes. The biography includes source notes for each chapter and a chronology of events in Mohandas Gandhi's life up until his assassination in 1948.

Glenn Alan Cheney's *Mohandas Gandhi* also emphasizes Gandhi's nonviolent crusade. In addition to providing information about Gandhi's life, Cheney relates Gandhi's beliefs to the civil rights movement in the United States. Doris and Harold Faber's *Mahatama Gandhi* is based on Gandhi's autobiography.

Demi's *The Dalai Lama: A Biography of the Tibetan Spiritual and Political Leader* is a biography of the Buddhist leader. Demi's highly illustrated text provides numerous insights into the search for the spiritual leader after the death of the thirteenth Dalai Lama in 1933. Through the description of this search, as well as descriptions of the Dalai Lama's later life, the biographer explores the values and beliefs associated with the man who in 1989 received the Nobel Peace Prize. By quoting the words given by the Dalai Lama at this ceremony, notice how Demi reveals the important Buddhist values: "Because we all share this small planet earth, we have to learn to live in harmony and peace with each other and with nature. Live simply and love humanity. For as long as space endures and for as long as living beings remain, until then may I, too, abide to dispel the misery of the world" (unnumbered).

Ken Mochizuki's *Passage to Freedom: The Sugihara Story* is a highly acclaimed biography of the Japanese consul to Lithuania who helped many Jewish refugees escape from the Holocaust. The biographer presents a strong character who continues to grant visas for refugees to pass through the Soviet Union to Japan, even though the Japanese government denied Sugihara's requests to issue visas. The biographer chose an interesting style by telling the story through the voice of Sugihara's five-year-old son. An afterword by Sugihara's son places the heroic actions of his father into a contemporary context.

Mary Malone's *Connie Chung: Broadcast Journalist* is part of the Contemporary Women Series published by Enslow. This biography of the television journalist begins with the experiences of Chung's family as they leave a dangerous situation in China in the 1940s and immigrate to the United States. The major portion of the book focuses on Chung's various experiences in journalism including the Watergate affair and her experience as an anchor for television. The text includes black-and-white photographs that depict her life. Many of these photographs include other well-known journalists such as Edward R. Morrow, Walter Cronkite, and Dan Rather. The biography includes a chronology of Chung's life, as well as a list of further reading and an index.

Historical Fiction with More Contemporary Settings

Asian and Asian American literature set in more contemporary times frequently focuses on experiences during World War II, especially on those of Japanese Americans. For example, several books center their settings and plots on the internment of Japanese Americans. Many children are surprised to read stories about the treatment of Japanese Americans during World War II.

Two books by Yoshiko Uchida tell about a Japanese American family's experiences after the bombing of Pearl Harbor. (Although the stories are fictional, they are based on what happened to Uchida and her family.)

In Uchida's *Journey to Topaz*, the police take away Yuki's father, a businessman in Berkeley, California, and send Yuki, her mother, and her older brother to a permanent internment center in Utah, called Topaz. Uchida creates vivid pictures of the internment camp. She describes, for example, latrines without doors, lines of people waiting to use them, and the wind blowing across the desert into the barracks. The fear of the interned people and their wardens climaxes when the grandfather of Yuki's best friend goes searching for arrowheads and is shot by a guard who believes that he is trying to escape.

Yuki's story continues in *Journey Home*. The family returns to Berkeley, only to discover distrust, difficulty finding work, and anti-Japanese violence. The family feels hope and strength more than bitterness, however. Yuki discovers that coming home is having everyone she cares about around her. An interesting study may be made by comparing Uchida's historical fiction novels with her *Invisible Thread,* in which she tells about her own experiences.

Laurence Yep's *Hiroshima* is set in Japan in 1945, during the time of the nuclear bombing of Hiroshima. Yep includes descriptions of both the crewmen on the

Enola Gay, from which the atomic bomb was dropped, and the children in a Hiroshima classroom. Yep describes the various aspects of the bombing including the mushroom cloud and the destruction of the city. A section on the aftermath of the bombing covering the arms race and the peace movement should provide a springboard for interesting classroom discussions.

The setting for Graham Salisbury's *Under the Blood Red Sun* develops the historical time period associated with the Japanese bombing of Pearl Harbor on December 7, 1941. The following quote develops the sights and sounds of the actual bombing:

> Huge, awful black clouds of smoke rolled up into the sky from Pearl Harbor. You could barely see the ships, which were lined up in neat rows like chips of gray metal. The smoke was so thick you couldn't even see the mountains. Hundreds of planes circled the sky like black gnats, peeling off and dropping down to vanish into the boiling smoke, then reappearing, shooting skyward with engines groaning, circling back, sunlight flashing when they turned. (p. 106)

Throughout the book, Salisbury describes settings that allow readers an opportunity to vicariously experience the time period and the conflicts present during the war years.

The setting for Sook Nyul Choi's *Year of Impossible Goodbyes* is Japanese-occupied Korea at the close of World War II. The author develops the person-versus-society conflict experienced by Sookan, a ten-year-old Korean girl and her family, who experience the oppressive treatment of both the Japanese and Russian occupation of North Korea. The author uses many small details and incidents to make concrete the oppression experienced by the family and the family's longing for freedom. For example, the family is forbidden to grow flowers. In one incident, when the family manages to have a tiny patch of flowers, the Japanese police captain and his men trample the flowers. After many dangerous experiences, the children and their mother escape to South Korea. In her endnotes, the author states her reasons for writing this book: "Having lived through this turbulent period of Korean history, I wanted to share my experiences. So little is known about my homeland, its rich culture and its sad history. My love for my native country and for my adopted country prompted me to write this book to share some of my experiences and foster greater understanding" (unnumbered). You may find it useful to compare the settings, values, and themes in *Year of Impossible Goodbyes* with those developed by Helen Kim in *The Long Season of Rain,* which is set in Seoul Korea during the 1960s.

The themes in children's historical fiction with settings during World War II resemble themes in books describing other times of great peril. The stories written about the Japanese American experience frequently develop themes related to the beliefs that prejudice and hatred are destructive forces and moral obligation and personal conscience are strong forces.

Informational Books About World War II and Asian Experiences

There are several informational books that focus on true experiences of Japanese during World War II. Tatsuharu Kodama's *Shin's Tricycle* focuses on experiences during the nuclear bombing of Hiroshima. This story is told by a teacher who survived the bombing but saw his child die. It tells about a boy who receives a longed-for tricycle for his fourth birthday, only to be riding the tricycle at the time of the bombing. When Shin dies during the bombing, his parents bury him with the tricycle. The tricycle has recently been recovered and is now found in the Peace Museum in Hiroshima. The impact of this book could be compared with Toshi Maruki's *Hiroshima No Pika* which also depicts the consequences of the bombing.

Books that describe or depict nuclear war also vary depending on the intended audiences and the messages to be related. Compare the highly visual and personalized descriptions in Maruki's *Hiroshima No Pika* with Carl B. Feldbaum and Ronald J. Bee's historical and scientific descriptions in *Looking the Tiger in the Eye: Confronting the Nuclear Threat*. Using a picture-storybook format, Maruki relates the experiences of seven-year-old Mii on August 6, 1945, as the child and her mother pass by fire, death, and destruction. Maruki, who actively campaigns for nuclear disarmament and world peace, concludes her book on a hopeful note: "It can't happen again if no one drops the bomb" (p. 43, unnumbered). Feldbaum and Bee's text includes the history of nuclear weapons and discusses decisions made by political, scientific, and military officials.

Jerry Stanley's *I Am an American: A True Story of Japanese Internment* describes the events that led up to the internment of Japanese Americans living on the West Coast and the effects of this experience on the people. Ellen Levine's *A Fence Away from Freedom: Japanese Americans and World War II* includes personal narratives in which Japanese Americans describe their experiences. The text includes a bibliography, a glossary of terms, a chronology of major events, and a map of internment centers.

Contemporary Asian American Stories

The widest range of Asian American experiences in current children's literature is found in the works of Laurence Yep, who writes with sensitivity about Chinese Americans who, like himself, have lived in San Francisco, California. His characters overcome the stereotypes sometimes found in literature about Asian Americans, and his stories integrate information about Chinese cultural heritage into the everyday lives of his characters. We have already discussed several of his historical fiction novels set in the United States and his collection of folklore collected from Chinese Americans.

In *Child of the Owl*, Yep develops the story of a heroine, twelve-year-old Casey, who discovers that she knows more about her father's world of racehorses than about her own Chinese heritage. It is only after she is sent to live with Paw-Paw, her grandmother in San Francisco's Chinatown, that she makes discoveries about, and learns to understand, her Chinese heritage. The author uses a story about the Owl Spirit to help Casey make discoveries about her history.

Yep uses the owl as a symbol throughout the book. In an afterword, Yep states that he presented the owl story, "which is based upon stories of filial devotion once popular among the Chinese and upon Chinese folklore concerning owls and other animals" (p. 217). In *Thief of Hearts,* Yep has written another novel in which the main character gains cross-cultural understanding. Yep's *Later, Gator* develops themes related to sibling rivalry, as well as insights into Chinese American and white attitudes.

Betty Bao Lord, the author of *In the Year of the Boar and Jackie Robinson*, creates a story that reflects her own experiences and beliefs. Like her protagonist Shirley Temple Wong, Lord was a Chinese immigrant to the United States. Lord says: "Many feel that loss of one's native culture is the price one must pay for becoming an American. I do not feel this way. I think we hyphenated Americans are double blessed. We can choose the best of both" (endcover). Like Lord, her heroine Shirley discovers that she can adore baseball, the Brooklyn Dodgers, and Jackie Robinson and still maintain the bond of family and the bond of culture.

Memory, seeds, and traditional beliefs are very important in Sherry Garland's *The Lotus Seed*, a book written for younger children. In this story, a Vietnamese family resettles in the United States. During happier days in Vietnam, the grand-mother picks a seed from a lotus plant in the emperor's garden to remember a special occasion. Throughout her life, she looks at this seed during important moments in her life or when she feels sad. The seed is so important that she brings it to the United States when her family escapes the war. Years later, a grand-son carelessly throws out the seed, which saddens his grandmother tremendously. Luckily, the seed is thrown where it eventually grows into a lotus plant. When the blossom fades, the grandmother gives a seed to each of her grandchildren. Garland develops a universal theme about how small things and memories that they evoke are important in our lives.

Adjusting to a new culture and developing understanding of oneself and others are problems faced by many new Americans. Lensey Namioka's *Yang the Youngest and His Terrible Ear* is a humorous contemporary realistic fiction story that speaks to the needs of many readers. The author develops a protagonist, nine-year-old Yingtao, who is out of place in his musical family. Although he has a great eye, he has a terrible ear. Students of children's literature can analyze Yingtao's reactions to both learning English and trying to make his family understand that he is not, and will never be, a talented musician. The author helps readers visualize the prob-lems by relating them to Yingtao's Chinese background. In a satisfying ending, both the family of his American friend and Yingtao's own family realize the impor-tance of honoring one's gifts. *Yang the Third and Her Impossible Family* is a humor-ous sequel in which Yingmei Yang, the family's third daughter, tries her best to learn to be an American.

Trying to adjust to new classmates is a common plot developed in many of the Asian American stories. Michele Maria Surat's *Angel Child, Dragon Child* is a con-temporary realistic story about a young Vietnamese girl's difficulties developing associations with her classmates after her family moves to the United States. Phyl-lis Shalant's *Beware of Kissing Lizard Lips* is a humorous story about a Korean American boy who is trying to gain both self-confidence and acceptance by his classmates. The plots, characters, and themes in these books may encourage dis-cussion and promote understanding.

Picture books written for younger children frequently focus on young Asian American children as they become familiar with various aspects of their culture. For example, in *Chin Chiang and the Dragon's Dance*, Ian Wallace creates a satisfac-tory conclusion for a person-against-self conflict. Young readers can understand Chin Chiang's conflict. He has practiced for and dreamed of dancing the dragon's dance on the first day of the Year of the Dragon. The time arrives, but he runs away because he fears that he will not dance well enough to make his grandfather proud. With the help of a new friend, Chin Chiang discovers that his dream can come true. Full-page watercolor paintings capture the beauty of the celebration and depict Asian influences on the city of Vancouver. Kate Waters and Madeline Slovenz-Low's *Lion Dancer: Ernie Wan's Chinese New Year* is a photographic essay that follows a boy as he prepares to take part in the very important lion dance. Readers can make interesting comparisons between these two books.

Numerous experiences in the life of a Vietnamese American are shown through a photographic essay in Diane Hoyt-Goldsmith's *Hoang Anh: A Vietnamese-Ameri-*

APPLYING KNOWLEDGE OF CULTURAL VALUES AND BELIEFS TO *THE SUNITA EXPERIMENT*

Mitali Perkins's *The Sunita Experiment* has been named on several lists for outstanding books including New York Public Library Books for the Teen Age Reader, 1994; ALA Recommended Books for Reluctant Readers, 1994; and IRA-CBC Notable Books in the Field of Social Studies. The book about a family from India who now live in California, provides strong literary elements of character, conflict, and theme, as well as examples of cultural beliefs. Consequently, the book provides a good source for identifying the values and beliefs that are implicit or explicit in the story and relating those values and beliefs to the plot and characterization.

The Sunita Experiment is a story about a thirteen-year-old girl whose life in California changes when her grandparents come for a visit from India. The text provides many insights into both the Indian culture and the Indian American culture. Three generations are represented in the story: the grandparents, who have come to visit; the parents, who were originally from India but who have become quite "Westernized"; and their daughter, Sunita, who is totally "Westernized" and wants to remain that way. The clash of cultures is the main conflict of the story as Sunita struggles to understand her grandparent's culture.

As you read the following descriptions of Indian life-styles, values, and beliefs found in the book, try to authenticate them with what you know or have learned about the Indian culture. Also consider if and how these various beliefs might cause friction for an American teenager:

> Husbands have authority over their wives.
>
> Girls should not invite boys to their homes.
>
> Teaching is a preferred profession for women.
>
> Children stay with their parents until they are married.
>
> Marriages are arranged by the families.
>
> A woman's place is in the home.
>
> The education of women is becoming more acceptable.
>
> Respect for elders is important.

As you read the book, you may also trace the changes in Sunita as her character progresses from rejection of her cultural roots to acceptance of and appreciation for her cultural identity. For example, early in the book she experiences conflict in school because she does not want to identify her "roots" on a *National Geographic* map (p. 7) and then experiences additional feelings of person-versus-self conflict when most of the class identifies European ancestry. There are only three students who are not of European heritage: one identifies China, one identifies Africa, and Sunita reluctantly identifies India. After her grandparents arrive, Sunita is embarrassed by the differences between her home and the homes of her friends (pp. 12–14). Sunita resents the playing of Indian music in her home because the "twanging sitar music that grated on her nerves and made their house sound like a mecca for aging hippies. A grumpy neighbor had already complained three times since Sunita's grandparents had arrived" (p. 19). Sunita unfavorably contrasts her mother's normal tailored suits with the traditional saree she wears after her grandparents arrive (pp. 21–22). She is ashamed of her family's cultural differences (pp. 24–27). Sunita experiences embarrassment when her essay on arranged Indian marriages is read before the class (pp. 48–50). By the end of the book, however, Sunita respects her Indian heritage as demonstrated when she wears a saree because of her own choice and feels like an Indian princess (pp. 177–179).

As you authenticate the life-styles, values, and beliefs identified in the book, try to decide if the book is or is not authentic for the portrayal of Indian culture. As you read the book for portrayal of Sunita's characterization and conflict, decide if the author develops plausible characterization of, and conflict for, a girl living in two cultures.

can Boy. Lawrence Migdale's photographs show the daily activities of Hoang Anh and his family in San Rafael, California, as they work on their fishing boat, live and play at home, prepare for the New Year, and experience the Tet Festival. Patricia McMahon's *Chi-Hoon: A Korean Girl* is a photographic essay that presents one week in the life of a girl.

Although Takaaki Nomura's picture storybook *Grandpa's Town* is set in Japan rather than North America, the themes of the story relate to the universality of loving relationships between grandfathers and grandsons, possible loneliness after the death of a loved one, and preferences for staying with old friends. This story, written in both Japanese and English, includes a great deal of cultural information. A young boy accompanies his grandfather around town, meets his grandfather's friends, and discovers that his grandfather is not willing to leave these friends to move in with the boy and his mother.

The importance of even small cultural artifacts, such as eating utensils, stimulates a humorous plot in Ina R. Friedman's *How My Parents Learned to Eat*. Friedman suggests the solution to a problem on the first page of this picture storybook: "In our house, some days we eat with chopsticks and some days we eat with knives and forks. For me, it's natural" (p. 1, unnumbered). The rest of the story tells how an American sailor courts a Japanese girl, and each secretly tries to learn the other's way of eating. The couple reaches a satisfactory compromise because each person still respects the other's culture.

 ## SUMMARY

In this chapter, we have discussed the folklore of several Asian cultures including China, India, and Japan.

The discussion of Chinese folklore showed that Confucian and Taoist philosophies may influence tales from that culture. Popular elements in Chinese folklore include the importance of the emperor and gods that control life in the home. Scholarship is one of the highest values in the folklore, along with loyalty, patience, and obedience.

The discussion of folklore from India showed that it is influenced by two great belief systems: Hindu and Buddhist. The Jakarta tales are among the most important for revealing Buddhist beliefs and values. These tales also highlight the importance of helping others and of living in harmony.

Folklore from Japan is also influenced by religion and belief systems, especially Buddhism. Folktales often include supernatural monsters and beasts. The fox is one of the greatest tricksters in Japanese folklore.

There are numerous informational books about the early history and cultures of the Asian peoples. Books about trade routes are especially popular. There are historical fiction books that are set in early China or Japan. Historical fiction authors may place their characters in a setting in which Asian people immigrate to the United States.

Poetry with Asian or Asian American roots reflects ancient values and beliefs, as well as contemporary concerns. Literature reflecting more contemporary times may focus on various leaders, such as biographies of Indira Gandhi or Mohandas Gandhi. Contemporary authors of Asian American literature provide insights into conflicts faced by contemporary Asian Americans as many of the characters rediscover their Asian heritages and also live within the contemporary U.S. culture.

1. Choose one of the cultural groups discussed in this chapter. Read a number of myths, legends, and folktales from that culture. Summarize the traditional beliefs and values. Provide quotations from the tales to show the beliefs and values. Try to identify those same beliefs and values in other genres of literature depicting the same culture. What conclusions can you reach about the importance of traditional literature?

2. After you have read a number of folktales from China, India, Japan, or another Asian country, identify the story openings, storytelling style, and story endings that are the most common for the culture.

3. Choose a religious belief such as one from the Buddhist or Hindu tradition and locate folklore that reflects that belief.

4. Folklore may be "rewritten" to emphasize the important beliefs of a political or a religious group. Choose a country in which the political or religious climate has changed over the years. Try to find evidence of these different beliefs in the folklore.

5. Choose an outstanding author of Asian or Asian American literature such as Laurence Yep, and read several books by that author. What makes the plots and the characters memorable? What are the themes in the writer's work? Is there a common theme throughout the writing?

6. Search a social studies or history curriculum and identify Asian Americans who have made contributions during the time periods or areas being studied. Identify literature selections that include additional information about those individuals and their contributions.

7. Compare an autobiography of an Asian or Asian American personage with biographies about the same person written for children or young adults.

8. Compare the themes and conflicts in poetry written by Asian Americans with the themes and conflicts in contemporary realistic fiction about Asian Americans.

9. Read an article on Asian art such as Andrew Solomon's "Don't Mess with Our Cultural Patrimony!" (1996). What is the importance of traditional art in the culture?

Involving Children with Asian Literature

 ## PHASE ONE: TRADITIONAL VALUES IN FOLKLORE

Many of the examples provided in this section are from Chinese folklore. The techniques, however, may be used with folklore from any of the Asian countries.

Using a Web to Develop a Unit Around Chinese Folklore

As we have already discovered, students can learn a great deal about a country and its people by investigating a number of the traditional tales from that country. Such an investigation also increases students' understanding of the multicultural heritage of the United States and develops understanding of, and positive attitudes toward, cultures other than one's own.

The web in Figure 5–1 (Norton, 1999) uses traditional tales from China to analyze personal values, important symbols, and disliked human qualities in the Chinese culture. It also looks at supernatural beings. Finally, it lists motivating introductions to the study of traditional tales, as well as stimulating activities to accompany the study.

This web was used as a structure for a successful study of folktales from China by the teacher of a fifth-grade class. Objects displayed throughout the classroom stimulated students' interest. A large red paper dragon met the students as they entered the room. Other objects included joss sticks (incense), lanterns, Chinese flutes, a tea service, fans, statues of mythical beasts, lacquered boxes and plates, silk, samples of Chinese writing, a blue willow plate, jade, and reproduction of Chinese paintings. Many Chinese folktales were displayed on the library table. Chinese music played in the background. The chalkboard contained a message, written in Chinese figures, welcoming the children to China. (Examples of useful reference books on Chinese art are included in the bibliography.)

The students looked at the displays, listened to the music, tried to decipher the message, and discussed what they saw and heard. They located China on a map

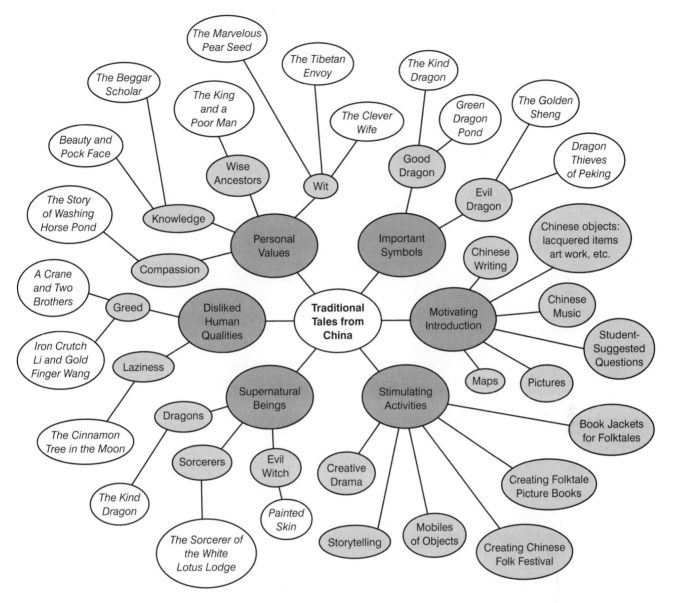

FIGURE 5–1 Web of a Unit of Study on Chinese Folklore

and a globe. Then they listed questions they had about China—questions about the people, country, values, art, music, food, houses, animals, and climate.

The teacher shared several of her favorite Chinese folktales with the group. They included Marilee Heyer's *The Weaving of a Dream: A Chinese Folktale*, Margaret Mahy's *The Seven Chinese Brothers*, Demi's *The Empty Pot*, and tales found in Neil Phillip's *The Spring of Butterflies and Other Chinese Folktales*, as well as other collections of Chinese folktales. The teacher and students searched for values, symbols, and negative human qualities in these tales. The teacher also provided brief introductions to other tales to stimulate the children's interest in reading the tales. The children then chose tales to read independently. As they read, they considered their questions about China; when they discovered information about the culture and the people, they jotted it down so that they could share it with the class.

After collecting their information, the children discussed ways of verifying whether or not the information was accurate. They compared the information with library reference materials and information in magazines such as *National Geographic*. They also invited to the classroom several visitors who were either Chinese or had visited China.

The students used their knowledge about the people, culture, and literature of China in their own art, creative drama, and writing. They drew travel posters as well as book jackets and illustrations for folktales. They also made mobiles of folk-literature objects.

One artistic activity was to create picture storybooks from single folktales. The group chose a favorite tale not already in picture-book format, illustrated it with drawings, and bound the pages together. Because many of the published picture books contained information about the origins of their tales, the students included similar information inside their own front covers. Because published book jackets often tell about the illustrator and the research to provide authentic pictures, the students' books contained this information. The students told about themselves and the ways in which they prepared for their drawing assignments. They described the mediums they used for their illustrations. Then they shared their books with one another and other classes and proudly displayed the books in the library.

The class also chose some stories for creative drama. The teacher divided the class into groups according to favorite folktales. Each group then chose a method for sharing the story with the rest of the class. Some groups re-created the stories as plays, others chose puppetry, and one group used pantomime with a narrator who read the lines.

This unit about one country led to an interest in folktales from other countries. The students next read folktales from Japan and other Asian countries. They discovered the similarities among many of Asian tales, especially in the symbolic animals found in both Chinese and Japanese tales.

Listening to Asian Literature to Predict Outcomes

Books in which the authors use questions at the close of the chapters or include considerable details offer numerous opportunities for students to predict outcomes about the continuing story. Lloyd Alexander's *The Remarkable Journey of Prince Jen* is a fantasy quest with an Asian setting. Although the book is a fantasy, Alexander integrates numerous details and beliefs from the traditional Chinese culture. The writing style motivates predicting outcomes because each chapter concludes with comments and questions that can be used to ask students to hypothesize about what will happen in the next chapter or to write their own next chapter.

You may introduce the setting by asking students to view and discuss the map at the beginning of the novel. As students look at the map, they can predict the type of setting for the book and the genre of literature. For example, they will find names such as the Kingdom of T'ien-Kuo and the cities of Chai-sang and Ch'angan. They will notice that all of these place names sound Chinese. However, they will also notice that there is a mountain called the Mountain of Sorcerers. This name should lead them to believe that the story may be a fantasy.

Next, introduce the book in such a way that encourages students to make predictions. For example, you might ask questions such as these: Have you ever thought about the consequences of your choices? If you had two choices, what would have happened if you had done ____ instead of ____? Would things have been different? You can use the following script to introduce the activity:

> As you read Lloyd Alexander's *The Remarkable Journey of Prince Jen,* you will learn just how important choices can be. You will also discover some important objects that at first seem quite ordinary. The author also uses an interesting technique at the close of each chapter to involve your responses and to have you predict outcomes. As you listen to or read this book, you will stop at the end of each chapter and try to answer the author's questions before proceeding to the next chapter.

After introducing and discussing the book, read the first chapter. Stop at the end of the chapter and read Alexander's statement and question: "Our hero is eager to start his journey, but Master Wu seems to be casting a dark shadow on a bright prospect. What can be the difficulty? To find out, read the next chapter" (p. 8). Ask the students to predict what they think the difficulty is and to speculate about the conflict that will be developing in the next chapter. After they have made their predictions, read the second chapter to verify and compare their predictions with Alexander's plot. You may continue reading this book orally and asking questions to encourage students to predict outcomes, or the students may read the remainder of the book on their own and write their own predictions at the close of each chapter.

Choices and questions are also very important in the text. Students can respond to these choices by considering this question: If the character had done ____ instead of ____, which things have would have been different? They can speculate about such differences.

As students read the book they should also identify details and beliefs that are characteristic of the Chinese culture. Even though this book is a fantasy, they can identify and discuss details that seem to be appropriate to an Asian setting.

ADDITIONAL ACTIVITIES TO ENHANCE PHASE ONE

Here are some activities for children or young adult students related to this phase:

1. Chinese culture influenced Japanese culture; consequently, many of the Japanese tales are similar to Chinese tales. Compare the values in Japanese folklore with ones in Chinese tales. Here are some Japanese tales that might be used in the study: Katherine Paterson's *The Tale of the Mandarin Ducks*, Anne Laurin's *The Perfect Crane*, Robert D. San Souci's *The Samurai's Daughter: A Japanese Legend,* and Odds Bodkin's *The Crane Wife.*
2. Research the Buddhist and Hindu religions and search for evidence of the associated cultural beliefs in the folklore. For example, search for Hindu beliefs in Aaron Shepard's *Savitri: A Tale of Ancient India* and Madhur Jaffrey's *Seasons of Splendour: Tales, Myths, and Legends of India.* Search for Buddhist beliefs in Demi's *Buddha Stories* and in Judith Ernst's *The Golden Goose King: A Tale Told by the Buddha.*

 PHASE TWO: FOLKLORE TOLD IN THE UNITED STATES

You may develop a web similar to the one developed for Chinese traditional literature and compare the values and beliefs found in folklore collected from Chinese

Americans. For this activity, you may use Laurence Yep's *The Rainbow People*, a collection of twenty folktales collected from Chinese Americans in the United States. The text is divided into tales about tricksters, fools, virtues and vices, Chinese America, and love.

Share and discuss with the students information from Yep's introductory comments. For example, folktales "are strategies for living. At the very least, the stories offered consolation and more often hope. But beyond that, the stories also expressed the loneliness, anger, fear, and love that were part of the Chinese-American experience" (p. x).

As part of this activity, students will discover in the trickster tales that keeping one's wits could save one's life, that loyalty is important, and that treachery is evil. In the tales about fools, readers discover that misinterpretations and bad luck can cause serious consequences. In the tales about virtues and vices, readers discover the positive worth of kindness and the negative worth of greed and impatience. In addition, one must be moderate in desires. Before students read the tales under "In Chinese America," share Yep's introduction to the section in which he describes the work of the Chinese in North America as they built railroad lines and worked in industry and agriculture. Ask the students to identify any examples or reflections of this work that they find in the literature.

Students might also analyze the folklore components and the new cultural setting in Paul Yee's *Tales from Gold Mountain: Stories of the Chinese in the New World*. These are literary tales created by Yee that reflect both the traditional values and the conflict the Chinese faced as they overcame prejudice and adversity in North America.

ADDITIONAL ACTIVITIES TO ENHANCE PHASE TWO

Here are some activities for children or young adult students related to this phase:

1. Add the folktales retold in the United States to the unit about China.
2. Interview someone living in the United States who originally came from an Asian country. Ask them to tell their favorite folktales.
3. Investigate the influence of the railroad in North America in the 1800s and early 1900s on Asian people.

 ## PHASE THREE: HISTORICAL NONFICTION

Integrating Literature and Geography.

Many of the multicultural books discussed in this text lend themselves to an analysis using five themes from geography. Geographers have developed a procedure that allows readers to inquire about places on the earth and to analyze their relationships to the people who live there. The following five fundamental themes in geography were developed by the Committee on Geographic Education (1983) and are also discussed in GEO News (1990):

1. *Location, including where and why:* Where does the story take place—as far as city, country, continent, longitude, latitude, and so forth? Why does the story take place in this location?

2. *Place, including physical and human characteristics:* What are the physical features and characteristics? What are the characteristics of the people, including distinctive cultural traditions?
3. *Relationships within places, including cultural and physical interactions and how relationships develop:* How do human-environmental relationships develop and what are the consequences? What is the primary use of land? How have the people altered the environment? Where do most people live?
4. *Movement, including people, ideas, and materials:* How are the movements of people, ideas, and materials influenced and accomplished? What are the consequences of such movements?
5. *Regions, including how they form and change:* What are the major languages? What are the vegetation regions? What are the country's political divisions? How do the regions change?

Introduce these five themes of geography and how the themes will be used to analyze books. Allow students to discuss information that would be included under each of the categories.

You may develop a chart for each of the books that you will be using for the activity. On this chart, place the five themes of geography. As students read or listen to each book, ask them to identify and discuss the information that would be appropriate for each of the categories.

The following activity is developed around John S. Major's *The Silk Route: 7,000 Miles of History*. Before students read this book, provide some historical background about the time period and the locations. For example, show and discuss the map at the beginning of the book on which the silk route is traced from Chang'an, China, to Byzantium during the Tang Dynasty (A.D. 618–907). Discuss the geographical locations through which the Silk Route extends as well as the importance of trade routes during this time period. The following type of information may be placed on a chart. The listings show a few of the examples that were identified, discussed, and analyzed with a class of students using *The Silk Route: 7,000 Miles of History*:

Location: Chang'an, China, the largest city in the world in A.D. 700. The Silk Route, or ancient trade route between China and Byzantium.
Oasis town of Dunhuang is an important trading and supply center.
The oasis city of Kashgar provides dried dates, raisins, and jade to bring back to China.
Pamirs are a range of mountains in eastern Afghanistan.
Market of Tashkent marks eastern edge of Persian cultural world.
Transoxiana is a wild area in which bandits attack caravans.
Herat is a thriving city of artisans.
Baghdad is the greatest city of the Islamic world and a hub of trade.

Place: Network of caravan tracks cross the steppes and deserts of Central Asia.
Conditions on the caravan route include heat, hunger, thirst, and bandit raids.
Buddhist temples are seen in China.
Each different city specializes in goods that are made and traded.

Relationships within Places: Emperors of Tang Dynasty brought China to a high point of power and culture.
The importance of silk to the ancient Western world brought trade with China.
In China, men grow grain; women produce silk.
Trade goods from China include porcelain, herbal medicines, and silk cloth desired by Islamic and Byzantine worlds.

Movement: The world of Islam expanded rapidly after its founding by Muhammad in 622.

Silk was used as money.

Materials brought to trade changed hands several times along the route.

Buddhist religion came to China from India along the Silk Route about A.D. 100.

In Heart, there are Muslim imams, Zoroastrian priests, Nestorian Christian priests, and Buddhist monks.

Regions: China includes farmland suitable for growing grains.

China has groves of mulberry trees whose leaves feed the silkworms.

Taklamakan, one of the world's driest deserts, has sand dunes, rocky flats, and dry riverbeds.

The Silk Route crosses the Pamirs, a range of high mountains in eastern Afghanistan.

As students identify and discuss these themes in geography, ask them to consider the importance of each of the themes to the development of the Silk Route and the movement of ideas across its 7,000 miles. They could compare the various categories found in this early time period and compare the contemporary routes and countries that are discussed in this book. Which categories would change? How would they change? Which categories would be similar to this earlier time period in history? Why would they be similar?

Many additional books may be used for a similar activity. The informational books discussed in the previous sections provide excellent sources for selecting appropriate literature.

ADDITIONAL ACTIVITIES TO ENHANCE PHASE THREE

Here are some activities for children or young adult students related to this phase:

1. Choose two books that provide information about the same place in Asia in the same time period. Compare the information found in the books. Evaluate the informational books according to the accuracy of the facts and the organization of the books.
2. After investigating the history of one of the Asian countries, choose a time in the history of the country during which you would have liked to live. Write stories or journal entries that describe your life during that time period. Include your reasons for selecting the time period.

 ## PHASE FOUR: HISTORICAL FICTION

Identifying Traditional Values and Historical Happenings

Books set in feudal Japan, in early China, and in earlier periods in the United States provide opportunities for students to search for continuing cultural threads and to authenticate historical happenings. For example, you could ask students to read Erik Christian Haugaard's *The Boy and the Samurai*. Have them search for cultural information and describe the depiction of the settings. Have them evaluate the author's ability to include cultural traditions and beliefs throughout the text. How does the author create vivid settings and believable conflicts?

Two books that may be used for comparisons of settings, conflicts, and characterizations are Laurence Yep's *The Serpent's Children* and Katherine Paterson's *Rebels of the Heavenly Kingdom*. Both of the books have settings during the time of the Taiping Rebellion in nineteenth-century China. Laurence Yep's *Dragon's Gate* and *Dragonwings* may be used to analyze the impact of a foreign culture on Chinese immigrants and to evaluate the author's ability to develop characters who retain their traditional values, overcome stereotypes, and face conflicts associated with their new experiences.

ADDITIONAL ACTIVITIES TO ENHANCE PHASE FOUR

Here are some activities for children or young adult students related to this phase:

1. Jean Merrill's *The Girl Who Loved Caterpillars*, a picture book set in twelfth-century Japan, provides an interesting stimulus for creative writing. The author states that the second chapter to the original scroll has been lost. Consequently, you can speculate about what happened to the subject of the story—a wise woman who was interested in nature. Write your own version of the missing chapter and decide if the woman became a scientist or a philosopher, or if she became alienated from her family and society, or if she has some other fate.

2. Trace the molding of two cultures in two picture storybooks by Allen Say. *Grandfather's Journey* is an immigration story that focuses on a character's journeys: the first one from Japan to California and then a later one that takes him back to visit the Japan of his youth. *Tree of Cranes* is set in Japan and develops a story as the boy's mother, who was born in the United States, prepares a Christmas celebration that combines the Japanese and U.S. cultural traditions.

 PHASE FIVE: CONTEMPORARY LITERATURE

Compare Biographies of One Biographical Character

Studying several biographies of the same individual allows students to evaluate and compare the accuracy of characterization in biographies. Students can also analyze "plot," setting, and theme in biographies. For example, they could compare three biographies of Gandhi: Victoria Sherrow's *Mohandas Gandhi: The Power of the Spirit*, Glenn Alan Cheney's *Mohandas Gandhi*, and Doris and Harold Faber's *Mahatama Gandhi*.

To analyze "plot" in biographies have students identify the pattern of action, locate examples of specific types of conflicts (person against self, person against person, person against nature, person against society), analyze why the biographer emphasizes those types of conflicts, consider why and how the conflicts relate to the biographer's purpose in writing, and locate examples of ways in which the biographer develops the readers' interest.

To evaluate setting in biographies, ask students to identify the various settings; identify the ways in which the biographer informs readers about the important details related to the time period; analyze how much influence the setting has on the plot and characters; find specific locations mentioned in the biography and locate these places on a map, in geography texts, or in other nonfiction sources; evaluate the authenticity of settings by comparing the information in various non-fiction sources; check the accuracy of dates and happenings in other nonfiction sources; and draw a setting as if it were a backdrop for a stage production (first evaluating whether or not there is enough information about the setting to complete a drawing).

To evaluate theme in biography, ask the students to find the primary, or main, theme in a biography and several secondary themes. Ask the students to consider how these themes are integrated into the biography, analyze whether or not the title of the biography reflects the theme, search for evidence of the biographical subject's ability to triumph over obstacles, identify and compare the themes developed in several biographies written about the same person, and compare the themes in biographies written for younger children with those written for young adults.

ADDITIONAL ACTIVITIES TO ENHANCE PHASE FIVE

Here are some activities for children or young adult students related to this phase:

1. Laurence Yep is one of the most prolific authors of Chinese American literature for young readers. His books integrate information about Chinese cultural heritage into the everyday lives of his characters. In addition to Yep's historical fiction books already discussed, read books such as *Child of the Owl; Star Fisher; Thief of Hearts;* and *Later, Gater*. Identify important recurring themes that are developed by the author. Are there any similarities in characterization, conflict, and setting? If so, what are these similarities? How does the author develop cultural knowledge and beliefs within his stories? Read information about the author and try to decide why he writes his stories.
2. Poetry with Asian or Asian American roots may be found that reflects traditional values and beliefs or contemporary concerns. Many of the Japanese poems, for example, reflect close relationships with nature. Using a poetry collection such Demi's *In the Eyes of the Cat: Japanese Poetry for All Seasons,* discuss the various images of nature and various animals that live in nature. Are there similarities in the feeling about nature in the poetry and in the traditional literature? This book of poetry could also introduce a study of haiku. Search for and share additional examples of haiku and write your own haiku poetry.

BIBLIOGRAPHY

Asian Art Museum of San Francisco. *Tomb Treasures from China: The Buried Art of Ancient Xi'an*. San Francisco: Asian Art Museum and Fort Worth: Kimbell Art Museum, 1994.

Cai, Mingshui. "Images of Chinese and Chinese Americans Mirrored in Picture Books." *Children's Literature in Education*. 25 (1994): 169–191.

Committee on Geographic Education. *Guidelines for Geographic Education*. Washington, D.C.: National Council for Geographic Education and the Association of American Geographers, 1983.

Council on Interracial Books for Children. "Criteria for Analyzing Books on Asian Americans." In *Cultural Conformity in Books for Children*, edited by Donnarae MacCann and Gloria Woodard. Metuchen N.J.: Scarecrow, 1977.

Dugger, Celia. "Queens Old-Timers Uneasy As Asian Influence Grows." *The New York Times* (Sunday, March 31, 1996): 1, 18.

Freeman, Nancy K. "Look to the East to Gain a New Perspective, Understand Cultural Differences, and Appreciate Cultural Diversity." *Early Childhood Education Journal* 26 (1998): 79–82.

Gandhi, Indira. *My Truth*. New York: Grove Press, 1980.

GEO News Handbook (November 11–17, 1990): 7.

Guirand, Felix, edited by. Translated by Richard Aldington and Delano Ames. *New Larousse Encyclopedia of Mythology*. New York: Crescent Books, 1987.

Gurjar, Nandita. "Literature from India." Paper presented at Texas A&M University, College Station, Texas, December 12, 1995.

Harada, Violet H. "Caught Between Two Worlds: Themes of Family, Community, and Ethnic Identity in Yoshiko Uchida's Works for Children." *Children's Literature in Education* 29 (March 1998): 19–30.

Hickey, M. Gail. "'Back Home, Nobody'd Do That:' Immigrant Students and Cultural Models of Schooling." *Social Education* 62 (November/December 1998): 442–447.

Holzman, Donald. "The Place of Filial Piety in Ancient China." *Journal of the American Oriental Society* 118 (April-June 1998): 185–199.

James, Grace. *Green Willow and Other Japanese Fairy Tales*. New York: Avenel, 1987.

Jenyns, R. Soame. *Chinese Art: Gold, Silver, Later Bronzes, Cloisonné, Cantonese Enamel, Lacquer, Furniture, Wood*. Oxford: Phaidon, 1980.

_____. *Chinese Art: Textiles, Glass and Painting on Glass, Carvings in Ivory and Rhinoceros Horn, Carvings in Hard Stones, Snuff Bottles, Inkcakes and Inkstones*. Oxford, Phaidon, 1981.

Kao, Karl S. Y., edited by. *Classical Chinese Tales of the Supernatural: Selections from the Third to the Tenth Century*. Bloomington: Indiana University Press, 1985.

Khorana, Meena. *The Indian Subcontinent in Literature for Children and Young Adults: An Annotated Bibliography of English-Language Books*. New York: Greenwood, 1991.

Kuo, Louise, and Yuan-his Kuo. *Chinese Folk Tales*. Celestial Arts, 1976.

Leach, Maria, edited by. *Funk & Wagnalls Standard Dictionary of Folklore, Mythology, and Legend*. New York: Harper & Row, 1972.

Levenson, Jay A., edited by. *Circa 1492: Art in the Age of Exploration*. Washington: National Gallery of Art and New Haven: Yale University Press, 1991.

Lion-Goldschmidt, and Jean-Claude Moreau-Gobard. *Chinese Art: Bronzes, Jade, Sculpture, Ceramics*. Oxford: Phaidon, 1980.

Mackenzie, Donald. *India: Myths and Legends Series*. London: Mystic Press, 1987.

Marcus, Leonard S. "Talking with Authors." *Publishers Weekly* 247 (February 14, 2000): 98–101.

Nivendita, Sister, and Anandak Coomaraswamy. *Hindus and Buddhists: Myths and Legends Series*. London: Mystic Press, 1987.

Norton, Donna E. *Through the Eyes of a Child: An Introduction to Children's Literature*. 5th ed. Upper Saddle River, N.J.: Merril/Prentice Hall, 1999.

Onishi, Norimitsu. "Affirmative Action: Choosing Sides." *The New York Times* (March 31, 1996): Section 4A, 26–29; 32–35.

Ramanujan, A. K., edited by. *Folktales from India: A Selection of Oral Tales from Twenty-Two Languages*. New York: Pantheon, 1991.

Reza. "Pilgrimage to China's Buddhist Caves." *National Geographic*, (April 1996): 52–63.

Roberts, Moss. *Chinese Fairy Tales and Fantasies*. New York: Pantheon, 1979.

Seeger, Elizabeth, retold by. *The Five Sons of King Pandu: The Story of the Mahabharata*. Illustrated by Gordon Laite. New York: William Scott, 1967.

Solomon, Andrew. "Don't Mess with Our Cultural Patrimony!" *The New York Times Magazine* (March 17, 1996): 30–37, 44, 52, 58, 64.

Stokstad, Marilyn. *Art History*. Volumes One and Two. New York: Abrams, 1995.

Swaraji, Paul. *Indira Gandhi*. London: Robert Royce Limited, 1985.

Tyler, Royal, edited and translated by. *Japanese Tales*. New York: Pantheon Books, 1987.

Wyndham, Robert. *Tales the People Tell in China*. New York: Messner, 1971.

CHILDREN'S AND YOUNG ADULT LITERATURE REFERENCES

Chinese Literature

Alexander, Lloyd. *The Remarkable Journey of Prince Jen*. Dutton, 1991 (I: 10 + R: 6). Revealing many traditional values, this book has a hero who goes on a quest.

Allen, Judy. *Tiger*. Illustrated by Tudor Humphries. Candlewick, 1992 (I: 5–8 R: 4). A hunter saves a South Chinese tiger by taking its picture rather than killing it.

Armstrong, Jennifer. *Wan Hu Is in the Stars*. Illustrated by Jennifer Armstrong. Tambourine, 1995 (I: 4–8 R: 5). An absentminded poet tries to travel to the stars.

Asian Cultural Centre for UNESCO. *Folktales from Asia for Children Everywhere*. Vol. 3. Weatherhill, 1976 (I: 8–12 R: 6). The folktales are from Afghanistan, Burma, Indonesia, Iran, Japan, Pakistan, Singapore, Sri Lanka, and Vietnam.

Chang, Margaret, and Raymond Chang, retold by. *The Beggar's Magic: A Chinese Tale*. Illustrated by David Johnson. Simon & Schuster, 1997 (I: 5–10 R: 5). A folktale in which kindness is rewarded.

Chrisman, Arthur Bowie. *Shen of the Sea*. Dutton, 1925 (I: 8 + R: 4). Winner of the 1926 Newbery Medal.

Conger, David. *Many Lands, Many Stories: Asian Folktales for Children*. Illustrated by Ruth Ra. Tuttle, 1987 (I: 8 + R: 5). Fifteen folktales are identified by their countries of origin.

Czernecki, Stefan, retold by. *The Cricket's Cage: A Chinese Folktale*. Hyperion, 1997 (I: 5–8 R: 4). This is an illustrated version of the legend of the Forbidden City.

Demi. *Chingis Khan*. Henry Holt, 1991 (I: all). This is a highly illustrated biography of the Mongol leader who conquered Persia and China.

_____, adapted by. *Dragonkites and Dragonflies: A Collection of Chinese Nursery Rhymes*. Harcourt Brace, 1986 (I: all). A collection of twenty-two traditional nursery rhymes.

_____, *The Empty Pot*. Holt, 1990 (I: 5–9 R: 4). This folktale shows that honesty is important.

Fang, Linda. *The Ch'i-lin Purse: A Collection of Ancient Chinese Stories*. Illustrated by Jeanne M. Lee. Farrar, Straus & Giroux, 1995 (I: 10 + R: 5). This is a collection of nine stories.

Fritz, Jean, Katherine Paterson, Patricia McKissack, Fredrick McKissack, Margaret Mahy, and Jake Highwater. *The World in 1492*. Illustrated by Stefano Vitale. Henry Holt, 1992 (I: 10 +). The section on "Asia in 1492" by Katherine Paterson presents information on leaders of China, Japan, Korea, Southeast Asia, and India.

Heyer, Marilee. *The Weaving of a Dream: A Chinese Folktale*. Viking, 1986 (I: 8 + R: 5). This is a retelling of "The Chuang Brocade."

Hong, Lily Toy. *The Empress and the Silkworm*. Whitman, 1995 (I: 4–8 R: 4). The text includes a legend about the discovery of silk as well as other information about silk.

_____, retold by. *Two of Everything*. Whitman, 1993 (I: 5-8 R: 4). A Chinese folktale in which a magical pot duplicates everything that is put into it.

Kimmel, Eric A., retold by. *Ten Suns: A Chinese Legend*. Illustrated by Yongsheng Xuan. Holiday, 1998 (I: 6–10 R: 6). The tale was told in the Shang Dynasty.

Kuo, Louise, and Yuan-hsi Kuo. *Chinese Folk Tales*. Celestial Arts, 1976 (I: 8 + R: 6). This is a collection of folktales from China.

Lewis, Elizabeth Foreman. *Young Fu of the Upper Yangtze*. Henry Holt, 1932 (I: 10 + R: 5). This story depicts life in China in the 1920s.

Lord, Bette Bao. *In the Year of the Boar and Jackie Robinson*. Illustrated by Marc Simont. Harper & Row, 1984 (I: 8–12 R: 4). Baseball helps a Chinese girl make friends.

Louie, Ai-Lang. *Yeh Shen: A Cinderella Story from China*. Illustrated by Ed Young. Philomel, 1982 (I: 7–9 R: 6). This ancient Chinese tale has many similarities with versions from other cultures.

I = Interest age range

R = Readability by grade level

Mahy, Margaret, retold by. *The Seven Chinese Brothers*. Illustrated by Jean and Mou-Sien Tseng. Scholastic, 1990 (I: 5–8 R: 4). Watercolors complement this traditional folktale.

Major, John S. *The Silk Route: 7,000 Miles of History*. Illustrated by Stephen Fieser. Harper-Collins, 1995 (I: 8–12 R: 6). The text and illustrations discuss different cities along the ancient Silk Route.

Malone, Mary. *Connie Chung: Broadcast Journalist*. Enslow, 1992 (I: 10 + R: 5). This is a biography of the television journalist.

Namioka, Lensey. *Yang the Third and Her Impossible Family*. Illustrated by Kees de Kiefte. Little, Brown, 1995 (I: 8 + R: 4). This is a sequel to *Yang the Youngest and His Terrible Ear*.

_____. *Yang the Youngest and His Terrible Ear*. Illustrated by Kees de Kiefte. Little, Brown, 1992 (I: 8 + R: 4). A nine-year-old boy moves with his musical family from China to Seattle.

Paterson, Katherine. *Rebels of the Heavenly Kingdom*. Lodestar, 1983 (I: 10 + R: 6). This work of historical fiction is set in China during the Taiping Rebellion.

Phillip, Neil. *The Spring of Butterflies and Other Chinese Folktales*. Lothrop, Lee & Shepard, 1986 (I: 9 + R: 6). These tales are from northern China.

Reid, Struan. *Cultures and Civilizations: The Silk and Spice Routes*. Discovery/Macmillan, 1994 (I: 9 + R: 6). This informational book describes the culture of the trade routes.

Roberts, Moss. *Chinese Fairy Tales and Fantasies*. Pantheon, 1979 (I: 10 + R: 6). Folktales in this collection tell about enchantment, greed, animals, women, ghosts, and judges.

Seeger, Elizabeth. *Pageant of Chinese History*. Longmans, 1934 (I: 8 + R: 5). Winner of the 1935 Newbery Honor.

Strathern, Paul. *Exploration by Land: The Silk and Spice Routes*. Discovery/Macmillan, 1994 (I: 9 + R: 6). The text presents information on the Silk Route.

Wallace, Ian. *Chin Chiang and the Dragon's Dance*. Atheneum, 1984 (I: 6-9 R: 6). A boy dreams of dancing on the first day of the Year of the Dragon.

Wang, Rosalind C., retold by. *The Treasure Chest: A Chinese Tale*. Illustrated by Will Hillenbrand. Holiday, 1995 (I: 8–12 R: 5). A widow's son earns the gratitude of the Ocean King.

Waters, Kate, and Madeline Slovenz-Low. *Lion Dancer: Ernie Wan's Chinese New Year*. Photographs by Martha Cooper. Scholastic, 1990 (I: 5–8 R: 4). A six-year-old boy performs his first lion dance.

Wong, Janet S. *Good Luck Gold and Other Poems*. Macmillan, 1994 (I: all). The poetry of this Chinese American author reflects her experiences.

Yacowitz, Caryn, adapted by. *The Jade Stone: A Chinese Folktale*. Illustrated by Ju-Hong Chen. Holiday, 1992 (I: 4-8 R: 4). A stone carver goes against the wishes of the emperor.

Yee, Paul. *Tales from Gold Mountain: Stories of the Chinese in the New World*. Macmillan, 1990 (I: 10 + R: 5). Eight original stories are based on the experiences of Chinese immigrants.

Yep, Laurence. *The Amah*. Putnam's, 1999 (I: 10 + R: 6). A girl tries to confirm her identity in the family.

_____. *Child of the Owl*. Harper & Row, 1975 (I: 10 + R: 7). Casey learns to respect her heritage and to look deep inside herself.

_____. *Dragon's Gate*. HarperCollins, 1993 (I: 10 + R: 6). This historical fiction novel takes place during the construction of the transcontinental railroad in the 1860s.

_____. *Dragonwings*. Harper & Row, 1975 (I: 10 + R: 6). In 1903, eight-year-old Moon Shadow helps his father build a flying machine.

_____. *Later, Gator*. New York: Hyperion, 1995 (I: 8–12 R:5). This is a story of sibling rivalry.

_____. *The Man Who Tricked a Ghost*. Illustrated by Isadore Seltzer. Troll, 1993 (I: 5–8 R: 4). Set in medieval China, the story tells about a boy who outwits a ghost.

_____. *The Rainbow People*. Illustrated by David Wiesner. Harper & Row, 1989 (I: 9 + R: 5). These twenty Chinese folktales were collected from Chinese Americans.

_____. *The Serpent's Children*. Harper & Row, 1984 (I: 10 + R: 6). In nineteenth-century China, a girl finds that she has strength to protect her family.

_____. *Star Fisher*. Morrow, 1991 (I: 10 + R: 6). In 1927, a Chinese American family experiences prejudice when they move to West Virginia.

_____. *Thief of Hearts*. HarperCollins, 1995 (I: 10 + R: 7). In this is sequel to *Child of the Owl*, Casey faces issues related to cross- cultural understanding.

_____. *Tiger Woman*. Illustrated by Robert Roth. BridgeWater, 1995 (I: 5–8 R: 5). This is a retelling of a folktale from China in which a woman is transformed into several different forms.

Young, Ed, translated by. *Lon Po Po: A Red-Riding Hood Story from China*. Philomel, 1989 (I: all R: 5). The girls outwit the wolf in this version of the folktale.

_____. *The Lost Horse*. Harcourt Brace, 1998 (I: all). The folktale includes puppets.

_____. *Mouse Match*. Harcourt Brace, 1997 (I: all). The telling is done on a background that resembles a scroll.

Zhang, Song Nan, retold by. *Five Heavenly Emperors: Chinese Myths of Creation*. Tundra, 1994 (I: all). Creation myths from China.

India

Butler, Francelia. *Indira Gandhi*. New York: Chelsea House, 1986 (I: 12 + R: 7). This biography of India's leader emphasizes how history, politics, and culture shaped her career.

Chatterjee, Debjani. *The Elephant-Headed God and Other Hindu Tales*. Illustrated by Margaret Jones. Oxford University Press, 1992 (I: 8 + R: 5). This is a collection of twelve Hindu myths.

Cheney, Glenn Alan. *Mohandas Gandhi*. Watts, 1983 (I: 11 + R: 7). This biography emphasizes Gandhi's ideas as well as presenting information about his life.

Chodzin, Sherab, and Alexandra Kohn, retold by. *The Wisdom of the Crows and Other Buddhist Tales*. Illustrated by Marie Cameron. Tricycle, 1998 (I: 8 + R: 6). A collection of Buddhist stories.

Cumming, David. *The Ganges*. Raintree Steck-Vaughn, 1994 (I: 8 + R: 5). The text provides an overview of one of the largest waterways in the world.

Dalal-Clayton, Diksha. *The Adventures of Young Krishna: The Blue God of India*. Illustrated by Marilyn Heeger. Oxford University Press, 1991 (I: 10 + R:6). This is a collection of myths about the Hindu deity.

Demi. *Buddha Stories*. Henry Holt, 1997 (I: all). A collection of Jataka tales that reveal the teachings of the Buddha.

_____. *The Dalai Lama: A Biography of the Tibetan Spiritual and Political Leader*. Henry Holt, 1998 (I: all). A highly illustrated biography of the Tibetan spiritual leader.

Dhanjal, Beryl. *Amritsar*. Dillon Press, 1993 (I: 9 + R: 5). This informational book presents important information related to the sacred city in India.

Dharma Publishing Staff, retold by. *Courageous Captain: A Jataka Tale*. Illustrated by Rosalyn White. Dharma, 1989 (I: 6–9 R: 5). Young sailors discover that kindness, wisdom, and courage are the secrets to success.

_____. *The Rabbit in the Moon: A Jataka Tale*. Illustrated by Rosalyn White. Dharma, 1989 (I: 6–9 R: 5). A rabbit is placed in the moon to show the world the power of selflessness and a pure heart.

Eaton, Jeanette. *Gandhi, Fighter Without a Sword*. Morrow, 1950 (I: 10 + R: 6). Winner of the 1951 Newbery Honor.

Ernst, Judith. *The Golden Goose King: A Tale Told by the Buddha*. Parvardigar, 1995 (I: 10 + R: 5). A goose's wisdom helps a king learn to rule wisely.

Faber, Doris, and Harold Faber. *Mahatama Gandhi*. Messner, 1986 (I: 10 + R: 6). The authors focus on the nonviolent philosophy of Gandhi in this biography.

Fishlock, Trevor. *Indira Gandhi*. Illustrated by Karen Heywood. London: Hamish Hamilton, 1986 (I: 9–12 R: 5). The biography places Indira Gandhi's life in the context of Indian history.

Gandhi, Indira. *Remembered Moments*. New Delhi: Indira Gandhi Memorial Trust, 1987 (I: 10 + R: 7). This text includes selections from Gandhi's autobiographical writings and interviews.

Ganeri, Anita. *Benares*. Dillon, 1993 (I: 9 + R: 5). Color photographs accompany this informational book about one of the Holy Cities of India.

_____. *Exploration into India*. New Discovery, 1994 (I: 8 + R: 5). This informational book presents a history of India, beginning with early civilization and extending into modern India.

_____. *I Remember India*. Raintree Steck-Vaughn, 1995 (I: 7–9 R: 4). This is a brief introduction to the land, people, and daily life of the people from India.

_____, and Jonardon Ganeri. *India*. Raintree Steck-Vaughn, 1995 (I: 8 + R: 4). This is a source of general information and key facts about the country.

Greene, Carol. *Indira Nehru Gandhi: Ruler of India*. Childrens Press, 1985 (I: 8 + R: 4). This is a highly illustrated biography written for younger readers.

Haskins, James. *India Under Indira and Rajiv Gandhi*. Enslow, 1989 (I: 10 + R: 5). This nonfiction book chronicles the history of India as these leaders try to build a strong nation.

Hermes, Jules. *The Children of India*. Carolrhoda, 1993 (I: 8 + R: 4). The photographs and text present the lives of children from different regions and social levels.

Hewitt, Catherine. *Buddhism*. Thomson Learning, 1995 (I: 9 + R: 5). The illustrated text presents history and beliefs associated with Buddhism.

Jafa, Manorama. *Indira Priyadarshini*. Illustrated by Bodhraj. New Delhi: Frank, 1988 (I: 9–12 R: 5). Events in this biography are presented from the perspective of Indira Gandhi.

Jaffrey, Madhur, retold by. *Seasons of Splendour: Tales, Myths and Legends of India*. Illustrated by Michael Foreman. Atheneum, 1985 (I: 8 + R: 4). This is a collection of tales from the Hindu tradition.

Jendresen, Erik, and Joshua M. Greene. *Hanuman*. Illustrated by Li Ming. Tricycle, 1998 (I: 8 + R: 6). A tale based on Valmiki's "Ramayana."

Kalman, Maira. *Swami on Rye: Max in India*. Viking, 1995 (I: all). Max the dog goes to India in search of the meaning of life.

Kamel, Aleph. *The Bird Who Was an Elephant*. HarperCollins, 1990 (I: 8 + R: 5). There is Hindu belief reflected in this story.

Karpin, Florence. *The Prince in the Golden Tower*. Penguin, 1989 (I: 8 + R: 5). This fantasy has foundations in the same sources as folklore.

Laure, Jason. *Enchantment of the World: Bangladesh*. Childrens Press, 1992 (I: 8 + R: 5). The color photographs and text provide an introduction to the country.

Lewin, Ted. *Sacred River*. Clarion, 1995 (I: 6–10 R: 5). Watercolors depict a pilgrimage to Benares.

Masani, Shakuntala. *The Story of Indira*. Vikas, 1974 (I: 10 + R: 6). This is a carefully researched biography of Indira Gandhi.

McNair, Sylvia. *Enchantment of the World: India*. Childrens Press, 1990 (I: 8 + R: 4). The color photographs and text present the geography, history, people, and culture of India.

Mipham, Lama, retold by. *Great Gift and the Wish-Fulfilling Gem: A Jataka Tale*. Illustrated by Terry McSweeney. Dharma, 1990 (I: 6–9 R: 5). A good-hearted child searches the world for a gem that will bring happiness to the people of the world.

Perkins, Mitali. *The Sunita Experiment*. Little, Brown, 1993 (I: 12 + R: 6). An eighth-grade girl discovers understanding of and respect for her Indian heritage.

Roth, Susan L. *Buddha*. Doubleday, 1994 (I: 6–9 R: 5). This picture book tells about the life of Prince Siddhartha, who became the Buddha, the Enlightened One.

Rothfarb, Ed. *In the Land of the Taj Mahal: The World of the Fabulous Mughals*. Henry Holt, 1998 (I: 10 + R: 6). The text presents an extensive history.

Shepard, Aaron. *Savitri: A Tale of Ancient India*. Illustrated by Vera Rosenberry. Whitman, 1992 (I: 8–10 R: 5). This story appears within the Mahabharata, India's national epic.

Sherrow, Victoria. *Mohandas Gandhi: The Power of the Spirit*. Millbrook Press, 1994 (I: 12 + R: 7). This biography chronicles the life of the man who believed in peaceful resistance.

Singh, Nikky-Guinder Kaur. *Sikhism: World Religions*. Facts On File, 1993 (I: 9 + R: 5). The text describes the origins and history, central beliefs, and rituals of Sikhism.

Wangu, Madhu Bazaz. *Hinduism: World Religions*. Facts on File, 1991 (I: 9 + R: 5). This informational book presents the history, customs, and beliefs associated with Hinduism.

Japan

Bang, Molly. *The Paper Crane*. Greenwillow, 1987 (I: 8 + R: 5). A paper crane brings success.

Blumberg, Rhoda. *Commodore Perry in the Land of the Shogun*. Lothrop, Lee & Shepard, 1985 (I: 8 + R: 6). This informational book describes Commodore Perry's diplomatic mission to open Japan to trade in the 1850s.

Bodkin, Odds, retold by. *The Crane Wife*. Illustrated by Gennady Spirin. Harcourt Brace, 1998 (I: all). Greed is punished.

Carlson, Lori M., edited by. *American Eyes: New Asian-American Short Stories for Young Adults*. Holt, 1994 (I: 12 + R: 7). This collection of stories from writers whose roots are from Japan, China, Korea, Vietnam, or the Philippines.

Coerr, Eleanor. *Mieko and the Fifth Treasure*. Putnam, 1993 (I: 8 + R: 5). A young Japanese girl almost loses her gift for drawing when her hand is cut during the bombing of Nagasaki.

Demi, selected by. *In the Eyes of the Cat: Japanese Poetry for All Seasons*. Translated by Tze-si Haung. Holt, 1992 (I: all). The poems are divided according to the seasons.

Feldbaum, Carl B., and Ronald J. Bee. *Looking the Tiger in the Eye: Confronting the Nuclear Threat*. Harper & Row, 1988 (I: 12 + R: 7). This book tells the history of nuclear weapons.

French, Fiona. *Little Inchkin*. Dial, 1994 (I: 4–8 R: 4). A small hero is rewarded by Lord Buddha.

Friedman, Ina R. *How My Parents Learned to Eat*. Illustrated by Allen Say. Houghton Mifflin, 1984 (I: 6–8 R: 3). This humorous story is about eating with chopsticks or knives and forks.

Gollub, Matthew. *Cool Melons—Turn to Frogs!: The Life and Poems of Issa*. Illustrated by Kazuko G. Stone. Lee & Low, 1998. (I: 8 +). This is a combined biography and poetry collection.

Hamanaka, Sheila, retold by. *Screen of Frogs*. Orchard, 1993 (I: 5–10 R: 5). A Japanese folktale in which a man is rewarded for saving the land for the frogs.

Haugaard, Erik Christian. *The Boy and the Samurai*. Houghton Mifflin, 1991 (I:11 + R: 6). In feudal Japan, a young orphan helps a Samurai rescue his wife from a warlord.

_____. *The Revenge of the Forty-Seven Samurai*. Houghton Mifflin, 1995 (I: 11 + R: 6). Historical fiction set in Japan.

Hoobler, Dorothy, and Thomas Hoobler. *The Ghost in the Tokaido Inn*. Philomel, 1999 (I: 10 + R: 6). Historical fiction set in eighteenth-century Japan.

Ichikawa, Satomi. *Here a Little Child I Stand: Poems of Prayer and Praise for Children*. Philomel, 1985 (I: all). The collection includes a Japanese and Hindu prayer.

James, Grace. *Green Willow and Other Japanese Fairy Tales*. Illustrated by Warwick Goble. Avenel, 1987 (I: 10 + R: 6). This is a large collection of Japanese folktales.

Kodama, Tatsuharu. *Shin's Tricycle*. Illustrated by Noriyuki Ando. Translated by Kazuko Hokumen-Jones. Walker, 1995 (I: all R: 5). This story is set in World War II at the time of the bombing of Hiroshima.

Laurin, Anne. *The Perfect Crane*. Illustrated by Charles Mikolaycak. Harper & Row, 1981 (I: 5–9 R: 6). A Japanese tale tells about the friendship between a magician and the crane he creates from rice paper.

Levine, Arthur, retold by. *The Boy Who Drew Cats: A Japanese Folktale*. Illustrated by Frederic Clement. Dial, 1994 (I: 5–9 R: 5). The cats come to life to defeat a giant rat.

Levine, Ellen. *A Fence Away from Freedom: Japanese Americans and World War II*. Putnam, 1995 (I: 12 + R: 7). The book describes the experiences of Japanese Americans during this period.

Maruki, Toshi. *Hiroshima No Pika*. Lothrop, Lee & Shepard, 1982 (I: 8–12). A powerfully illustrated picture book shows the aftereffects of the first atomic bomb.

Melmed, Laura Krauss. *The First Song Ever Song*. Illustrated by Ed Young. Lothrop, Lee & Shepard, 1993 (I: 4–8). The illustrations and poetic text follow a boy as he poses the question, What was the first song ever sung?

Merrill, Jean, adapted by. *The Girl Who Loved Caterpillars*. Illustrated by Floyd Cooper. Putnam, 1992 (I: 5–8 R: 5). The story is set in twelfth-century Japan.

Mochizuki, Ken. *Passage to Freedom: The Sugihara Story*. Illustrated by Dom Lee. Lee & Low, 1997 (I: 8 + R: 5). A biography of a Japanese man who saved many Jewish people.

Mosel, Arlene. *The Funny Little Woman*. Illustrated by Blair Lent. Dutton, 1972 (I: 6–8 R:6). In a Japanese folktale, a woman steals a magic paddle.

Nomura, Takaaki. *Grandpa's Town*. Translated by Amanda Mayer Stinchecum. Kane-Miller, 1991 (I: 3–7 R: 4). The text written in both Japanese and English follows a boy and his grandfather as they go around the grandfather's town.

Paterson, Katherine. *The Tale of the Mandarin Ducks*. Illustrated by Leo and Diane Dillon. Lodestar, 1990 (I: 5–10 R: 6). A couple is rewarded for their kindness to a pair of ducks.

Salisbury, Graham. *Under the Blood Red Sun*. Delacorte, 1995 (I: 8 + R:5). A Japanese American boy and his best friend find their lives are disrupted by the bombing of Pearl Harbor.

San Souci, Robert D. *The Samurai's Daughter: A Japanese Legend*. Illustrated by Stephen T. Johnson. Dial, 1992 (I: 5–8 R: 5). The heroine slays a sea monster.

Say, Allen. *Grandfather's Journey*. Houghton Mifflin, 1993 (I: all). The immigration story of a Japanese American.

_____.*Tree of Cranes*. Houghton Mifflin, 1991 (I: 5–8 R: 4). A Japanese boy's mother shares her California Christmas.

Snyder, Dianne. *The Boy of the Three-Year Nap*. Illustrated by Allen Say. Houghton Mifflin, 1988 (I: all R: 6). A Japanese woman tricks her lazy son into working.

Stamm, Claus. *Three Strong Women*. Illustrated by Jean and Mou-sien Tseng. Viking, 1990 (I: 5–9 R: 4). Three women teach a wrestler lessons about the true meaning of strength.

Stanley, Jerry. *I Am an American: A True Story of Japanese Internment*. Crown, 1994 (I: 10 + R: 5). The author examines the experiences of Japanese Americans during World War II.

Tyler, Royal, edited and translated by. *Japanese Tales*. Pantheon, 1987 (I: 12 + R: 7). This is a large collection of tales.

Uchida, Yoshiko. *Invisible Thread*. Messner, 1992 (I: 10 + R: 6). A Japanese American tells her own experiences.

_____. *Journey Home*. Illustrated by Charles Robinson. Atheneum, 1978 (I: 10 + R:5). In a sequel to *Journey to Topaz*, twelve-year-old Yuki and her parents return to California.

_____. *Journey to Topaz*. Illustrated by Donald Carrick. Scribner's, 1971 (I: 10 + R: 5). A Japanese-American family is held in an internment camp in Utah during World War II.

_____, retold by. *The Magic Purse*. Illustrated by Keiko Narahashi. Macmillan, 1993 (I: 6–9 R: 4). In this folktale, a courageous act brings rewards.

_____, retold by. *The Wise Old Woman*. Illustrated by Martin Springett. McElderry, 1994 (I: 8–10 R: 5). This folktale develops the theme that wisdom comes with age.

Whipple, Laura, selected by. *Eric Carle's Animals Animals*. Philomel, 1989 (I: 5–9). Several of the poems in this anthology are haiku from Japan.

Yagawa, Sumiko. *The Crane Wife*. Illustrated by Suekichi Akabas. Morrow, 1981 (I: all R: 6). A traditional Japanese tale depicts the consequences of greed.

Yep, Laurence. *Hiroshima*. Scholastic, 1995 (I: 10 + R: 5). The text describes the nuclear bombing.

Literature from Other Asian Cultures

Asian Cultural Centre for UNESCO. *Folktales from Asia for Children Everywhere*. 3 vols. Weatherhill, 1976, 1977 (I: 8–12 R: 6). These folktales come from many Asian countries.

Choi, Sook Nyul. *Year of Impossible Goodbyes*. Houghton Mifflin, 1991 (I: 10 + R: 5). A ten-year-old tells about her Korean family's experiences during the Japanese occupation in World War II.

Conger, David. *Many Lands, Many Stories: Asian Folktales for Children*. Illustrated by Ruth Ra. Tuttle, 1987 (I: 8 + R: 5). Fifteen folktales are identified by their countries of origin.

Garland, Sherry. *The Lotus Seed*. Illustrated by Tatsuro Kluchi. Harcourt Brace Jovanovich, 1993 (I: 5–8 R: 4). A Vietnamese woman brings an important lotus seed with her to America.

Han, Suzanne Crowder. *The Rabbit's Escape*. Illustrated by Yumi Heo. Holt, 1995 (I: 5–8 R: 5). The text is told in both Korean and English.

_____. *The Rabbit's Judgment*. Illustrated by Yumi Heo. Holt, 1994 (I: 5–8 R: 5). This is an adaptation of a Korean variant of "The Tiger, the Brahmin, and the Jackal."

Hoyt-Goldsmith, Diane. *Hoang Anh: A Vietnamese-American Boy*. Photographs by Lawrence Migdale. Holiday, 1992 (I: 5–9 R: 4). The activities of a boy who now lives in California.

Hyun, Peter, edited by. *Korea's Favorite Tales and Lyrics*. Illustrated by Dong-il Park. Tuttle/Seoul International, 1986 (I: 5–10 R: 6). This is a collection of folktales, poems, and stories.

Jaffe, Nina. *Older Brother, Younger Brother: A Korean Folktale*. Illustrated by Wenhai Ma. Viking, 1995 (I: 4–8 R: 5). Goodness is rewarded and cruelty is punished.

Kim, Helen. *The Long Season of Rain*. Henry Holt, 1996 (I: 10+ R: 5). The setting is Seoul, Korea, in the 1960s.

Koch, Kenneth, and Kate Farrell, selected by. *Talking to the Sun: An Illustrated Anthology of Poems for Young People*. Metropolitan Museum of Art and Holt, Rinehart, and Winston, 1985 (I: all). This anthology includes poems from several Asian peoples.

Lee, Lauren. *Korean Americans*. Cavendish, 1995 (I: 10+ R: 5). The author celebrates the contributions of Korean Americans.

McMahon, Patricia. *Chi-Hoon: A Korean Girl*. Photographs by Michael O'Brien. Caroline House, 1993 (I: 8+). The text presents one week in the life of a Korean girl.

Nye, Naomi Shihab. *This Same Sky: A Collection of Poems from Around the World*. Four Winds, 1992 (I: all). This anthology includes poems from China, India, Japan, South Korea, and Vietnam.

Rhee, Nami, retold by. *The Magic Spring: A Korean Folktale*. Putnam, 1993 (I: 7–10 R: 5). A magic spring changes the lives of an elderly couple.

Shalant, Phyllis. *Beware of Kissing Lizard Lips*. Dutton, 1995 (I: 10+ R: 6). A sixth-grade Korean American faces the challenges of his first boy-girl party.

Surat, Michele Maria. *Angel Child, Dragon Child*. Illustrated by Vo-Dinh Mai. Carnival/Raintree, 1983 (I: 6–8 R: 4). A young Vietnamese child learns to adjust to her American home.

Vuong, Lynette Dyer. *The Golden Carp and Other Tales from Vietnam*. Illustrated by Manabu Saito. Lothrop, Lee & Shepard, 1993 (I: 8+ R: 5). The book includes six folktales.

Zimmermann, Robert. *Enchantment of the World: Sri Lanka*. Childrens Press, 1992 (I: 8+ R: 5). Color photographs and text describe the geography, history, culture, and industry of this country.

Jewish Time Line

1743 B.C.E.	The Covenant with Abraham, beginning important period in Jewish history
11th century A.D.	Rashi's commentary on the Pentateuch (first five books of Bible)
1492	Expulsion of 200,000 Jewish people from Spain during the Spanish Inquisition
1580	The *Maaseh Buch,* a popular book incorporating Talmudic tales and legends, which remained the most popular book in Yiddish for three centuries
1600	Elaboration on five books of Moses (Pentateuch) compiled
1700s / 1800s	Awakening interest in the study of Jewish folklore
1884	Joseph Jacobs's application of principles of anthropology and folklore to Jewish literature, in articles published in the *Jewish Encyclopedia* and in *Studies in Biblical Archaeology*
1887	Moses Gaster's collecting and publishing of *Jewish Folklore in the Middle Ages*
Late 1800s and early 1900s	Years of emigration when many Jewish families sought to escape political, economic, and religious restrictions in Eastern Europe
1938	Archives of Yidisher Visnshaftleker Institute contained over 100,000 items of Yiddish folklore
1938–1939	Abraham Berger's early survey of Jewish folklore
1933–1945	Years of the Holocaust: 1933, Hitler took power in Germany; 1935, Hitler reintroduced conscription; 1938, Hitler's armies began moving across Europe and the imprisonment of the Jewish people began; 1945 Allies forces defeated Germany
1973	Newbery Honor: Johanna Reiss's *The Upstairs Room*
1977	Caldecott Honor: Artist Beverly Brodsky McDermott, *The Golem: A Jewish Legend*
1982	Newbery Honor: Aranka Siegal's *Upon the Head of the Goat: A Childhood in Hungary, 1939–1944*
1985	Mildred L. Batchelder Award: Uri Orlev's *The Island on Bird Street*
1986	Mildred L. Batchelder Award: Roberto Innocenti's *Rose Blanche*
1990	Newbery: Lois Lowry's *Number the Stars*
1990	Caldecott Honor: Illustrator Trina Schart Hyman for *Hershel and the Hanukkah Goblins*
1992	Mildred L. Batchelder Award: Uri Orlev's *The Man from the Other Side*
1993	Children's Book Award: Karen Hesse's *Letters from Rifka*
1994	Children's Book Award: Nancy S. Toll's *Behind the Secret Window: A Memoir of a Hidden Childhood During World War Two*
1995	*Anne Frank: The Diary of a Young Girl: The Definitive Edition,* including materials not found in the earlier diary
1996	Hans Christian Andersen International Medal: Uri Orlev
1996	Mildred L. Batchelder Award: Uri Orlev's *The Lady with the Hat*
1997	Caldecott: David Wisniewski's *Golem*

6

Jewish Literature

To begin our exploration into Jewish literature, we must first understand the importance of literature to the Jewish people and then answer the question, What does it mean to be Jewish? Gloria Goldreich in her introduction to *A Treasury of Jewish Literature from Biblical Times to Today* (1982) provides a historical background that stresses the importance of literature to a people who were denied a homeland for twenty-five centuries. From the time they were exiled by the Babylonians to the creation of the modern state of Israel in 1948, they were dispersed throughout the world. During this time, Goldreich emphasizes the importance of the prose and poetry of the people:

> [It] sustained them and ensured their survival as a people. The written word was the portable homeland of the Jews. They carried their precious books from country to country. Each generation added to this wondrous literature and taught it with gentleness and love. Reading and writing, the study of books, the weaving of words, are a form of worship for the Jewish people. To read the story of one's people means to become united with that people. (pp. 1–2)

In this chapter, we will explore early writings inspired by the Torah and the Talmud (interpretative writings on the Bible), as well as the folklore of Yiddish-speaking people. We will discuss the history texts and the historical fiction stories that present the history of the people. We will examine contemporary stories that focus on Judaism today. Through folklore, historical fiction, biography and autobiography, poetry, and informational books, we will discover the values, the beliefs, and the history of the Jewish people. Through the literature, we will discover characteristics of the writing as well as the authors who bring this literary heritage to us.

WHAT DOES IT MEAN TO BE JEWISH?

Who are the approximately 13 million Jewish people who live in the world today? Rabbi Morris Kertzer (1993) provides three definitions for Jewish people: religious, spiritual, and cultural definitions. Kertzer's religious definition is, "A Jew is one who accepts the faith of Judaism." The spiritual definition is, "A Jew is one who seeks a spiritual base in the modern world by living the life of study, prayer, and daily routine dedicated to the position that Jewish wisdom through the ages will answer the big questions of life—questions like, Why do people suffer? What is life's purpose? Is there a God?" The cultural definition is, "A Jew is one who, without formal religious affiliation, and possibly with little Jewish practice, regards the teachings of Judaism—its ethics, its folkways, its literature—as his or her own" (p. 7). Rabbi Kertzer adds to these definitions the fact that Judaism is not a race.

As we explore the literature, we will discover the role of each of these definitions. As you read the various genres of literature, you will also discover basic Jewish values that thread through the literature. For example, Jewish people place considerable value on life. One of their sayings, l'Chayim, means "to life." Much of the literature from the Biblical stories of the Exodus to the World War II Holocaust stories emphasize the importance of freedom. As a way to gain freedom, however, there is a focus on the need for human action. Rabbi Kertzer emphasizes that Judaism strikes a balance between human rights and the rights of other creatures, and even Earth itself.

FOLKLORE AND ANCIENT STORIES OF THE JEWISH PEOPLE

The folklore of a culture transmits the culture's essential values. Folklorists who study Jewish literature contend that the folklore provides a portrait of the people, an understanding of the Jewish heritage, and a link to both the biblical and historical past. In this section, we will consider the history of the collection of Jewish folklore, explore the types of folklore available, and identify the characteristics of the folklore.

History of the Collection of Folklore

In a survey of Jewish folklore, Abraham Berger (1938, 1939) presents a history of the collecting, scholarly studying, and publishing of Jewish folklore. This history begins with Rashi's commentary on the Pentateuch (the first five books of the Bible), written in the 11th century A.D. An elaboration on the five books of Moses was compiled around 1600. The most popular book of this early period was the *Maaseh Buch*, first edited in 1580. This text incorporated Talmudic tales and legends. For three centuries, the *Maaseh Buch* remained the most popular book written in Yiddish.

Yiddish, according to David Bridger in *The New Jewish Encyclopedia* (1976) is second only to Hebrew as the most important of all languages spoken by Jewish people. Bridger states:

> The history of the Yiddish Language dates back to the 10th or 11th century when in the German provinces of the Rhineland, Jews speaking the local German dialects intermingled Hebrew expressions for religious and intellectual concepts. Yiddish has since undergone its own development, especially after the migration of the Jews from the German provinces and their subsequent settlement in Poland, the Ukraine, and other east European countries. In addition to the numerous Hebrew elements (about 20 per cent) contained in Yiddish, some other elements from the languages of the countries where the Jews lived (mainly Slavid words) were gradually adopted. Printed and written in Hebrew characters, Yiddish became the vernacular of the Jewish masses.

According to Berger, the awakening interest in the study of Jewish folklore reached its height in the seventeenth and eighteenth centuries. In the nineteenth century, Moritz Steinschneider conducted extensive studies of Hebrew and Yiddish tales.

In the late nineteenth century, Joseph Jacobs applied principles of anthropology and folklore to Jewish literature in articles published in the *Jewish Encyclopedia* and in his *Studies in Biblical Archaeology* published in London in 1884. In 1887, Moses Gaster collected and published *Jewish Folklore in the Middle Ages*. Berger emphasizes that a strong interest in Jewish legends was found throughout the nineteenth century. The Talmud and Midrash were cited as demonstrating moral lessons or as unveiling important events and divine truths.

The romantic interest in folklore in Russia and Poland and the growing Jewish nationalism aroused additional interest in collecting Jewish folklore and using folklore to preserve the spirit of the Jewish people.

According to Weinreich (1988), considerable work in collecting and publishing Yiddish folklore is credited to the establishment of the Yidisher Visnshaftleker Institute—VIVID (The Institute of Jewish Research). By 1938, the archives of the institute contained over 100,000 items including 32,442 proverbs, 4,989 folk beliefs, 4,673 children's tales, 4,411 folk songs, 3,807 anecdotes, 2,340 folktales, 1,000 customs, 630 songs without words, and 79 Purim plays.

Scholars choosing to conduct research, teachers selecting stories for telling, and retellers choosing materials have a rich source of literature. As we approach a study of Jewish folklore, we should heed Berger's (1938/1939) advice, "The Jewish folklorist of the future will have to be versed not only in the methods of general folklore, but also in the historic past of the people, so that he may be able to interpret Jewish folklore both as part of its environment and as a continuation of the traditional pattern" (p. 49).

Types of Folklore

Folklore is sometimes categorized by who tells the stories and for what purposes they are told. When evaluating tales of the Yiddish-speaking peoples of Eastern Europe, Weinreich (1988) identifies several of these important types and purposes. For example, comic and sentimental tales were told at weddings by entertainers known as badkhomin. Stories about the Jewish patriarchs and Elijah the Prophet were told by grandfathers to their grandsons as they waited in synagogues between early and late-evening prayers. Wonder and magic tales were told by mothers and grandmothers to children in the home. Students told scary ghost and demon tales after their teachers left for evening prayers. Teachers told stories of God's wonders, while rabbis told parables to illuminate truths.

Folklorists and collectors of Jewish folklore such as Weinreich (1988), Ausubel (1975), and Sherman (1992) have identified various types of tales and characteristics of the tales. For example, when analyzing Yiddish folktales, Weinreich identified the following types of tales: parables and allegorical tales that give listeners moral or spiritual instruction; children's tales or kinder-mayselekh; wonder tales or vunder-mayses, which have supernatural figures and helpers such as Elijah the Prophet who acts like a fairy godmother; pious tales, which contain ethical messages or reflect the persecution of the Jews; humorous tales, which reflect absurd and inappropriate behavior especially of nitwits and pranksters; legends, which are mainly religious stories about spiritual leaders; and supernatural tales about ghosts, golems, and elves. Weinreich maintains that the inclusion of a Yiddish proverb or a citation from the Bible, Talmud, or Book of Prayers is one of the ways of changing a universal tale into a Jewish story.

Considerable Jewish traditional literature is based on sacred writings. Ausubel (1975) emphasizes the influence of this early literature when he states, "sacred writings, such as the Talmud and Midrash, are almost inexhaustible repositories of the legends, myths, and parables of the Jewish people" (p. xviii). As we discuss the literature, notice how each of the types of literature are represented and how the literature may be influenced by the sacred writings.

Examples of Jewish Folklore

In a review of Jewish folktales, Rahel Musleah (1992) identifies four elements that are found in Jewish folktales. First, a Jewish folktale includes reference to a Jewish place such as a synagogue or a wedding canopy. Second, the characters in a Jewish folktale include important historical characters such as King Solomon rather than an unknown king. Third, the stories are frequently set in a "Jewish time" such as a holiday or life-cycle event. Finally, the story includes a Jewish message that reveals values such as faith, learning, remembrance, hospitality, and family. The following sections give some examples of types of Jewish folktales. As you read them, look for the four elements cited by Musleah.

Wonder Tales   Jewish wonder tales, like wonder tales from other cultures, are filled with supernatural characters and magical objects. The stories, however, may contain Jewish proverbs and characters or "markers" that identify them as Jewish. For example, in "How Much Do You Love Me?" in Beatrice Silverman Weinreich's *Yiddish Folktales* or Nina Jaffe's *The Way Meat Loves Salt: A Cinderella Tale from the Jewish Tradition,* readers will find characteristics of Cinderella tales, as well as Jewish markers. Cinderella characteristics include supernatural beings, attendance at a special function, a girl dressed in rags, a person of high regard, a search for the maiden, a test for the rightful owner of a shoe, and a magical object. There are, however, also various Jewish markers such as the importance of the rabbi and the rabbi's son, the character of Elijah the Prophet, the blessing over wine, the importance of cleanliness, and the reliance on visions seen through dreams.

Elijah the Prophet appears in these two variants of the Cinderella story. Elijah is found in numerous Jewish wonder tales: he takes the place of a fairy godmother or another supernatural helper. There are several folktales in Howard Schwartz and Barbara Rush's *The Diamond Tree: Jewish Tales from Around the World* that illustrate the importance of the powers of Elijah the Prophet and the magical characteristics of wonder tales. For example, in "Katanya," Elijah in disguise helps a worthy person in need. The title of this tale from Turkey means, "God's little one" in Hebrew. In "The Magic Sandals of Abu Kassim," Elijah the Prophet, disguised as an old man, gives a generous, but needy man a pair of remarkable shoes.

Magical objects and moral lessons are found in many Jewish wonder tales. "The Magic Pitcher," which is also included in Howard Schwartz and Barbara Rush's *The Diamond Tree: Jewish Tales from Around the World*, features a magical object that keeps refilling with olive oil. The authors' sources and commentary include valuable information for scholars interested in comparative studies and in researching Jewish folklore. The commentary includes the collector of the tale, the location in which the tale originated, the original source, and the variant number. Additional information helps readers interpret the importance of the tale. For example,

Schwartz and Rush state, "Olive oil was and still is a precious commodity in the Middle East, a fact that is reflected in this story. The miracle of the olive oil echoes the biblical accounts of Elisha found in II Kings 4:1–7. 'The Magic Pitcher' also recalls the journey of the little girl to her grandmother's house in 'Little Red Riding Hood' from Grimms' Fairy Tales" (p. 116).

Other tales in *The Diamond Tree: Jewish Tales from Around the World* illustrate morals. "The Giant of Og and the Ark" teaches the importance of cooperation. "Chusham and the Wind" emphasizes that there is a right and a wrong way of doing almost everything. "The Water Witch" develops the importance of charity freely given. "A Tale of Two Chickens" develops the virtues of honesty. "The Bear and the Children" offers assurance that parents will help their children in times of danger.

Humorous Tales and Fools and Simpletons   Many of the Jewish folktales are pious and moralistic, as well as witty and ironic. They frequently make an ethical point and present a lesson of right conduct. Examples of this characteristic are found in Margot Zemach's *It Could Always Be Worse* and in Steve Sanfield's *The Feather Merchants and Other Tales of the Fools of Chelm*. Zemach relates the story of nine unhappy people who share a small one-room hut. The father desperately seeks the advice of the rabbi, who suggests that the father bring a barnyard animal inside the hut. A pattern of complaint and advice continues until most of the family's livestock is in the house. When the rabbi tells the father to clear the animals out of the hut, the whole family appreciates its large, peaceful house. Sanfield's *The Feather Merchants and Other Tales of the Fools of Chelm* is a collection of thirteen traditional Eastern European Jewish tales about the good and decent people of Chelm, who can also be silly and foolish.

In the stories of fools and simpletons, the characters demonstrate innocent stupidity. This type of character is found in several selections in Isaac Bashevis Singer's *Stories for Children*. For example, in "The Elders of Chelm and Genendel's Key," the elders including Gronam Ox, the head of the community council, and Dopey Lekisch, Zeinvel Ninny, Treitel Fool, Sender Donkey, Shmendrick Numskull, and Feivel Thicwit solve the problem of the lack of sour cream by passing a law that from then on water will be called sour cream and sour cream will be called water.

Advice from a rabbi is a frequent story plot technique that both develops the ridiculous situation and leads to the moral of the story. Joan Rothenberg's *Yettele's Feathers* is a cautionary tale against spreading rumors and gossip. When the situation becomes extreme and no one will speak to Yettele Babbelonski, she asks the rabbi for advice. When Yettele declares that words are like feathers and not like rocks because words and feathers cannot hurt anyone, the rabbi tells her to cut off the top of her largest goose-feather pillow and bring it to him. When the wind snatches the pillow from her arms, she is lost in a blizzard of feathers. Now the rabbi tells her that he will help her after she retrieves all of the feathers. After Yettele becomes extremely fatigued trying to gather the feathers, she concludes that in a lifetime she could never put all the feathers back into the pillow. Now the rabbi uses her own words to teach the moral of the story: "And so it is with those stories of yours, my dear Yettele. Once the words leave your lips, they are as impossible to put back as those feathers" (p. 31).

Weinreich's *Yiddish Folktales* (1988) is another good source of humorous stories about fools and simpletons. Stories such as "Next Time That's What I'll Say," "Why Khelmites Lighted Up the Night," "The Rolling Stone," and "A Cat in Khelm" all depict foolish actions and the humorous consequences of these actions.

Jewish folklore is life-affirming. Even though many of the people lived through persecution and the poverty of ghettos, their stories are an affirmation of life and a defiance against the world's cruelties. Many stories such as Isaac Bashevis Singer's *Mazel and Shlimazel, or the Milk of a Lioness* illustrate a moral triumph even in what appears to be certain defeat. The story ends optimistically and teaches an important lesson for life. Singer's *Mazel and Shlimazel, or the Milk of a Lioness* pits Mazel, the spirit of good luck, against Shlimazel, the spirit of bad luck. To test the strength of good luck versus bad, the two spirits decide that each of them will spend a year manipulating the life of Tam, a bungler who lives in the poorest hut in the village. As soon as Mazel stands behind Tam, he succeeds at everything he tries. Even Princess Nesika is in love with him. Just as Tam is about to complete his greatest challenge successfully, Mazel's year is over, and an old, bent man with spiders in his beard stands beside Tam. With one horrible slip of the tongue encouraged by Shlimazel, Tam is in disfavor and condemned to death. Shlimazel has won. But wait! Mazel presents Shlimazel with the wine of forgetfulness, which causes Shlimazel to forget poor Tam. Mazel rescues Tam from hanging and helps Tam redeem himself with the king and marry the princess. Tam's success is more than good luck, however: "Tam had learned that good luck follows those who are diligent, honest, sincere and helpful to others. The man who has these qualities is indeed lucky forever" (p. 42).

Tales in Singer's *When Shlemiel Went to Warsaw and Other Stories* reflect both human foibles and folklore themes. For example, "Shrewd Tidie and Lyzer the Miser" pits foolish, greedy actions against cunning and trickery. To his discomfort, the miser learns, "If you accept nonsense when it brings you profit, you must also accept nonsense when it brings you loss" (p. 12). Notice how the story concludes with an important moral value and a lesson.

Tales of Ghosts and Goblins   Supernatural spirits in Jewish folktales range from restless spirits known as dibbuks to enormous human-made creatures, or golems, created to protect the Jewish community of Prague. Many of these stories include holy people who are able to cast demons into uninhabitable places or foil evil spirits. Some of the supernatural beings like goblins and demons are evil, while others like some ghosts and the golem are beneficial.

Eric Kimmel's *Hershel and the Hanukkah Goblins* is an example of a frightening tale in which spiritual forces overcome evil. In addition, the story contains many characteristics of Jewish folktales: the setting is a village synagogue during a Jewish holiday; there are Jewish symbols including a menorah, Hanukkah candles, and potato latkes; there are Jewish names such as Hershel and Queen Esther. In this scary tale, Hershel outwits a series of menacing goblins until he finally faces the dreaded King of the Goblins. Now Hershel uses the power of the menorah and the Hanukkah candles to outwit the goblin and remove his frightening power. The theme of the story reveals the triumph of Hanukkah.

A section titled "Tales of Ghosts and Other Strange Things" in Josepha Sherman's *Rachel the Clever and Other Jewish Folktales* contains several ghost tales. Some of the stories develop beneficial ghosts, while in others, the ghosts are frightening or even evil. Many of these ghost stories, however, reflect strong Jewish values such as the importance of keeping a promise and the need for a rabbi to say proper funeral prayers.

"The Golem of Prague" is one of the best-known stories about a beneficial supernatural being. The story set in Prague, Czechoslovakia, tells about the chief rabbi who fears for his congregation and creates a giant man out of clay. This golem, a huge silent creature, protects the Jewish people until King Rudolf issues a decree that "None of his people was ever again to spread rumors about the Jews, on the pain of banishment" (p. 96). At the point in the tale when the golem is no longer needed, the rabbi speaks holy and magical words over him. After this prayer, the golem returns to lifeless clay and is hidden under a pile of books. The tale ends with a feeling of hope for future times when the Jewish people might need assistance: "And who knows? For all anyone can tell, the golem is sleeping there still, waiting for the time when he will be needed once more" (p. 97). You may compare this version of the tale with Barbara Rogasky's *The Golem*, Isaac Bashevis Singer's *The Golem*, and David Wisniewski's *Golem*.

Clever Folks and Survivors   Stories focusing on clever folk may have complicated bits of argumentation, puzzles, and word play. Riddle stories are popular among Jewish storytellers. For example, "The Clever Daughter: A Riddle Tale," in Weinreich's *Yiddish Folktales*, is a tale in which a nobleman asks three questions: What is the fastest thing in the world? What is the fattest thing in the world? And what is the dearest thing in the world? It is only the innkeeper's daughter who can help her father answer the questions.

"The Bishop and Moshke: Another Riddle Tale" is also found in *Yiddish Folktales*. In this tale, Moshke saves himself from a thrashing by the bishop by answering three questions given by the king: Where is the middle of the earth? How many stars are in the sky? What will I be thinking when you come back to see me? Moshke tricks the bishop, dresses in the bishop's clothes, and presents himself before the king where he answers the king's questions in such a clever way that the king allows Moshke to thrash the bishop. Now Moshke becomes the king's chief counselor. Many of the Jewish tales show that clever characters tend to survive.

Nina Jaffe and Steve Zeitlin's *While Standing on One Foot: Puzzle Stories and Wisdom Tales from the Jewish Tradition* retells stories in two parts. The problem is developed in the first part, and the resolution is provided in the second. The two parts are separated with a question that reinforces the role of wisdom in Jewish folklore.

The importance of keeping a promise, respecting the Sabbath, and believing in the power of prayer are characteristics of Howard Schwartz and Barbara Rush's *The Sabbath Lion: A Jewish Folktale from Algeria*. In this story of faith and survival, a ten-year-old boy named Yosef crosses the desert with a caravan to claim his family's inheritance from a relative who dies in Egypt. The caravan leader breaks a promise that Yosef will be able to rest on the Sabbath and fulfill his Sabbath ceremonies. When Yosef refuses to break the Sabbath, he is left alone in the dangerous desert. The importance of faith is shown as Yosef carries on the ceremonies and says his prayers. When a large lion approaches, Yosef is not attacked but instead is carried across the desert to Egypt and then returned to his mother who awaits him in Algiers. According to the author's commentary, this story is told in North Africa, Iran, and Bukhara.

Legends with Biblical Sidelights   Many of the stories in Jewish legend include biblical characters. According to Ausubel (1975), "In the entire history of the Jewish people there was no personality that left its stamp on the Jewish consciousness as indelibly as Moses. The folk regarded him not only as its greatest hero, its supreme prophet, its lawgiver and its ruler, but also as its teacher. That is why for three thousand years Jews have referred to him as Mosheh Rabbenu (Moses, Our Teacher)" (p. 477).

Golem is a highly illustrated tale about a rabbi who brings to life a clay giant to help the people of Prague.

Source: Cover from GOLEM by David Wisniewski. Copyright © 1996 by David Wisniewski. Reprinted by permission of Clarion Books/Houghton Mifflin Company. All rights reserved.

Therefore, it is not surprising that many Jewish stories include the heroic character of Moses. Miriam Chaikin's *Exodus* is adapted from the Biblical story. The text dramatizes such occurrences as discovering Moses in the bulrushes, the voice of God in the burning bush, the ten plagues sent to the Egyptians, the parting of the Red Sea, and the giving of the Ten Commandments. Warwick Hutton's *Moses in the Bulrushes* is a heavily illustrated retelling of the finding of the infant Moses by the pharaoh's daughter. Mordicai Gerstein's *The Shadow of a Flying Bird* is adapted from the literature of the Kurdistani Jews. The story presents an account of Moses during his last days on earth and his discovery that "[a] man or woman's life is like the shadow of a flying bird." The various stories of Moses reflect a strong Jewish theme about the importance of freedom.

Two collections of literature are retellings of Midrash stories, a collection of Biblical events and stories. Jan Mark's *God's Story: How God Made Mankind* progresses from the first seven days of creation through the story of King Solomon and the promise of the Messiah. The author's introduction provides valuable information about the background of the stories. This collection may be compared with Miriam Chaikin's *Clouds of Glory: Legends and Stories about Bible Times*. Chaikin emphasizes the elements of a story that make up a Midrash.

Several recent texts focus on women in Biblical times. Yona Z. McDonough's *Eve and Her Sisters: Women of the Old Testament* includes stories about fourteen women of the Bible. Sandy Eisenberg Sasso's *But God Remembered: Stories of Women from Creation to the Promised Land* includes legends about Lilith, who tradition tells us was Adam's first wife, and other little known female figures such as Serach, the granddaughter of Jacob, and the five daughters of Zelophehad, who come to Moses after their father dies and ask to inherit their father's land. The characteristics of these women reflect many of the important values found in Jewish folklore: the love for family; the desirable characteristics of grace and wisdom; the importance of music and Psalms to impart knowledge and understanding; the role of hope, forgiveness, and God in Jewish history; and the requirement of kindness to a stranger, as well as the importance of freedom.

Jose Patterson's *Angels, Prophets, Rabbis and Kings from the Stories of the Jewish People* includes stories about the patriarchs, heroes and heroines, kings, and prophets. The anthology concludes with a useful discussion about the symbols in the illustrations that introduce each of the chapters. In the following example, notice how the author helps readers understand some of the cultural components of the illustrations and the stories about the patriarchs:

> Pagan idols smashed by Abraham. The idol here is based on a Canaanite clay statue and is thought to represent a mother goddess from Iron Age Palestine (12 century B.C.E.). Below: a nomadic tent with sheep and goats. The design of these tents has probably changed little since Bible times. The bowl of lentil stew from which Esau exchanged his birthright. Bottom: Joseph's dreams—the dreams that enraged his brothers, above these, the two dreams he interpreted in Pharaoh's prison. (p. 141)

The folklore discussed in this section reflects the values and beliefs of the people. Most of the stories include a message that shows the importance of such values as faith, learning, hospitality, knowledge, cooperation, and charity. We will conclude our discussion of the folklore of the Jewish people by applying some of the insights into an example in which we authenticate a folklore selection that does not include source notes. To authenticate this example, we will need to apply the values, beliefs, and characteristics discovered through our study of Jewish folklore.

Folklore in which the original sources are not identified may be authenticated, at least partially, by analyzing the authenticity of the values, beliefs, situations, and characteristics of characters found in the folklore. For example, in an effort to authenticate the values, beliefs, situations, and believability of characters found in Isaac Bashevis Singer's "A Tale of Three Wishes" from *Stories for Children*, we can identify the important cultural elements in Singer's tale and then search for these elements in other sources such as Rabbi Joseph Telushkin's *Jewish Wisdom* (1994), Nathan Ausubel's commentaries in *A Treasury of Jewish Folklore* (1975), and Rabbi Irving Greenberg's *The Jewish Way: Living Holidays* (1993).

An analysis of Singer's tale reveals that the story is philosophical in nature with both moralistic and witty elements. The story takes place in a town that has all of the things a town should have, including a synagogue, a study house, a poorhouse, a rabbi, and a few hundred inhabitants. The main characters are named Shlomah, Esther, and Moshe. The three wishes in the story include a desire to be as wise and rich as King Solomon, to be as learned in religion as the famous Rabbi Moshe Maimonides, and to be as beautiful as Queen Esther. Part of the story takes place on Hoshanah Rabbah, the last day of the feast of Tabernacles. On this miraculous night, the children see angels, seraphim, cherubim, fiery chariots, and the ladder from Jacob's dream. When the children squander their wishes, they discover the consequences of foolish actions. They also discover the most important lessons of all: how to gain wisdom, scholarship, and beauty of the soul. The sources for their growing wisdom include the Bible, the Talmud, and the Torah.

All of these features found in "A Tale of Three Wishes" can be authenticated using other sources. For example, according to Ausubel (1975) the features of Jewish folklore that distinguish it from other bodies of folklore include the following: (1) it is philosophical and subtle, pious and moralistic, witty and ironic; (2) it is almost always ethical, pointing a lesson of right conduct, ceaselessly instructing, even when the tale is being entertaining or humorous; (3) it is life-affirming; and (4) it includes mention of Heaven and Earth, natural and supernatural, and spiritual and material.

"A Tale of Three Wishes" has all of these qualities. The three characters learn a moral lesson in a witty and ironic manner. There is a strong moral lesson when the characters misuse their wishes in a foolish way. In "A Tale of Three Wishes," the moral lesson is developed through the knowledge of an old man, when he states:

> You were the ones who tried to play tricks on heaven. No one can become wise without experience, no one can become a scholar without studying. As for you, little girl, you are pretty already, but beauty of the body must be paired with beauty of the soul. No young child can possess the love and the devotion of a queen who was ready to sacrifice her life for her people. Because you three wished too much, you received nothing. (p. 11)

EARLY HISTORY OF THE JEWISH PEOPLE

Both nonfiction books and historical fiction texts available for children and young adults provide a vivid history of the Jewish people. The books also reinforce the strands of cultural beliefs and values developed through the study of Jewish folklore. For example, Yaffa Ganz's *Sand and Stars: The Jewish Journey Through Time* provides detailed historical information and relates history to many of the values and beliefs developed in Jewish literature. In his introduction, Ganz stresses the importance of the Torah in Jewish history:

As a consequence of their foolish actions, the three characters in the story finally discover the true and moralistic means of attaining their desires—wisdom, scholarship, and beauty. "For those who are willing to make an effort, great miracles and wonderful treasures are in store. For them the gates of heaven are always open" (p. 14). The values and beliefs expressed in these quotes from "A Tale of Three Wishes" are similar to the Jewish values and beliefs identified in other sources.

Biblical and historical references are found in the story: including Jewish names and the mention of holy days. The characters in "The Tale of Three Wishes" include Shlomah, Esther, and Moshe. All of these names are found in Jewish history and legend. The Jewish Queen Esther is known in literature for both her beauty and her virtue. Portions of "The Tale of Three Wishes" are set on the holy night of Hoshanah Rabbah. According to Rabbi Greenberg (1993), Hoshanah Rabbah (Great Hosannas) is the final day of Sukkot and is a special day of rejoicing in the temple. This holy night is also associated with the studying of the Torah. The custom grew for the people to stay up all night learning the Torah. This is also the day when the people begged for forgiveness from the king and the king finally granted them mercy. In "The Tale of Three Wishes," it is this holy night on which wishes may be granted.

The lessons discovered and the morals developed in "The Tale of Three Wishes" are characteristic of Jewish culture. As a consequence of foolish actions, the characters finally discover that they must work to gain wisdom, scholarship, and beauty of the soul. Jewish scholars testify to the importance of all three characteristics. According to Rabbi Telushkin (1994), wisdom and scholarship are of the utmost importance because, "[i]n traditional societies, elders are respected for their ties to the past and for the wisdom they transmit. . . . As regards scholars, the older they become the more wisdom they acquire. . . . But as regards the ignorant, the older they become, the more foolish they become" (pp. 249, 250).

Wisdom and virtue are also characteristics eventually gained by the characters in "A Tale of Three Wishes." Ausubel (1975) also emphasizes the importance of wisdom and virtue. He states that the wise man has always been the ideal of Jewish tradition and folklore. It is knowledge and reason that lead him to wisdom, and virtue is the highest wisdom. According to Ausubel, "This pattern was laid down by Moses and the Prophets and it is remarkable how many Jews have attempted to emulate them ever since" (p. 30). Ausubel stipulates that knowledge comes before wisdom and that he who lacks knowledge lacks everything. In addition, knowledge of the Talmud and the Torah are of vital importance.

All of these cultural beliefs and values are found in "A Tale of Three Wishes." Even though there is no information about the original source identified in the text, the cultural authenticity of the story may be authenticated through other sources.

[For] "the Jews, the Torah and God are indivisible. Our heroes are not warriors, but men of God. Our courage is not limited to physical strength; it is nurtured in our hearts and minds. Our wealth is not measured in gold, but in the wisdom of the Torah. Our goal is neither power nor fame, but a world of holiness, godliness, and love. Therefore, on our long and difficult journey across the face of the earth, we brought untold blessings to the peoples of the world." (p. iii)

This history then proceeds from 1743 B.C.E. through the seventeenth century. Each chapter is introduced with a time line of important people and happenings. An index and a glossary add to the usefulness of the text. The text is a valuable source for authenticating historical fiction.

Many of the informational books, especially those written for younger readers, focus on specific times or places. Interesting comparisons may be made by analyzing picture books that focus on a common subject. For example, Karla Kuskin and Neil Waldman have written books associated with the history of Jerusalem. Kuskin's *Jerusalem, Shining Still* begins with the building of the temple by King David and proceeds through the tumultuous history of the city. The author includes the role of Babylonians, Greeks, Romans, Persians, Muslims, Egyptians, Turks, and Crusaders in the history of the city. The author concludes with the Six-Day War that returned Jerusalem to the Jewish people. Notice how the author concludes the book on a positive theme: "For three thousand years this city has been battered and burned, and then built up, rebuilt and built again. Tonight, spreading across the tops of stony hills, it sits at peace beneath the moon. Three thousand years have passed, and still Jerusalem shines. King David would be proud" (p. 27).

In *The Golden City: Jerusalem's 3,000 Years*, Waldman also focuses on this sacred city. Waldman includes information about the early conflicts. To trace historical change, Waldman's watercolor illustrations are labeled with both time and place. He also includes Biblical texts. Like Kuskin, Waldman concludes his book on a positive note:

> Just as in centuries past, thousands of people from faraway places come to visit Jerusalem each year. They are drawn by the splendor of the place, the magnificent domed mosques and the narrow alleyways, the delicate carvings and the massive ramparts, the ancient shrines and modern museums. But hidden beneath all these visible things is the mysterious feeling that, as you pass through the city gates, you are actually drifting back past the days of fabled knights and prophets, to the time when a young boy slew a giant with a slingshot. (pp. 25-26 unnumbered)

As you analyze these books, consider the impact of the different types of illustrations, the content covered, and the moods created by each of the texts and the illustrations.

Another time period that had great impact on Jewish history is 1492. Norman H. Finkelstein's *The Other Fourteen Ninety-Two: Jewish Settlement in the New World* details the history of the Jewish people who were expelled from Spain in 1492. There is information about the Spanish Inquisition, anti-Semitism during the period, and the movement of people and ideas as the Jewish people searched for a new location in which to live. The author stresses that during the expulsion, 200,000 Jewish people left Spain with only their religion and their culture. The final chapter chronicles the positive Jewish experience in the American colonies. The text includes a bibliography of books and articles and an index. Additional information about the Jewish experience in 1492 and a comparison with life in other parts of the world is available by reading *The World in 1492* by Jean Fritz, Katherine Paterson, Patricia and Fredrick McKissack, Margaret Mahy, and Jamake Highwater. For example, topics related to Judaism are discussed in sections on Europe, Asia, and Africa.

Elizabeth George Speare's Newbery winner, *The Bronze Bow*, is the most highly acclaimed historical fiction novel written for children about the early Jewish people. Speare's text focuses on Israel during Roman rule. She portrays the harshness of the Roman conquerors by telling the story through the eyes of a boy, Daniel bar Jamin, who longs to avenge the death of his parents. (The boy's father was crucified by Roman soldiers, and his mother died from grief and exposure.) Daniel bar

Jamin's bitterness intensifies when he joins a guerrilla band and nurtures his hatred of the Romans. His person-against-self conflict comes to the turning point when he almost sacrifices his sister because of his hatred. Speare encourages readers to understand Daniel's real enemy. When Daniel talks to Jesus, both Daniel and readers realize that hatred, not Romans, is the enemy. In fact, the only thing stronger that hatred is love. Speare shows the magnitude of Daniel's change when he invites a Roman soldier into his home at the close of the story. It is interesting that this theme, along with the importance of wisdom, is also stressed by Yaffa Ganz's introduction to *Sand and Stars: The Jewish Journey Through Time* and many of the selections of folklore discussed earlier.

YEARS OF EMIGRATION AND IMMIGRATION

The next important time period developed in Jewish literature focuses on the years of emigration in the early 1900s, when many Jewish families sought to escape the political, economic, and religious restrictions placed on them. Books written about this time period emphasize the search for sanctuary, freedom, and a better life. The literature also develops the destructive forces associated with anti-Semitism and the horrors and dangers experienced by many Jewish people as they sought freedom. The characters and themes show the importance of inner strength, which allows families to take great risks to escape persecution and to create new lives.

According to Dorothy and Thomas Hoobler's *The Jewish American Family Album*, about 2.5 million Jewish immigrants arrived in the United States between 1880 and 1924. Most of these immigrants came from Eastern Europe, particularly Russia. This nonfiction book provides descriptions of families as they leave Europe, arrive in the United States, begin new lives, and become part of U.S. life. Historical photographs and firsthand descriptions add to the authenticity of the book. Notice in the following quote from Elizabeth Hasanovitz's experiences how her description of life in Russia before World War I and her desire for education and freedom mirror the conflicts, settings, and themes found in many historical fiction books written about this same time period:

> Those long years of struggle for an education! At 14 I was already giving lessons to beginners so as to earn money to pay for my books and teacher, so that I might be less a burden to my father. . . . Many times the chief (of police) and his guards would disturb us in the middle of the day, interrupting our work and frightening the children, who feared the uniforms as if they concealed devils and who were thrown into frenzy at their approach. . . . After each visit days of misery followed. Many, many times my father and I sat through the night thinking and thinking how to better our condition, what future to provide for my brothers and sisters. . . .
> Freedom, freedom!
> Freedom I wanted. (p. 19)

There are many excerpts from this book that may be used for comparisons and for authentication of historical fiction.

Several authors of historical fiction focus on the dangerous times for, and the persecution of, the Jewish people living in Russia during the early 1900s. Authors who develop credible person-against-society conflicts must describe the values and beliefs of the time period or the attitudes of a segment of the population so that readers understand the nature of the antagonist. In Kathryn Lasky's *The Night Journey*, deadly anti-Semitism is the antagonist that forces a Jewish family to plan and execute a dangerous flight from czarist Russia. The story seems more credible because the modern-day family in this book believes that these memories would be so painful that their great-grandmother should not be encouraged to remember the experiences.

In Karen Hesse's *Letters from Rifka*, a Jewish family flees Russia in 1919. The plot unfolds as Rifka writes letters to her cousin Tovah. The details reveal that degrading experiences and terror do not overcome the family's will to escape and survive. The author develops the theme that people need political and religious freedom and will go through considerable danger to obtain it. It does this by describing the often dangerous experiences the family goes through, including months of separation, before being reunited in the United States. The story may be believable because it is based on the true experiences of the author's great-aunt.

 ## THE HOLOCAUST IN CHILDREN'S AND YOUNG ADULT LITERATURE

In 1933, Adolf Hitler took power in Germany, and Germany resigned from the League of Nations. In 1935, Hitler reintroduced conscription of German soldiers and recommended rearmament, contrary to the Treaty of Versailles. Along with a rapid increase in military power came an obsessive hatred of the Jewish people. In March 1938, Hitler's war machine began moving across Europe. Austria was occupied, and imprisonment of Jews began. World War II became a reality when the Germans invaded Poland on September 1, 1939.

The 1940s saw the invasions of Norway, Belgium, and Holland; the defeat of the French army; and the evacuation of British soldiers from Dunkirk. The literature written from the start of the invasions through the defeat of Hitler's forces in 1945 includes many tales of both sorrow and heroism.

This period from January 30, 1933—beginning with the rise of the Nazis to power—through May 8, 1945—ending with the Allied defeat of Nazi Germany—is considered the most tragic period of Jewish history and is called the Holocaust. Approximately six million Jews—including one million Jewish children under the age of 18—were killed during this period.

Authors who write informational books, biographies and autobiographies, and historical fiction set in World War II often focus on the history of the Holocaust and the experiences of Jewish people in hiding and concentration camps. Because the literature is frequently written by people who lived similar experiences to those they are writing about, the stories tend to be emotional. The authors often create vivid conflicts as they explore the consequences of war and prejudice by having characters ponder why their lives are in turmoil, by describing the characters' fears and their reactions to their situations and to one another, and by revealing what happens to the characters or their families as a result of war. As might be expected, the themes of these stories include the consequences of hatred and prejudice, the search for religious and personal freedom, the role of conscience, and obligations toward others.

Educational and Political Background of the Time of the Holocaust

Several of the biographies and autobiographies as well as historical fiction novels discussed in this chapter mention the importance of education in the lives of the protagonists. This is especially true in the autobiographies of persons who were in hiding. For example, Nelly S. Toll in *Behind the Secret Window: A Memoir of a Hidden Childhood During World War Two* dreams of and draws pictures associated with attending school. She hopes that one day she will attend school like her mother.

Eleanor H. Ayer's *Parallel Journeys* allows readers to understand the role of books and education, especially through the viewpoint of Hitler youth: one is Jewish, and the other a member of a German youth organization. By using alternating chapters to tell the story of each, Ayer allows readers to understand two very different experiences. Notice in the following example how Ayer introduces attitudes toward school and books. Alfons Heck, the German youth, introduces his memories in this way:

> Unlike our elders, we children of the 1930's had never known a Germany without Nazis. From our very first year in the Volksschule or elementary school, we received daily doses of Nazism. These we swallowed as naturally as our morning milk. Never did we question what our teachers said. We simply believed whatever was crammed into us. And never a moment did we doubt how fortunate we were to live in a country with such a promising future. (p. 1)

Later, he describes the massive book burning during which "[m]ore than 70,000 books with messages said to be 'threatening' to the Reich were destroyed. Thousands of onlookers cheered. Without these 'threatening' books, the Nazis had tighter control over what was taught in their schools" (p. 7). He also describes how the Jewish children were singled out for special treatment by the teachers and then were no longer permitted to attend school.

To get a better understanding of what authors describe in books, let us go back to Germany in the 1930s and 1940s, and try to re-create the educational climate during the Nazi rule. As we progress through these examples, try to picture what was happening in German education that also encouraged the Nazi attitude toward the Jewish people and, consequently, helped to lead to the Holocaust. You might consider what your attitudes would be if you were a Nazi youth or if you were a Jewish student before the Jewish students were no longer permitted to attend school.

According to Hans Mauer in *Jugend und Buch im Neuen Reich* (1934), the goals of the Reich Youth Library and Hitler Youth Organization included the following: First, books should arouse an enthusiasm for the heroes of sagas, legends, and history; for the soldiers of the great wars; and for the Fûhrer and the New Germany. These books should strengthen youth's love of the fatherland and give them ideals by which to live. Second, books should show the beauty of the German landscape. Third, books should focus on the fate of children of German ethnic groups living abroad. Such books should emphasize that German youth yearn for the Third Reich. Fourth, books should deal with the love of nature and promote nature crafts. Fifth, books should relate old German myths, folktales, and legends in a language reflecting the original folk tradition. Sixth, books should give practical advice and help to the Hitler Youth.

Christa Kamenetsky (1984) researched the role of literature in developing the National Socialist (Nazi) indoctrination, the literature plan for the seventh grade, and censorship principles of Hitler's Germany. Each of these findings provide broader insights into the role of books in Nazi Germany and the increasing prejudice against the Jewish people. As you read each of these descriptions, try to imagine the impact on education and the children.

In order to indoctrinate youth in the National Socialist Movement, the Reformed School Curriculum in literature for German schools included Nordic themes in literature, poetry, drama, and ritual with an emphasis on folktales, myths, legends, and sagas. In language, the curriculum emphasized the wisdom of the ancestors through such sources as proverbs, sayings, and place names. In geopolitics, the curriculum focused on the historical rights for eastward expansion and the spiritual character of the Nordic race. In history, the curriculum included heroic themes in German history, German fighters, German thinkers, German conquests, and German peasants and settlers.

The most revealing of these areas is the list of censorship principles advocated by the Nazi party. As you read this list, please pay particular attention to these principles and think about how the principles would have affected the Jewish people:

1. Removal of books that contradict the Nordic Germanic attitude. This includes books that show unheroic Germanic characters, pacifistic themes, or weaknesses in German history

2. Removal of books that develop the wrong attitude toward Jews. Books should not portray Jewish people as noble protagonists or Germans as treacherous villains

3. Removal of books that present cooperation among different races or interracial marriages

4. Removal of books that accept the imperialism of the Pope or place the monastic life over the value of a life dedicated to the service of Germany

5. Removal of books written by Jewish authors or by people who express views that dissented with those of the Nazi regime (The works of seventy Jewish writers were withheld from children. The works of forty dissidents were withheld.)

6. Removal of books for reasons of national self-preservation and national security (The Nazi party determined these security risks.)

7. Removal of books that represent sentimental clichés and moralistic tales because these books had no bearing upon promoting the heroic ethics needed for the young team of the future

As you read examples of the literature discussed in the next sections, consider how these censorship rules could influence students. You will also have a greater understanding of Ayer's biographical character in *Parallel Journeys* when he mentions that more than 70,000 books that were burned and that might be considered threatening.

Informational Books About the Holocaust

In this section, we will discuss the informational books, historical fiction, and biographies and autobiographies written about the Holocaust. According to Leslie Barban (1993), this is a very important subject that may be ignored by parents, teachers, and librarians. She stresses the consequences of silence about the subject, citing the growth of neo-Nazi groups and the apparent increase in anti-Semitism feelings. Her article titled "Remember to Never Forget" includes lists of recommended informational books, fiction and picture books, biographies and autobiographies; discussion suggestions; and activities to accompany Holocaust literature. It provides a valuable resource for anyone using Holocaust literature in a classroom.

As for evaluations of any informational books, the accuracy of the facts is extremely important in evaluations of informational books about the Holocaust. Highly emotional periods in history are difficult to present objectively. Many of the books on the Holocaust rely heavily on photographs that depict the horrors of the time period. Photographs are often more appropriate than drawings because they clarify the text and illustrate the happenings described in the text. For example, Chana Byers Abells's *The Children We Remember* presents black-and-white photographs from the Yad Vashem Archives in Jerusalem. The photographs contrast people's early lives with their later experiences in the Holocaust. The photographs leave little question about the fate of the Jewish people and the horrors that they suffered.

David A. Adler's *We Remember the Holocaust* is based on remembrances of survivors of the Holocaust, most of whom were children and teenagers at the time. The chapter headings provide a vivid introduction to the text that follows. For example, "I remember people carrying around tremendous bundles of money"; "They wanted everyone to know who the Jews were"; "Tell them I was there, I'm real. It happened." Michael Leapman's *Witnesses to War: Eight True-Life Stories of Nazi Persecution* is another source of stories about Holocaust experiences.

The information in Susan D. Bachrach's *Tell Them We Remember: The Story of the Holocaust* was researched using materials, photographs, and documents from the United States Holocaust Memorial Museum. The text is divided into three parts: Nazi Germany; the "Final Solution"; and Rescue, Resistance, and Liberation. In addition to photographs and detailed information, the text includes maps, a chronology of events associated with the Holocaust, suggestions for further reading, a glossary, and an index. The suggestions for further reading are divided according to general overviews, specialized nonfiction topics, biographies, fiction, memoirs, and art. This list is also divided into two sections: one for younger readers and one for more advanced readers.

Seymour Rossel approaches his book *The Holocaust* with an historian's detachment. He traces Adolf Hitler's rise to power; describes the harassment, internment, and extermination of many Jewish people; and discusses the Nuremberg trials of the Nazis. Rossel effectively quotes from original sources, such as diaries and letters, to allow readers to visualize the drama and draw their own conclusions

Barbara Rogasky's *Smoke and Ashes: The Story of the Holocaust* begins with the history of anti-Semitism and proceeds to the 1933–1945 experience. This text shows life in the concentration camps and explores such questions as these: Why and how did the Holocaust happen? and Didn't anyone try to stop the Holocaust? Photographs add to the feeling of tragedy.

Milton Meltzer's *Rescue: The Story of How Gentiles Saved Jews in the Holocaust* develops another side of the Holocaust and shows that many people risked their lives to help the Jewish people. This book is very important to help readers authenticate historical fiction stories such as Louis Lowry's *Number the Stars,* which is based on the resistance movement.

There are several valuable reference books that are not written for children or young adults. The information in the books, however, can easily be shared with students. For example, Sharon Keller's *The Jews: A Treasury of Art and Literature* (1992) includes beautiful reproductions of Jewish paintings. A section of the book includes art and literature that is associated with the Holocaust. *Marc Chagall and the Jewish Theater* (Guggenheim Museum, 1992) provides reproductions of Chagall's works that were first displayed in the Jewish Theater and were then left to decay in basements as the Holocaust continued.

Informational books about the Holocaust experience written for younger children may relate the experience of a loved relative who survived. For example, David Adler's *The Number on My Grandfather's Arm* is a photo essay in which a grandfather explains the meaning of his concentration camp number to his granddaughter. Even though the telling presents the sad experiences associated with his life in Poland, the warm relationship between the grandfather and granddaughter are revealed in photographs.

Shelley Tanka's *One More Border to Cross* follows the Kaplan family as they escape from Europe and eventually reach Canada. By describing the role of the Japanese consul in helping them gain visas, the author develops the theme that many people helped the Jewish people, even at the risk to their own lives and reputations.

Historical Fiction

A considerable portion of Holocaust literature written for children and adolescents is classified as historical fiction, although the stories may be based on experiences of the author or experiences of family or friends. The authors of these books usually encourage readers to see, feel, and experience the frightening person-against-society conflicts in which they place their heroes and heroines.

Although most of the books written on this subject are for slightly older readers, there are three interesting picture storybooks that are appropriate for all readers. These three books provide an introduction to the Holocaust and allow interesting comparisons. The setting for Roberto Innocenti's *Rose Blanche* is a time in Germany when a young girl's curiosity leads her to the country outside of her town where she discovers a concentration camp and the people who live behind barbed wire. The somber-colored illustrations and text depict a time of danger and hardship but also a time when the girl's unselfish actions lead her to try to help the Jewish people.

Margaret Wild's *Let the Celebrations Begin!* is also set in a concentration camp as the prisoners prepare for liberation. Julie Vivas's illustrations, drawn in pastels, and the lighter mood of the story have received some criticism.

The third picture storybook, Jo Hoestlandt's *Star of Fear, Star of Hope* is a book of friendship and terrible memories. The text begins in a compelling style: "My name is Helen, and I'm nearly an old woman now. When I'm gone, who will remember Lydia? That is why I want to tell you our story" (p. 2 unnumbered). The narrator tells her story set in France during the German occupation. Her best friend is Lydia, a Jewish girl who must wear a star. Unfortunately, the close relationship of the two girls ends on Helen's birthday when Lydia, fearing for her parents, goes home to warn them about the Nazis who are rounding up the Jews. Unable to understand why Lydia leaves her on her birthday, Helen calls out, "You're not my friend anymore." This is Helen's last encounter with Lydia because the family then disappears. The story concludes on a note of both hope and sadness: "Now I'm old. I only hope with all my heart that Lydia lived to become like me, a grandma, somewhere in the world. Maybe one day she'll read this story to her granddaughter and she'll recognize herself in it and remember me. Then she'll call me on the telephone. 'Hello, Helen?' she'll say. 'It's me, Lydia.' It would make me so happy to hear her voice. . . . I'll always have hope. . . . " (p. 27, unnumbered).

As you examine these three picture books about the Holocaust, compare the themes, the style, and the illustrations. What are the messages? Which ones seem the most appropriate to you? Why?

Most of the historical fiction selections about the Holocaust are written for older students. These stories have strong person-versus-society conflicts. For example, Uri Orlev in *The Island on Bird Street* uses actions of the character and descriptions of the society to encourage readers to understand the nature of that society. Notice in the following quote how Orlev uses actions to let readers understand the danger that the Jewish boy faces in the Warsaw ghetto:

> I walked on the dark side of the street, away from the moonlight, trying to hug the walls of the houses as closely as I could. "Stop to listen now and then," Father had told me. "Look around you and behind you. Danger doesn't only strike from the front." . . . We always took a different way back, entering at the rear of the building through a window whose bars had been sawed. (p. 36)

In this next quote, notice the descriptions of the men who come to the hidden bunker and the reactions of the boy and the people who have been hiding in the bunker:

> Its inhabitants began to come out. It took a long while for the last of them to emerge. The Germans and the policemen kept shouting, and footsteps kept crossing the ruins from the cellar to the front gate. Now and then someone stumbled. . . . Somebody fell once or maybe twice. A shot rang out. Nobody screamed, though. Even the children had stopped crying. The last footsteps left the building. I heard voices in the street and an order to line up in threes. The same as had been given us. Then they were marched away. A few more shots. Finally the car started up and drove away. . . . It was strange to think that those people had been hiding with me in one house without us even knowing about each other. . . . They'd never take me away like that. (p. 81)

Trust in and loyalty toward a parent are strong motivational forces in *The Island on Bird Street*. It is a survival story set in the Jewish ghetto of Warsaw, Poland. The book chronicles Alex's experiences as he turns a bombed-out building into a refuge, while he waits for his father's return. Orlev develops the symbolism of a lonely island, on which Alex, like Robinson Crusoe, must learn how to survive, and the terrifying historical background of the Holocaust, in which Alex witnesses the capture of his Jewish family and friends, experiences fear and loneliness, and nurses a resistance fighter's wounds. The book concludes on a note of hope. Alex's father returns, finds Alex where he promised to wait, and takes Alex to the forests to be with the partisans who are resisting the Nazis. Like Orlev's hero, Orlev spent the years 1939–1941 in hiding in the Warsaw ghetto.

Orlev's *The Man from the Other Side* is based on true experiences of a journalist who helped his stepfather smuggle food through the sewer to sell to Jewish people in the Warsaw ghetto. This is another vivid book that allows readers to glimpse the Jewish experience during World War II.

The Warsaw ghetto and the forests surrounding Warsaw are the settings for two books by Christa Laird. The author reveals the nature of the antagonist by describing the actions of a boy in *Shadow of the Wall*: "When Misha first heard the sound of marching, he was still some distance from the orphanage. He imagined the boots: black bully boots. He pressed himself into the dark shadow of the wall and waited, holding his breath as if afraid that the very bricks might betray his presence" (p. 9).

In addition to the person-versus-society conflicts that are developed as the author describes the danger from the Nazi soldiers, there are also person-versus-self conflicts. These include the torment expressed by relatives who know that their young sons and daughters are risking their lives to keep people in the ghetto alive, the fear described by the young people as they escape the ghetto through the sewers, and the conflict expressed as they realize they have a dwindling supply of physical courage. Throughout the book, the author highlights Jewish values and beliefs through the characters. For example, the need for prayer is shown as children are taught the Jewish prayers so that they will remember "an echo from a lost world"; the importance of taking part in Hebrew classes is emphasized, even in the times of fear; and a code of laws is developed so that there will be no unjust verdicts within the ghetto. Laird's *But Can the Phoenix Sing?* is a sequel to *Shadow of the Wall* as Misha, escaping from the Warsaw ghetto, joins the resistance movement and lives in the forest of Parczew near Warsaw.

The importance of trying to keep the family together is an important theme in Holocaust novels such as Edith Baer's *Walk the Dark Street*. The author, the only member of her immediate family to survive the Holocaust, vividly depicts this time as she focuses on concerns such as searching for missing relatives.

Carol Matas's *Daniel's Story* was published in conjunction with an exhibit called "Daniel's Story: Remember the Children" at the United States Holocaust Memorial Museum in Washington, D.C. Although the story is fictional, it is based on the real experiences of many children who were first required to live in a ghetto and then moved to a concentration camp.

Several historical fiction books focus on the Jewish people and the Gentiles who helped them during the Holocaust. Johanna Reiss tells a fictional version of her own life in *The Upstairs Room*. Reiss allows readers to glimpse the varying consequences of prejudice and hatred as a young girl, Johanna, hears news of the war and asks why Hitler hates her people. Reiss shows people heroically fulfilling the obligations of one human to another when a Dutch family offers, in spite of great danger, to hide Johanna and her sister on their farm. The farmer builds a secret space in an upstairs closet to provide a hiding place for the two girls. At first, Johanna does not understand why she and her sister must hide, but gradually, she realizes their serious predicament, as word of the Holocaust spreads.

In several scenes, Reiss's style and first-person point of view make the children's fear seem immediate and direct; for example, as the children hide in the cramped closet, here is the tense description:

> Footsteps. Loud ones. Boots. Coming up the stairs. Wooden shoes. Coming behind. Sini put her arms around me and pushed my head against her shoulder. Loud voices. Ugly ones. Furniture being moved. And Opoe's protesting voice. The closet door was thrown open. Hands fumbled on the shelves. Sini was trembling. She tightened her arms around me. I no longer breathed through my nose. Breathing through my mouth made less noise. (p. 149)

Iva Vos's *Hide and Seek* presents the cruel world of the Holocaust as it changes the lives of Jewish people living in the Netherlands under German occupation. Through characterization and developing conflict, the author encourages readers to understand both the courage of the Jewish people and the determination of the Dutch Gentiles who risked their lives for their neighbors. This book can be compared with Lois Lowry's *Number the Stars*, set in Copenhagen in which the Danes try to save their Jewish citizens. As you read these two books, compare Vos's and Lowry's motivation for writing their books. Are there any similarities in these motivations?

The Jewish characters in *Hide and Seek* and *Number the Stars* survive their terrifying experiences. Another strong survivor is developed in Uri Orlev's *Lydia, Queen of*

Palestine. This is a lighter story than the previously discussed novels. In this story, ten-year-old Lydia escapes from Romania to Palestine, where she becomes a resident of a kibbutz. Readers enjoy this often humorous story of a free-spirited child who considers herself "a terror." During her life in the kibbutz, she causes three nannies to be discharged, copes with her parents' divorce by inflicting tortures on a doll that she considers the "other woman," and creates a dream world in which she marries a Romanian prince and later becomes Queen of Palestine. Lydia has many of the characteristics needed to be a survivor.

Biography and Autobiography

First-person accounts of an incident are among the most powerful portrayals of the Holocaust experience. Certainly, *Anne Frank: The Diary of a Young Girl: The Definitive Edition* is among the most widely read autobiographies of the Holocaust. The diary, written by Anne Frank while she was in hiding in the attic of a house in Amsterdam, provides an intimate view of family life during the Holocaust.

The following entry from the diary is an excellent example of the power of Anne Frank's story:

Friday, October 9, 1942

Dear Kitty,
Today I have nothing but dismal and depressing news to report. Our many Jewish friends and acquaintances are being taken away in droves. The Gestapo is treating them very roughly and transporting them in cattle cars to Westerbork, the big camp in Drenthe to which they're sending all the Jews. Miep told us about someone who'd managed to escape from there. It must be terrible in Westerbork. The people get almost nothing to eat, much less to drink, as the water is available only one hour a day, and there's only one toilet and sink for several thousand people. Men and women sleep in the same room, and women and children often have their heads shaved. Escape is almost impossible; many people look Jewish, and they're branded by their shorn heads. (p. 54)

Through her diary, Anne Frank reflects not only growing fear but also love for life. This ability is highlighted in Patricia Hampl's review of the book published in *The New York Times Book Review* (1995). Hampl states, "The 'Diary,' now 50 years old, remains astonishing and excruciating. It is a work almost sick with terror and tension, even as it performs its miracle of lucidity. . . . All that remains is this diary, evidence of her ferocious appetite for life. It gnaws at us still" (p. 21).

You may compare the impact of, and the content covered in, Anne Frank's autobiography with two biographies of Frank written for younger readers: Johanna Hurwitz's *Anne Frank: Life in Hiding* and Ruud van der Rol and Rian Verhoeven's *Anne Frank: Beyond the Diary*. Both authors develop strong feelings of advocacy for Anne Frank and the Jewish people, as well as attacks against the developing attitudes of anti-Semitism and the experiences of the Jewish people in the concentration camps. You may also consider how these two books may differ because the authors know more about the outcomes of the Holocaust than were known by Anne Frank when she wrote her autobiography.

You may also compare Anne Frank's autobiography with Livia Bitton-Jackson's *I Have Lived a Thousand Years: Growing Up in the Holocaust*. The autobiography focuses on the life of a thirteen-year-old Hungarian girl and the experiences of her family as they live in ghettos, forced labor camps, and in both Auschwitz and

Dachau. Readers understand the severe consequences of the experiences when she is finally liberated and someone assumes that Livia is sixty years old.

Nelly S. Toll's *Behind the Secret Window: A Memoir of a Hidden Childhood During World War Two* is another interesting personal account of the Holocaust. For thirteen months, eight-year-old Nelly and her mother were hidden from the Nazis by a Gentile couple in Lwow, Poland. During this time, Nelly kept a diary that she later used to write her memoir. Although the text tells about the frightening occurrences that are part of her life, the illustrations in the text are reproductions of paintings that she drew while she was in hiding. The paintings allowed her to create the world of a normal childhood filled with happy families and school friends.

Ilse Koehn's *Mischling, Second Degree: My Childhood in Nazi Germany* provides valuable insights into history and the values of both the Jewish and German people. The title of the book is based on one of the three basic designations of Jewish people under the Nazis. The first is Jew—anyone with three racially full Jewish grandparents, or a person belonging to the Jewish religious community. The second is Mischling, first degree—anyone with two Jewish grandparents. The third is Mischling, second degree—anyone with one Jewish grandparent and not of the Jewish faith or married to a Jew. Additional history is revealed as Ilse discusses German philosophies. Many of these are similar to those discussed earlier under the German curriculum for Hitler Youth. For example, she talks about "Blood and Soil," which means old German soil soaked with German blood. There is a description of the big bonfire in front of the Berlin University after Hitler ordered the burning of books that were "un-German." The response of her Jewish father to this incident reveals his love of books when he buries his forbidden literature in the garden. By contrasting the German and Jewish side of her family, the author reveals many Jewish values that were not as respected by her German relatives such as the value of books and studying: "'Sure, he's good-looking, charming, plays the guitar,' Mutter Dereck said to her neighbor, 'but what does that get you? And books, books, books.' She sneered. "Studies after work, he does. If he has so much energy left over, why doesn't he come here to help? God knows we could use an extra pair of hands'" (p. 3).

Although Ilse is not placed in a concentration camp, she experiences the farewell of her grandmother and describes her courage as she is placed on the train heading for Theresienstadt concentration camp. The book is filled with the need for secrecy even for a young girl as she discovers that her motto is: "Stay alive! Stay alive! Stay alive!" (p. 207).

An effective author's style may be one of the most important literary elements used to increase understanding of the Jewish experience during World War II. In *No Pretty Pictures: A Child of War*, Anita Lobel, the future Caldecott Honor winner, develops her own life experiences during the years in Krakow, in hiding in the countryside, while living in the ghetto, and during internment in various concentration camps. Lobel does not complete her autobiography, however, with liberation. Instead, she tells about her life of recuperation in Sweden following her imprisonment by the Nazis. Lobel uses an especially effective writing style to allow readers to understand the full meaning of the changes in her life.

In the second part of her autobiography—which is set in Sweden—Lobel uses contrasting descriptions of settings, personal responses to food, and emotional reactions to help readers understand the differences. For example, notice in the following quote how Lobel helps readers visualize the changes in her life by contrasting settings:

> At first I had spent a lot of time in bed, getting up only to go to the toilet and to wash in the bathroom down the corridor. I don't know how soon I came to take for granted

Three important issues are discussed in journals and in informational books written for adults in relation to the topic of the Holocaust: (1) How should authors write about the Holocaust? (2) How should the Holocaust be taught in schools? (3) How can people be prepared to answer the claims of those who deny the Holocaust?

Hazel Rochman (1992) provides an interesting discussion about how authors should and should not approach writing about the Holocaust. In a review of Ruth Minsky Sender's *The Holocaust Lady* (1992), Rochman maintains that even though this book is much discussed, it is an example of how authors should not write about the Holocaust. Rochman states, "The writing here is sentimental and self-centered, full of cliché about 'horror, pain, and degradation.' On almost every page, at least once, her tears glide, glisten, or roll gently down her cheeks, and/or her heart skips a beat; people read her work with quivering hands, their faces distorted with pain" (p. 46). In contrast, Rochman discusses books such as Ida Vos's *Hide and Seek* (1991) and

Maus Spiegelman's *Maus: A Survivor's Tale* (1991), which are written in a controlled style that has greater power. As you study books about the Holocaust, decide which styles are most effective for presenting this time period.

Two other authors present issues that are important when reading and discussing Holocaust literature. Wilson Frampton (1991) argues that although Holocaust education is vital to our understanding of both the past and the future, the subject is not found in many school curricula and is inadequately covered in history textbooks. Frampton states:

> In summary the issue of Holocaust education will continue to percolate. It's a topic identified by many but comprehended by few. The revisionists are producing massive literature that denies the Holocaust ever existed. When a student is confronted with this 'type' literature will he or she have the ability to recognize the underlying message or will the student fall prey and assume the revisionist point of

view? The literature of the revisionists is dedicated toward discrediting the Holocaust as nothing more than a 'Jewish myth.'" (pp. 34-35)

In her book, *Denying the Holocaust: The Growing Assault on Truth and Memory*, Deborah Lipstadt (1994) presents the strategies that people use when they deny the existence of the Holocaust and discusses the claims of the deniers. She concludes her book with a chapter on "Twisting the Truth." The section in which she discusses the documentation of *The Diary of Anne Frank* and the strategies that deniers use to claim that the book was written after the war are of particular interest to anyone interested in literature about the Holocaust.

As you read these articles and books, ask yourself these questions: What is your viewpoint on the writing style of Holocaust literature? How is the Holocaust taught in schools today? How should the Holocaust be taught? What is your answer to people who would deny the existence of the Holocaust?

---

the luxury of the flushing toilet, the sink to wash in, the fresh towels. I had no lice in my stubby hair anymore, no lice in the seams of my pajamas. The sheets on my bed were so white, so clean. . . . These were miraculous pleasures after the filthy bunks barely filled with hay and burlap. For years my body, my skin had not felt the wrappings of such comfort. (p. 130)

Lobel contrasts the memories brought on by such simple things as smells, sounds, bus rides, gates, weather, and announcements. Through these contrasts, readers also gain an understanding of the fear and suspicion that became a part of Lobel's life and how difficult it was for her to overcome her suspicious reactions. Lobel creates a many-sided character by contrasting and describing her own reactions and conflicting person-versus-self conflicts. By the conclusion of the autobiography, the author has developed a strong character who understands her own need for self-realization, especially through her artwork.

Jewish poetry ranges from the words of the Psalms and Proverbs found in the Writings (the third section of the Hebrew Bible) to expressions of fear, horror, and hope for life written during the Holocaust, as well as to contemporary poetry that expresses longings for peace and stability.

The best-known poetry is probably the poetry written in Psalms and Proverbs. When writing about this poetry, Gloria Goldreich (1982) declares that the Psalms and Proverbs offer advice on how individuals can live moral and just lives. She states:

> In the Book of Psalms, it is Israel and the human heart that speak. The individual psalmist, speaking either for himself or for the Jewish people, expresses sorrow, disappointment, and suffering, as well as gratitude, exaltation, and blessing. The lyric words of the verses convey the inner mood of the individual and give voice to the vast sweep of human emotions. The pathos of sorrow, the thrill of victory, the despair of defeat, and the affirmation of hope all find voice in wondrously linked words, alleged to have been penned by King David, the poet-warrior, "the sweet singer in Israel." (p. 26)

Herbert G. May and Bruce M. Metzger (1973, 1977) provide the following classifications for the Psalms: hymns, in which individuals express acts of praise; laments, in which individuals seek deliverance from illness or false accusation, or the nation asks for help; songs of trust, in which an individual expresses his confidence in God's readiness to help; thanksgiving, in which an individual expresses gratitude for deliverance; sacred history, in which the nation recounts the story of its past; royal psalms, which are used during special occasions such as coronations or royal weddings; and wisdom Psalms, in which the individual meditates on life.

One of the most famous Psalms is Psalm 100. As you read this poem notice that it is a hymn calling for all nations to praise the Lord:

Psalm 100

Make a joyful noise to the Lord, all the lands!

Serve the Lord with gladness!

Come into his presence with singing!

Know that the Lord is God!

It is he that made us, and we are his;

We are his people, and the sheep of his pasture.

Enter his gates with thanksgiving, and his courts with praise!

Give thanks to him, bless his name!

For the Lord is good;

His steadfast love endures for ever,

And his faithfulness to all generations.

Many of the values and beliefs presented in earlier literature in this chapter are apparent when reading the Proverbs, which are attributed to Solomon, the son of David. The quest for wisdom and knowledge are found throughout Proverbs. For example, Proverbs 1, verse 2, admonishes "That men may know wisdom and instruction." Proverbs 2, verse 2 teaches the need to be "attentive to wisdom" and include "your heart to understanding." Chapter 2, verses 8, 9, and 10 states that those who guard the paths of justice and preserve the way of God's saints can expect the following:

> Then you will understand
>> righteousness and justice
>> and equity, every good path;
> for wisdom will come into your
>> heart,
> and knowledge will be pleasant
>> to your soul; . . .

David's Songs: His Psalms and Their Story, selected by Colin Eisler and illustrated by Jerry Pinkney, provides an attractive introduction to both the Psalms and the history of David. To provide additional clarification, Eisler introduces each of the Psalms with a few sentences that explore the meaning of the poem.

Just as the Psalms include hymns of praise, there are songs that are sung during traditional Jewish holidays. Jeanne Modesitt's *Songs of Chanukah* is a collection of fourteen songs that are sung during this eight-day holiday. The book includes an introduction to each song that states when it would be sung or explains the meaning of the song. The text includes musical arrangements for piano and chords for guitar.

Some of the Jewish poetry is similar in nature to the Yiddish folktales presented in this chapter. For example, Mani-Leib's *Yingle Tsingl Khvat* is a humorous poem that tells the story of a shtetl, a little village, in which the rainy autumn continues until the village is so muddy that neither people on foot or on horseback can reach the market. The poem reveals how Yingle Tsingl solves the villagers' problem by bringing winter to the town. The poem contains many elements of Yiddish folktales, including a synagogue; a rebbe, who is a plucky and daring hero who is brave and adventurous even though he is small; and a magic object.

Poetry written during the Holocaust contains similar themes as those found in the historical fiction and biography with Holocaust settings. One of the best collections of poetry written by children during this period is . . . *I Never Saw Another Butterfly . . . : Children's Drawings and Poems from Terezin Concentration Camp, 1942-1944,* edited by Hana Volavkova. As you read the following poem, notice what the child misses and how the child expresses the desolation of the ghetto:

The Butterfly
The last, the very last,
So richly, brightly, dazzling yellow,
Perhaps if the sun's tears would sing
    against a white stone. . . .
Such, such a yellow
Is carried lightly 'way up high.
It went away I'm sure because it wished to
    kiss the world good-bye.
For seven weeks I've lived in here,

Penned up inside this ghetto.

But I have found what I love here.

The dandelions call to me

And the white chestnut branches in the court.

Only I never saw another butterfly.

That butterfly was the last one.

Butterflies don't live in here,

   in the ghetto.

1942 Pavel Friedmann (p. 39)

Notice in this next example, that even though there is a feeling of fear, there is still a strong feeling of Jewish pride and dignity:

I Am a Jew

   I am a Jew and will be a Jew forever.

Even if I should die from hunger,

   never will I submit.

I will always fight for my people,

   on my honor.

I will never be ashamed of them,

I give my word.

I am proud of my people,

   how dignified they are.

Even though I am suppressed,

I will always come back to life.

Franta Bass (p. 57)

Contemporary poets continue to develop themes that are similar ones in the earlier poems as searching for God and the need for peace. Sandy Eisenberg Sasso suggests in her poem *In God's Name* that people may call God by different names, but all of the names such as "Creator of Light," "Shepherd," and "Redeemer" are all really the same name.

In *The Matzah That Papa Brought Home*, Fran Manushkin uses the structure of a cumulative rhyme to tell about a family preparing for and celebrating the Passover Seder. The poem begins with the matzah (unleavened bread) that Papa brought home and is expanded with new verse elements relating to the Passover Seder as they shared: the asking of the four questions; the counting of ten plagues; the singing of the "Dayenu," which has fourteen verses; the dipping of bitter herbs; the sipping of the matzah ball soup; the hunting for and finding the afikoman, which is a piece of matzah hidden at the start of the Seder; the opening of the door for Elijah in the hope that the prophet will come and bring peace to the people of the earth; and the hugging and saying "Next year in Jerusalem." The poem ends on this joyous note, which has a special meaning to Jewish people who were scattered around the world for centuries and could not return to Israel. Both the cumulative poem and the illustrations convey feelings of family closeness, as well as of excitement as the family looks forward to the days of the Passover and to the experiences they will remember.

Several of the poems included in Naomi Shihab Nye's anthology *This Same Sky: A Collection of Poems from Around the World* are written by authors from Israel. These poems reflect contemporary conflicts, especially the conflict between war and peace. Poet Yehuda Amichai declares that he is influenced by the ethics of his father and by the cruelties of war. This conflict is developed in his poem "Wildpeace" as he searches for a peace that comes quickly like wildflowers and in "Jerusalem," in which he considers the two sides of the conflict and what people do to try to convince each other that they are happy.

Poet Dahlia Ravikovitch, who was raised on a collective farm, voices her independence and her creativity in "Magic" as she visualizes herself today as a hill and tomorrow the wondering sea. Throughout her poem, she thinks of both today and tomorrow. The poem ends on a strong feeling for hope because she knows that tomorrow, she will be tomorrow.

CONTEMPORARY JEWISH LITERATURE

The literature written about Jewish experiences after the Holocaust differs considerably depending on the age of the intended audience. Picture storybooks develop themes about relationships and the importance of family or depict important holidays in the life of the Jewish community. Books written for older audiences may describe the experiences of survivors from the Holocaust as they learn to live in a new land, follow characters who experience anti-Semitism, or develop the conflicts felt by Jewish characters when they live in non-Jewish environments.

Picture Storybooks

The Keeping Quilt, by Patricia Polacco, develops a strong symbol of family history and unity in the object of a family quilt. The quilt is made from the old clothes of family members in the hope that the quilt will help the family remember their previous home in Russia. The text and illustrations describe the various ways in which the quilt is used by the family through the generations: a tablecloth for the Sabbath, a wedding canopy, a blanket for a newborn baby. Finally, the quilt is used to wrap the latest member of Polacco's own family. There is a feeling of continuity as Polacco suggests that the new baby will use the quilt as she grows and take the quilt with her when she leaves home.

Many of the books for younger readers explain the importance of various Jewish customs, holidays, and celebrations. Both Barbara Goldin and Patricia Polacco authored books about Sukkot, also called The Feast of Tabernacles or the Festival of Booths, a week-long holiday in September or October that is a reminder of generations of homelessness. To celebrate Sukkot, Jewish people build little huts, or sukkot. Sukkot marked the forty years that Israelites wandered in the desert, before they entered the Promised Land. In Goldin's *Night Lights: A Sukkot Story,* a young boy helps the family build the sukkah. Through the preparation, the author reveals the history of the celebration. Two of the main characters, Daniel and Naomi, also overcome their fear as they look through the branches and stalks that form the roof of the hut and realize that the stars and moon that light the night are the same stars and moon that the early wanderers in the desert and farmers in the field saw through their sukkah roofs.

In *Tikvah Means Hope* by Patricia Polacco, two children and an elderly man build a sukkah. After the children spend the night in the hut, they go with the man to the market to buy food for the festive meal. This story becomes a story of miracles when a fire ravages Oakland, California. The miraculous experience occurs when both the sukkah and Tikvah, the pet cat, are saved from destruction.

A prayer shawl is a symbol of continuity between generations in Sheldon Oberman's *The Always Prayer Shawl*. Ted Lewin's illustrations reinforce the idea of different generations because the illustrations of the early history of the prayer shawl and the grandfather are painted in black and white. When the younger boy, Adam, grows into manhood the artwork changes to color. When Adam becomes a grandfather himself, he tells the story of the prayer shawl to his own grandson who is also named Adam. Notice how the story concludes on a sense of continuity as "Adam's grandson whispered into his ear. 'I am going to be just like you. I will have a grandson whose name will be Adam. And someday I will give him this Always Prayer Shawl.'" (p. 32).

The Sabbath traditions are developed in both text and illustrations in *Starlight and Candles: The Joys of the Sabbath* by Fran Manushkin. The text uses the Sabbath traditions of one family to introduce various aspects of the Sabbath such as baking the Challah bread, telling the origins of the first Sabbath, lighting of the candles, saying the Sabbath blessings, welcoming of the Sabbath Bride, attending the synagogue, and carrying the Torah.

Books written by Roni Schotter, Jenny Koralek, and Eric A. Kimmel focus on the Passover and Hanukkah. Schotter's *Passover Magic* follows a family and their relatives as they prepare for and celebrate the Passover with the traditional Seder. The author's note presents additional information about the Passover and the history of the Jewish people as they escaped from slavery. This information includes the significance of various symbolic foods. Koralek's *Hanukkah: The Festival of Lights* presents the history of the holiday and discusses the symbolism of the Hanukkah candles. Kimmel's *A Hanukkah Treasury* includes stories, recipes, and games.

Hanukkah and Christmas both feature in Michael J. Rosen's *Elijah's Angel: A Story for Chanukah and Christmas*. In this story of friendship between Michael, a nine-year-old Jewish boy, and Elijah, an elderly African American wood carver, the person-versus-self conflict develops when Elijah gives Michael a carved angel as a gift for Christmas. Michael now tries to decide if it is all right to have a Christmas angel in a Jewish home. The story has an ecumenical ending as the boy's parents tell him that the angel represents friendship, "And doesn't friendship mean the same thing in every religion?" (p. 21). The ecumenical theme is strengthened at the close of the story when Michael gives his friend a menorah and the Jewish family finds candles lit on the menorah that is placed in the window of Elijah's shop.

Books for Older Readers

Novels for older readers may focus on the lives of characters and their families after they escape from the Holocaust and settle in a new country. Some of these stories are filled with happy experiences, while others include the tragic outcomes of prejudice and anti-Semitism.

Research studies reported by Tamar Shoshan (1989) and William B. Helmreich (1990) highlight the viewpoints of many survivors and children of survivors. These are interesting reports because many of the research findings are also found in novels. For example, Shoshan concludes:

> Findings from dozens of in-depth interviews with Holocaust survivors indicate that the shock and pain of the violent, often sudden, separation from their closest family members, more than any other of their dreadful experiences, determined the extent of their individual traumas. These survivors seem to be in a state of permanent, incomplete mourning, expressed in somber states of mind, which their children, the second generation, have absorbed almost from birth. A unique kind of mutual dependence developed between these children and their parents. (p. 206)

Shoshan maintains that children of survivors long for memories they are unable to acquire, especially for a sense of connectedness with family members from the pre-Holocaust past.

In another study that looks at Holocaust survivors, Helmreich (1990) identifies two different types of responses by those who came to the United States. In the early responses are a buoyant quality in which the refugees want to emulate the spirit of earlier "pioneers" who came to the United States. In contrast, journal entries of social workers tell about immigrants who had difficulty adapting to the relatives and friends who welcomed them to the new land and to the struggle to find adequate housing and decent jobs. In addition, some of the immigrants experienced anxiety, depression, and paranoia. These survivors were surrounded by a broad cross section of the U.S. population who knew little about the Jewish culture and their previous experiences. Helmreich points out that the Jewish immigrants faced two problems as they tried to assimilate into life in the United States: (1) they had been weakened physically and psychologically by their experiences and (2) they had little or no English and were unfamiliar with U.S. culture. The survivors brought with them, however, a desire to preserve Jewish culture and to raise the level of Jewish consciousness to new heights. Many of these immigrants brought with them a need to remember the Holocaust and a strong support for Israel.

Many of the characteristics identified by Shoshan and Helmreich are also found in realistic fiction. Sonia Levitin's characters in *Silver Days* and *Annie's Promise* face severe changes in their lives as Papa works desperately hard to make a living and Mama, formerly a lady from a well-to-do background, takes on menial jobs to help support her family. The author uses contrasts between life in pre-war Germany and life as Jewish immigrants in the United States to develop the understanding of changes in their life.

The trauma experienced by Kathryn Lasky's heroine in *Pageant* is of a lighter and more humorous nature. Her conflict occurs in situations such as playing a shepherd in the annual Christmas pageant and trying to survive Stuart Hall, an exclusive girls school with predominately Christian students.

Nonfiction books for older audiences may focus on important celebrations or on other cultural information. Books about the Jewish coming of age have been written by Eric A. Kimmel and Barbara Diamond Goldin. Kimmel's *Bar Mitzvah: A Jewish Boy's Coming of Age* describes the importance of being thirteen, the history of the bar mitzvah, and the responsibilities that accompany this ceremony.

In the following quote, notice how Kimmel develops the meaning of the bar mitzah experience and the history associated with it:

> Suddenly you are aware that there are other people standing with you. You cannot see them, but you feel their presence—aged rabbis bent over yellow pages of the Talmud;

old women lighting Sabbath candles; a family standing together on the edge of a corpse filled pit, looking not at the bodies below, but at the sky above; young pioneers, men and women, building a new nation in an ancient land with hands on the plow and rifles on their shoulders. They are all here—people of the book and people of the sword; dwellers in tents and dwellers in palaces, those who spoke with peasants and those who conversed with kings. (p. 103)

Kimmel tells his readers that now they understand what it means to become bar mitzvah and become part of the ancestors who go back to the time of Abraham. In *Bat Mitzvah: A Jewish Girl's Coming of Age*, Barbara Diamond Goldin uses a similar approach to describe the ceremony and preparation for the Jewish girl's coming of age.

How Do You Spell God? Answers to the Big Questions from Around the World is an interesting comparative text designed to answer questions about different religions. Rabbi Marc Gellman and Monsignor Thomas Hartman answer questions in nineteen chapters. The title of each chapter is based on a question that is then answered in that chapter. Some of these questions include: What's a religion? How are religions the same? How are religions different? How do you spell God? What questions does each religion want to answer the most? Can I talk to God? In addition to Jewish and Christian answers, the book provides basic information on other organized religions including Hinduism, Buddhism, Confucianism, Shinto, and Islam.

 ## SUMMARY

In this chapter, we have analyzed the folklore and ancient stories of the Jewish people and identified the values, beliefs, and types of stories found in the literature.

Many of the folklore selections reflect the values and beliefs of the people including messages that show the importance of such values as faith, learning, hospitality, knowledge, cooperation, and charity. Various examples of Jewish folklore were discussed, including wonder tales, humorous tales, tales of ghosts and goblins, clever folks and survivors, and legends with Biblical sidelights.

We considered literature, both nonfiction and fiction, that provided a vivid history of the Jewish people and the years of emigration and immigration. The nonfiction books cover important periods in Jewish history and may focus on historical change in locations such as Jerusalem. Books that create vivid images of fleeing Europe in the early 1900s depict the importance of and trauma associated with developing a new life in a new land.

We discussed literature about the Holocaust including historical fiction, biography, and autobiography. The most emotional literature of the Holocaust is told through the point of view of authors who either lived through the experience or had friends or family members who told their stories to the authors.

Finally, we considered contemporary works. Through this literature, we discovered threads that proceed from the earliest folklore through poetry and contemporary literature.

SUGGESTED ACTIVITIES FOR DEVELOPING UNDERSTANDING OF JEWISH LITERATURE

1. Develop a time line of Jewish history. Identify literature that relates to important occurrences. Discuss why you believe that the literature is a good example of the period.

2. Choose a value found in Jewish folklore and collect examples of literature that exemplify that value. Discuss how the value is developed through the folklore.

3. Two examples of a Cinderella-type tale were discussed in the chapter ("How Much Do You Love Me?" in Beatrice Silverman Weinreich's *Yiddish Folktales* and Nina Jaffe's *The Way Meat Loves Salt: A Cinderella Tale from the Jewish Tradition*). Locate additional tales that are similar to those found in other cultures. How is the variant similar to the tales from other countries and how does the tale develop a Jewish perspective?

4. Read Eleanor Ayer's *Parallel Journeys* and compare the points of view of the Jewish girl who survived the Holocaust and the German youth who grew up as part of the Hitler Youth Organization. Discuss how the goals of the Reich Youth Library and the school curriculum discussed in this chapter might have influenced German youth.

5. Compare the information revealed in an adult source about hidden children during World War II such as Jane Marks's *The Hidden Children: The Secret Survivors of the Holocaust* (1995) with that found in a version written for juvenile audiences such as Howard Greenfeld's *The Hidden Children*. If possible, interview a survivor of the Holocaust. How is the survivor's story similar or different from those personal narratives revealed in the literature?

6. Read personal narratives about an experience during the Holocaust such as Adina Blady Szwajger's *I Remember Nothing More: The Warsaw Children's Hospital and the Jewish Resistance* (1990) and compare Szwajger's point of view and experiences with those expressed in historical fiction. For example, Chapter 18, "Children in Hiding," reflects sentiments similar to those expressed by Christa Laird in *Shadow of the Wall* and *But Can the Phoenix Sing?*

7. Research newspapers and magazines to locate articles on pro-Jewish sentiment and anti-Semitism. Discuss your findings and the possible consequences of these sentiments or actions.

8. Choose a Jewish person who is the subject of biographies and, if possible, who has also written an autobiography. Compare the information in the literature. What are the points of view expressed? Analyze the authenticity of each title.

9. Compare the values and beliefs developed in Jewish folklore with the values and beliefs expressed in Jewish poetry. What similarities do you find? If there are differences, how do you account for the differences?

Involving Children with Jewish Literature

 PHASE ONE: TRADITIONAL LITERATURE

As discussed in this chapter, the Jewish folklore transmits the essential values of the culture, provides a portrait of the people, offers an understanding of the Jewish heritage, and furnishes links to both the biblical and historical past.

Webbing the Values Found in Jewish Folklore.

Begin this webbing activity by acquiring as many examples of Jewish folklore as possible. As students read the folklore, have them develop a web showing its important characteristics. Figure 6–1 is an example of a partial web about Jewish folklore developed with students.

As students add to the web, ask them to discuss the importance of the values, the historical characters, and the references to places and people.

Comparing Three Versions of the Golem

Students may read and compare the illustrations and the texts in three versions of The Golem story: David Wisniewski's *Golem*, Barbara Rogasky's *The Golem*, and Isaac Bashevis Singer's *The Golem*. Students may read all three texts and compare the power of the writing, consider the quality of the information provided in the author's or illustrator's notes, and view and discuss the impact of the illustrations. They may also consider why Wisniewski's illustrations were chosen as one of the ten best-illustrated books of the year and presented with the Caldecott Medal, and why the Isaac Bashevis Singer's text (Singer was a recipient of the Nobel Prize) was chosen as an American Library Association "Notable Book," a *School Library Journal* "Best Book of the Year," a *New York Times Book Review* "Notable Children's Book of the Year," and a *New York Times* "Outstanding Book of the Year."

FIGURE 6–1 Web Showing Traditional Jewish Values Found in Folklore

ADDITIONAL ACTIVITIES TO ENHANCE PHASE ONE

Here are some activities for children or young adult students related to this phase:

1. Compare Nina Jaffe's *The Way Meat Loves Salt: A Cinderella Tale from the Jewish Tradition* with Cinderella stories found in other cultures. What are the similarities? What are the differences? What makes Jaffe's retelling a Jewish folktale?

2. Make an annotated bibliography of tales that may be categorized as parables and allegorical tales, children's tales or kinder-mayselekh, wonder tales, pious tales, humorous tales, legends, and supernatural tales. What are the characteristics of each type of tale that make it appealing to the reader? What are the cultural contributions of each type of tale?
3. Many of the humorous Jewish tales are especially appealing to children. Choose a favorite humorous tale and prepare it as a readers' theater.

PHASE TWO: ADAPTATIONS OF TRADITIONAL LITERATURE

Developing a Person-Against-Person Plot Structure with a Literary Folktale

Literary folktales include many of the characteristics of traditional tales told through the oral tradition. For example, Eric A. Kimmel's *Hershel and the Hanukkah Goblins* is similar to many of the traditional Jewish folktales. In addition, the plot structure provides an excellent source for developing a person-against-person plot structure that is found in many of the folktales.

Plots in stories frequently follow a triangle, a structure in which the beginning of the story identifies the problem, introduces the characters, and describes the setting. Increasing conflict is then developed until the story reaches a climax. Following the climax there is usually a turning point incident, followed quite rapidly by an end of conflict or a resolution of the problem. To show this conflict, you might present students with a plot diagram similar to that in Figure 6–2.

Ask the students to think about some stories they know that follow this type of plot structure. For example, they can retell "The Three Billy Goats Gruff" or "Goldilocks and the Three Bears" and decide how the story follows this diagram. Asking students to act out one of these stories will help them understand and appreciate the developing conflict. After students have retold or acted out a familiar story, have them place the incidents from the story on the plot diagram.

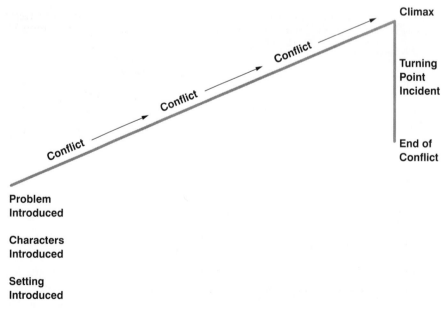

FIGURE 6–2   A Plot Diagram

Select a Jewish folktale—a traditional or a literary retelling—that has a strong plot development that can be shown on such a plot structure. For example, *Hershel and the Hanukkah Goblins* is a literary folktale similar to many Jewish folktales. The story is set in a village during Hanukkah. Hershel, the main character, enters the village and discovers that the people are unable to celebrate Hanukkah because wicked goblins haunt the synagogue. To rid the village of goblins, someone must spend eight nights in the old synagogue, light the Hanukkah candles each night, and convince the king of the goblins to light the candles on the eighth night. Hershel declares that he is not afraid of the goblins and offers to rid the village of them. The plot develops as Hershel uses his wits and common materials to trick increasingly fearsome goblins and light the candles. The progression continues until on the eighth night, Hershel tricks the king of the goblins into lighting the Hanukkah candles. At this point the spell is broken and all of the households celebrate Hanukkah in their homes. The author develops the theme that even common materials may be used in uncommon ways if a person uses those materials with wit and intelligence.

Introduce *Hershel and the Hanukkah Goblins* to the students. Show the illustrations and ask the students to respond to the mood of the story and to consider what type of problem and conflict might be in the story. If desired, you may read the author's endnote, in which he provides information about the Hanukkah celebration.

Read the story aloud to the students. Before placing the incidents on the plot diagram, encourage the students to provide their personal responses to the story. Now draw a blank plot diagram on the board or an overhead transparency and ask the students to identify elements from the story that can be placed on the plot diagram. For example, a group of third-grade students identified the information found in Figure 6–3 (Norton & Norton, 1999).

Plot Diagram for Hershel and the Hanukkah Goblins

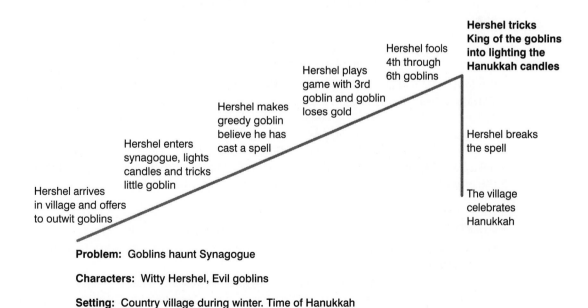

Hershel tricks King of the goblins into lighting the Hanukkah candles

Hershel fools 4th through 6th goblins

Hershel plays game with 3rd goblin and goblin loses gold

Hershel makes greedy goblin believe he has cast a spell

Hershel enters synagogue, lights candles and tricks little goblin

Hershel arrives in village and offers to outwit goblins

Hershel breaks the spell

The village celebrates Hanukkah

Problem: Goblins haunt Synagogue

Characters: Witty Hershel, Evil goblins

Setting: Country village during winter. Time of Hanukkah

FIGURE 6–3 A Plot Diagram of *Hershel and the Hanukkah Goblins*

After the students complete the plot diagram, ask them to consider what they think the theme is or the message that the author is giving. The third-grade students who completed this activity decided that the themes were (1) it is important to use one's wits and intelligence and (2) even common objects may be used to outwit the enemy if they are used with intelligence. Have the students defend their choice of themes by identifying what happened in the story to make them important. For example, all of Hershel's actions show the importance of wit and intelligence. In a search for common objects that are used to outwit the enemy, Hershel crushes a hard-boiled egg, which is part of his lunch to make the little goblin believe that he can crush rock. He uses pickles and the second goblin's greed to make it believe that he has cast a spell on the pickle jar in which the goblin has caught its fist. He uses a dreidel and his wits to play a game with the third goblin and force the goblin to lose gold. He uses Hanukkah candles to trick the king of the goblins into lighting some candles so that Hershel will believe that the goblin really is fierce and the king.

ADDITIONAL ACTIVITIES TO ENHANCE PHASE TWO

Here are some activities for children or young adult students related to this phase:

1. Search for cultural evidence related to the Jewish tradition in Trina Schart Hyman's illustrations for Eric A. Kimmel's *Hershel and the Hanukkah Goblins*.
2. Select important motifs, themes, and values found in Jewish folklore, and create your own literary folktale.

PHASE THREE: HISTORICAL NONFICTION

Historical nonfiction includes books that depict the early centuries of the Jewish people, biographies and autobiographies, and the early years of immigration and emigration.

Prepare Time Lines and Maps Showing Early Jewish History

Students might read books such as Yaffa Ganz's *Sand and Stars: The Jewish Journey Through Time;* Karla Kuskin's *Jerusalem, Shining Still;* and Neil Waldman's *The Golden City: Jerusalem's 3,000 Years*, and then develop a time line showing important dates and happenings in Jewish history.

Following the reading of Norma Finkelstein's *The Other Fourteen Ninety-Two: Jewish Settlement in the New World*, ask students to prepare a world map that shows the expulsion routes of some of the 200,000 people who left Spain.

ADDITIONAL ACTIVITIES TO ENHANCE PHASE THREE

Here are some activities for children or young adult students related to this phase:

1. Get heavily illustrated adult sources such as Sharon R. Keller's *The Jews: A Treasury of Art and Literature* (1992) or Therese and Mendel Metzger's *Jewish Life in the Middle Ages: Illuminated Hebrew Manuscripts of the Thirteenth to the Sixteenth Centuries* (1982). Develop shadow boxes, collages, or other pictorial representa-

tions of various time periods. For example, using *Jewish Life in the Middle Ages*, focus on topics depicted and illustrated in the following chapters: "The Jewish Quarter," "The House," "Costume," "The Professional Life of the Jewish Community and Its Place in the Medieval City," "Family Life," and "Religious Life."

2. Two highly illustrated informational books, Neil Waldman's *The Golden City: Jerusalem's 3,000 Years* and Karla Kuskin's *Jerusalem, Shining Still* provide a history of the city. Compare and evaluate the books by answering these questions: (1) Are the facts accurate? How do you know if the facts are accurate?; (2) What are the qualifications of the author to write the book or of the illustrator to illustrate the book?; (3) How do the illustrations help or not help readers understand the subject?; (4) How does the organization of the book help or not help the reader develop understanding of the subject?; and (5) Does the author encourage the readers to become involved in the subject?

3. Informational books about Jerusalem frequently include information about the Western Wall, which are the remains of an outer wall of the Second Temple, destroyed twenty-five hundred years ago. Conduct research to discover the history of and the importance of this wall. This activity could be expanded to include other walls that have been important in history. For example, *The Talking Walls* by Margy Burns Knight includes the Western Wall in Jerusalem, in addition to the Great Wall of China, the granite walls of Great Zimbabwe in Africa, and the Cuzco walls in the Andes of Peru, and the Vietnam Veterans Memorial in Washington, D.C. In addition, the book discusses other kinds of walls, such as carvings in the cliffs near India's Bay of Bengal, paintings on the outside walls of an Egyptian house, and the paintings of Diego Rivera found on walls throughout Mexico. This comparative study allows students to discover the importance of walls throughout history and within a diverse group of cultures.

 PHASE FOUR: HISTORICAL FICTION

The majority of historical fiction books written for children and young adults focus on the Holocaust. This topic is found in both picture storybooks and in novels. You may choose to combine a study of historical fiction with that of biography and autobiography to help students develop a clearer understanding of this time period.

The majority of recent published articles on teaching Jewish literature also focus on developing instructional strategies and units around the subject. For example, Samuel Totten (1998) stresses the need for establishing a foundation for the study of the Holocaust; Hilarie B. Davis, William R. Fernekes, and Christine R. Hladky (1999) emphasize Internet resources for studying the Holocaust; Geoffrey Short (1997) discusses learning about the Holocaust through literature; and Paul Kaplan (1998) identifies appropriate Holocaust literature.

The modeling activity developed in this section presents considerable background information. Providing background information is frequently necessary because students may not have enough prior knowledge to understand the conflict in the books.

Developing Understandings of Holocaust Literature Through Modeling

Reading researchers identify modeling as one of the most effective ways to increase comprehension of text. For example, Dole, Duffy, Roehler, and Pearson

(1991) emphasize modeling to help teachers explain the mental reasoning involved in performing various reading tasks. Early and Ericson (1988) declare that research shows that teachers neglect modeling the process and explaining or describing what students should do during a comprehension lesson. They stipulate that modeling is especially important when teaching students to make inferences. Modeling encourages readers to think about why they are responding personally to literature or a question in a certain way. Norton (1992, 1999) has developed modeling approaches designed to help students understand the inferences authors use when developing characterization and applying figurative language. Making inferences about the characters through their actions, dialogues, and thoughts is difficult for many students.

Developing the Modeling Strategy   To prepare for the modeling lesson, first identify a skill and analyze the requirements needed to implement it. For example, gaining meaning through inferred characterization requires that readers go beyond the information provided in the text; use clues from the text to hypothesize about a character's feelings, actions, beliefs, values, and so on; and use background knowledge gained from other experiences. Next, you need to identify a text and portions of the text from which characterization can be inferred.

Using the text, you need to plan ways to review the students' prior knowledge (schema) related to both the literary element and the setting, conflict, or historical happenings for the book. For example, you could develop a "review" to illustrate how authors imply characterization in literature through such devices as narration, dialogue, character's actions and thoughts, and even more subtle ways such as symbolism and figurative language. To introduce the setting or time frame for a story, use supports such as maps, pictures, films, historical time lines, picture books, and news articles that encourage students to identify prior knowledge, develop new understandings, and increase their abilities to respond to the characters and conflicts developed in the story. Activities such as brainstorming what is known, identifying images or feelings associated with a word or topic, and listing and answering questions about topics are additional ways to activate prior knowledge.

When you teach the modeling strategy you introduce or review the specific literary element that will be modeled and introduce the text. Then you model the whole sequence by reading from the text, stopping at an appropriate place and asking the inference question, answering the question, providing evidence that supports the answer, and exploring your reasoning process. This last part is extremely important because it allows you to explain how the task was approached. It also allows for an aesthetic response as you explain your personal feelings, past experiences, and previous knowledge that entered into the thought processes. Finally, when the students understand the process, they join in by answering questions, citing evidence, and exploring their own thought processes.

Modeling Example of Inferring Characterization   The book example in this modeling lesson focuses on the 1990 Newbery Award book, Lois Lowry's *Number the Stars*. This historical fiction novel is set during the Holocaust. As you prepare this modeling activity, first identify the requirements for effective reasoning so that students understand those requirements. For this lesson, students must be aware that effective inferencing requires them to go beyond the information the author provides in the text. They must use clues from the text to hypothesize about a character's emotions, beliefs, actions, hopes, and fears. Students must also be aware that authors develop characters through dialogue, narration, and characters' thoughts and actions. Share examples from literature or create your own and then ask the students to provide examples that show how they can make discoveries about characters.

Explain to the students that they will first listen to you read an excerpt from a book, ask a question, answer the question, provide evidence from the story that supports the answer, and share your reasoning process. You should also explain that after students listen to you proceed through the sequence, they will use the same process to answer questions, identify evidence, and explore their own reasoning process. You should discuss the meanings of evidence and reasoning and encourage students to consider how they use evidence and reasoning in their own lives. Students should realize that their own experiences, prior knowledge, emotions, and reactions are important parts of their reasoning process.

Then emphasize the importance of this activity by asking students to explain why it is important to be able to make inferences about characters in literature. Encourage students to discuss how understanding characterization makes a story more exciting, enjoyable, and believable. Students should also understand that they can employ characterization in their own writing.

Next, plan a way to introduce the story *Number the Stars* to students. The review of prior knowledge or the development of new knowledge about the Holocaust is extremely important for students in order for them to understand the settings and conflicts presented in *Number the Stars*. For example, to introduce the setting you can use a map of Europe on which students locate the important places in World War II. Ask students to locate the countries of the European Allies and the Axis Powers. They should locate the setting for the book (Copenhagen, Denmark) and the route taken by 7,000 Jewish people who were smuggled by the Danish Resistance across the sea to Sweden.

Students will also require background information about the events in the 1940s that created the plot and conflict developed in *Number the Stars*. To provide additional background information about the Holocaust, you could read excerpts from Barbara Rogasky's *Smoke and Ashes: The Story of the Holocaust* and Milton Meltzer's *Rescue: The Story of How Gentiles Saved the Jews in the Holocaust*. These books reinforce the reasons for the actions and terror expressed by the characters in *Number the Stars*.

Provide the first modeling example. Read orally from the beginning of the book through the section:

> Annemarie looked up, panting, just as she reached the corner. Her laughter stopped. Her heart seemed to skip a beat. "Halte!" the soldier ordered in a stern voice. The German word was as familiar as it was frightening. Annemarie had heard it often enough before, but it had never been directed at her until now. (p. 2)

Ask, "What do Annemarie's actions and feelings reveal about her?" Provide your own answer such as the following: "I think that Annemarie is normally a happy girl. I think that Annemarie is also experiencing a time when she feels considerable fear." Then provide the evidence from the text: "Annemarie's actions and responses when she races her friends indicate that she normally responds with laughter and enjoys the activities associated with playing with her friends and exploring the neighborhood. When she hears the soldier use the German word,

'Halte!', her reactions change from laughter and joy to those associated with fear. The descriptions such as her heart seemed to skip a beat are associated with this fear." Now, provide your own reasoning to reach the answer: "As I read this story, I could first feel the joy associated with carefree children as they race laughingly through their familiar neighborhood. I know from my own experience, the feelings of joy and happiness that occur when winning such a race. The author, however, develops a total change of attitude as within two paragraphs Annemarie goes from the normal laughing girl to one of such fright that her heart seems to skip a beat. The mood changes so drastically that I believe that Annemarie is experiencing extreme fear. I believe that Annemarie may be experiencing this fear for the first time because she does not remember such words being directed at her."

At this point, verify that the students understand the procedure. If they do not, model another example. When the students understand the process, let them join the discussion by providing answers, evidence, and reasoning. It is advisable to let older students write brief answers to the questions, evidence, and reasoning before the discussion. These notes will increase the quality of the discussion that follows each question. This procedure should be flexible and encourage students to provide numerous responses and reasons.

Continue reading the book orally until you come to the next logical discussion point. Interesting inferences and discussions result following the interaction with the soldiers and response to the encounter:

> The two soldiers turned away. Quickly Annemarie reached down again and grabbed her sister's hand before Kirsti could resist. Hurrying the little girl along, she rounded the corner. In a moment Ellen was beside her. They walked quickly, not speaking, with Kirsti between them, toward the large apartment building where both families lived. When they were almost home, Ellen whispered suddenly, "I was so scared." (p. 5)

Ask these questions: "What do the soldiers' actions reveal about them? What do Ellen and Annemarie's responses reveal about them and the nature of the conflict?" Ask the students to answer the questions, provide the evidence, and explore their reasoning processes. You should encourage a range of ideas. The students may use background information gained from the introduction to the book to expand their reasoning processes.

Number the Stars includes numerous additional opportunities for inferred characterization activities. Longer stories, such as *Number the Stars*, lend themselves to discussions according to chapters. Students can read or listen to and discuss several chapters each day. After each session, ask the students to summarize what they know about the characters and their developing conflict. Ask them, "What do you want to know about these characters?" To increase interactions with the text, you may ask students to write personal responses to each of the characters or to consider how they might have reacted if they were in the same position.

After students have been involved in modeling and discussion activities, they should have many opportunities to read, discuss, and respond to additional books in which the authors use inferences to develop characterization. The following books are useful for extending understanding of both the Holocaust and for modeling characterization. Shorter picture storybooks include Jo Hoestlandt's *Star of Fear, Star of Hope* and Margaret Wild's *Let the Celebrations Begin!*. Longer novel-length books include Uri Orlev's *The Island on Bird Street*, Johanna Reiss's *The Upstairs Room*, and Ida Vos's *Hide and Seek*.

ADDITIONAL ACTIVITIES TO ENHANCE PHASE FOUR

Here are some activities for children or young adult students related to this phase:

1. Historical fiction is a means of translating the information in textbooks into vivid spectacles of human drama. Choose a social studies or history text appropriate for students of a certain age. Compare the coverage of the Holocaust in the history or social studies textbook with that found in historical fiction. If possible, find passages in historical fiction that develop similar settings and conflicts described in the social studies or history textbooks. Discuss the impact of two different presentations.

2. Current newspaper articles frequently stress the courage of German citizens who helped Jewish people during World War II. Search for articles that express this point of view. For example, Peter Schneider (2000) introduces an article titled "Saving Konrad Latte" in *The New York Times Magazine,* in this way: "For every Jew who was saved, dozens of Germans performed everyday acts of heroism to make it possible. This man's saviors proved that obedience wasn't the only option" (p. 53). Read the articles, and then discuss various options that might have been possible during this period and the consequences of these options.

 ## PHASE FIVE: CONTEMPORARY LITERATURE

Informational books, biographies and autobiographies, and fictional titles are all found in contemporary literature. Some of the biographies and autobiographies provide literature that may be related to the Holocaust. Several of the contemporary fiction stories develop the lives of characters after they survive their experiences and move to Israel or to the United States.

Analyzing Author's Style to Develop an Understanding of the Holocaust

In *No Pretty Pictures: A Child of War*, Anita Lobel uses such literary devices as symbolism, similes, metaphors, and comparisons to develop both a believable and vivid autobiography. As students read *No Pretty Pictures: A Child of War*, ask them to identify and discuss examples of especially vivid writing style. Ask them to relate the appropriateness of various examples of author's style to their knowledge of the Holocaust. The following section illustrates this process.

Symbolism   To have students explore symbolism, ask questions such as the following: What is the importance of the missing furs and empty cupboards in this quote?

> The heavy wardrobe where we hung our coats was wide open. "They took my furs," Mother said. "And all the silver." The open cupboards of the dining room armoire were bare. The holiday candlesticks and the fancy silver coffeepot and teapot were gone. (p. 6)

The author uses many even more powerful but more subtle symbols. For example, ask students to consider what the author means by each of these terms and the symbolism of no light, leafless trees, and no blue in the sky in the following passage:

> Now in the whispering of the grown-ups I began to hear over and over again the words transported, deported, concentration camp. And liquidation. Somewhere there must be a terrible place. A barren area with no light. With leafless trees and no blue in the sky. Where these words stopped being just words and became real things. (p. 9)

Similes and Metaphors   Ask the students to consider what the author means by each of these examples of figurative language:

"a bunch of smelly Jewish strangers. For hours we were like the contents of a boiling pot on the stove. Waiting for the lid to be lifted and the stew to be ladled out." (p. 47)

"He was startled, I looked up into furious blue eyes. . . . I knew he had intended to kick me away. Then he shook me off as if I had been a yelping, not especially dangerous dog." (p. 81)

"I found a big book. Reading it, slowly turning page after page, the new words in my new language were like so many sleeping beauties, captured behind layers of brambles and thorns. Gradually they began to come forward, detaching from their thorny underbrush. Shedding their moss. Slowly at first, the words on the pages began to cooperate and perform." (p. 132)

There are many additional activities that may be accomplished to study Lobel's writing style. For example, students can find and discuss the author's use of contrasting settings and emotions as she compares her life after liberation with that in captivity or in hiding. They can trace her use of war words and peace words and how these words reflect the conflict and her changing attitudes.

ADDITIONAL ACTIVITIES TO ENHANCE PHASE FIVE

Here are some activities for children or young adult students related to this phase:

1. Identify common themes found in Jewish poetry and trace the themes through folklore and other types of literature. Develop an oral presentation of favorite poems.
2. Study poetry, using Samuel Totten's (1998) suggestions for using reader-response.
3. Develop an illustrated dictionary or encyclopedia that develops the importance of various Jewish customs, holidays, and celebrations. If possible, interview Jewish people about the importance of these subjects and include these first-hand reports in the texts.
4. Investigate the role of the bar mitzvah and the bat mitzvah in the lives of thirteen-year-old Jewish youth.

BIBLIOGRAPHY

Ausubel, Nathan, edited by. *A Treasury of Jewish Folklore.* New York: Crown, 1946, 1975.

Barban, Leslie. "Remember to Never Forget." *Book Links* 2 (March 1993): 25–29.

Berger, Abraham. "The Literature of Jewish Folklore: A Survey, With Special Reference to Recent Publications." *Journal of Jewish Bibliography* 1 (October 1938/January 1939): 12–20, 40–49.

Bridger, David, edited by. *The New Jewish Encyclopedia.* New York: Behrman House, 1976.

Davis, Hilarie B., William B. Fernekes, and Christine R. Hladky. "Using Internet Resources to Study the Holocaust: Reflections from the Field." *The Social Studies* 90 (January/February 1999): 34–41.

Dole, J. G., L. Duffy, L. Roehler, and P. D. Pearson. "Moving from the Old to New: Research on Reading Comprehension Instruction." *Review of Educational Research* 61 (1991): 239–264.

Early, Margaret, and Bonnie O. Ericson. "The Act of Reading." In *Literature in the Classroom: Readers, Texts, and Contexts,* edited by Ben F. Nelms, pp. 31–44. Urbana, Ill.: National Council of Teachers of English, 1988.

Frampton, Wilson. "Holocaust Education and the Need for Consistency." *Jewish Education* 59 (Spring/Summer 1991): 31–35.

Goldreich, Gloria, edited by. *A Treasury of Jewish Literature: From Biblical Times to Today.* New York: Holt, Rinehart and Winston, 1982.

Greenberg, Rabbi Irving. *The Jewish Way: Living Holidays.* New York: Touchstone, 1993.

Guggenheim Museum. *Marc Chagall and the Jewish Theater.* New York: Guggenheim Museum, 1992.

Hampl, Patricia. "A Review of *The Diary of a Young Girl: Anne Frank, the Definitive Edition.*" *The New York Times Book Review* (March 5, 1995): 21.

Helmreich, William B. "The Impact of Holocaust Survivors on American Society: A Socio-Cultural Portrait." *Judaism* 39 (Winter 1990): 14–27.

Kamenetsky, Christa. *Children's Literature in Hitler's Germany.* Columbus: Ohio University Press, 1984.

Kaplan, Paul. "Exploring the Holocaust." *School Library Journal* 44 (November 1998): 40–41.

Keller, Sharon. *The Jews: A Treasury of Art and Literature.* New York: Macmillan, 1992.

Kertzer, Rabbi Morris, revised by Rabbi Lawrence A. Hoffman. *What Is a Jew?* New York: Macmillan, 1993.

Lipstadt, Deborah. *Denying the Holocaust: The Growing Assault on Truth and Memory.* New York: Plume/Penguin, 1994.

Marks, Jane. *The Hidden Children: The Secret Survivors of the Holocaust.* New York: Ballantine, 1995.

Mauer, Hans. *Jugend und Buch im Neuen Reich.* Leipzig: Lehmanns Verlag, 1934.

May, Herbert G., and Bruce M. Metzger. *The New Oxford Annotated Bible with the Apocrypha: An Ecumenical Study Bible.* New York: Oxford University Press, 1973, 1977.

Metzger, Therese, and Mendel Metzger. *Jewish Life in the Middle Ages: Illuminated Hebrew Manuscripts of the Thirteenth to the Sixteenth Centuries.* Secaucus, N.J.: Chartwell Books, 1982.

Musleah, Rahel. "Rediscovering the Jewish Folktale." *Publishers Weekly* 239 (September 21, 1992): 42–43.

Norton, Donna E. *The Impact of Literature-Based Reading.* Upper Saddle River, N.J.: Merrill/Prentice Hall, 1992.

_____. *Through the Eyes of a Child: An Introduction to Children's Literature.* 5th ed. Upper Saddle River, N.J.: Merrill/Prentice Hall, 1999.

_____, and Saundra E. Norton. *Language Arts Activities for Children.* 4th ed. Upper Saddle River, N.J.: Merrill/Prentice Hall, 1999.

_____, and Saundra E. Norton. "Document Authentication of Folklore." *Encyclopedia of Library and Information Science* 61 (1998): 109–121.

Rochman, Hazel. "How Not to Write About the Holocaust." *Booklist.* 89 (October 15, 1992): 416.

Schneider, Peter. "Saving Konrad Latte." *The New York Times Magazine* (February 13, 2000): 52–57, 72–73, 90, 95.

Sender, Ruth Minsky. *The Holocaust Lady.* New York: Macmillan, 1992.

Sherman, Josepha. *A Sampler of Jewish American Folklore.* Little Rock: August House, 1992.

Short, Geoffrey. "Learning Through Literature: Historical Fiction, Autobiography, and the Holocaust." *Children's Literature in Education* 28 (December 1997): 179–190.

Shoshan, Tamar. "Mourning and Longing from Generation to Generation." *American Journal of Psychotherapy* XLIII (April 1989): 193–207.

Spiegelman, Maus. *Maus: A Survivor's Tale.* New York: Pantheon, 1986, 1991.

Sutherland, Robert D. "Hidden Persuaders: Political Ideologies in Literature for Children." *Children's Literature in Education* 16 (Autumn 1985): 143–157.

Szwajger, Adina Blady. *I Remember Nothing More: The Warsaw Children's Hospital and the Jewish Resistance*. Translated by Tasja Darowska and Danusia Stok. New York: Touchstone/Simon & Schuster, 1990.

Telushkin, Rabbi Joseph. *Jewish Wisdom: Ethical, Spiritual, and Historical Lessons from the Great Thinkers*. New York: Morrow, 1994.

Totten, Samuel. "The Start Is As Important As the Finish: Establishing a Foundation for Study of the Holocaust." *Social Education* 62 (February 1998): 70–76.

Totten, Samuel. "Using Reader-Response Theory to Study Poetry About the Holocaust with High School Students." *The Social Studies* 89 (January/February 1998): 30–39.

Vos, Ida. *Hide and Seek*. Boston: Houghton Mifflin, 1991.

Weinreich, Beatrice Silverman, edited by. *Yiddish Folktales*. Translated by Leonard Wolf. New York: Random House/YIVO Institute for Jewish Research, 1988.

CHILDREN'S AND YOUNG ADULT LITERATURE REFERENCES

Abells, Chana Byers. *The Children We Remember*. Greenwillow, 1986 (I: all). Photographs are from the archives of Yad Vashem, Jerusalem, Israel.

Adler, David A. *Chanukah in Chelm*. Illustrated by Kevin O'Malley. Lothrop, Lee & Shepard, 1997 (I: 5–8 R: 5). A humorous story about finding a tale for the menorah.

_____. *Child of the Warsaw Ghetto*. Illustrated by Karen Ritz. Holiday, 1995 (I: 7 + R: 5). A biography of Froim Baum who lived in the Warsaw ghetto and survived the Dachau concentration camp.

_____. *The Number on My Grandfather's Arm*. Photographs by Rose Eichenbaum. UAHC, 1987 (I: 6–8) In a photobiography, a man tells his granddaughter about his experiences in Auschwitz.

_____. *We Remember the Holocaust*. Holt, 1989 (I: 10 + R: 7). Survivors of the Holocaust describe their experiences.

Ayer, Eleanor, with Helen Waterford and Alfons Heck. *Parallel Journeys*. Atheneum, 1995 (I: 12 + R: 7). A biography of a Jewish Holocaust survivor and a German youth.

Bachrach, Susan D. *Tell Them We Remember: The Story of the Holocaust*. Little, Brown, 1994 (I: all). Information from the United States Holocaust Memorial Museum.

Baer, Edith. *Walk the Dark Streets*. Farrar, Straus & Giroux, 1998 (I: 12 + R: 7). This historical fiction novel is set during the Holocaust

Bitton-Jackson, Livia. *I Have Lived a Thousand Years: Growing Up in the Holocaust*. Simon & Schuster, 1997 (I: 12 + R: 6). An autobiography based on the author's experiences in ghettos, labor camps, and Auschwitz.

Boudalika, Litsa, edited by. *If You Could Be My Friend: Letters of Mervet Akram Sha'ban and Galit Fink*. Orchard, 1998 (I: 8 +). The book is based on correspondence between two twelve-year-old girls, one from Jerusalem and one from Palestine.

Bresnick-Perry, Roslyn. *Leaving for America*. Illustrated by Mira Reisberg. Children's Book Press, 1992 (I: 7–10). A Jewish Russian family comes to America in the 1920s.

Chaikin, Miriam. *Clouds of Glory: Legends and Stories about Bible Times*. Illustrated by David Frampton. Clarion, 1998 (I: 9 + R: 5). This is a retelling of Midrash stories.

_____, adapted by. *Exodus*. Illustrated by Charles Mikolaycak. Holiday, 1987 (I: all R: 5). This adaptation follows Moses as he leads his people from slavery in Egypt.

_____. *A Nightmare in History: The Holocaust 1933–1945*. Clarion, 1987 (I: 10 + R:7). This informational book traces the history of anti-Semitism and the annihilation of the Jews.

Cooper, Ilene. *The Dead Sea Scrolls*. Illustrated by John Thompson. Morrow, 1997 (I: 8 + R: 5). The author discusses this important archaeological find.

Crosby, Ruthann. *Miracle in the Glass*. Illustrated by Richard A. Cook. Frozen Chosen, 1998 (I: 8 + R: 6). The author includes an index of Hebrew and Yiddish words used in this Holocaust and Hanukkah story.

I = Interest age range
R = Readability by grade level

David, Jo, and Daniel B. Syme. *The Book of the Jewish Life*. UAHC, 1998 (I: 10 R: 5). This is a nonfiction book about Jewish life.

Dillon, Ellis. *Children of Bach*. Scribner's, 1992 (I: 10+ R: 6). A group of talented Hungarian Jewish children escape persecution.

Drucker, Olga Levy. *Kindertransport*. Henry Holt, 1992 (I: 8+ R: 5). A Jewish girl tells about her own experiences when she was evacuated to England during World War II.

Eisler, Colin, edited by. *David's Songs: His Psalms and Their Story*. Illustrated by Jerry Pinkney. Dial, 1992 (I: all). These psalms were chosen because they reflect David's life and faith.

Finkelstein, Norman H. *Friends Indeed: The Special Relationship of Israel and the United States*. Millbrook, 1998 (I: 10+ R: 6). This informational book develops the history of American and Israeli relationships.

_____. *The Other Fourteen Ninety-Two: Jewish Settlement in the New World*. Scribner's, 1989 (I: 10+ R: 6). This book describes the story of Jewish people as a consequence of their expulsion from Spain in 1492.

Fishman, Cathy Goldberg. *On Hanukkah*. Illustrated by Melanie W. Hall. Simon and Schuster, 1998 (I: 6-8 R: 4). The book focuses on the Jewish holiday.

Frank, Anne. *Anne Frank: The Diary of a Young Girl: The Definitive Edition*. Edited by Otto H. Frank and Mirjam Pressler. Translated by Susan Massotty. Doubleday, 1995 (I: 12+ R: 6). This autobiography of Anne Frank's years in hiding in the Netherlands contains material not included in the earlier diary.

Frank, Rudolf. *No Hero for the Kaiser*. Translated by Patricia Crampton. Illustrated by Klaus Steffens. Lothrop, Lee & Shepard, 1986 (I: 10+ R: 7). This historical novel with an anti-war theme was censored by Hitler.

Fritz, Jean, Katherine Paterson, Patricia McKissack, Fredrick McKissack, Margaret Mahy, and Jake Highwater. *The World in 1492*. Illustrated by Stefano Vitale. Henry Holt, 1992 (I: 8+). This book includes sections written by different authors.

Ganz, Yaffa. *Sand and Stars: The Jewish Journey Through Time*. Shaar, 1994 (I: 10+ R: 6). This history proceeds from early history through 1650.

Gellman, Rabbi Marc, and Monsignor Thomas Hartman. *How Do You Spell God?: Answers to the Big Questions from Around the World*. Morrow, 1995 (I: 10+ R: 7). This informational book provides basic information on various organized religions.

Gelman, Rita Golden. *Queen Esther Saves Her People*. Illustrated by Frane Lessac. Scholastic, 1998 (I: 5-8 R: 4). The illustrations depict the Persian setting.

Geras, Adele. *My Grandmother's Stories: A Collection of Jewish Folktales*. Illustrated by Jael Jordan. Knopf, 1990 (I: 8+ R: 4). The ten tales are based on the family history of Eastern European Jewish immigrants.

Gerstein, Mordicai. *The Shadow of a Flying Bird*. Hyperion, 1994 (I: all). This is an account of Moses during his last days on earth.

Goldin, Barbara Diamond. *Bat Mitzvah: A Jewish Girl's Coming of Age*. Illustrated by Erika Weihs. Viking, 1995 (I: 10+ R: 5). This informational book describes the ceremony that marks a Jewish girl's coming of age.

_____. *Night Lights: A Sukkot Story*. Illustrated by Louise August. Harcourt Brace, 1995 (I: 4-8 R: 5). A boy overcomes his fears as he learns about the meaning of Sukkot.

Greenfeld, Howard. *The Hidden Children*. Ticknor & Fields, 1993 (I: 10+). The author interviewed survivors of the Holocaust.

Harber, Frances. *The Brothers' Promise*. Illustrated by Thor Wickstrom. Albert Whitman, 1998 (I: 4–6 R: 4). Two brothers help each other in a time of need.

Hautzig, Esther. *The Endless Steppe: A Girl in Exile*. Harper, 1968 (I: 12+ R: 7). In a true story, a Jewish girl and her parents are exiled to Siberia during World War II.

Hesse, Karen. *Letters from Rifka*. Henry Holt, 1992 (I: 10+ R: 6). A Jewish girl and her family flee Russia in 1919.

Hoestlandt, Jo. *Star of Fear, Star of Hope*. Translated from the French by Mark Polizzotti. Illustrated by Johanna Kang. Walker, 1995 (I: 7–10 R: 3). Nine-year-old Helen tells the story of the disappearance of her friend during the Holocaust.

Holliday, Laurel. *Children in the Holocaust and World War II: Their Secret Diaries*. Washington Square, 1995 (I: 12 +). This is an anthology of diaries written by children.

Hoobler, Dorothy, and Thomas Hoobler. *The Jewish American Family Album*. Oxford University Press, 1995 (I: 10 +). A nonfiction book focuses on the lives of many Jewish immigrants.

Hurwitz, Johanna. *Anne Frank: Life in Hiding*. Illustrated by Vera Rosenberry. The Jewish Publication Society, 1988 (I: 8–12 R: 5). This is a simpler version of the life of Anne Frank.

_____. *Faraway Summer*. Morrow, 1998 (I: 10 + R: 5). Set in 1910, a Jewish girl takes part in a Fresh Air Fund summer vacation in Vermont.

Hutton, Warwick, adapted by. *Adam and Eve: The Bible Story*. Macmillan, 1987 (I: 4–8). A story of creation.

_____. *Moses in the Bulrushes*. Atheneum, 1986 (I: 4–8). This picture book version focuses on the discovery of the infant Moses by the pharaoh's daughter.

Innocenti, Roberto. *Rose Blanche*. Stewart, Tabori & Chang, 1985 (I: all). A young German girl discovers a concentration camp outside of her town.

Jaffe, Nina. *The Way Meat Loves Salt: A Cinderella Tale from the Jewish Tradition*. Illustrated by Louise August. Holt, 1998 (I: 5–8 R: 4). A musical score is included in this version.

_____, and Steve Zeitlin. *While Standing on One Foot: Puzzle Stories and Wisdom Tales from the Jewish Tradition*. Illustrated by John Segal. Holt, 1993 (I: 10 + R: 5). Problems and resolutions are presented in two-part stories.

Kaplan, William, and Shelley Tanaka. *One More Border: The True Story of One Family's Escape from War-Torn Europe*. Illustrated by Stephen Taylor. Douglas & McIntyre, 1998 (I: 8 + R: 4). This photobiography tells of a family's escape.

Kerr, Judith. *When Hitler Stole Pink Rabbit*. Coward, McCann, 1972 (I: 8–12 R:3). Anna and her family escape from Hitler's Germany.

Kimmel, Eric A. *Bar Mitzvah: A Jewish Boy's Coming of Age*. Illustrated by Erika Weihs. Viking, 1995 (I: 10 + R: 5). This informational book describes a Jewish boy's coming of age.

_____. *Be Not Far from Me: The Oldest Love Story: Legends from the Bible*. Illustrated by David Diaz. Simon & Schuster, 1998 (I: 9 + R: 5). The stories are about heroes and heroines from the Bible.

_____. *Days of Awe: Stories for Rosh Hashanah and Yom Kippur*. Illustrated by Erika Weihs. Viking, 1991 (I: 10 + R: 5). This is a collection of three tales about the Jewish holy days.

_____, edited by. *A Hanukkah Treasury*. Illustrated by Emily Lisker. Holt, 1998 (I: all). This is a collection of stories and activities.

_____. *Hershel and the Hanukkah Goblins*. Illustrated by Trina Schart Hyman. Holiday, 1989 (I: 4–9 R: 5). Hershel outwits the goblins that haunt the synagogue.

Knight, Margy Burns. *Talking Walls*. Illustrated by Anne Sibley O'Brien. Tilbury House, 1992 (I: all). The text and illustrations introduce important ancient walks from around the world, including the Western Wall in Jerusalem.

Koehn, Ilse. *Mischling, Second Degree: My Childhood in Nazi Germany*. Puffin, 1990 (I: 10 + R: 6). The autobiography of a girl growing up in Germany during World War II.

Koralek, Jenny. *Hanukkah: The Festival of Lights*. Illustrated by Juan Wijngaard. Lothrop, Lee & Shepard, 1990 (I: 5–8). Illustrations and text explain the Hanukkah celebration.

Kurtz, Jane. *The Storyteller's Beads*. Harcourt Brace, 1998 (I: 10 + R: 6). Two young people overcome their antagonism as they are both uprooted from their homes.

Kuskin, Karla. *Jerusalem, Shining Still*. Illustrated by David Frampton. Harper & Row, 1987 (I: 8–10). This picture book provides historical information about Jerusalem.

Laird, Christa. *But Can the Phoenix Sing?* Greenwillow, 1995 (I: 12 + R: 6). A seventeen-year-old boy works for the Jewish underground.

_____. *Shadow of the Wall*. Greenwillow, 1990 (I: 12 + R: 6). A boy in the Warsaw ghetto joins the resistance.

Lasky, Kathryn. *The Night Journey*. Illustrated by Trina Schart Hyman. Warne, 1981 (I: 10 + R: 6). A girl learns about her great-grandmother's escape from Czarist Russia in 1900.

_____. *Pageant*. Macmillan, 1986 (I: 10 + R:6). A Jewish teenager goes to school with Christian students.

Leapman, Michael. *Witnesses to War: Eight True-Life Stories of Nazi Persecution*. Viking, 1998 (I: 10 +). This informational book focuses on real-life experiences.

Levitin, Sonia. *Annie's Promise*. Atheneum, 1993 (I: 12 + R: 6). This is the third book about the Platt family.

_____. *Journey to America*. Illustrated by Charles Robinson. Atheneum, 1970 (I: 12 + R: 6). A Jewish family escapes from Nazi Germany. This is the first book in the story of the Platt family.

_____. *Silver Days*. Atheneum, 1989 (I: 12 + R:6). These are additional experiences of the family introduced in *Journey to America*.

_____. *The Singing Mountain*. Simon & Schuster, 1998 (I: 12 + R: 6). This is a contemporary realistic fiction novel.

Lobel, Anita. *No Pretty Pictures: A Child of War*. Greenwillow, 1998 (I: 10 + R: 6). This is an autobiography written by the author of many children's books.

Lowry, Lois. *Number the Stars*. Houghton Mifflin, 1989 (I: 10 + R: 6). The Danes try to save their Jewish citizens in 1943.

Mani-Leib. Translated by Jeffrey Shandler. *Yingle Tsingle Khvat*. Illustrated by El (Lazar) Lissitzky. Mt. Kisco, Moyer Bell Limited, 1986 (I: all). This poem is written in Yiddish and English.

Manushkin, Fran. *The Matzah That Papa Brought Home*. Illustrated by Ned Bittinger. Scholastic, 1995 (I: 3–8). This cumulative rhyme describes the Passover Seder.

_____. *Starlight and Candles: The Joys of the Sabbath*. Illustrated by Jacqueline Chwast. Simon & Schuster, 1995 (I: 4–8). This picture book tells about the Sabbath traditions.

Mark, Jan, retold by. *God's Story: How God Made Mankind*. Illustrated by David Parkins. Candlewick, 1998 (I: all). These stories are retellings from the Old Testament.

_____. *The Tale of Tobias*. Illustrated by Rachel Merriman. Candlewick, 1996 (: all). The biblical story is retold.

Matas, Carol. *Daniel's Story*. Scholastic, 1993 (I: 12 + R: 6). A fourteen-year-old describes his imprisonment in a concentration camp.

McCaughrean, Geraldine, retold by. *God's People: Stories from the Old Testament*. Simon & Schuster, 1997 (I: 9 + R: 5). The text includes many of the stories from the Bible.

McDonough, Yona Z. *Eve and Her Sisters: Women of the Old Testament*. Illustrated by Malchah Zeldis. Greenwillow, 1994 (I: 8 +). Stories about fourteen women are included.

McSwigin, Marie. *Snow Treasure*. Illustrated by Mary Reardon. Dutton, 1942 (I: 8–10 R:4). This is a retelling of a real adventure fighting the Nazis in World War II Norway.

Meltzer, Milton. *Rescue: The Story of How Gentiles Saved Jews in the Holocaust*. Harper & Row, 1988 (I: 10 + R: 6). Non-Jewish individuals help Jewish people during World War II.

Modesitt, Jeanne, compiled by. *Songs of Chanukah*. Illustrated by Robin Spowart. Musical arrangements by Uri Ophir. Little, Brown, 1992 (I: all). A collection of fourteen songs.

Morpurgo, Michael. *Waiting for Anya*. Viking, 1991 (I: 10 + R: 6). Set in southern France during World War II, a Jewish man works to smuggle children over the Spanish border.

Napoli, Donna Jo. *Stones in Water*. Dutton, 1997 (I: 9 + R: 6). Set in World War II, best friends are abducted by German soldiers and taken to a work camp.

Newman, Leslea. *Matzo Ball Moon*. Illustrated by Elaine Greenstein. Clarion, 1998 (I: 4–8 R: 4). A young girl helps her grandmother prepare for Passover.

Nicholson, Michael, and David Winner. *Raoul Wallenberg: The Swedish Diplomat Who Saved 100,000 Jews from the Nazi Holocaust Before Mysteriously Disappearing*. Gareth Stevens, 1989 (I: 10 + R: 6). A biography of the man whose mission was to protect Hungarian Jews.

Nye, Naomi Shihab, selected by. *This Same Sky: A Collection of Poems from Around the World*. Four Winds, 1992 (I: all). This collection of poems from sixty-eight different countries includes four poems from Israel.

Oberman, Sheldon. *The Always Prayer Shawl*. Illustrated by Ted Lewin. Boyds Mills, 1994 (I: 6–9). A prayer shawl is passed from grandfather to grandson.

Orlev, Uri. *The Island on Bird Street*. Translated by Hillel Halkin. Houghton Mifflin, 1984 (I: 10 + R: 6). A twelve-year-old Jewish boy survives in the Warsaw ghetto.

_____. *The Lady with the Hat*. Houghton Mifflin, 1995 (I: 12 + R: 5). A Holocaust survivor moves to Israel.

_____. *Lydia, Queen of Palestine*. Translated from the Hebrew by Hillel Halkin. Puffin, 1995 (I: 10 + R: 6). A ten-year-old girl describes her life in a kibbutz in Palestine.

_____. *The Man from the Other Side*. Houghton Mifflin, 1991 (I: 10 + R: 6). A boy and his father help bring supplies to the Jewish people in the Warsaw ghetto.

Paterson, John, and Katherine Paterson. *Images of God*. Illustrated by Alexander Koshkin. Clarion, 1998 (I: 10 + R: 5). The authors use both Hebrew and Christian Bibles to discuss depictions of God.

Patterson, Jose. *Angels, Prophets, Rabbis and Kings from the Stories of the Jewish People*. Illustrated by Claire Bushe. .Peter Bedrick, 1991 (I: 10 +). This anthology includes forty-six tales and a commentary about the symbols in the stories.

Podwal, Mark. *The Menorah Story*. Greenwillow, 1998 (I: all). An informational book.

Polacco, Patricia. *The Keeping Quilt*. Simon & Schuster, 1988 (I: 5–8 R: 5). This picture story-book tells the story of the importance of the quilt to four generations of Jewish women.

_____. *Tikvah Means Hope*. New York: Doubleday, 1994 (I: 4–9 R:5). This story about the Sukkot celebration has a contemporary message of hope and rejoicing.

Rael, Elsa Okon. *When Zaydeh Danced on Eldridge Street*. Simon & Schuster, 1997 (I: 4–8 R: 4). Set in Manhattan during the 1930s, an eight-year-old stays with her grandmother and makes discoveries about her Jewish faith.

Reid, Barbara. *Two by Two*. Scholastic, 1992 (I: 2–6). Plasticine figures illustrate a retelling of the flood story of Noah's ark.

Reiss, Johanna. *The Upstairs Room*. Crowell, 1972 (I: 11 + R: 4). This is based on a true story of a Jewish girl's experience hiding from the Nazis.

Rochman, Hazel, and Darlene Z. McCampbell, compiled by. *Bearing Witness: Stories of the Holocaust*. Orchard, 1995 (I: 12 + R: 6). This anthology of Holocaust stories includes short stories, remembrances, letters, and poetry.

Rogasky, Barbara, adapted by. *The Golem*. Illustrated by Trina Schart Hyman. Holiday, 1996 (I: 10 + R: 5). A clay giant is brought to life.

_____. *Smoke and Ashes: The Story of the Holocaust*. Holiday, 1988 (I: 10 + R: 6). This is a history of the 1933–1945 Holocaust.

Rosen, Michael J. *Elijah's Angel: A Story for Chanukah and Christmas*. Illustrated by Aminah Brenda Lynn Robinson. Harcourt Brace Jovanovich, 1992 (I: 5–8). A Jewish boy is in conflict over accepting a Christmas gift.

Rossel, Seymour. *The Holocaust*. Watts, 1990 (I: 12 + R: 7). This history proceeds from the Treaty of Versailles to the rise of Hitler to the Nuremberg trials.

Rothenberg, Joan. *Yettele's Feathers*. Hyperion, 1995 (I: 5–8 R: 6). A highly illustrated folktale about a widow who learns a lesson about gossiping.

Sanfield, Steve. *The Feather Merchants and Other Tales of the Fools of Chelm*. Illustrated by Mikhail Magaril. Orchard, 1991 (I: 8 + R: 5). This anthology includes thirteen Jewish tales about the humorous residents of Chelm.

Sasso, Sandy Eisenberg. *But God Remembered: Stories of Women from Creation to the Promised Land*. Illustrated by Bethanne Andersen. Jewish Lights, 1995 (I: 8 + R: 7). The text includes legends about four women who lived during Biblical times.

_____. *In God's Name*. Illustrated by Phoebe Stone. Jewish Lights, 1994 (I: all). Written in poetic form, this book describes a diverse group of people's search for the name of God.

Schotter, Roni. *Passover Magic*. Illustrated by Marylin Hafner. Little, Brown, 1995 (I: 5–8). A young girl and her family celebrate Passover.

Schrier, Jeffrey. *On the Wings of Eagles: An Ethiopian Boy's Story*. Millbrook, 1998 (I: 6–9 R: 4). A picture book about the Ethiopian Jews.

Schwartz, Howard, and Barbara Rush, retold by. *The Diamond Tree: Jewish Tales from Around the World*. Illustrated by Uri Shulevitz. HarperCollins, 1991 (I: 8 + R: 5). This collection of fifteen tales includes sources and commentary on each tale.

_____. *The Sabbath Lion: A Jewish Folktale from Algeria*. Illustrated by Stephen Fieser. HarperCollins, 1992 (I: 6–9 R: 5). A highly illustrated folktale that explores the importance of the Sabbath and keeping a promise.

Schweiger-Dmi'el, Itzhak. *Hanna's Sabbath Dress*. Illustrated by Ora Eitan. Simon & Schuster, 1996 (I: 4–6 R: 4). A moral tale in which kindness is rewarded.

Sherman, Josepha, selected and retold by. *Rachel the Clever and Other Jewish Folktales*. August House, 1993 (I: 9 + R: 5). This is a collection of forty-six tales.

_____. *A Sampler of Jewish American Folklore*. August House, 1992 (I: 12 + R: 7). This anthology of folklore includes source notes and a useful bibliography.

Siegal, Aranka. *Grace in the Wilderness: After the Liberation, 1945–1948*. Farrar, Straus & Giroux, 1985 (I: 10 + R: 7). This is a sequel to *Upon the Head of the Goat*.

_____. *Upon the Head of the Goat: A Childhood in Hungary, 1939–1944*. Farrar, Straus & Giroux, 1981 (I: 10 + R: 7). Nine-year-old Piri experiences the Holocaust.

Silverman, Maida. *Israel: The Founding of a Modern Nation*. Dial, 1998 (I: 8 + R: 5). This informational book includes a time line.

Singer, Isaac Bashevis. *The Golem*. Illustrated by Uri Shulevitz. Farrar, Straus & Giroux, 1982, 1996 (I: 10 +). A giant is shaped from clay.

_____. *Mazel and Shlimazel, or the Milk of the Lioness*. Illustrated by Margot Zemach. Farrar, Straus & Giroux, 1967 (I: 8–12 R: 4). The spirit of good luck and bad luck have a contest.

_____. *Stories for Children*. Farrar, Straus & Giroux, 1984 (I: 10 + R: 5). This is a collection of thirty-seven stories retold by the Nobel Prize winning author.

_____. *When Shlemiel Went to Warsaw and Other Stories*. Illustrated by Margot Zemach. Farrar, Straus & Giroux, 1968 (I: 10 + R: 4). This collection includes both traditional and literary folktales.

Speare, Elizabeth George. *The Bronze Bow*. Houghton Mifflin, 1961 (I: 10 + R: 6). A Jewish boy rebels against Roman rule during the time of Jesus.

Tames, Richard. *Anne Frank*. Watts, 1989 (I: 8–10 R: 4). This is a brief biography that includes numerous photographs.

Tarbescu, Edith. *Annushka's Voyage*. Illustrated by Lydia Dabcovich. Clarion, 1998 (I: 4–8 R: 4). This picture book recounts an immigrant's journey from Russia to America.

Toll, Nelly S. *Behind the Secret Window: A Memoir of a Hidden Childhood During World War Two*. Dial, 1993 (I: all R: 5). The text and illustrations tell the autobiography of a girl in Poland.

Van der Rol, Ruud, and Rian Verhoeven. *Anne Frank, Beyond the Diary: A Photographic Remembrance*. Translated by Tony Langham and Plym Peters. Viking, 1993 (I: 8 +). Photographs and maps provide a graphic accompaniment to the biography.

Volavkova, Hana, edited by. *. . . I Never Saw Another Butterfly . . . Children's Drawings and Poems from Terezin Concentration Camp, 1942–1944*. Schocken, 1993 (I: all). This collection of poems was written by children during the Holocaust.

Vos, Ida. *Hide and Seek*. Translated by Teresse Edelstein and Inez Smith. Houghton Mifflin, 1991 (I: 8 + R: 5). A Jewish girl describes her years of hiding in Nazi-occupied Holland.

Waldman, Neil. *The Golden City: Jerusalem's 3,000 Years*. Atheneum, 1995 (I: 8–12 R: 5). This illustrated nonfiction book traces the history of Jerusalem from the time of King David through the Six-Day War in 1967.

_____. *The Never-Ending Greenness*. Morrow, 1997 (I: all). Set in the Holocaust of World War II.

Weinreich, Beatrice Silverman, edited by. *Yiddish Folktales*. Translated by Leonard Wolf. Pantheon, 1988 (I: 12 + R: 6). This is a large collection of Yiddish folklore that includes annotations to the tales, notes, bibliography, and glossary.

Wells, Rosemary. *Streets of Gold*. Illustrated by Dan Andreasen. Dial, 1999 (I: 5 + R: 5). A biography of a girl who leaves the Soviet Union in 1894.

Wild, Margaret. *Let the Celebrations Begin!* Illustrated by Julie Vivas. Orchard, 1991 (I: all). Lighter colors project a less somber mood for a Holocaust story.

Williams, Laura E. *Behind the Bedroom Wall*. Illustrated by A. Nancy Goldstein. Milkweed, 1996 (I: 8 + R: 5). A thirteen-year-old discovers that her parents are hiding a Jewish woman and her daughter.

Winter, Kathryn. *Katarina*. Farrar, Straus & Giroux, 1998 (I: 8 + R: 5). A girl experiences religious conflict during the Holocaust.

Wisniewski, David. *Golem*. Clarion, 1996 (I: all). This 1997 Caldecott Medal winner includes notes about the origins of the legend.

Zalben, Jane Breskin. *Pearl's Eight Days of Chanukah*. Simon & Schuster, 1998 (I: 4-8 R: 4). The text includes directions for making menorahs and dreidels as well as other projects.

Zemach, Margot. *It Could Always Be Worse*. Farrar, Straus & Giroux, 1977 (I: 5–9 R: 2). A small hut seems larger when all the animals are removed.

Middle Eastern Time Line

3000 B.C.	Myth of "Isis and Osiris": Great myth of ancient Egypt for over 3,000 years
2500 B.C.	Egypt's Old Kingdom and the construction of the pyramids
9th century B.C.	"Iblis": Creation story explaining the beginning of humankind (Islamic version of Adam and Eve later found in work of Jarir at-Tabari, famous Islamic scholar who was a religious authority and historian born about A.D. 839)
A.D. 610	Founding of Islam by Muhammad, the Prophet of Allah (570–632)
700s	Collection of Islamic folklore centered in Baghdad: purpose to expand knowledge about Muhammad's time and to write scholarly commentaries on the Koran
1500s	Mosques built in Istanbul, Turkey, designed for Sultan Suleyman the Magnificent, ruler of Ottoman Empire
1704	*The Arabian Nights or the Thousand and One Nights,* translated from Arabic to French by Antoine Galland
1885–1888	Translation of *The Thousand Nights and a Night* from Arabic to English by Sir Richard Francis Burton
1900–1910	Increased interest in collecting folklore and publishing tales in academic journals to be studied by Arab specialists
1910	Publishing of Arabian two hundred tales by Hans Schmidt
1914	Edmund Dulac's illustrations for *Sindbad the Sailor and Other Stories from the Arabian Nights,* inspired by Persian miniatures of the fifteenth century
1922	Opening of Tutankhamun's tomb (pharaoh of Egypt, mid-1300s B.C.)
1971	Mildred L. Batchelder Award: Hans Baumann's *In the Land of Ur: The Discovery of Ancient Mesopotamia*
1974	Hans Christian Andersen International Medal: Illustrator Farshid Mesghali (Iran)
1980	Caldecott Honor to artist Chris Van Allsburg's *The Garden of Abdul Gasazi*
1985	*The Ancient Egyptian Book of the Dead* translated by R. O. Faulkner
1987	Palestinian uprising
1987	World population of Muslims estimated as ranging from 555 million to one billion
1990	Newbery Honor: Suzanne Fisher Staples's *Shabanu, Daughter of the Wind*
1991	Mildred L. Batchelder Honor Award: Rafik Schami's *A Handful of Stars*
1991	Persian Gulf War
1995	Mildred L. Batchelder Honor Award: Vedat Dalokay's, *Sister Shako and Kolo the Goat: Memories of My Childhood in Turkey*
1997	Importance of Islamic values in literature emphasized by numerous scholars in publications such as *Islamic Horizons*
1998	*The Space Between Our Footsteps: Poems and Paintings from the Middle East,* a large anthology of poems and paintings from the Middle East selected by Naomi Shihab Nye

7 *Middle Eastern Literature*

$\mathcal{W}$hen readers think about the Middle East, the term may cause them to visualize such diverse settings and people as vast areas of oil-rich deserts, Bedouin people living nomadic lives, exotic personages from the Arabian Nights, or ancient Egyptians floating down the Nile River on their way to the pyramids. All of these images may be found in the literature of the Middle East.

Ian A. Morrison in his informational book *Middle East* provides a definition for the Middle East that also emphasizes the diversity of the area:

> The "Middle East" is a strange name to use for an area. It was invented by Europeans, to mean somewhere between Europe and the countries of eastern Asia, which is known as the Far East. Although the people who live in the Middle East did not give it that name themselves, they have found it convenient to use it in the same way that people use the Midwest in America. In Arabic it is called Sharq al Awsat or East-the Middle, because there is such variety to the region that it is difficult to find any other single term to describe all the differences there are. (p. 5)

On a map, we can trace the Middle East from Egypt and Turkey in the west, to Saudi Arabia and Yemen on the south, to Iran on the east. There is another strong influence, however, that binds many of the Middle Eastern countries with people from throughout the world. From the Atlantic coast of Africa to the Indian Ocean, from the Sahara to Smarkand, from immigrants to the United States and Canada, there is a bond of religion. Meena G. Khorana (1997) describes the impact of this religious bond: "It is awesome to contemplate that Muslims all over the world—whether in Delhi or Timbuktu or London—turn to Mecca five times daily to pray. This powerful image symbolizes both the diversity and oneness of the Islamic world" (p. 2).

As we read the literature, we cannot forget the strong influence of Muslim beliefs in both Arabic and non-Arabic countries. Frederick M. Denny (1987) states, "There are more than 160 million Arabic speakers, of whom well over 90 percent are Muslim" (p. 13). Denny estimates that the world population of Muslims ranges from 555 million to one billion. He states, "A very significant factor in current and future Muslim populations is the annual rate of growth. Among the twenty-five fastest growing nations in the world, eleven have majority Muslim populations (e.g., Pakistan, Bangladesh, Saudi Arabia, Syria, Egypt, Iran, Morocco, and Iraq). . . . For the first time, Islam is becoming a significant minority religion in Western nations, especially France, Britain, West Germany, Canada, and the United States" (pp. 14–15).

As you noticed in the above quote, Denny uses both terms Muslim and Islam. Islam, according to Denny, means "Submission to God, the name of the true religion, according to the Qur'an; one who submits is a Muslim" (p. 131). Consequently, as we discuss the literature that is influenced by the Islamic faith, we will use both terms. In addition, Denny identifies three important dimensions of Islam: history, religion, and culture. This history includes the continuing power of Arabic traditions, symbols, personages, moral ideals, and social attitudes. As we analyze the literature, we will discover that all of these dimensions are found.

In this chapter, we will discuss the rich folklore from the Middle East and the Arabic world and identify the various values and beliefs found in the literature. We will evaluate the nonfiction sources, including both informational books and biographies. We will also discuss poetry and contemporary realistic fiction as we search for cultural threads across genres.

 ## HISTORICAL PERSPECTIVES

The lack of literature about the Middle East is of concern to many students of children's literature. The major portions of the Middle East collections in most libraries are informational books about the geography and the people. In addition to a lack of books in a variety of genres, there is also the issue of stereotypes that may be found in many of the books.

Stereotypes

In a study of children's literature relating to the Middle East, Rita M. Kissen (1991) is extremely critical of the stereotypes found. She states, "Both in the media and in the classroom American children have been presented with an image of Arabs and Palestinians as stupid and lazy at best, or terrorists and rapists at worst" (p. 112). Through her survey of Arabs in juvenile and young adult literature, she drew several conclusions: children's writers do not suggest that the nomadic existence has any value as a way of life; hostile Arab characters seem to proliferate the literature published after 1976; the emphasis on Arab hatred for the Jewish people occurs especially in books set during the 1967 War; and there is an image of Arabs as brutal terrorists.

Sylvia Iskander (1997) emphasizes this problem when she states "relatively few books depicting Arabs in a nonstereotypical fashion have appeared on the literary scene" (p. 11). When analyzing picture books, Iskander found the following stereotypes and cultural inaccuracies: behaviors that suggest characters are ignorant or cruel, appearances that depict similar appearances in all characters, inaccuracies in clothing and cultural depictions, and names that reveal lack of knowledge of Arabic. In a contrasting view of some of the literature and the stereotypes, Greta Little (1997) analyzed recent changes in books that she identified as "hostage dramas." Although the characters may be involved in such dramas, she concluded that the authors in more recent books develop fewer negative stereotypes and include in-depth character development rather than stock representations.

As you read and analyze books with Arab subjects, keep these stereotypes in mind. Also try to develop your own list of books and authors whose works do not develop stereotypes, provide erroneous information about various cultures, or suggest that all cultural groups within the Middle East are identical.

AUTHORS WHO WRITE AND ILLUSTRATE BOOKS

The lack of children's books with Middle Eastern subjects is dramatically shown when the Newbery and Caldecott winners are analyzed. The one example of a Newbery Award winner with a Middle Eastern subject is *Shabanu, Daughter of the Wind*, a story by Suzanne Fisher Staples set in the Bedouin culture, which won the Newbery Honor Award in 1990. Virginia Hamilton's *In the Beginning: Creation Stories from Around the World* includes "God Ra the Creator," a myth believed to be from ancient Thebes and taken from the Egyptian Mortuary Texts. This book, which includes myths from many cultures, won the Newbery Honor Award in 1989. In the Caldecott winners, there are no books about Middle Eastern characters and cultures unless one includes Chris Van Allsburg's *The Garden of Abdul Gasazi*, winner of the 1980 Caldecott Honor Award. Abdul Gasazi is a dog-hating retired magician who seems to have the power to cast spells.

*I*SSUE   *Evaluating Literature*

Most of the children's books relating to Middle Eastern culture available have settings in the Middle East rather than the United States. There are very few books about Americans of Arabic descent. When evaluating the literature, students of children's literature should consider both the literary quality and the authenticity of the story. Hazel Rochman (1993), however, provides some cautions to consider when evaluating books with foreign settings. She states:

Stories about foreign places risk two extremes: either they can overwhelm the reader with reverential details of idioms, background, and custom; or they can homogenize the culture and turn all the characters into mall babies. There's always that tension between the particular and the universal, between making the character and experience and culture too special, and making them too much the same. (pp. 25–26)

In addition to evaluating the books for literary quality, you may consider the following questions:

1. Does the book transcend stereotypes especially in political and social descriptions? Does the depiction of characters and lifestyles lack any implication of stigma? For example, is there an image that all Arabs are brutal terrorists?
2. Is the culture authentically portrayed? Is the culture treated with respect? Are the customs and values accurately portrayed without showing the culture as overly exotic or romanticized?
3. Are social issues and problems depicted frankly and accurately, without oversimplification?
4. If the book is a biography, are both the personality and the accomplishments of the main character shown in accurate detail and not oversimplified?
5. Are the illustrations authentic and nonstereotypical in every detail?
6. Does the author avoid offensive or degrading vocabulary?
7. Is the setting of the book accurately portrayed whether the book is historical or contemporary?

Students of children's literature will need to look for sources other than the New-bery and Caldecott books to discover quality literature. For example, journal articles such as Tasneema Khatoon Ghazi's "Islamic Literature for Children Adopts the English Language" (1997) include highly recommended books. The *School Library Journal's* "Best Books for 1998" list includes Susan Fletcher's *Shadow Spinner,* a novel set in the time of Shahrazad in ancient Persia.

Discovering the backgrounds of authors who place their stories in Middle Eastern settings illustrates how closely many of them base their stories on firsthand experiences. For example, Suzanne Fisher Staples, author of *Shabanu: Daughter of the Wind* and the sequel *Haveli,* worked as a UPI correspondent in Asia, including Pakistan and Afghanistan. While she was in Pakistan, she became involved with the nomads of the Cholistan Desert. This is the setting for the characters and plots developed in her books.

Gaye Hicyilmaz, author of *Against the Storm,* lived in Turkey for many years. Her book was inspired by a true incident reported in the Turkish press. Rafik Schami, author of *A Hand Full of Stars,* was born in Damascus, Syria. Judith Heide Gilliland, co-author of *Sami and the Time of the Troubles* and *The Day of Ahmed's Secret,* lived in Beirut for several years. Many of the authors of the adult texts, such as the folklore sources discussed later in this chapter, are literature and folklore scholars. Some of these books, however, have been criticized for cultural inaccuracies in either text or illustrations (Iskander, 1997).

 ## VALUES IDENTIFIED IN THE CULTURE AND LITERATURE

One of the ways to help us evaluate and to authenticate the literature from a culture is to identify some of the values that scholars from the culture believe are important. Because the current scholarship emphasizes values of Islamic literature, in this section we will discuss these values. For example, when discussing Islamic literature for children, Tasneema Khatoon Ghazi (1997) stresses the importance of stories about khalifahs, prophets, and scholars that teach values related to respect for parents and teachers, kindness to servants, and the rewards of perseverance. After identifying how these values are developed in several books, she concludes: "The values introduced in these stories, however, are universal and can be taught to any child. They emphasize the importance of truth, generosity, leading an unpretentious life, and finding pleasure in simple things" (p. 9).

Writers who stress the importance of Islamic values in literature frequently emphasize the ethical concerns that are included in books. For example, Khorana (1997) states, "books for children serve as integrating forces and are intended to provide an ideological base for youth" (p. 3). She emphasizes the need for literature that transmits the traditions to the next generation.

Several writers in current issues of the journal *Islamic Horizons* also mention the need for retaining and teaching Islamic values especially as Muslims move into non-Islamic nations. Abdul Basit's (1998) article in which he stresses integration without losing Muslim identity identifies the following Islamic values: extended family systems in which parents and others in this family exercise control over the young, strong sexual mores, adherence to religious faith anchored in a belief in one God and traditional moral values, and importance of family or community goals over personal goals. Khaliijah Mohammad Salleh (1997) emphasizes the roles of men and women in the value system of society and how these roles are defined by religion and tradition. For example, "men are the protectors and maintainers of women because Allah has given them more strength. While men are reminded of their responsibility, the women too are reminded of theirs: that the righteous women are devoutly obedient and guard their chastity in their husband's [sic] absence" (p. 57).

Several scholars stress the importance of folklore in developing both cultural identity and value systems. For example, Mansooreh Rai (1997) states that in Iran there is now a search for cultural identity through the study of Iranian folklore, music, painting, sculpture, and architecture. Rai also emphasizes her belief in the need for authentic cultural literature in order: "To prevent cultural invasion from Western countries through music, movies, and books, and to establish a peaceful dynamic society in harmony with Islamic values, we should trust in the miracle of children's literature to effect change and the implication of its rise and fall on the cultural development of a nation" (p. 33).

As you read and evaluate literature from the Middle East, especially literature that includes Muslim people and Islamic values, search for these values. If the values are there, how do authors develop these values? How are they shown in literary elements associated with conflicts, plots, characterization, and themes?

 ## FOLKLORE AND ANCIENT STORIES FROM THE MIDDLE EAST

From our definition of the Middle East and the various countries that lie within this region it is understandable that the folklore comes to us from many different sources and time periods and is influenced by various religions.

History of Collection

The influence of Muhammad and his followers is apparent in the purposes for collecting Arabic folklore. According to Inea Bushnaq in *Arab Folktales* (1986), the collection of Arab tales began as early as the eighth century when Arab philologists of the Abbasid era, who were centered in Baghdad, collected tales and poetry recited by professional bards. Bushnaq states: "The collectors' purpose was to equip themselves with all the knowledge to be had about the prophet's time, the better to write scholarly commentaries on the Koran" (p. xxiii). Problems resulted, however, because of differences between written language, the language of the Koran, and spoken Arabic, which often did not include words found in dictionaries.

In 1704, *The Arabian Nights or The Thousand and One Nights* was translated from the Arabic into French by Antoine Galland (Leach, 1972). This translation introduced the Persian tales into Europe. Between 1885 and 1888, Sir Richard Francis Burton, the British Consul in Trieste, translated *The Thousand Nights and a Night* from Arabic to English and published the tales in sixteen volumes (Burton, 1985). Burton's translation is a primary source for many retellings in English. (Susan Fletcher identifies Burton's book as her guide for the writing of *Shadow Spinner*, discussed later in this chapter.)

An increased interest in collecting the tales occurred in 1900 when Enno Littman, an archaeologist on an expedition, collected tales through an Arab friend. In 1910, Hans Schmidt published two hundred tales. Collections of Arabic tales began to appear in French, English, German, and Italian academic journals. These journals were intended for study by Arab specialists and linguists (Bushnaq, 1986).

Types of Tales

Collectors of the folklore categorize the stories according to specific types. For example, Burton (1985) identifies the following three types of stories found in *The Thousand Nights and a Night*: classic fables, fairy tales based on some supernatural agency, and stories based on historical fact or anecdote.

When discussing tales that reflect the mystical tradition of Islam known as Sufism, Mojdeh Bayat and Mohammad Ali Jamnia (1994) identify three types of Sufi stories: those dealing with one's relationship to oneself and one's personal growth, those dealing with one's relationship to society and other people, and those dealing with one's relationship to God. According to Bayat and Jamnia, Sufi stories "may seem to be quite simple, their deeper significance may, depending on the student's level of understanding, be subtle and very difficult to grasp" (p. 3).

The purposes for Sufis stories are also related to their types. Bayat and Jamnia discuss the importance of the stories as teaching and training tools because many stories are used to convey messages of loving care or to teach particular codes of conduct. "If a pupil is ready to cross a barrier, a properly timed story gets the message across" (p. 4).

Bayat and Jamnia also warn, however, that many of the stories are difficult for Westerners to understand because the themes need to be clarified in the light of the culture from which the stories come. For example, misunderstanding may result because Islamic culture and Sufism reflect a masculine bias. In Sufi symbolism, woman stands for one who pursues worldly desires, while man symbolizes the true lover of God. In their book *Tales from the Land of the Sufis*, Bayat and Jamnia present a history of Sufism and examples of stories that reflect Sufi beliefs.

In *Arab Folktales*, Bushnaq (1986) provides the following categories of Arabic tales: Bedouin tales told by desert nomads; tales of magic and supernatural or household tales that include djinn, ghouls, and afreets; animal tales, which include fables and anecdotes; famous fools and rascals; religious tales and moral instruction; and tales of wit and wisdom that tell about clever men and wily women. In our discussion of folklore, we will use Bushnaq's categories because much of the folklore published for children falls under these categories.

Specific types of tales may also have specific openings. For example, tales of magic and the supernatural that are household tales—considered the entertainment of women—may have a story opening like the following: "There was, there was not, In the oldness of time" or "This happened, or maybe it did not. The time is long past, and much is forgot."

Some of the tales have Arabic closings that are the equivalent to "they lived happily ever after." For example, an Arabic tale of magic and the supernatural might end with, "We left them happy and back we came. May Allah make your life the same!"

In this next section, we will discuss examples that reflect these types of tales and identify values and beliefs that are found in the tales.

Bedouin Tales *Arab Folktales,* edited by Inea Bushnaq, discusses characteristics of Bedouin folktales and provides examples of the tales collected from nomadic peoples of the desert. As you read Bedouin folktales, you may look for characteristics such as generosity in which a person's worth is counted not by what he owns but by what he gives to others; hospitality to those who enter the home and encampment (traditionally the period of Bedouin hospitality is three-and-one-third days); the importance of ancestry and birth in a culture in which the family is the most important social unit; and pride, independence, and self-sufficiency of the nomadic characters. Many Bedouin tales reflect these values when the storyteller concludes with a sentence such as "So it is when men are noble."

Generosity and hospitality are the major values depicted in Bushnaq's "The Last Camel of Emir Hamid." In this tale from Saudi Arabia, a reward is given for generosity. Hospitality is important in "The Boy in Girl's Dress," a story from Syria that shows the importance of hospitality in a treeless, waterless region in which to deny food and shelter could mean denying life. This tale shows that the traditional period of Bedouin hospitality is so binding that even an enemy, once having eaten salt under one's roof, will be protected as a guest. In this tale, the heroine hurries to feed her lover before the return of her father, whom he has offended.

Tales of Magic and Supernatural   Eric A. Kimmel's *The Three Princes: A Tale from the Middle East* has characteristics of both magic and wit and wisdom. The story has a characteristically vague, contradictory opening: "Once there was and once there was not a princess who was as wise as she was beautiful" (p. 1 unnumbered). The princess challenges her three suitors to bring back the rarest things that they find in their year-long travels, and she will marry the prince who returns with the greatest wonder. In a dramatic ending, the prince who returns with the orange that cures any illness uses the fruit to heal the princess and thus wins her for his wife. The importance of generosity, sacrifice, and wisdom are revealed as the princess chooses the prince who sacrificed the most.

In an Egyptian version of the Snow White tale, Eric A. Kimmel's *Rimonah of the Flashing Sword: A North African Tale*, the queen wishes for a child with skin as dark as a pomegranate, eyes as bright as pomegranate seeds, and a voice as sweet as pomegranate juice. As you read the following summary of the story, identify the motifs that make it similar to other Snow White stories and the motifs that make this variant Arabic:

> When the child is seven-years-old, her mother falls ill. Before the mother dies she gives her daughter a crystal vial with three drops of her blood and tells her to wear it around her neck. If it turns red and liquid, she will know that danger threatens. A sorceress casts a spell that causes the queen's death and bewitches the king so he will marry her. When the evil queen looks into her magic bowl and asks who is the fairest of all she is told Rimonah. When a huntsman is ordered to take Rimonah to the desert and kill her, Rimonah pleads for her life and escapes to the desert where she lives with a Bedouin tribe. As she grows she becomes a fearless young horsewoman who is skilled with dagger and sword. Finally the queen discovers the deception and tries to kill the girl with a scorpion. Now Rimonah flees again and enters the cave of 40 thieves. She stays with the thieves until the queen discovers her and rides to the home of the 40 thieves on her carpet. The queen tricks Rimonah into accepting a ring. When Rimonah slips the ring on her finger she goes into a deathlike swoon. The vial around her neck protects her from the queen's deadly spell. The 40 thieves place her into a glass coffin where she stays until a prince kisses her and she is revived. When they decide to return to the city and seek revenge on the queen, they find Rimonah's father in a casket in the desert. He is not dead, however, and when he awakens he is out from under the spell. The queen gets on her carpet and tries to escape. She leaves without her magic bowl which Rimonah throws after her. The queen is destroyed. The story ends, "And so, all that was sorrowful ended in joy and all that was wrong was made right again. So may it be forever. (p. 30 unnumbered)

There are several magical tales in Neil Philip's *The Arabian Nights,* including a variant of the Cinderella story. This variant includes both motifs related to Cinderella and motifs that are characteristic of Arabic folklore. Notice how the following motifs suggest that this is an Arabic story: a pot with a jinni provides the heroine with whatever she fancies, including beautiful clothes. For example, the pot provides gold anklets studded with diamonds. The heroine enters the King's harem where the women's part of the entertainment was held. In her haste to leave the feast, she drops the diamond anklets. The queen organizes a search party for the person who can wear the anklet. After the girl is found, she is taken back to the palace where the celebration lasts for 40 days and 40 nights while the wedding is prepared. The evil sisters learn the secret of the jinni and turn their younger sister into a white dove by jabbing her with diamond pins. The prince sends out search parties. Without the heroine, he begins to sicken and waste away. Every day the white dove comes to the prince's window and the prince grows to love the bird. The prince finds the diamond pins, pulls them out, and the bride reappears.

The ending of this Cinderella variant concludes with a characteristic Arabic ending that points out respected values and despised human actions: "The prince and his love lived many years in happiness, blessed by children as beautiful and kind as themselves. But the two sisters died of jealousy poisoned by their own spite" (p. 37).

Additional stories in this collection include characteristic Arabic sayings and beliefs. In "The Fisherman and the Jinni," the fisherman says "Allah be praised" as the net is cast. He catches a jar of copper with the seal of King Solomon the Great. When he pries open the jar, a monstrous jinni emerges.

A. E. Jackson's *Ali Baba and the Forty Thieves and Other Stories* includes three stories told by Shahrazad during the thousand and one nights: "Ali Baba and the Forty Thieves," "The Enchanted Horse," and "Sindbad the Sailor." These stories include magical spells, magicians, sultans, princesses, and exotic adventures. "The Enchanted Horse" presents several of the values that are important in the folklore. For example, the princess uses her wits to escape a forced marriage, and the sultan discovers the importance of providing protection for one who is in his care. This honoring of protection is developed as the prince rescues the princess and calls out to the sultan: "The next time the Sultan of Cashmere thinks of marrying a princess who has come to him for protection, let him make sure that he has the lady's consent" (p. 64). The story closing is characteristic of Arabic tales and also reinforces the importance of obtaining a father's permission for a marriage and living in honor: "The King of Persia at once sent an ambassador to the father of the princess, who had for months been mourning the mysterious disappearance of his daughter, to request his consent to her marriage with Prince Feroze-shah. When that was given, the marriage was celebrated with much magnificence, and the Prince and Princess of Persia lived in honor and happiness for many years" (p. 64). You may compare Jackson's retelling of the tale with Eric A. Kimmel's *The Tale of Ali Baba and the Forty Thieves*.

Animal Tales "The Duty of the Host" in Inea Bushnaq's *Arab Folktales* develops both the importance of hospitality and provides a reason for animal behavior. In this tale from Saudi Arabia, a guest is robbed and the moth is so ashamed of having failed in hospitality that she throws herself into the nearest flame. This becomes a *pourquoi,* or why, tale because it reveals why the fireflies' descendants go towards the flame; namely, because they choose death over disgrace.

Stories such as Bushnaq's "Who Has the Sweetest Flesh on Earth?" from Palestine are elaborate accountings for the idiosyncrasies of animals. The story opens with a characteristically vague opening and proceeds to a question pertaining to animal behavior: "Have I told you, or have I not, why the serpent is the least loved of the creatures of the earth?" (p. 223).

According to Bushnaq, the favorite type of animal story in Arabic is a trickster tale in which two animals, or a human and an animal, try to outwit each other. These tales usually end with a punch line that is wise and witty. For example, "The Cat Who Went to Mecca," an animal tale from Syria, concludes: "The king of the mice jumped back into his hole and rejoined his subjects. 'How is the king of the cats after his pilgrimage?' they asked. 'Let's hope he has changed for the better.' 'Never mind the pilgrimage,' said the king of the mice. 'He may pray like a Hajji, but he still pounces like a cat'" (p. 216).

One of the fables in David Kherdian's *Feathers and Tales*, "The Camel and the Mouse," is an example of a fable told by Jalal-uddin Rumi (1207–1273), who was a mystic, a poet, and a founder of the Sufi order called the Mevlevi dervishes, known for their whirling dances of ecstasy. This fable reveals the importance of planning ahead and understanding the characteristics of a leader. The fable develops this lesson when a mouse designates himself the leader by guiding a camel across the wilderness. This arrangement works until the two reach a river. When the mouse asks to be carried across the river so that he will not drown, the camel responds, "'You should have thought of this before you tried to become a leader,' the camel answered, and marched across the river by himself" (p. 24). Many of the animal fables from India and Greece were assimilated into the Arabic tradition.

Religious Tales and Moral Instruction   One of the oldest tales from Egypt emphasizes the cycle of life, death, and rebirth. The story of Isis and Osiris was the great myth of ancient Egypt for over three thousand years, from about 3000 B.C. to the second century A. D. In the foreword to Jules Cashford's *The Myth of Isis and Osiris*, the reteller states:

> The appeal of the myth of Isis and Osiris lay in the fact that people could identify with them by sharing the fate of human beings, yet they also transcended the limitations of the human condition. Isis lost her husband but found and revived him. She brought her child up alone, overcame his sickness, and he grew up to take his father's place. When the ancient Egyptians lost their loved ones, they mourned like Isis, and they imagined that when they died they became like Osiris, continuing to live in another realm as he did. So the Egyptians also saw in the death and revival of Osiris an analogy for human life after death. (p. viii)

This book provides additional insights into the ancient Egyptian culture because the book is illustrated with pictures of early Egyptian art.

The Egyptian myth "The Sun-God and the Dragon: God Ra the Creator" is found in Virginia Hamilton's *In the Beginning: Creation Stories from Around the World*. According to Hamilton, the myth "is taken from Egyptian Mortuary Texts and is part of a temple ritual. Some of the ritual was a dramatic presentation of the conflict between God Ra and the dragon Apophis. The myth is thought to come from ancient Thebes. . . . Instead of riding in a chariot, the sun-god Ra traveled the heavens in a boat called Millions of Years, starting in the morning in the east, and at sunset, disappearing into the underworld of the Underneath Sky. The lesser god Osiris was the moon-god and the Judge of the Dead. Isis was Osiris's sister and the patron goddess of women. Horus was the son of Osiris and Isis and the savior of mankind.

Some of the religious tales reflect the common ground between Islam and Christianity. Shulamith Levy Oppenheim's *Iblis* is a retelling of a story thought to date back to the ninth century B.C., is both a creation story explaining the beginnings of humankind and our troubles, and a cautionary tale showing the dangers of disobeying God's orders. The author tells us about an Islamic version of this Adam and Eve story:

> [It] can be found in the work of Jarir at-Tabari, a famous Islamic scholar who was a religious authority and historian. Born about 839 A.D. in Amul, a city near the southern shore of the Caspian Sea, he traveled throughout the Islamic world as a young man and finally settled in Baghdad, in what is now Iraq. He acquired material for his history of the world from oral storytelling and literary sources, as well as from the Koran. (author's note, unnumbered)

You may compare this variant of the Adam and Eve story with the Christian story. In the Islamic version, the teller reveals that Adam and Eve lived in Paradise for five hundred years during which time Iblis, the great Satan, tried to enter Paradise, but the entrance to Paradise was protected by the flaming sword of the angel Ridwan. In his desire to enter Paradise, Iblis flatters the peacock, who sends out a serpent who was created a thousand years before man and was Eve's favorite companion. Iblis tricks the serpent into allowing him to enter Paradise and convinces Eve that she should eat from the forbidden tree. After they eat the fruit, God commands that Adam, Eve, and the animals that led them into disobeying God depart from Paradise. The peacock lost his melodious voice, the serpent lost her feet, and Iblis was cast back into the torments of all eternity. Adam was expelled from Paradise through the gate of Repentance so that he would never forget how Paradise might be regained. Eve was expelled through the gate of Grace. The serpent and the peacock were exiled through the gate of Wrath. Iblis was hurled out through the gate of Damnation.

Tales of Wit and Wisdom   "The Clever Minister's Daughter," in Inea Bushnaq's *Arab Folktales,* is an example of a tale of wit and wisdom. In this story from Syria, a minister's daughter answers two series of three questions asked by the king. In so doing, she proves her worth and she marries the king. The three questions are "What is the most precious of all stones? What is the sweetest of all sounds? What, after God, gives us life?" (p. 354). To these questions, she answers, "the most precious of all stones is the millstone, the sweetest of all sounds is the call to prayer, and the most lifegiving after God is water" (p. 354). After she solves another series of tasks, she saves her father's life, "And so the first minister continued to stand at the king's right shoulder, and now he was also father of the queen" (p. 355).

As you read additional tales, try to discover some of the characteristics, values, and beliefs discussed in this folklore. For example, you may discover that many of the Bedouin tales reflect generosity, hospitality, the importance of family, ancestry and birth. The characters frequently show pride, independence, and self-sufficiency. Tales of the magical and the supernatural frequently develop the importance of wit and wisdom and the importance of Allah. Enchanted characters, magical spells, and trickster animal characters are found in many of the tales of magic. Many tales from Egypt include the cycle of life, death, and rebirth. Religious tales frequently suggested a common ground between Islam and Christianity.

Early editions of Arabic folktales and more modern editions provide the basis for interesting comparisons. The various versions of "The Thousand and One Nights" provide interesting comparisons of their illustrations. For example, a facsimile edition of *Arabian Nights: The Book of a Thousand Nights and a Night* translated by Sir Richard Burton was published in 1985. This edition includes sixteen illustrations by Albert Letchford that were included in the first edition published in the late 1800s. The illustrations in this adult version of the tales may be compared with Edmund Dulac's illustrations for *Sindbad the Sailor and Other Stories from the Arabian Nights* first published in 1914 and reissued in 1986. According to the text, Dulac's art was inspired by Persian miniaturists of the fifteenth century.

Illustrations in the older editions may also be compared with more recent editions of various stories from "The Arabian Nights." For example, comparisons might include Sheila Moxley's illustrations for Neil Philip's *The Arabian Nights*, Eric A. Kimmel's illustrations for *The Tale of Aladdin and the Wonderful Lamp: A Story from the Arabian Nights*, and A. E. Jackson's illustrations for *Ali Baba and the Forty Thieves and Other Stories*.

You might consider the following evaluation criteria for the illustrations (Norton, 1999, p. 180):

1. The illustrator's use of visual elements—line, color, shape, texture—and certain artistic media should complement or even extend the development of plot, characterization, setting, and theme in the text.
2. The design of the illustrations—individually and throughout an entire book—should reinforce the text and convey a sense of unity that stimulates aesthetic appreciation.
3. The artistic style chosen by the illustrator should enhance the author's literary style.
4. The illustrations should help the readers anticipate the unfolding of a story's action and its climax.
5. The illustrations should convincingly delineate and develop the characters.
6. The illustrations should be accurate in historical, cultural, and geographical detail, and they should be consistent with the text.

This final point dealing with historical, cultural, and geographical detail is especially important when evaluating the illustrations if the books are to provide accurate cultural information. Nonfiction books showing art from the ancient cultures may be used to help with this authentication process. These books are discussed in this next section.

EARLY HISTORY

Nonfiction informational books provide excellent sources for learning about a culture and for authenticating the illustrations and texts in fictional works. There are numerous books written for juvenile audiences that provide interesting information about the early history of the people living in the Middle East. Some of the books written for adult audiences provide excellent sources for authenticating illustrations and texts.

Books about the ancient Egyptian culture are especially valuable and informative if they include both historical information and photographs of architecture and artifacts. For example, the adult book *The Ancient Egyptian: Book of the Dead,* translated by R. O. Faulkner and edited by Carol Andrews (1985), provides valuable information to accompany the folklore about Osiris and Isis and other gods and goddesses of ancient Egypt. The translations in this text came from the collection of Egyptian funerary papyri found in the British Museum. The text explains the purposes for the sheets of papyrus covered with magical texts and illustrations, which the Egyptians placed with their dead. They were used to help the dead pass through the dangers of the Underworld and attain an afterlife in the Field of Reeds, the Egyptian heaven. The text traces the dates of the papyri and discusses the purposes for the various spells found on the papyri. Many of the accompanying illustrations are in full color and provide a visual interpretation of the beliefs of early Egyptians.

David M. Rohl's *Pharaohs and Kings* (1995) provides another adult source for the history, culture, and geography of ancient Egypt. The photographs may be used to supply useful information for any age group.

Informational books about ancient Egypt written for juvenile audiences may present the history of the people or focus on specific subjects such as the building of the pyramids, creating mummies, or exploring the tombs. Because there are several sources that discuss the same subjects, readers may compare the effectiveness of each of the books. As you read informational books, consider such areas as the accuracy of the facts and the ability of the author to separate facts and theory; the quality of the illustrations and the ability of the illustrations to clarify the text; the organization of the text; the ability of the text to increase interest in the subject and to encourage analytical thinking; the style of the writing; and the quality of the aids such as maps, graphs, indexes, glossaries, and lists for further reading.

Ancient Cultures of Egypt

Informational books should encourage analytical thinking by allowing young readers to become involved in solving problems and observing carefully. Books by Judith Crosher and by Andrew Haslam and Alexandra Parsons contain features that encourage reader involvement. Crosher's *Ancient Egypt* is a highly illustrated book that presents the history of ancient Egypt and its people. Captioned, color photographs and illustrations provide helpful information. The book has a unique interactive feature in which readers view a scene on see-through cutaways: they can turn the transparent page and discover what is inside each of four structures—a home, the king's palace, a burial tomb, and the Temple of Khons.

Andrew Haslam and Alexandra Parsons's *Ancient Egypt* encourages reader involvement because the text includes step-by-step directions for making models, clothing, objects, and foods related to Ancient Egypt. In addition, the text provides a brief introduction to ancient Egypt and then examines different aspects of the civilization such as religions, family life, communications, and geography.

Time lines are another feature that authors use to clarify information about historical times. Viviane Koenig's *The Ancient Egyptians: Life in the Nile Valley* includes a time line, as well as an introduction to the people including their work, social and economic lives, and religious traditions. Readers obtain a feeling for the different types of people who made up ancient Egypt—including craft workers and artists, scribes and scholars, and pharaohs who ruled the land. The text includes a list of further reading, a glossary, and an index.

Geraldine Harris's *Ancient Egypt: Cultural Atlas for Young People* explores the history of ancient Egypt through text, maps, charts, illustrations, and photographs. The text is divided into two parts: The History of the Pharaohs and A Journey Down the Nile. The text is highlighted with labeled photographs and illustrations, maps, glossary, further reading, and index.

Building the Pyramids

Books on building the pyramids provide insights into Ancient Egyptian beliefs in the ancient gods and the afterlife.

Anne Millard's *History Highlights: Pyramids* is a highly illustrated text that provides information on the following topics: the types of pyramids constructed over 4,500 years ago during Egypt's Old Kingdom, the purposes for the pyramids as permanent tombs for Egypt's kings, the appearance of a pyramid complex, the god kings of Egypt, the building of the pyramids, the craft workers who help make the pyramids, and the daily lives of various people who worked on the pyramids. One of the most interesting sections discusses the religious beliefs that caused the change from pyramids built like staircases to those built with straight sides. (Step pyramids were built as staircases to heaven which allowed the king to climb to reach the stars. The change in religious beliefs occurred during Dynasty IV when straight-sided pyramids began to be built as sunbeams of stone up which the king would walk to join the gods.) The author's discussion of Osiris and other gods will help readers understand the folklore the includes these Egyptian deities. The text helps readers understand the close relationship among ancient Egyptians, their religious beliefs, and their architecture. The text includes an interesting date chart that compares activities in Africa, Asia, the Americas, and Europe.

Two other books that provide information about the pyramids are Carter Smith's *The Pyramid Builders* and Jacqueline Morley, Mark Bergin, and John James's *An Egyptian Pyramid*. Smith's text includes topics such as the mystery of the pyramids, the seeds of civilization, and Egyptian culture. The author's afterword discusses how various researchers and scholars are rediscovering ancient Egypt. *An Egyptian Pyramid* includes illustrations that are labeled and numbered to help clarify the text, which shows the process of being pyramids: from the laying of the foundations, to quarrying stones, to building the pyramid itself, and finally to the sealing of the pyramid as the king's tomb. The text includes a glossary and an index.

Mummies and Searching the Tombs

Ideas in informational books should be broken down into easily understood component parts. Authors often use an organization that progresses from the simple to the more complex, or from the familiar to the unfamiliar, or from early to later development. In *Into the Mummy's Tomb: The Real-Life Discovery of Tutankhamun's Treasures*, Nicholas Reeves introduces the topic with a prologue that relates history to more current events. This prologue introduces a mystery in which two secret, locked cupboards in Highclere Castle in England reveal ancient Egyptian treasures that were hidden after the discovery of Tutankhamun's tomb. The text then proceeds in chronological order, beginning with "The Hidden Steps, Cairo, Egypt, 1907" and concluding with "The Tomb's Secrets, Hampshire, England, 1988." Numerous photographs and maps complement this historical progression.

James Putnam's *Mummy* describes the principles, history, and ceremonies associated with the preservation of bodies. The text includes numerous labeled photographs that illustrate topics covered including what mummies are, the Egyptian Book of the Dead, the process for creating mummies, and Egyptian concepts of the afterlife. The section on the mummy and the god Osiris can help in understanding the folklore. The author includes comparisons with other mummies such as Greek and Roman mummies, mummies from the Andes, and animal mummies. An interesting section Putnam discusses the treasures of Tutankhamum and the curse of the mummy. *Mummies and Their Mysteries* by Charlotte Wilcox also discusses the process of mummification and introduces readers to mummies found in different parts of the world.

James Cross Giblin's *The Riddle of the Rosetta Stone: Key to Ancient Egypt* describes the process used to decipher the hieroglyphs found on the Rosetta Stone,

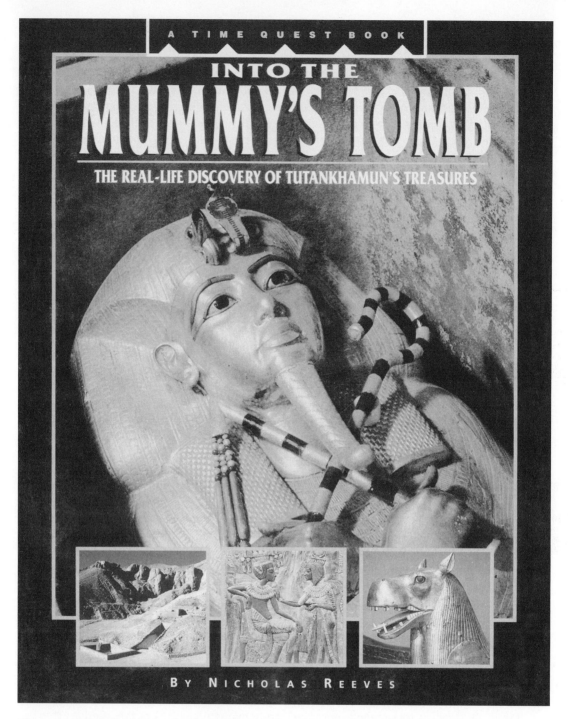

A TIME QUEST BOOK

INTO THE MUMMY'S TOMB

THE REAL-LIFE DISCOVERY OF TUTANKHAMUN'S TREASURES

BY NICHOLAS REEVES

The text of *Into the Mummy's Tomb* proceeds from the discovery of Tutankhamun's tomb to the treasures that were hidden.

Source: Into the Mummy's Tomb, Nicholas Reeves, Madison Press Books, 1992.

which had been written in Greek, hieroglyphs, and another Egyptian script. It was the finding of this stone that eventually made possible the translations of the ancient hieroglyphs. The illustrations clarify the text by showing the techniques used by the scholars. For example, Giblin shows how Champollion assigned letters to all of the hieroglyphs and thus made it possible to read the ancient symbols. Notice in the following quote how Giblin helps readers follow a spatial organization as they also view the stone:

> What makes this stone so special? Step closer, and you'll see. Spotlights pick out markings carved into the surface of the stone, and close up you can tell that these markings are writing. At the top are fourteen lines of hieroglyphs—pictures of animals, birds, and geometric shapes. Below them you can make out thirty-two lines written in an unfamiliar script. And below that, at the bottom of the slab, are fifty-four more lines written in the letters of the Greek alphabet. (p. 7)

Ancient Cultures of Other Middle Eastern Areas

Just as for the early Egyptian culture, there are informational books that allow readers to glimpse the arts, architecture, and life-styles of other cultures in the Middle East. For example, several adult sources provide excellent illustrations and accompanying text that could be valuable for any age group. *The Art and Architecture of Islam 1250–1800* by Sheila S. Blair and Jonathan M. Bloom (1994) is a comprehensive text that includes sections on the architecture and arts in Iran under the Ilkhanids, the Timurids, and the Safavids and Zands. The text is organized in chronological order and divided into two major periods: 1250–1500 and concluding with 1500–1800. The photographs, many in color, provide a source for authenticating the illustrations in juvenile books.

Three additional adult sources include sections on ancient Middle Eastern cultures. Jay A. Levenson's *Circa 1492: Art in the Age of Exploration* (1991) includes a section on the art from Islamic empires. Color photographs and accompanying text present such artifacts as a Turkish lantern, a Koran binding, a Koran fragment, a Koran chest, a ceremonial kaftan, and various swords from the Ottoman empire. This text is especially useful because it allows readers to compare the art in different cultures of the world including Europe and the Mediterranean, the Orient, and the Americas. H. W. Janson's *History of Art* (1995) includes sections on ancient Persian art and Islamic art. The Islamic art chapter includes photographs of mosques, mausoleums, statuary, drawings, and manuscripts. David Piper's *The Illustrated History of Art* (1994) includes sections on Iranian art and Islamic art from Syria, North Africa, and Turkey. These sources are valuable for identifying characteristics of the early art of these cultures.

Juvenile Informational Literature

Several books written for younger audiences present the history of peoples of the Middle East and their cultures. Fiona Macdonald's *A 16th Century Mosque* provides detailed information about the architecture in the ancient Arabic world and yields insights into the role of religion in art and architecture. The text describes the mosques built in the sixteenth century in and around Istanbul, Turkey. Most of these mosques were built for Sultan Suleyman the Magnificent, the ruler of the Ottoman empire; they were designed by the architect Sinan Pasha, who lived from 1491–1588. The text discusses Sinan's career at Suleyman's court and his accomplishments in building the mosques, which are considered some of the finest achievements of Islamic art. Detailed colored drawings with labels help readers follow the text. The text includes topics such as the first mosque, mosque styles, workers' lives, and the Ottoman Empire. The text concludes with an overview of mosques around the world.

Mokhtar Moktefi and Veronique Ageorges's *The Arabs in the Golden Age* presents the history, social life, and customs of Islamic peoples. In the introduction, the authors emphasize the importance of the Islamic religion on daily life, culture, and art:

> Islam was the creative force behind the religious, military, and cultural prominence of the Arabic empire during the Golden Age, which began with the spread of the teachings of the prophet Muhammad in the early eighth century and endured roughly into the mid-thirteenth century. Decorative arts—weaving, glassmaking, tile-work, pottery, inlaid carvings in stone, plaster, and metal—had never been so beautiful. Many people, for the first time, could read. Thousands of handtooled, leather-bound books were filled with calligraphy so well executed that it rivaled the beauty of the miniatures accompanying the stories, poems, religious teachings, and learned treaties. (p. 5)

This text helps students realize the importance of the arts in the Islamic world, as well as providing illustrations demonstrating their beauty.

Peter and Ruth Mantin's *The Islamic World: Beliefs and Civilizations 600–1600* provides an informative introduction to the beliefs associated with the Islamic religion, the rise of Islam, and the founding of Islam by Muhammad, the Prophet of Allah. For example, the text introduces the belief of the Muslims by identifying and defining the five pillars or main duties of Islam. Because these pillars support the Muslim way of life, they are important for authenticating the beliefs found in other genres of literature. The authors introduce the Muslim faith by stating: "Muslims are united in their belief that God's teachings have been revealed through the Prophet Muhammad. By following these teachings Islam offers a complete way of life to all Muslims" (p. 8). Next the authors define the five pillars of Islam including:

First, Shahadah: To bear witness that there is one God, Allah and Muhammad is His Prophet.
Second, Prayer: Muslims should pray to Allah five times a day. (Before prayer Muslims remove their shoes and wash. They stand on a carpet or prayer mat, facing in the direction of Mecca.)
Third, Zakah or alms: A part of what Muslims earn every year should be given to the poor and sick.
Fourth, Fasting: Muslims should fast from dawn to sunset every day of the holy month of Ramadan. Ramadan was the month in which God's teaching began to be revealed to Muhammad.
Fifth: Pilgrimage: Muslims should try to go on a pilgrimage to the holy city of Mecca at least once in a lifetime.

Maps, photographs, and illustrations clarify the discussion about different aspects of Islam. The accuracy of information in this text written for juvenile audiences may be authenticated through such adult sources as John Alden Williams's *The Word of Islam* (1994) and Mostafa Vaziri's *The Emergence of Islam: Prophecy, Imamate, and Messianism in Perspective* (1992).

Authors of informational books may use a style that heightens and encourages readers' interest. In *Mysterious Places: The Mediterranean*, Philip Wilkinson and Jacqueline Dineen encourage interest by asking questions about locations, several of which are found in the Middle East. For example, notice how the authors capture interest when they introduce the city of Leptis Magna in Libya, 46 B.C.–A.D. 211: "Why did the Romans build this splendid city on the edge of the arid Sahara Desert? And why was Leptis Magna, with its wonderful classic buildings, abandoned to the encroaching desert sands?" (p. 61). The text uses a similar approach for introducing Hagia Sophia in Istanbul, Turkey, built from A.D. 360 to 537 and the Topkapi Palace, Istanbul, Turkey, built from A.D. 1465 to 1853. A hint of mystery and intrigue is developed through the questions associated with the Topkapi Palace: "What evil schemes were plotted and murders committed behind the closed doors of this luxurious palace, home of the fabulously wealthy Ottoman sultans and their harems of power-hungry women?" (p. 83). After asking each of the questions, the authors discuss the various mysteries surrounding the location. There is a list of sources for additional information including museums that may be visited to learn more about Mediterranean region, specific sites that may be visited to help answer questions, and further reading. This text may be used for a comparative study of ancient places.

Another text that includes several ancient civilizations is *The Visual Dictionary of Ancient Civilizations*, edited by Emily Hill. The illustrations and text present a wide range of objects from ancient worlds including Egypt, Assyria, and Persia. The text includes a time line and an index, and it serves as a good reference source.

Kathryn Lasky's *The Librarian Who Measured the Earth* is a biography of Eratosthenes, the chief librarian in Alexandria, Egypt. His calculations made over two thousand years ago provided a measurement for the size of the earth that is only two hundred miles different from our calculations today. This biography describes a man who strove for knowledge and used his curiosity to make remarkable discoveries. Kevin Hawkes's illustrations give a flavor of this time period. The author's notes, an afterword, and an author's bibliography, and an illustrator's bibliography provide additional information and add to the authenticity of the text.

Fictional Storybooks Set in the Ancient Middle East

Authors of fictional picture storybooks with settings in the ancient Middle East frequently focus on people from early cultures or develop stories that are similar to the folklore set in the ancient civilizations. For example, in *The Stone Carver: A Tale of Ancient Egypt*, Mary Stolz uses an actual monument—the Sphinx—built to honor the ruler, Khafre, Pharaoh of Egypt, as the basis for a fictional story about a stone carver who may have worked on the monument. Deborah Nourse Lattimore's illustrations enhance the information about the art and architecture of ancient Egypt presented in the text. Each double-page spread is surrounded by hieroglyphs that retell the story of the stone carver who may have conceived of and supervised the carving of the Sphinx. The end pages add to the note of authenticity. The artist, who is a student of Egyptology and a member of the American Research Center in Egypt at Columbia University and the Egypt Exploration Society in London, includes labeled hieroglyphs that add to the comprehension of the drawings that surround each of the pages within the story.

Robert Sabuda's *Tutankhamen's Gift* is a fictionalized biography about the life of the son of Pharaoh Amenhotep III, ruler of Egypt. In the notes on the text, the author states that facts from such ancient civilizations as Egypt are both difficult to determine and debated by scholars. In this tale of Tutankhamun's ascendancy to pharaoh in the mid-1300s B.C., the author highlights the role of the young ruler, who proclaims, "I, Tutankhamen, am pharaoh, ruler of Egypt. I shall rebuild the temples and fill them with monuments to the gods so the people will again have faith. I shall lead the people of Egypt through their suffering and tears so they believe in themselves once more. This will be my promise to you and my gift to the gods" (p. 25 unnumbered).

Shulamith Levy Oppenheim's *The Hundredth Name* is similar to a folktale because it is set "far back in time" in Muslim Egypt. This literary folktale has an emphasis on Allah as its young hero tries to discover, through his camel, the hundredth name for Allah. The spiritual quality of the tale is reinforced through the hazy illustrations, painted in acrylics on gessoed linen canvas, that allow the grain to show through the paint.

Appointment is a picture storybook adaptation of W. Somerset Maugham's "Appointment in Samarra." In this Arabic tale set in Baghdad, death in the disguise of an old woman searches for Abdullah the servant. There is a strong sense of fate when Abdullah tries unsuccessfully to escape death by leaving Baghdad to travel to Samarra. In a surprise ending, Maugham shows that we cannot escape death, or our fate. Death's appointment with the servant is actually in Samarra and not in Baghdad. Roger Essley's double-page illustrations in desert tones add to the feeling of a hot, dry country.

Historical Fiction Set in the Ancient Middle East

Susan Fletcher's *Shadow Spinner* is set in ancient Persia during the time of Shahrazad and the telling of the tales for "The One Thousand and One Nights." The author's note reveals that she used Richard F. Burton's English translation of *The Book of the Thousand Nights and a Night* as her guide. The heroine of her story is Marjan, a crippled serving girl who has the ability to spin her own stories. Marjan becomes involved with Shahrazad's problems when Marjan is overheard telling a story that is new to Shahrazad. At this point, Marjan enters the harem to assist Shahrazad in her quest for new stories; subsequently, Marjan is forbidden to leave the harem and becomes part of palace intrigue. Through the descriptions of the palace, the city, and the harem, readers discover many of the details associated with the setting in the Ancient Middle East.

Fletcher uses an interesting technique to introduce both the themes in the book and the importance of storytelling. Each chapter is introduced with a section titled "Lessons for Life and Storytelling." For example, notice in the following quote how Fletcher develops the power found in words and stories: "In the old tales, there is power in words. Words are what you use to summon a jinn, or to open an enchanted door, or to cast a spell. You can do everything else perfectly, but if you don't say the right words, it won't work. If you know how to use words, you don't have to be strong enough to wield a scimitar or have armies at your command. Words are how the powerless can have power" (p. 194). Many of these chapter introductions would be interesting to use as part of a storytelling project.

Fletcher also provides additional information in the author's note when she discusses the background of the book. For example, she states:

> Since the names in the tale of Shahrazad are of Persian derivation, I have given my story a Persian inflection. Where I have made up characters not included in the original tale, I have given most of them Persian names. Shahrazad, Dunyazad, and their father, as well as Shahryar and his brother are introduced in the original tale. Marjan, Ayaz, Mitra, the bazaar storyteller, and most other characters are my own inventions. Zaynab was inspired by one of the stories Shahrazad told, "The Wily Dalilah and Her Daughter Zaynab." (pp. 218–219)

Nonfiction children's literature that emphasizes the Middle East typically focuses on religious aspects of the culture, the geography and the people, and conflicts. Poetry and fictional literature often focuses on the human struggle as characters overcome conflicts with society or within themselves.

Informational Books

Informational books by Richard Wormser and Dianne M. MacMillan provide information about contemporary religious practices associated with the Islamic faith. Wormser's *American Islam: Growing Up Muslim in America* focuses on the lives of American teens who follow the Islamic religion. MacMillan's *Ramadan and Id-al-Fitr* presents the importance of Ramadan, the ninth month of the Islamic calendar and Id-al-Fitr, the festival of the first day of the tenth month following the fast of Ramadan. The text provides insights into fasting from dawn to sunset, Muhammad, the Pillars of Islam, and other practices associated with these two important religious periods.

Matthew S. Gordon's *Islam: World Religions* provides an overview of Islam that includes both its historical and modern context. The text begins with Muhammad and the founding of Islam and proceeds to subjects such as the spread of Islam, the Koran and the law, religious life in Islamic countries, and Islam and the modern world. There is a useful glossary and an index.

There are numerous informational books that present the economies, the cultures, the history, and the geography of different countries in the Middle East. Full-color photographs of children and their families from various backgrounds add to readers' knowledge of the diversity of a country. Books by Matti A. Pitkanen and Jules Hermes focus on children and their families. Pitkanen's *The Children of Egypt* begins with an introduction to ancient Egypt, and then it pictures and discusses the lives of contemporary children. Readers are introduced to Said, the son of a boatman, who is learning how to sail; Hamed, who lives on the banks of the Nile; Aziza, whose family raises food on a small plot of land; and Muhammad, who lives on the Fayyum Oasis. The text includes a fact sheet, a pronunciation guide, and an index. Unfortunately, the large color photographs are not captioned. Hermes's *The Children of Morocco* follows a similar format and approach. This text also shows a diversity of life-styles and ethnic backgrounds. There is a commonality among the children, however, because of the influence of Islam in their daily lives.

Several books provide information about the desert and the inhabitants of the desert. John King's *Bedouin: Threatened Cultures* describes the Bedouin way of life as it has survived for centuries in the Arab world and discusses threats to the continued existence of this nomadic people's culture. Labeled color photographs, a glossary, a list of further reading, an index, and addresses for further information add to the value of the book. This book could be used in association with Bedouin folktales or when authenticating portions of Suzanne Fisher Staples's fictional story *Shabanu: Daughter of the Wind*. Simon Scoones's *The Sahara and Its People* describes life in a wide area of the desert of northern Africa.

There are numerous titles in the "Enchantment of the World Series" that discuss history, culture, geography, agriculture, and art of various countries. For example, Mary Virginia Fox's *Enchantment of the World: Bahrain*, *Enchantment of the World: Iran,* and *Enchantment of the World: Tunisia* present a history of each country and then discuss topics related to its culture and natural resources. Each book includes a tour of cities and villages, a mini facts page, and an index. Labeled color photographs and maps help clarify the texts.

Additional examples of books in this series include Leila Merrell Foster's *Enchantment of the World: Iraq, Enchantment of the World: Jordan,* and *Enchantment of the World: Saudia Arabia* and Marlene Targ Brill's *Enchantment of the World: Algeria*. Because there are a number of books in this series written by different authors, they provide a source for comparative studies. Which books are more effective and why? Do any of the books develop stereotypes, as suggested in the earlier studies that analyzed textbooks?

These books from the "Enchantment of the World" series may also be compared with other books that focus on specific countries such as Susannah Honeyman's *Saudi Arabia*, Sean Sheehan's *Pakistan*, and Jabeen Yusufali's *Pakistan: An Islamic Treasure*.

Several of the informational books about the Middle East focus on the various conflicts among Arab countries or the conflicts between Arab countries and Israel. Consequently, these books may be compared for type of coverage, biases if any, issues covered, and depth of coverage. For example, you could compare Zachary Kent's *The Persian Gulf War: "The Mother of All Battles"* with Leila Merrell Foster's *The Story of the Persian Gulf War*.

Books by John King and Cathryn J. Long explore wider conflicts, such as the conflicts between Arab and Jewish people. King's *Conflict in the Middle East* discusses the causes of conflicts in the countries of the Middle East and the impact of this conflict on the contemporary world. He includes discussions of lands and peoples, including differences in economic resources. Events and incidents are presented in chronological order, and topics covered include religions, the results of World War I and World War II, Arab nationalism, the 1948 foundation of Israel as a state, and the Palestinian uprising of 1987. Cathryn J. Long's *The Middle East in Search of Peace* also explores Jewish–Arab relations and the origins of conflicts.

Elizabeth Ferber's biography *Yasir Arafat: The Battle for Peace in Palestine* provides added insights into the conflict in the Middle East. The biography traces Arafat's political career and provides background information on the history of the Arab–Israeli conflict. The biography includes chapter notes and a chronology. Black-and-white photographs illustrate the text.

As you read these contemporary books, consider the views on stereotypes identified by William Griswold et al. (1975) and Rita M. Kissen (1991). Do you find the stereotypes identified by these researchers? Has the literature changed since the study conducted by Griswold et al.? How are the conflicts depicted? What, if any, are the biases in reporting these conflicts?

Poetry

One of the more extensive sources of poetry from the Middle East for children is Naomi Shihab Nye's anthology *This Same Sky: A Collection of Poems from Around the World*. In her introduction, Nye states her motivation for editing this collection:

> Poetry has always devoted itself to bringing us into clearer focus—letting us feel or imagine faraway worlds from the inside. During the Gulf War of 1991, when the language of headline news seemed determined to push human experience into the 'sanitized' distance, I found myself searching for poems by Iraqi poets to carry into classrooms. Even if the poems had been written decades earlier, they helped to give a sense of human struggle and real people living behind the headlines. (p. xii)

Two issues seem to dominate the discussions about contemporary Islamic cultures and consequently may influence the literature. First, what is the role of women in the culture? For example, might new publications and the accompanying discussions help lead to more rights for women? Second, what will be the impact of industrialism and Westernization?

Barbara Crossette (1996) discusses women's rights under Islam and the possible impact of a new publication, "Claiming Our Rights: A Manual for Women's Human Rights Education in Muslim Societies." This manual, according to Crossette, will be tested in Bangladesh, Jordan, Lebanon, Malaysia, and Uzbekistan. The objective is to assemble discussion groups and to exchange ideas that may lead to self-awareness among women. Crossette states, "Sometimes at great risk to themselves, women are making gains, though frequently small and fragile" (p. 5). In addition to containing instructions for conducting grass-roots discussions, the manual includes "provocative passages from the Koran," Arab proverbs, and pro-

files of four women who are identified as "the first heroines of Islam." As you consider the role of women in the Islamic world and in Islamic literature, you may wish to debate the possible impact of such a manual and the accompanying women's rights movement.

Houston Smith (1994) identifies the related issues of industrialism and Westernization that could influence the culture and the literature. He states:

[T]here are indications that Islam is emerging from several centuries of stagnation which colonization no doubt abetted. It faces enormous problems: how to distinguish modern industrialism (which on balance it welcomes) from Westernization (which on balance it doesn't); how to realize the unity that is latent in Islam when the forces of nationalism work powerfully against it; how to hold on to Truth in a pluralistic, relativizing age. But having thrown off the colonial yoke,

Islam is stirring with some of the vigor of its former youth. From Morocco on the Atlantic, eastward across North Africa, through the Indian sub-continent (which includes Pakistan and Bangladesh) on to the near-tip of Indonesia, Islam is a vital force in the contemporary world. As there are some 900 million Muslims in the global population of five billion, one person out of every five or six belongs today to this religion which guides human thought and practice in unparalleled detail. And the proportion is increasing. (p. 177)

As you read Smith's quote, consider the possible impact of both industrialism and Westernization on the Islamic culture and literature. Also consider the impact of the ever-increasing numbers of Islamic worshippers in the world. How could this influence literature? What consequences do you believe might result from Crossette's concerns about women's rights?

This collection includes poetry from Saudi Arabia, Kuwait, Pakistan, Iraq, and Lebanon, as well as from many other countries throughout the world. Many of the themes in the poetry are universal. For example, in "A Sailor's Memoirs," a poem by Muhammad al-Fayiz from Kuwait, the poet longs to give peace—peace to the Gulf breeze, peace to sandy shores, peace to returning ships, and peace to quiet dwellings. In "A Dream of Paradise in the Shadow of War," a poem by Muneer Niazi from Pakistan, the poet remembers the poignant melodies of the nightingale's song, people returning home, and a village wilderness turned into a perfumed garden. In "A Pearl," a poem by Fawziyya Abu Khald from Saudi Arabia, the poet remembers a gift, symbolic of truth and love, passed down from grandmother to mother and finally to the poet. The fact the poems in the anthology reflect universal needs is highlighted by the titles of the anthology's sections: Words and Silences, Dreams and Dreamers, Families, The Earth and Sky in Which We Live, Losses, and Human Mysteries.

The Space Between Our Footsteps: Poems and Paintings from the Middle East, a collection of poetry also selected by Naomi Shihab Nye, includes both poems and paintings from the Middle East. The selections represent the works of more than one hundred poets and artists from nineteen Middle Eastern countries. In her introduction to the anthology. Nye provides considerable information about the importance of poetry in the Middle East. She states:

> This book in your hands offers a medley of voices and visions from the twentieth century. Consider *The Space Between Our Footsteps* to be like the mezza tables of hors d'oeuvres spread out all across the Middle East, which often precede a greater feast. . . . Subjects include an immense affection for childhood and children, a tender closeness to family, a longing for early, more innocent days, a passion for one's homeland, grief over conditions of exile, a reverent regard for the natural world, and a love for one another and for daily life. Do any of these concerns sound alien to us? (p. viii)

As you read the poems and look at the art, try to identify these themes.

Several additional anthologies of poetry include at least a few poems from the Middle East. Satomi Ichikawa's *Here a Little Child I Stand: Poems of Prayer and Praise for Children* includes an Islamic prayer to Allah by Add Al'Aziz Al-Dirini. Ruth Gordon's anthology *Under All Silences: Shades of Love* includes several poems from Egypt and Persia. The Egyptian poems are translated from ancient hieroglyphic texts written about 1500 B.C. The Persian texts are also translated from ancient sources in the 1200s. In one of these ancient Persian poems, the poet wonders about Solomon and all his wives and the Soul. Two poems from ancient Egypt are also included in Kenneth Koch and Kate Farrell's *Talking to the Sun: An Illustrated Anthology of Poems for Young People.*

Contemporary Realistic Fiction

Picture storybooks written for younger children include stories about personal development and pride, trying to live in a city when there is conflict, and keeping the memory of a beloved brother alive. These books may be criticized for inaccuracies or stereotypes, or they may be acclaimed for positive representations. For example, as you read *The Day of Ahmed's Secret* by Florence Parry Heide and Judith Heide Gilliland, set in Cairo, Egypt, analyze the content and illustrations to decide which is more important: the themes of personal development and pride in work or Sylvia Iskander's (1997) analysis that "the flaw lies in the lack of cultural accuracy in text and illustrations?" (p. 13)

In contrast, Iskander's analysis of Heide and Gilliland's *Sami and the Time of the Troubles* concludes that this text and the illustrations by Ted Lewin "present an accurate portrait of life in war-torn Lebanon" (p. 15). This story depicts a family trying to survive in the basement shelter as guns and bombs shake the walls. Notice how the authors introduce the conflict and suggest the influences on a young boy's life:

> My name is Sami, and I live in the time of the troubles. It is a time of guns and bombs. It is a time that has lasted all my life, and I am ten years old. Sometimes, like now, we all live in the basement of my uncle's house. Other times, when there is no fighting, when there are no guns, we can be upstairs. We can go outside: my mother can take my little sister Leila to market, my grandfather and uncle can go to work, and I can go to school. (p. 1)

As the family huddles in the basement, Sami thinks about the quiet days when it is safe to be outside and he remembers all of these pleasant experiences. Ted Lewin's illustrations allow readers to visualize the contrasts between the basement shelter and the pleasant times when there are no bombs. The front and endpapers introduce the true nature of the conflict by showing the results of a car bomb in a once-quiet neighborhood.

The Bedouin folktales reflected the pride, independence, and self-sufficiency of the nomadic characters. These same characteristics are found in Sue Alexander's *Nadia the Willful*. Nadia is the young daughter of a Bedouin sheik who lives with her family in the desert. The Bedouin values of pride and independence are especially strong in Nadia when she refuses to allow the family to forget her favorite brother who has been lost in the desert. Nadia does not obey when her father tries to hide his grief by decree that no one will utter Hamed's name again. In a satisfying ending, Nadia makes her father realize that the only way that he can retain his son Hamed is to remember him and talk about him. Nadia's actions not only stress determination, they also develop the power of love and remembrance.

Books for older readers develop themes related to the importance of childhood memories and friendships, the necessity for surviving in a dangerous world, and the searching for personal identity within a culture that may not respect women's roles.

The theme of the importance of memories and friendship is developed in Vedat Dalokay's *Sister Shako and Kolo the Goat: Memories of My Childhood in Turkey*. This book, which won the 1995 Mildred Batchelder Honor Award, is a personal remembrance of the former mayor of Ankara, Turkey. In it, he lovingly recalls his childhood in rural Turkey and his special friendship with a widow and her remarkable goat, Kolo. The author develops many of the values and beliefs identified in the folklore. For example, the importance of hospitality is shown when the new goat comes into the family unexpectedly and is considered a "Guest of God" because "[i]f a traveler needs shelter or food, he knocks at the door of any house along the way. The host offers him whatever he needs, because the traveler is considered a guest sent by God. This is a very old Turkish tradition that is still practiced today" (p. 14).

Dalokay develops many of these Turkish values as he remembers Sister Shako's thoughts and advice about subjects such as holy places and death. For example, Sister Shako states her beliefs about death: "Now I am here in this hut; but after death, I shall be in the caterpillar on the black earth, I shall be in the rain seeping into the earth. Blowing winds and rapid rivers will carry me around this world. May death come nicely, smoothly, without pain, without suffering" (p. 58). To clarify understanding, the text includes footnotes that describe various customs and beliefs presented in the story. The cultural nature of the text is reinforced by regional words, idioms, sayings, and descriptions of traditions of eastern Turkey.

Surviving in a dangerous world is a theme developed in several books set in the Middle East. Rafik Schami's *A Hand Full of Stars* places the hero in the political turmoil of modern Damascus. Showing how dangerous society can be, the story follows a teenager who wants to become a journalist within this suppressed society. His wishes come true when he and his friends begin an underground newspaper. After reading this book, you may speculate about the symbolism in the title. The author states at the end of the book what *A Hand Full of Stars* means: "The Hand is the hand of Uncle Salim, always there to guide the narrator; in the saddest moments, it points the way out of despair. Like the stars that illuminate the dark night sky, the Stars in the hand stand for hope" (endnote).

Inner-city survival provides the setting and conflict in Gaye Hicyilmaz's *Against the Storm,* set in Ankara, Turkey. This story shows the consequences of urban poverty when Mehmet and his family arrive in Ankara and find themselves trapped in a shantytown that is quite different from the wonderful city the family has heard

APPLYING KNOWLEDGE OF CULTURAL VALUES AND BELIEFS TO SHABANU: DAUGHTER OF THE WIND

The 1990 Newbery Honor Book, Suzanne Fisher Staples's *Shabanu: Daughter of the Wind,* provides strong literary elements of character, conflict, and theme, as well as examples of cultural beliefs. Consequently, the book provides a good source for identifying values and beliefs and for relating those values and beliefs to the plot and characterization in the story. Two articles may help students of children's literature as they read and analyze this book: Suzanne Fisher Staples's "Writing About the Islamic World: An American Author's Thoughts on Authenticity" (1997) and Laurie A. Brand's "Women and the State in Jordan" (1998).

Shabanu: Daughter of the Wind is a story about a Muslim family who lives in the Cholistan Desert in Pakistan. The main character, Shabanu, is the youngest of two daughters in a nomadic extended family. She has learned that she cannot determine the direction of her life, and this causes her person-against-self and person-against-society conflict. As a Muslim, her father has complete authority over her, and she is struggling to accept his decisions regarding her future.

As you read the following list of life-styles, values, and beliefs found in the book, try to authenticate them with what you have learned about an Islamic culture that is influenced by the Quran (Koran) and the threads of the culture identified in the folklore. The family in this story closely adheres to the mandates of their religion. Some of the life-style descriptions, values, and beliefs that are mentioned in the story include the following:

Sons are more important than daughters.

Marriages are arranged by the families, and are encouraged to take place as soon as a girl reaches puberty.

Poetry has a strong history in this culture.

Girls must be veiled once they reach puberty.

A woman can be killed for tarnishing the family's honor.

When children are small, they can go anywhere.

Sexual segregation begins at puberty.

A girl who is not married by age 16 is a disgrace.

Wrestling is an acceptable recreational activity for men.

The ritual of the dead includes facing the body toward Mecca, washing the body, and wrapping it in a shroud.

Burial must be quick, to send the soul on its way.

Children do not fast during Ramadan, the month of fasting.

During Ramadan, no eating or drinking is allowed until sundown.

Muslims must be up before the sun rises.

Parents decide what is best for their children.

A child's happiness is less important than the family's honor.

A bride price is a common practice with arranged marriages.

Muslim men are permitted four wives; women, one husband.

A woman's place is in the home.

Parents are due the utmost respect.

A child is not to question a father's decision.

A "light beating" is permissible if a woman is disobedient.

As you authenticate the life-styles, values, and beliefs identified in the book, try to decide if the book is or is not authentic for a nomadic people of the Islamic faith. What is your evidence that the book is or is not authentic?

about. This becomes a story of friendship and determination when Mehmet receives the help of a streetwise orphan and uses his own courage to find a way out of this environment. Hicyilmaz's story is vivid because she lived in Turkey for many years. According to the endnotes, "It was here that she was struck by the way children in particular are forced to suffer the effects of poverty and how poverty destroys the very fabric of society. Her novel was inspired by a true incident reported in the Turkish press" (endnotes).

SUMMARY

In this chapter, we have discussed the traditional literature and identified values and beliefs found in the folklore from various cultures and countries in the Middle East. For example, we found that the Bedouin tales reflect generosity, hospitality, the importance of family, ancestry, and birth. Pride, independence, and self-sufficiency are important values. In this chapter, folklore was discussed in the following categories: Bedouin tales, tales of magic and supernatural, animal tales, and religious tales and moral instruction.

We discussed informational and fiction books that depict the ancient cultures. Books about the ancient cultures are especially valuable and informative if they include both historical information and photographs of ancient architecture and artifacts. Informational books that encourage analytical thinking by allowing young readers to become involved in solving problems and observing are especially meaningful. Fictional books about ancient cultures either typically focus on stories about people who might have lived in the ancient Middle East, such as a stone carver, or are fictionalized biographies of early rulers. Authors of fiction frequently build stories upon the folklore such as found in "The One Thousand and One Nights."

Poetry is an important part of the literature from the various Middle Eastern countries. Many of the values found in the folklore, such as closeness of family and love for homeland, are reflected in the poetry. The poetry discussed is from both ancient and contemporary cultures.

We concluded the chapter with a discussion of contemporary literature, both fictional and informational books, and an application of the knowledge gained by analyzing Suzanne Fisher Staples's *Shabanu: Daughter of the Wind*. This final application identified life-styles, values, and beliefs found in the book, including the mandates of religion.

SUGGESTED ACTIVITIES FOR DEVELOPING UNDERSTANDING OF LITERATURE FROM THE MIDDLE EAST

1. Compare the values and beliefs found in folklore from ancient Egypt and from Islamic cultures. Find examples of folklore that depict these values and beliefs.
2. Trace the emergence of Islamic beliefs in the folklore.
3. Locate an article about the exploration of ancient Egyptian tombs and artifacts such as Terence Walz's "The American Experience in Egypt: A Retrospective Chronicles Two Centuries of Exploration" (1996). How does an article like this one written by the executive director of the American Research Center in Egypt compare to the information found in other informational books about ancient Egypt?

4. Locate a picture storybook in which the illustrator has depicted the early Islamic culture. Authenticate the illustrations by referring to art books that include photographs of Islamic art and architecture. Does the illustrator of the picture storybook develop an accurate feeling for the culture? Why or why not?

5. Read a novel written for adults such as Jean P. Sasson's *Princess: A True Story of Life Behind the Veil in Saudi Arabia* (1992). Compare the novel with Suzanne Fisher Staples's *Shabanu: Daughter of the Wind*, a book written for younger readers. What are the similarities and what are the differences in the culture, values, and life-styles depicted?

6. Read Suzanne Fisher Staples's *Haveli*, the sequel to *Shabanu: Daughter of the Wind*. Develop a list of the life-styles, values, and beliefs developed in the sequel. How do they compare with those listed in this chapter and with those identified in informational books and in folklore?

7. Collect news articles about the Middle East. Do you identify any of the stereotypes reported in the earlier study discussed in this chapter?

Involving Children with Literature from the Middle East

*A*s discovered in the previous sections, literature from the Middle East includes literature from a wide range of countries—from Egypt and Turkey to Saudi Arabia, Yemen, and Iran. The literature also includes the influences of the Islamic faith. In this section, we will follow the same five phases used with literature from other cultures in previous chapters.

 ## PHASE ONE: TRADITIONAL VALUES IN FOLKLORE

You may begin your study of the cultural characteristics of folklore from the Middle East by collecting a number of folktales, myths, and legends from the various countries. As you read the literature, you may identify the geographic location of the tale on a map. Developing a web of the folklore and the respected values and disliked qualities is an excellent way to begin this study. The web in Figure 7–1 is an example of one developed by students following the reading of the folklore.

Study the information on the web. The respected values include wit and wisdom, generosity, hospitality, friendship, and protection for those in your care. The disliked qualities include jealousy and disobeying God's orders. The beliefs include a belief in Allah, a belief in death and revival, and a belief in fate. The motifs include magical spells, trickster animals, and moral instruction. Also notice that by identifying locale, students can compare both similarities and differences. For example, they will discover that the ancient Egyptians believed in fate and revival after death as reflected in such myths as the myth of Isis and Osiris. They will also discover that many respected values are closely related to the geography of the culture. For example, the Bedouin people who lived a nomadic life in the desert emphasized the importance of hospitality and generosity especially to those who are under their care. Lead discussions in which students consider each of these values and motifs.

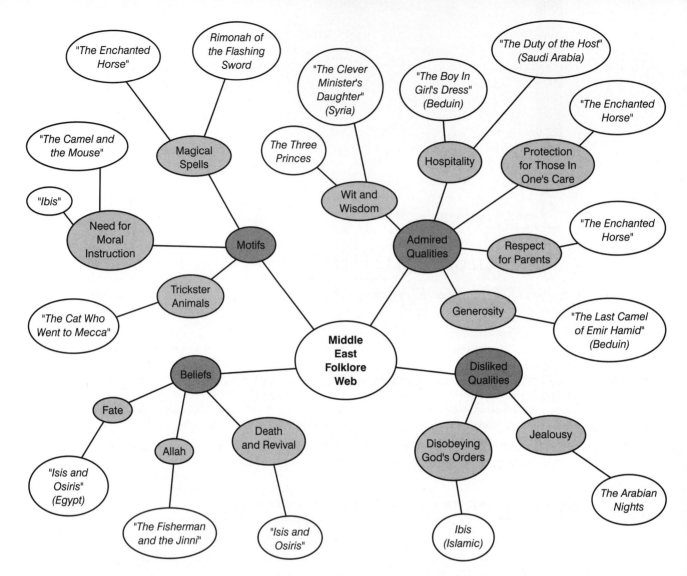

FIGURE 7–1 Web Showing Traditional Values Found in Folklore from the Middle East

Additional Activities to Enhance Phase One

Here are some activities for children or young adult students related to this phase:

1. Compare Eric A. Kimmel's Egyptian version of Snow White, *Rimonah of the Flashing Sword: A North African Tale*, with Snow White tales from other cultures. What are the characteristics of this tale that make it Egyptian? What are the characteristics that make it similar to other Snow White tales?

2. Compare Neil Philip's variant of the Cinderella story in *The Arabian Nights* or Rebecca Hickox's *The Golden Sandal: A Middle Eastern Cinderella Story* with Cinderella tales from other cultures. What are the characteristics of the tale that make it Arabic? What are the characteristics that make it similar to other Cinderella tales?

3. Ehud Ben-Ezer's *Hosni the Dreamer: An Arabian Tale* is described as being based on an old Arabian folktale. Read and analyze the tale and evaluate Uri Shulevitz's illustrations. What evidence can you find that this is based on an Arabian folktale? Are the illustrations authentic for the culture and the location?
4. Make a collection of openings and closings found in folklore from various areas of the Middle East. Are there any generalizations that can be made about the folklore style?
5. Using the religious tales such as Shulamith Levy Oppenheim's *Iblis*, search for the common ground between Islam and Christianity. What are the Islamic influences depicted in *Iblis*?

 ## PHASE TWO: NARROWING THE FOLKLORE TO THE LITERATURE OF ONE COUNTRY

If desired, you may develop separate webs for topics such as "Folklore from Egypt," "Bedouin Folklore," or "Arabic Folklore." Now students can do an in-depth study of one of the areas. They should locate the places where the folklore originated on a map. They could also relate the themes and motifs in the folklore to the geography of the locations.

They may choose illustrated versions of folktales from one area and authenticate the cultural, geographical, and historical accuracy of the illustrations. Another excellent activity that provides a pleasurable culminating activity for a study of the folklore of the culture is to develop a storytelling activity in which students prepare stories for telling by investigating the background of the stories, discovering the traditional storytelling styles, and telling the tales to an audience.

Additional Activities to Enhance Phase Two

Here are some activities for children or young adult students related to this phase:

1. Find folktales from a specific country of the Middle East that do not have extensive author's notes, or your teacher will provide them for you. Develop author's notes or illustrator's notes that might accompany each of the books. Several books provide examples of source and author's notes developed by authors or retellers of folklore. For example, in Eric A. Kimmel's *The Tale of Ali Baba and the Forty Thieves,* Kimmel provides background information about the tale, including a reference to an eleventh century sheikh and a location in modern Teheran where the tale might have taken place. Lise Manniche's *The Prince Who Knew His Fate* includes extensive notes, maps, and sketches of figures in the Egyptian Museum, Cairo. There is also a listing of meanings of terms from the early Egyptian culture. This latter book includes eight pages of supporting information titled "About the Story and the Illustrations."
2. Extend the storytelling activity into a "Storytelling Festival from _____." Ask students to focus on the stories from one area, practice the stories using an appropriate storytelling style, and include music that might provide background for the stories.
3. Ask students to choose a folktale from a specific area that does not include illustrations. Have students either draw authentic illustrations or choose illustrations from art books that could be used to illustrate the text.

There are numerous nonfiction informational books about various locations in the Middle East; consequently, the books provide excellent sources for evaluating informational books and comparing texts written about the same subjects. Guidelines developed by the National Science Teachers Association (1992) provide selection and evaluation criteria for informational books that may be used for this activity. For example, this organization recommends the following criteria:

1. All facts should be accurate.
2. Stereotypes should be eliminated.
3. Illustrations should clarify the text.
4. Analytical thinking should be encouraged.
5. The organization should aid understanding.
6. The style should stimulate interest.

Before students discuss and apply these criteria to informational books, you may ask the students to suggest their own guidelines for selecting and evaluating nonfiction books. After they provide their suggestions and reasons for the guidelines, you may compare their guidelines with those developed by the science association.

Next, select a group of informational books that develop similar topics and tell the students that they will use the guidelines to evaluate each of these books. For example, you might choose Judith Crosher's *Ancient Egypt*, Andrew Haslam and Alexandra Parsons's *Ancient Egypt*, Geraldine Harris's *Ancient Egypt: Cultural Atlas or Young People*, and Viviane Koenig's *The Ancient Egyptians: Life in the Nile Valley*. Another group of books might include Anne Millard's *History Highlights: Pyramids*; Carter Smith's *The Pyramid Builders*; and Jacqueline Morley, Mark Bergin, and John James's *An Egyptian Pyramid*.

Another group of books for comparisons and evaluations might include informational books about the Islamic world such as *A 16th Century Mosque* by Fiona Macdonald, *The Arabs in the Golden Age* by Mokhtar Moktefi and Veronique Ageorges, and *The Islamic World: Beliefs and Civilizations 600–1600* by Peter and Ruth Mantin.

Students could develop a chart with the evaluative criteria and then include information from the text that show if the text meets or does not meet the guidelines. For each book, they may summarize the coverage found in the books, as well as how well it meets each of the criteria. As students develop and use their evaluative criteria, they should compare the accuracy of the facts found in the texts. If they discover discrepancies, they have an opportunity to use other references to try to discover which text is correct.

Additional Activities to Enhance Phase Three

Here are some activities for children or young adult students related to this phase:

1. Several of the informational books encourage reader involvement by including step-by-step directions for making models or other items. Choose a book such as Andrew Haslam and Alexandra Parsons's *Ancient Egypt,* and follow the directions for making models, clothing, objects, or foods. Give a demonstration to the class or to a group.

2. Develop a list of criteria for evaluating maps in informational books. Select a group of informational books that include maps and evaluate the maps. Rate them and qualify the texts from best to worst. Provide your reasoning for each rating.

3. Select several nonfiction books that present the art and architecture of the Islamic world. Identify characteristics of the art. Search illustrated folklore, and identify any similarities between the art and architecture in the nonfiction books and those found in the folklore.

 ## PHASE FOUR: HISTORICAL FICTION

Many of the historical informational books just discussed may be used to provide sources so that students can write fictional accounts of people's lives. According to Robert Sabuda in the author's note to *Tutankhamen's Gift*, a fictionalized biography about the life of the Egyptian ruler who came to the throne as a child during the mid-1300s B.C., "Historical facts from ancient civilizations such as Egypt's are often difficult to determine and are much debated by scholars" (notes on the text). Consequently, Sabuda uses information that he could find on ancient Egypt to write a fictionalized biography about the young ruler.

After students have researched the early periods of the Middle Eastern cultures, ask them to select a time period and a location. Then have them write a historical fiction story about the time period and a person who may or may not have actually lived during this period. For example, Mary Stolz uses an actual monument built to honor a pharaoh of Egypt to write a fictional story about a stone carver who may have worked on the Sphinx. After the students have written their fictionalized stories, ask them to write an author's note that provides historical background and that supports the actual historical information in the book.

Additional Activities to Enhance Phase Four

Here are some activities for children or young adult students related to this phase:

1. Many of the poems selected by Naomi Shihab Nye in *The Space Between Our Footsteps: Poems and Paintings from the Middle East* provide glimpses into the history of either a person or a people. Some of the poems provide happy memories while others focus on cultural conflicts caused by war or consequences of political disagreements. Choose a poem and use the poem to develop a historical fiction or an illustrated book that uses ideas developed in the poem.

2. Compare the characteristics of and the themes developed in Shulamith Levy Oppenheim's *The Hundredth Name* with folklore that has Islamic characteristics.

 ## PHASE FIVE: CONTEMPORARY LITERATURE

Many of the contemporary realistic stories can be used to encourage students to search for themes developed in the books. They can then look for support for the themes they have identified. For example, after reading Florence Parry Heide and

Judith Heide Gilliland's *Sami and the Time of the Troubles,* they may search for support for themes such as it is important to retain memories, especially in times of troubles, and it is important to retain determination. Students may also search for cultural information in the book, which is set in Beirut, the capital of Lebanon.

It is difficult but possible to survive in a dangerous world is a theme developed in several books written for older readers. Students can analyze the books to find important characteristics of the literature, which may mirror international headlines about new dangers in today's world. In the person-against-society conflicts of this survival literature, the protagonists are usually innocent children and the antagonists are terrorist groups, oppressive military governments, or mass violence. For example, Rafik Schami the author of *A Hand Full of Stars,* places his hero in the political turmoil of modern Damascus. Showing how dangerous a society can be, the story follows a teenager who wants to become a journalist within a suppressed society. His wishes come true when he and his friends begin an underground newspaper.

Surviving in urban poverty provides the setting and conflict for Gaye Hicyilmaz's *Against the Storm*. The story is set in Ankara, Turkey. There is a strong theme that friendship and determination help to overcome problems in times when survival seems almost impossible. Ask students to summarize the characteristics that make survival possible.

After students have read, analyzed, and discussed the conflicts and the characters in these books, ask them to search news sources such as newspapers, newsmagazines, and television to identify if these survival stories could take place in real life. You might share with them the information that the author of *Against the Storm* was inspired to write her novel by a true incident that was reported in the Turkish press.

Many of the books discussed in this chapter could be used to integrate activities from various areas of the curriculum. For example, there are a number of ways that Suzanne Fisher Staples's *Shabanu: Daughter of the Wind* could be used with various areas:

Art, Music, and Poetry Interpretations
1. Create a model of Shabanu's home.
2. Make a shadowbox showing the safari.
3. There are several references to desert poems. Develop a collection of such poems and then write a poem.

Characterization
1. Identify the evidence that suggests that Shabanu has an independent character.
2. Identify the evidence that suggests that Shabanu is strong willed. How do her characteristics cause her person-against-self conflicts?
3. Why does Shabanu believe that happiness is fragile?
4. What are the most important lessons about life that Shabanu learns?

Clarification of Values
1. Investigate and discuss the importance of a dowry, sons, veiling, and arranged marriages in this Muslim culture.
2. Contrast the role of men and women in the book.
3. Contrast the role of young girls with that of older women.
4. Investigate and discuss the importance of the religious beliefs developed in the book. For example, what is the importance of Mecca and Ramadan?

Conflict

1. Develop a person-against-society plot development for Shabanu.
2. Develop a person-against-self plot development for Shabanu.

Setting

1. Locate Pakistan on a map and research the characteristics of the Cholistan Desert. Locate the surrounding countries and describe the characteristics of those countries.
2. Contrast the life of people who live in the desert with those who live in the cities of Pakistan.

Written Responses

1. Write a personal response that tells your reaction to the incident when Mama slapped Shabanu because Shabanu did not want to marry an older man with three wives (p. 193).
2. Write a personal response to Rehim's gifts (pp. 195–197).
3. Write your personal reaction to Sharma's argument about Shabanu's marriage (p. 205).
4. Write your personal response to Sharma's gift of wisdom (p. 217).
5. Write your personal response to Sharma's advice (p. 225).
6. Write a poem that provides the characteristics of Shabanu or the desert setting.

To relate this last series of activities using Staples's book to contemporary roles in Muslim populations living in the United States, students could compare the roles of the characters in *Shabanu: Daughter of the Wind* with the experiences described by Richard Wormser in his informational book *American Islam: Growing Up Muslim in America*.

Before leaving the literature of the Middle East, ask students to summarize the information that they have learned about the various cultures and countries in the Middle East. Ask them to consider what they would still like to learn about these cultures and countries. This list of additional questions and areas of interest could easily expand the research into the culture.

Additional Activities to Enhance Phase Five

Here are some activities for children or young adult students related to this phase:

1. Newspapers such as the Sunday edition of *The New York Times* include many features that could be used to model a newspaper about contemporary Middle Eastern cultures. For example, search through a newspaper and list the various features that might be in a newspaper, such as the following: international, national, and state news; editorials; arts and leisure; travel; magazine; business; and sports. There could also be special features such as in-depth coverage of education, fashions, foods, and book reviews. Students can choose features they would like to investigate, select editors and reporters for each feature, and publish the newspaper.
2. Use a book such as Richard Wormser's *American Islam: Growing Up Muslim in America* as an example of a book that describes the lives of young people in the United States. If possible, interview people who came to the United States from one of the Islamic countries. Compose a list of questions, conduct interviews, and share these responses with the class.

BIBLIOGRAPHY

Basit, Abdul. "Islam in America: How to Integrate Without Losing Muslim Identity." *Islamic Horizons.* Vol. 27 (March/April 1998): 32–34.

Bayat, Mojdeh, and Mohammad Ali Jamnia. *Tales from the Land of the Sufis.* Boston: Shambhala, 1994.

Blair, Sheila S., and Jonathan M. Bloom. *The Art and Architecture of Islam 1250–1800.* New Haven: Yale University Press, 1994.

Book of the Dead: The Ancient Egyptian, translated by R. O. Faulkner and edited by Carol Andrews. New York: Macmillan, 1985.

Brand, Laurie A. "Women and the State in Jordan," in Yvonne Yazbeck Haddad and John L. Esposito, eds., *Islam, Gender and Social Change* pp. 100-123. New York: Oxford University Press, 1998.

Burton, Sir Richard F., translated by. *Tales from the Arabian Nights: Selected from the Book of a Thousand Nights and a Night.* New York: Excalibur, 1985.

Bushnaq, Inea, edited by. *Arab Folktales.* New York: Pantheon, 1986.

Crossette, Barbara. "A Manual on Rights of Women Under Islam." *The New York Times* (Sunday, December 29, 1996): p. 5.

Denny, Frederick M. *Islam: Religious Traditions of the World.* New York: HarperCollins, 1987.

Foster, Leila Merrell. *The Story of the Persian Gulf War.* Childrens Press, 1991 (I: 8 + R: 5). A highly illustrated depiction of the Gulf War of 1991.

Ghazi, Tasneema Khatoon. "Islamic Literature for Children Adopts the English Language." *Bookbird* 35 (Fall 1997): 6–10.

Griswold, William J, et al. *The Image of the Middle East in Secondary School Textbooks.* New York: Middle East Studies Association, 1975.

Iskander, Sylvia. "Portrayals of Arabs in Contemporary American Picture Books." *Bookbird,* 35 (Fall 1997): 11–16.

Janson, H. W. *History of Art,* 5th ed. New York: Abrams, 1995.

Khorana, Meena G. "To the Reader." *Bookbird* 35 (Summer 1997): 2–3.

Kissen, Rita M. "The Children of Hagar and Sarah." *Children's Literature in Education* 22 (1991): 111–119.

Leach, Maria, edited by. *Funk & Wagnalls Standard Dictionary of Folklore, Mythology, and Legend.* San Francisco: Harper & Row, 1972.

Levenson, Jay A. *Circa 1494: Art in the Age of Exploration.* New Haven: Yale University Press/Washington: National Gallery of Art, 1991.

Little, Greta. "The Changing Image of Arabs in Hostage Dramas." *Booklist* 35 (Fall 1997): 28-30.

National Science Teachers Association. "Criteria for Selection—Outstanding Science Trade Books for Children." *Science and Children* 29 (March 1992): 20–27.

Norton, Donna E. *Through the Eyes of a Child: An Introduction to Children's Literature,* 5th ed. Upper Saddle River, N. J.: Merrill/Prentice Hall, 1999.

Piper, David. *The Illustrated History of Art.* New York: Crescent Books, 1994.

Rai, Mansooreh. "The Iranian Revolution and the Flowering of Children's Literature." *Bookbird* 35 (Fall 1997): 31–33.

Rochman, Hazel. *Against Borders: Promoting Books for a Multicultural World.* Chicago: American Library Association, 1993.

Rohl, David M. *Pharaohs and Kings.* New York: Crown, 1995.

Salleh, Khaliijah Mohammad. "Islam in America: The Role of Men and Women in Society." *Islamic Horizons* 26 (January/February 1997): 57.

Sasson, Jean P. *Princess: A True Story of Life Behind the Veil in Saudi Arabia.* New York: Morrow, 1992.

Smith, Houston. *The Illustrated World's Religions: A Guide to Our Wisdom Traditions.* New York: HarperCollins, 1994.

Staples, Suzanne Fisher. "Writing About the Islamic World: An American Author's Thoughts on Authenticity." *Bookbird* 35 (Fall 1997): 17-20.

Vaziri, Mostafa. *The Emergence of Islam: Prophecy, Imamate, and Messianism in Perspective.* New York: Paragon, 1992.

Walz, Terence. "The American Experience in Egypt: A Retrospective Chronicles Two Centuries of Exploration." *Archaeology* 49 (January/February 1996): 70–72, 74-75.

Williams, John Alden. *The World of Islam.* Austin: University of Texas Press, 1994.

CHILDREN'S AND YOUNG ADULT LITERATURE REFERENCES

Alexander, Sue. *Nadia the Willful.* Illustrated by Lloyd Bloom. Pantheon, 1983 (I: 7–10 R: 5). A Bedouin girl teaches her father about the importance of remembering a lost son.

Ben-Ezer, Ehud. *Hosni the Dreamer: An Arabian Tale.* Illustrated by Uri Shulevitz. Farrar, Straus & Giroux, 1997 (I: 6-8 R: 5). The author identifies the story as being based on an old Arabian folktale.

Brill, Marlene Targ. *Enchantment of the World: Algeria.* Childrens Press, 1990 (I: 9+ R: 5). Geography, history, people, and culture of this Northern African country are presented in an informational book.

Bushnaq, Inea, edited by. *Arab Folktales.* Pantheon, 1986 (I: 12+ R:7). This is a large collection of Arabic folklore.

Cashford, Jules, retold by. *The Myth of Isis and Osiris.* Barefoot Books, 1993 (I: all). An Egyptian myth that is based on the cycle of life, death, and rebirth.

Crosher, Judith. *Ancient Egypt.* Viking, 1993 (I: 9+ R: 5). This highly illustrated book presents the history of ancient Egypt and its people.

Dalokay, Vedat. *Sister Shako and Kolo the Goat: Memories of My Childhood in Turkey.* Translated by Guner Ener. Lothrop, Lee & Shepard, 1994 (I: 10 R: 5). In this 1995 Mildred Batchelder Honor Book, the former mayor of Ankara recalls his childhood and his friendship with a widow and her goat.

Dulac, Edmund, illustrated by. *Sindbad the Sailor and Other Stories from the Arabian Nights.* Hertfordshire, England: Hodder and Stoughton, 1914; Omega, 1986 (I: 12+). This is a reissue of a book published in 1914.

Ferber, Elizabeth. *Yasir Arafat: The Battle for Peace in Palestine.* Millbrook, 1995 (I: 12+ R: 7). This is a biography about the Palestinian leader.

Fletcher, Susan. *Shadow Spinner.* Atheneum, 1998 (I:10+ R: 6). This historical fiction novel is set in the time of Shahrazad.

Foster, Leila Merrell. *Enchantment of the World: Iraq.* Childrens Press, 1990 (I: 9+ R: 5). This book discusses the geography, history, people, and culture of Iraq.

_____. *Enchantment of the World: Jordan.* Childrens Press, 1991 (I: 9+ R: 5). This book introduces the geography, history, government, religion, and culture of Jordan.

_____. *Enchantment of the World: Saudi Arabia.* Childrens Press, 1993 (I: 9+ R: 5). This book presents the history, geography, and culture of the largest country on the Arabian Peninsula.

Fox, Mary Virginia. *Enchantment of the World: Bahrain.* Childrens Press, 1992 (I: 9+ R: 5). The history, geography, culture, government, and industry of this island in the Persian Gulf.

_____. *Enchantment of the World: Iran.* Childrens Press, 1991 (I: 9+ R: 5). The history, modern life, and culture of Iran.

_____. *Enchantment of the World: Tunisia.* Childrens Press, 1990 (I: 9+ R: 5). Geography, history, people, and culture of Tunisia.

Giblin, James Cross. *The Riddle of the Rosetta Stone: Key to Ancient Egypt.* Crowell, 1990 (I: 10+ R: 6). The informational text follows the process used to decipher the ancient hieroglyphs.

I = Interest age range
R = Readability by grade level

Gordon, Matthew S. *Islam: World Religions*. Facts on File, 1991 (I: 10 + R: 6). This informational book provides an overview of Islam.

Gordon, Ruth, selected by. *Under All Silences: The Many Shades of Love*. Harper & Row, 1987 (I: 9 +). The anthology includes several Egyptian and Persian poems.

Hamilton, Virginia, retold by. *In the Beginning: Creation Stories from Around the World*. Illustrated by Barry Moser. Harcourt Brace, 1988 (I: 8 +). This collection of myths includes "The Sun-God and the Dragon," a tale from Egypt.

Harris, Geraldine. *Ancient Egypt: Cultural Atlas for Young People*. Facts on File, 1990 (I: 9 + R: 5). The history of ancient Egypt is explored through charts, illustrations, and maps.

Haslam, Andrew, and Alexandra Parsons. *Ancient Egypt*. Thomas Learning, 1995 (I: 8–12 R:4). This informational text includes directions for making models related to Ancient Egyptian civilization.

Heide, Florence Parry, and Judith Heide Gilliland. *The Day of Ahmed's Secret*. Illustrated by Ted Lewin. Lothrop, Lee & Shepard, 1990 (I: 6–9 R: 4). A picture storybook set in Cairo.

_____. *Sami and the Time of Troubles*. Illustrated by Ted Lewin. Clarion, 1992 (I: 6–9 R: 4). A Lebanese boy and his family live in a basement shelter.

Hermes, Jules. *The Children of Morocco*. Carolrhoda, 1995 (I: 8 + R: 5). Full-color photographs and text describe the homes, work, and ways of life of children and their families.

Hickox, Rebecca. *The Golden Sandal: A Middle Eastern Cinderella Story*. Illustrated by Will Hillenbrand. Holiday, 1998 (I: all). A tale from Iraq.

Hicyilmaz, Gaye. *Against the Storm*. Little, Brown, 1992 (I: 10 + R: 6). A boy learns about survival in Ankara.

Hill, Emily, editor. *The Visual Dictionary of Ancient Civilizations*. Dorling Kindersley, 1994 (I: all). The illustrations and text identify a wide range of objects from ancient worlds.

Honeyman, Susannah. *Saudi Arabia*. Raintree Steck-Vaughn, 1995 (I: 8 + R: 5). This informational book provides an introduction to the land, climate, daily life, and culture of Saudi Arabia.

Husain, Shahrukh. *Mecca*. Dillon, 1993 (I: 8 + R: 4). Color photographs and text present important aspects of this religious city of the Muslims.

Ichikawa, Satomi. *Here a Little Child I Stand: Poems of Prayer and Praise for Children*. Philomel, 1985 (I: all). A collection of prayers from many countries and cultures.

Jackson, A. E. *Ali Baba and the Forty Thieves and Other Stories*. Derrydale, 1994 (I: 10 + R: 5). This folklore text includes three tales.

Kent, Zachary. *The Persian Gulf War: "The Mother of All Battles."* Enslow, 1994 (I: 10 + R: 6). This informational book begins with descriptions of bombing and concludes with the aftermath of the war.

Kherdian, David, retold by. *Feathers and Tails*. Illustrated by Nonny Hogrogian. Philomel, 1992 (I: 5–9 + R: 4). This collection of folklore includes an example of a Sufi fable.

Kimmel, Eric A., adapted by. *Rimonah of the Flashing Sword: A North African Tale*. Illustrated by Omar Rayyan. Holiday House, 1995 (I: 5–9 R: 5). An Egyptian version of the "Snow White" tale.

_____. *The Tale of Aladdin and the Wonderful Lamp: A Story from the Arabian Nights*. Illustrated by Ju-Hong Chen. Holiday, 1992 (I: 6–9 R: 5). Retold from the Arabian Nights.

_____. *The Tale of Ali Baba and the Forty Thieves*. Illustrated by Will Hillenbrand. Holiday House, 1996 (I: 6–9 R: 5). The folktale is from the Arabian Nights.

_____. *The Three Princes: A Tale from the Middle East*. Illustrated by Leonard Everett Fisher. Holiday House, 1994 (I: 6–9 R: 5). A princess challenges three princes.

King, John. *Bedouin: Threatened Cultures*. Raintree Steck-Vaughn, 1993 (I: 9 + R: 5). This informational book describes the social life and customs of these nomadic peoples.

_____. *Conflict in the Middle East*. New Discovery, 1993 (I: 9 + R: 5). This informational book discusses the causes of conflict in the countries of the Middle East.

_____. *Kurds: Threatened Cultures*. Thomas Learning, 1993 (I: 9 + R: 5). This informational book discusses the problems of the Kurds, who live predominately in Iraq, Iran, and Turkey.

Koch, Kenneth, and Kate Farrell, selected by. *Talking to the Sun: An Illustrated Anthology of Poems for Young People*. Metropolitan Museum of Art and Holt, Rinehart and Winston, 1985 (I: all). This anthology of poems illustrated with works of art includes two poems from ancient Egypt.

Koenig, Viviane. *The Ancient Egyptians: Life in the Nile Valley*. Illustrated by Veronique Ageorges. Millbrook, 1992 (I: 8 + R: 5). The informational book discusses the people, including their work, social and economic lives, and their religious traditions.

Lasky, Kathryn. *The Librarian Who Measured the Earth*. Illustrated by Kevin Hawkes. Little, Brown, 1994 (I: 9 + R: 5). This is an illustrated biography about the chief librarian in Alexandria.

Long, Cathryn J. *The Middle East in Search of Peace*. Millbrook, 1994 (I: 10 + R: 6). This book explores the origins of Arab–Israeli conflict.

Macdonald, Fiona. *A 16th Century Mosque*. Illustrated by Mark Bergin. Peter Bedrick, 1994 (I: all). Detailed illustrations show the mosques built in Istanbul.

MacMillan, Dianne M. *Ramadan and Id al-Fitr*. Enslow, 1994 (I: 8 + R: 5). The text and photographs present Ramadan.

Manniche, Lise. *The Prince Who Knew His Fate*. Philomel, 1981 (I: all). The story is translated from hieroglyphs.

Mantin, Peter, and Ruth Mantin. *The Islamic World: Beliefs and Civilizations 600–1600*. Cambridge, England: Cambridge University Press, 1993 (I: 10 + R: 7). This informational book includes formation on the rise and influence of Islam.

Maugham, W. Somerset. *Appointment*, adapted by Alan Benjamin. Illustrated by Roger Essley. Simon & Schuster, 1993 (I: all). A servant cannot escape a fateful death.

Millard, Anne. *History Highlights: Pyramids*. Gloucester, 1989 (I: all). The types of pyramids, the purposes for pyramids, and the building of pyramids in Egypt are discussed.

Moktefi, Mokhtar, and Veronique Ageorges. *The Arabs in the Golden Age*. Millbrook, 1992 (I: 9 + R: 5). This book presents the history, social life, and customs of Islamic peoples.

Morley, Jacqueline, Mark Bergin, and John James. *An Egyptian Pyramid*. Peter Bedrick, 1991 (I: 8 + R: 4). The text and illustrations describe the construction of the pyramids.

Morrison, Ian A. *Middle East*. Steck-Vaughn, 1991 (I: 9 + R: 5). This book surveys the geography, languages, history, and culture of the region.

Nye, Naomi Shihab, selected by. *This Same Sky: A Collection of Poems from Around the World*. Four Winds, 1992 (I: 9 +). This anthology includes poetry from Saudi Arabia, Kuwait, Pakistan, Iraq, and Lebanon.

_____, selected by. *The Space Between Our Footsteps: Poems and Paintings from the Middle East*. Simon & Schuster, 1998 (I: all). An anthology of poems and paintings.

Oppenheim, Shulamith Levy. *The Hundredth Name*. Illustrated by Michael Hays. Boyds Mills, 1995 (I: 4–8 R: 4). An Egyptian boy tries to discover the hundredth name for Allah.

_____, retold by. *Iblis*. Illustrated by Ed Young. Harcourt Brace, 1994 (I: all). This is an Islamic version of Adam and Eve.

Philip, Neil, retold by. *The Arabian Nights*. Illustrated by Sheila Moxley. Orchard, 1994 (I: 8 + R:5). Shahrazad saves her life by telling the king a different story every night.

Pitkanen, Matti A. *The Children of Egypt*. Carolrhoda, 1991 (I: 8 + R: 4). The focus is on the day-to-day lives of Egyptian children.

Putnam, James. *Mummy*. Photographs by Peter Hayman. Knopf, 1993 (I: 9 + R: 5). The book describes the principles and ceremonies associated with the preservation of bodies.

Reeves, Nicholas. *Into the Mummy's Tomb: The Real-Life Discovery of Tutankhamun's Treasures*. Scholastic, 1992 (I: 8 + R: 5). This book traces Howard Carter's discovery of the tomb.

Sabuda, Robert. *Tutankhamen's Gift*. Atheneum, 1994 (I: all). This highly illustrated text gives a fictionalized account of the possible childhood and early life of the man who became leader of Egypt.

Schami, Rafik. *A Hand Full of Stars*. Translated by Rika Lesser. Dutton, 1990 (I: 12 + R: 6). In this story set in Damascus, a boy becomes involved with an underground newspaper.

Scoones, Simon. *The Sahara and Its People*. Thomson Learning, 1993 (I: 8 + R: 4). Color photographs and text provide information about the Sahara.

Sheehan, Sean. *Pakistan*. Marshall Cavendish, 1994 (I: 9 + R: 5). This is a history and geography of this country.

Smith, Carter. *The Pyramid Builders*. Silver Burdett, 1991 (I: 9 + R:5). This informational book describes the construction of the pyramids and the culture of ancient Egypt.

Staples, Suzanne Fisher. *Haveli*. Random House, 1993 (I: 12 + R: 6). This is a sequel to *Shabanu: Daughter of the Wind*.

_____. *Shabanu: Daughter of the Wind*. Knopf, 1989 (I: 12 + R: 6). A girl in Pakistan asserts her independence.

Stolz, Mary. *The Stone Carver: A Tale of Ancient Egypt*. Illustrated by Deborah Nourse Lattimore. Harcourt Brace, 1988 (I: all). This story tells how the Sphinx may have been carved.

Van Allsburg, Chris Van. *The Garden of Abdul Gasazi*. Houghton Mifflin, 1979 (I: 5–8 R: 5). A boy enters a magic garden.

Wilcox, Charlotte. *Mummies and Their Mysteries*. Carolrhoda, 1993 (I: 8-12 R: 5). This informational book introduces readers to mummies found in different parts of the world.

Wilkinson, Philip, and Jacqueline Dineen. *Mysterious Places: The Mediterranean*. Illustrated by Robert Ingpen. Chelsea House, 1994 (I: 9 + R: 5). The text includes several locations from the Middle East.

Wormser, Richard. *American Islam: Growing Up Muslim in America*. Walker, 1994 (I: 12 + R: 6). The book describes the lives of American teens who follow the Islamic religion.

Yusufali, Jabeen. *Pakistan: An Islamic Treasure*. Dillon, 1990 (I: 9 + R: 5). The history, culture, and life-styles of Pakistan.

Author/Title Index

Subject Index